SELECTIONS
FROM THE
LETTERS DESPATCHES AND OTHER STATE PAPERS

PRESERVED IN
THE MILITARY DEPARTMENT OF THE GOVERNMENT OF INDIA

1857-58

SELECTIONS
FROM THE
LETTERS DESPATCHES AND OTHER STATE PAPERS

PRESERVED IN
THE MILITARY DEPARTMENT OF THE GOVERNMENT OF INDIA

1857-58

EDITED BY
George W. Forrest
DIRECTOR OF RECORDS, GOVERNMENT OF INDIA

WITH A MAP

VOLUME IV

JHANSI
CALPEE
GWALIOR

ASIAN EDUCATIONAL SERVICES
NEW DELHI ★ MADRAS ★ 2001

ASIAN EDUCATIONAL SERVICES
* 31, HAUZ KHAS VILLAGE, NEW DELHI - 110016
  Tel : 6560187, 6568594 Fax : 011-6852805, 6855499
  e-mail : asianeds@nda.vsnl.net.in
  website : www.aes-books.com

* 5, SRIPURAM FIRST STREET, MADRAS - 600 014,
  Tel : 8115040 Fax : 8111291
  e-mail : asianeds@md3.vsnl.net.in

Price : Rs. 1195
First Published: Calcutta, 1912
AES Reprint : New Delhi, 2001.
ISBN : 81-206-1551-4

Published by J. Jetley
for ASIAN EDUCATIONAL SERVICES
31, Hauz Khas Village, New Delhi - 110 016.
Processed by AES Publication Pvt. Ltd., New Delhi-110 016
Printed at Subham Offset Press DELHI - 110 032

SELECTIONS

FROM THE

LETTERS, DESPATCHES AND OTHER STATE PAPERS

PRESERVED IN

THE MILITARY DEPARTMENT

OF

THE GOVERNMENT OF INDIA

1857-58

EDITED BY

GEORGE W. FORREST, B.A.

DIRECTOR OF RECORDS OF THE GOVERNMENT OF INDIA
FELLOW OF THE BOMBAY UNIVERSITY

WITH A MAP

VOLUME IV

CALCUTTA
SUPERINTENDENT GOVERNMENT PRINTING, INDIA
1912

PREFACE

THE first volume of the Selections from the Letters, Despatches and other State Papers in the Military Department of the Government of India, 1857-58, contained the documents from the first outbreak of disaffection to the siege and storming of Delhi by the English troops. The second and third volumes contained in a similar form all papers relating to the mutiny at Lucknow and the defence of the Residency by the garrison; General Havelock's march from Allahabad and the first relief of Lucknow; General Outram's defence of Lucknow; Sir Colin Campbell's relief of Lucknow in November 1857; General Outram's defence of the Alumbagh; General Windham's defence of Cawnpore; Sir Colin Campbell's storming and capture of Lucknow; all documents relating to the outbreak at Cawnpore, the defence of the intrenchment, and the massacre of the survivors. The present volume contains in a similar form all papers relating to Sir Hugh Rose's campaign in Central India from the capture of Rathghur and the action at Barodea to the siege and storming of Jhansi, 3rd April 1858; all the documents detailing the operations attending the capture of Calpee on the 24th May 1858; all the despatches and reports relating to the Gwalior operations, from the march from Calpee on the 6th of June to the capture of the Rock of Gwalior, held to be one of the strongest and most important fortresses in India.

In the introduction to the present volume the history of the Central Indian Campaign, one of the most glorious achievements in the military annals of England, is told from the despatches of Sir Hugh Rose and the respective commanders and brigadiers. They have been collated with diaries and letters, and certain errors rectified and obscure points cleared. In the Central Indian Campaign no army, but a small body of good fighting men, led by a chief always ready to face tremendous risks, marched in the hottest and most deadly season of the year from the confines of Western India to the waters of the Jumna, a distance of a thousand miles. They made their way across rugged plateaux where roads were mere tracks and towns few and far between; they toiled through dense jungles where the Bhil hunter roamed undisturbed; they crossed broad rivers, swollen with the rain which fell on the mountains; they forced formidable passes; they fought and won pitched battles, and they stormed the strongest forts. The capture of Jhansi must rank with the great actions recorded in British annals. A force consisting of an incomplete division had laid siege to a strong fortress and a walled city, defended by a desperate and disciplined garrison more than double its number, and supplied with all the munitions of war. The Bombay Sepoy and the Madras Sapper vied with the British soldier in patience, endurance of privation, and fatigue. Then, in light of day, this handful of men stormed the lofty walls, and, after four days' strenuous fighting, the city was captured. The taking of Calpee, a natural fortress on a high bald rock rising from the Jumna, completed the plan which the Government of India had drawn up for the Central India Field Force. But the occupation of Gwalior by Tantia Topee and the Ranee of Jhansi compelled Sir Hugh Rose, leaving a small garrison at Calpee, to make a very rapid march in summer heat to Gwalior with the remainder of his troops, and to fight and gain two actions on the road, one at Morar Cantonments, the other at Kotah-ka-Serai. They arrived, from great distances and by bad roads, at their posts before Gwalior on the day appointed, the 19th of June; and on that same day carried by assault all the enemy's positions on strong heights and in most difficult ground; taking one battery after another, twenty-seven pieces of artillery in the action, twenty-five in the pursuit, besides the guns in the fort, the old city, the new city, and finally the rock of Gwalior.[1] On the 28th of June Sir Robert Napier marched from Gwalior in pursuit of the enemy, and by a daring feat of arms closed the Central Indian Campaign.

Miss L. M. Anstey has rendered me great service in the correction of the proofs of the Introduction and the State Papers—a tedious and difficult task when dealing with printers who do not know a word of English. She has also collated the proofs with the despatches published in the Government of India Gazette, the London Gazette and the Parliamentary Papers of the time, and has assisted me in reconciling many discrepancies in the contemporary narratives. Mr. F. G. Stokes, besides making many suggestions, has contributed the exhaustive index, which will be of service to the students of war.

The sources of the narrative as in the previous volumes are State documents, but the Introduction has no official character or authority.

GEORGE WILLIAM FORREST.

IFFLEY, OXON ;
June 1912.

---

[1] Sir Hugh Rose's Despatch, 13th October 1858.

CONTENTS

Chap.		Pages
	Introduction	
I	Central India.—Jhansi	1
II	Calpee	81
III	Gwalior Despatches	128
Appendix A		i
,, B		xv
,, C		xxxvii
,, D		xlii
,, E		lxvii
,, F		xciv
,, G		cxiii
Map		*In pocket*

LIST OF ABBREVIATIONS USED

Adjt.	For	Adjutant.
Arty.	,,	Artillery.
Asst.	,,	Assistant.
Beng.	,,	Bengal.
B. E. R.	,,	Bombay European Regiment.
B. N. I.	,,	Bombay Native Infantry.
Brig.	,,	Brigade.
Brigr.	,,	Brigadier (General).
Bvt.	,,	Brevet.
Cav.	,,	Cavalry.
C. I. F. F.	,,	Central India Field Force.
cmdg.	,,	commanding.
cmds.	,,	commands.
Co., Coy.	,,	Company.
Col. Sgt.	,,	Colour-sergeant.
Com. Gen.	,,	Commissary-general.
Commr.	,,	Commissioner.
Contgt.	,,	Contingent.
Corp.	,,	Corporal.
D. A. A. G.	,,	Deputy Assistant Adjutant-General.
Dep.	,,	Deputy.
Dept.	,,	Department.
Div.	,,	Division.
Dragns.	,,	Dragoons.
Ens.	,,	Ensign.
F. F.	,,	Field Force.
Gen.	,,	General.
Gnr.	,,	Gunner.
H. A.	,,	Horse Artillery.
H. C.	,,	Hyderabad Contingent.
H. M.	,,	Her Majesty's.
Hyd.	,,	Hyderabad.
Inf.	,,	Infantry.
kld.	,,	killed.
Lc.	,,	Lance.
Lt.	,,	Lieutenant, light.
Maj.	,,	Major.
Mil.	,,	Military.
mtd. in desp.	,,	(honourably) mentioned in despatches.
N. I.	,,	Native Infantry.
Pte.	,,	Private.
Punj.	,,	Punjaub.
Q. M. G.	,,	Quartermaster-General.
Qr.-Mr., Q. M.	,,	Quartermaster.
R.	,,	River.
R. A.	,,	Royal Artillery.
R. E.	,,	Royal Engineers.
recmd.	,,	recommended.
Reg., Regt.	,,	Regiment.
Rev.	,,	Revenue.
Sgt.	,,	Sergeant.
S. M.	,,	Sappers and Miners.
s.-s.	,,	sun-stroke.
Surg.	,,	Surgeon.
Tpr.	,,	Trooper.
wd.	,,	wounded.

INTRODUCTION

BUNDELCUND or the country of the Bundelas* is a strip of country about half the size of Scotland, lying south or south-west of the Jumna, and separated by that river from the wide open Gangetic plain. Both on physical and ethnical grounds it should naturally be included among the states of Central India. During the expiring convulsions of the Muhammadan Empire one of the Mahratta free lances seized the state of Jhansi, a fragment of Bundelcund, and had his claim by conquest confirmed by a Sanad from his Master, the Peshwa. He and his successors governed it under the title of Subahdar as a vassal of the Peshwa. In 1817 the Peshwa ceded the state of Jhansi to the British, and its new rulers acknowledged the hereditary title of the local ruler, and fifteen years later advanced him to the dignity of Rajah. In 1835 he died after having adopted a son. Sir Charles Metcalfe, then Governor of Agra, however decided that in the case of chiefs who may hold lands or enjoy revenues under grants such as are issued by Sovereigns to subjects, the power which made the grant had a right to resume it on failure of heirs male. The British Government refused to recognise the adopted son and selected a great uncle to succeed to the principality. He was an incapable leper and, having oppressed and misgoverned for three years, he died childless. After an investigation by a Commission of the pretensions of several claimants, the British Government selected the brother of the deceased Rajah to be his successor. Meanwhile oppression and disorder had become so rampant in the state that the British Government had to do what they have had to do in the case of many Native States—undertake its direct management. And with the same result. After establishing

*Bundelas, a tribe who claim to be Rajputs. They give a name to the province of Bundelkhand (corruptly Bundelcund). They are descended from the Garhwars of Kantit and Khairagarh, and first settled in Bundelkhand in the 13th or 14th century. *Balfour's Cyclopædia of India.*

order and reforming every branch of the administration and developing the revenues of the State, they handed over the immediate control of the principality to the Rajah whom they had selected. He governed for eleven years with little ability and less energy. No son was born to him, but on his death bed (1853) he adopted a son. His widow, who united the martial spirit of the Mahratta soldier with the subtlety of the Deccan Brahmin, demanded the succession for the boy. Colonel Low, one of the Members of Council who had opposed the annexation of the great central tract of India known as Nagpore, clearly pointed out in a Minute the distinction between Sovereign Native States and dependent Native States. "The Native rulers of Jhansi," he wrote, "were never Sovereigns, they were only subjects of a Sovereign, first of the Peshwa, and latterly of the Company, the Government now had a full right to annex the lands of Jhansi to the British administration." Lord Dalhousie declared in an official paper that "as the Rajah had left no heir of his body, and there was no male heir of any Chief or Rajah who had ruled the principality for half a century, the right of the British Government to refuse to acknowledge the present adoption was unquestionable." The Governor-General had also to consider the wide-spread misery brought upon the people of the state by the two first rulers we had placed in power, and he held "that sound policy combines with duty in urging that the British Government, in the case of Jhansi, should act upon its right, should refuse to recognise the adoption, and should take possession of Jhansi as an escheat." The Court of Directors, who had laid down the principle that the right of adoption, while creating a right to inherit the private property and personal status of a deceased dependent Native Prince, did not carry with it the right to succeed to his political functions nor to the Government of the State except by the consent of the Paramount Power, concurred in the views of the Governor-General and Jhansi was brought under the direct administration of the Government of India. An ample pension* was granted to the widow of the late Rajah : and she was called upon to pay the debts of her late husband. The Ranee protested in vain against the decision of the Government, and the Mahratta Queen, tall in stature,

---

* "The British Government regarded her anger and her remonstrances with careless indifference. They did what was worse, they added meanness to insult. On the confiscation of the State they had granted to the widowed Ranee a pension of £6,000 a year. The Ranee had first refused, but had ultimately agreed to accept this pension. Her indignation may be imagined when she found herself called upon to pay out of a sum which she regarded as a mere pittance the debts of her late husband." *History of the Indian Mutiny, Kaye and Malleson.* Six thousand pounds per annum can be hardly regarded as a mere pittance. Eight thousand was the sum granted to the Peshwa.

handsome in person, young, energetic, proud and unyielding, from that moment indulged the stern passions of anger and revenge. The news of the Mutiny at Meerut on the 18th of May inspired her with the hope of gratifying them. She dexterously employed religious mendicants, the dark engines of fanaticism always to be found in India, to fan among the people the embers of religious hate caused by the open slaughter of kine for the purpose of food amid a Hindu population. She used them to increase the fear and religious passion which had been aroused among the sepoys by the question of the greased cartridges and to scatter among them the seeds of disloyalty and contention. Though we had lately annexed a country with a brave and turbulent population, there were no English troops to guard its capital. There was a detachment of Foot Artillery, the left wing of the 12th Regiment of Native Infantry, the head-quarters and the right wing of the 14th Irregular Cavalry. Captain Dunlop of the 12th commanded the garrison, and Captain Alexander Skene was the Political Officer in charge of the State. The troops were cantoned a little distance from the walled city which was overlooked by a fortress on a high granite rock or kopje. Near the walls of the town were several large temples and groves of tamarind trees, and on the east and west were belts of high basalt hills. A short distance away to the south lay the bungalows of the officials, the gaol, the Star fort occupied by the Artillery who guarded the treasure-chests, and the lines of the men. On the afternoon of the 1st of June, a company of the 12th Regiment of Native Infantry " raised the standard of revolt and invited all men of the *deen* (religion) to flock to their standard offering to remunerate each man for his services at the rate of twelve rupees per month."* They marched into the Star Fort and took possession of it. Captain Dunlop, of whom Sir Hugh Wheeler had reported that " he was a man for the present crisis "† at once paraded the rest of the 12th and the cavalry, and they said they would stand by him. That night Captain Turnbull, Ensign Taylor, Quarter Master Sergeant Newton, and Lieutenant Turnbull of the Revenue Survey slept in the lines of the 12th regiment Native Infantry, and Lieutenant Campbell slept in the lines of the Irregular Cavalry. Nothing occurred. The men were again paraded in the morning and renewed their professions of devotion to their officers. Captain Dunlop spent the morning at the quarter guard preparing shells for his intended assault on the Star Magazine. In the afternoon, as he was returning from the Post Office

---
* *Written deposition of a Native of Bengal, Appendix A.*
† *Captain P. G. Scot's Report, Appendix A.*

accompanied by Ensign Taylor,* he was saluted on nearing the parade by shots from some men of his regiment. Dunlop fell dead and Taylor severely wounded. "Two havildars and a sepoy hid the latter under a charpoy (bed) but to no purpose.†" The troopers, following the lead of the infantry, shot Lieutenant Campbell who was attached to them.‡ "But though wounded he kept his seat on his fleet charger which enabled him by overleaping a gate to escape into the fort without further injury."§ Lieutenant Turnbull "so warmhearted and anxious to do good and to benefit others was on foot and failed to reach the fort. He took refuge in a tree, was seen to climb it and was shot down." The mutineers breaking up into bands proceeded to set fire to the bungalows and to release the convicts from the gaol. A party consisting of 50 sowars and 300 sepoys then approached the town with two guns and a number of Customs and Police chuprassees ‖ led by the gaol daroga ¶ in their train and the doors of the Orcha gate were thrown open to them to the cry of *deen ka jai*.** The Ranee placed guards at her gate and shut herself up in her palace. Captain Gordon sent an urgent message soliciting her assistance at this crisis, but this was refused, as the mutineers threatened to put her to death and to set fire to her palace in case of her compliance with Captain Gordon's request. The Ranee's guards then joined the mutineers. The whole body now marched towards the Town Fort with the intention of taking it by assault, but when they drew near it, the garrison received them with such a well-directed fire that they fell back in confusion.

The garrison, including women and children, were only 55 in number. Lieutenant Burgess of the Revenue Department and some of his European and Eurasian subordinates resided in the fort. When the mutineers seized the Star Magazine and to stay in cantonments was fraught with

---

* The young lad had been with his brothers, and had made great haste to rejoin on the Mutinies breaking out at other stations. He reached Jhansi a few days before he was slain.

† *Written deposition of a Native of Bengal, Appendix A.*

‡ "Lieutenant Campbell of the 15th Native Infantry, the only officer present with the 14th Irregulars." *Captain P. G. Scot's Report, Appendix A.*

§ *Written deposition of a Native of Bengal, Appendix A.*

‖ Chuprassy. H. *Chaprase*, the bearer of a *Chaprās*, i.e., a badge plate inscribed with the name of the officer to whom the bearer is attached. The *chaprāsī* is an office messenger or henchman bearing such a badge on a cloth or leather belt. *Hobson-Jobson, by Colonel Henry Yule, R.E., C.B., and A. C. Burnell, Ph.,D. C.I.E.*

¶ Daroga, P. and H. *Dārogha*. "The chief Native Officer in various departments under the native government, a superintendent, a manager, but in later times he is especially the head of a police, customs, or excise station." *Ibid.*

** *Deen ka jai*, i.e., Victory to the faith !

considerable danger, the permanent residents were joined by Major Skene, his wife and two children, Captain Gordon of the Madras Native Infantry, Dr. McEgan, 12th Bengal Native Infantry, and his wife, Lieutenant Powys, 61st Bengal Native Infantry on Civil Employ in the Canal Department, his wife and child, Mrs. Browne, wife of Dr. Browne, Deputy Commissioner of Jalowan, * and her child and sister, and the English and Eurasian subordinates in the different departments of the Government. Dunlop and his comrades immediately proceeded to lay in provisions, arms and ammunition. They piled up huge stones behind the gates to prevent their being burst open. The women assisted the men " in cooking for them sending them refreshments, and casting bullets." The scanty garrison were able by skilful concentration and a well-directed volley to scatter their assailants when they made their first assault, but they had neither guns nor provisions to withstand a regular siege. The besiegers were busy during the night in planting their guns for their next attack. The besieged held a council of war. It was decided to send three of the garrison to the Ranee to ask her to use her influence to enable them to proceed unmolested to some place of refuge within British territory. The following morning Messrs. Andrews, Purcell and Scott issued from the fort, disguised as Mussulmans, with the intention of seeing the Queen and obtaining her aid, but the feint being discovered, the gentlemen were taken to her palace. She did not even condescend to honour them with an interview, but ordered them to be carried before the mutinous resseldar† for orders. Her words were to the effect "she had no concern with the English swine." This was a signal of death. " The three gentlemen were then dragged out of the palace. Mr. Andrews was killed before the very gates of the Ranee's residence by Jharoo Comar's son supposed to be a personal enemy of his, and the other two were despatched beyond the walls of the town." In the afternoon a second attempt was made to surprise the fort by breaking open a gate, but the besieged succeeded in repelling the invaders who retreated after stationing guards at the gateway as they had done the preceding day.

The mutineers now began to plunder indiscriminately not only the houses of Europeans but also of some of the leading natives in the town.

* " Jalaun is the Northern District of the Jhansi Division, situated in the tract of country west of the Jumna, known as Bundelkhand." *Hunter's Imperial Gazetteer of India.*

† "Resseldar," Ar. P. H. *Risāladār.* Now applied to the native officer who commands a *ressala* or troop in one of our regiments of Irregular Horse. *Hobson-Jobson, by Yule and Burnell.*

"The Bengalees were specially singled out for vengeance because one of them, the post office writer, had concealed Mr. Fleming in his house, and the mutineers had succeeded in tracing him out, and murdering him in the Baboo's house." They threatened with instant death, as the Bengalee witness tells us, the Ranee if she refused to throw in her lot with the rebels. "She accordingly consented and supplied them with a reinforcement of 1,000 men and two heavy guns which she had ordered to be dug out of the earth. They had been buried three years ago." During the night they and the guns of smaller calibre from the cantonment were placed in position and all opened next morning, but they made little impression on the walls of the fort. The marksmen however so galled the garrison that "Captain Gordon was shot through the head when he exposed himself at the parapet." * The besieged answered vigorously and, Skene and Burgess being good shots, their rifles laid many low. For hours the little band held their foes at bay. Then they had to contend not only against the enemy without but with traitors within their gates. A native who was inside the fort states "that Lieutenant Powys was found by Captain Burgess and others lying bleeding from a wound in the neck, and was able to say that four men beside him had attacked him, the four were immediately put to death." The native informant who was in the city says that Lieutenant Powys saw a Khitmutgar (table servant) of Captain Burgess attempt to pull down the stones that closed the fort gates and shot him, that this man's brother cut Lieutenant Powys down with his tulwar, and was instantly shot down by Lieutenant Burgess.†

---

* "A native who was in the fort said he was kneeling over pulling up a bucket, some syce (groom) in the lower enclosure had filled with wheat. A native who was in the city at the time said he was firing at the assailants; but both agreed that he (Captain Gordon) was shot in the head when exposing himself at the parapet.' Captain P. G. Scot's Report. Appendix A.

Mrs. Mutlow in her statement writes "Monday, about eight o'clock in the morning, Mr. Gordon was shot, the Regiment Subadar wrote to Captain Skene to come out of the fort saying, 'we will not kill any of you, we will send you all to your own country'; so Captain Skene wrote to the Ranee to tell the sepoys to take their oath and to sign her name on the letter, all the Hindoos took their oath :- 'if any of us touch your people just as we eat beef'; and those Mussulmans took their oath, 'if any of us touch you just as we eat pork.' And the Ranee signed her name on the top of the letter and it was given to Captain Skene. As soon as he read the note every one was agreed to it." Appendix A.

† The Bengalee says, "then a Kherkie or secret door was treacherously thrown open by the natives within. Captain Powys shot and killed one of the traitors, but was shot dead in return by the brother of the man he had slain. The handful of Europeans in the fort were now for a moment paralysed—they knew not how to overcome such odds from within and without. They, however, mustered courage, and when they observed that a rush was made from outside through the passage, they all ascended the terrace of a high building in the fort, and thence kept firing on the enemy below. The latter then proposed a parley, promising to allow the Europeans to quit the fort unmolested provided they surrendered themselves and their arms to them." Appendix A.

The supply of ammunition was now nearly exhausted and the stock of provisions seriously diminished. There was no hope of succour. The men might die fighting their way out. But the women and children had to be considered. Reluctantly they " were induced to open the gates relying on the most solemn promises made to Major Skene that the lives of all would be spared."* About 4 or 5 P. M. the news spread through the town that the garrison were coming down from the fort. " I also went to the gateway," says a native servant, " when my master with mem sahib and other officers came down, I saluted him and could not help weeping. The sowars and sepoys pelted us with stones and obliged us to separate. All the officers went to one side and the servants joined me." Men, women and children were taken to a garden near the city and all were slaughtered without mercy. Three days after the bodies were gathered together and buried in a pit. Skene, while he was awaiting the last stroke, told a sepoy who was standing beside him " that it was idle for the mutineers to hope that England would be denuded of all her bold sons by the destruction of the handful of men that were now at their mercy." On the accursed city which had sinned with the sepoys the wrath of the bold and patient British Soldier was not long in falling.

About two hundred miles eastward of Jhansi lies the station of Nowgong which was garrisoned at the time by the Right Wing and headquarters 12th Regiment Native Infantry (strength about 400 bayonets), the Left Wing of the 14th Irregular Cavalry (strength about 219 men) and the 4th Company 9th battalion of Native Artillery (strength about 66 men) with No. 18 Light Field Battery attached. The force thus mainly consisted of regiments which had one wing stationed at Jhansi. At the end of April, the disaffection shewed itself as at Barrackpore and Meerut in incendiary fires. Thirteen days after the outbreak at Meerut (10th May), the Native Officer Commanding the Cavalry told Major Kirke, who commanded the station, that his corps had learned by letter from Delhi that every Christian there had been murdered. " He appeared to wonder at the little the Europeans knew of affairs in Delhi while his men and himself were in communication with the place. His neglect, or disobedience of orders, a few hours after was very suspicious ; and from that night the men and officers, by their demeanour, awoke strong distrust in our minds." No sign of it was however shewn to the

Nowgong.

---

* *Captain P. G. Scot's Report, Appendix A.*

troopers. The officers visited their pickets and during the day went to the lines, and talked with the native officers : " they were received with freezing politeness." The 12th native infantrymen and the artillery, however, " liked the arrangements very much ; they were greatly gratified by the confidence in them shewn by the officers who slept among them." Major Kirke reported to Major-General Sir Hugh Wheeler, Commanding the Division, that the men were well disposed and pleased. The General replied that the report was highly satisfactory. On the 30th of May, it was reported to Major Kirke that mutiny was being openly plotted in the Artillery lines. Four men, who were named by the Native Officer as being most active in propagating sedition, were dismissed from the Company's service and the Commandant ordered that the guns of the battery should be placed every night in front of the quarterguard of the 12th Native Infantry. "I think" writes an officer "that the men of the company felt affronted and humiliated by this measure."

On the 4th of June four out of the five companies of the wing of the 12th Native Infantry sent a petition stating they were anxious to be led against the rebels. At 11 A.M. a letter brought by express was put into the hands of Major Kirke. It was from Dunlop at Jhansi, written at 4 P.M. the previous afternoon. " The artillery and infantry have broken into mutiny and have entered the Star Fort. No one has been hurt yet. Look out for stragglers." Kirke at once summoned the native officers of the 12th Native Infantry : he expressed his pleasure at the receipt of the petition and told them that he would report their loyalty to the Governor-General. The native officers, having again warmly asserted their fidelity, were told of the mutiny at Jhansi. They at once wrote a letter to their regimental comrades reproaching them for their conduct, imploring them to return to their allegiance and informing them that they intended to fight against the rebels. "The letter was at once despatched by express." That afternon the troops were paraded in undress, the right wing at its own lines, the artillery company half way between its lines and those of the 12th, the wings of the irregulars in their lines. "The 12th and artillery were then separately asked if they would stand by the Government : when it came to the turn of the artillery company the old subahdar* expressed at once his loyalty to Government with a boldness and enthusiasm that did him high honour. It was a fine sight to see that old man of fifty years' service, struggling with the difficulty of

---

* Subahdar. *Sūbah*, a province—*Sūbahdār*, the governor of a province. As a military term, Subahdar is the highest grade of native officer.

weakened lungs and organs of speech time had impaired to proclaim loudly a loyalty most of those about him had no great sympathy with; they however followed his example, and seized hold of the Queen's colour of the 12th, which was at hand, and said they would be loyal; on their return to their lines, they embraced their guns, and were enthusiastic about their loyalty. During their absence from the guns, Seetaram (a non-commissioned officer) stood beside them with spikes and a hammer ready to spike them in case of the company mutinying ".* The officers were much gratified at the conduct of the men, and word of it was sent to Jhansi. Two parties of the 14th Irregulars consisting of forty sowars each under a native officer were also despatched to Jhansi and Fatehpore, the chief town of a district of the same name in the Jhansi division. On the 7th of June a report was received from the Officer Commanding the Jhansi Detachment stating that he had halted at Mowraneepore (thirty miles from Nowgong) on hearing that all the Europeans at Jhansi had been murdered. Two days later a shepherd came into the cantonment and told them that Dunlop and Taylor had been shot on the Jhansi parade. "The 12th men at Nowgong seemed horrified at the news: most certainly many of them were sincerely so; and that night the men of the artillery volunteered to serve against the rebels." The next morning a letter came from the Native Magistrate at "Mowraneepore saying that he had heard of the murder of every European at Jhansi, that he had received a perwannah (order) to the effect that the Ranee of Jhansi was seated on the guddee (throne) and that he was to carry on business as hitherto". At sunset the six artillery guns were according to the recent order brought before the quarter-guard of the infantry. The new guards were being marched off to relieve the old ones, when a number of the men began to load, and three Sikhs stepped to the front. Kana, "a tall dare devil," fired at the native non-commissioned officer and shot him dead. They then made a rush at the guns. "The sergeant, Raite by name, drew his sword and was fired at; I think one of the artillerymen interceded to save him." The native gunners not only did nothing to protect their guns, but in about a minute's time they fired grape at the tents on parade that the officers slept in, and subsequently two rounds more at the officers.

The officers, who were assembled at the mess-house, instantly hurried down to the lines. They found groups of panic-stricken sepoys. They

---

* *Letter from Captain P. G. Scot*, dated Rewah, August 16th, 1857, *Appendix B*.

could not induce them to advance on the guns. A party of the mutineers assembled in front of the mess-house with one gun, and Major Kirke, finding that the men who were with him would not act on the offensive, ordered the officers to abandon the cantonment. Accompanied by a large number of women and children and some eighty sepoys who had remained faithful to their Colours, they set forth for Chutterpore, the capital of a small state of the same name. They had not gone far when they took the wrong road. It however soon fell dark and, as they were concealed from the cantonment by a hill, they made an attempt to regain the main road by striking across country, but they found the ground impassable. This was the luckiest incident that happened to them. The troopers, after they had burnt the bungalows, had gone forth in quest of them and were scouring the main thoroughfares for them. "They had reproached the infantry for not having slain us." Guided by a native boatman, the fugitives made their way through the solid blackness of the night and arrived at Chutterpore as the dawn began to break. The state was governed by a Ranee who treated them with considerable kindness, though some of her chief officers were Muhammadans and seemed to sympathise with the rebels. "They told us that a message had come from Nowgong that the troops had risen for *deen* (religion) and that the Ranee must not shelter us." But the Ranee remained firm in her determination. She not only sheltered them but also sent out troops to protect them when there was an alarm that the rebels were approaching. After enjoying her hospitality for two days the fugitives set forth for Allahabad. On the morning of the 15th they reached Mahoba. "The Rajah was very kind and hospitable to us. Next morning we left under an escort furnished by the Ranee of Nowgong." During the day, news, having reached them of the mutiny at Banda and at Hamirpore, the chief town of a district in the Allahabad division, they determined to change their route. On the night of the 17th, they started for Mirzapore or Chanar, and, after a long tramp, they encamped under some hills near a pass which ran through two hills. Their guide had led them into a trap. A body of bandits held the pass and demanded a round sum of money before they would let them go through it. By the advice of the native officers it was paid. Next morning, however, as they were on the point of leaving their camp, the bandits opened fire on them. "The sepoys, numbering from eighty to ninety men replied for a few minutes with a wild fire, as they could scarcely see an assailant; and at length ten or twelve fell back, and coul not be got to advance. Lieutenant Townsend waited with Lieutenant Ewart, myself and two or three sepoys at a tree, firing at any men we could see. He shewed the most perfect courage amid the confusion and the fire, which was brisk; and I regret very greatly to say that he was shot through the heart, and died in about half a minute, merely exclaiming, 'O God I am hit'. The main body was far off, in a hopeless and rapid retreat, that the officer was vainly trying to stop or slacken; and I had to leave this brave young man's body where it fell."* The small band fell back keeping the bandits who pursued them at a distance by turning on them frequently. When they again crossed the Chutterpore border the pursuit ceased. The fugitives pressed forward but their progress was slow as the women and children were on foot. "Before two o'clock, Major Kirke, the Sergeant-Major Lascar and Mrs. Smalley, the wife of the band-master, all died of sunstroke or apoplexy." The Major alone was buried "the sepoys helping with their bayonets to dig his grave." At 3 p.m. they entered the village of Kabrai. "The men gave out that they were rebels, taking us to the Banda Nawab to be killed by the King of Delhi's orders; they feared to escort us otherwise." † When dusk fell, the sepoys told their officers that the ruse had been discovered, that they could protect them no further, and that they must make their way by themselves. "This was said sadly and respectfully." As soon as it was dark the majority of the party again set forth for Banda. ‡ On the morning of the 25th of June they were attacked by some villagers. They had only nine horses amongst them and "we were all crippled for action by having some one behind us or a child before." Scot's horse was struck by a spear and instantly set off at full gallop. He had Mrs. Mawe's child before him and the Bandmaster behind and so was unable to stop him. He was followed by Lieutenant Remington and Ensign Franks. They wandered under the glare of a June sun in the glittering heat of a brown parched land till they saw a ravine with some water. "We all rode towards it; the descent was very steep, we all dismounted and had a drink." The horses were getting water when two armed villagers appeared and bade them be

---

* *Captain P. G. Scot's Report, dated Rewah, August 16th, 1857, Appendix B.* This Report differs in some respects from the *Report, dated Nagode, July 28th, 1857.*

† *Captain P. G. Scot's Report, dated Nagode, July 28th, 1857, Appendix B.*

‡ Some of the Europeans and all the Eurasians elected to remain behind. "The party that moved on consisted of (Captain Scot) Lieutenants Ewart, Barber, Jackson, Remington and Franks; Dr. Mawe, 12th Native Infantry, and Mrs. Mawe and child; Mr. Harvey Kirke, Mrs. Smalley and child; and Sergeant Kerchoff and his wife." *Captain P. G. Scot's Report, dated Nagode, July 28th, 1857, Appendix B.*

off. Mounting their horses they rode away. Dr. Mawe and his wife however fell off their horse as he was starting and were left behind. "We sat down on the ground awaiting our death, for we felt sure they would come and murder us; poor fellow he was very weak, and his thirst frightful; I said I would go and bring some water in my dress and his cap Just as I was leaving him the two villagers came down; they took 80. rupees from him which he had round his waist, and his gold watch. I had on a handsome guard-ring which they saw. I went towards the nullah and drew off my wedding ring and twisting it in my hair, replaced my guard; they came to me and pulled it off my finger. I tore part of the skirt of my dress to bring the water in, but it was of no use, for when I returned my beloved's eyes were fixed, and though I called and tried to restore him and poured water into his mouth, it only rattled in his throat; he never spoke to me again. I held him in my arms till he sank gradually down. I felt frantic but could not cry; I knew the being I had idolized nearly fifteen years was gone, and I was alone; so I bound his head and face in my dress for there was no earth to bury him."* The pain in her hands and feet was intense and she went down to the ravine and sat down on a stone in the water. When night fell she would stagger forth into the darkness and seek her child. In about an hour she was found by some villagers who took her out of the water. They made her walk to a neighbouring village and that night they sent her in a dhooly to Banda. "She was met on the way by a palkee the Nawab had sent out when he heard of her being in the village. The Nawab had sent orders to all the villagers round not to injure Europeans." The trooper who accompanied the palkee told her that a little child and three gentlemen were at Banda. "How I hoped it was Lottie. On arrival I found my poor little one; she was greatly blistered from the sun; the officers were Captain Scot and the two young men† and the Bandmaster." Soon after Dr. Mawe was left behind, Lieutenant J. H. Barber fell dead from his horse. Two days later Lieutanant Ewart also died of sunstroke. As the remainder were drinking water at a village, they observed a signal given by one of the rustics. Sergeant Kerchoff was too slow in mounting and he was stunned with blows

---

* *Mrs. Mawe's Narrative of the Mutiny of the 12th Regiment, Native Infantry, at Nowgong.*

† Lieutenants Frank and Remington.

Of the men left behind at Kabrai, forty-one persons, drummers, buglers and their families ultimately reached Banda in safety.

and left for dead. Lieutenant Jackson, Mr. Harvey Kirke and Mrs. Kerchoff were able to get away. They were well treated when they entered the Adzighur territory; and after resting some days were sent on to Nagode * which they reached on the 29th of June. It was due to the protection and kindness of the Ranee of Adzighur and the Nawab of Banda that the fugitives from Nowgong owed their lives. The Nawab had a most difficult part to play. Banda was a military station garrisoned by detachments from regiments quartered at Cawnpore. At the time of the outbreak at Meerut three companies of the 1st Regiment Native Infantry, had recently arrived there from the great military cantonment on the borders of Oudh. On the 14th of June news reached Banda of the revolt at Cawnpore and the men on detachment duty at once exhibited their mutinous intention at head-quarters. An attempt was made to disarm them by the aid of the Nawab's troops and it failed. The Nawab had, at his peril, given shelter to the women and children in his palace. It was now determined that the Europeans should retire to British territory, which they reached, safely guarded. The mutineers, after plundering and burning the bungalows, started with the treasure and ammunition to join their comrades at Cawnpore. Throughout the little territory of Banda, the revolt swiftly spread and all signs of British supremacy vanished. Never was revolution more rapid, never more complete. Anarchy, murder and plunder raged in the adjacent districts. The Nawab attempted to frame a government and maintain order, but like Scindia and many other chiefs he was unable to extinguish the flames of religious passion and hate which had been kindled. Left isolated, without power to deal with the threats and the inducements that were held out to him, he was drawn into the vortex of revolt.

In the heart of Hindustan about eighty miles north of Jhansi and sixty-five miles south of Agra rises from a wide and arid veldt a vast block of basalt capped with sandstone. On it stands bold and definite, three hundred feet above the plain, the fortress of Gwalior. The ramparts, built above the steep sides perpendicular by nature or art, conform to the outlines of the summit, which is a table-land about a mile and three quarters in length and half a mile in breadth. "The area within," says an old writer, "is full of noble buildings, reservoirs of water, wells and

---

* Nagode.—A military station in the Central Indian Agency, distant a hundred and eight miles from Allahabad. The regiment quartered there in 1857 was the 52nd Native Infantry which remained loyal till the end of August. They then plundered and burnt the station but a few sepoys escorted the officers and their families to Mirzapore.

cultivated land, so that it is really a little district in itself." At the northeast of the plateau is the magnificent palace of the ancient Kings of Gwalior whose lofty bastions and curtain walls break the line of the ramparts. Here is the main approach, protected on the outside by a massive wall. Seven monumental gates, placed at intervals, guard the steep ascent which rises from the ancient city that nestles below. Protected by a wall encircling the mountain base, it was in olden days a large and prosperous settlement. Standing in the principal road leading from Agra to Malwa, Gujarat and the Deccan the Fortress of Gwalior was of great strategic importance. The early English travellers used to speak of it as the Gibraltar of the east. Hindu and Muhammadan Chiefs contended for the citadel the possession of which " was deemed as necessary to the ruling Emperors of Hindustan as Dover Castle might be to the Saxon and Norman Kings of England." It was won by stratagem by one of Babar's Generals and the Moghul Emperors used it as " the Bastille of Hindustan." On the disruption of the Moghul Empire it fell into the hands of a petty Jat Prince known as the Rana of Gohud. From him it was wrested by the Mahrattas, but, in February 1780 Warren Hastings sent a detachment under Major Popham, a gallant and daring officer, to protect the small principality of Gohud from the encroachments of Mahadjee Scindia, the greatest and most active of the Mahratta leaders whose formidable army, organized under French officers, made him virtual master of Hindustan. Popham, after expelling the Mahrattas from Gohud, assaulted and captured the fortress of Lahar, without a battering ram, by the sheer pluck of his men. He had set his heart on "the glorious object" as he called it of taking the fortress of Gwalior. He lay about the fort for two months maturing his plan. On the 3rd of August in the evening Popham ordered a party to be in readiness to march under the command of Captain William Bruce, and put himself at the head of two battalions which were immediately to follow the storming party. "To prevent, as much as possible, any noise in approaching or descending the rock a kind of shoes, of woollen cloth, were made for the sepoys and stuffed with cotton." At eleven o'clock the whole detachment moved out from their camp eight miles from Gwalior. Guided by some neighbouring banditti, they proceeded through unfrequented paths and reached their goal a little before daybreak. Just as Captain Bruce arrived at the foot of the rock, he saw the lights which accompanied the rounds moving along the ramparts and heard the sentinels cough. When the lights were gone, the wooden ladders were placed against the rock. One of the bandits first mounted and returned with an account that the guard had retired to sleep. "Lieutenant Cameron, our Engineer, next mounted, and tied a rope ladder to the battlement of the wall, this kind of ladder being the only one adapted to the purpose of scaling the wall in a body (the wooden ones only serving to ascend the crag of the rock, and to assist in fixing the rope ladder)." Captain Bruce and twenty sepoys scaled the wall and assembled beneath the parapet. Three sepoys, however, incautiously fired at some of the garrison who lay asleep near them. Instantly an alarm was raised and many of the garrison ran to the spot. But they were stopped by the warm fire kept up by the small party of grenadiers until Major Popham with reinforcements came to their aid. The garrison then retreated to the inner buildings and discharged a few rockets, but soon afterwards retreated precipitately to the gate; whilst the principal officers thus deserted assembled together in one house, and hung out a white flag. Major Popham sent an officer to give them assurance of quarter and protection; "and thus in the space of two hours this important and astonishing fortress was completely in our possession; we had only twenty men wounded and none killed." Warren Hastings told the House of Lords that Gwalior was "taken by a manœuvre which for the secrecy and boldness of its execution equals anything to be met with in history." The Rana claimed possession of the fort and we gave it back to him. He, however, proving unfaithful to the British Government was abandoned to his fate. In 1784 Mahadjee laid siege to the fortress, bribed the garrison, and marched into it. From that time, Gwalior became the home of the Scindia family and the capital of their kingdom. Ten years later, Mahadjee Scindia died and was succeeded by his grand-nephew, Daulat Rao Scindia, who by the strength and discipline of his army became the most formidable member of the Mahratta confederacy. The Treaty of Bassein (31st December 1801), by which the English engaged to restore the Peshwa to power on condition of his becoming a subsidiary prince, was a grave blow to the power of the confederacy and sorely wounded the Mahratta pride. The Mahratta Chief of Nagpore (commonly called the Raja of Berar) and Daulat Rao Scindia could not tolerate the abandonment of the Mahratta independence, and on the 3rd of August 1803 began the second Mahratta war. The well-contested and hardly won victories of Assaye and Laswari broke the power of Scindia, and both in Upper and Central India he was compelled to enter into a defensive treaty and make a large cession of territory. When the war broke out, the Governor of Gwalior undertook to surrender the fortress to the English, but secretly instigated the Commandant not to deliver it up at the appointed time. It was therefore invested by British troops and on the 5th of February 1804 they gained possession of it. But Scindia had concluded the treaty of peace under the hope that by the words of the treaty the fort of Gwalior would remain in his possession. The Marquis of Wellesley, by a not wholly inadmissible interpretation of the letter of the treaty, declared that justice did not require us to surrender the fort, while sound policy imperatively called upon us to keep it out of Scindia's hands. General Wellesley considered that "the argument is on our side"; but he wrote to Malcolm "I would sacrifice Gwalior, or every frontier of India, ten times over, in order to preserve our credit for scrupulous good faith, and the advantages and honours we gained by the late war and the late peace; and we must not fritter them away in arguments drawn from overstrained principles of the laws of nations, which are not understood in this country. What brought me through many difficulties in the war and the negotiations of peace? The British good faith and nothing else." *

In 1805 Lord Cornwallis again landed in India as Governor-General and on the 22nd of November a fresh treaty was concluded which ceded Gwalior and Gohud to Scindia. The camp which Daulat Rao pitched in a small circular valley surrounded by barren hills to the south of the fort grew into a handsome town and retains at the present day its old name Lashkar, the camp. In March 1827 Daulat Rao died leaving no son, but in accordance with his last wishes, a youth of eleven years, belonging to an obscure branch of the family, was adopted and placed on the Guddee under the title of Ali Jah Jan Khwájah Rao Scindia. In 1843 he also died without leaving a son, and his widow, a wayward, passionate but clever girl of twelve years of age with the concurrence of the chiefs of the state and the army, adopted a lad of about eight years of age, the nearest, though a very distant relative of the late Maharajah. Disorders arose in the state and the insolence of an overgrown mutinous army compelled Lord Ellenborough, then Governor-General, to take prompt action with regard to Gwalior. On December 28th, 1843, at Maharajpore, the English once more encountered the Mahrattas. They fought with all their ancient valour, but had to retreat after a desperate resistance. Three thousand of the enemy lay dead on the field and fifty-six superb bronze guns were the prize of the victors. The same day another British force encountered another portion of the

---

* *Despatches of the Duke of Wellington*, Vol. II, page 1106.

Mahratta army at Punniar, twelve miles from Gwalior, and gained a complete victory. The victorious forces met beneath the walls of the ancient stronghold which on the 4th of January was taken possession of by the contingent force commanded by British officers. On the 13th of January a fresh treaty was signed and ratified. The administration of the State was entrusted to a Council of six nobles. "The Council of Regency," wrote Lord Ellenborough to the Duke of Wellington, "cannot be changed without our consent. It is to act according to our advice during the Maharajah's minority, which terminates, when he becomes eighteen, on the 19th of January 1854." Two years before the stated interval the British Government dissolved the Council of Regency, declared the minority of the young sovereign at an end, and with his consent appointed Dunker Rao, a young Brahmin of great ability and integrity, who had already proved his talent for administration, Diwan or Prime Minister.* Dunker Rao though young in years was worthy of his high office and will always hold a high rank among the eminent Indian Statesmen who have done so much to consolidate our Indian Empire by their able management of a great Feudatory State. He improved the revenue and judicial administration, and with a firm hand he attempted to put down bribery and extortion. The natural consequences followed. In May 1854, Colonel Malcolm, the Political Agent at Gwalior, having been appointed Resident at Baroda, Captain Macpherson,† Resident at Bhopal, was appointed to succeed him. Two months however elapsed before the new Resident could reach Gwalior. During that time the low courtiers and dexterous intriguers who surrounded the young Rajah persuaded him that he should take into his own hands the administration of the State and dismiss his Prime Minister. But Scindia was a born soldier, not an administrator. "His education had been nearly confined to the use of his horse, lance, and gun, whence his tastes were purely and passionately military. He seemed to enjoy no occupation save drilling,

---

* "I have seldom seen a man of greater intelligence and refinement of manners, or one who impressed me so favourably as did the Prime Minister of Gwalior. There was that in his serene, half sad yet intellectual countenance which would have made a noble study for Fra Angelica." *Campaigning Experiences in Rajpootana and Central India during the Suppression of the Mutiny, 1857 and 1858, by Mrs. Henry Duberly, page 159.*

Colonel Grove Somerset wrote—"I look upon Dunker Rao as a gentleman, an honest and faithful man and my friend."

† He attained about this time, by brevet, the army rank of Major. "In his regiment the good health enjoyed by his seniors prevented him from ever rising above the rank of Captain." *Memorials of Service in India From the Correspondence of the late Major Samuel Charters Macpherson, C.B., edited by his brother William Macpherson, qage 297.*

C

dressing, ordering, transforming, feasting, playing with his troops, and the unwearied study of books of evolution, and he grudged no expenditure connected with that amusement." Scindia had the Mahratta quickness of apprehension but the lad was impatient of public business, and when Macpherson reached Gwalior, public affairs had drifted into the utmost confusion. The new Political Agent had a difficult and delicate game to play, but no man was better adapted by nature and training to play it.

Samuel Charters Macpherson. Samuel Charters Macpherson is one of the many sons of England who have gone forth for her, not only conquering and to conquer, but saving and to save*. He was the second son born (6th January 1806) to Dr. Hugh Macpherson, Professor of Greek in the University of Aberdeen. In consequence of delicate health in childhood, he learnt his rudiments at his father's knee but growing tall and strong, he was sent to the College of Edinburgh. Here he busied himself, not only with classic and moral philosophy but also with botany, chemistry and geology. At seventeen he was entered at Trinity College, Cambridge. But, as a systematic course of study has always been considered necessary for the legal profession in Scotland, he left Cambridge after a residence of two years to read for the Scotch bar. Nobler destinies were in store for him. His eyes, always weak, were over-taxed by too close a study of Political Economy and Civil law: they became subject to an affection which interfered seriously with his studies. It was necessary that he should choose another profession. A cadetship in the East India Company's service was obtained for him and he sailed for Madras early in 1827. On his arrival, he was posted to the 8th Regiment of Native Infantry. After four years of regimental duty, he was appointed to the Staff as Assistant Surveyor General—an office which gave him ample opportunity for continuing his favourite scientific studies. He wrote to a young friend at Cambridge, "The temple of written knowledge has been inexorably shut against me since I was the age you are. I catch but passing and desultory glimpses of what goes on within, but I am a worshipper without the gate, and improve my uncommon opportunities of studying this strange race, and the land which it inhabits, and so keeping my mind active and enlarged in physical and moral views, and ready for any march that fortune may assign to it." While engaged on the geographical survey of the land and acquiring a knowledge of the people by timely intercourse with all classes, Macpherson was summoned to join his regiment, which had been engaged for some time in operations

---

* *Bibliotheca Pasterum, Vol. IV, collated by John Ruskin.*

against a native chief, the Rajah or Zemindar of Goomsar. Fortune had assigned to the highly educated Scotch lad a long career among the barbarous aboriginal tribes who occupy the hill tracts of Orissa on the south-west frontier of Bengal. It was a life full of peril, full of anxiety and responsibility, full of wild adventure and barbarism, and it was also full of noble accomplishment. Among these tribes human sacrifices prevailed. Macpherson studied the religion, which was the foundation of the cruel rite, and the social institutions which contributed to its power. He visited the tribes in their mountain homes; he mixed familiarly and conversed freely with them. They soon became attached to him by personal regard, by their knowledge of his justice, and their experience of his sympathy and kindness. By a well-devised and judicious series of conciliatory measures and by the introduction of a system of pure justice, the extinction of the enormity was effected among two of the most important tribes. The good work begun by Macpherson was carried on by worthy successors till the barbarous rite became extinct throughout all the tracts of the Orissian hills. In 1848, the malaria of the jungles having sunk deep into his system, he was obliged to take leave to England to recruit his health. On his way home, at Cairo, Outram introduced himself to Macpherson as one who had "long watched his career with the deepest interest and admiration." Soon after his return to India (1853), he was appointed Political Agent at Bhopal, "a very pretty and pleasant country," from whence he was transferred to the more important office of Resident at the Court of Gwalior. There is little need to point the moral of such a story as the Indian Mutiny, but of its many morals there is one chief arrowhead of which we should not lose sight. In the offices vital to our safety, it is not sufficient to have clever administrators, but men of sense, courage, honour and sympathy. Such in truth were John Lawrence, Henry Lawrence and Charters Macpherson, holding at the time of the outbreak three of the most vital posts in India.

On assuming office at Gwalior, Macpherson did not attempt to play the role of ruler under a thin veil. He considered it his first duty to conciliate the friendship of both the Prince and his Minister, and to offer, in a mode that could not injure the impression of their power, every advice and admonition. His main aim was to raise the young Maharajah as high and make him as useful in independent action as he was capable of being made. Between the Deccan Brahmin and the son of the Scotch Professor there quickly arose a friendship, and their relations, rightly accepted, aided and increased the vigour and authority of both many reforms in the administration of the State were introduced, and cultivation and prosperity increased. Over the young Rajah Macpherson exercised a strong influence, and led him to extend his thoughts beyond his pleasures and the means of providing for them. In the spring of 1857, Scindia, accompanied by the Resident, the Diwan and several of the Gwalior Chiefs, paid a visit to Calcutta. Scindia and Dunker Rao inspected the colleges and schools as models to be reproduced at Gwalior. The Maharajah went down the Hughly and saw a spinning-mill at work. " On his way he was particularly boastful, until he passed the house occupied by the Viceroy of Oudh. The sight sobered him in an instant and his zeal for civilization instantly increased." * Lord Canning, however, at his last audience, allayed any fears that may have arisen in his mind with regard to the permanence of his own dynasty. The Governor-General complimented him on the successful administration of his territories and the wise introduction of useful reforms, and added that, if such measures were persevered in and he died without male issue, the Government would follow the ancient Hindu custom of recognising an adopted successor. The remark made a deep impression on the Maharajah and the courtesy and generosity of Lord Canning were powerful factors in winning the fidelity of Scindia.

The Maharajah returned to his capital in April and, shortly after his arrival, gave a grand fête. " The last grand military display we had, " wrote a lady, " was the blowing up of a mud fort ; it was a very striking sight." Three weeks pass, and, on the 16th of May, tidings reached Gwalior from Agra of the outbreak at Meerut. " It burst on us at Gwalior like a thunder-clap and paralysed us with horror ". † They were a handful of Englishmen and women in the capital of a Native State garrisoned entirely by native troops. The Chief was a young Mahratta. His army consisted of ten thousand men. In addition there was the Gwalior Contingent, one of those bodies of troops which the British Government had insisted on certain Native Princes and Chiefs maintaining, in addition to their own armies necessary for the civil administration of their respective territories. They were recruited from the same class as the Bengal sepoy and also from the same country—Oudh. The Chiefs had no control over the troops enlisted in their name and paid out of their

---

*The Times. (From our own Correspondent.)

† "We did not see the terrible details till a day or two afterwards, when we were dining with the Stuarts : I remember our gloomy forebodings, and how we talked of what had happened. Little more than a month after, out of the nine people assembled together that night, there were only three survivors ". A Lady's escape from Gwalior by R.M. Coopland.

coffers, so the men had not the usual ties of mercenary troops, for while they received the money of one master, they obeyed another. In May 1857, the Gwalior Contingent was composed of four field batteries of artillery, a small siege train, two regiments of cavalry and seven of infantry, aggregating eight thousand three hundred and eighteen men. The sepoys were of great stature, admirably disciplined. The artillery were thoroughly trained, the cavalry well mounted and the horses well groomed. The greater portion of the force was stationed at Gwalior with outposts at Sipri, Garoli, and Agra. The same day that tidings reached Gwalior of the outbreak at Meerut, came a message from the Lieutenant-Governor of the North-West Provinces asking if a Brigade of the Gwalior contingent could be spared to Agra. The Resident promptly placed at his disposal a Regiment and a half of Infantry, on e hundred horse, and a battery—being one-half of the force at Gwalior. On the evening of the 12th, Macpherson had a long conversation with the Maharajah who was deeply distracted by the accounts and rumours which filled his capital of outbreaks throughout the Northern Provinces and Rajputana. He had closely watched the outbreaks in Bengal ; he must have learnt a good deal when he was at Calcutta, and he apprehended a widespread mutiny of the Sepoy army. "He said that from the greased cartridges, the belief had arisen in the army that the Government intended to strike at the Hindu and Muhammadan religions. That the enemies of our rule had found in that belief a pretext and opportunity. That the confidence of the army in the Government was at an end, and that a wide-spread belief had arisen that they would overthrow it ". But Scindia begged that his troops, his personal services, all his resources might be considered at the disposal of the Governor-General. Morning came, and at the earliest dawn of day, the young Sovereign, with a dark foreboding on his heart, went to the Resident. He earnestly warned him against the expectation that the Contingent troops, if sent to our Provinces, would act against their brethren or abstain from joining them should they revolt. He also urged that "the internal peace of Gwalior, the obedience of the reduced Princes and Thakurs " depended upon the Contingent. Macpherson replied that the first object was simply to gain time for the European force to assemble to crush the rebels, and as they agreed that the Contingent "would not mutiny at least until our Regiments did so," they might meanwhile be useful in cting against plunderers and maintaining our communications. The Resident took the opportunity of suggesting that the domination of the sepoys and the Moghul Emperor must shake the foundation of authority not only in

British Provinces but in every State of Hindustan. " Should the Contingent revolt but above all should our Power be shaken, the Princes and Chiefs of the Rajput, Jat and other ancient races of Gwalior would unite to cast off the Mahratta yoke." Scindia quite understood the force of the suggestion. Thus fortified, Macpherson urged him to influence by his example the surrounding Princes and to counteract the movement of the Contingent and of his sympathizing troops towards rebellion, and to do this by demonstrating, by every act devisable, that he discredited the religious pretext of the movement, that he held that our power must triumph, and that he was, therefore, necessarily one with us. Scindia agreed with the Resident that " at whatever immediate risk to Gwalior, the Lieutenant-Governor's wish for aid from the Contingent should be complied with." The young Maharajah at the suggestion of the Resident summoned Dunker Rao the next day from his country residence. The Prime Minister, though he did not underrate the magnitude and importance of the struggle, " was perfectly confident that it would be at once stamped out by the European force assembling under the Commander-in-Chief, provided that every semblance of ground for the cartridge grievance and cry should be at once removed."

On the 13th of May, the Lieutenant-Governor requested the despatch to Agra of the 18th Regiment of Cavalry and a Battery. The Resident telegraphed to him that, "although their officers considered them still sound, yet if associated with disturbed Corps no one would answer for a moment for their soundness." This warning does not seem to have had much effect, for that day Lieutenant Cockburn started with two hundred horse and six guns. After a rapid march they reached Agra. The horse were, however, mostly detached to strengthen the position at Allygurh, an important city about eighty miles from Meerut and sixty from Agra. * It arrived there just as a wing of the 9th Native Infantry mutinied and carried off the treasure. It returned to Hattras † and behaved well against a body of plunderers, but on the 23rd, a hundred men, shouting *Deen*, moved off to Delhi. They had been corrupted, as Scindia said they would be, by contact with rebellion. Macpherson thought it of

---

* Allygurh, a district containing about 1,900 square miles. The chief town, also called Allygurh, is defended by a famous fortress. It lies on the high road between Cawnpore and Meerut.

† "Hathras (*Hattras*). Town in Aligarh District, North-Western Provinces, and headquarters of Hathras *tahsil*— a well-built and prosperous trading centre, with numerous rick and stone houses." *Hunter's Imerial Gazetteer.*

the highest importance that Scindia should at once, by some act whose profound significance could not be mistaken, demonstrate that he had thrown in his lot with the English. He therefore urged the Maharajah to send the Body Guard of 400 horse and a horsed Battery to Agra. "For it was notorious that the formation of that Guard had been for years, the object next to Scindia's heart, that its Cavalry, composed of Mahrattas of his own caste or kindred, were his companions by day and by night, inseparable from his pleasures and his State; that although pampered soldiers, their fidelity to Scindia might be relied on, and their despatch would certainly import more unequivocally than any other act then possible his co-operation with us." The Maharajah cordially adopted the suggestion, but he requested that his guard might be accompanied by a British officer. He, however, omitted nothing to make the despatch palpably his own act or to heighten its effect. "With high apparent exultation, he made them over next day to Captain Campbell * in the presence of the officers of the Contingent and myself. The day after he marched out with them to their Camp."† Scindia was highly gratified by the Governor-General acknowledging its despatch as a mark of attachment and confidence. On the 22nd of May, at the request of the Lieutenant-Governor, the 1st Contingent Infantry under Major Hennessy moved from Gwalior to Etawah, a civil station about thirty miles away, from which the Magistrate had been compelled to retire by the mutiny of another portion of the 9th Native Infantry. ‡

The following day, the Lieutenant-Governor requested the despatch to Agra of a reserved troop of the 1st Cavalry. Macpherson submitted a repetition of the warning that the Contingent would not act against our troops, their brethren, although he trusted they would still act against broken hordes of plunderers or mutineers. "All believed in the truth of the cartridge grievance, but it affected the Sepoys alone. The great object of the leaders of the revolt, as shewn in every proclamation and newspaper, was to lead the mass of the population to regard the contest as a religious one. Whence they laboured from Calcutta to Lahore to spread the belief that, to destroy Caste the Government had mixed

---

* Captain Campbell was Superintendent of the Durbar Public Works.

† *Report on Gwalior by Major Macpherson, 10th February 1858.*

‡ "Major Hennessy in a very difficult position restored order while the Lieutenant-Governor thanked and promised to reward his corps. Yet it was understood to be in the van of the movement, and, on the mutiny of the Contingent its Soobadar Major assumed command of the whole." *Report on Gwalior by Major Macpherson, 10th February 1858.*

pigs and bullock bones with the peoples food." * An attempt was now made in Gwalior to excite disturbances by the cry that flour, sugar, etc., so polluted had been brought from Agra!! Dunker Rao tried, by a searching enquiry, to expose the falsehood of the malicious rumours. This roused the ire of the sepoys and, on the 26th of May, about the end of the feast of Ramzan, their fanatical zeal ran so high that they insulted the Diwan on his venturing to visit the Resident in cantonments, where he had gone to reside in order to be near the electric telegraph and the Brigadier. The attitude of the sepoys was so threatening that Dunker Rao, afraid of personal violence, had to leave his carriage and return to the town by a by-path on horse-back. Major Macpherson on hearing what had occurred, arranged to return to the Residency next day. The following morning the Resident visited Scindia at his request and found him oppressed with anxiety. He spoke long of the state of affairs. "He observed that amongst the most affected of the Contingent, and some of his own men from our provinces, nightly meetings for administering pledges—as on Ganges Water—amid infinite boastings of the destruction of the English power and of all Christians were very rife." He then said the feelings evinced by the sepoys towards the Diwan when he attempted to visit the Resident in Cantonments made his going there impossible. "For with his life, in fact, was imperilled our great object to avoid giving to the leaders of the revolt the least pretext for forcing on an outbreak while we expected the fall of Delhi to change the whole aspect of things." He therefore begged, as essential to the security of their intercourse, that Major Macpherson should live at the Residency, or anywhere else the Resident pleased save in cantonments beyond Scindia's jurisdiction. The Resident told him that he had anticipated his wishes. Scindia then asked permission to guard the Residency and large storehouse with his own instead of the Contingent troops, "when," he added, "the Residency may also become, as you desire, a place of refuge for the ladies of the Cantonments, such as has been provided in Agra and Jhansi and is most essential here." Major Macpherson consented to the Residency being guarded by His Highness' troops alone. He, however, informed the Maharajah that, though he agreed generally with his views regarding the Contingent, its officers confided very strongly in their men. Scindia said that, their confidence was to him wholly incomprehensible, and added emphatically "The Contingent Sepoys have entirely ceased to be servants of your Government, and this I say expressly with a

---

Report on Gwalior by Major Macpherson, 10th February 1858.

view to acquit myself of responsibility." * The Resident at once informed the Brigadier of Scindia's formal warning.

Brigadier Ramsay who commanded the Contingent at Gwalior was, like John Hearsey at Barrackpore and Hugh Wheeler at Cawnpore, a gallant old soldier, with a large knowledge of the sepoy, of his habits and of his language, and, perceiving in his men little evidence of change from the old discipline, manners and shew of personal devotion, could not understand the transformation which the blind fury of fanatical zeal had wrought in them. He considered that the removal of the ladies, unless imperatively necessary, would indicate want of confidence in the fidelity of the troops, and he "determined to say nothing on the subject." The next day there was, however, a strong rumour that the troops were to mutiny that night, set fire to the lines and massacre their officers. The Brigadier reluctantly consented to the women and children being sent to the Residency. The Diwan was with the Resident when the women arrived. He instantly rode off to inform His Highness. " He came straight at speed with a strong body of horse and posted parties of it, and of foot so as to make safe the Residency and the roads from Cantonments both to it and to his Palace lest the officers should need either." That night the infantry and cavalry officers slept in their lines and the artillery officers and the old Brigadier before the guns. The belief of the officers of the Bengal Army in the loyalty of their men was too often a grievous mistake. But the calm courage and high sacrifice by which, standing upon their views of duty, they illustrated their generous error must command admiration for ever.

<small>Brigadier Ramsay.</small>

Next morning, at the earnest request of Scindia, who could no longer confide their safety to those of his troops recruited from our Provinces, the ladies were sent from the Residency to one of his palaces. "The natives of Gwalior," says one who was present, "crowded to a sight such as had never been seen in their streets before. Fifteen or sixteen carriages dashing through, surrounded by hundreds of wild Mahratta horsemen, filled with English ladies and children. A gallop of four or five miles through heat and dust brought us to the Rajah's palace." Major Macpherson at once sent a telegram to Mr. Colvin informing him what had taken place and that it was his intention "to send the ladies under escort of a body of horse to Agra." He asked that Scindia's body-guard should meet them at Dholpore, the capital of a Native State of the same name

---

Report on Gwalior by Major Macpherson, 10th February 1858.

on the high road to that city. The Brigadier, on reading the telegram, took a fatal step. "I took on myself," he writes, "to report to Mr. Colvin that we had slept in the lines the previous night, that all was quiet and confidence increasing, and that I considered Scindia was disposed to enhance his own services at the expense of the contingent." The Brigadier also wrote to Major Macpherson that he apprehended no outbreak and that he thought the ladies should return. "Two ladies, Mrs. Meade and Mrs. Murray, in opposition to the most urgent solicitations of Major Macpherson, returned to Cantonments late in the afternoon, and the news of their having done so immediately spread through the station, and had the most beneficial effect on the men generally, who it was reported to me had been greatly hurt at the distrust implied by their leaving the Cantonments. Many enquiries were made of the other officers, whose wives and children had not returned, and voluntary offers of protection and even of rescue were made to their officers by many other men." It was never clear whether in this instance, as in many others, there may not have been as much of weakness and apprehension as of wicked purpose in the conduct and speeches of armed men angered by false rumours which had been spread with a systematic endeavour to sow distrust and ill-feeling between them and their officers. The Brigadier added—"I am happy to say that the rest of the ladies returned to Cantonments this morning, and I consider that the excitement caused by the above occurrences has, so far as this Cantonment is concerned, subsided."* On the 1st of June, the Governor-General telegraphed to Gwalior, "Convey my thanks at once to Scindia for his kind and thoughtful attention, as well as his energetic measures for the security of the ladies in the Cantonment. It gives me the greatest pleasure to have to acknowledge these repeated proofs of his attachment to the British Government."

On the 7th of June, the Officer Commanding at Jhansi requested aid from Gwalior. He merely wished to reduce to submission fifty men of the 12th Native Infantry who had seized the treasure. The rest of the troops he considered continued loyal. Captain Murray, with a wing of the 4th Contingent Infantry and a Battery, was sent to quell the handful of mutineers at Jhansi. However, they had not marched three days, when news reached Murray that every Christian, man, woman and

* "Scindia expressed intense concern on hearing that they were not to remain with him, at least until Delhi fell." *Report on Gwalior by Major Macpherson, 10th February 1858.*

child, had been killed at that city; and he at once returned to Gwalior. The awful extent of the catastrophe soon became known in Scindia's capital. Early on the morning of the 11th, His Highness, "excited and distracted," visited the Resident. He was accompanied by the Diwan. "They said that, from the nearness of Jhansi and the intimacy between its population and that of Gwalior, the atrocity of the massacre and the amount of treasure seized, the Contingent and all in Gwalior were stirred to the very uttermost. All save a very few believed that our Empire was in its last hour." Scindia, the Diwan, and the Mahratta officers, "survivors of the old war" still believed that we should triumph. But their belief was sorely tried. News came daily of fierce and murderous risings. Delhi did not fall. It sore pressed its besiegers. The people of Gwalior shewed by their manner full of insolence, of exaggerated deference or of pity, their ripe conviction that our rule was over. The only question to the soldiery and people was— when Scindia, blinded by the Resident and the Diwan, would accept and act upon the conviction. *[margin: 11th June, Massacre at Jhansi deeply stirred Gwalior.]*

On the 13th, at the Durbar's urgent request, Major Macpherson requested the Brigadier to despatch half a regiment and two guns to two districts near the river Chumbul. The 2nd Regiment was selected for this duty. Major Blake, their Commander, "an Officer who, beyond most well informed, experienced and beloved of his corps" reported "that it would not move though he still hoped that it would come right." But the time had come when Blake would no longer be left in his illusion.

On Sunday morning, the 14th of June, the English attended divine service in the Gwalior Church and took the sacrament of the Lord's Supper. The hot Indian day wore away in misery. All was quiet, but "It was a dread foreboding stillness," says the wife of the chaplain, "I read the lines 'while drooping Sadness enfolds us here like mist' in the *Christian Year* and felt comforted."* They had heard the particulars of the Jhansi massacre and did not know how soon they might meet the same fate themselves. "The dread calm of apprehension was awful. We indeed drank the cup of bitterness to the dregs. The words — 'O death in life, the days that are no more' kept recurring to my memory like a dirge." Noon came. The husband, worn out by his morning's work, lay down to rest; the wife read home letters — "one from my sister on her wedding tour." Suddenly the servants entered with scared faces, and exclaimed that a bungalow was on *[margin: The outbreak at Gwalior, 17th June 1857.]*

"I afterwards recovered that very book." A Lady's escape from Gwalior. By M. Coopland, page 112.

fire and the wind was blowing the flames towards them. When the Chaplain and his wife went out, they saw all the residents were taking the furniture out of their houses and pouring water on the roofs. " The heat was dreadful, the wind high, and the Mess House was soon also a mass of flames. When the sun began to set the wind fell and the flames ceased to spread but the Mess House was a heap of burning fuel." All was again calm : the smoke drifted away and the stars rolled over in their eastern majesty. Nine o'clock and the evening gun is fired. No sooner was its sound lost when the bugles rang out an alarm, followed by the cries of many voices, "To arms! to arms! the Feringhees (Europeans) are come." The artillerymen rushed to their guns, the infantry seized their muskets, and the sepoys, possessed with the spirit of bigotry and maddened with fear, proceeded to destroy all that came in their path. Major Blake, Commandant of the Second Infantry Regiment, a gallant officer much beloved by his men, on hearing the bugles, took a hasty leave of his wife and galloped to the lines. On arriving at the quarter-guard he and his charger were mortally wounded. Lieutenant Pearson, Adjutant of the same regiment, was roused from his bed by the news that the troops had risen and "lined all the roads with the determination of killing all Europeans they could lay their hands on." He quickly mounted his horse and left his wife in charge of a native servant. " I knew what I had to expect," he writes, " and yet it was my duty to go and do my best ; so I went away from my home which I never saw again." No sooner had he got out into the road than he was met by Dr. Mackellar and Lieutenant Ryves (12th N. I.), who had just escaped from Jhansi, and they were hustled down the parade by a mob of sepoys. " Before we got 100 yards we sustained three volleys from men not fifteen yards off, but were not touched. The fourth volley saluted us just as we passed the head of the grenadier company, one ball of which shot my poor charger right through the heart. He fell dead on me, and I had the greatest difficulty in extricating myself expecting a bayonet in my back every moment. In getting from under him I tore off my boot, so proceeded to parade without it, as retreat was hopeless." On reaching the parade, Pearson saw Blake lying shot through the lungs. "His horse lay near him quite dead." The sepoys saw it was useless even to unfasten his coat, " but I insisted on it, and did it myself placing his head on my shoulder, and trying to make him speak ; but it was no good—the poor fellow was dying fast." They were surrounded by hundreds of mutineers but none laid hands on them. The sepoys of Blake's regiment vented their sorrow and anger, declaring vehemently that the foul deed had been done by the men of the Fourth. Some of them made an attempt to carry their wounded Commander to the hospital. But he soon died, and the Brahmin sepoys, to whom the touch of a corpse is deadly pollution, buried him. Meanwhile, Pearson and his two comrades made their way to the Cavalry lines. But here the bullets flew fast. Mackellar and Ryves, being mounted, made a rush for it, forded the river and galloped off towards Agra: and Pearson stood alone barefooted. "Just at this moment three sepoys caught hold of me, and said they would try and save me. They threw off my hat, tore off my trousers and the remaining boot, covered me as well as they could with my horse-cloth, which my groom had brought along with us, and, putting me between the two, the third walked in front; and what between knocking up one man's musket, whose bayonet was just at my back, and declaring I was one of their wives we got through all the sentries and crossed the river. They then wanted me to make the best of my way off, saying that the chances were ten to one that my wife was killed by that time, but I told them plainly I would not try to escape without her. After a great deal of persuading, they took me down the banks of the river (the opposite side of which was regularly lined with sentries to prevent escape) till we came opposite our house, where they set me down, and one man said, ' Now I will go and bring your wife to you if she is alive'; so off he went, and after about twenty minutes of the most agonizing suspense dear M—and I met again. I must say the three sepoys with us behaved splendidly. Seeing poor M—was unable to walk, they tied my horse-cloth in a sort of bag fashion on to a musket, put her into it, and placing the butt and muzzle on their shoulder, carried her this way seven miles till we reached the Residency, by which time I could hardly put my feet to the ground from walking barefoot over the thorny ground. On arriving there we met three other people just escaped, and I got an elephant, on which we all mounted, intending to seek further protection in the Lushkur, with the Maharajah, to whom lots of people had gone; but before we had got half a mile we met nearly a dozen carriages, all in full gallop, accompanied by the body-guard in full retreat back to the Residency." They swiftly turned back, and a few sowars being left to protect them, they soon reached the Residency. The other party of fugitives on the road consisted of Major Macpherson and his sister Mrs. Innes,* Brigadier Ramsay, Captain and Mrs. Maude and child,

---

* Mrs. Innes, wife of General McLeod Innes, V.C.

Captain and Mrs. Murray and two children, and several other persons of whom the majority were women and children.

Brigadier Ramsay and Captains Meade and Murray, finding it useless to attempt reaching the lines, had proceeded with their families under the escort of some faithful sepoys to the Phoolbagh (Flower Garden),* Scindia's palace in the Lashkar. When news was brought to the Residency of the outbreak at the cantonment, Macpherson set off at once to see the Maharajah. He found him at the Phoolbagh surrounded by his troops under arms. Dunker Rao was with his master. Both knew the temper of the rebels and of their own troops, and they declared it was impossible to protect the fugitives. They had already ordered carriages and palanquins to convey them to Agra, and an escort of Scindia's bodyguard to guard them. Macpherson, with noble courage and self-devotion, wished to remain at his post, but Scindia, feeling that his presence would be a source of grave embarrassment and that his life would not be safe, wisely protested against his stay. The young sovereign realised the magnitude of a catastrophe which might even threaten his throne and, anxious and agitated, he had to face a most difficult position. His troops might coalesce with the rebels and demand that he should lead them against the English. If he refused they might, having powerful artillery, bombard his city and fort. His first idea was, by means of his treasure, to purchase the departure of the rebels from his territory. But Major Macpherson urged the Mahratta Chief to make, for the sake of the British Government, a splendid effort to retain them until Agra could be reinforced or Delhi fall. He must rely on British strength and British generosity to reward him for any temporary sacrifice or peril to his more immediate interests. Dunker Rao asked, if it were necessary for the detention of these rebels to receive them into the Maharajah's service, would the Governor General approve of the step? The Political Agent said, if no other means might avail, the measure might be adopted.† The Maharajah, through his Minister promised that every effort should be made and every stratagem adopted to detain the contingent, and right well did Scindia keep his promise.

Macpherson, after his interview with Scindia, set forth with his party for Agra. After proceeding about eighteen miles, they halted during the hot hours of the day, and about four o'clock started again for Dholpore.

---

*" This residence is more princely than the town palace, it has such wealth of space, with handsome lofty rooms, pillars, fountains terraces and gardens of flowers." *Campaigning Experiences by Mrs. Henry Doberley, page 159.*

† " *Memorials of Service in India* ", edited by William Macpherson, page 317.

The sun had almost done his work when they entered a village eight miles from the river Chumbul (which divides Scindia's territory from Dholpore) and found two hundred Ghazis drawn up under the Command of a Muhammadan who had once been a native officer in the Gwalior Contingent. "After long parley he protested that he did not wish to injure the Europeans and came to visit them arrayed in green, fingering his beads unceaseless." The commander of the bodyguard, however, discovered that a party of bandits was posted in the ravines fringing the river and he and his men wisely refused to walk into the trap. Having got through the village, the fugitives halted near it for the night. Macpherson now determined to abandon the carriages and to send the ladies at midnight on horseback by a bridle path to cross the river lower down. As they were on the point of starting, the camp was startled by the arrival of Thakoor Buldeo Sing and a strong band of followers. He was a Brahmin, the chief of a warlike clan in the neighbourhood. The wise Diwan, who knew the country and people well, had asked him to come to their aid and he had gladly obeyed the summons. He reminded the Resident of a visit he had once paid them and of his intercession with the Diwan regarding some tanks and wells for his people. "We have not forgotten this," he said "and we will defend you with our lives." Buldeo Sing set half of his men to watch the Ghazis and, with the rest of his band, conducted the fugitives to the river. At the edge of the ravines the bodyguard left them "under orders it was said from Gwalior".* The Thakoor guided them through the rough country, avoiding a band of mutineers by changing the route, and by his aid they crossed the Chumbul. On the opposite bank, a body of the Rana's troops and some elephants was ready to receive them. At 10 A.M. they reached Dholpore, and were treated by the Chief with great kindness.† At dusk they started again for Agra, "the ladies and children in native carts, and the gentlemen on elephants escorted by some of the Rana's troops. We had two or three alarms during the night, but at length got to the end of our journey, and reached the Cantonment of Agra about 10 A.M. Most thankful were we to be again in safety after all that had occurred."

* "At the edge of the ravines the bodyguard, despite of remonstrances and reproaches, turned their back upon the party." It is however quite possible that the Diwan ordered them back because he did not want a conflict between the Mahrattas and Jats. He knew Buldeo was quite capable of conducting them safely.

† The Chief was a Jat, the descendant of the Rana of Gohud who had made Gwalior over to us.

On Friday the 19th another body of fugitives, consisting entirely of women and children, made their way from Gwalior to Agra. At the first outbreak of the mutiny in that Cantonment, Dr. and Mrs. Kirke, Mr. and Mrs. Coopland and Mrs. Raikes took shelter in Major Blake's bungalow, where they found his wife. As the roads were soon guarded and planted with guns and the cavalry rode to and fro, it was impossible for them to make their escape. Straggling shots were heard and an evil din came ever onwards. The guards rushed into the house and said the mutineers had been joined by the ruffians of the bazaar and were coming to loot the house. They advised them to go into the garden, for, if they were discovered, they would assuredly be slain. A faithful Muhammadan servant of Mrs. Blake's guided them to a spot where they lay concealed behind a bank well covered with bushes. The night was clear and they understood the meaning of the red glare in the sky. "The moon (which had now risen) looked calmly down on our misery, and lighted the heavens, which were flecked with myriads of stars." An ominous crackling was heard and shouts of glee and triumph. The mob was burning and plundering the bungalow next door. Presently the din grew louder : clouds of smoke and shafts of flames swept over them. Major Blake's house was on fire. Then footsteps were heard coming towards them. The sepoys were searching for them. " I saw the moonlight glancing on their bayonets as they thrust aside the bushes, and they passed so close by us that we might have touched them."* Mirza stood by his mistress. The faithful sentry came and told her that " the sahib was shot." She had now no desire to escape for " the bitterness of death seemed past,"† but Mirza and the sepoy dragged her to Mirza's hut at the corner of the garden. Dr. and Mrs. Kirke with Mrs. Raikes and her nurse and baby took refuge in a stable. Mr. Coopland and his wife followed Mrs. Blake. They all crouched down in the hut not daring to move and scarcely to breathe. Mirza then barred the door and fastened it with a chain. Half an hour crept on. Then they heard the sepoys again searching for them. They came outside and asked Mirza, " Have you no Feringhis (Europeans) concealed." He swore the most sacred oath in the *Koran* that there were none in his house. They were not satisfied. They hit the door with the butt end of their muskets. The chain fell with a clang, and as the door burst open the full moon shed its light on their bayonets. " We

* *A Lady's escape from Gwalior by R. M. Coopland,* page 122.
† *Mrs. Blake's Narrative.*

thought they were going to charge in upon us: but no; the hut was so dark they could not see us. They called for a light; but Mirza stopped them and said, 'You see they are not here: come and I will show you where they are.' He then shut and fastened the door and they again went away." Silence awhile. Mirza returned and softly said, "They will be here again soon, and will kill me for concealing you, when I swore you were not here; so I will take you to the bearer's hut *: he will not betray you." He then opened the door and they went out. "Day was beginning to dawn, and the air felt cool after the close atmosphere of the house we had been in for so many hours." Mirza guided them to his fellow-servant's hut, one of a cluster built of mud and very low and small. They lay on the ground quite worn out with watching and terror. "Our lips were parched, and we listened intently to hear the least sound: but a brooding silence prevailed." Here they were joined by Mrs. Raikes and her baby. Day grew apace and a party of sepoys returned to search for the officer. They heard the baby cry, and they told the native nurse who was standing near the door to shew them the child. As she brought it out a shout arose, *Feringhee ke baba* (It is an European child). The mother's shriek rent the air. The sepoys began to pull off the roof of thatch. They did not dare to enter for fear of the rifle and revolver. The wretched fugitives stood up close together in a corner of the hut: each of us took up one of the logs of wood that lay on the ground as some means of defence. When the roof was off the sepoys began to fire down upon them. At the first shot they dropped the wood and Coopland exclaimed ," Let us rush-out, and not die like rats in a hole."† "We all rushed out; and Mrs. Blake, Mrs. Raikes and I clasped our hands and cried, *Mut maro, mut maro*, (do not kill us)." The sepoys said, "We will not kill thē mem-sahibs, ‡only the sahib."§ Instantly they

* Bearer. The word has two meanings in Anglo-Indian colloquial: (*a*) A palanquin-carrier, (*b*) (In the Bengal Presidency) a domestic servant who has charge of his master's clothes, household furniture, and (often) of his ready money. *Hobson-Jobson by Colonel Henry Yule*, R.E., C.B., and A. C. Burnell, PH.D., C.I.E.

† *Mrs. Blake's Narrative.*

‡ *Mem-Sahib.* This singular example of a hybrid term is the usual respectful designation of a European married lady in the Bengal Presidency; the first portion representing *Ma'am. Hobson-Jobson, by Col. Henry Yule and A. C. Burnell.*

§ *Sahib.* The title by which, all over India, European gentlemen, and it may be said Europeans generally, are addressed, and spoken of, when no disrespect is intended, by natives. It is also the general title (at least where Hindustani or Persian is used) which is affixed to the name or office of a European, corresponding thus rather to *Monsieur* than to Mr. For *Colonel Sahib, Collector Sahib, Lord Sahib,* and even *Sergeant Sahib* are thus used, as well as the general vocative *Sahib!* 'Sir!' In other Hind. use the word is equivalent to 'Master'; and it is occasionally used as a specific title both among Hindus and Musulmans, *e.g., Appa Sahib, Tipū Sahib*; and generically is affixed to the titles of men of rank when indicated by those titles, as *Khān Sahib, Nawāb Sahib, Rājā Sahib*. The word is Arabic and originally meant 'a companion,' *ibid.*

D

dragged the ladies back into a hut. "I saw no more," writes the Chaplain's wife, "but volley after volley soon told me all was over."* They lay on the ground in the hut "and the stillness was such, that a little mouse crept out and looked at us with its bright eyes and was not afraid." Mrs. Campbell, the wife of Captain Campbell, rushed in with her hair falling about her shoulders in profusion and in a native dress. She had been alone all that dread night and was half wild with fear. Mrs. Kirke with her little son joined them. Her husband, who was much beloved by the officers and sepoys under his care, had just been slain before her eyes. A crowd of natives now began to gather round the hut and the unfortunate women became the centre of much curiosity. Mrs. Campbell, known as the Rose of Gwalior, they greatly admired, and remarked how well her feet looked in Indian slippers. Mrs. Blake they said was already dying. Then a party of the 2nd Infantry came and carried them to their lines. On arriving there, several of the sepoys said with deep emotion to Mrs. Blake, "We will take you to the Sahib." A dead charger lay on the road near the Quarter Guard and, passing beyond all possibility of doubt, she was overcome with a deadly weakness. They placed her on a rough native bed and gave her some water. When she recovered, a native officer of her husband's regiment bent on one knee before her and said the Colours were gone. The bruised heart felt no fear and anger rose in her bitter and momentary. "It is your own fault": she said, "Where is he? and why did you kill him?". The native officer replied that the Major had been killed by the 4th Foot and that his own men had buried him. Mrs. Gilbert and her child and Mrs. Procter now joined the little group.

Lieutenant Procter had staying in his bungalow when the outbreak began Mrs. Gilbert, the wife of an absent officer. He and his wife might have made their escape on foot but "Mrs. Gilbert was helpless, she was daily expecting her confinement. She could not run and how could he leave her."† All night Procter, his wife, Mrs. Gilbert and her child lay crouched up in a dark corner of the butler's hut. As day broke they were discovered. A sepoy came into the hut, and having got from them all the little money they had, "to bribe the rest he said to let us escape"

---

* "The Chaplain, Mr. Coopland, wholly unknown to the troops, was pursued with volleys through cantonments and cut down." *Report on Gwalior,* dated *February 10th, 1858.*

† *Mrs. Procter's manuscript Narrative of her escape from Gwalior.* It has never before been printed.

he told them the sepoys had made a vow that the women and children would not be hurt. "It was only my poor husband they sought." When the sepoy had gone, Procter "moved from his corner and lay down behind a bed, I covered him with a counterpane and lay over him, but oh! we knew well all was now in vain." Soon after, seven or eight sepoys came in and searched around. They brought wheaten cake and water and told the women not to be afraid. They did not want to touch them. "A dread unnatural calm came over me. I could have done anything then. I spoke to them all quietly, ate and drank what they brought, and told them I was not afraid. They asked me who I was, I told them, they said at once, ' Where is your Sahib'? I said 'Oh! if you could tell me I should be so happy.' ' Where is he?' Ah they knew too well. After two or three hours of this agonising suspense I could take no heed of time— Mrs. G. and nurse were taken out of the hut. I sat still, and dreadful men came in and said, get up, and go out, they came quite close to me with their muskets. I said 'don't kill me, what will you do with my sahib if you find him?' ' Kill him' was the reply at the same time telling me to rise. All hope was now gone. I knew not what I did as I went out, one thought alone possessed me that they were going to kill him! The compound was full of sepoys loading their muskets. I threatened, entreated, promised all was in vain. They only laughed and told some of their comrades to take me by the hand and lead me out. I heard shots—I turned and saw him running some 40 yards without being hit. I could look no longer and just as I turned away they said ' fallen '(Gera) Oh that awful moment." The unfortunate Procter, on his wife leaving the hut, rushed out and ran with his best speed followed by the bullets of his men. He reached a low mud bank. "There a Sowar was standing with his Tulwar concealed, the moment the sahib came within reach he cut him across the head and face. He fell instantly heaved one sigh and all was over. One ball entered his leg." The next day three native servants buried their master's body in the graveyard.

A few of the sepoys took Mrs. Procter to the lines of the 2nd Regiment, where she found Mrs. Gilbert and the other ladies surrounded by mutineers. About five minutes later, the men of her husband's regiment insisted on taking Mrs. Procter and Mrs. Gilbert to their lines, and the men of the 2nd ordered their dead commander's carriage to be got ready in order to take his widow where she pleased. Seven women, two children and a nurse were packed into it. The faithful Mirza drove, and two sepoys escorted it as far as the town. On reaching the palace of the Maharajah he forwarded them at once in bullock carts to the Chumbul*. They were joined on the road by Mrs. Gilbert, Mrs. Procter and Mrs. Queck, a Sergeant's wife. They toiled slowly onwards the whole of that long hot afternoon : " the dust rising in clouds, and the hot wind parching us. The men who drove the bullocks could hardly make them move." When the red sun was low they had gone but a few miles, and the ever faithful Mirza told them they were being pursued by some troopers. On reaching a station where the horses for the mail were kept, Mirza told them to get out of the carts and hide themselves. We all sat on the ground and Mirza said, " Only pretend to go to sleep : but I fear I cannot save you as they are bent on killing you." Presently they heard the clatter of iron-shod hoofs and five troopers rode up armed with matchlocks and swords. As soon as they saw the carts they stopped and dismounted. Mirza went towards them and began talking to them. " We heard him say, See how tired they are ; they have had no rest. Let them sleep tonight you can kill them to-morrow : only let them sleep now." They retired a short distance. But when darkness had fallen they came forward again and began loading their muskets and unsheathing their swords. Mirza begged the women to give him their trinkets to bribe the ruffians to spare their lives. " Mrs. Blake was the only one who had any, Mrs. Campbell and Mrs. Kirke having been stripped of theirs, and I [Mrs. Procter] had left mine behind. I instantly took off my wedding ring and tied it round my waist as I was determined to save it if possible." Mrs. Blake gave her ornaments to Mirza who handed them to the sowars. They were disappointed at the smallness of the booty, and holding a loaded pistol at Mirza's breast, made him swear there were no more articles. Mrs. Campbell who knew the vulgar tongue came forward and offered them £40 if they would take a note to her husband at Agra. The villains at first consented and went for some paper, but returned and said it was a plot to betray them into the hands of the authorities. They again threatened to kill the women. At that moment was heard the tramp of horse and the clang of arms. It was the Maharajah's bodyguard returning from escorting Major Macpherson and his party. The ruffians disappeared. The women begged the bodyguard to escort them to Agra. But they refused as they had no orders from their Sovereign. They too went off. " We then lay down, and some of us went to sleep : the poor children did, at least."

With the first glint of dawn, they again set forth. About noon on

---

*" To have attempted more had been their certain destruction he being very hardly pressed to save the lives even of the Christian families in his hereditary service furiously demanded by the fanatics." *Report on Gwalior, dated February 10th, 1858.*

Tuesday they reached the second *dâk* bungalow on the way to Agra. Here they halted during the day. In the evening they again started in the carts. Mirza had procured some chuddars, or large veils which native women wear, in which they wrapped their heads so as to look like them on a journey. " The oxen slowly dragged their weary limbs along, hanging their heads and stopping every instant." At night they reached a large village. They got out of the carts and huddled together by the road side. The rustics came to see them and remarked about these wearied draggled women, " Well, they are not worth a pice (farthing) each." But to the Rose of Gwalior they said, " you are worth an anna (three half pence)." The next day they reached the Chumbul, and leaving their carts, they crossed it in a rude boat. Soon after reaching the opposite bank a trooper on a camel rode up and gave Mrs. Campbell a note. It was from her husband and addressed to Scindia. She read it. Believing that all in Gwalior not of Major Macpherson's party had been slain, he begged His Royal Highness that the bodies should be decently interred—especially his own wife's. The trooper offered to take her to her husband. He had come a few miles out of Agra determined to learn at any risk the fate of his wife : and was now the trooper said at the *dâk* bungalow at Mannea. The Rose of Gwalior generous, chivalrous, and brave, refused to desert her companions. Taking a pin she pricked on the back of her husband's note—" We are here, more than a dozen women and children send us help." The trooper went off and the poor creatures rallied their courage and " pounded over the burning sands facing a scorching hot wind without even a rag to cover our heads." When they had crossed the sands, Mrs. Queck, the Sergeant's wife, fell down in a fit of apoplexy and in a quarter of an hour she was dead. As her companions trudged on, they begged some villagers to bury her body. So died one of " the most gentle and kind-hearted creatures that ever existed." Soon after the party were met by elephants and carts which took them to Dholpore. Here they rested for the night. As daylight was coming on them, they started in country carts for Mannea which they reached in safety and found Captain Campbell. Here Mrs. Gilbert gave birth to a daughter. The mutineers were, however, hovering around looking for Feringhees, and after a few hours halt they again set forth. The mother and child were placed on a native cot and carried, while the rest travelled in their country carts. " Having got a strong guard from the Rana of Dholpore we proceeded in safety all night, and arrived next morning at 9 o'clock in Agra. Forlorn and desolate indeed was our condition."

Indore.   In Central India two Mahratta Military leaders, Scindia of Gwalior and Holkar of Indore alternately held the fore-eminence. After the Marquis of Hastings had crushed the wandering bandits of Central India and brought to a successful close the Pindari war (1817), which gave a death blow to Mahratta supremacy, Scindia and Gwalior both became Protected Native States: and Indore, Holkar's capital, was selected as the Head-quarters of the Agent to the Governor-General for Central India. On the 16th of June, news reached Indore that the Gwalior Contingent had risen and Scindia's capital was in the hands of the mutineers. The Agent to the Governor-General at the time was Henry Marion Durand, a gallant soldier of eminent abilities and, in the full sense of the word, a good man.

Henry Marion Durand was born on the 6th November 1812. His father, an officer of cavalry of powerful build and great courage, had served on the staff of Sir John Moore, had accompanied his chief in the famous retreat through the mountains of Galicia, was by his side when he fell at Corunna and helped to bury him at the dead of night. He afterwards took part in the crowning victory of Waterloo, but his early death put an end to a career full of promise. When his son had the choice of a nomination to Haileybury and the career of a civil administrator or a cadetship to Addiscombe, he chose the profession dignified by danger. Henry Marion Durand was but a lad of thirteen when he entered the Company's Military Seminary which gave to the Empire so many gallant and illustrious soldiers. Eldred Pottinger, Vincent Eyre and Napier of Magdala were at the time among the cadets. In June, 1828, Durand left Addiscombe having won many prizes, the sword for good conduct and a commission in the Bengal Engineers. In October, 1829, he sailed for India in the *Lady Holland*. Among his fellow-passengers was Alexander Duff, the first missionary from the Kirk of Scotland, and a friendship sprang up which lasted through life. When the cadet became Lieutenant-Governor of the Punjab, Dr. Duff wrote to congratulate him. Durand answered that when he looked back upon his career and contrasted it with that of the Scotch missionary, he felt it had been a mere flash in the pan. Like Henry Lawrence, Henry Durand presented the rare combination of practical activity and military valour with high culture and a serious interest in great questions. The wreck of the *Lady Holland* on the Dassan island, a small strip of rock and sand some forty miles from Table Bay, gave the young cadet an opportunity of shewing the same calm courage which he displayed at the storming of Ghazni. After a stay of some weeks in a little cottage near Cape Town, he again set sail, and landed at Calcutta about the end of May. Three months later, he was ordered to report himself to the Chief Engineer at Cawnpore. On arriving there, he was directed to proceed to Meerut, where he was attached to the Department of Public Works. During the next fifteen months, he was employed in surveying stations for European troops upon the outer spurs of the Himalayas, and in constructing barracks for the Himalayan sanatorium of Landaur.* Next we find him, always ardent and diligent, superintending the construction of canals, surveying for new works of irrigation, and giving his spare hours to the study of military history and languages. "I am reading Persian," he writes to a friend, "and what do you imagine I have hit upon to translate? Paley's 'Moral and Political Philosophy.' My Moonshee, I suspect, thinks me mad." Cæsar, "who at school was read without pleasure or amusement," he enjoyed vastly. "Many of his descriptions now strike me as interesting in the extreme, and make my blood tingle in the same manner that some parts of Napier's 'Peninsular War' effect. The latter work, I think I before told you, I rank as the first of English military works. Sallust, Virgil, and Horace are also in Camp; but as I am now fagging at the 'soft bastard Latin' in case I should by any great and unexpected good luck obtain permission to go to Italy to visit the canals of that country, I have very little time for my own friends. In fact my duty is so eternal and never-ending that I have to steal a few hours from night to enable me to get through a little Italian, that too when I often would much sooner sit and idle in consequence." Some years later (1835), his rich discovery of fossils on the Siwalik hills, a low range, lying at the foot of and parallel to the Himalayas, led him to the study of palæontology and he wrote several papers descriptive of the most interesting specimens for the *Journal of the Bengal Asiatic Society*. In 1837, he was placed by Lord Auckland on special duty in connection with a project for draining and reclaiming the Najafgarh swamp near Delhi.* The knowledge he had acquired of the people and of their land tenures during his out-door work on the canals led to the young engineer officer being offered the post of Secretary to the Agra Board of Revenue. He was about to accept it when news of an advance into Afghanistan reached him. His strong military instincts led him to volunteer for military service, and he was attached to the army of the Indus as one of the two engineer officers

* *The life of Major-General Sir Henry Marion Durand, K.C.S.I., C.B., by H.M. Durand, Vol. I.*

charged, in addition to their ordinary duties, with the work of the Topographical Department. At the capture of the renowned fort of Ghazni, he discovered a feeling of genuine chivalry and complete intrepidity. He had been selected to command the party which was to blow in the Kabul Gate, but knowing that Captain Peat, who was his senior, expected the command, he requested that it might be given him. Durand *craved* that to him should be entrusted the hazardous operation of placing the powder and firing the train. The boon was granted. Close to the massive portal the native sappers piled the bags containing nine hundred pounds of powder. Durand and Sergeant Robertson laid the hose and a port-fire attached to it along the foot of the scarp to a sally-port, into which they stepped. The port-fire would not light, and Durand * was some time blowing at the slow match and port-fire before the latter caught and blazed. But it went out. Durand and the sergeant lit it again, and after watching it burn steadily for some moments, they retired to the sally-port. The enemy, expecting a general escalade, had manned the wide circumference of the walls and sent forth from the ramparts a brisk fire of musketry. But they knew not the real danger. "Anxious, however, to discover the cause of the bustle which they partially heard in the direction of the important entrance, they now displayed a large and brilliant blue light on the widened rampart immediately above the gate. But they had not time to profit by its glare, when the powder exploded, shivered the massive barricade in pieces, and brought down in hideous ruin into the passage below masses of masonry and fractured beams." The fire from the ramparts swept the front companies under Colonel Dennie and the reserve column under Brigadier Sale drawn up on the road, who awaited the bugle signal to advance from Peat's covering party. But the bugler had been shot through the head. Peat, "a cool brave soldier," returned to the column and reported the entrance was blocked. Above the sighing of the boisterous wind and the rattle of the musketry, Durand heard the bugler's signal of retreat. He had, with a keener observation, seen that no failure had taken place and, unable himself by illness and an accident to run, sent the good tidings by a

---

* Years afterwards Lord Clyde, then Sir Colin Campbell, ascertained from my father the truth of this story of which he had heard. His comment was a characteristic one. "By God, Durand," he exclaimed after a moment's silence, bringing his hand down with an emphatic slap upon his knee, "By God, Durand, I would not have done that for my own father."—*Life of Major-General Sir Henry Marion Durand, K.C.S.I., C.B. By H. M. Durnad, C.S.I., Vol. I, p. 53.*

brother officer.* The bugle lifted its gallant note; the storming party advanced and Ghazni was won. Shortly after the occupation of Kabul, Durand returned to India with Sir John Keane.

Durand's part in the Afghan campaign had greatly increased his reputation. It had also enabled him to acquire a considerable amount of information regarding Scinde, Afghanistan and the Punjab. After his return he was mainly occupied in preparing a number of maps, plans and reports connected with the campaign. In the spring of 1841, after eleven years passed in the East, he sailed for England. There was no cloud on the Indian horizon. Dost Muhammad had come into Kabul and surrendered. "Once more," Durand writes in his journal, "Lord Auckland's luck is beyond calculation, and promises to carry him through everything." Soon after reaching home, Durand was introduced to Lord Ellenborough, who had been nominated to succeed Lord Auckland. Ellenborough asked him to write a military memoir on the Punjab for the Duke of Wellington, and offered him an appointment as aide-de-camp on his staff. Towards the close of November, he sailed for India with his chief. At the end of February the ship approached Madras. No news from India had reached them since October. The future Governor-General asked if they were near enough to communicate with the shore. "I was told," says Lord Ellenborough, "we were, and I desired them to inquire whether there was any news. I took the telegraph book in my own hand to take down the answer. It came, 'Yes, very distressing from the North-West, the army destroyed.'† This was the first intimation I had on my arrival of the actual state of things then existing."

Lord Ellenborough arrived at Calcutta on the 28th of February 1841 and immediately assumed the office of Governor-General of India. Shortly before landing, he had appointed Durand to the post of Private Secretary, an office of great labour and responsibility, requiring sound judgment, considerable method and power of work. As the confidant of the ruler of an Empire, a Private Secretary must be brave and faithful, capable of executing orders punctually, of keeping secrets inviolably, of observing facts vigilantly and of reporting them truly; and such a man was Marion

---

* Keane, who was created a G.C.B. and Baron Keane of Ghazni, afterwards did ample justice to the gallantry and presence of mind of the young subaltern. "Had it rested with me," he said, I would have handed over to you my Cross of the Path as the rightful owner of it." And forty years later the "Ghazni" medal was founded by some of the officers of my father's corps in remembrance of him."—*Life of Major-General Sir Henry Marion Durand, K.C.S.I., C. B., By H. M. Durand, C.S.I., Vol. I, p. 57.*

† Speech in the House of Lord delivered on the 10th August 1860.

Durand.* But he was of too commanding a spirit, too little of a diplomat to be a popular Private Secretary. The essence of his character, being loyalty and obedience, two of a soldier's cardinal virtues, he identified himself with the views and policy of a master the great energy and decision of whose character were obscured by vanity. Lord Ellenborough found the business of the Government conducted on a bad system, and he attempted to improve it. He wrote to the Duke of Wellington : "The most trifling things come before the Governor-General in Council and occupy the time while the Empire may be in danger. Lord Auckland told me I should find a great want of *instruments* : I could find them more easily in the army than in the Civil Service." And when he found better instruments in the army for appointments hitherto reserved for the protégés of the Court, he had to contend against the whole influence of the Court and of the Civil Service. Durand, as Private Secretary, also made many bitter foes on account of his master's honest and patriotic distribution of patronage. Lord Ellenborough was, however, too occupied with war and foreign policy to be able to effect any great improvement in the internal administration. Durand accompanied the Governor-General throughout the Gwalior Campaign and was by his side at Maharajpore 28th December 1843, where the English once more encountered the Mahrattas. Ellenborough was in the thick of the fight which he "thoroughly enjoyed and seemed utterly regardless as to danger." For Maharajpore, Durand received the star which was made from the metal of the captured guns.

In June, 1844, Lord Ellenborough heard the news of his recall by the Court† and on the 1st of August he embarked for England. Durand asked permission to accompany his chief, but the application having been refused, he accepted the post of Commissioner of the Tenasserim province offered him by Sir Henry Hardinge, the new Governor-General. On the 18th of November, 1844, George Broadfoot, the head of the illustrious garrison of Jalalabad, wrote to Lord Ellenborough—" Captain Durand, I was delighted to find my successor in Tenasserim, the fittest man in

---

* See *The History of England.* By *Thomas Babington Macaulay, Vol. II, p. 171.*

† On the 2nd of July 1844 Lord Ellenborough wrote to the Duke of Wellington :—

"I was perfectly prepared for my recall by the Court which I learnt by the last mail, the report I had received of their conduct having satisfied me that they intended to proceed to that extremity ; but even knowing, as I have long done all your generous kindness, I was hardly prepared for your speech, of which you sent the report to the *Times,* a speech which would console me for much greater injustice and wrong than I have experienced at the hands of the Court."

India for the situation, able and benevolent."* Durand continued the good work begun by Broadfoot, who had, in spite of strenuous opposition swept away many abuses, and introduced sound measures of reform. Durand was benevolent, but against evil-doers hard as flint. He was by nature incapable of making a compromise. He found that the valuable teak forests of the province were being rapidly destroyed by the European and Native speculators abusing their licenses to cut timber. The agents of a Calcutta firm were convicted by the Conservator of Forests of wanton destruction of timber in a portion of the forests held by them. The policy of the Commissioner was the substitution of Government management for the licensing system. The Moulmein merchants and the Moulmein press stormed against it. The Conservator of Forests brought a criminal charge against the editor of a paper for a gross libel, and a charge against a European for fraudulent conduct in timber transactions. Both cases were tried by Durand, who convicted the prisoners and sentenced the editor to imprisonment and fine. They sent a petition to the Deputy-Governor of Bengal, Sir Herbert Maddock, who, in the absence of the Governor-General in the Punjab, was the President in Council. The Deputy-Governor requested that the Calcutta Judges would report on the case, and they reported against it on a purely technical point of the conviction. The Deputy-Governor as President in Council removed Durand from his post.† It would have been more chivalrous and decent, as he was dealing with a man to whom he was personally hostile, if he had left the final decision to the Governor-General. Methodical, with a firm and lofty soul and the purest motives for his guides, Durand had carried on the administration of the province steadily and ably, heedless of the calumnies of envy and avarice, but he had not that superficial sympathy and buoyant nature which furnish the power to reform abuses with the minimum of friction.

Lord Hardinge, on his return to Calcutta, offered Durand the situation of Chief Engineer at Lahore, the advanced post of the army. "This at all events will show," the Governor-General said, "that I am not displeased with him." This offer was refused in a letter, which Lord Hardinge rightly characterised as "cold." Having declined the appointment in the Punjab, Durand sailed for England to lay his case before the Court of Directors. He obtained opinion of Counsel as to the legality of his views

---
* *The career of Major General Broadfoot, C.B. By Major W. Broadfoot.*

† As Director of Records I had an opportunity of reading the whole case. Durand behaved as a strong, honourable man, but his reply to the Bengal Secretary's letter was more warm than discreet.

in the two Tenasserim cases, and, armed with their opinion, he presented his appeal. The Court had already approved of the orders of Sir Herbert Maddock and he got the stereotyped reply which fresh proof can seldom modify. The Court saw no reason to alter their determination. The President of the Board of Control, Sir John Hobhouse, afterwards Lord Broughton, however, told him that when he went back to India he should be employed exactly as he had been before and should be no sufferer in any respect from what had passed. Durand sought consolation from the keenest of vexations, the vexation of injustice, in composition. He employed the winter and spring in writing his valuable Sketch of the First Afghan War which was published thirty years later, when the lessons of the first Afghan War had been forgotten and when we were engaged in a second campaign in that country.

In June, 1848, news reached England of the murder, by the direction or under the authority of Moolraj, the governor of the district of Multan, of Mr. P. Vans Agnew, the Political Assistant, and Lieutenant Anderson who commanded the Sikh Escort. Durand knew that the Sikhs had been defeated but not crushed in the first Sikh War, and that to grant them, after their defeat, the right to govern themselves was a generous but dangerous experiment. He felt certain that the outbreak at Multan would spread and that the Sikhs would try another fall with their old antagonists. In July, he sailed from England, but, as the steamers were full, he went in a sailing vessel and did not reach Calcutta till the beginning of December. Three weeks later, he joined the Commander-in-Chief's army. At the sanguinary battle of Chillianwala he was throughout the day by the side of Lord Gough. At the crowning victory of Gujerat he served " with a very good officer," he writes, seven days after the action, " General Campbell of the 98th. He is a friend of Sir C. Napier, and as cool, brave and judicious an officer as you can wish to see for a hot day's work." And Colin Campbell, who proved himself so cool and brave at Alma and Lucknow, warmly acknowledged Durand's important services in his despatch. For his services in the campaign, Durand was made a Brevet-Major and received the war medal with two clasps. At the close of the war, he was anxious to be again appointed Commissioner of Tenasserim, the post having become vacant. But it was impossible for Lord Dalhousie to pass such a slur on the government of his predecessor. The offer of the charge of a district in the Punjab was made to him, but it was at once refused on the ground that " it would be very painful to enter upon the execution of duties of a subordinate

15th February 1849.

character and under men, without intending the remotest reflection on any of them, to most of whom I have held superior appointments." This roused the ire of the great Viceroy, and Durand was informed that by his refusal of a Deputy Commissionership he had excluded himself altogether from employment in the Punjab. He was, however, offered the political post of Assistant Resident at the Court of Gwalior, which he accepted. About the time that Durand went to Gwalior, Sir Charles Napier landed at Calcutta (6th May 1849), as Commander-in-Chief. Soon after his arrival, he offered Durand the command of the Sappers and Miners. "I want to know," he wrote, " if this will suit your book. * * * If it does, do let me hear from you directly. Nothing will gratify me more than that the first thing in my gift should go to one of Lord Ellenborough's friends, and *no job*, for that I do for no man living, intentionally. If I did, I could never look Lord Ellenborough in the face. Your claims appear to me to be stronger than those of any man above you." But Durand considered a grave wrong had been done him and he was determined to have a clear recognition of the fact, by the bestowal of a post equivalent to the one of which he had been deprived. He refused the command of the Sappers and Miners, and, shortly after, when the offer of the Political Agency at the Muhammadan Court of Bhopal was made to him, he merely wrote a few lines expressing his readiness to "serve wherever the Governor-General might be pleased to employ him." A milder ruler than Dalhousie would have been moved to high resentment by such a provocation. The Commander-in-Chief wrote to Durand a letter which only Charles Napier could write: "You had no cause to give such an answer to the Governor-General as you have done. His desire has been to serve you. If he had not this desire, he might have left you to vegetate and taken no notice of you at all. * * * Were I in Lord Dalhousie's place I tell you honestly I would throw you overboard on receiving your answer. Had he done so, you could not have complained. His desire to serve you has been evident, and in return your answer is very little short of insult. I have never read a word on the subject, but you and others think Hardinge ill-used you. Well *tell him so*! I think Lord—ill-used me, and I told him so in *my* plain English; but I did not make a quarrel with his successor, because he did not make up to me for Lord—'s foul treatment. * * * * If one man insults you, you have no right to insist on an apology from another who has no concern with the quarrel, especially if he tries to make up to you for the ill-usage you have received. I repeat to you, my dear friend, you are *wrong* and were I in your place, I would say to Lord Dalhousie that I was sulky at the mischief done me by Lord Hardinge and had in a fit of temper replied to Lord Dalhousie's kindness very improperly and that I accepted his offer with gratitude to him."* Such an appeal it was hardly possible to disregard. Durand wrote a letter to Lord Dalhousie expressing his obligation to him. The imperious Governor-General was emphatically a great man, whose spirit was raised high above the influence of any small passion. He told Napier, " Major Durand shall be Agent at Bhopal and stand as fair with me as ever he did." Again, " You are aware already that I think Major Durand an able and good man." During Durand's tenancy of the Agency at Bhopal, improvements were made in the judicial and revenue administration of the State; the financial disorder was converted into a surplus and turbulent subjects were brought under control. The Agent won the goodwill and confidence of the famous " Secunder Begum," who conducted, under his supervision, the administration as regent during the minority of her daughter. The friendship between the Muhammadan Begum and Durand was of service in the hour of peril. When the flames of insurrection raged round her and she was threatened by her own fanatical subjects, Secunder Begum never tottered in her loyalty to the British Government. The British Resident, when at her Court, found time to carry on his studies and to labour eagerly on his essays dealing with the great questions of the time. Durand's style, a mirror of his own personality, was plain, terse, pure and effective. Time has revealed faults in his papers, but they are not the faults of a vulgar and mechanical administrator. Scattered through them are passages which reveal that he could elevate his mind to the greatness of that trust to which the order of Providence has called the English in India. " Renowned as conquerors, and not unknown as tax-gatherers, it would not be wise to count, as yet, on having realized any great capital of popularity. The Anglo-Saxon in India moves upon the surface; darkness is on the face of the deep beneath him ; and it remains to be seen whether he will be given that spirit and wisdom which can alone enable him to form, enlighten, and mould into a higher state of moral, intellectual, and physical civilization the chaotic mass of people—ay, of nations—which acknowledge his supremacy."†

During the Bhopal days there was, however, little hope and cheerfulness, and Durand determined to resign his appointment and return to England. After two years at home, mainly spent in vainly attempting

* Life of Major-General Sir Henry Marion Durand, K.C.S.I., C.B. By H. M. Durand, C.S.I., Vol. I, p., 134.
† Life of Major-General Sir Henry Marion Durand, K.C.S.I., C.B. By H. M. Durand, C.S.I., Vol. II, p. 144.

to get an appointment at the Board of Control or the War Office, he returned to Calcutta on the 2nd of January 1856. He found himself, after eight and twenty years of distinguished service, without any appointment. The writings of so robust a thinker as Durand laid the foundation of many important reforms, but they did not conduce to the official advancement of the writer. He was considered a dangerous man, and there was no room in the Political Department for a person of that description. After remaining three months without any employment, Henry Durand had to accept a subordinate post in the department in which he first made his mark. He was appointed Inspecting Engineer of the Presidency Circle. The post had one advantage—its head-quarters was the capital. Durand came into personal contact with Lord Canning, who became impressed with a sense of his ability and power. The Governor-General asked him to write Memoranda on the great questions of the time—the occupation of Quetta, the war with Persia. Durand, as was his wont, expressed his views clearly without diplomatic subtilty. The march of events has proved the fallacy of many of the arguments used in these State Papers, but they contain lessons and warnings which time cannot efface. "The gleam of empire is from British bayonets, but if a fixed and a small quantity of these has to cope with ever-expanding and diverging spheres of action, there must eventually come a limit of success." A few months before the fountains of the great deep of revolution were broken loose, he warned the Governor-General, and deprecated the proposed expedition to Herat, through Afghanistan; and he warned against a perennial danger—the danger of denuding India of British troops.* Lord Canning, slow and cautious, but a man of infinite tenacity and will, by degrees became convinced that Durand was strong and genuine, and in March, when Sir Robert Hamilton had, on account of his health, to go to England, he appointed him as Governor-General's Agent in Central India, one of the most important political posts in the Empire.

The territory known as the Central India Agency is a section of the triangular plateau that lies to the south-west of the Jumna, a territory whose history has been strongly influenced by its physical features. A land of rugged basalt hills and fertile valleys watered by noble streams, {.sidenote The Central India Agency.}

---

* "Lord Canning was at the time distinctly disposed to go the other way. He had in fact written home that he could spare six regiments of European infantry for any operations out of India. These regiments were to have been drawn from our northern stations, mainly from the Punjab, upon the stability of which province, a few months later, so much depended."—*Life of Major-General Sir Henry Marion Durand, Vol. I, p. 193.*

it was marked off by nature to become the home of states founded by the younger son of a Rajput chief, the Moghul adventurer, or the Mahratta freebooter. When the Pindaris were crushed and British supremacy established in Central India, a multitude of petty states, whose territory varied from a few square miles to two or three thousand, were placed under the supervision of the officers of the British Government, whose chief was "the Agent of the Governor-General in Central India." Besides the petty states, there are in Central India six substantive or protected states who, having vitality enough to preserve peace and order, were allowed to retain their independent powers of administration These states are Gwalior, Indore, Bhopal, Dhar, Dewas, and Jowra, of which two (Bhopal and Jowra) are Muhammadan and the rest Mahratta.*

The scattered dominions of Scindia are bounded on the north by the British districts of Agra and Etawah, and the protected states of Dholpore and Rajputana are conterminous with them on the north-west. Along the whole of these frontiers the river Chumbul forms the boundary line. To the north-east the Gwalior State extends almost to the point where the Chumbul and the Jumna are joined by a smaller tributary, known as the Sind, which divides it from the protected States of Bundelcund. On the south-east the river Betwa separates it from the British districts. To the south, between the Gwalior State and British territory, lies the Muhammadan State of Bhopal. To the west of Bhopal is the dominion of Holkar, which stretches beyond the Nerbudda, hardly less sacred in the eyes of the Hindu than the holy Ganges. About forty miles north of the Nerbudda, on a plateau some two thousand feet above the sea, is situated in an isolated fraction of the state, Indore, the capital. Indore is an artificial and not a geographical capital, and as the state was built up by a series of spoliations, the capital is separated from the remaining parts of the dominion by the smaller states which, though robbed, survived. To the north and north-east lies, separating it from a portion of its territory, the Mahratta state of Dewas, which before the British occupation was sorely oppressed by Scindia and Holkar and plundered of many districts. To the west, the Mahratta state of Dhar separates it from territory plundered from the noble Puar family. To the north of the state lies Jowra. But in this case the Mahratta chief had to bestow a fief on a Moslem adventurer. To the north of Jowra, the dominion of Holkar stretches into Rajputana, by which it is surrounded on three

* *A Collection of Treaties, Engagements, and Sunnads relating to India and Neighbouring Countries.* By C. U. Aitchison, Vol. IV.

sides. Gwalior, Indore, and the other States of the Central India Agency are geographical expressions, being merely names given to portions of the great triangular peninsula divided by no marked natural boundaries. The geographical position of the peninsula was itself, however, during the mutiny of vital importance. Through it, from the Nerbudda on the south to the river Chumbul on the north, ran the great highway which connected Bombay with Madras. It was also the chief route for telegraphic communication between Calcutta and the Bombay and Madras Presidencies.

On the 5th of April, Sir Henry Durand assumed charge of the office of Agent to the Governor-General. The Chief of the State was Tookajee Rao Holkar, like Scindia, a young man. He owed his accession to the throne to the Resident, Sir Robert Hamilton, who, on the failure of lineal heirs, had placed him on the Musnud without waiting for direct instructions from the Government. His conduct surprised them and called forth a severe censure. The Resident was informed that by his proceedings an opportunity had been lost to Government of marking an important line of policy. In a letter to the young Chief, the Governor-General laid down the conditions on which the State was conferred on him. Nine quiet years followed, nine years during which the lad was educated with care and learnt to read and speak English, but never could write it with any ease. The education was purely literary and superficial. Tookajee Rao remained a Mahratta cultivator endowed with all the cunning of a rustic. In 1852, he was entrusted with the entire management of the affairs of the State. It was a grave misfortune that Sir Henry Durand did not have time before the outbreak to impress his robust personality on the young Chief and to gain his confidence as he had gained the confidence of the Begum of Bhopal.*

---

* "It was the habit therefore at the Indore Durbar when Hamilton returned to England, not without some mental inquietude as to the results of his absence to speak out freely—to ventilate grievances and to expound the supposed means of remedying them. But Durand could not tolerate this. A man of an imperious temper, with a profound belief in the immense inferiority of the Asiatic races, he esteemed it to be the worst presumption in a Mahratta prince or noble to openly express an opinion of his own in the presence of the representative of the British Government. And, for this, or for some other reason which I cannot even conjecture, he seems never to have had any feeling of personal kindness towards the young Maharajah. There was an antipathy which, perhaps, was reciprocated."— *A History of the Sepoy War in India, 1857-1858, Vol. III, p. 327.* A British Resident of less imperious temper than Durand would not tolerate a native ruler ventilating his grievance against the Government of which he was the representative in the presence of his chief people. Durand was a man of iron. His will, like his frame, was cast in an heroic mould. But as Sir Auckland Colvin says, the combination of extreme strength and tenderness was his extreme charm. When Lord Mayo announced his death he wrote that the sad intelligence "will be received in every part of the Empire with feelings of the keenest regret not only among the brethren of the service but his many friends."

Three weeks after he entered on his duties at Indore, news reached Durand that a sepoy of the 37th Bengal Native Infantry was caught in the act of carrying a treasonable message to the Rewah Durbar. There was reason to believe that he was one of several emissaries sent to test the fidelity of the Native Chiefs.

Immediately after, there came tidings of the mutinous behaviour of the 3rd Cavalry at Meerut, then a report that the 7th Oudh Regiment, stationed seven miles from the Oudh Cantonments, had refused to bite the cartridge. The wind of mutiny was growing. But on the 11th of May, Durand wrote to Lord Canning, " I have no reason to suppose that any of the contingents of Central India have as yet shown any disposition to sympathise with the disaffected movement. Rumours of an uncomfortable feeling existing among the Mhow native troops I have heard, but nothing definite and nothing to which I attach any importance." Mhow is an important military station between thirteen and fourteen miles south-west of Indore. The garrison at the time consisted of one company of artillery, Europeans 91, Natives 93; Right Wing of the 1st Light Cavalry, Europeans 13, Natives 282; the 23rd Bengal Native Infantry, Europeans 16; Natives 1,178. Colonel Platt of the 23rd Native Infantry, who commanded the station, had served for more than thirty years in that regiment, and, in the previous year, when an opportunity occurred for his joining a European corps, the men had unanimously entreated him not to leave them.

Two days after Durand despatched his letter to the Governor-General, he received an unintelligible telegram from Agra regarding the outbreak at Meerut and the massacre at Delhi. The next day he received a more definite account. It was a critical situation. The revolt of the Native Infantry at Mhow might or might not follow. The first aim of the Resident was to protect the Residency, to guard the treasure which was considerable, and to prevent the contagion of mutiny spreading from the men of the regular army to the sepoys of the Contingent. The only troops stationed in Indore, for the protection of the treasure and other buildings, was a regiment of the Malwa Contingent, two hundred strong. This contingent was supported at the expense of the various dependent Princes and Chiefs of Malwa. It was mainly recruited from the same class as the Bengal sepoy and was practically part and parcel of the Bengal Army. It was, like the Gwalior Contingent, paid by one master, governed by another master, and owed allegiance to no one. Holkar's troops, the number and payment of which were regulated by treaty, consisted of about 642 artillerymen, 3,820 cavalry and 3,145 infantry, including the contingent of horse which he was bound to furnish to the British Government. At Sirdarpore, about forty miles from Indore, was stationed the Malwa Bhil Contingent, recruited from the wild tribes of Western and Central India which Outram had reclaimed. Durand now summoned to his aid two hundred and seventy of these Bhils. From Sehore, the head-quarters of the Bhopal Contingent, he ordered two troops of cavalry, two hundred and seventy infantry and two guns.

On the 15th of May, the Resident paid a visit to the Maharajah. "The visit was private, we were received with no show, and our object ostensibly was to see the Gardens of the Lallbagh. Colonel Durand and the Maharajah had a strictly private interview, I being the only other person present. Colonel Durand applied to the Maharajah for the aid of his troops in the event of a mutiny breaking out at Mhow before the force sent from Sehore* could arrive. The Maharajah readily promised every assistance, but at the same time stated that his men were not equal to cope with regular troops, that he had but little ammunition, and that he would require three hours' notice to enable him to move his troops from their lines up to the Residency."† Durand ordered the ammunition to be sent to him from the Mhow magazine.

The following day news arrived that the officers of the 23rd Bengal Native Infantry were doubtful of their men, and a native was sent to the Maharajah with a request for troops. "These were almost immediately after countermanded, but not before the orders had been issued by the Maharajah. This of course caused no slight commotion in the city."‡ On the 30th, the detachment of the Bhopal Contingent and the Malwa Bhil Corps arrived at Indore. So the month of May wore to a close.

On the 1st of June, news reached Indore of the mutiny at Nusseerabad, fifteen miles from Ajmere, the head-quarters of the Rajputana Field Force. The following day Durand went to Mhow in order to make a requisition in person for the European Battery. "But on his return he stated that Colonel Platt's arrangements were so satisfactory there, that he had no fear of the Native regiments there escaping punishment if they attempted to mutiny and he had therefore not applied for the Battery." On the

---

* About one hundred miles from Indore.

† From Captain W. R. Shakspear, Officiating 1st Assistant Agent to the Governor-General for Central India, to Sir Robert Hamilton, British Agent to the Governor-General for Central India, 16th January 1858.

‡ Ibid.

6th of June, there came tidings of the mutiny at Neemuch, an important military station situated on the border of Scindia's territory to the north-west of Indore. The conflagration had spread from Nusseerabad to Neemuch. When the story of the Neemuch outbreak reached Mhow, it was bound to create a profound impression among the sepoys and sowars. The leaders of the Neemuch mutiny belonged to the left wing of the First Cavalry. That day Durand ordered the Bhopal Contingent's two guns to be moved up to the west face of the Residency, a double-storied house built of stone, situated in a park about four hundred yards east of the Khan river and about two miles south-east of the town. On the north-western side of the park ran the Mhow road, which crossed the river by a bridge. Within the park were houses for the Political Assistants to the Agent, the post-office, the telegraph-office, and the treasury and bazaar. Durand posted the cavalry of the Bhopal Contingent in the square of the Residency stables situated to the north of the house, and the infantry in tents between the post-office and the stables. "The Maharajah was like-wise applied to for troops and he furnished three guns (six pounders, after-wards changed for nine pounders), a company of infantry and two troops of cavalry. The infantry and guns were placed near the opium godown at the entrance to the bazaar, the cavalry in the Nawab of Jourah's compound."* On the 9th, Durand wrote to Colonel Platt expressing his gratification at hearing that the 23rd Bengal Native Infantry had volun-teered against the mutineers. He accepted their offer, and if the First Cavalry likewise volunteered, he was ready to accept theirs. The follow-ing day news reached Indore of the revolt of the United Malwa Contin-gent Cavalry, and of the murder of their Commanding Officer and Adjutant. Durand went to see the Maharajah at his palace in the city. " He was evidently much distressed at the news and told Colonel Durand that his own cavalry and the United Malwa Contingent Cavalry were as one, and that he feared his would now revolt, that he had no confidence in them. He begged Colonel Durand's advice and counsel which it was promised should be sent the Maharajah afterwards in writing."† It was suggested to Durand that the treasure should be moved into the Resi-dency, for then they would have only one place to defend in case any attack was made. " Colonel Durand objected on the score of such a move caus-

---

* The Nawab's compound was to the north-west of the Residency.

† *From Captain W. R. Shakspear, Officiating 1st Assistant Agent to the Governor-General for Central India, to Sir Robert Hamilton, Bart., Agent to the Governor-General, for Central India.*

ing a panic and that the sight of so much treasure in the open would be too great a temptation to the troops." It was also proposed that the Maharajah's three guns should be brought up to the Residency, as they would then be more under British control. "The cause of this proposition was that the Sikh cavalry stationed in the Stable Square had more than once brought to notice that of a night the Maharajah's three guns were shifted and had been brought to bear on the square, so as to rake it diagonally. The officer in charge of these lines, I believe, refused to move them from their position unless their own company of infantry was allowed to accompany them." Durand vetoed the proposal on the ground that to move the guns would cause a panic. Captain Ludlow, Superintending Engineer Saugor and Narbudda Territories, and Captain Cobbe, Executive Engineer at Mhow, "then proposed to entrench the Residency; this also was not permitted by Colonel Durand."[*] It would not have been easy to entrench the Residency, for, as Lieutenant-General Travers states, "it stands upon ground not having an inch of soil in depth."[†] The attempt to fortify the place would, Durand felt, increase the fears and suspicions of the sepoys which had already been aroused by the news that the Governor of Bombay, Lord Elphinstone, was sending a column under the command of Major-General Woodburn to Mhow. "I wish," he wrote on the 13th of June, "that I could give you a satisfactory account of the state of the troops at Mhow. The Twenty-third Native Infantry is, I think, more disposed to remain quiet than the wing of the First Cavalry. The troopers of the latter are said to be taunting and urging the Infantry to rise. Both, however, are in fear of the European battery, and also of the guns and troops here. They are in fear, too, of the Column from Bombay, which they suspect to have a punitive mission for themselves. The officers are endeavouring to assure them that they have nothing to dread, provided they remain orderly and quiet. If the Mhow troops rise, it will probably be as much owing to the apprehensions so insidiously spread amongst them, of stern measures being in store for suspected corps, as to anything else. We sadly want the capture of Delhi to act as a sedative on Chiefs and people and the smouldering spirit of revolt." The day before, he had received information from Agra that Delhi had fallen. Three days later, there came the

---

[*] *From Captain W. R. Shakspear, Officiating 1st Assistant Agent to the Governor-General, for Central India, to Sir Robert Hamilton, Bart., Agent to the Governor-General for Central India, 16th January 1858.*

[†] *"The Residency stands upon ground not having an inch of soil in depth."—The Evacuation of Indore, 1857. By Lieutenant-General Jas. Travers, V.C., C.B., p. 63.*

evil tidings that the Gwalior Contingent had mutinied and that Scindia's capital was in their hands. Communication with Agra by the main road was cut off. The news was a grave blow to the hopes of Durand, but there remained the expectancy of the arrival of Woodburn's column. And Delhi he believed had fallen. On the 28th, Lord Elphinstone telegraphed to him that Woodburn could not advance. He wished to know what effect it would have on Central India. Durand promptly replied that he could not answer one hour for the safety of the country if the fact became known that the column was not marching on Mhow. He urged the Governor of Bombay to push on the force without delay. Lord Elphinstone telegraphed in reply that Woodburn's advance had not been countermanded. But the mischief had been done. The contents of the first telegram had become known in the bazaar and were eagerly discussed. At the same time, it also became known in the town that Delhi had not fallen.*

On the morning of the 1st of July, Durand received a letter from Agra, dated the 20th of June, stating that the report of the fall of Delhi was not true. The British position had been repeatedly attacked: it was all our slender force could do to hold their own: and no assault would be made till reinforcements had arrived. Durand was busy framing a telegram to convey the contents of the letter to the Governor of Bombay, when a native messenger rushed into the room and said there was a tumult in the bazaar. A great noise approaching nearer and nearer confirmed the intelligence. Durand left his desk and walked to the steps of the Residency. At that moment he heard the roar of guns. Holkar's three nine-pounders, which had been brought down for the protection of the Residency, were "pouring rounds of grape into the Bhopal Contingent Cavalry at its *pickets* and the infantry in their *tents*—all of course quite unprepared—many cooking, others bathing."† A little after eight that morning, Saadat Khan, a man of weight in Indore and an officer in Holkar's Cavalry, followed by eight troopers had galloped from the direction of Indore to the Durbar troops posted between the city and the Residency shouting—"Get ready, come on kill the Sahibs: it is the order of the Maharajah." The Durbar troops turned out at once and, screeching their religious cries, formed up. The gunners placed their guns in position and opened fire. The infantry, joined by

---

* *Life of Major-General Sir Henry Marion Durand.* By H. M. Durand, C.S.I., Vol. I, p. 212.

† *Annals of The Indian Rebellion*, p. 842.

the rabble of the town, eager for blood and plunder, murdered thirty-nine British subjects, European and Eurasian women and children who had remained in their homes.

Travers was about to enter the orderly room, when the grape came whistling through the lines. He at once hastened to the picket in the Residency stable square and placed himself at the head of the few cavalry ready, though not properly formed. It was a great moment. Less than twenty sabres against three guns and infantry supporting them. He gave the order to charge. "As I cast my eye back, and found only six or seven following me, and not in good order, much as I despise the Mahrattas as soldiers I saw we could not by any possibility make an impression. Still at it I went; to draw rein or turn after giving the order to charge was too much against the grain. I came in for a large share of the most polite attention. My horse was wounded in three places; I had to parry a sabre-cut with the back of my sword; but God, in his great mercy, protected me, and the dastardly gunners threw themselves under their guns. Had I had thirty or forty good sowars at the time, with their hearts in the right place, I would have captured their three guns and cut their 200 infantry to pieces; but what could half a dozen do against so many."* The enemy now moved the guns into the place in front of the Residency. Meanwhile, Durand had made hasty preparations for its defence, and had written to Colonel Platt, "Send the European battery as sharp as you can. We are attacked by Holkar." On Travers' return from the charge, it was despatched to Mhow by a trooper. The two Bhopal guns were pushed forward to the right flank of the Residency and ordered to open fire. They were worked so effectively by the fourteen native loyal gunners under Sergeants Orr and Murphy † that they disabled a field-piece of the enemy and drove back their supports. The rest of the cavalry now came up and asked to be led to the charge. Travers could find no bugler nor could he get the men into proper order. "They seemed uncertain whom to trust—who were friends or who were foes; and to lead them on as they then were would have been destruction. They would have been taken in flank by Holkar's numerous cavalry and overthrown." News now reached Travers that

---

* *Letter from Major Travers, 4th July 1857.*

† " Captain Cobbe of the Madras Artillery had at first tried to take command. Though so prostrated by illness that the Agency Surgeon told him it was as much as his life was worth to move, Cobbe managed to crawl to his guns; and there he remained for a time, too weak to stand, but showing a noble example of soldierly spirit and courage.—" *Life of Major-General Sir Henry Marion Durand. By H. M. Durand, C.S.I., Vol. I, p. 214.*

the infantry were in a state of mutiny. The Bhopal Contingent levelled their muskets at their officers and drove them off. The Mehidpore Contingent refused to obey orders and remained sullenly aloof. The Bhils were formed, but they would not fight. Travers then posted them in the Residency in the hope that under cover they would at least fire their muskets. But when the cannon-balls of the enemy came crashing into the building, they abandoned their posts and rushed into the inner room. There were now only fourteen faithful native gunners, eight combatant officers, two doctors, two sergeants and five European civilians to defend a vast building which was by its construction almost incapable of defence. The forces were unequally matched. Durand had only two guns, the enemy had three nine-pounders, and Durand knew that some twenty-nine other guns might at any moment be brought against him. Holkar's infantry was about two thousand strong. His cavalry mustered fourteen hundred sabres, and this mass of trained men would be aided by the rabble of the city. Two hundred mutinous sepoys were within the Residency enclosure. The cannonade had now lasted two hours. " Holkars's horse and foot with additional guns came crowding down to support the attack." The battery summoned from Mhow could not arrive for two hours, and if it fought its way into the Residency against " overwhelming numbers," it could only prolong the defence for a short time. There could be no question of standing a siege, for there was no food and only one well, exposed to the fire of the enemy who occupied the enclosures and buildings immediately in front of the Residency. " No field artillery," writes General Travers, "could drive the enemy from such a position; infantry could alone do this." The infantry consisted of five hundred mutinous sepoys within the Residency enclosure, who at any moment might join the foe. The Bhopal Contingent were staunch, but beyond the control of their officers. Then Captain Mayne, their Commander, brought a short and formal message. They had heard that some of Holkar's guns and cavalry were moving round to cut off the retreat and they were going to consult their own safety by leaving at once. They begged that this last chance might be taken of saving the women and children. Durand had blown open the gates at Ghazni. In such a man a soldier's death was gain. He had now to make the greatest sacrifice which a soldier can offer up to duty. It was not his own life or his fair fame that he had to consider; it was the lives of the women and children. It would have been an act of folly to continue the vain conflict. " Although he could have held the Residency for a few hours longer," wrote Colonel

Travers, "we should have been unable to withdraw the poor helpless women and children."* Durand, Travers, and every officer present knew that, even if they held out for a few hours, the position was ultimately hopeless. And if they delayed there was a certainty of their retreat being cut off. Durand decided to abandon the Residency. It was the most miserable morning of his life. "First," he wrote, "came the humiliation of being forced to withdraw before an enemy that I despised, and who, could I have got anything to fight, would have been easily beaten back. As it was, with only fourteen Golundauze who would stand by their guns we not only held our own for about a couple of hours, but beat back their guns and gained a temporary advantage. So that we retired unmolested in the face of the superior masses, whose appetites for blood had been whetted by the murder of unarmed men, women and children. Of all the bitter, bitter days of my life, I thought this the worst, for I never had had to retreat, still less to order a retreat myself, and though the game was up, and to have held on was to insure the slaughter of those I had no right to expose to such a fate, without an adequate hope or object, still my pride as a soldier was wounded beyond all expression, and I would have been thankful if any one had shot me." The women and children retired to the back of the Residency while the guns were raking the front. The carriages and horses were in the hands of the mutineers. "We mounted the gun-waggons," writes a brave woman, "sitting upon the shot and powder boxes and were slowly dragged by bullocks. The guns with the few cavalry and some infantry who did not desert us followed with the officers. As we retreated over the plain we saw the smoke of the burning bungalows and for some time heard heavy firing, the shot from the enemy's guns passing close among us; mercifully not a soul was hit." As the withdrawal was being effected, the Bhopal Contingent cavalry closed in, and Travers experienced no difficulty in getting the men in line and in hand "sufficiently at any rate to allow of our assuming a threatening attitude which might prevent pursuit, and give our people a start of some miles."† It was impossible for Durand to make his way to Mhow, for his handful of men, women and children would have, at the first portion of their journey, to run the gauntlet of the

---

* "I had carefully reviewed our position," General Travers, V.C., writes, "and was turning to inform Durand I considered it was hopeless, and that I could do no more, when he came and gave me his opinion which was identical with my own, and as I afterwards learnt, with that of every officer present." *Letter from Colonel Travers, dated Sehore, 4th July 1857.*

† *The Evacuation of Indore, 1857. By Lieut.-General Jas. Travers, V.C., C.B., p. 17.*

enemy's fire, and he determined to wend his way on the line of Woodburn's advance. The imminent danger which must have beset the European battery if they had left Mhow was, however, a source of grave anxiety. Travers wrote two notes stating that Durand * had evacuated Indore, and that they were endeavouring to effect a retreat by the Simrole Ghat. † Two troopers in a quarter of an hour's interval were despatched with these notes. On arrival at the village of Tellore, ten miles from Indore, the inhabitants informed the fugitives that a considerable body of Holkar's troops with guns had occupied the Simrole Ghat. The men of the Bhopal Contingent now declared that they must return to Sehore, their head-quarters. "The Seikhs said that unless they did so their families would be dishonoured and slaughtered by the Mussulmans, while the latter professed a like dread of the former. Both urged our accompanying them. They assured us they would escort us with their lives in safety to Sehore, be loyal to us there, and should we desire to leave Sehore, they would escort us to any station we might name. Durand reluctantly changed his route, and set forth for Sehore. On the 3rd of July, he reached Ashta in Bhopal territory. "The guard drawn up upon the banks of the Parbati and across our road and the crowd with it made many think their last hour had come. The women and children were dismounted from the limbers, and the guns got ready for action, when a messenger arrived to announce it was the Guard of Honour! It was a relief." On the 4th of July, Durand, with the guns and every European who had reached the Residency at Indore on the morning of the outbreak, arrived at Sehore. His old friend the Begum still ruled Bhopal and was loyal to the core, but she told him "that the whole of India is now at enmity with us, that our remaining here is a source of weakness to her and endangers the State and her." After a day's stay Durand, with the view of getting into communication with General Woodburn, set forth for Hoshangabad, on the southern bank of the Nerbudda. On his arrival there, he heard what had taken place at Mhow.

Mhow.

On the morning of the 1st of July, about 11 A.M., Colonel Platt called at Captain Hungerford's bungalow and handed him Durand's note,

* "I mentioned his name purposely to intimate that he, the British Representative, had not been killed.—*The Evacuation of Indore, 1857. By Lieut.-Genl. Travers, V.C., C.B., p. 17.*

† "I did not mention Sehore, and whatever the trooper added was obviously his own invention."—*The Evacuation of Indore, 1857. By Lieut.-Genl. Travers, V.C., C.B., p. 17.* Sir John Kaye is inaccurate when he states that the pencil notes from Travers stated that Durand and other Europeans had evacuated the Residency and were retreating upon Sehore.—*Kaye, vol., III, p. 338.*

requesting that the European battery should be sent to his aid. Hungerford rode down to the barracks and turned out the battery. As no escort was ordered to accompany it, two men, armed with muskets, mounted on the limber boxes, were told off for each gun and waggon. In his letter to the Brigade-Major, dated Saugor, the 2nd of July, Hungerford states he left Mhow "at about half-past eleven." The battery had trotted half-way to Indore when a sowar rode up to him with a note in pencil from Colonel Travers stating, " We are retreating on Simrole, on the Mundlaysir road from Indore." "The sowar added that Colonel Durand and the officers and ladies from the Residency were with Colonel Travers; that Colonel Durand had not retired on Mhow, as Mhow was in Holkar's territories, and would be attacked by Holkar's troops either that night or the following morning. There being no road to Simrole which I could follow, the battery was brought back to Mhow as quickly as possible."*

Besides sending the European battery to Indore, Colonel Platt "despatched the two flank companies of the 23rd regiment, native Infantry, under command of Captain Trower and accompanied by Lieutenant Westmacott, down the road to Bombay, with orders to bring back into cantonments, at all hazards, two 9-pounder brass guns, belonging to the Maharajah, which had passed through Mhow two hours previously."† A troop of 1st Light Cavalry under Captain Brooke was also sent with the detachment; on overtaking the guns, they "charged them and the capture was effected without any loss on our side.‡ Some of Holkar's gunners were killed. About 3 P.M. the guns were brought into the fort. Meanwhile, Colonel Platt was devoting his care to the task of defending the cantonments against any attack by Holkar's troops

---

* *Letter to the Secretary to Government, Bengal, Mhow Fort, 17th July 1857. Appendix D.*

† *Report of Brevet-Major Cooper, 23rd Native Infantry Headquarters, Mhow, July 9th, 1857, Appendix D.*

‡ "Some of my men demurred at being sent to this duty and lagged behind; but on the whole I was satisfied with their conduct, especially when, on nearing the guns (two brass 9-pounders, manned by about twenty-five artillerymen), they charged them, and the capture was effected without any loss on our side." *Letter from Captain Brooke, I.B.C., to the Deputy Adjutant General.*

"On the 1st of the month, news came in from Indore that the Rajah's troops had arisen and slaughtered every European, forty in number. I heard nothing of it; but the Commanding Officer came to my bungalow, saying, 'You are on duty, to go and retake some guns with the 3rd troop.' We went; and most marvellous to say, took them the first charge, Brooke and I together. The men demurred at first, but afterwards followed well. We were all surprised, as we knew they were in an unsettled state. The guns were brought to the fort." *Letter from an officer, Fort Mhow, 6th June.*

from Indore. In the loyalty of his own men the gallant old soldier had the most profound belief. A picket of Light Cavalry was thrown out about five miles on the Indore road under two Lieutenants, and another of fifty sepoys under Lieutenant Simpson to the north of the cantonments near a ravine. The women and children who had taken refuge in the Artillery barracks were moved into the arsenal, or fortified square; and the European battery sent to guard it.* "All officers were ordered to proceed to the lines of their men and remain there all night, ready to turn out at a moment's notice and the men were kept accoutred. The arsenal guard was increased by thirty men; and everything was ready to resist the attack if possible."†

About 9.30 p.m. the officers of the 1st Cavalry, after having dined at mess, went to their lines. Captain Brooke and the subaltern who had accompanied him in the morning expedition had a tent pitched two or three yards in front of the main guard. After seeing that their horses were ready for action, they went to the tent and tried to sleep. About ten o'clock a small bungalow in front caught fire. Brooke's companion went out to see the cause of this. On reaching the guard, he found Lieutenant Martin, the Adjutant, in the centre of the men talking to them. "I joined him, and observed one man in my troop—a villain; he had his carbine, and began to cavil with Martin about some men Brooke and I had killed in the morning. I feeling sleepy said to Martin, 'I'll turn in,' but good God! I had hardly turned my back, and got to Brooke's side, when an awful shriek arose from the men, and the

* Captain Hungerford writes—"Colonel Platt met me on re-entering cantonments. I gave him Colonel Travers' note, and told him what the sowar had said, requesting permission at the same time to take my battery into the Fort, as the Fort could be defended for any length of time. Colonel Platt would not hear of it. At the artillery barracks all the wives and families of officers and men had taken refuge. The barracks could not be well defended, from their extent and position. I urged repeatedly on Colonel Platt, during the afternoon, the advisability of defending the Fort; but only at the very last moment could he be persuaded to allow me to enter it. At half-past 6 p.m. Colonel Platt rode down to the artillery barracks and told me to enter the Fort." *Letter to the Secretary to Government, Bengal, 17th July, 1857. Appendix D.*

Captain Trower, 23rd Native Infantry, writes—"Fort, July 6th. However in riding away from the lines I saw the men collected in groups talking and some with muskets in their hands; this made me more suspicious, and I went and reported it to the Colonel; he, poor man, thanked me, but evidently did not doubt the good faith of the regiment * * * However, thank God, my representations coupled with the assistance of the officer commanding the artillery made him give orders for the occupation of the place we are in now."

† Captain Hungerford writes—"He had strengthened the guard at the gateway to fifty men from his own regiment." *Letter to the Secretary to Government, Bengal, 17th July, 1857. Appendix D.*

bullets whizzed round us in torrents." The Subaltern leapt out of the tent and saw Martin rushing across the parade amid wild yells. He reached him and Brooke followed. " We felt our last moment had come, but we ran for it. I led to the fort, a mile off. The men kept following us, and the bullets fell thick. Having got across the parade-ground about 500 or 600 yards, we came to the hill with the church at the top: and when at the top, Martin caught hold of me exclaiming, ' For God's sake stop!' I caught hold of his arm and said, ' Only keep up and follow,' but at this moment I felt I was done. We parted, as I thought, only to meet in death."* Brooke and the officer of the 1st Cavalry rushed on. " By this time the infantry had all risen; and as I ran, the ground was torn up with bullets and they fell thick around me. Their lines were in a direct line between the fort and ours, so that we poor fellows had to run the gauntlet of both fires." On approaching a bungalow about a quarter of a mile from the fort, he saw two natives and rushed up to them. He "simply took their hands, barely able to speak, and said, ' Save me.' They did—to them I owe my life." The men of the infantry regiment were fast advancing, screeching their religious cry, and the two natives hid him in a small house. Some sepoys came to it, but they could not find him. Then there was a lull. His native friends had disguised him in their clothes. He opened the door and ran for the fort. " Can I ever make you feel the deep thankfulness that was in my heart as I ran across the open plain up the hill to the fort. The artillerymen were manning the walls, and the sentry's call was never more thankfully received; and I cried friend! friend! and found myself inside."*

The officers of the 23rd regiment dined that night at the Sergeant-Major's house close to the lines. After dinner they sat in a group outside to enjoy the cool of the night. Then it was proposed that they should go to their beds at the bell tents of each of their companies. As they were moving away, some one said, "The report is, the regiment will rise at ten to-night." The Major answered, "Oh, very well; let's wait and see." The words were hardly uttered when they heard shots in the cavalry lines, and rushed towards their companies. They were received with shots and with difficulty made their way to the fort. On the arrival of the fugitives at the fort, Colonel Platt, who commanded, ordered the native guard to be disarmed and turned out of the fort. He also ordered the European battery to turn out. He then called upon the officers to follow him and do what they could to stop the outbreak. Fagan knew it

* *Letter from an officer belonging to 1st Cavalry, Fort Mhow, July 6th.*

was hopeless, for he had been obliged to run the gauntlet of the men's fire; but he at once responded, and mounted his horse, remarking only that it was too late. Platt replied, "You are the man I always took you for." Half an hour passed before the battery moved out. The horses were knocked up by their morning's work and several of the drivers had deserted. As it advanced up the infantry parade, it was several times fired upon, but no rebel could be seen. The blazing bungalows illuminated the ground, but the huts of the sepoys were in darkness. When opposite the centre of the infantry lines, Hungerford halted, expecting to be joined by the Colonel and the Adjutant. No sign of them. The sepoys again opened fire. Hungerford unlimbered and fired several rounds of grape and round shot into the lines. "There was some groaning and noise, but nothing visible; and in a few minutes everything was perfectly quiet."* The whole of the cavalry had trotted away in regular file and taken the road to Indore: the infantry had also fled in the greatest disorder across country towards Holkar's capital.

At day-break, an officer who had been hiding in the bazaar all night, crept into the fort and told them that Colonel Platt and Captain Fagan had been killed in their lines, and Major Harris was lying dead in the road shot by his own troopers. A detachment, consisting of two guns, ridden by gunners (Europeans) and escorted by volunteers, was sent out under Captain Brooke to search for the bodies of the missing officers. They were found much mutilated.† The British blood was roused. "We all vow vengeance"—writes one of them. That very morning two men of the 23rd Native Infantry who were with Lieutenant Simpson on picket duty escorted him safely to the fort. Major Cooper, their Commander, promised to reward their fidelity by promotion to the rank of Havildar, but they subsequently deserted and joined their comrades. The struggle in the sepoy breast between fidelity and regard for his officer and the wild Bacchic impulse to fight for his faith is one of the most tragic features of the mutiny. The mutilated bodies of the officers

---

*From Captain T. Hungerford to the Secretary to Government, Bengal, Mhow Fort, 17th July, 1857. Appendix D.

†"When we found him (Colonel Platt) next morning both cheeks were blown off, his back completely riddled with balls, one through each thigh; his chin smashed into his mouth, and three sabre-cuts between the cheek-bone and the temples; also a cut across the shoulder and the back of the neck."

Major Harris was found dead on the parade ground the next morning, with a frightful sabre-cut in the shroat.

were brought into the fort and buried "in the corner of the bastion, all three in one grave."

The officers now formed themselves into a volunteer corps and relieved the artillerymen of their night watches, snatching sleep and food when and where they could. The women, most of them of gentle birth, " were huddled together and they had to do everything for themselves, and employ all their time in sewing bags for powder for the guns, well knowing the awful fate that awaits them if the place is taken; there has not been a sign of fear, they bring us tea or any little thing they can, and would like to keep watch on the bastions if we would let them."

On the 3rd of July, Hungerford was informed that Holkar's troops, accompanied by the mutineers from Mhow, meant to attack the fort. Every preparation was made to meet it, and Hungerford, having been left alone at Mhow without any political officer, assumed political authority and wrote to the Maharajah as follows:—

"I understand, from many natives, that you have given food to the mutinous troops. I have heard also, but do not know whether to believe, that you have lent them guns and offered them irregular cavalry, as assistance. These reports are probably very much exaggerated; I do not believe them. You owe so much to the British, and can be so utterly ruined by showing enmity towards them, that I do not believe you can be so blind to your own interest as to afford aid and show friendship to the enemies of the British Government. Let me understand therefore from yourself what your wishes are. From your not throwing obstacles in the way of the mutinous troops passing through your territory, and not punishing them, as a power friendly to the British would do, many may suppose that you are not so much the friend of the British Raj as I believe you to be. Write, therefore, and let me understand your intentions. I am prepared for everything, alone and without assistance; but with the assistance I very shortly expect, I can act in a manner that you will find, I fear, very injurious to your interests; and if you will take my advice, you will write to me at once, and let me know what I am to think of the reports which have reached me."

Early in the forenoon of the 5th of July, arrived Holkar's Prime Minister, Bhao Rao Ramchunder, and his treasurer Khooman Sing accompanied by Captain Fenwick, an East Indian in the service of the Maharajah. Holkar wrote:—

"No one in the world regrets more than I do the most heart-rending catastrophe which befell at Indore and at Mhow. My troops, probably under the influence of the Mhow mutineers, mutinied openly on the morning of the 1st instant; and the very companies and guns that were sent to protect the Residency picked up a general quarrel with some one, and began at once to fire upon the Residency house. The mischief done was great; many lives were lost. No companies of the contingent, etc., assisted the British officers; but it is cheering to hear that Colonel Durand, Mr. Shakespear and family and others went away quite safe. The rascals then plundered the whole Residency. The next morning the Mhow troops, after committing similar brutalities arrived here; the whole town was in a panic. A greater part of my troops were in open mutiny, and what remained could not be trusted. The Mahomedans raised a standard of "Deen," and the disorder was complete. Under these sad circumstances the mutineers exacted their own terms. They not only demanded the heads of a few Europeans whom I had concealed in my own palace, but also of a few officers of the court who were supposed to be in the British interest. They prepared to plunder and destroy all, if I myself did not come out. I had no alternative left but to offer them my own person, but I would not allow the poor Europeans to be touched before being killed myself. After plundering the British treasury, and the carriage from the town, and taking with them all the guns which had gone over to them in a state of mutiny, all the mutineers of this place and Mhow have marched off last night in a body towards Dewass. The tale is a painful one, and will be described to you in detail by Rao Ramchunder and Bukshee Khooman Sing, who are bearers of this to you. I have not even in a dream, ever deviated from the path of friendship and allegiance to the British Government. I know their sense of justice and honour will make them pause before they suspect, even for a moment, a friendly chief, who is so sensible of the obligations he owes to them, and is ready to do anything for them; but there are catastrophes in this world which cannot be controlled, and the one that has happened is one of the kind.

The deputation from Indore confirmed the statement in the letter that the Maharajah had been unable to control his mutinous troops, and expressed on his part deep regret at the occurrences which had taken place in his capital. They offered also to send over the remaining treasure from the Residency to Mhow, and were prepared to carry out any measures which Hungerford might advise for opening up communication through and tranquillising the country. On the evening of the 6th, the treasure, amounting to 4 lacs besides nearly $23\frac{1}{2}$ lacs in Company's paper, arrived in the fort. The same day news reached Mhow that Captain Hutchinson, an Assistant to the Resident, had been taken prisoner by the Rajah of Amjhera, a petty Rajput state in Malwa. Mrs. Hutchinson was the daughter of Sir Robert Hamilton, and the following shows that Holkar had not forgotten what he owed to his former guardian.

"His Highness the Maharajah has learnt with great regret the astounding account of Captain and Mrs. Hutchinson and parties' detention at Amjhera. He looks upon Mrs. Hutchinson as his sister, and the whole family as his own relations; and though not crediting that the Rajah of Amjhera could be so blind to his own interests, he has, however, lost no time in ordering Bukshee Khooman Sing, with three companies of infantry, two guns, and 200 sowars, towards Amjhera, with orders to blow up the town, and bring in the Rajah dead or alive, should he have proceeded to any extremities with the party. Amjhera, it must be recollected, is not a tributary to Holkar, but to Scindia; but in this emergency His Highness thinks hesitation as to its being a foreign state inadmissible."*

---

* *From Captain T. Hungerford to the Secretary to Government, Bengal, Mhow Fort, 17th July 1857. Appendix D.*

The news of the attack on Indore Residency by Holkar's troops spread like wild fire throughout the country around. It was stated that the Maharajah had joined in the revolt, and the petty chiefs were ready to follow the example supposed to have been set by the great Mahratta sovereign. The Rajah of Amjhera immediately sent his troops to attack the small town of Bhopawar where a detachment of the Bhil Corps was stationed. News of their approach reached Dr. Chisolm, who was in medical charge of the cantonment. "I immediately assembled the men of the Bhil Corps, about 180 in number (the headquarters as you know being away), got out two small guns which we had, helped to load them with my own hands, and posted them in a good spot. I then sent to Lieutenant Hutchinson, the Political Officer, who was living three miles away, and told him what I had done, recommending him to join me and make a stand at the lines of the Bhil Corps. He accordingly came down with his family. All this occurred on the evening of the 2nd July." Night fell without any appearance of the enemy. The men lay down at their posts and the two officers slept at the quarter-guard. When dawn broke, they discovered that only twenty Bhils remained in the lines; the others had stolen away from fear: and it was evident from their conduct that these twenty did not mean to fight. Resistance was now hopeless, and the women and children had to be considered. On the morning of the 3rd of July, Lieutenant and Mrs. Hutchinson and child, Mrs. Stockley and four children, and Dr. Chisolm started for Jhabua, a small subsidiary native state between Indore and Amjhera. In the afternoon they arrived within its boundary, and had halted to rest their cattle when they were overtaken by a small body of horse and foot, who had been sent in pursuit of them. "We gave ourselves up for lost; but Lieutenant Hutchinson and myself prepared to sell our lives as dearly as we could. Fortunately, we were well armed, having five guns between us." Though worn out with fatigue, Hutchinson and Chisolm kept watch all night, each awaking his companion (if he slept) at the slightest cause for alarm. "You may imagine how dreadful a night the poor ladies passed; indeed few of our party will be disposed, I fancy, ever to forget it. Nothing but jungle all round; one miserable hut within sight, belonging to some *dâk* runners, deserted again by the few people who accompanied us so far from Bhopawar; and a band of assassins at hand thirsting for our blood." When daylight returned, a small party belonging to the Jhabua state conducted them to an adjacent town. At first they treated them with civility, but towards evening they grew insolent and began to plunder them. "We saw our position had but little improved, and we prepared again to sell our lives as dearly as we could." At this moment, an escort sent by the Chief to conduct them to his capital arrived, and the next morning (5th July) they reached their goal and found shelter and safety. The young Chief, a good-looking youth of sixteen, received them with marked kindness. In consequence of his minority, the management of affairs rested in the hands of his grandmother; and she, in the true chivalrous spirit of her race, did all she could for the safety and comfort of her way-worn guests. "To protect us," Dr. Chisolm says, "was as much as she could do; for there were a number of Arabs and men of that class in the employ of the Chief; and these fanatics loudly demanded our surrender that they might put us to death. The family themselves are Rajputs, and had fortunately a number of Rajput retainers about them. To these they assigned our protection; and faithfully did they execute their trust. Not a Mussulman sepoy was allowed to approach our quarters in the palace." Five days did they enjoy the hospitality and protection of the young Rajput Chief. Then, escorted by some troopers whom Holkar had sent for their rescue, they returned to Bhopawar, where they remained for a couple of days. "From Bhopawar," Dr. Chisolm writes, "we intended to go into Indore, where Holkar had kindly prepared rooms for us in his palace. But, hearing that many of his troops were still in a very agitated state, and that the Mussulmans in the city were ripe for mischief, we turned off and came in here, thinking it more prudent, both on Holkar's account and our own. We arrived on the night of the 16th July, thanking God for His mercy to us during so many days of danger." The next day Hungerford wrote to the Bengal Government:—" The country is perfectly quiet, the Maharajah of Indore most anxious for opportunities to prove his friendship and fidelity to the Government. This Fort is strengthened and provisioned in such manner as to enable us to hold it for any length of time against any native force; trade and business are carried on as usual in the towns in Holkar's states. The Maharajah's tributaries having discovered the mistake they first fell into of thinking Holkar inimical to the British, have suppressed all disorders in their own districts, and are willing to assist in maintaining order. Some of the Maharajah's troops alone show a bad spirit, and are still mutinous and disaffected; but they will, I think, be restrained from any further excess, and on the arrival of European troops the Maharajah will at once disarm and punish them."

It was due to the courage with which Hungerford assumed responsibility, and the tact and firmness he displayed, that Mhow was saved from falling into the hands of the mutineers, and tranquillity was preserved throughout Holkar's wide territories.

While at Hoshangabad, news reached Durand which made him very anxious. There had come to the Commissioner of Nagpore false reports that the fort at Mhow had fallen into the hands of the mutineers and that all the Europeans had been massacred. He thereupon ordered all the officers commanding the military posts on the northern line of his territory to fall back if the Indore mutineers threatened to march towards the south, and he wrote to General Woodburn urging him to march eastward towards Nagpore. Durand felt that the line of the Nerbudda must be held in order to prevent the conflagration in the north spreading to the south. He wrote to the Commissioner of Nagpore and to the Government of India pointing out the grave political and strategic error involved in the proposed change of operations. He also wrote to General Woodburn expressing his strong disapproval of it. He went further. He took upon himself the grave responsibility of authorizing the officers commanding the military posts to disregard the orders they had received. Fearing that written words might not confirm Woodburn's wavering purpose, he again set forth southward to reach him and to exercise his own strong will over him. On the way, glad tidings reached Durand that his vigorous requests for the advance of the column had been successful. General Woodburn had been forced by ill-health to resign his command, and Brigadier General Stuart, who had succeeded him, was ordered to march direct for Mhow by way of Assarghur.

On the morning of the 12th of July, the column, consisting of the 14th Light Dragoons, Woolcomb's Field Battery, the 25th Bombay Native Infantry, and a Pontoon Train, left Aurungabad and made its way over the rough pass of Chowker. Eight days later they were encamped on the south bank of the river Tapti. Cholera now broke out in the camp and, in a few hours, many died. "Major Follett, Commanding the 25th Regiment, Bombay Native Infantry, died here about 9 P.M. He was a fine man and much beloved of his regiment." Before the first streak of dawn, the column moved slowly down the high banks covered with trees to the ford. Once upon the shingle at the water's edge, the infantry, taking off shoes and stockings, waded across and formed up on the opposite bank. "Then down comes the artillery, gun after gun, dashing the stream about in a thousand rainbows as they pass through; there are the dragoons and gaudily dressed irregulars in groups quietly watering their horses; there dhooly-bearers carrying the sick man across, sprinkling their heads and dhoolies with the precious water as they go, yonder is a long line of camels jingling with bells, stalking over, there is the great unwieldy elephant sucking up gallons of water for his capacious stomach (with a huge bunch of leaves tucked up between his trunk and tusk) or blowing it over his heated body and limbs. When he has quenched his thirst he takes down his leaves and fans the flies away as he carefully moves off." After crossing, they marched through the town of Burampore and encamped on the north side. "Here the body of Major Follett was buried; and as a proof of the love his men bore for him, they carried his body, dug his grave, and heaped up a rude mound of stones over the spot when the ceremony was ended; and these were *high caste* men too! * But that their regiment should do such an act seems only natural, they are such fine soldiers and commanded by such superior officers."† The touching of a corpse involved the loss of caste. To the Brahmin sepoy the loss of caste meant becoming an outcast, an object of loathing and disgust.

On the morning of the 22nd of July, the column encamped to the north of the fort of Assarghur on a little plateau surrounded by dense jungle. That evening Colonel Durand came into camp from the fort, and from that time he impressed his strong character on the movements of the column.

On the 24th of July the column set forth for the Nerbudda, and on the evening of the fourth day the broad and rapid stream lay before them. The monsoon rain had fallen on the hills, and the stream was running fast. In a few hours it rose several feet. "High and large boulders rapidly disappeared; the current increased in rapidity, while huge trunks of trees, bushes, and logs of wood came floating down." The river must be crossed at once. Large boats of a rude description were ready, and upon them the troops, artillery and baggage were taken across. The whole of the 3rd Hyderabad Cavalry under the command of Captain Orr had now joined them.

On the 1st of August, crags hewn from the solid rock in prismatic pillars, or hills mantled with dense jungle, looked down on the long column as it made its way through the pass of Simrole to Central India. They encamped at night in a town of that name, and in the morning,

---

* The 25th Regiment, Bombay Native Infantry.
† *Central India, by Thomas Lowe, p 44.*

fine and cold, they began their last march to the relief of Mhow. Rain had fallen all night in torrents, and it was difficult to drag the guns through the black loamy cotton soil. "The elephants sank knee-deep into the mire, but this was nothing to them." Slowly the column made its way along. At length the cantonment and town of Mhow appeared in sight, and, as they neared it, fresh horses came out to assist the artillery along the still heavy roads. "As we drew nearer there was the sound of a heavy gun, another, and another, until twenty-one were counted. What could this be for? Has Delhi fallen? It must be so! But no! though perhaps it was an equally important thing to the people here; the salute was fired from the fort for the 'relief of Mhow.'" After firing the salute, the small garrison came out to meet the column as they marched into Mhow, "the 25th band playing rejoicingly." Three days later, the force was strengthened by the arrival of 250 bayonets of H. M. 86th.

Stuart's Column enters Mhow, 2nd August.

The timely relief of Mhow saved the line of the Nerbudda, and it gave us an important base for military operations. But every hand was now against the English—from Neemuch to Saugor, from Gwalior to Mhow—and the force at Durand's disposal was extremely inadequate to the restoration of order and the stay of anarchy. The Gwalior contingent had become our most powerful foe; the Bhopal contingent was in open mutiny, and no trust could be put in the Malwa contingent. Holkar's force, which had supplied the troops who had attacked and burnt the Residency, consisted of 30 guns of various calibre, about 1,400 horse and five battalions of disciplined infantry; and Holkar's capital contained a turbulent population ready to burn and slay. Durand's force was sufficient to disarm Holkar's force at Indore and maintain order in the city. But he could not at the same time disarm Holkar's troops stationed in separate cantonments. He was weak in infantry and the rain had rendered the country impassable. He therefore wisely determined to leave Indore alone for the present and to make preparations for operations against the enemy who were openly defying our power and spreading rebellion over the whole state of Malwa. In July, a number of Scindia's revolted troops had seized Mundesore, an important town near the Rajputana frontier, about a hundred and twenty miles north-west of Indore. All the turbulent Afghans and foreign mercenaries in the surrounding districts joined them. Firoz Shah, of the Delhi royal family, placed himself at their head and raised the Mussulman

Insurrection in Malwa.

standard. But Durand had to possess his soul in patience. The heavy rains continued and rendered the black cotton soil impassable. He made the best use of the delay. "The hammer and forge were going night and day in the fort, gear for elephants and siege-guns was making, untrained bullocks were being taught the draught of guns, and commissariat stores were being prepared." In September, the rebel force had risen to some seventeen or eighteen thousand. As Easter in Western lands marks the awakening of spring, so in India the Dasahra—like Easter a moveable festival, occurring in September or the early days of October—marks the close of the season when the rain waters the parched plains, and the arrival of dry winter when the fields are green with young corn. Some intercepted letters informed Durand that at the close of the great Hindu festival a general rising would take place in Malwa. On the 12th of October, when the rains had barely ceased, news reached Mhow that a body of Rohillas was about to move on the town of Mandlesar on the Nerbudda. The 3rd and 4th Troops of the 3rd Hyderabad Cavalry Contingent under Lieutenant Clark were sent at once to the village of Goojeeree to intercept them on their way. Another detachment of the 3rd Cavalry was sent to the town of Mandlesar, to Captain Keatinge, the political agent there. Two days later, three companies of the 25th Bombay Native Infantry, three guns, and fifty sabres of H. M. 14th Light Dragoons were ordered to proceed without delay to the support of Lieutenant Clark. On the 19th, orders were issued for the column to march, and all Europeans left behind to go into the fort. The cantonment was to remain in charge of a detachment of H. M. 86th., a portion of the 25th Native Infantry, and the detachment of the Bombay Sappers under Lieutenant Dick, Bombay Engineers. On the 20th, the bulk of the column set out for Dhar, and early the next morning the siege train followed.

Stuart's Column leaves Mhow, 19th October.

The State of Dhar.

The small state of Dhar is situated about thirty-two miles west-south-west of Indore. The first Peshwa, Bajee Rao, assigned the principality with some adjoining districts and the tribute of some Rajput chiefs, to Assund Rao, a member of the Puar family, one of the most distinguished in the early Mahratta history. Assund Rao died in 1748, and was succeeded by his son, who was one of the great Mahratta leaders that fell on the fatal plain of Panipat (1761). For twenty years before the British conquest of Malwa, the Dhar State was subjected to a continued series of spoliations, chiefly at the hands of Scindia and Holkar, and was only saved from destruction by Meena Bae, the mother of the reigning chief, who had the talents and courage which distinguish the Mahratta woman. By a treaty, concluded on 18th January, 1819, the Rajah of Dhar agreed "to act in subordinate co-operation with the British Government, and to have no intercourse or alliance, private or public, with any other State, but secretly and openly to be the friend and ally of the British Government; and at all times when that Government shall require, the Rajah of Dhar shall furnish troops (infantry and horse) in proportion to his ability." In May, 1857, Anand Rao Puar, then thirteen years of age, succeeded his half-brother. When news of the attack on the Residency at Indore reached Dhar, some four hundred mercenaries, mainly Arabs and Afghans, who had been enlisted by the Prime Minister, plundered and burned two British stations, and on their return they took possession of the fort of Dhar. On the 15th of October, Captain Hutchinson, the Political Agent, reported that the mother and uncle of the young Chief had instigated the rebellion and outrages of the mercenaries, and that the Durbar had received with marked attention and civility emissaries from Mundesore, where the insurgents, under the Imperial Prince, had become a formidable force. Durand determined to attack at once the fort at Dhar, and, having crushed rebellion there, to march north against the Shahzada and disperse the Mundesore army.

On the 22nd of October, after a wearisome march over a broken and muddy country, the column sighted the fort of Dhar. The enemy had taken steps to attack them outside the citadel. On a hill south of the fort, they had planted three brass guns, and from this battery they extended in force along the east face, "skirmishing in splendid style." The 25th Native Infantry rapidly engaged the skirmishers and compelled them to retire. Then Major Robertson, their commander, gave the word, and the gallant Bombay sepoys hurled themselves on the guns, captured them, and turned them upon the enemy. At this moment the 86th Regiment and the sappers in the centre, with the dragoons under Captain Gall on their right, and the Nizam cavalry under Major Orr on their left, were advanced against the centre of the enemy's position. "They made a rapid move to turn our right and get round to the baggage. But the dragoons, led by Gall, and the native cavalry by Orr and Macdonald, Deputy Quartermaster-General of the forces, charged and drove them back into the fort."*

---

* "The 3rd Cavalry charged home with fiery energy, and one of Orr's troopers was found lying dead with five of the enemy slain around him." *Life of Sir Henry Durand.* By H. M. *Durand, C.S.I., Vol. I, p. 230.*

The Fort of Dhar.

On the 24th, the siege-train arrived at the camp at Dhar, which was pitched in an enormous ravine surrounded on all sides by heights broken by gigantic fissures. About a mile and a half to the north, on a mound some thirty feet above the plain, stood the fort with its massive walls built of fine-grained red granite, some thirty feet high, having at intervals fourteen bastions and two square towers. To capture this citadel by coup de main was impossible. The walls must be breached, and to establish a breaching battery, a position must be taken up as near as practicable. The south-east and north faces were quite unapproachable from the plain, upon which there was little or no cover, and the approaches on all these sides were almost perpendicular, while the walls and bastions were considerably higher on account of the fall of the hills. The west face was defended by thick zig-zag loop-holed walls, strengthened by bastions, running up from the lower gate to the curtain. In the centre was an intricate, almost impregnable, eastern gateway, flanked by massive bastions. Opposite the west face, and only three or four hundred yards distant from it, was a long high mound terminating at a large lake. It was determined to take advantage of this natural parallel and to erect a breaching battery on it at a spot opposite the corner curtain. Strong cavalry and infantry pickets were thrown out on the east and on the northern faces, and as the lake was unfordable it was considered that there was no escape for the enemy. On Sunday morning, 25th October, the 86th and Madras sappers marched through a gorge leading from the camp to Dhar. As the troops neared the fort, a very smart fire of musketry, gingalls and round shot was kept up by the enemy. "The artillery dashed along in splendid style and speedily opened fire upon the bastions, while the 8th with their rifles subdued the heat of the fire from the matchlock men. All this time the mortar battery which had been constructed on a hill some two thousand yards south of the fort kept sending shells into it." About noon, the long mound was occupied. During the night the breaching battery was thrown up, and next day the heavy guns opened fire upon the curtain of the fort. "For a long time little or no effect was produced. But, by and by, the thundering weight of metal continuously battering at one spot had the inevitable result. Little by little the stone work crumbled as the eighteen pounders continued to pour their contents on

Siege of Dhar.

it.". On the 27th October, Major Woolcomb, Lieutenants Strutt and Christie, and some men of the Bombay Artillery, Lieutenant Fenwick and a company of the 25th Regiment Native Infantry volunteered to enter the town, which lay between the battery and the fort, and to fire it. About 9-30 P.M., they crept down from the front of the battery, crossed over the valley below, skirted the water's edge, and were then lost to sight among the trees and huts. "A blaze soon sprang up from one spot, then another, and another, and we could see the burning port-fire flung through the air to other houses. The conflagration spread faster and faster, and the whole town was enveloped in flames flickering high and broad; then arose a din of voices, amid volleys of musketry, rattling, and screams, and howling of dogs. Roof after roof tumbled in, and soon the village was one huge pile, overshadowed by curling clouds of smoke dancing high above the flames and darkening the bright starry sky. It was a gorgeous sight, and if beauty could accompany such a picture, it was there, as every flame, and cloud, and burning timber lay reflected, bright and changing, on the still bosom of the lake below." The party rushing through the scorching flaming streets returned in safety to the battery. By the morning of the 29th, the 18-pounders and 24-pounder howitzer had made a considerable hole in the curtain. The next day the enemy hoisted a white flag and a messenger was sent to them, but after some conversation they drove him away. It was only a ruse on their part to gain an opportunity of examining the breach. All through the day of the 31st the British batteries kept up an unremitting fire, while that of the enemy slackened. At sunset, a storming party was ordered to be in readiness for the night, and Corporals Hoskins and Clarke volunteered to examine the breach for them. About ten o'clock, the two soldiers started, reached the top, made their examination, and returned. The breach was practicable and easily ascended. The skirmishing party was advanced, mounted the breach, and entered the fort unopposed by a soul. The rebels, foreseeing an assault, had left the fort by the main gateway, and taking advantage of the cover afforded by plantations of high-grown sugar-cane and gigantic cereals and darkly shaded groves of mango and tamarind trees, they had made their escape unobserved by the outlying pickets.*

Major Woolcomb, Lieutenants Strutt, Christie, and Fenwick.

Burning of the Town.

Corporals Hoskins and Clarke.

---

* "The jemadar commanding the irregular picket was placed in arrest, but it would appear from the evidence adduced on enquiry that he was not much to blame. The trooper sent by him to warn the picket of dragoons, after it was known that the enemy were off, fell with his horse on the way and was at once disabled; at the same time the European picket, which had been there for some days, and knew the whole locality well, happened to have been changed the very day of the escape." *Central India, by Thomas Lowe, p. 82.*

The Governor General's Political Agent ordered the fort of Dhar to be demolished and the state to be confiscated pending the final decision of Government.* At five o'clock on the morning of the 8th of November, the column started from its encamping-ground at Dhar. They left the once stately fort a heap of ruins, the palace and gates burning piles. " The flames shot up from the crackling masses beneath them in wild luridity, and glimmered upon the departing masses in ghastly beams, as they threaded along in silent tramp beneath the shadows of the dismantled bastions and walls." As they continued their march through western Malwa towards Mundesore, news reached them of the evil deeds done by the enemy who had preceded them. " In several of Scindia's villages and towns they had plundered the inhabitants, beaten them, and carried away the women." On the 8th of November, a large body of the Afghan mercenaries or Velayuties, as they were called, attacked the station of Mehidpore, garrisoned by a portion of the Malwa contingent, commanded by Major Timmins. The infantry and artillery of the contingent were drawn up near the artillery lines, and the guns opened on the enemy, who were under cover of the bungalows and their enclosures. The majority of the contingent infantry, however, refused to attack when led on by their officers. " The Subah-dar-Major opened his jacket as the rebels approached, took out a green flag and hoisted it." Only a portion of the artillery stood to their guns, and at noon the rebels attacked and took them. " The contingent troops then fled, and their officers were forced to escape, escorted by a faithful band of the 2nd Gwalior Cavalry."† On the 9th of November, they arrived in our camp. That night, Major Orr, with three hundred and thirty-seven sabres, drawn from the 1st, 3rd, and 4th Regiments started for Mehidpore.

Mehidpore, 8th November.

On the morning of the 12th, after a march of sixty miles, Orr arrived at Mehidpore and found it had just been evacuated, the enemy having taken with them two 12-pounders, four 9-pounders, and sixty cartloads of ammunition and plunder. " Orr after watering and feeding his horses set forth in pursuit. After a ride of twelve miles he came

---

* " It was subsequently restored to Rajah Anand Rao Puar with the exception of the Bairsea Pergunnah, but was retained under British management till the Chief should attain the age of eighteen years, or until he should become competent to manage his own affairs. The management of the state was entrusted to the Chief in October, 1864." *A Collection of Treaties compiled by C. U. Aitchison, B.C.S., Vol. III, p. 380. Parliamentary Papers on Dhar, April 8th, 1859.*

† *Telegram from Captain Mayne to the Governor General, Camp, Jehampore, November 13th, 1857.*

in touch with their rear-guard at the village of Rawal. They were well posted, having their right resting on the village and their front covered by a nullah or rivulet. Orr immediately crossed the rivulet and, braving the fire of the guns, Abbot and Johnstone with their troopers charged. As they rode up to them the enemy fired, and the grape passed over their heads with a rushing noise like a covey of birds." In another instant they were right upon the battery sabring the gunners. And then began a mortal tussle. The Afghans standing up manfully, made a desperate resistance. An English officer came up with one of the Rohillas. " He was a fine fellow, and perhaps a leader. He was requested to surrender, this he refused to do ; he was then told that unless he did so, death would assuredly be his portion. Then ensued the struggle for life in deadly conflict, which he manfully maintained upon foot till the cold sharp spear of his antagonist pierced his breast ; he then fell upon the field, cast one agonised withering look of a still unvanquished spirit on his foe, threw his arms across his eyes, and died without a groan." The combat continued until darkness fell and the enemy vanished in the tall crops of sugar-cane and jowaree. But the guns were retaken with all their ammunition, and one hundred and fifty of the enemy lay dead on the field. The British loss was one hundred killed and wounded.

On the 14th of November, Durand received a despatch from Major Orr informing him of the defeat of the mutineers at Mehidpore. The news was important, not merely on account of the success gained, but because it proved the loyalty and gallantry of the Hyderabad contingent. Durand continued his march through western Malwa towards Mundesore as fast as the roads would permit. On the 19th of November, the camp was pitched at Hornia on the banks of the Chumbul. Spies stated that a large rebel force was now only twenty miles away and that the rebels had determined to give the British battle in the open field. They had spread in Mundesore the report that they had defeated the English at Dhar and that they were now going to destroy utterly the few remaining Feringhees who had the temerity to follow them so far. But, with oriental carelessness they neglected, what was most vital to their success—the defence of the great natural barrier. To cross the Chumbul without opposition was a business of no light nature, for the banks were rugged and almost perpendicular, the stream was rapid and deep, and its bed broken by enormous boulders of basalt. The sappers had cut a road down the bank for the artillery and then the passage began. "It was a beautiful picture," says an eye-witness. "The steep, verdant, shrubby banks covered with our varied forces, elephants, camels, horses, and bullocks; the deep flowing clear river reaching on and on to the far east to the soft deep blue tufted horizon; the babble and yelling of men, the lowing of cattle, the grunting screams of the camels, and the trumpeting of the weary heavily-laden elephant; the rattle of our artillery down the bank, through the river, and up the opposite side; the splashing and plunging of our cavalry through the stream—neighing and eager for the green encamping-grounds before them; and everybody so busy and jovial, streaming up from the deep water to their respective grounds; and all this in the face, almost, of an enemy." The crossing of the force, ammunition, and baggage occupied nearly the whole day.

On the morning of the 21st of November, the column encamped four miles south of Mundesore. In the afternoon, the enemy came out from the town and occupied in force a village upon the British left, and formed up into considerable masses upon the extensive plateau in front of their line. The accurate fire of the British guns caused the masses to waver; the order was given for the sappers and Hyderabad infantry to occupy the village, which was speedily done, for as they advanced, the enemy evacuated it and fled. "The cavalry pursued and cut up a good number of them; the main body then fled into Mundesore. By 5 o'clock the field was ours."

The spies had informed Durand that the rebel force, some five thousand in number, who had been besieging Neemuch, had raised the siege, and were hastening to join their comrades at Mundesore. He, therefore, determined to occupy a position which would enable him to prevent their junction. The next morning he crossed the river, and, making a flank movement to the left, he encamped to the west of the town within two thousand yards of the suburb. He was just in time. A cavalry movement showed that the Neemuch rebels were posted in considerable force five miles away on the high road to that station. At dawn, Durand struck his camp and went forth to meet them. There was a small branch of the river to be crossed, and before all the baggage could be got over, the enemy came out from Mundesore to fall upon the rear. The dragoons and two guns soon drove them back. The march continued, unmolested. When they had gone about five miles, and approached the spot where the enemy was said to be posted, a halt was sounded. A few officers rode ahead, when they saw in front of them what seemed like moving masses and flags, waving above the high crops of grain. "They became more and more distinct and presently we could see a large body of horsemen and two bodies of infantry." It was the enemy from Neemuch in force. They had selected a very strong position upon the road, their right resting on the village of Goorariah, their centre on a long hill, and their left well covered by fields, of uncut grain, with broken ground and nullahs in their front full of water and mud.

The troops took up their position for the battle. The artillery rattled to the front, the men cheering and waving their hats as they flew past to open fire. The 86th formed into double line on the right of the guns; the 25th, with the Madras sappers *en échelon* on their left, moved up under a sharp and heavy fire in double line, "as beautifully as on a parade ground," to the enemy's centre. To the left of these was the Hyderabad infantry, and on either flanks were the dragoons and irregular cavalry. The Hyderabad Contingent artillery opened fire from the British left centre. During the artillery duel, the enemy's infantry came down from their heights and with banners and flags of all colours flying, advanced to within a few yards of the infantry. The 25th Bombay Native Infantry, led by Major Robertson, charged and drove them back. Lieutenant Martin of the Bengal Cavalry, with some score of dragoons, flung himself on the enemy's guns and cut down the gunners. But the dashing charge was not supported, and he had to retire, having received a wound in the knee. The horsemen, however, again fell on the guns and captured them. The enemy, contesting every inch of the ground, retired to the village.* The 86th and 25th Bombay Native Infantry now moved on it: and the men fell fast, because they had to pass a good many nullahs filled with sepoys who, from these ambuscades, plied their muskets with effect. But keeping well together, they surmounted the difficulty of the ground and attacked the village. The walls of the houses and the enclosures were pierced with loopholes through which the rebels commenced a well sustained fusillade. The British soldier and the Bombay sepoy fought their way into the village, but as the enemy were under shelter and aimed so coolly that every shot told, the assailants were ordered to withdraw. During this combat, the

---

* "Those who had not the chance of doing so fled along the Neemuch road and in other directions through fields. The cavalry cut up great numbers in these fields." *Central India, by T. Lowe, p. 112.*

rear-guard was attacked by a strong body from the city of Mundesore. The Hyderabad Cavalry, commanded by Captains Abbott and Murray, with two guns and three companies of infantry, were sent to reinforce it. The two guns opened on the enemy, and when they began to waver, the Hyderabad Cavalry and a troop of the 14th Dragoons, commanded by Lieutenant Leith, charged them and drove them back to a point where a small pond of water and some shallow pits or stone quarries joined. Lieutenant Redmayne who was leading, wheeled round the pond, being closely followed by Lieutenant Chapman and a few dragoons. A tremendous concentrated fire of musketry from the quarry dashed nearly the whole to the earth. Lieutenant Redmayne, whose horse had carried him far ahead of his men, was, while lying on the ground, hacked to pieces by the rebels. "When his body was brought in, no feature could be recognised." At this moment Captain Abbott appeared on the other side of the pits, and the enemy retreated into the Mundesore fort. Sable night fell, and the Rohillahs held the village—a flaming fire. The British loss was great—upwards of sixty officers and men wounded.

About 10 o'clock next morning, the 18-pounder and 24 pounder howitzers were brought up to within two hundred and fifty yards of the village and poured forth a storm of shot and shell. The houses were reduced to a mass of ruins and the fire consumed all that would burn. But the gallant garrison still held out. Towards 4 P.M., the 86th Regiment, the 25th Bombay Native Infantry, and some Madras sappers stormed the burning village. The heroic Rohillas defended the burning sheds with dogged bravery, and, from the tops of the charred ruins, sent a deadly fire on their assailants as they rushed through the streets. "The Madrassees with their huge blue turbans, behaved gloriously, as they always do. They were rushing about like salamanders in the flames and smoke." The Bombay sepoys, always patient, faithful and brave, also shone that day. Many of them were wounded as they charged the village, or in the furious hand-to-hand struggles. When they were brought into the field hospital with arms and legs shattered by round shots, limbs and body perforated by musket bullets, and flesh wounds of no slight nature, their general observation was, "Ah well, never mind, we have eaten the Sircar's salt for many years; this has been good work, and the Sircar will be good and take care of us, or our families if we die." "One poor fellow, whose blood was welling away profusely from a wound near the shoulder joint, was offered a little brandy-and-water as a stimulant, when he nobly said 'Give it to my brother first,' who sat next to him groaning in agony; he then drank and said he did not mind his wound, for he knew Government would not forget him."* During that dreadful conflict, the County Downs had to freely use their bayonets as they drove the Rohillas, contesting every inch of the ground, out of the houses. The Irish lads not only fought manfully, but their conduct increased the lustre of the soldiers' heroism. "Occasionally a son of the sister isle, all covered with sweat and dust, his face blackened by powder and smoke, would be seen leading tenderly outside the walls a woman or a child." When evening came, only a few rebels remained in strongly built houses at the upper end of the village. Cavalry pickets were thrown around them and the troops returned to camp. "The next day not a living soul remained in Goorariah."

The capture of Goorariah was a mortal blow to rebellion in Western Malwa. During the attack on the village, the Shahzada and his Afghan mercenaries evacuated Mundesore, and as they fled through the country, the population attacked them and drove them into the jungles. After a large breach had been made in one of the walls of the Mundesore fort by the Madras Sappers, in order to render it untenable by a foe, the column marched for Indore. Major Orr was left behind with his force of Hyderabad troops and Captain Keatinge was appointed political agent of Western Malwa.† No better choice could have been made. He had, before the outbreak at Indore, controlled his own district with courage and energy, and during the operations he had rendered good service by raising and managing some native levies in the small states north of Indore. On the 15th of December, the column marched through the suburbs of Indore and pitched their camp in front of the Residency. The massive walls of the stately home of the Governor-General's Agent at Indore stood, but the inside had been completely gutted. The church, "a pretty little village-like sanctuary," had been rifled and defiled. Of the hospitals and other buildings nothing remained but blackened tumble-down walls. But the British representative, cruelly and treacherously driven away, had returned supported by British bayonets. The court

---

* "Not a man refused to take what was offered to him as drink—even then, all shunned—wine was willingly accepted by them; and when an amputation was performed they bore it with heroic fortitude, for although chloroform was not administered, scarcely a groan escaped while the dreadful knife was severing the member from its body. In action they were cool, gallant, and intrepid; under the painful ordeal of the surgical operation they displayed patience, cheerfulness, and fortitude." *Central India, by T. Lowe, p. 120.*

† Afterwards Colonel Keatinge, V.C., Chief Commissioner of Assam.

astrologer had said, " Though every European save one were slain, that one would remain to fight and reconquer." On the afternoon of the 15th, Holkar's mutinous troops laid down their arms. At 5 o'clock, all officers of the force attended, at an invitation from the Maharajah, an open durbar. Holkar told the Brigadier he " was very glad to see him and his victorious army." Durand informed the Maharajah that the British Government expected that all who had taken part in the attack on the Residency and on Mehidpore should be punished. Holkar promised that a Commission which he had previously appointed would make full enquiries into the matter. But Durand had grave doubts whether justice would ever be done. He had not much faith in the fidelity of the Indore chief. The precise nature and amount of Holkar's loyalty has been discussed at considerable length and with considerable acrimony. But the facts are few and simple. The British Residency was attacked by Holkar's mutinous troops; Europeans were murdered, and the Resident was compelled to evacuate it. Holkar knew what was taking place. Saadat Khan rode up wounded to Holkar's palace and told him that he had wounded a sahib and attacked the Residency. For three days Holkar remained in his palace in constant communication with the mutineers. He then visited the Residency and onversed with Saadat Khan, with the commander of the infantry which had led the attack, and with the subahdar of the 23rd Native Infantry who was a party to the murder of his commanding officer. On the other hand, it must be remembered that he refused to hand over to the Mhow mutineers the Europeans and other Christians who had taken refuge in his palace, and when he had recovered from the shock of the revolt of his troops, he acted with energy, consideration, and loyalty to the British cause. But the fact remains that at the critical moment when the Residency was attacked, Holkar hesitated and did nothing. If he had appeared at the Residency, with such troops as he could depend upon, to overawe his mutinous soldiers, the outbreak would at once have been put down. He was careless of the lives of English officers, and in the hour of trial violated his duty to the Government to which he owed allegiance, and which from a cottage had placed him on a throne. If Holkar had been deposed and his state confiscated and divided among our faithful allies, there is not a native chief who would not have admitted the justice of our decision. But the Government of India, taking into consideration his subsequent conduct, treated him with marked leniency and generosity. Sir Robert Hamilton, who had hastily and improperly placed Holkar on the throne, advocated his claim for territorial reward for mutiny services. But Lord Canning, when he understood the whole question, deliberately recorded that Holkar's services were not such as to entitle him to a reward; and his decision was endorsed by successive Viceroys.

On the 16th, Durand ceased to be Agent to the Governor-General. Sir Robert Hamilton had returned to Indore and resumed charge of his duties. He was accompanied by Sir Hugh Rose, who took command of the force which then assumed the name of the Central India Field Force. Thus ended the Malwa Campaign, a brilliant episode in the history of the Indian Mutiny. Durand had overcome by patience and courage the varied obstacles which beset his path, and had proved himself a skilful and daring commander. "His conduct," as Lord Canning recorded in a minute, "was marked by great foresight and the soundest judgment as well in military as in civil matters." He had many points to guard, and the trustworthy force at his disposal was almost hopelessly small; but by a judicious use of it, and by the closest personal supervision of its movements, Colonel Durand saved our interests in Central India until support could arrive.

When Sir Colin Campbell was in Calcutta, a general plan of campaign was designed, by which the resources of the three Presidencies, after the arrival of reinforcements from England, should be made available for combined action. A Bombay column, called the Central India Force, supported by the Rajputana Field Force on one side and the Madras force called the Saugor and Nerbudda Field Force on the other side, was to march through the heart of Hindustan to restore order, and, by distracting the attention of the insurgents in that quarter, obviate the risk of Sir Colin Campbell being attacked by the formidable Gwalior Contingent and other rebels, whilst engaged in the reduction of the Doab, Rohilcund, and Oudh. The Central India Field Force was to make Mhow its base of operations. After capturing Jhansi, the stronghold of the mutineers in Central India, it was to march to Calpee situated on the Jumna, where Sir Colin hoped to come in touch with it. The Madras column, starting from Jubbulpore and clearing the line of communication with Allahabad and Mirzapore, was to march across Bundelcund to Banda, also situated on the Jumna some ninety-five miles south-west of Allahabad. It was a well-conceived plan and showed a broad grasp of the science of war. The officers appointed to carry out the operations, under the instructions of the Commander-in-Chief, were Major-Generals Sir Hugh Rose to

Plan of Campaign.

command the Central India Field Force, and Whitlock and Roberts to command the Madras column and Rajputana Field Force respectively.

It would be difficult to imagine two men more different in their characters and their lives than Colin Campbell, the son of a Scotch carpenter, and Hugh Rose, the son of the Minister Plenipotentiary at the Prussian Court. Colin Campbell was a brave soldier endowed with a vigorous intellect, Scotch homely sense and Scotch caution; Hugh Rose was a clever, impulsive soldier, whose operations were marked by skill, daring, and determination, but a lack of caution which nearly ended in disaster. Genius, however, attached to everything he did: we see it in his despatches, we see it in his conduct of war. To Colin Campbell the mounting of the ladder of success was a long and tedious process; to Hugh Rose promotion came rapidly. Entering the army in 1820 as an Ensign in the 93rd Sutherland Highlanders, he was transferred to the 19th Regiment, and, in recognition of the gallantry he had displayed under critical circumstances in Ireland, he was given, on the special recommendation of his commanding officer, an unattached majority by purchase, after a little more than six years' service. Soon after obtaining his majority, Major Rose was appointed to the 92nd Gordon Highlanders and served with them eleven years. In the year 1840 he was attached, with the rank of Lieutenant-Colonel and Deputy Adjutant-General, to Omar Pasha's Brigade in Syria during the operations against Mehemet Ali. Soon after his arrival, and in a brilliant exploit, the fiery courage of the sabreur was displayed. As Rose was wandering accidentally in the direction of the Egyptian outposts, he noticed that a large body of their cavalry was about to surprise the camp of Omar Pasha. Putting himself at the head of a regiment of Arab cavalry, he charged down on the Egyptian horse. "In the hand to hand encounter that followed Colonel Rose received two or three slight wounds, but he succeeded in completely routing the enemy, killing several of them. He himself, with his own hand, wounded and captured the leader." For this "dashing and gallant conduct," to use the words of his superior officer, "Colonel Rose, besides receiving a sabre of honour from the Sultan and the order of the *Nishan Iftehan* in diamonds, had bestowed upon him by his sovereign the insignia of the Military Companionship of the Bath. Soon after the termination of the war in the Levant, Colonel Rose was appointed Consul-General in Syria. The state of affairs in the country was most critical. The Consul-General had to uphold Turkish and

British interests in Syria against the intrigues of rival powers and to preserve the peace between the Christian Maronites and Muhammadan Druses. In carrying out this policy, Hugh Rose showed rare ability, adroit adaptation of means to ends and a bold bearing up against powerful antagonists.. He also displayed courage of the truest temper and a spirit of active and warm benevolence towards his fellow-creatures. When the American missionaries at Abaye on Mount Lebanon sent an urgent appeal to the Consul for assistance, Rose rode there accompanied only by two Kavasses. He found the castle in flames and the Druses with drawn swords watching outside to sabre the Christians as they were driven out of the fire. The imperious Consul so exercised his dominion over the Druses that they not only refrained from slaying the Christians but allowed them to go to Beyrout under his charge. The Druses had laid waste the country with fire and sword, and, beset by fanatics thirsting for blood, he conducted in safety seven hundred Christians to Beyrout. During the journey, he and his two Kavasses gave up their horses to the women to ride. When cholera raged with great fury in Beyrout, and "the terror-stricken Christian population abandoned their houses and fled to the country" he alone of all the Europeans, with the exception of one medical officer and some sisters of charity, remained behind to visit the huts of those smitten with the mortal disease. "Language faintly conveys," says the address presented to him by grateful eye-witnesses, "the impression created by conduct so generous and humane; but the remembrance of it will never be effaced from the hearts of those who were the objects of such kindness, nor will such devotion easily be forgotten by those who witnessed it."*

For the good work he did in Syria, Lord Palmerston, in January 1851, appointed Hugh Rose Secretary of the Embassy at Constantinople. The same year he was promoted Brevet-Colonel. In June 1852, Sir Stratford Canning went to England and was absent for some eight or nine months, during which time Rose, as chargé d'affaires, showed that a slender authority in the hands of a strong man may be of the greatest service at a grave crisis. One morning the Turkish Minister for Foreign Affairs and the Grand Vizier informed Rose that Prince Menchekoff, a personal favourite of the Czar and a man of an over-bearing demeanour who had been sent as a special envoy to Constantinople, demanded that the Sultan should sign a Secret Treaty which would virtually give the Czar the

---

* *Clyde and Strathnairn.* By Major-General Sir Owen Tudor Burne, K.C.S.I., p. 93.

protectorate of all the Christian subjects of the Porte. No sovereign having a proper regard for his own dignity and independence could admit such a proposal. The Sultan's independence and the integrity of his dominions had been guaranteed by England and the other Powers, and the Grand Vizier asked Hugh Rose what material pledge he could give that England would support them in opposing the Russian demand. It was a difficult and delicate position. Rose was not the appointed representative of England at the Ottoman Porte, and for him to give a material guarantee might well be regarded as acting outside the sphere of his duty. Rose informed the Grand Vizier that it was for the Porte to specify the assistance required, and he would immediately send off an express message to Belgrade or Vienna, or a steamer to Malta with the intelligence to Her Majesty's Government. "Oh," replied the Grand Vizier, "special messengers and steamers are too late. We must sign the Secret Treaty by sunset this evening, or Prince Menchekoff will demand his passports. We wish to see the British fleet in Turkish waters." Rose stated that he had no power to order the British fleet to Constantinople, but he would inform the Admiral at once of the gravity of the situation and the serious responsibility he would incur if he were to refuse to bring the fleet. The Grand Vizier was satisfied. That night the Sultan's Ministers declined to sign the treaty.* Admiral Dundas did not feel justified in sending the fleet into Turkish waters without directions from home, and the ministry approved of his decision. But as the historian of the Crimean War remarks, "Although he was disavowed by the Government at home, and although his appeal to the English Admiral was rejected, it is not the less certain that his mere consent to call up the fleet allayed the panic which was endangering at that moment the very life of the Ottoman Empire."†

Russia drifted into war with England and France, and Rose was appointed Queen's Commissioner at the Head-Quarters of the French Army, with the local rank of Brigadier-General. At Alma when, during three sunny hours a French and an English army fought side by side,

---

* Major-General Sir Owen Tudor Burne, who states that he gives "Sir Hugh Rose's own account of the incident," writes, "Not long after sunset, the Porte's Chief Dragoman came to Colonel Rose at Therapia to inform him that Prince Menchekoff had presented his demand for their signature of the treaty, and that they had refused it. The despatch sent to Admiral Dundas, though not acted on, had gained its object." *Clyde and Strathnairn By Major-General Sir Owen Tudor Burne, K.C.S.I.*, p 95.

† *The Invasion of the Crimea.* By A. W. Kinglake, Vol. I, p. 106.

General Rose was with the 1st Regiment of the Zouaves while they, under a heavy artillery fire, captured the Telegraph Height. The following morning, when he was visiting with General Canrobert La Maison Brulée upon which the Russians had concentrated a heavy artillery fire, Rose was wounded by the splinter of a shell. At the Mount of Inkerman, where England fought the gathered strength of the Czar, he offered a striking instance of coolness and daring. In order to reconnoitre the ground between the left of General Canrobert and the right of General Pennefather, he rode leisurely down the Tchernaya road under the withering fire from the whole line of pickets. " The horseman turned neither to the right nor to the left nor could the Russians hit him. Suddenly, they saw him fall headlong with his horse. After a few minutes, paying no attention to the firing, the mysterious horseman got up, shook himself, patted his horse, and led the animal leisurely back up the road. The Russians were so awe-struck that an order was sent along the line to cease firing on the man, who ' we afterwards learnt,' said the Russian officer, ' was Colonel Rose.' " General Canrobert, who himself was always ready for an act of brave self-devotion, recommended Hugh Rose for the Victoria Cross for gallant conduct on three different occasions, but, having the local rank of Brigadier-General, he was considered not to be eligible, as the regulations expressly excluded General Officers from this decoration. He was, however, on the 12th of December 1854, promoted "for distinguished conduct in the field" to be Major-General, and on the 16th of October 1855 he received the degree of Knight Commander of the Bath.*

Soon after the tidings of the revolt of the Bengal Army reached England, the Duke of Cambridge, who " personally had an opportunity in the Crimea of seeing what manner of man my gallant friend was, and of what stuff he was made," gave him the important command of the Poona Division of the Bombay Army. It was the command which Charles Napier held before he went to conquer Sind. On the 19th of September 1857, Hugh Rose landed at Bombay. Lord Canning had intended to give the command of the Central India Force to General John Jacob, the daring leader of cavalry who had subdued the proud and warlike mountaineers of the Afghan and Beloochee frontier, but John Jacob, who commanded the cavalry during the Persian Campaign,

---

* *London Gazette, 6th February 1855.*

86   INTRODUCTION

25th November 1857.

was detained at the desire of the British Minister in Persia, and the command was given to Sir Hugh Rose.*

On the 17th of December, he assumed command of the Central India Field Force, which consisted of two brigades. The 1st Brigade, recently the Malwa Field Force, was at Mhow; the 2nd Brigade was at Sehore. The left or 1st Brigade at Mhow under the command of Brigadier C. S. Stuart of the Bombay Army was composed of :—

    1 Squadron, 14th Light Dragoons.
    1 Troop, 3rd Bombay Light Cavalry.
    2 Regiments, Hyderabad Contingent Cavalry.
    2 Companies 86th Regiment ;† 25th Bombay Native Infantry.
    1 Regiment, Hyderabad Contingent Infantry.
    3 Light Field Batteries (one belonging to the Royal Artillery, one to that of Bombay, the third to Hyderabad).
    Some Sappers.

The right or 2nd Brigade at Sehore under the Command of Brigadier Steuart, 14th Dragoons, was composed of :—

    Head-Quarters, 14th Light Dragoons.
            3rd Bombay Light Cavalry.
    1 Regiment, Hyderabad Contingent Cavalry.
            3rd Bombay European Fusiliers.‡
            24th Bombay Native Infantry.
    1 Regiment, Hyderabad Contingent Infantry.
    1 Battery, Horse Artillery.
    1 Light Field Battery.
    1 Battery, Bhopal Artillery.
    1 Company, Madras Sappers.
    A detachment of Bombay Sappers and a siege train.

On the morning that he assumed command, the Major-General rode from Indore to Mhow, reviewed the 1st Brigade and inspected the

---

* Outram wrote to John Jacob from Calcutta on the 6th of August, the day he left for Allahabad.—" I have urged the Governor-General to give you command of that army (Central India) and he appears most highly to approve of the idea, satisfied as he is that you of all men are best fitted for the great military and political responsibilities which must rest on that commander. As the Commander-in-Chief of all India will, I presume, command the Eastern army, yours will be the highest command in India next to his. My own part in the campaign will be very secondary, merely preserving the country up to Cawnpore, and maintaining the Commander-in-Chief's communications."

†The remainder of the companies of this regiment joined before the attack on Chanderi.
‡Now the 2nd Battalion, Leinster Regiment.

hospitals. On visiting the hospital of the Madras Sappers, he told the men how pleased the Government were at their gallant conduct, and on a wounded sapper begging not to be left behind, Sir Hugh said that every attention should be given to him. Sir Hugh possessed great energy and it was taxed to the utmost in making the necessary numerous arrangements for his force to take the field. He gave himself entirely up to the business, labouring day and night, thinking of nothing else. "He was laughed at and called a griff by a good many, and a good many others asked who he was and what he had done." But the griff swiftly proved that he knew well the business of war, and the London dandy, after the longest march spruce and neat, won the confidence and affection of his men. On Christmas day the General and his staff dined with the officers at Mhow. The banners captured from the enemy in the Malwa Campaign, and green leaves in the place of holly and mistletoe, decorated the room. "The maids of merry England were not forgotten, nor were the heroes who had gone gloriously to their graves in the conflicts in Bengal and other parts of India. It was a happy meeting; few, however, who were present then met together to celebrate another Christmas." The new year came, and with it the cheering news of the relief of Outram and Havelock at Lucknow by Sir Colin Campbell. But grave tidings from Saugor also reached them. A large force of mutineers were moving towards that cantonment with the view of attacking the fort whose garrison consisted of one weak company of European Artillery and about forty officials. To this small body of men was entrusted the protection of a large and important arsenal and the lives of some one hundred and seventy European women and children. In the cantonments were one thousand Bengal sepoys and about one hundred irregular cavalry. They had behaved well, but would they continue to be loyal when they came in touch with their mutinous brethren? They were now mistrusted and not allowed to do duty in the fort, and to remain loyal under the circumstances would indeed be a hard and trying exercise of faith. The importunities of their deluded comrades, who were wild with bigotry and flushed with success, the dread of being outcasts if their masters were driven into the sea, were incentives strong enough to draw the most faithful into the vortex of rebellion. No praise is too high for the sepoy who remained true to his colours.

To Brigadier Whitlock had been assigned the task of relieving Saugor, but Sir Hugh Rose knew that the Madras column could not reach

Saugor for two months, and, taking upon himself the responsibility of diverging from the plan of campaign, he determined to march rapidly, with a portion of his force, to its relief. On the 6th of January, accompanied by Sir R. Hamilton, he left Mhow to join the 2nd Brigade at Sehore. On the morning of the 8th of January the siege train commenced its march from Indore,* and six days later joined the force at Saugor. On the 10th, the 1st Brigade left Mhow. It was marching in a parallel line to clear the Grand Trunk Road and ultimately join the other brigade in the attack on Jhansi. On the morning of the 16th, Sir Hugh Rose with the 2nd Brigade left Sehore, and after passing over a rich plateau, they ascended a range of hills and saw below them the city of Bhopal spreading itself in the form of an amphitheatre, on the declivity of a hill, the foot of which is bathed by a fine lake surrounded by a circle of large trees. The Begum of Bhopal, who had put off the mutinous solicitations of her people from day to day by assuring them that the proper time for the expulsion of the British had not yet arrived, welcomed the British force, furnished it with supplies, and placed at the disposal of Sir Hugh Rose 600 or 700 of her troops. On the morning of the 16th the brigade left Bhopal. The siege train followed the next day. But it was no easy task to transport the heavy guns through jungle and nullahs, over rough ground and hills. On the afternoon of the 24th, the siege train reached a tributary of the river Beena, where hundreds of baggage wagons were found jammed together and unable to gain the opposite bank. "The sappers piled arms and went to work in good earnest, felling trees, cutting the road, and carrying dry sand to cover the slippery path. The carts were got over after immense labour, then came the 18-pounders, and when they arrived at the slippery incline, the elephants struck—they would not move an

---

* We had scarcely gone four miles on the road when a violent explosion was heard in our rear. For an instant we imagined ourselves fired on from an ambush, but on turning round we saw a great column of smoke among the artillery of the Hyderabad Contingent and the men rushing wildly about here and there. The halt was sounded and we galloped to the spot, and a most melancholy scene presented itself. A limber of 9-pounder was filled with loaded shells and these had exploded through some accident in packing. There lay a human-foot in one spot, pieces of flesh in another, burning cloth in a third; a wounded man here, another dying there, a third with the hair of his face and head singed off, and jaw broken. Two men were blown to atoms, the head with the right arm attached being all that was found. The limber had disappeared and the gun, with its trail broken, was driven some yards back covered with blood. The oxen stood still as death also wounded. The driver who sat upon the box was only blown off, while the second ahead of him was killed."

inch further with their charge, so the heavy guns were pulled up the incline by the Madras Sappers."*

It was 3 o'clock in the morning before the work was done. The sappers bivouacked in the jungle, and after a short rest of three hours, they set forth in advance of the guns to overcome fresh obstacles. About 1 P.M. on the 25th, the siege train joined the force at Rathghur. On the previous morning, when Sir Hugh Rose with the advanced guard reached the encamping-ground, he discovered that the leading flankers had, by taking a wrong road, got into a skirmish with the enemy posted in the suburbs of the town. He promptly advanced and covered with the infantry and guns, their return from a position so unsuited to cavalry. "In rectifying this mistake, I had gained a good deal of ground to the right front, and a company of the 24th Native Infantry had taken, with spirit, one or two houses and gardens ; on reconnoitring, I found that they were at the commencement of the suburbs, and that to keep all this would compromise my right, and plan of attacking the fort from the left flank. I therefore ordered the troops back to their Camp†". The next day Sir Hugh Rose made, with Major Boileau, commanding Engineers, and a small party of the 3rd Europans and 3rd Light Cavalry, a complete reconnaissance of eighteen miles of the whole country round the fort, which is situated on the spur of a long high hill. "The east and south faces were almost perpendicular, the rock being scarped and strengthened by a deep rapid river, the Biena, running close beneath from east to west; the north face looked along the densely jungled hill, and was strengthened by a deep ditch some twenty feet wide; the west face overlooked the town and Saugor road : on this face was the gateway, flanked by several square and round bastions. The wall to the north side was strengthened by an outwork looking like a second wall. Along each face were strong bastions commanding various points, and also in the four angles ; approach from the east and south was next to impossible, approach from the west or town side almost as difficult."‡

The reconnaissance having confirmed in all essentials the information on which Sir Hugh Rose had formed his plan of attack, he carried it

Siege of Rathghur.

---

* "I am convinced that no men in the world could have done better (few so well) than did the Madras Sappers in their voluntary labour in this instance. They had it all their own way." *Central India, by T. Lowe, p. 172.*

† *From Major-General Sir Hugh Rose, K.C.B., commanding Central India Field Force, to the Adjutant-General of the Army Head-Quarters, Bombay, dated Camp Saugor, 7th February 1858.*

‡ *Central India, by Thomas Lowe, pp. 173-174.*

out by investing, the same evening, the rock of Ráthghur as closely as the great extent, hills, thick jungle, and a difficult river would allow. He requested the commander of the Bhopal force to invest the south-west of the fort, as it was the one which faced the Bhopal territory.* On the north and north-east were the 3rd Bombay Light Cavalry and the cavalry of the Hyderabad Contingent. The remainder of the force occupied the plain across which runs the Saugor road.

Early on the morning of the 26th, Sir Hugh Rose with the 3rd European Regiment, followed by the 18-pounder howitzers and mortars and the guns of the Hyderabad Contingent, arrived at the jungle at the foot of an open plateau which Major Boileau had selected for the breaching batteries. The sappers who had been sent forward to prepare fascines fell in, and the troops entered the jungle towards the foot-path that led to the summit. When they had made their way well into the wild growth, they suddenly found themselves in the midst of fire. "The jungle grass before, behind, and on both sides of us was in a blaze! What with the heat of the sun and the fire we were pretty nearly roasted. The guide had lost the path, so we halted; the order to 'right about face' was given, and by-and-by we came upon the track. We had not gone far when we found ourselves jammed—progress, save by single file, was impossible. The order 'sappers to the front' was given and away they went to cut a road up this hill for the guns. The ascent, however, was so rugged and steep that much labour was required ere they could be dragged up the summit." The enemy, on seeing the position the English had occupied, opened fire on it from their gingalls and small guns. It was, however, kept down with the fire of the 6-pounder of the Hyderabad Contingent and the $5\frac{1}{2}$ mortars. Sir Hugh Rose writes, "I beg to mention for his devotion on this occasion, Quartermaster Thompson, commanding a half battery of the Artillery of the Hyderabad Contingent, who has completed thirty-two years of meritorious service. Twice hit, he continued to fight his guns successfully to the close of the day. I thanked his battery on the ground."† At 4 P.M. the

---

* *From Major-General Sir Hugh Rose, K.C.B., commanding Central India. Field Force, to the Adjutant-General of the Army, Head-Quarters, Bombay, dated Camp Saugor, 7th February 1858.*
Dr. Lowe writes, "On the east were about a thousand of the Bhopal troops." (*Op. cit. 174.*)

† "The Quarter-Master of the Hyderabad Contingent, M. Thompson, had two narrow escapes. One musket ball struck his leathern helmet, and a second struck him in the chest, upon a pocket-book. Several others were wounded by musket balls." *Central India, by Thomas Lowe, p. 177.*

two 18-pounders with elephant draught were brought up the hill, "the 3rd Europeans dragging them up the steep where the elephants could not go."

Meanwhile, the firing against the town had driven the enemy into the fort and enabled Brigadier Steuart to take possession of a mosque opposite the north face, commanding the town, and within range of the main gate of the fort. On this height and another to the left he placed Captain Lightfoot's 9-pounder battery, one 8-inch howitzer and two 8-inch mortars. These batteries forming the right, or town attack, kept up, night and day, an effective fire on the line of defences and buildings of the fort. "During the pay the General was in front the whole time, choosing sites for the breaching and mortar batteries, and had numerous escapes from being killed." The next day, the 28th, the General, who was constantly between the two attacks which were two and a half miles apart, changed the 8-inch howitzer from the right to the left attack, in order to enfilade with its fire the palaces and defences of the north face. He also directed that from the right an attack should be made on a low massive tower close to the main gateway. The storming party, led by Captain Lightfoot who volunteered to accompany it, entered the tower under a heavy fire from the walls of the postern which were only fifty yards distant. It was found on a thorough examination to be of no value as an offensive and the troops were withdrawn from it before daylight.*

At 8 A.M. on the 28th, the sand-bag batteries of the left attack having been completed, the two 18-pounders and the 8-inch howitzer were brought up to them and commenced their fire against the outer wall of the east curtain of the fort. It soon began to crumble into the ditch. Sir Hugh Rose had just returned to the camp from the battery, when the rebels were seen coming in force out of the thick jungle in the British rear with standards flying. They crossed the river and attacked the vedettes on the right rear of the camp. At this moment another large body appeared on the opposite bank. These two forces, amounting to 1,500 or 2,000 men, consisted mainly of sepoys and Afghan mercenaries. They were led by the Rajah of Banpore, who hoped, by acting in concert with the garrison, to raise the siege, by making a strenuous attack upon the British rear. Hugh Rose, however, as soon as he heard the news of their approach, moved rapidly with an outlying picket of Her Majesty's 14th Light Dragoons, "who in less than a minute were in their saddles," to meet

* "Captain Lightfoot recommends Private Davies of the 3rd Europeans for his gallantry and intelligence on this occasion." *From Major-General Sir Hugh Rose, K.C.B., commanding Central India Field Force, Camp Saugor, 7th February 1858.*

them, ordering two guns and the rest of the picket to follow in support. The enemy, who were skirmishing with a picket of the 3rd Light Cavalry, on seeing their approach, fired a discharge of muskets and rockets at them and ran into a gorge of the Biena and up its rocky bank. Brigadier Steuart who had been called up, advancing from the mosque, unlimbered, and, with a few rounds of artillery, sent the rebels on the other side of the river into the jungle. Then the whole rebel force retreated rapidly to a precipitous ridge four miles to the north-west of Rathghur from whence they had started in the morning. However, Captain Hare of the Hyderabad Contingent with some of his troopers came up with their rear before they reached their coign of vantage and sabred several of them.*

While the fray was going on in the plain, the garrison redoubled their fire from the fort. But the two batteries continued to pound away at the wall. Then the rebels saw their friends retreat into the jungle and their fire became far less effectual. The English batteries continued to pour forth their shot and shell every quarter of an hour. At 10 P.M. a breach appeared which seemed practicable. It was decided to examine it. " Corporal Linahan, Subadar Seloway, and two privates of the Madras Sappers examined the breach under a very heavy fire from the enemy who were evidently on the *qui vive.*" All night the cannonade continued. At daylight the guns in the fort were silent. Lieutenant Strutt of the Bombay Artillery and Dr. Lowe of the Madras Sappers, noticing how quiet all was, thought they would go to the breach. " We went, not a shot was fired. Lieutenant Strutt jumped down into the ditch, scrambled over the rubble and up the breach, I followed. On looking into the fort not a soul was to be seen. The birds had flown ; how, was a mystery." They had fled in the dead of night by a precipitous path where no footing could be seen. "One or two mangled bodies lay at the bottom, attesting the difficulty of the ascent." Crossing a ford over the Biena under the Bhopal camp they passed through the Bhopal lines into the jungle.† The 3rd Europeans when they entered the fort

---

*" Captain Hare and Lieutenant Westmacott attached to the Hyderabad Cavalry did good service on this occasion, and Lieutenant Moore of the 3rd Bombay Light Cavalry, who on account of the few artillerymen served a gun with effect, deserves also to be mentioned."

†" The reports of all the officers on duty state that these rebels, crossing a ford over the Biena to the south-west, under the Bhopal camp, passed through the Bhopal lines into the jungle ; the Bhopal troops fired a few shots at the fugitives, two or three of their dead baggage animals in this ford showed the track they had taken. The Bhopal troops have been and are still so useful to me that I merely mention this circumstance, which is nothing out of the way amongst Oriental troops, out of justice to my own force." *From Major-- General Sir Hugh Rose, K.C.B., commanding Central India Field Force, to the Adjutant General of the Army, Head-Quarters, Bombay, dated Camp Saugor, 7th February* 1858.

"treated the women and numerous children of the rebels who were left there, with the humanity which was to be expected from their discipline and their faith. I enjoined the troops, for the honour of their country and the Army, not to harm a woman or a child."

On the 30th the sappers and miners occupied the fort and commenced mining and demolishing the buildings. News now reached Sir Hugh Rose that the garrison of Rathghur, strengthened by rebels from Bundelcund, had concentrated at Barodia on the left bank of the Beena—a strong village with a " gurrie," or small fort, with dense jungle on each side, about 12 miles from Rathghur. At midday on the 31st, the General, with five guns Horse Artillery, four guns Captain Lightfoot' battery, two 5½-inch mortars with fifteen men of Captain Woolcomb's battery under the command of Lieutenant Strutt, three troops 14th Light Dragoons, two troops 3rd Bombay Light Cavalry, twenty-five men Madras Sappers, 3rd European Regiment, and a detachment Hyderabad Contingent Field Force marched for Barodia. As they approached the river Biena the enemy were observed on the left, well concealed by long grass and nullahs. Hugh Rose immediately ordered Turnbull's two guns to come into action, but before they could open fire, there came a crash of musketry. Lightfoot's four 9-pounders were called up and opened with grape and round shot. It was too close for shrapnel. The 3rd Europeans were in skirmishing order in front of the flanks of the guns, and musketry replied to musketry. The fire of the rebels diminished, but it could not be silenced Then the order to attack was given. The 3rd Europeans charged, drove the enemy out of the thick jungle and twisting nullahs, and took possession of the bank of the river commanding the ford to Barodia. The Afghans and Pathans fought with their accustomed courage, several of them, even when dying, springing from the ground and inflicting mortal wounds with their broad swords.*

Hugh Rose turned the advantage gained by the 3rd Europeans immediately to account. He sent the Hyderabad Irregular Cavalry, supported by the 3rd Bombay Light Cavalry under Captain Forbes, to cross the ford covered by the skirmishers. He himself followed with four guns of the Horse Artillery and a troop of Her Majesty's 14th Light

---

* 'Lieutenant-Colonel Liddell, Captain Neville, Royal Enginers, Captain Campbell, 3rd Europeans, Captain Rose, my Aide-de-Camp, and Lieutenant Macdonald, Assistant Quarter Master General, were conspicuous in this advance; Lieutenant Macdonald was slightly wounded and his horse twice wounded." *From Major-General Sir Hugh Rose, K.C.B., commanding Central India Field Force, to Colonel Green, C.B., Adjutant-General of the Army, P. 12.*

Dragoons in support under Lieutenant-Colonel Turnbull. The rest of the force was ordered to march as swiftly as possible after them, with the exception of a detachment of the Hyderabad Contingent Field Force (infantry and guns) under Captain Hare, which remained at the ford to protect the rear. Forbes, a fine soldier, as daring as he was skilful, found the enemy's flanks posted in thick jungle, their centre in comparatively open ground. Without a moment's hesitation he charged and broke their centre. The enemy found safety behind their guns, well-placed in front of the village. It was a strong position. On three sides it was surrounded by thick jungle, in which matchlock men were posted, and before them ran a wet nullah whose banks were lined with infantry. Turnbull, who had rapidly taken his guns across the ford, unlimbered in front of the village and opened fire on the enemy's position. They answered with guns and rockets. Captain Neville of the Royal Engineers, who had joined the force the day before and was acting as the General's Aide-de-Camp, was struck by a round shot in the head. He fell dead from his horse. He had passed days and nights in the trenches before Sebastopol without being touched. The night before, he had written a letter to his mother expressing the certainty he felt of death in the coming action, yet he pressed Sir Hugh Rose with much earnestness to let him act as his Aide-de-Camp at Barodia.*

<small>Captain Neville.</small>

Driven from their position by the fire of the British guns, the enemy retreated into the village and jungle. Sir Hugh Rose, crossing the nullah, seized the wall round the hamlet and surrounded it with the skirmishers and a troop of the 3rd Light Cavalry. Soon after, the village itself and the little fort was occupied, but the enemy, except a few Afghan skirmishers who were killed, had fled into the jungle. Their losses, according to their own statement, were four or five hundred. Their ablest military leader was killed and the Rajah of Banpore was wounded.

---

*" Knowing what excellent service he had done as an Engineer Officer before Sebastopol I had brought him up by forced marches to assist in the reduction of the forts in this country; during the action he was most useful to me, exhibiting to the last the courage and intelligence which had obtained for him so honourable a reputation." *From Major-General Sir Hugh Rose, K.C.B., Commanding Central India Field Force, to Colonel Green, Adjutant-General of the Army, p. 13.*

" The loss of this officer was much lamented by the General. He had been all through the Crimean war—had passed days and nights in the trenches before Sebastopol, and had escaped with much honour, and in so short a time to have met death in such a manner after such a career was indeed lamentable. He was buried the after day in a little mound near the camp, all the officers of the force having followed him to his grave." *Central India, by T. Lower, p. 184.*

Two British officers were killed and six wounded, and the casualties among the men were seven.

About 2 A.M. the force returned to camp. The capture of the fort of Rathghur and the defeat of the rebels at Barodia had completely opened Hugh Rose's communications with the west and Saugor. He now issued his orders for the last march on the city, which for eight months had been surrounded by thousands of insurgents. As the British troops passed by the villages, peasants, who had been robbed and maltreated by the insurgents, ran to the wayside to greet them.* At daylight on the 3rd February the fort of Saugor, which is situated on a hill in the heart of the town, was seen. When they drew near the city, some of the Europeans came out to meet them, and on each side of the road there were swarms of natives in their bright and many-coloured dresses, who gazed with wonder at the unexpected apparition of a British regiment.† The 14th Dragoons and the large siege guns dragged by elephants were a source of much curiosity and awe to them. As the troops marched beneath the walls of the fort, they saw the ramparts crowded with men, women, and children. For many a week, during eight weary and anxious months, they had heard of relief being near, till "we grew sick with expecting and watching for its realisation." Then there came the faint sound of distant guns. After three days it grew more sharp and quick and they knew that Rathghur was being bombarded. "The rebels inside the fort, among whom were some of the most daring and troublesome leaders, could not have had a wink of sleep from this constant booming which was distinctly heard at Saugor. But to us it brought sweet slumbers and a happy sense of approaching security. At last, to our joy it was reported that the fort had been taken and that Sir Hugh Rose was close at hand." The troops, after marching through the city in a long line and skirting its beautiful lake, encamped on the right of the road beneath a barren belt of hills.

Sir Hugh Rose had opened communications with the west and north and the time had now come for him to clear the way, towards the east. On the eastern flank, about twenty miles from Saugor, was the

Saugor.

Siege and capture of Garhrakote.

---

* "The villagers about Sanoda appeared to be in the deepest distress. They had been plundered of everything by mutinous sepoys and Bundeelahs for months past, and were reduced to such an extreme condition of poverty as to wander through our camp seeking the undigested grains from among the dung of our cattle and then and there to eat them!" *Central India*, by Thomas Lowe, p. 189.

† "A British regiment had never been seen at Saugor." *Central India*, by T. Lowe.

strong fortress of Garrakota standing on an elevated angle of ground. The wide deep river Sonar washes the east face. A tributary stream with precipitous banks flows around the west and northern faces; to the south is a strong gateway flanked by bastions and a ditch about twenty feet deep and thirty wide*. It was so well built by French engineers that when it was besieged by Brigadier Watson in the Pindari war (1818) with a force of 11,000 men and twenty-eight siege guns, he was unable to make a breach in the massive walls, and the garrison were allowed to evacuate the fort with all the honours of war. The fort was now held by the mutineers of the 50th and 52nd and by a large body of insurgents, and it had to be taken before Hugh Rose could advance on Jhansi.

On the 9th a small force went out to destroy the fort at Sanoda, about ten miles from Saugor, and to cut a road for the siege train to cross the river Beas. The Madras Sappers having done this work of distruction, the force set forth for Garrakota. After a trying march over hills and through a dense jungle, skirmishing and halting and stealing upon the enemy, they sighted the fort, and, late in the afternoon, they reached the encamping-ground. When the shadows grew longer, they got their tents pitched and " made the very best of a very rough dinner." It was somewhat interrupted by the enemy sending round-shots and rockets into the camp. Meanwhile, the General had been making, what he always did make, a thorough reconnaissance, and he did not return to camp till nearly 8 o'clock. " How he endured so much was surprising to every one, nor was it the most agreeable thing for his staff". The General had found that the enemy had erected some earthworks on the road to the south, by which they expected the British force to arrive, and that they were occupying in some force the village of Baseri near the fort. Despite the darkness, Hugh Rose determined to drive them at once from their position. The horse artillery, taking up position on an elevated spot in front of the British camp, poured upon them a destructive fire. The enemy sounded their bugles and advanced in force at a double upon the guns, but were driven back in disorder by the 3rd Europeans. They again formed up and advanced with unabated vigour, but as they got near the guns they were again beaten back and they retreated in disorder into the fort. During the night a breaching

---

*"This ditch ran round the west face also. On the opposite side of the river is the well-built town of Gurrakotta about one mile from the fort." *Central India, by T. Lowe*, p. 194.

battery was erected, opposite the west face. The next morning the 24-pound howitzer opened fire and, working all day, silenced the enemy's guns. "One large gun annoyed us a good deal. It was worked well, and we could see the enemy in their red coats loading and firing it. Lieutenant Strutt of the Bombay Artillery fought this gun admirably and at length knocked it from the embrasure. After this no further annoyance from them was experienced."* The 18-pounders played upon the fort all the evening and through the night. At dawn, the enemy could be seen escaping from it in great numbers. The order was given to cease fire, and the 3rd Europeans, on entering the citadel, found it deserted. Captain Hare with the Hyderabad Cavalry, two troops of the 14th Light Dragoons under Captains Need and Brown, and two guns of Horse Artillery under Lieutenant Crowe set forth in pursuit. After a rapid ride of twenty-five miles Hare found them the other side of the river Beas. Leading his guns and cavalry across the stream, he opened fire and swiftly charged them. "A great number were slain and made prisoners, as was also a good deal of their plunder captured. Thus the 51st and 52nd mutinous sepoys were punished, and the beautiful little fort of Garrakota fell into our hands."

After a short front had been destroyed by mines so as to leave a practicable breach in the *enceinte* of Garrakota, and a company of the loyal and gallant 31st Bengal Native Infantry † under Lieutenant Dickens placed in charge of it, the column rejoined the force in Saugor on the 17th Febuary. The General was anxious to move on Jhansi without delay. It was clearly his interest to strike another blow at the rebels before they recovered their *morale* and placed themselves in a strong position easy to defend. To his bold and aggressive spirit a period of enforced inaction was the sorest of trials. But, owing to the want of supply and transport, it was impossible to make at once a further advance. On the 29th of February, he wrote to the Governor of Bombay: "I am unfortunately detained by want of supplies and carriage, to the great disadvantage of the public service: I have lost nine precious days, doubly precious not only on account of the time at a season when every hot day endangers the health and lives of the European soldiers, but because every day has allowed the rebels to recover the *morale* they had lost by my operations, which I had made as rapidly and efficiently

---

* " Near the gun from which we had been so annoyed, and which was silenced by Lieutenant Strutt, were three bodies; one of these was the body of a havildar, the other two were privates. The last shot from the howitzer had killed these men." *Central India*, by T. Lowe, p. 193.

† *Military History of the Madras Engineers*. By Major H. M. Vibart Royal, (late Madras) Engineers, Vol. II, p. 331.

as possible, knowing that any success with orientals produces twice as good a result if one acts promptly and follows up one success with another. Nothing requires system so much as transport. Laying in supplies, as it is called, is perfectly easy in a fertile and peaceful country, but this will not do in my case, where a country has been devastated or is in the hands of the enemy. Then appears all the risk of a civil or occasional system of supply."

During this period of repose, Sir Hugh bestirred himself with his usual vigour to collect provisions and transport and to increase the efficiency of his force in every branch. He had the siege train resupplied from the arsenal with a large amount of ammunition and strengthened with other heavy guns and howitzers and large mortars. "Many more elephants were obtained, and the Ordnance and Engineering Parks were specially strengthened." The 3rd European regiment changed their uniform for a dress more suited to a tropical climate, a loose stone-coloured cotton blouse and trousers and a puggree of the same colour. The officers and men enjoyed their brief rest and there was great and constant conviviality in the various messes and camps. "We were on the eve of a long and trying march north—months would pass away ere another such respite could be dreamed of, and if we could place any reliance on the reports in camp of the work in store for us, we certainly had every reason to take pleasure by the hand and 'be merry while we may,' so there was music and feasting in all due order; and days of promotion and days of receipt of gratuity for service wounds, and birthdays, and other memorable occasions, were celebrated with rejoicings." A few days after came the long march in a scorching season and wasted country and night bivouac in the jungle.

Sir Hugh Rose's Force leaves Saugor for Jhansi, 27th January.

On the evening of the 26th of February, Sir Hugh Rose despatched Major Orr's column of the Hyderabad Contingent to march on a route parallel to his own and to reconnoitre the passes through the range of hills, which were serious obstacles to the forward movement of his force and to the union of the 1st and 2nd Brigade, without which the attack could not be made on Jhansi. At 2 A. M. on the morning of the 27th, Sir Hugh Rose's force was again put in motion. As the troops marched away from Saugor, rockets were seen to shoot up into the dark sky from the centre of the city. "The enemy had evidently had their spies in our camp who were now telegraphing the departure of our troops to their friends north of us." After moving over a belt of hills through a narrow pass, the force halted. The next morning, while the stars were still out, the column was again in motion, and it had not gone a mile when rockets again were seen shooting up into the sky at regular intervals in front of them. As they moved on and on, beacon fires warning the enemy of their approach shone out of the dark masses of jungle on the different hills. But when the dawn had at last brought the full light of the day the fires were no longer seen. Then, when the sun's rays began to be felt, they halted near the village of Rijwas and pitched camp on a flat surrounded on three sides by high hills. Here Sir Hugh Rose was joined by Major Orr, who had reconnoitred the passes and gathered important information regarding them. The pass of Narut was the most difficult, and the enemy, thinking that the British force must pass through it, had increased its natural difficulties by barricading the road with abatis and parapets made of large boulders of rock 15 feet thick; all passages by the sides of the road being made impracticable by the almost precipitous hills covered with jungle which came down to the edge of the road. The Rajah of Banpore " who is both enterprising and courageous, " defended this pass with 8 or 10,000 men. The next most difficult pass was Dhamooney, which lay on Sir Hugh Rose's right. About the third pass, Mudinpore, twenty miles from the Narut, very little was known except that in the ordnance map it was described "as good for guns." Acting on the information gathered by Major Orr, the General determined to force his way through the pass of Mudinpore and so gain the table-land above the hills. But before he could advance, it was necessary to capture, in order to preserve his communication with Saugor, the fort of Barodia which lay about two miles north of the camp and immediately commanded the road to the pass. On the afternoon of the 2nd of March a few guns, a couple of mortars, infantry and cavalry were sent out to drive the enemy out of the little citadel. " After some shelling and knocking open the gate, the enemy were seen escaping over the fort wall into a jungle hill." Lieutenant Prendergast, Madras Engineers, with a section of the Madras Sappers and a company of the Khoonds, a semi-barbarous, undisciplined body of levies recently raised from the hill districts, took possession.*

Capture of the Fort of Barodia.

---

*These Khoonds were most extraordinary fellows. When they marched they seemed to keep on the jog-trot, laughing and joking and carrying their arms as one would imagine of a wild Irish mob; they seemed possessed of no scruples of caste, and were always willing to go anywhere and do anything where there was a chance of looting a rag or a lota (brass drinking vessel). They appeared to be the very best of material from which to mould a useful corps, but at present, as might be expected,' were in the roughest possible form. *Central India*, by *Thomas Lowe*, pp. 210-211.

In order to deceive the enemy as to his intention, and prevent the Rajah of Banpore from coming from the pass of Narut to the assistance of the Rajah of Shaghur who defended Mudinpore, the General determined to make a serious feint against Narut. About two o'clock on the morning of the 3rd of March, he sent Major Scudamore, commanding Her Majesty's 14th Light Dragoons, with two Troops of that regiment, one Troop 3rd Light Cavalry, 100 Irregular Cavalry, one 24-pounder howitzer, three Bhopal 9-pounders, and the 24th Regiment Bombay Native Infantry to the fort and town of Malthon just above the pass of Narut. Three hours later, Sir Hugh Rose marched with the main body * against the pass of Mudinpore. For about five or six miles, the column moved along the foot of a long range of hills, and then it entered the almost pathless route which led to that pass. As it approached the gorge, the enemy's skirmishers fired on the advanced guard from the hills on the right, but they were soon driven back. The column moved steadily forward with the batteries, and at about eight hundred yards from the edge of the plateau, where the road suddenly descends into a glen, thickly wooded, they found the enemy posted on the rocky and precipitous hills which lined the left of the defile. Major Orr opened fire on them with round-shot and spherical case. At this moment an officer, filled with the zeal of battle, galloped his guns to the right front with the view of

* It consisted of—
Advance Guard.
500 Hyderabad Cavalry.
200 Hyderabad Infantry.
4 Guns, Artillery.
1 Company, 3rd Bombay Europeans.
Centre.
1 Troop, Her Majesty's 14th Light Dragoons.
Sappers and Miners.
4 Guns, Horse Artillery.
Right Wing, 3rd Bombay Europeans.
3 9-pounder Guns, Captain Lightfoot's Battery.
2 5½-inch Mortars.
1 8-inch Mortar.
1 8-inch Howitzer.
Left Wing, 3rd Bombay Europeans.
Siege Train.
3rd Bombay Light Cavalry.
Baggage and Convoy.
Rear Guard.
125 Hyderabad Infantry.
Howitzer and 1 Gun, Horse Artillery.

pouring an enfilading fire into the enemy. "But he had not taken into consideration that this movement brought him to within fifty or sixty yards of the edge of the glen in which lay concealed some hundred sepoys who, before he could unlimber, opened a very heavy fire on his guns which he was unable to depress on them." So unexpected was the attack, so rapid and hot the fire,* that the artillerymen had to take shelter behind their guns. Several were wounded. The General had his spur shot off and his favourite charger struck. He ordered the guns to be retired out of the range of the enemy's musketry. The sepoys hailed this little reverse with shouts. But their success only brought on their more rapid defeat. Sir Hugh Rose, now knowing their exact position, ordered a hundred of the Hyderabad Contingent Infantry to charge into the glen and sweep the rebels down into the road. At the same time he sent a company of the 3rd Europeans against their front. The rebels, driven with loss from the glen, crossed the road and ascended a hill on its left. Not giving them time to breathe, the General directed Captain Macdonald, Assistant Quartermaster-General, to storm the heights with two companies of the 3rd Europeans. " Captain Macdonald conducted them ably and gallantly up the almost precipitous height, and extending the Grenadier company from the right, and supporting them with the other company, drove them from the first to the second line of hills. As soon as Lieutenant-Colonel Liddell had come up, with the rest of the 3rd Europeans, I moved him up the hill, in support of his two companies, directing him to advance, and drive the enemy successively from all the hills commanding the pass. He performed this movement entirely to my satisfaction."† The glens and hills which protected the pass having been taken, the 4th Hyderabad Cavalry drove in the enemy's front and cleared the pass. Their main body, repulsed in flank and front, retired to the village of Mudinpore, situated at the end of a long lake along which the road through the pass ran. Behind the strong masonry dam, they had planted their few guns, which had played on the 3rd Europeans as they advanced up the hill. The 8-inch howitzer and the 9-pounders were brought to the head of the lake, and a few rounds drove the enemy from their strong position behind the dam. The troops advanced through the village and then stayed their march to

---

* " As rapid and hot a fire as ever I saw," wrote Sir Hugh Rose to Sir Colin Campbell.

† *From Major-General Sir Hugh Rose, K.C.B., commanding Central India Field Force, to Major-General Mansfield, Chief of the Staff, Cawnpore, dated Camp before Jhansi, the 26th March 1858.*

breathe awhile and quench their thirst. After a short halt, the Hyderabad Cavalry were sent in pursuit, and, coming up with the tail of the enemy, cut up a great number and captured many, among others the Astrologer of the Rajah of Shaghur. He confessed that he had been mistaken in his prediction of the fitting day for the destruction of the Feringhees. When the sun was wending to the time of bringing home the cattle, the troops, after a long march, weary and footsore, parched and exhausted, halted near the deserted village of Pepeeria and encamped within sight of the fort of Sorai, a little well-built keep on a hill commanding an extensive view of the surrounding plains. The lines of the sappers were pitched in the beautiful garden of the Shaghur Rajah. "In the centre of this extensive enclosure was the seraglio of the Rajah overshadowed by mango and guava trees, and embowered by groves of orange and citron trees, laden with golden fruit, and sweet-smelling blossoms."

The results of the successes at Mudinpore were as numerous as they were favourable. Sir Hugh Rose's force had got into the rear of the passes and the enemy's line of defences of which they thought so much. The pass of Narut, considered by them as impregnable, was turned. Sir Hugh Rose wrote to Sir Colin Campbell, "The great thing with these Indians is not to stay at long distances firing; but after they have been cannonaded to close with them. They cannot stand. By forcing the pass of Mudinpore I have taken the whole line of the enemy's defences in rear and an extraordinary panic has seized them. I hope I am not over-sanguine, but I think that matters as far as we have gone look well. All in our rear is really police work and all I want is a reserve to occupy the country I take, and prevent my flanks and rear being turned as I advance. A military police, organised on the Irish Constabulary system, is what is needed here, and in India generally." After rendering the fort of Sorai useless, the force marched upon Murrowra, about twelve miles north, where there was a large and important fort. On reaching the town, they found it deserted. On the 7th, the British flag was hoisted upon a bastion of the fort; a proclamation of annexation of the territory was read; the artillery fired a royal salute; the bands played "God save the Queen," and the Rajah of Shaghur was disinherited. Two days later, the force started for Banpore, and, as they neared the encamping-ground opposite the town, they heard the sounds of very heavy firing at regular intervals from the west. It was the siege guns of the 1st brigade breaching the fort of Chanderi. The palace of the Rajah of Banpore, a vast pile, was found to contain great quantities of property belonging to English officers, and orders were given to destroy it. On the evening of the 11th, part of it was blown down, and huge fires lighted in other apartments; by nightfall it was burning brilliantly, "like a great bonfire."

The start on the 14th was long before daylight, and, as the sun began to flood the heavens with crimson and gold, the troops marched along the border of the lake of Talbehat, "and the wild fowl flew in hundreds above it, screaming and darting into the quiet weedy waters." Above the lake, on the western side, rises boldly from the plain an extensive hill glorified with bastions, temples and towers, and crowned with a feudal castle. During the halt of two days, a breach was made in its old stout walls so as to render it incapable of defence. On the 16th of March, the General sent the Madras and Bengal sappers to the left bank of the Betwa, eight miles away, with instructions to build a bridge across the stream. The Chief Engineer, however, found it fordable, with a good shingle bottom. On the morning of the 17th of March, the whole force crossed the Betwa and encamped on the left (north) bank. By the execution of daring and delicate manœuvres, Sir Hugh Rose's inferior numbers had driven the enemy from their strongholds further and further north. His idea of strategy was to secure the initiative however inferior his force, to waste no time, and to give the enemy no rest. He had, as in Syria and the Crimea, proved himself absolutely fearless, and his fiery energy had aroused the enthusiasm of his soldiers. His successes had won their confidence, and, though a strict disciplinarian, he had gained their affection by the kindly word and by always sharing their hardships. He had led them, burning to avenge the massacre of the women and children at Jhansi, to within striking distance of the guilty city. On the 1st of March, the glad tidings reached him that the 2nd brigade, under Brigadier Stuart, had taken by storm the strong fortress of Chanderi. A formidable obstacle to his advance had thus been removed, and within a few days the two brigades would be concentrated for a final move on Jhansi.

To attack, with a handful of Europeans, a city surrounded by a wall twenty-five feet high, loopholed and bastioned, protected by a fortress built on a high granite rock, rendered almost impregnable by art, garrisoned by eleven thousand Afghan mercenaries animated by the spirit of fanaticism, was outside the bounds of ordinary strategy. Lord Canning and Lord Clyde were anxious that the stronghold of the rebel power should speedily fall, but they were constrained to face the possibility of a reverse. On the 11th of February, four days before the main portion of the army destined for the siege of Lucknow had crossed the Ganges, Sir Colin Campbell wrote to Sir Hugh Rose authorising him to pass by Jhansi for the moment, and, in accordance with the general plan of campaign, sweep the rebels before him by marching in two divisions, one on Calpee through Chirkaree and the other on Banda. Lord Canning wrote to Sir Colin Campbell, " I have written Sir R. Hamilton and Sir Hugh Rose, in the sense of your instructions to the latter, imposing upon them, that if for any reason, whether as being too strong for him, or for any other cause, it should be politic to pass by Jhansi for the moment, there is plenty of work for the Nerbudda field force in the neighbourhood of the Jumna." No ruler more strongly maintained the fact than Lord Canning that the soldier is the servant of the statesman. But Lord Canning, in his correspondence with military commanders, also recognised the important fact that some special knowledge and practical acquaintance with the working of the military machine is necessary to manœuvre armies. Hugh Rose on the spot saw better the strategical requirements of the situation. He too had always foreseen the difficulties of besieging Jhansi with an inadequate force, and he had fully understood the reasons which led the Viceroy and Lord Clyde to give him the option of not attacking it, " but it was impossible," he wrote in a public despatch, " to obey my orders to march to Calpee by Chirkaree, and leave such a stronghold as Jhansi untaken in my rear."

A month before Sir Colin Campbell wrote to Sir Hugh Rose that he should advance on Calpee through Chirkaree, the Commander of the Central India Field Force had despatched his 1st brigade from Mhow to march parallel with him as he advanced on Jhansi. It, therefore, proceeded on the road to Agra, clearing the country as far as Goona. Here it was met by Major Orr, with a detachment of the Hyderabad contingent of all arms, and Major Keatinge, the Political Officer who had advanced from Mundesore and done splendid service in re-establishing postal and telegraphic communication. Brigadier Stuart had orders from the Commander-in-Chief to march from Goona, about seventy miles to the westward, and take the important fort of Chanderi, whose capture was necessary in order that the 1st brigade on the west and the 2nd brigade on the east of the river Betwa should be concentrated for the attack on Jhansi. The sepoys, after their defeat by Hugh Rose, had gone to Chanderi, whose garrison had sworn to defend it as the Rajputs had defended it in the days of old.* To capture it was no easy task. The citadel, girt by a rampart of sandstone flanked by circular bastions, stands on the top of a hill, beneath which nestles the outer fort and the town, built entirely of stone. In the days of the great Akbar, it was said, " If you want to see a town whose houses are palaces, visit Chanderi." The rule of Mahratta bandits killed its commercial prosperity, and it became a city of splendid ruins.

On the 5th of March, Brigadier Stuart encamped six miles from the town. The next day he pushed a reconnaissance in force to clear the jungle that intervened. After a march of three miles, he came to a narrow pass between two high hills. The rebels, according to the wont of orientals, had not realised the necessity of defending it. Two miles further, however, he found the road barricaded, and when the engineers began to remove the obstruction, the enemy opened fire from a hill on the left. They were soon dislodged, and the artillery advanced with two companies of the 86th on the right, and the 26th Bombay Native Infantry on the left. They had reached within a mile of the fort, when suddenly they came on a wall, which extended from one ridge of hills to another opposite, the valley intervening. "The wall was loopholed, and furnished with bastions twelve or fourteen feet in height and several in thickness." From the loopholes the enemy sent a devastating fire into the small ranks of the advancing force. But it did not stop them. The men of the 86th, led by Lieutenant Lewin, and Major Keatinge of the Bombay Artillery, rushed forward. Lewin and Keatinge were the first to reach the top of the wall, and, jumping down, closely followed by the Irish lads, they drove the rebels back into the fort. The wall was

---

*In January 1528, the Emperor Baber took Chanderi by storm. In his memoirs he writes, "In a short time the pagans rushed out, completely naked, to attack us; put numbers of my men to flight; and leaped over the ramparts. Some of our troops were attacked furiously, and put to the sword. The reason of this desperate sally from the works was, that, on giving up the place for lost, they had put to death all their wives and women, and being resolved not to survive, had stripped themselves naked, in which condition they rushed out to fight, and engaging with ungovernable desperation, drove our people along the ramparts. Two or three hundred pagans had entered Medini Rao's palace, where numbers of them slew each other; one person taking his stand with a sabre in his hand, while the others pressed in one by one in succession, and stretched out their necks eager to die. In this way many went to hell, and by the favour of God, in the space of two or three geris, I gained this celebrated fort, without raising my standard or beating my kettle-drum, nd without exerting the whole strength of my arms."

destroyed, a force was left at the spot, and the brigade skirted round one of the ranges of hills which commanded the fort, and encamped. Next day, Stuart took possession of the woody ridge, which was divided only by a wide jungly ravine, "about as broad as the range of a 9-pounder," from the fort. Some field guns and mortars were dragged up with difficulty and opened fire on the palace, the most striking feature of the citadel. "But the enemy's guns replied well, and with good practice; neither could they be silenced." A road had to be constructed along the edge of the ridge in order to bring up the heavy guns of the besiegers, and this entailed much hard work and occupied many days. On the 20th, the 24-pounders were dragged up by the elephants, and, being placed in position, opened fire. "It was evident Chanderi had not been so disturbed for many a year. Most of the trees were of a flowering description, and covered with gorgeous blossoms; while flights of parrots screamed among them, monkeys chattered at the soldiery, an occasional panther was turned out of his lair, and wild ducks wheeled overhead."[*] On the breaching battery which was nearest the fort the enemy kept up an incessant artillery and musketry fire. "One individual, who possessed a European rifle, and had learnt to use it, caused much annoyance and many wounds, and the bullocks bringing up ammunition afforded them excellent marks."[†] Though the range was very short and point-blank, it was no easy matter to destroy the almost solid rock. After two days of constant bombardment, signs of a breach appeared in the round bastion. On the 15th, the Brigadier wrote to the officer commanding the remainder of the 86th, who had been left behind, that the breach would be practicable the following day, but he would defer the assault till the 17th if his men could join him before that time. The County Downs had marched fifteen miles that morning. Twenty-eight miles of a stiff road through a thick jungle remained to be done. They set forth, and by 10 o'clock next morning they marched into camp playing 'The British Grenadiers.'

Taking advantage of the darkness of the night, Captain Keatinge, accompanied by a native, crept barefooted along the scarp of rock, which connected the ridge with the hill on which the fort stood, till he came within a few yards of the debris of the battered bastion. An unexpected obstacle now stopped him. A deep trench had been cut in the rock and

---

[*] *Recollections of the Campaign in Malwa and Central India.* By Assistant Surgeon John Henry Sylvester.
[†] *Ibid.*

extended completely across it, being some fourteen feet wide and as many deep. But the knowledge he had gained of the ground was of the utmost service the next day.

About three o'clock on the morning of the 17th, the two storming parties assembled for the attack. The party accompanied by the Brigadier and staff, composed of Royal Engineers, Her Majesty's 86th Regiment and 25th Regiment, Bombay Native Infantry, was to assault the breach, while the other party, led by Captain Little, composed of Her Majesty's 86th Regiment and men of his own gallant corps (the 25th), was to make a false attack to draw away the resistance that might occur at the breach, and also, if practicable, to enter the fort. Silently the troops ascended to the batteries. As the grey dawn appeared, the British guns opened and sent out shells and rockets into the fort and showers of grape into the breach. The roar of the guns was the signal for attack. The stormers rushed forward. "Scaling ladders were thrown across the cutting at the base of the breach which in itself was as difficult to mount as could be conceived."* Under a mass of fire, the soldiers rushed up to the breach and a separate hand to hand fight took place. Keatinge fell severely wounded. He struggled up, and, as he led his men into the fort, was again struck down. The stormers went on, taking gun after gun, now shooting, now bayoneting the enemy, or dashing them over the height into the ravine below. The enemy exploded a mine and some men of the 86th were killed, others horribly burnt. "Their uniform, save the shoes, had been completely burnt away, and their bodies charred and blackened."† Little and his party had entered the fort about the same time as Keatinge, and the enemy, seeing themselves attacked on two sides, gave up resistance, and the great body of them escaped down through the town beneath, "and were seen in full flight in the jungle beyond, for it was now bright daylight." Every rebel that remained was shot or bayoneted by the Royal County Downs. It was St. Patrick's day and the Irishmen swore by their Patron Saint that they would avenge "the little babbies and the poor ladies who were butchered in Cawnpore and Jhansi." Chanderi was taken, together with a vast number of guns, and the stormers marched into camp through the deserted town, " the bands playing, of course, St. Patrick's Day." Sir Colin Campbell wrote that the success at Chanderi was mainly owing to

* *Recollections of the Campaign in Malwa and Central India. By Assistant Surgeon John Henry Sylvester.*
† *Ibid.*

the officers, whose really brilliant gallantry he considered was equalled by their ability and devotion.

On the 20th of March, the 2nd brigade, under the command of Sir Hugh Rose, having marched fifteen miles, reached their encampment, about eight miles from Jhansi. After a rest of two hours, Brigadier Stewart, with the cavalry and artillery, was sent to invest the city.* Sir Robert Hamilton, in a memorandum written (20th March 1862) four years after this event, states, "As the infantry were about to follow, an express arrived with a dispatch to me from Lord Canning desiring that I would move on Chirkaree to relieve the rajah who was besieged by Tantia Topee and the Gwalior Contingent in his fort, General Whitlock's force not being within reach. There came also a dispatch from the Commander-in-Chief, Lord Clyde, to Sir Hugh Rose ordering him to proceed to Chirkaree to save the loyal rajah of that State." It is hardly probable that Sir Hugh Rose would have moved his infantry from their encampment after a march of fifteen miles, before he had heard the result of the reconnaissance which he had sent Major Boileau to make as to where the batteries should be established. On the 15th of March, the Secretary to the Government of India, Military Department, wrote from Allahabad to General Whitlock, "From intelligence which has reached the Right Honourable the Governor-General from Chirkaree, it cannot be doubted that the fort of that place has, by this time, fallen into the hands of the insurgents, who were laying siege to it, and who were already masters of the town, part of which was burnt. Punnia and Rewah are also threatened. It is of urgent importance that support should be given to the loyal Chiefs of Bundelcund as soon as possible, and as no troops can be moved into the Bundelcund States from this side of the Jumna, the Governor-General desires me to request that you will proceed at once with the column under your command in the direction of Punnia, Chirkaree, or such other point as you may judge expedient, with the object of supporting the Chiefs who may be threatened by the insurgents, and freeing them from the danger to which they are now exposed." A copy of the letter was forwarded "for the information and guidance of Major-General Sir Hugh Rose, K.C.B., Commanding Central India Field Force." Sir Hugh Rose, in acknowledging the receipt of the letter, writes, "On the left bank of the River Betwa, 19th March 1858. I have the honour to say that, I shall pay the strictest attention to these

---

* *From Major-General Sir Hugh Rose, K.C.B., Commanding Central India Field Force, to the Chief of the Staff.*

instructions and be careful to shape my own course so as to give, in combination with Major-General Whitlock, confidence and support to these Chiefs. I may, I hope, be permitted to say that I have received, with sincere pleasure, these instructions; strategically and politically speaking, they are calculated to produce the best effect on this part of India; and they develop and complete a plan of operations, which Sir Robert Hamilton and myself had agreed yesterday that it would be advantageous to carry out after the reduction of Jhansi, for the reliefs of the Chiefs in question, and the defeat of the rebel army concentrated at Chirkaree and Nowgong, whose numbers, Sir Robert Hamilton says, amount to 60,000 men according to the last reports received."

Sir Robert Hamilton, in his memorandum, states that he received on the 20th a dispatch from Lord Canning desiring that he would relieve the Rajah of Chirkaree who was besieged by Tantia Topee, but, in his letter on the same day, the 20th, he acknowledges the receipt of a dispatch dated 13th March, and on that date the Governor-General had written to General Whitlock that " it cannot be doubted that the fort of that place has fallen." Sir Robert Hamilton, in his letter to the Governor-General of the 20th, gives the cogent strategical reasons why Sir Hugh Rose should capture Jhansi before he proceeded to Chirkaree.* He closes his letter as follows:—" In conclusion, I beg to state that Sir Hugh Rose desires me to express his entire concurrence in the views and reasonings above expressed and his hope they will be considered sufficient to allow of a slight delay in giving effect to his Lordship's wishes." Sir Robert Hamilton in his memorandum (20th March 1862), however, states. " Sir Hugh Rose considered the order of the Commander in-Chief imperative." Sir Hugh Rose had, on the 19th, informed the Governor-General in Council, the supreme military authority in India, that he would carry out his instructions after the reduction of Jhansi, and it is hardly possible that the next day he would consider the order of the Commander-in-Chief imperative, as the order was bound to be written before the 13th of March. From the 27th of February to the 17th of March Lord Clyde was occupied in the capture of Lucknow. On the 11th of February, Lord Clyde had offered to Sir Hugh Rose the option of not attacking Jhansi, and it is hardly likely he would have sent an imperative order on that date. Sir Robert Hamilton also states in his memorandum, " There was not anything left to my discretion in my letter to the Governor-General."

---

* *From Sir R. Hamilton, Agent to the Governor General in Central India to G.F. Edmonstone, Esq , Secretary to Government of India, Foreign Department, dated March 1858.*

But the orders conveyed to General Whitlock and forwarded to Sir Hugh Rose, dated the same day as the letter to Sir Robert Hamilton, were of the most discretionary kind. Sir Robert Hamilton adds, " And I therefore took on myself the responsibility of proceeding with our operations." Sir Robert Hamilton, as Agent to the Governor-General, had no military authority, and Sir Hugh Rose was the last man who would have allowed him to assume " the responsibility of proceeding with our operations." The statements have gained for Sir Robert Hamilton the credit " of giving a decided character to the campaign." But they are entitled to as much credence as the claim that the original plan of the military operations of the Madras and Bombay divisions was mainly due to Sir Robert Hamilton and not to Lord Clyde and the Chief of his staff, and that the strategic merits of the campaigns below the Jumna were also due to him. The course of action which Sir Hugh Rose adopted and Sir Robert Hamilton considered best received the frank approval of the Governor-General. The Secretary to the Government of India with the Governor-General wrote, " In reply, I am desired by his Lordship to inform you that under the circumstances represented, and with advertence to the fact of Sir Hugh Rose's force having been already committed before Jhansi, the decision taken in respect of the prior reduction of that place was unquestionably right and is therefore entirely approved."

At 2 A.M. on the morning of the 21st of March, the day that Lucknow was finally taken by Sir Colin Campbell, Sir Hugh Rose, with the remainder of his brigade, marched upon Jhansi and arrived before the city about seven o'clock. " The troops piled arms on the right of the road about a mile and a half from the fort, and the General and his staff rode off for the purpose of reconnoitring the city and surrounding country. They did not return till past 6 P. M." The General had no plan or even correct description of the fort and the city, and before the siege operations could begin, he had for some days to make long and repeated reconnaissances in order to ascertain the enemy's defences. A fair apprehension of the nature of the conflict, which Sir Hugh Rose with an incomplete division undertook, must be based upon some acquaintance with the features of the ground and the nature of these defences. The fort presented the most formidable aspect. Built on a huge granite rock, it had walls of solid masonry, in thickness from sixteen to twenty feet, and extensive and elaborate outworks of the same solid construction with front and flanking embrasures for artillery, and loopholes, of which in some places there were five tiers, for musketry. Guns placed on the high towers of the fort, commanded the country all around. One of these towers, called the "white turret," had been raised in height by the rebels and mounted with heavy ordnance. From it floated the red standard of the Ranee. Except on the west and part of the south, the fort abutted on the city, which was surrounded by a fortified and massive wall from 6 to 12 feet thick, varying in height from 18 to 30 feet, with numerous flanking bastions armed as batteries with ordnance, and loopholes with a banquette for infantry. The steepness of the rock protected the west, and three flanking bastions protected by their fire the fort's east face. The most important of them was a high mound or mamelon, fortified by a strong circular bastion for five guns, round part of which was drawn a ditch 12 feet deep and 15 feet broad of solid masonry. On the east side, outside the city walls, was a large tank and a picturesque palace, numerous gardens and temples : on the west, another large tank, gardens, and temples. To the right of the British encampment, stretching to the north and east of the city, was a long belt of hills through which ran the road to Orchha, the ancient capital of Bundelcund, and the fortress of Calpee which, riring above the right bank of the Jumna, commanded the road from Jhansi to Cawnpore. To the left of the British encampment were other high hills and the road to Dutteah and Gwalior. Due north of the British forces was the fort. Between the camp and the city were the ruined cantonments, the jail, and the Star Magazine. Near the city wall were groves of tamarind trees and temples with their gardens, one the Jokhun Bagh, the scene of the massacre. Nine months had rolled on since the men, women and children had been slaughtered without mercy in that garden and their mangled bodies thrown into a pit. And now a day of vengeance had come.

On his arrival at Jhansi, Sir Hugh Rose, following the maxim of Vauban, proceeded to establish seven flying camps as an investing force around the city. He gave to one of the principal camps, commanded by Major Scudamore, half a troop of Horse Artillery, and later, to Major Gall, commander of another camp, two 9-pounders. "These camps detached to the front outposts and vedettes, which watched and prevented all issue from the city day and night ; each camp on any attempt being made to force its base was to call on the other to help." The General gave directions also that the road from the city should be obstructed with trenches and abattis. Many very formidable elements entered into the problem of the siege. There was no means of breaching the fort except from the south, but the south was flanked by the fortified city wall and the mound. The city, therefore, must be taken before attacking the fort, and the fortified mamelon was the key to the city, for it covered, not only the south side of the fort, but it also enfiladed two walls of the town and commanded the whole of the south quarter of it, including the palace. The capture of this great work must be an essential part of the plan of attack. Sir Hugh Rose determined to concentrate a heavy fire on the mamelon and on the south of the city, to breach the wall close to the mound and to dismantle the defences which protected it and opposed an attack. After careful reconnaissance, the General selected a rocky knoll (the right attack) on the eastern side, to the south of the lake opposite the Orchha Gate, and a rocky ridge (left attack) on the southern side as the best spots for his breaching batteries. But these batteries could not be completed till the arrival of the 1st brigade with its siege guns.

On the 22nd of March, Jhansi was invested, and about 9 P.M. that evening, the Madras and Bombay sappers moved silently from camp in company with two 18-pounders, howitzers and mortars, and a company of the 24th Native Infantry for the purpose of throwing up a battery, the first on the right attack near the Orchha road. In the night's dead silence they could hear the hum of voices in the city, and through its darkness they saw the glimmer of a torch or lantern passing to and fro on the ramparts. As the heavy guns neared their destination, the darkness was broken by a sudden flash before them. The men halted, prepared to resist an attack. Several officers pushed their horses forward: and they found that the light came from a detachment of the 3rd Europeans who had taken possession of the position where the battery was to be erected. In the night a mortar battery was thrown up on a little temple, and the heavy guns placed in batteries on the rocky ridge, about three hundred yards from the walls. When morning broke and the enemy caught sight of the opposing batteries, they opened fire from the guns of the fort and from two or three batteries on the city wall. "At first the shots passed over us, but by and by they got our range exactly and then their shots struck the sand-bags and the temple almost every time. There was generally time to bob one's head beneath the bags when they fired before the shot reached, but one of their guns which we named ' Whistling Dick ' never gave us time for this precaution, for the puff of smoke was scarcely seen before the shot whizzed over your head, or came with a heavy thud on the battery."

On the evening of the 24th, four batteries were ready on the right attack, and at daylight on the 25th they opened fire. On that day the siege train of the 1st brigade arrived. The next morning the Madras sappers marched, with a working party of the Royal Engineers, to erect batteries on the *left attack* upon a rough rocky eminence about four hundred yards from the fort. Below this rocky ridge was a small defile, and from it, nearer to the enemy, the ground sloped upwards to a small plateau. This was taken possession of under a very galling cross-fire from the guns of the fort, the bastions, and the city walls. The Royal Artillery, commanded by Captain Ommaney, soon got a ten-inch howitzer into position, and the Hyderabad Artillery brought up other guns. As the native artillerymen were laying the gun, a round shot from the fort killed a subahdar and a havildar. A sepoy of the contingent quietly remarked, "there is luck for somebody." All day and through the night of the 25th, the British troops were hard at work throwing up cover for their guns, and by morning they were placed in position. Two 18-pounders were to dismantle the defences of the fort, while the two 10-inch mortars destroyed it. Two 8-inch mortars and one 8-inch howitzer were to play on the mound and adjacent wall and city. One 18-pounder was to breach the wall near the bastion of the mound. On the morning of the 26th, the guns opened fire. At sunset the parapets of the White Turret, the Black Tower, and the Tree Tower, which faced the left attack, were knocked into shapeless heaps by the fire of the two 18-pounders. The mortars hurling their missiles into the air, to drop thence into the fort and there explode, created great havoc. The General, having pointed out to Lieutenant Pittman, Bombay Horse Artillery, the position of a powder magazine "respecting which I had information * he blew it up in the third shot, keeping up a well-directed fire on the fort." Eight days and nights from the right and left attack did the terrific storm of iron hail endure ; eight days and nights did the rebels maintain the fight, their guns being admirably managed by a Bengal artilleryman "who has been distinctly seen through a telescope laying them so as to make them bear on our positions."† Many guns were silenced, but the damage was swiftly repaired and the guns put once more in fighting condition. When the parapets were swept away, the

---

*" We have a fakir prisoner, who was present in Jhansi when the massacre of our country women and men took place : his life was spared on condition that he would point out where the magazine of the rebels was situated ; and I am glad to say his information has proved of some service already." *Letter from Camp before Jhansi, dated March 16th.*

†*Ibid.*

native women were seen working on the walls repairing them. Riflemen to fire at the parapets and the embrasures and loopholes were placed in all the batteries, with sand-bags to protect them. They also occupied various advanced positions behind boulders of granite, cottage walls, and temples, from whence they killed and wounded a considerable number of the enemy. But the rebels met wounds and death with a calm constancy. "Notwithstanding the damage done to their fort and works upon the wall, their vigilance and determination to resist abated not one iota; on the contrary, their danger appeared to add to their courage." It was now the hottest season of the year and the British gunners continued their work in the scorching sun "as though it were winter time." During the mid-day heat, the rebels, however, scarcely fired a shot. In the afternoon they opened a tremendous fire of every kind. "Round shots of various sizes bounded over our heads, and matchlock balls whizzed like hail above us. From this hour till sunset was always a dangerous time and our poor fellows were severely tried." In the cool of the evening, the Ranee of Jhansi with her hand-maids, wrapped in bright radiant vesture, went to the batteries and roused the zeal of her soldiers by her presence and her fiery words.* When sable night came, the shells, climbing the sky, dropped into the city, lurid gleams rose from the buildings and cheer upon cheer burst forth from our batteries.

The Garden Battery on a rock in rear of the west wall of the city and the Wheel Tower on the south greatly annoyed the left attack. The two 8-inch mortars and occasionally the two 10-inch mortars of the left attack answered the former.† To silence the latter a new battery called the Kaho Tehree or East Battery was established to the east of

* "A bombardier in charge of one of the breaching guns reported to Sir Hugh Rose on one occasion that 'he had covered the Queen and her ladies with his gun,' and asked permission to fire on them; but he was told that that kind of warfare was not approved." *Clyde and Strathnairn, by Major-General Sir Owen Tudor Burne, K.C.S.I., p. 116.*

† "No one considered the left attack a desirable spot. Any one ran a considerable risk of being hit going in, and as great coming out, and almost as large a one when in the batteries. It was situated on a rising ground opposite their chief battery, the mamelon, and very close to it; there were no trees for shelter from the sun, and only large fragments of rock well heated through, under which to take shelter from the enemy's fire. The men working the guns and mortars here were necessarily much exposed, and we lost a good many, chiefly gunners of the Hyderabad Contingent. Captain George Hare, commanding a regiment of infantry of that service, held this attack during the greater part of the siege. Any kind of ease when not actually engaged was totally out of the question. The rock was so hot no one could sit or lie on it without feeling scorched, and when standing upright the head of the individual was exposed to the enemy's fire." *Recollections of the Campaign in Malwa and Central India. By Surgeon John Henry Sylvester, p. 91.*

the rocky ridge. But the two 5½-inch mortars, with which it was armed, not proving sufficient, Sir Hugh Rose substituted for them two 8-inch mortars and a 9-pounder. "Before the sand-bag battery could be made for the 9-pounder, Acting Bombardier Brenna, of Captain Ommaney's Company, Royal Artillery, quite a lad, commanded and pointed the 9-pounder in the open, and silenced the enemy's gun in battery on the bastion destroying besides its defences. I praised him for his good service on the ground, and promoted him."

On the 30th, our batteries had disabled and dismantled the defences of the fort and city and disabled the enemy's best guns. The wall, however, was so solid and the masonry so hard that the two breaching guns made but little impression the first two days. Only a small breach near the mound could be seen. The ammunition was giving out. It was evident there would not be sufficient to multiply breaches in the town wall, or to establish a main breach in the south double wall of the fort. Under these circumstances, the officers commanding the Artillery and Engineers called to the General's notice the necessity of having recourse to escalade, to which he gave his consent, requiring, however, that the breach near the mound should form an important and principal point of attack.* In order to widen the breach, Sir Hugh Rose concentrated on it day and night an overwhelming fire from the 18-pounder and the 8-inch howitzer. From the mortar batteries also, in the centre and left attacks, shells were poured day and night into the mound and adjoining houses. But, with many guns disabled, many men killed and wounded, the enemy maintained the fight.

With the view to acquire rapid information respecting the enemy's movements, Sir Hugh Rose had established a telegraph upon one of the hills east of Jhansi, which commanded an extensive view of the country north and east. On the afternoon of the 31st, the General was in the battery on the right completing his arrangements for storming the next day, when an aide-de-camp rode up, and informed him that flags were flying from the signal, indicating that the enemy were coming in great force from the north. "He rode off as quietly as though nothing of importance awaited his orders." But Sir Hugh Rose knew he was in

---

* " Both of these officers," writes Sir Hugh Rose, " entertained a mistrust of the breach, thinking that it was mined and not practicable." *From Major-General Sir Hugh Rose, K.C.B., Commanding Central India Force, to the Chief of the Staff, dated Camp Mote, the 30th April 1858.*

imminent danger. Before him was a strong fortress garrisoned by 11,000 desperate men; behind him, close to him, within hail of their friends at Jhansi, was an army of 20,000 strong, chiefly consisting of the redoubtable Gwalior Contingent who had fought Sir Colin Campbell at Cawnpore. They were commanded by Tantia Topee, the ablest leader the mutineers had produced. It was a supreme moment. If Sir Rose withdrew his troops from the investment of the siege, the *morale* of the besieged would be improved and he might be overwhelmed by a combined attack. His alternative was victory or ruin. Hesitation or doubt had no part in his nature. He resolved at once to meet the enemy, while not relaxing the siege or withdrawing a single man from the pickets. The force at his disposal for the battle did not number over 1,500 men of all arms, and of these not 500 were British infantry.

Hugh Rose's dispositions were swiftly made. Soon after he left the battery, the 1st brigade, or as many of them as could be spared, struck camp and moved along the Calpee road, on the Jhansi side of the Telegraph hill. It was now dark, and they marched on over against the right flank of the enemy unobserved, and remained there under arms all night. " By and by elephants came silently up to the battery and took off two 24-pounders, which were placed upon the Orchha road near the hill, so as to check the enemy making for the city this way."* The 2nd brigade remained under arms in their camp and the pickets along the whole British line were strengthened and ready for action. About 8 P.M. the enemy reconnoitred in force, and, deceived as to our numbers by the removal of the 1st brigade, took up a position close in front of our camp, and their watch-fires burned in multitudes. When the besieged saw from the walls the fires burning in the plain, they raised a loud shout and fired a salute. All night their drums beat, their bugles sounded, and their riflemen poured their fire into the batteries. All night our batteries threw their shot and shell into the city.

Battle of the Betwa, 1st April.

Between 4 and 5 A.M., when it was still dark, the British pickets began to fall back on their support, and so soon as early dawn shone forth, dense masses of infantry, accompanied by numerous batteries and many hundred cavalry were seen pouring over a knoll. On they came, their long line spreading far beyond the British flanks, waving innumerable banners of all colours and devices, beating drums, and their bayonets

Central India by Thomas Lowe, p. 245.

gleaming in the sun. Opposed to them was a short thin line consisting of fifteen hundred men. In the centre were the heavy guns, supported by the 3rd Europeans, the 24th Bombay Native Infantry, and the Hyderabad Infantry; on the right of the line a troop of 14th Dragoons and one of the Hyderabad Cavalry with the Eagle Troop Horse Artillery; and on the left Captain Lightfoot's field battery and two troops of Her Majesty's 14th Light Dragoons. No sooner had the enemy reached within six hundred yards of the British line than they unlimbered, and their guns began with the roar of thunder to pour forth a storm of fire which was at once answered. Musketry replied to musketry, and as their superior fire began to tell on our close ranks around the big guns, the infantry were ordered to lie down. The battle was now fully developed, and dense blue clouds of smoke covered the vast plain, through which could be seen dark bodies moving on our left flank. Sir Hugh Rose knew that if he were outflanked the small party that were investing the city would be literally between two fires, and they must fight for life. An attack in front against the enormous disproportion of forces would not succeed even if he sacrificed his last man in the attempt to stop the enemy. But their flanks were capable of being rolled together if well struck. He acted without hesitation. He ordered the artillery from both flanks of the line to advance, the Eagle Troop Horse Artillery to the right so as to crush the enemy's gunners by an enfilading fire. As the movement on the right was being accomplished, one of the guns was knocked over and disabled. The enemy raised a loud yell of triumph. Hugh Rose directed Lieutenant Clarke of the Hyderabad Cavalry to charge the enemy's battery. They went forward at full gallop, but showers of grape and volleys from the Afghan matchlock-men mowed them down and checked their advance. Again and again they charged, but their attempts on that battery proved vain. Their gallant leader fell severely wounded. When Hugh Rose saw the enemy following up the Hyderabad Cavalry, he felt the supreme moment had arrived. Placing himself at the head of Need's troop of dragoons, he dashed into the enemy's left and at the same time Prettyjohn and MacMahon charged their right. "This was a magnificent sight," says an eyewitness, "and in a moment the enemy's ranks were a mass of confusion. The British infantry, seeing the confusion, sprang up, poured into the mass before them one deadly volley, and with level bayonets plunged on them. The rebels broke and fled. The British force followed the flying herd. Many of the enemy, however, preserving their resolution and courage, gathered in masses in the ravines and behind rocks and fought desperately hand to hand.* The cavalry charged through and through them, and the plain was covered with single fugitives. The horsemen pursued them, slashing with their swords, and the rebels hid behind stones and bushes to have one dead shot before they died. The vigorous chase was continued until the cavalry suddenly found themselves confronting a long line of infantry, artillery, and cavalry drawn up on some jungly ground. It was the third division of the Peshwa's army under the personal command of Tantia Topee. He at once opened his guns on the cavalry, and Turnbull's and Lightfoot's batteries replied.

Meanwhile Brigadier Stuart, with the 1st brigade, had moved round the hill on the plain on the enemy's right and encountered the large detachment of the enemy which Tantia had sent the previous night to enter Jhansi from the north. After a short tussle, Stuart drove them before him, and the 86th, the 25th Native Infantry, and the Cavalry pursued.

Tantia Topee, on seeing his front line broken, his right flank turned, and our troops moving on his second line, determined to retreat across the Betwa. He caused the jungle to be set on fire, and then, under cover of the smoke and flame, moved rapidly towards the river, his artillery constantly pouring shot into our advancing columns. "It now became," says Sir Hugh Rose, "a Cavalry and Horse Artillery affair." Sir Hugh Rose himself with the guns of the Eagle Troop and the Field Battery under Captain Lightfoot galloped through the ravaging fire and caught up the enemy at a small village near the river, "which is broad, shallow, and strong here." They at once opened on the enemy as they were recrossing the Betwa. Tantia's infantry attempted to arrest the progress of the British troops by volleys of musketry, and his guns sent forth a heavy fire. But the cavalry continued the pursuit with undiminished ardour until all the enemy's guns were captured. Tantia Topee himself fled to Calpee. His army of 20,000 men had been broken and dispersed, and a thousand of them lay dead on the field of Betwa. By sunset, the small band of victors returned to camp. The enemy's guns had ceased firing and they kept deep silence in the city. That morning

* "I saw one sergeant of the Horse Artillery hewn in pieces in one of these nullahs, while numbers of our troops were close at hand. He had cut down two of the enemy and was then attacked by others from behind; he fell in the ditch and was there sadly cut up, while numbers of the enemy were being slain beside him. The man who had cut him down then ran amongst us and figured away like a mad dog, first stepping one way, then another, brandishing his bloody tulwar, until he fell shot by a 3rd European."
Central India. By T. Lowe, p. 250.

when the booming of Tantia's artillery was heard, the rebels in the fort and town opened a tremendous fire on our batteries. " They mounted the bastions and the walls, and shouted and yelled, and poured down volleys of musketry until it was thought they intended to make a sortie, while every tower of the fort was enveloped in flame and smoke." A few moments of fervent joy and then they saw from the fort Tantia's host fleeing across the plain. All hope of relief was gone. All day the batteries of the besiegers poured in their shot and shell. The tottering defences were wasting away under the breaching guns. Great numbers tried to escape from the northern gate of the city, but were all cut up by our line of cavalry pickets or fell by the rifle. But the spirits of the more brave remained unsubdued. They must make their stand and they must die, if they could not preserve Jhansi from falling into the hands of the infidels.

On the 2nd of April, Major Boileau, the Chief Engineer, having reported that all the necessary preparations had been made for the escalade, the General issued a division order for the assault of the defences of the city wall the following morning, and a copy of the order with a plan of attack was furnished to the officers in command. That afternoon Sir Hugh rode down to one of the batteries on the right attack to look to the ladders which lay below under the cover of the hill. He then went to the left attack, and inspected, as far as possible, the condition of the breach The order to attack was known only to the commanding officers. At two o'clock in the morning the men were awoke with the words, " Assault immediately." An hour later, the storming parties moved in dead silence to the positions marked out for them to wait for the signal. It was to be three guns fired in succession by Captain Ommaney, on the western side. A feint attack was also to be made on the west wall by a small detachment under Major Gail, 14th Light Dragoons. The assault column of the 1st brigade, under Brigadier Stuart, who were to make the left attack, consisted of 21st Company, Royal Engineers, the 86th Foot, and 25th Bombay Native Infantry. They were divided into two parties, one party, commanded by Lieutenant-Colonel Lowth, 86th Regiment, was to storm the breach ; the other party, led by Major Stuart, 86th Regiment, was to escalade the rocket tower and the low curtain immediately to the right. The brigade under Brigadier Stewart, 14th Dragoons, consisted of the Madras and Bombay sappers, the 3rd Bombay Europeans, and the infantry of the Hyderabad Contingent. They were also divided into two parties, the right commanded by Lieutenant-Colonel Liddell, the left by Captain Robinson, both of the 3rd Europeans, who were to escalade the town wall at the points indicated.

Storming of Jhansi. Left attack.

The stormers waited for some time in suspense for the signal. The moon was very bright and at any moment they might be discovered by the enemy. It was not till dawn began to shine forth that the order to advance was given in a voice a little above a whisper. The ladders were hoisted upon the shoulders of the sappers, and, preceded by the 3rd Europeans and Hyderabad Infantry, they moved from their cover. No sooner did the stormers of the left attack turn into the road leading towards the gate than the enemy's bugles sounded, and a fearful storm of missiles poured upon them from the long line of the wall and the towers of the fort. "For a time it appeared like a sheet of fire out of which burst a storm of bullets, round shot, and rockets destined for our annihilation." More than two hundred yards to march through this fire deluge. And they did it. The sappers planted the ladders in three places for the stormers to ascend. But the rebels sent down upon them from the walls volleys of musketry, rockets, earth pots filled with powder, logs of wood, every sort of missile on which they could lay their hands. Many of the stormers fell, and the living sheltered themselves behind stones. But the native sappers, animated by the heroism of their officers, kept firm hold of the ladders. Major Boileau, the Chief Engineer, proceeded in hot haste to the Brigadier, who was in command of the reserve, reported that the ladders were without protection, and asked for some Europeans. Stuart gave him a hundred men of the 3rd Bombay Europeans that were with the reserve. The stormers, reinforced again, rushed at the ladders. In a few moments, Lieutenant Dick of the Bombay Engineers was at the foot of one of the ladders, and ran up, calling on the 3rd Europeans to follow him. He fell from the walls, bayoneted, and shot dead. Lieutenant Meicklejohn and a man of the 3rd Europeans had reached the wall when their ladder, owing to the crush of men that followed, broke, and, left alone on the walls, they were literally hewn to pieces. Lieutenant Bonus mounted another ladder, and was hurled down, struck by a stone in the face,[*] and Lieutenant Fox, Madras Sappers, was shot through the neck. Corporal

---

[*] "Lieutenant Bonus, Bombay Engineers, has also been specially brought to my notice for the gallant manner in which he led up and maintained his position on the ladder until disabled and knocked over by the blow of a stone." *From Brigadier C. Stuart, C. B., Commanding 2nd Brigade, Central India Field Force, to the Assistant Adjutant-General, Central India Field Force, dated Camp Jhansi, the 29th April 1858.*

Hard, Privates Rogers and Archibald, all of the Grenadier Company, and Private Drummond, No. 1, and Private Doran, No. 3 Company of the 3rd European Regiment, all fought gallantly till the ladder gave way. Lieutenant-Colonel Liddell, on finding the ladders of no service, ordered Lieutenant Goodfellow, Bombay Engineers, to try a bag of powder at a postern.* Assisted by a few native sappers, the gallant young engineer carried it, under a shower of bullets, to the postern gate, fired it, and out flew the door in fragments. The soldiers made a rush into the cloud of smoke to get through the entrance, but even that failed: it was filled by huge blocks of stone and masonry. Nothing remained now but to bring away the dead and wounded. "Ensign Newport and Private Gillman of No. 1 Company, 3rd Bombay European Regiment, assisted by Corporal Hard of the Grenadiers, carried off the body of Lieutenant Fox of the Madras Sappers and Miners through the hottest fire." The baffled column moved back to the rifle pits. Meanwhile, Captain Robinson, 3rd Bombay European Regiment, having been informed that some of the 86th Regiment had entered by the breach to his left, "doubled some of his party round to that point, at which he effected an entrance, and cleared the ramparts so as to enable the remainder to mount the ladders unopposed."

Before the first grey of morning filled the east, the stormers of the right attack had got unobserved within 350 yards of the wall, "which was about twenty-three feet high." The three guns were heard and both parties tramped forward steadily. When about one hundred yards from the Rocket Tower and the low curtain immediately to the right, Stuart of the 86th, who commanded the escalading party, roared out, "Now, lads, for an Irish yell," and the Irish yell rose high above the storm of musketry which brust on them.† They dashed forward, and with them went the gallant sepoys of the 25th. Many fell. When they came beneath the walls, stink-pots, rockets, and red-hot balls were poured down upon them. More fell. But the ladders were placed. Up rushed Dartnell (86th), Fowler (86th), Webber (R. E.), and Stuart (86th), followed by the men. Dartnell was the first man up, and for a moment he was alone. The Afghans hacked at him, and he saved his life

Right attack

---

* *Recollections of the Campaign in Malwa and Central India under Major General Sir Hugh Ross, G.C.B. By Assistant Surgeon John Henry Sylvester.*
† *From Brigadier C. Stuart, C. B., Commanding 2nd Brigade, Central India Field Force, to the Assistant Adjutant-General, Central India Field Force, Camp Jhansi, 29th April 1858.*

by protecting his head from their sabres with his arms, which were frightfully cut. Fowler, now reaching the wall, shot one or two of Dartnell's opponents and so saved his life. After a great death-wrestle, the mamelon was gained, and the soldiers, running down the incline to the street leading to the palace, were joined by the stormers of the breach, who, led by Captain Darby, " in the most gallant manner had carried it with little loss."*

Sir Hugh Rose, who had entered the breach with the troops, now determined to take the palace. The street ran close under the fort walls and a large open space, exposed to a flanking musketry fire from an outwork of the fort and from the houses and the palace in front, had to be crossed. But, though staggered by this double fire on front and flank, the little band were not stayed in their course, and, led by the General, they went steadily on. Darby, Sewell, and Holroyd, all of the 86th with many of their men, fell wounded. " Sewell was badly hit, but young Jerome and a man named Burnes of the 86th carried him off at the risk of their lives." A position in the street was gained, and here Dr. Stack was shot through the heart while attending the wounded.† The General now directed loopholes for riflemen to be made through the houses, which brought a fire to bear on the outwork of the fort, a large house to be occupied close to the palace, and covered communication to be made to the mound.‡ " During the whole of this time General Rose was walking about among the men as cool and unconcerned as if nothing was taking place." The skirmishers of the 86th penetrated gallantly from the house into the palace. The men who held it were few in number, but their resistance was desperate. Every room was defended with the most determined fury. But it was of no avail. From room to room they were driven at the point of the bayonet, neither asking nor giving quarter. As they fell back, they set fire to trains of gunpowder and perished with their assailants in the explosion. But the palace was taken by the British soldier.

While the work of death was going on in the palace, the General, having received no reports from the right attack, set forth with his staff to

---

* The foregoing is taken from an account written at the time by one who was present.

† " A doctor's duty with the storming party is a dangerous one. Dr. Stack of the 86th was shot through the heart on the left attack, and Dr. Miller severely wounded on the right attack." *Central India by Thomas Lowe*, p. 256.

‡ *From Major-General Sir Hugh Rose, K.C.B., Commanding Central India Field Force, to the Chief of the Staff, dated Camp Mote, the 30th April 1858.*

discover them. He found them in the south-east corner of the city fighting their way through the streets to the palace. The enemy smote them with a deadly fire from the houses. The assailants burst open the doors: the contest was furious, but it was short. Shouts and groans were heard in every quarter, and the street was wet with dark blood. Every inch of ground was contested until the palace was reached. Many a brave man fell. Among them was one whose death came home to Sir Hugh Rose. Turnbull, who commanded the artillery, had been with him in all his actions, and in all he gave instances of an invincible courage and fearlessness in danger. At Betwa he had, during the day, often exposed himself to the fire of the enemy in order to choose the best position for his guns, and the skill with which he placed and worked them materially helped to win the day. He had that morning entered the breach with Sir Hugh Rose and was sent by him to bring guns into the city to batter the houses which the rebels held. From a window of one of them he was shot through the abdomen. " The blood welled out from his wound, and I knew he would die."* Thus fell that fine soldier, and " his premature fate," wrote Sir Hugh Rose, " prevented his receiving the reward which was his due."

The right and left attacks being concentrated in the palace, the General gained possession of a large portion of the city by advancing the 3rd Europeans to the north-east while the 86th held the palace. The two regiments occupied with picquets commanding houses to their front. Thirty or forty Afghan troopers, the chosen body-guard of the Ranee, occupied the palace stables under the fire of the fort. Detachments of Her Majesty's 86th and 3rd Europeans were sent to take them. Sergeant Brown was the first to dash boldly into the stable-yard closely followed by his comrades. The sowars sent through windows and loopholes a well-sustained fusillade. The Afghans, when some of the 86th attempted to enter the stables, cut at them with their swords, " and the wounded men," says a surgeon who was present, " came staggering out with the most terrible sword cuts I ever saw in my life." Driven from the stables by the bayonet, they retreated behind the houses, still firing, or fighting with their swords in both hands till they were shot or bayoneted, struggling, even when dying on the ground, to strike again. " A

---

* *Central India by Thomas Lowe*, p. 357. Dr. Lowe is incorrect in saying that he was shot from a window of the palace.

party of them remained in a room off the stables which was on fire till they were half burnt; their clothes in flames, they rushed out hacking at their assailants and guarding their heads with their shields."* All the sowars were killed, but not without several casualties on our side. Captain Sandwith, who "commanded with spirit the Europeans on this occasion,"† was among the wounded. In the quarters of the Ranee's body-guard was found an English Union Jack of silk, which Lord William Bentinck had given a former Rajah of Jhansi.‡ "And when it was brought out into the yard, how the Royal County Downs yelled and cheered!" The General granted the soldiers their request to hoist on the palace the flag of their country which they had so bravely won. "It was instantly taken to the top of the palace by the adjutant of the 86th, and put up, under a heavy fire from the fort."§ Meanwhile, the fighting from house to house went on. And Jhansi was a slaughter-pen reeking under the hot eastern sun.

Sir Hugh Rose, while present at the attack on the stables, received a report that about four hundred of the enemy had tried to force a picquet, had been driven back, and had occupied a high and rocky hill to the west of the fort. The General immediately ordered out from the camps of the two brigades the available troops of all arms against the hill. The force consisted of Woolcomb's battery, some companies of the 24th Native Infantry and Hyderabad Contingent Infantry, with a few dragoons under the command of Major Gall. The hill was an isolated rock with paths or shelves on it. It was surrounded, and round shot and shell was sent into the midst of the rebels to bring them down. But they knew death awaited them below. Then the infantry was sent to attack them, and sweeping steadily on, killed all of them fighting to the last, except about twenty who gained an eminence difficult to approach. They there blew themselves up. The Ranee's father who

---

* *From Major-General Sir Hugh Rose, K.C.B., Commanding Central India Field Force, to the Chief of the Staff, dated Camp Mote, the 30th April 1855.*

† *Ibid.*

‡ The gallant soldiers captured in the quarters of the sowars the Ranee's standards, three standards of the body-guard, three kettle-drums and horses, and an English Union Jack of silk, which Sir Robert Hamilton tells me Lord William Bentinck had given to the grandfather of the husband of the Ranee, with the permission to have it carried before him as a reward for his fidelity, a privilege granted to no other Indian Prince. *From Major-General Sir Hugh Rose, K.C.B., Commanding Central India Field Force, to the Chief of the Staff, dated Camp Mote, the 30th April 1858.*

§ *Central India by Thomas Lowe,* p. 259. Dr. Sylvester writes that it "was hoisted on the palace by Captain Darby under a heavy fire from the fort."

was amongst the rebels on the hill, was wounded. Better if he had died sword in hand. But not better for justice; for he was a chief instigator of that enormous crime which led to the vast and bloody tragedy of Jhansi. He was taken prisoner a few days afterwards and hanged on a tree in the garden where the women and children were slain.

When the long eastern summer day was closing, the signalling party telegraphed from the observatory that the enemy were approaching from the east. Sir Hugh Rose had to re-occupy with all the force he could collect the field of action of the Betwa, " the devoted troops marching to a fresh combat after thirteen hours' fighting in a burning sun with as much spirit as if they had not been engaged at all." The alarm, however, proved to be a false one.

The next day the General and Brigadier Stuart occupied by a combined movement the rest of the city. They were assisted by Major Gall " who spiritedly scaled the bastion at the Onao gate from his flying camp, and capturing the gun that was there threw it down the bastion." A large number of soldiers was killed that day in the street fighting that still went on. During the night there was heard a good deal of firing at the cavalry pickets outside. At dawn on the morning of the 5th, it was reported that the fort was evacuated.* " Brigadier Stuart, his staff, and Colonel Louth with some thirty men of the 86th Regiment, the adjutant of that corps carrying the Union Jack, left the palace and marched through the gate of the fort. They then planted the colours in the Queen's name with three times three on the square tower." Then was discovered the full strength of the citadel. "There was only one part of the fortress," writes Sir Hugh Rose, "the south curtain, which was considered practicable for breaching. But, when inside, we saw this was a mistake, there being at some distance in rear of the curtain a massive wall fifteen or twenty feet thick, and immediately in rear of this a deep tank cut from the live rock."

---

*" On the morning of the 5th, Lieutenant Baigrie, 3rd Europeans, went up to the fort gate and found it open; he went on from gate to gate, peeping and seeing no one, and at length found himself in the possession of the fort of Jhansi." *Central India by Thomas Lowe,* p. 260.

"A picket of the 86th Regiment, being near the gateway of the fort, saw it was open, and as the men were not fired on, they cautiously approached, and finally, with some officers, entered, and found it evacuated to a man. The red flag now gave place to the Union Jack." *Recollections of the Campaign in Malwa and Central India. By Assistant Surgeon John Henry Sylvester,* p. 113.

During the night, "the first really dark night since our arrival," the Ranee's horse had been brought into the fort-ditch. Let down from a window in the turret, she was mounted, with her step-son in her lap, and accompanied by three hundred Afghans and twenty-five troopers she stole away from the fort.* On reaching one of the pickets the party was headed back and separated. The Ranee with a few troopers rode as fast as their horses could speed for Bhandara, twenty-one miles from Jhansi. In the morning, a wounded Mahratta retainer of the Ranee was despatched from a flying camp to convey the news to the General. He immediately sent off strong detachments of Her Majesty's 14th Light Dragoons, 3rd Light Cavalry, and Hyderabad Cavalry to pursue, with guns to support them, as it was said that Tantia Topee had sent a force to meet the Ranee. When they came in sight of Bhandara the cavalry discerned the Irregular Horse sent to meet her. They immediately separated, probably with the view to mislead her pursuers as to her real course. Captain Forbes sent Lieutenant Dowker through Bhandara whilst he, with the 3rd Light Cavalry and 14th Light Dragoons, passed it by on the left. As Dowker rode through the town, he saw traces of the Ranee's hasty flight and her tent, in which was spread an unfinished breakfast. On the other side of the city he came up with forty of the enemy, consisting of Rohillas and Bengal Cavalry, and after a short sharp tussle they were slain. Pressing on, he caught sight of the Ranee on her grey horse accompanied by four attendants. The Mahratta Queen was as much at ease galloping a horse as in the zenana listening to her favourite minstrel, and a stern chase ensued. The British subaltern was fast gaining on her, when a shot was fired and he fell from his horse severely wounded and had to abandon the pursuit.

Meanwhile, Sir Hugh Rose caused the outskirts of the city to be scoured by cavalry and infantry, and there was many a desperate struggle. The carnage was terrible, for the Afghan and Rohilla sold his life to the British soldier hand to hand. Forty of them barricaded themselves in a house with vaults and a courtyard. A detachment of infantry, without knowing its strength, dashed forward to the assault. But the Afghans aimed coolly, and every shot told. They could not scale the wall, and in vain they tried to break open the massive door with the butts of their

---

* *Clyde and Strathnairn.* By Major-General Sir Owen Tudor Burne, K.C.S.I., p. 123.

muskets. Reinforcements were brought up, and several pieces of siege artillery, but, even when the house had been breached and knocked to pieces, the rebels continued to resist in the passages and vaults. And after they had slain and wounded many of their deadly foemen, they all perished. It was the last of a series of combats, which terminated the siege of Jhansi, so boldly undertaken and so desperately finished.

The capture of Jhansi must rank with the great actions recorded in British annals. A force consisting of an incomplete division had laid siege to a strong fortress and a walled city, defended by a garrison more than double their number, of desperate and disciplined men, supplied with all the munitions of war. It was the hottest season of the year, and from sunrise to sunset the infantry, artillery, and engineers had to conduct their operations without a morsel of shade to protect them, and amidst boulders which radiated all day an unbearable glare, and blasts of scorching heat. Many perished from the sun and the long unbroken toil. For seventeen days and nights the men of Scudamore's cavalry brigade never took off their clothes, nor let their horses stand unbridled. The Bombay sepoy and the Madras sapper vied with the British soldier in patience, endurance of privation, and fatigue. Then, in light of day this handful of men stormed the lofty walls, and, after four days' strenuous fighting, the city was captured. The loss of the victors amounted to 307 killed and wounded, of whom thirty-six were officers; that of the enemy was about 5,000. The British soldier fought to avenge the foul murder of the women and children, the rebels for existence. But though the British soldier is ready ever to strike an enemy and to take a stern revenge for innocent blood shed, there is in his conduct and character a great deal of gentleness and gallantry. When Jhansi was captured and the actual fight was over, a large number of the inhabitants were found to be in a complete state of destitution. "Both those reputed wealthy," to quote one among a number of witnesses, "and the very poor were all suffering alike, and it was strange to see our men serving out food for mothers and their children by the light of their blazing houses, and frequently beside the bodies of their slaughtered husbands or parents. Yet such assuredly was the case."

On the evening of the 15th of April, after the struggle was over and the battle fought and won, the British soldiers were assembled outside the city wall near the garden where the men, women, and children had been slaughtered. Sir Hugh Rose and his staff and the two chaplains who through all the storm, heedless of bullets, did their Master's work, ministering to the wounded and consoling the dying, stood over the pit where their bodies were buried. And there arose, as if from the slain that lay in the grave, the words, "Man that is born of a woman hath but a short time to live, and is full of misery." And then there came the closing note of victory—"I heard a voice from heaven saying unto me, Write, From henceforth blessed are the dead which die in the Lord: Even so saith the Spirit; for they rest from their labours."*

Jhansi, the great stronghold of the mutineers in Central India, had been taken, but Calpee, their well-fortified arsenal, full of warlike stores and ammunition on the right bank of the Jumna, remained to be captured. It was a place of great strategic importance, and, so long as Calpee remained in the hands of the rebels, the troops engaged in operations against the insurgents in the Doab, the line of the Ganges, Oudh and Rohilcund were exposed to attack from the line of the Jumna. "So long as Calpee was rebel, so long the enemy had it in their power to say that the East and West of India might be British but that the pivot of the centre was theirs." (1) To capture the pivot as soon as possible was of vital importance. But Sir Hugh Rose was checked in his advance by lack of food, transport and ammunition. For nearly three weeks he remained at Jhansi collecting these. He also could not move until he had secured Jhansi from attack by rebels from Kotah, a small Rajput principality of that name in Bundelcund. On hearing that Brigadier Smith's brigade was approaching from Rajputana and that Jhansi was secured from this danger, he sent, about midnight on the 22nd of April, Major Gall, 14th Light Dragoons, with a flying column along the road from Jhansi to Calpee to watch the enemy and obtain information of their movements. Leaving for a garrison at Jhansi part of the 2nd Brigade, Sir Hugh Rose with the 1st Brigade set forth for Calpee on the 25th of April. It was the hottest time of the year. "The country through which we passed was one continuous flat, the wells were almost dry and the water filthy. The heat became more and more oppressive, and the cattle began to emaciate and die."

---

* "As in the case of the massacre at Cawnpore, the darkest tints predominate, but the picture was not so black as it was painted." Captain Pinkney, Superintendent of the Jhansi district, in his official report writes, "The females were not taken before the Ranee, nor were their faces blackened, nor were they dishonoured as it has been erroneously reported."

(1) From Major-General Sir Hugh Rose, K.C.B., Commanding F. D. A. and Field Forces, to Major-General Sir Wm. M. Mansfield, K.C.B., Chief of the Staff of the Army in India, dated Gwalior, 22nd June 1858.

On the 1st of May Sir Hugh Rose found Major Gall's force at Poonth, sixteen miles from Koonch, a large intervening town about forty miles from Calpee. He now learnt that the garrison of Calpee, commanded by the Rao Sahib, a nephew by adoption of the Nana, (1) had been reinforced by five hundred Velaites under the Ranee of Jhansi, guns and troops from disaffected Rajahs, cavalry from the Kotah contingent and mutineers of Bengal cavalry. Leaving but a few troops in Calpee, Tantia Topee had marched with the remainder to Koonch, an open town but easy to defend because it was surrounded by woods, gardens and temples with high walls around them, every one of which was a defence. Tantia had also thrown up entrenchments which he had armed to defend the road to the town from Jhansi. Through secret reports from spies he was tolerably well informed of the small number of the British force and that the blaze of an Indian sun at its maximum heat was daily diminishing it. He determined to delay its advance by perpetual harassment during the day. Sir Hugh Rose felt that, in order to preserve the lives of his men, he must not undertake a long operation against Koonch, much less a siege, but by a bold and rapid stroke win a victory.

On the evening of the 5th of May, the 2nd Brigade, with the addition of four hundred men of the 71st, joined the camp. Orders were immediately issued for the 1st Brigade (accompanied by the division head-quarters) to march for the village of Lahorree, the road to which strikes off to the left and at nearly right angles with the Calpee road. (2) The 2nd Brigade was to march on the direct road to Koonch, and instructions were sent to Major Orr, who was already on the right flank, to close in towards the left and come in touch with the right of the 2nd Brigade " which he should find resting on the village of Oomree."(3) On the morning of the 6th the 1st Brigade reached Lahorree and halted there to rest during the heat of the day. The General, hearing that a body of Velaites held a strong fort of the same name six or seven miles on his left flank, sent Major Gall with a wing of the 3rd Europeans, some artillery and dragoons to attack and take it. But the fort was too strong to batter with field artillery, and the 3rd Europeans prepared to storm while the dragoons formed a ring around it to prevent the escape of the garrison. "The Major wished to lead the men into the fort, but was pulled back by some of the

---

(1) He was the adopted son of the second adopted son of the last Peshwa Bajee Rao.
(2) Letter from an officer in the 1st Brigade, dated Koonch, May 7th.
(3) From Major W. A. Orr, Commanding Field Force, Hyderabad Contingent, serving in Central India, to Colonel Wetherall, C. B., Chief of the Staff, C. I. F. F., p. 74

3rd regiment, having first received some ugly blows on the head with stones. Upon entering, every male was put to death, one fellow who attempted to effect an escape with his wife, finding it impossible to do so, severed the woman's head at a blow and then cut his own throat. This is desperate work and something more than fighting." In the desperate work two officers and several men were killed. A soldier named Whirlpool (1) received no less than nineteen wounds. "Take care lads," he said as they put him into the dhooly, "and don't shake my head, or else it will come off."

In the evening orders were issued to march on Koonch, about nine miles. "The men were worn out by the heat of the day and many fell out and had to be carried in the dhoolies. An occasional joke passes off among the older campaigners, and the hopes of meeting the foe keep up their flagging spirits." At dawn they arrived at a tope near the village of Nagoopura situated about a mile and a half from Koonch, where they halted and had grog and biscuits and some welcome rest. "The country about was beautiful; a dead level, and every yard turned up for cultivation. The town of Koonch stretching for about a mile, and nearly hidden by trees lay on our right, and from the centre rise the ruins of a fort with a flag flying from a height." Sir Hugh Rose's flank movement had been carried out with success. This was his posture on the morning of the 7th. His left, the 1st Brigade, resting its left flank on the village of Nagoopura, was on the North-west side in rear of the fort and town; his centre, the 2nd Brigade under Major Stewart, was in the village of Chomair masking the fortified front on the Jhansi road; his right, Major Orr's force, was in front of the village of Oomree. Sir Hugh Rose, having, as usual, first looked after the comfort of his men, rode across the wide plain to give Stewart and Orr his instructions and to view the ground. On his return he found the enemy had showed in force behind a low wall to our front and in the wood to the left of it. He sent the half troop of Artillery to shell them on the left. The enemy in return

---

(1) "He had been mentioned in despatches for saving the lives of two comrades who had fallen wounded from the broken ladders at the siege of Jhansi. He himself lived to receive the Victoria Cross and six pence a day beyond his usual pension. Sir Hugh Rose always thought that the name Whirlpool was assumed, and afterwards learnt that the man was a son of Major Conker, the Postmaster of Dundalk. When the General was in command in Ireland the parents came to thank him for his kindness to their son who was then in New South Wales." Clyde and Strathnairn by Major-General Sir Owen Tudor Burne, K. C. S. I., p. 128.

shelled the half troop and siege guns from a battery to our right. "Two of the guns were turned to the battery and soon silenced it."(1) At this moment the gallant Gall galloped into the wood and swiftly took a survey of the position. He reported that the infantry to the left had retreated further into the wood, having in their rear a large body of Cavalry, that the siege guns had driven the enemy from the cover of the wall, but that some way in rear of it was posted a large body of Infantry. Sir Hugh, according to his habits, instantly determined to drive the mutineers out of the wood, gardens and temples and storm the town. He threw the left wing of Her Majesty's 86th Regiment, under Major Stewart and the whole of the 25th Bombay Native Infantry, under Lieutenant-Colonel Robertson, into skirmishing order, the 86th on the left, the 25th on the right, their flanks supported by the half-troop Horse Artillery and a troop of Her Majesty's 14th Light Dragoons with Captain Ommaney's battery and Troops of Her Majesty's 14th Dragoons. The remainder of his force he drew up in a second line in reserve. Scarce was the order to advance given, when the 25th Skirmishers dashed into the woods, and, heedless of the fire of musketry and artillery, attacked and cleared the temples and walled gardens. The guns of the Royal Artillery opened fire on the houses of the town in their front and they were soon captured. (2) At the same time the 86th, covered by the three Horse Artillery guns and the Troops of the 14th Light Dragoons, making a circuit to their left, took all obstacles to their front " and then bringing their left shoulders forward advanced despite of artillery and musktry fire through the whole north part of the town and took the fort." (3) The enemy, finding their line of defence cut in two and their

---

(1) From Major-General Sir Hugh Rose, K.C.B., Commanding Central India Field Force, to Major-General Sir William Mansfield, K.C.B., Chief of the Staff, dated Camp Go'owlee, 24th May 1858, p. 67.

(2) "I expressed to Lieutenant-Colonel Robertson and the 25th on the ground may approbation of the gallantry with which they had gained their position." From Major-General Sir Hugh Rose, K.C.B., Commanding Central India Field Force, to Major-General Sir William Mansfield, K.C.B., Chief of the Staff, dated Camp Golowlee, 24th May 1858, p. 67.

(3) "The manner in which the 86th, ably led by Major Stuart, performed this movement which completed the cutting of the enemy's line in two, adds another claim to the obligation I owe this regiment for their very distinguished conduct on all occasions in the field." From Major-General Sir Hugh Rose, K.C.B., Commanding Central India Field Force, to Major-General Sir William Mansfield, K.C.B., Chief of the Staff, dated Camp Golowlee, 24th May 1858, p. 68.

right completely turned, retired in masses from Koonch to the extensive plains intersected by heavy ploughed land stretching towards Calpee. When the 1st Brigade, on making their way through the narrow and winding streets, emerged from the town, they found a Field Battery with Captain Thompson's and Gordon's Troops, Her Majesty's 14th Light Dragoons and a Troop of the 3rd Regiment Hyderabad Cavalry hotly engaged in attempting to dislodge a larger number of Rebel Infantry from a strong position in cultivated ground. On seeing the approach of some of the Infantry of the 1st Brigade from another direction, the enemy retreated. The Cavalry led by Gordon went at full speed at them and broke the mass. (1)

When the 1st Brigade came out of the town, the infantry for a short time searched the plains in pursuit of the enemy, but Sir Hugh Rose felt that it would be a "heartless and imprudent sacrifice" of men to continue the pursuit with that arm. The heat was intense and twelve men of the weak wing of Her Majesty's 71st had died from sunstroke. He therefore halted the infantry of the 1st and 2nd Brigade and Major Orr's force, which had advanced through the wood round the town to the plains, and sent the Cavalry of both Brigades and of Major Orr's rear force and the Horse Artillery and Field Guns in pursuit. (2) Slowly the enemy began their retreat across the plain in an irregular long line, five or six deep in some places. The line was "covered by skirmishers at close distances, who at intervals were in groups of small masses a mode of skirmishing peculiar to Indians; these groups act as a kind of bastion to the line of skirmishers." At every moment the skirmishers halted to rectify their line, two miles long, and to arrest in some degree the pursuit of the cavalry by a well-directed fire. "They fired and retired in perfect order," says an eyewitness, and, at the first charge of the 14th, coolly knelt down and delivered their fire at two yards. Of course the whole of that line was cut up." But a fresh line took their place. They

---

(1) From Major-General Sir Hugh Rose, K.C.B., Commanding Central India Field Force, to Major-General Sir William Mansfield, K.C.B., Chief of the Staff, dated Camp Golowlee, 24th May 1858.

(2) "The Cavalry of both Brigades, and of Major Orr's Force (except a party which I had left to watch the Jaloun road and my rear) one troop of Horse Artillery, Captain Field's guns and the four guns of the 18th Light Field Battery went in pursuit." From Major-General Sir Hugh Rose, K.C.B., Commanding Central India Field Force, to Major-General Sir William Mansfield, K.C.B., Chief of the Staff, dated Camp Golowlee, 24th May.

threw back the extreme right of their skirmishers so as to enfilade our line of pursuit. Sir Hugh Rose directed Captain Prettyjohn to charge with his squadron of 14th Light Dragoons and cut off the enfilading skirmishers, and they were completely shattered and separated. In the centre, the Artillery continued to advance, notwithstanding the heavy plough, and poured shrapnel upon the retreating line, and Blyth's troops and McMahon's squadron charged and charged its left and right. Blyth, through a heavy fire, fell upon a gun and captured it from the retreating foe. And Abbott, commanding the 3rd Regiment Hyderabad Cavalry, did the same. A heavy plough checked the pace of McMahon's squadron. " But the heavy ground was not broad, the squadron got through it, Captain McMahon leading the way, and cut to pieces the enemy who fought fiercely to the last. Captain McMahon received three sabre wounds but he continued the pursuit to the last."

For eight miles the skirmishers fought their pursuers. Then, the majority of them being killed, the remainder driven in, and their artillery captured, the main body got into confusion, lost their nerve and crowded into the road to Calpee, a long and helpless column of runaways. The scorching rays of the sun told even on them, " several fell dead on the road, struck by apoplexy, many exhausted threw away their arms, whilst others to quench their thirst rushed to the wells regardless if our Cavalry were upon them." But sun, fatigue and scarcity of water told still more on their pursuers. " The Horse Artillery and Cavalry were now so beat by sun and fatigue that they were reduced to a walk ; the guns were only able to rake the column in its depth with round shot and shell, but could not approach sufficiently close to give it grape." On arriving at the village where the enemy had broken into scattered flight across the country, the commanding officers informed the General that they were no longer able to pursue. He halted, and having watered the horses as well as he could, marched them back at sunset to Koonch. They had been in the saddle sixteen hours. The sun had made the greatest havoc amongst them that day. " While the action was going on dhooly after dhooly was brought into the field hospital with officers and men suffering from sunstroke, some dead, others prostrated, laughing and sobbing in weak delirium." Three days after the action Sir Hugh Rose wrote, " We should have destroyed the enemy, had not the dreadful heat paralysed the men. Eleven poor fellows were killed outright by the sun and many more were struck down. I was obliged four times to get off my horse from excessive debility. The doctor poured cold water over me and gave me restoratives which enabled me to go on again. I do not think I shall stay in India to pass such another torment as 110° in the shade. I have succeeded militarily better than I could have expected and that is all I wanted."

Immediately after his successful action Sir Hugh Rose marched from Koonch with the 1st Brigade. On account of the scarcity of water and forage on the line of march he had to leave behind the second Brigade, directing them to follow at one day's interval. But a storm of rain having rendered the tents too heavy for transport, the Brigade was delayed three days at Koonch. Delay was however fatal to Sir Hugh Rose's tactical plans. His attention was fixed on Calpee, but before Calpee could be attacked he had to effect a communication with Lieutenant-Colonel Maxwell who had been detached with the 88th Foot (1), some Sikhs and the Camel corps to co-operate with him against Calpee from the left bank of the Jumna. From Maxwell he was to receive a supply of ammunition to make good the large amount which his force had expended in the sieges of Churkere and Jhansi. He wrote to Colonel Maxwell that he would be on the Jumna a few miles below Calpee on the 14th of May. Having heard that the enemy had constructed elaborate lines of defence for the protection of Calpee, on the main road from Koonch to that fortress, he determined to turn them by breaking off to the right from the high road and to march to the village of Golowlee on the Jumna about 6 miles below Calpee. To mislead the enemy and mask this movement, he directed the 2nd Brigade to close up to the town of Oraye from Koonch, and, following the high road to Calpee, take up a position at the village of Banda. "This plan was foiled by the Brigade losing its way and, instead of going to Banda, making a double march, and following me to Sucalee." During this protracted march of twenty miles man after man went down smitten by the hot winds which blew across the dazzling white plains hard as flint. "We went on, a fearful hot wind blowing behind us all the time," says one who was present, "without being able to procure a drop of water, until the men began to cry out and our dogs to drop down dead. As we passed along we saw several camels, bullocks and tattooes (2) which had fallen dead from the heat but *there was no decomposition going on*. They seemed to be drying

---

(1) 2nd Connaught Rangers.
(2) Tattoo—a pony.

up like mummies in this intensely powerful sun! It was almost too much to endure, and as we marched on one felt obliged to gallop from bush to bush to gain a moment's shade, for one's mouth was parched, and one's head began to feel like a ball of fire, while rings of light danced before one's eyes." It was near two o'clock before the wretched march came to an end and a crowd of invalids reached Sucalee. Brigadier Stewart and the whole of his staff formed part of the sick list.

Above all things it was necessary that Sir Hugh Rose should reach the Jumna on the 14th as he had told Maxwell he would do. But the powers of movement of the 2nd Brigade were reduced to the lowest point. He could not push forward with vigour and leave it any distance behind, for it was weak, and the enemy had concentrated all their Cavalry, with Infantry and guns from their bivouacs, in the villages around Calpee for the purpose of unceasingly harassing his force. They knew full well how the sun and scarcity of water had told upon the Europeans, and it was part of their tactics to force them to be exposed at the hottest time of the day. A general order, issued by the rebel commander, stated that " as the European infidels either died or had to go into hospital from fighting in the sun, they were never to be attacked before ten o'clock in the day in order that they might feel its force." But these were not the only sources of trouble to the General. He now learnt that the Nawab of Banda had joined the rebels at Calpee, after being defeated by Whitlock, with an efficient body of Cavalry—the remnants of our mutinous regiments and some infantry and artillery also well trained.

On the 15th of March, General Whitlock was informed by the Military Secretary to the Government of India that it is of urgent importance that support should be given to the loyal chiefs of Bundelcund as soon as possible. But Whitlock was a man of extreme caution and his movements were slow. Setting out on the 22nd of March, he did not arrive before the town of Banda till the 19th of the following month. The Nawab had selected a spot in every respect well adopted to defend his capital. " His artillery commanded the main road on which my force was moving, enabling him to withdraw his guns if hard pressed. Broken ground with numerous ravines and nullahs covered his whole front, affording excellent cover to a swarm of skirmishers, who not only knew their value, but most skilfully availed themselves of them while every desired movement on my part on the enemy's flanks was impeded by ground most difficult for the combined operation of artillery and cavalry." The British force amounted to about nineteen hundred. (1) The enemy, commanded by the Nawab in person, were nine thousand in number, principally composed of mutineers of the three arms. On approaching within six hundred yards of the enemy's position, Colonel Apthorp, who commanded the advance guard consisting of three companies 3rd Madras European Regiment, two guns of Major Mein's European Troop of Horse Artillery, 1 Squadron of Hyderabad Cavalry under Captain Macintire, a few of the 12th Lancers and a detachment 1st Madras Native Infantry, formed up his troops into line. Macintire's Squadron was placed on the right. After the skirmishers had gone forward a short distance, Apthorp discovered that one or two of the enemy's guns were posted so as to enfilade the Infantry as they advanced. He therefore ordered Macintire to charge the guns, " and no men ever charged more nobly than the squadron of the 2nd Hyderabad Contingent Cavalry under their gallant leader Captain Macintire; one gun was captured, the other in the mêlée escaped for a time but the object was effected. The infantry advanced with comparatively small loss, but every nullah was filled with the enemy's infantry who made stiff dispute and there was many a hand-to-hand conflict in the ravines," where the bayonet did great execution. The advanced guard was hardly pressed when the main body came up, and by a flanking fire from the left, soon relieved them. The enemy slowly fell back, " occupying every available ground for opposition and our guns were in constant employment to dislodge them." Four hours passed before the Nawab fled, leaving on the field eight thousand of his men, and the firing ceased. The victors took possession of the Town and Palace and thirteen large guns, besides several of small calibre. A large quantity of ammunition and much valuable property belonging to the Nawab fell into their hands. General Whitlock took up his quarters at Banda, intending to wait there until

---

(1) A Troop Horse Artillery European	110
E ,, ,, Native	116
Her Majesty's 12th Lancers	227
1 Squadron Hyderabad Cavalry	136
Detachment Royal Artillery	111
Detachment Madras Foot Artillery	75
No. 1 Horse Battery	84
Detachment Sappers and Miners	101
3rd Madras European Regiment	518
1st Regiment Native Infantry	255
Detachment 50th Native Infantry	166
Total of all arms	1,899

the arrival of reinforcements should enable him to march towards Calpee to co-operate with Sir Hugh Rose. But the reinforcements did not arrive until the 27th May and by that time Calpee had been captured.

In order to give rest to the 2nd Brigade at Sucalee, Sir Hugh Rose delayed one day at the village of Etowa, a march in advance. He sent his own carriage to the sick for their assistance and called off the attention of the enemy from them by a diversion in an opposite direction. On the night of the 14th, the 2nd Brigade, under the command of Lieutenant-Colonel Campbell, 71st Highlanders, who had succeeded Brigadier Stewart, joined the 1st without molestation. A few hours afterwards Sir Hugh Rose marched with the 1st Brigade and Major Orr's force for Golowlee. "After our arrival in camp the cavalry of the enemy came down in force upon the baggage and rear guard. Several men of the 25th Native Infantry were killed and others wounded, and the enemy were driven off with loss. In the onslaught they were heard to say, "You have looted Jhansi, and now you are come to loot Calpee are you." On reaching Golowlee, Sir Hugh Rose sent two of the Hyderabad Cavalry across the Jumna to Maxwell who was about thirty miles off on the other side of it, requesting him to move up to the river without delay. Two Pontoon rafts, brought with great difficulty from Poona some eighteen hundred miles away, were floated by sunset on the Jumna and the junction with the Bengal army effected. "One of the most important of my instructions was now carried out. My force had marched from Bombay to the Jumna and had effected an union with the Bengal army, the immediate result of which was a combined operation of Bengal and Bombay troops against Calpee."

But it was no ordinary operation. Calpee stands on a high bald rock rising from the Jumna, and is a natural fortress. The only avenue by which the British could approach it from their camp on the Jumna was barred by a labyrinth of deep rocky ravines, every yard of them affording a dangerous obstacle or an ambush. To the south its front was covered by huge tombs, built as well as the walls round them of solid masonry, and capable of affording shelter to large masses of troops. There was no cover by which they could be approached. Save a few tamarind trees and bushes the country around was a sterile desert blighted by the fierce sun. At the foot of the fort was the town, also forming a formidable line of defence. The garrison consisted of the Gwalior Contingent, the best drilled and the best organised Native troops of all arms in India, mutinous Bengal regiments also well drilled, Rebel Cavalry from Kotah, a chosen band of fanatical Afghans, and the force of all arms of the Nawab of Banda. To take Calpee by a protracted operation was out of the question. "The prostration of the whole force had become a matter of arithmetical calculation. So many hours' sun laid low so many men." Sir Hugh Rose determined to beat the Rebel Army in one decisive action. "When I came near Calpee," he wrote, "I found that it was surrounded by a belt of ravines about two miles in breadth as difficult ground as could be seen, and that to attack the fort I must force the ravines, of which the enemy had entrenched the entrance, and afterwards the town which surrounded the fort. I always thought and hoped that I should have one good fight with the rebels for Calpee, and that, if they lost it, they would evacuate the town and fort."

On the morning of the 16th, the advanced guard and the centre of the 2nd Brigade reached the village of Diapoora without opposition, but the rear guard, under Major Forbes, was vigorously attacked by about 1,000 or 1,200 Cavalry besides a large body of infantry. Forbes, aided by Orr, after a stiff fight repulsed them, and brought safely the long and helpless line of baggage over difficult ground to the camp at Diapoora. Sir Hugh Rose, on hearing that Forbes was hard pressed, marched a body of troops to his assistance, and on reaching the camp, the 2nd Brigade found that the enemy had attacked in force a village, the possession of which by them would have rendered the camp untenable. The Officer Commanding in the village had felt himself so hard pressed that he had given orders for evacuating it. The enemy were pressing forward. Sir Hugh Rose immediately commanded the troops who were retiring to re-occupy the village and hold it at any price, and he sent the detachment he had brought with him to their support. Captain Lightfoot of the Bengal Horse Artillery placed his artillery skilfully on the left of the village, and the accurate fire of the shrapnel and round shot broke the Rebel Cavalry and drove them from their position in support of the infantry, who still held the deep and twisting ravines in front of the village. Sir Hugh Rose directed Captain Douglas, Commanding Artillery, Hyderabad Contingent, to post four 6-pounders on the right of the hamlet and burst shrapnel over the heads of the concealed foe. "This he did with his usual skill and devotion, under a heavy fire of the enemy's riflemen so effectually that the Rebels who were also suffering from the admirable fire of the 71st, retired from their ambuscades." Sir Hugh Rose did not pursue. The ground was difficult and the greater part of his men had been marching all night and engaged all day in fearful heat. "My game was a waiting one, and I abstained carefully from playing that of my adversary, which was to disorganise and prostrate my force by continued exposure to sun. I never yielded an inch to the enemy's attacks; but, on the other hand, husbanded the strength and health of my men for one great combat for Calpee. As it was, the intense heat made havoc amongst my troops, officers as well as men. Upwards of 200 out of less than 400 men of the Bombay Native Infantry fell out of the ranks on the line of march struck by the sun."

On the 17th instant, after noon, the enemy again attacked the 2nd Brigade at Diapoora and was repulsed. The same day Colonel Maxwell, leaving his column to take up their position opposite Calpee, arrived at Golowlee, and Sir Hugh Rose communicated to him his plan of attack and gave him the requisite directions. Maxwell was to construct, on the other bank of the Jumna, Mortar Batteries, one to shell the fort of Calpee and destroy its defences facing the British position, another to shell the part of the town facing the same way, and a third to be placed lower down the Jumna and opposite the village of Rehree, which stands on the edge of a small sandy plain situated between the belt of ravines and Calpee. Here the enemy had a force and battery which would awaken on the right column of attack when it debouched from the ravines. With the right (the 1st Brigade) Sir Hugh Rose intended to attack Calpee, whilst with his left (the 2nd Brigade) he intended to make a strong feint to be converted into a real attack if feasible. Orr's force at the village of Tehree in the right centre was to keep up the communication between the two Brigades and assist both as required---a skilful plan, but fresh and growing difficulties caused it to be altered. The wells in Diapoora began to fail. Troop horses and baggage animals died of drought. The 2nd Brigade, daily diminishing in numbers owing to sickness, was exposed to constant attack, and, on the morning of the 19th, these troops and the Hyderabad Field Force were removed to the camp on the Jumna. The enemy continued their tactics of harassing unceasingly the British troops and forcing them into the fierce sun which struck them down. "Out of the 36 men of the 14th Light Dragoons, forming part of our forage escort, seventeen were brought back to camp in dhoolies after only two hours' exposure to the sun." The hospital tents, where the temperature ranged from 109° to 117° and seldom fell under 100° at night, were crowded. On the 19th of May, Dr. Arnold, Superintending Surgeon, wrote in an official letter, "To illustrate better the state of health of all ranks, I may mention that we have now 310 Europeans in hospital, having lost in the week 21 by sunstroke; and there is scarcely an officer on the staff fit for duty. The Quarter Master General, Clergyman, the Adjutant-General, the Commissariat Officer, the Baggage Master, the Brigade Major and Brigadier of the 2nd Brigade are all sick . . . Thus paralysed as the force already is, and with the rest enfeebled and worn out by this long and arduous campaign, I cannot refrain from mentioning my apprehensions that, should the operations before Calpee be protracted and the exposure great, the force will be completely prostrated." But his labours, hardships and privations which had been incessant and severe, did not diminish the determination of the British soldier to fight.

At 3 A.M. on the 20th, Sir Hugh Rose crossed the river to select the sites for Maxwell's Mortar Batteries and to direct his attack on the city and fort. Sir Hugh Rose had hardly returned to camp when the enemy attacked with considerable determination the right flank, but, as he had fixed the 23rd for the attack on Calpee, he refused to be drawn into a general action. He directed the pickets merely to maintain the ground, "which they did steadily and gallantly, under the able command of Major Stewart, Her Majesty's 86th Regiment, until the enemy were beat back." On the night of the 20th, reinforcements, which Sir Hugh Rose ordered Maxwell to send across the Jumna, reached his camp. " They consisted of two companies Her Majesty's 88th Regiment, some Riflemen mounted on Camels with Sikh drivers, and two companies of Sikh Infantry—fine soldier-like looking fellows, and sensibly dressed, not imprisoned in British uniform." (1) On the 21st, Maxwell erected his Mortar Batteries opposite the village of Rehree and the town of Calpee. That day Sir Hugh Rose heard from his spies that the enemy intended to make a general attack on his position the next day. They had sworn to drive his force into the Jumna or to die.

The British force lay in the ground between the road from Calpee to Banda and the Jumna, the left nearly touching the Banda road and the

---

(1) Recollections of the Campaign in Malwa and Central India by John Henry Sylvester, p. 15 3.

" I sent across the Jumna on the night of the 20th two Companies of the 88th, the whole of the Camel Corps, and 124 of the Sikh Infantry." From Lieutenant-Colonel G. V. Maxwell, C. B., Her Majesty's 88th Regiment, Commanding Movable Column, Cawnpore District, to Colonel E. R. Whetherall, C.B., Chief of the Staff, Central India Field Force, dated Camp before Calpee, May 24th, 1858. Colonel Maxwell gives the strength of the Camel Corps at 682.

right resting on the ravines running down to the Jumna. In these stood the villages of Soorowlee and Golowlee, which were connected and held by strong pickets. On the morning of the 22nd, Brigadier Stewart, in compliance with instructions from the Major-General Commanding, proceeded to the Mortar Battery in front of our camp on the right. The picket at the Battery, consisting of one company of the 3rd European Regiment, also the picket on the bank of the Jumna, composed of one company of Her Majesty's 86th which guarded our extreme left flank, were reinforced by nearly the whole of Her Majesty's 86th Regiment, which, thrown into skirmishing order, covered almost the whole of our position to the right. In support were three guns of No. 4 Light Field Battery, one troop of Her Majesty's 14th Light Dragoons, a troop of the 3rd Bombay Light Cavalry and four companies of the 25th Bombay Native Infantry. On the Brigadier's left, the pickets of the right centre were supported by the other half of No. 4 Light Field Battery, the remainder of the 25th Bombay Native Infantry with the 21st Company Royal Engineers, the whole under the command of Lieutenant-Colonel Robertson of the 25th Bengal Native Infantry. In the centre were the Siege Guns, two 18-pounders, one 24-pounder, and two 8-inch Howitzers with the Madras Sappers under Lieutenant Gordon, supported by the wing of Her Majesty's 71st, one squadron of the 14th, a troop of the 3rd Light Cavalry and Captain Field's Royal Artillery 9-pounders. To the left of the centre, facing the plain and the village of Rehree, was posted No. 1 Bombay Troop Horse Artillery supported by two troops of the 14th. Beyond these were placed the Camel Corps and No. 18 Light Field Battery, supported by a detachment of the Sikh Corps, the Hyderabad Field Force covering the extreme left.

Shortly after 8 A.M., Sir Hugh Rose was informed by his videttes and outposts that the enemy were advancing in great force from Calpee and its environs towards the belt of ravines on the right, and along the Banda-Calpee road against the left. He commanded half of No. 4 Light Field Battery to move down to the Mortar Battery, and fire was immediately opened on the enemy, who were advancing in great numbers and with much spirit over ground most favourable to them. As Sir Hugh Rose was posting his siege guns, a message reached him from Brigadier Stuart that the right was no longer threatened. The attack on the left was now in full force, but Sir Hugh did not take away a man from the right. He had the power of foreseeing, which enables the born commander to discover the plans of his foe He felt that the enemy hoped, by arousing his anxiety for his left and centre, to induce him to impoverish his right. The stillness in the ravines was to him ominous, and he became convinced that in them the enemy lay concealed. He ordered a company of the 3rd Europeans to be pushed some hundred yards forward " into the network of ambushes." In a few moments the 3rd Europeans started the rebel host from their lair. From the deadly ravine labyrinths, there arose a curtain of fire and smoke, and the battle waged from the Jumna to the village of Tehree. From the left of the village Hugh Rose watched the determined attack made on his centre. He could meet it. He watched the enemy's movement on his left. It was intact. It was his right wing which caused him anxiety. The fire in that quarter grew slacker, and he sent a messenger to Brigadier Stuart to ask him if he would like to be reinforced by half the Camel Corps. The messenger returned to tell him that the Brigadier would be very glad to have them. At this moment Brigadier Stuart's fire became fainter and fainter, that of the enemy heavier. Hugh Rose knew what that meant ; his right, the key of his whole position, was in danger. He must deal with the affair himself, and he rode at once to its assistance, " with the whole of the Camel Corps at its best pace." On the way, he met an orderly coming to him at full speed from Brigadier Stuart. He was charged to say that the Brigadier wanted further reinforcements. " I knew that they were required, for the enemy's fire now came from within our position." (1) On reaching the foot of the rising ground on which the Mortar Battery and three guns had been placed, the British soldiers dismounted from their camels, and, led by Sir Hugh Rose and their Commander Major Ross, they " went up the rise in line at the double in perfect order." Volleys of musketry came over the crest and killed or wounded every horse of the Chief's Staff except one. On they went. The top was reached. A strange appalling sight burst upon them. The enemy, wild with opium and fury, were advancing in great numbers across a small piece of level ground against the Mortar Battery and the Field Guns. The seething mass poured in volley after volley as they approached, with loud yells of triumph, closer and closer to the guns. The English force could not reply. The Enfield rifles had become leaded. The slender chain of skirmishers,

---

(1) From Major-General Sir Hugh Rose, K.C.B., Commanding F. D. A., and Field Force to Major-Generel Sir Wm. M. Mansfield, K.C.B., Chief of the Staff of the Army in India, dated Gwalior, June 23rd, 1858, p. 97.

weakened by many having been struck down to the ground by sunstroke where they lay, had been pressed back by the superior weight of numbers. The guns had ceased firing. The Brigadier was on foot, bidding the gunners to draw their swords and defend them with their lives. Hugh Rose saw that the position was critical, almost desperate, but nothing could daunt his fiery courage. Without allowing his men to draw breath, he ordered the Rifles and the 80th to charge with their bayonets. The soldiers gave " one of those cheers which all the world over has been the herald of British successes," and, headed by their Chief and Major Ross, they at once charged down the steep, and attacked the dense lines of the mutineers, ten times superior to them in numbers. The rebels wavered, turned and fled, and were pursued by the British soldiers up and down the steep sides of the rocky ravines. (1)

At the same time as they made their determined attack on the right, the rebels, with equal vigour, attacked the right centre and the left centre. The right centre was guarded by four companies of the 25th Bombay Native Infantry who, after a most brave resistance, were forced back by the enemy's masses. At this moment Lieutenant Edwardes, commanding the 21st company of Royal Engineers, which had been moved in support of the 25th, charged with his small body, routed the foe and pressed the pursuit till they were out of reach. (2) On the left centre, the enemy advanced firing heavily. When they approached close to the remainder of the 25th which guarded it, they taunted them in the most foul language for their allegiance. The 25th answered the malediction of the mutineers in a manner worthy of their reputation and English discipline—a volley, a cheer and a charge of the bayonet.

---

(1) "The very important service rendered on this occasion by Major Ross, Commanding the Camel Corps, requires that I should make special mention of the ability and resolute gallantry with which he led his brave corps. This very promising officer is perfectly qualified to turn to the best account all the vast advantages of fleet or mounted infantry." From Major-General Sir Hugh Rose, K.C.B., Commanding Central India Field Force, to the Chief of the Staff, dated Gwalior, 22nd June 1858.

(2) " I beg to mention, specially, Lieutenant Edwardes for his prompt resolution on this occasion ; he is an enterprising and promising officer. The 21st Comp. fight as well in the field, as they work in the trenches, and are worthy of their distinguished corps." From Major-General Sir Hugh Rose, K.C.B., Commanding Central India Field Force, dated Gwalior, 23rd June 1858.

The enemy after a short tussle retreated. The 25th dashed through the ravines after them, came up with the rear near the village of Tehree, bayoneted them and continued the pursuit beyond the village. (1) The whole of the infantry on the left, covered by Captain Lightfoot's Troop of Horse Artillery, three guns of the Light Field Battery and the whole of the cavalry, made a converging attack on the enemy's right and the village of Tehree. They drove the rebels into it, through it, and over the plain towards the Calpee road. The enemy's retreat had spread from right to left over the entire line of battle. On the extreme right, Lieutenant-Colonel Louth with a few of the 86th and a Company of the Rifles moved forward through the ravines, and by a skilful manœuvre cut off and surrounded a large body of the enemy. " Part were killed on the bank of the Jumna, the rest were driven into the river, where they were shot or drowned." (2) On the left, the enemy's retreat became more and more a flight. Their infantry, cavalry and guns, all mingled together, rushed over the heights, up and down the ravines and along the high road to Calpee, closely followed by our cavalry and artillery. The pursuit lasted until horse and man could go no further and do no more. The majority of the rebels made their way towards Jaloun. Calpee afforded them no safe shelter for Maxwell's guns were pouring into it a stream of shot and shell.

The sweltering sun was sinking low when the fight, which was desperately maintained at every point throughout the day, came to a close and victory was secure. The plan of the enemy was well conceived and carried out with considerable energy of attack. Its failure was due to the pluck and discipline of the British soldier, the courage and loyalty of the Bombay sepoy and the intrepid genius of their commander. Never was the iron endurance of the British soldier more severely tested. All that summer day, beneath a burning sun, parched by suffocating hot winds, he fought without food or water. " Officers and men dropped

---

(1) " Lieutenant-Colonel Robertson, of whose gallantry and ability I have had so many proofs, and his devoted Regiment, whose loyalty and discipline have so often conquered treason and insubordination, deserve to be specially mentioned for their distinguished conduct on this occasion." From Major-General Sir Hugh Rose, K.C.B., Commanding Central India Field Force, to the Chief of the Staff, dated Gwalior, 22nd June 1858, p. 99.

(2) " I beg to mention especially Lieutenant-Colonel Louth for the good service he did on this occasion : he is a good and gallant officer who always leads his Regiment to success. He is well seconded by his admirable soldiers whom I canont eulogise more highly than by saying that they do credit to Ireland." From Major-General Sir Hugh Rose, K.C.B., Commanding Central India Field Force, to the Chief of the Staff, dated Gwalior 22nd of June 1858, p. 99.

down as though struck by lightning, in the delirium of a sunstroke, yet all this was endured without a murmur, and in the cool of the evening we were speculating upon the capture of Calpee on the morrow." But the hard-fought fight of the day had given us Calpee. The enemy began to evacuate the place during the night and it was, next morning, occupied without further fighting. Fifty-eight guns taken in the field or the fort; twenty-eight silk embroidered standards, and, what was of more importance, immense stores of ammunition fell into the hands of the victors. Outside the town in the shady park land surrounding the tombs, the British pitched their camp. "Early on the morrow the troops paraded and a royal salute was fired, for it was the 24th of May—our Queen's birthday, and the troops rejoiced in the prospect of going into quarters and the sick and wounded of going Home." On the 24th of May Lord Canning telegraphed to Sir Hugh Rose : " Your capture of Calpee has crowned a series of brilliant and uninterrupted successes. I thank you and your brave soldiers with all my heart." (1)

The capture of Calpee completed the plan which the Government of India had drawn up for the Central India Field Force. Instructions had been conveyed to Sir Hugh Rose that, after its capture, the Force should be broken up and part of it should be sent to Gwalior and the rest to Jhansi, as garrisons for those places. He had submitted to the Governor-General the distribution of troops for these two services and proceeded at once to make the necessary arrangements for their transfer. He himself was strongly advised by his medical officer to return at once to Bombay. He had had three attacks of sun during the assault and capture of Koonch, a fourth in an intermediate reconnaissance and a fifth in the general action of the Jumna on the 22nd of May. (2) The powerful remedies administered to enable him to rise again, ride, and retain his command in the field, " which I never left," and the duties of the

---

(1) " It is impossible to record the numerous individual acts of gallantry displayed that day when but one spirit animated the whole line—how the Brigadier prepared to die at his guns rather than yield an inch, how the natives of the force withstood the taunts and gibes hurled at them by their own kith and kin for their adherence to the British cause ; but half this credit may be fairly given to their officers and Commandant, Colonel Robertson, Captain Lightfoot and Lieutenant Strutt who shed lustre on the Bombay Artillery; and the casualties among the horses ridden by them showed they had not spared themselves." Recollections of the Campaign in Malwa and Central India by Assistant Surgeon John Sylvester, p. 157.

(2) During the day our gallant General, again almost beaten by the sun, would not return to camp, but sought the shelter of a tree to recover sufficiently to proceed with his anxious work. *Ibid.*, p. 163.

command, which had daily become more onerous owing to the sickness of his staff, had depressed his vital energies. A competent witness wrote : " The General was very ill ; his Chief of the Staff, General Wetherall, was in raging fever; his Quarter Master General, Captain Macdonald, worn out ; the Chaplain of the Force had lost his reason, and was apparently sinking fast." (1) Sir Hugh, having carried out his instructions, now followed the urgent advice of his physician ; he resigned his command and applied for leave on medical certificate. On the 1st of June he issued his farewell orders, and in glowing phrase addressed the men whom he had led to victory upon victory :—

" The Central India Field Force being about to be dissolved, the Major General cannot allow the troops to leave the immediate command without expressing to them the gratification he has invariably experienced at their good conduct and discipline, and he requests that the following general order may be read at the head of every corps and detachment of the force.

" Soldiers ! You have marched more than a thousand miles, and taken more than a hundred guns ; you have forced your way through mountain passes and intricate jungles and over rivers : you have captured the strongest forts, and beat the enemy, no matter what the odds, whereever you met him ; you have restored extensive districts to the Government, and peace and order now reign where before, for twelve months, were tyranny and rebellion ; you have done all this, and you have never had a check.

" I thank you with all sincerity for your bravery, your devotion and your discipline.

" When you first marched I told you that you, as British soldiers, had more than enough of courage for the work which was before you, but that courage without discipline was of no avail, and I exhorted you to let discipline be your watchword ; you have attended to my orders—in hardships, in temptations, and in dangers you have obeyed your General, and you never left your ranks.

" You have fought against the strong, and you have protected the rights of the weak and defenceless, of foes as well as of friends ; I have seen you in the ardour of the combat preserve and place children out of harm's way.

---

(1) Central India by Thomas Lowe, p. 297.

"This is the discipline of Christian soldiers and this it is which has brought you triumphant from the shores of Western India to the waters of the Jumna, and establishes, without doubt, that you will find no place to equal the glory of our arms."

After the defeat at Koonch, Tantia Topee went straight to Gwalior and concealed himself in the bazaar. It is the difficulty of ascertaining facts which is the greatest obstacle to the governing of an Oriental state. Neither Scindia nor Dunker Rao, nor the two chief officers of the army knew anything of the visit of Tantia Topee. Tantia had been to Gwalior in September 1857 to gain the Contingent to the Nana and move it upon Cawnpore. He succeeded. The main body of the Contingent left Gwalior and, reinforced by rebels from Banda and from Oudh, they pressed General Windham's force into their entrenchments at Cawnpore and occupied most of the city until they were routed by the force under Sir Colin Campbell on the 6th of December. (1) Tantia, who commanded the rebels, fell back with the remnant of his force on Calpee where he was joined by many mutineers. He did not venture to again cross the Jumna but he was always on the watch. His great aim was not to fight Sir Colin Campbell but to make a dash for the south—to raise a revolt in the Deccan and establish once again the power of the Peshwa. Scindia, influenced by Dunker Rao, was the main obstacle to the realisation of the plan. His chief agent declared, "Scindia being one with the English, does not regard the Peshwa. His Raj is great. Seeing his course, all the Rajahs, great and small, are cowed and side with the English. On account of him we have been unable to get an opportunity. Wherefore we must gain his troops, and get him into our hands when the Peshwa shall rule." Tantia was secretly plotting in the bazaar at Gwalior to get possession of Scindia when news reached him that Jhansi, their last great stronghold south of the Jumna, had fallen into the hands of the English, and that the Rao and the Ranee had fled in wild haste to a village fifteen miles from Gwalior where his own family lay. On the 26th of May, Tantia, unaccompanied by any followers, left Gwalior and joined the Rao, the Ranee and the Nawab of Banda. The next day a council was held to determine their future course. The Ranee was there, but not the Nawab of Banda. A sepoy from each company was present. "The Rao," says his Secretary, who was present and afterwards turned informer, "asked of the

---

(1) Selections from State Papers, Military Department, Volume Lucknow and Cawnpore, Introduction, pp. 340, 344.

council, whither shall we go? The Ranee demanded that they should move straight to Kurara in Jhansi. Tantia Topee said, "that even Bundelcund would be better." The Rao said, "There we should find the Boondelas hostile and no supplies. Our only course is to make for the Deccan where all will join us. But we must go first to Gwalior where the army is gained, and take it with us by the Sipree road. When that army shall come over, the Maharajah and the Baiza Baee will join us, and all the Princes of Hindostan will rise. (1)" The Sepoys however desired strongly to retire to Oudh. The council broke up without anything being settled. That night, however, an order was issued to march next morning across Scindia's Frontier, the Scinde River.

On the 28th of May the rebel force entered Gwalior territory and halted at Amean where they found posted 400 Scindian Foot, 150 horse and 4 guns. Scindia's Chief Political Officer told the Rao, "It is the order of the Maharajah and the Dewan that you retire." "And who," replied the Rao, "are you? A ten rupee underling of a Soobah drunk with bhang? And who are the Maharajah and Dinkur Rao? Christians? We are the Rao and Peshwa. Scindia is our slipper-bearer. (2) We gave him his kingdom. His army has joined us. We have letters from the Baiza Baee. Scindia himself encourages us. Tantia Topee has visited Gwalior and ascertained all. He having completed everything, I am for the Lushkur. Would you fight for us? All is mine!!" (3) Scindia's detachment did not attempt resistance. The next day the Rao continued his march, and on the 31st he encamped at Burragaon within eight miles of Gwalior.

A thorny and difficult task had confronted Scindia after the mutiny of the Contingent on the 14th of June 1857. The men of the Contingent were not his troops though he paid for them. They now demanded that he should enrol them and lead them against Agra. They would make Agra over to him, with such Provinces as he desired, then move on to Delhi.

(1) The grandmother of Scindia by adoption, known by her title of the Baiza Baee, was a person of considerable ability and influence in the Gwalior State.
Report on the Affairs of Gwalior, from the 24th of May to the 20th of June 1858. By Major S. Charters Macpherson, Political Agent.

(2) Ranajee, the first member of the Scindia family of note, commenced his career as the carrier of the slippers of Balajee Rao Peishwa. His care in the performance of this menial duty attracted his master's attention who appointed him to a command in the Pagah or stable horse. From this his rise to the first rank of Mahratta Chiefs was rapid.

(3) Report on the Affairs of Gwalior from the 24th of May to the 20th of June 1858. By Major S. Charters Macpherson, Political Agent.

But Scindia had no desire that the Moghul Emperor should overshadow the Mahratta Princes, and he relied on the strength and generosity of the British Government to uphold and reward him for his loyalty. The mutineers proposed, as an alternative, that he should hand over to them the 4½ lacs which the Resident had left in his charge; that he should give them 12 or 15 lacs more and provide them with supplies and carriage to move. "If he declined either alternative they would bombard and plunder his palace and city, empty his treasury, seize his fort and place himself in confinement or at their head." But Scindia had the courage of a soldier and the pride of a king. Threats did not shake his resolution Policy, however, demanded that he should send them no definite answer. To prevent them from moving at once on Agra, he gave them a donation of three months' pay and the promise of service, "which," he wrote, "I was obliged to give them instead of a destructive volley." Scindia's greatest apprehension was lest his troops, 10,000 in number, should coalesce with the contingent. They now clamoured loudly for the donation given to the rebels. He appeased them by fair promises. And so the game went on. The mutineers menaced, beseeched, dictated, wheedled and insulted Scindia. He confronted, defied, flattered and deceived them : and the political resources of an Oriental monarch are very great. He bribed their officers, their priests, and every man who could sow discord among them. "He ordered the removal of the wheels of carts within the range of the rebels, and sent all elephants and camels to distant jungles. He maintained that field operations were folly in the monsoon. After it, his course and that of all would be clear."(1)

News now began to reach Gwalior of Havelock's victories. One day there returned to the city the small remains of a wing of the 6th Contingent of infantry, who had joined the Nana. Their comrades had been left on the field of battle. They declared it was madness to face the Europeans. Scindia's belief in the foresight of Dunker Rao and the Resident, and in the wisdom of the line which he was following according to their advice, was strengthened. Dangers and perplexities, however, thickened about him. On the last day of July there arrived at Gwalior the rebel force from Mhow and Indore, who were on their way to Agra. "It excited the Contingent afresh," said the Dewan, "like oil thrown on the fire." The force comprised, not only the mutinous regiments from those stations, but 600 men of Holkar's army, with seven guns and 1,000

---

(1) Report on Gwalior, dated 10th of February, 1858.

Ghazees, led by a person styling himself Feroz Shah, Prince of Delhi, and also the 5th Contingent Infantry Regiment which had mutinied at Augur (1) and joined it on the march. The Contingent and Scindia's own troops demanded that they should move with the Mhow and Indore rebels on to Agra. Scindia told the Contingent that he could only communicate his plan to them after the Mhow and Indore mutineers had left. He knew it was no longer possible to retain them, and he hoped they would take with them the most mutinous and fanatical of the Contingent and his own soldiery.

On the 5th of September Scindia let the rebels go. Two days later, having collected some boats, they crossed the Chumbul with their baggage. Scindia had no desire that they should return, and by a clever secret movement, he swept in a night both banks of the river of its boats. The Contingent discovered that his smooth language and appearance of concession were no sufficient guarantee of his intentions. They were now determined to test his sincerity. On the 7th, their officers and 300 men went to his Palace Gardens and Scindia asked what they wished. The sepoys said that they had resolved to take Agra at once and destroy the Christians there, when they would carry Scindia's banner where he pleased: Scindia replied resolutely that they therefore did not await his orders. He declared that any movement made by them until after the monsoon would be against his will, and they should receive from him neither pay nor supplies. Exasperated at his reply, the sepoys declared that they had been betrayed. They returned to camp, planted the green flag of Islam and the white flag of Hinduism and prepared their batteries.

The night of the 8th of September Scindia passed in sleepless anxiety. All his troops save the Mahrattas seemed inclined to join the green and white standards. Then he would have no alternative save to become a puppet in their hands or fly to the English. Had but a bugle sounded or an alarm gun fired in the lines that night, his troops had risen uncontrollably. He had every bugle brought to his palace and every gun watched.

At break of day Scindia paraded his whole force. He understood the disposition of his own men. He addressed each corps and he exhorted the Mahratta officers not to let their sovereign suffer the degradation of being coerced by troops that were not recruited from their race. The appeal was successful. Scindia, assured of the loyalty of his troops,

---

(1) Augur is a large town in the dominions of Scindia, about thirty-six miles from Oojein. The 5th Contingent Infantry mutinied about the 5th of July and killed one officer.

moved out his whole force and himself arranged every battery and picket to meet an attack. The Contingent, however, lost heart and withdrew their guns. At the close of September Scindia heard of the capture of Delhi by the British and he exulted in their triumph and his own foresight.(1) On the 10th of October, the Mhow and Indore mutineers, reinforced by several bodies from Delhi, attacked the British camp at Agra and were routed by Colonel Greathead's column.(2) On the 14th of October Major Macpherson advised Scindia to let the Contingent go to Cawnpore, "as Greathead's column was ordered to press thither and a powerful force was rapidly assembled there." The following day the Contingent, accompanied by the emissaries of the Nana, left Gwalior. "In a spirit of bitter malignity they utterly destroyed and defaced, by cutting down, every tree in the cantonments at Gwalior; and then on their route wasted fiercely Scindia's country, denouncing him as the great enemy and betrayer of their cause."(1)

On hearing of the near approach of the rebels, on the 31st May, Scindia sent one of his most influential favourites and leader of the party opposed to the Dewan to watch and report on their movements. He talked with the leaders. The Rao maintained his old arrogant tone. "What does the Maharajah mean by thinking to fight with us? We are not here to fight, but to rest a few days, get supplies and money, and go to the Deccan. Upon what do you rely? Your army is with us and will certainly join us. Depend upon that. We have from Gwalior two hundred letters of invitation and assurance. What can the Maharajah and the Dewan possibly do alone?"

But the Maharajah and his Prime Minister were divided in their opinions how to face the crisis. The Dewan advised strongly to delay by money and every possible device the advance of the rebels so as to enable the force which had been sent in pursuit from Calpee to arrive, and to entrench at Morar Scindia's own body-guard and the Gwalior men, which he considered were sufficient to check the rebels for a time if they advanced. Dunker Rao, like Scindia, was ignorant of Tantia Topee's secret visit and knew not to what extent he had seduced from their allegiance the Mahratta troops. The officers of Scindia's own body-guard, partisans of the rebels, told their sovereign that the minister's advice was

---

(1) Macpherson's Report on Gwalior, February, 1858.
(2) Selections from the State Papers preserved in the Military Department of the Government of India, edited by G. W. Forrest, Volume I, Delhi.

derogatory and absurd. He could disperse the rebels by a single round from his gun. Scindia was a proud and headstrong youth. On the night of the 31st the Mahratta favourite returned from the rebel camp. He stated that the rebels were so dispirited and disorganised that "he could disperse them with his raw levy of 500 men." Scindia at once issued orders for the troops to assemble, and at break of day, without the knowledge of the Dewan, he led 8,000 men and 24 guns to fight the rebels. But there was no fight. "Scindia's right was carried by a single Sepoy who ran up to it waving his sword and shouting Deen. No one would fire at him. The mass of the rebels now came on. They and Scindia's men shouted Deen together, while many congratulated and embraced, and very many went to eat water melons in the bed of the Morar." The Body-guard alone made any resistance, and about sixty of these were killed or wounded. Scindia made for an adjacent hill on the right, saw his whole force marching homewards, and galloped straight with some fifteen attendants to the Phoolbagh. He there quickly changed his dress, remounted, and rode towards Agra. The Dewan, on hearing of His Highness' flight, advised the Private Secretary, if the Baiza Baee, the Maharanee and other ladies could not go to Agra, to make for Brigadier Smith's camp beyond Sipree; he himself then sped after the Maharajah with a few Sowars. He caught him up eight miles upon his road. Avoiding the highway, they reached Dholepore before midnight, and the Rana paid the fugitive monarch every possible attention. (1) On the following morning, the 3rd of June, Scindia reached Agra and, "as directed by the Governor General," was received there with every mark of honour and sympathy. Not one of Scindia's pampered favourites and boon companions followed him.

The Ranees with the chief Sirdars proceeded to the Fort of Nurwa, thirty miles from Gwalior. One Ranee did not accompany them. "The Gujja Rajah, mother of the Maharanee, believing that Scindia was beleaguered at the Phoolbagh, seized a sword, mounted her horse, and rode to the Palace, summoning all to her aid, until she found that he was certainly gone. She followed the other ladies on the third day. And with them went, alone of all Scindia's troops, 500 or 600 men, who chanced to be present, of his old Irregular Horse."

The Rao, Tantia Topee and the Ranee of Jhansi entered the city in triumph and declared the Nana as Peshwa or Chief of the Mahratta Confederacy. The Rao refused to assume any state. That he reserved,

---
(1) Report on the affairs of Gwalior from the 24th of May to the 20th of June 1858, by Major S. Charters Macpherson.

said he, " for the Musnud at Poona." He behaved with considerable tact and restrained the ravages of war as well as the hand of the spoiler. He confiscated and gave to plunder only the houses of the Dewan and of the two chief military officers. He gave to Scindia's troops the three months' pay due to them and two months' pay as gratuity, amounting in all to nine lacs. He distributed among his own troops about seven and a half lacs. The Jail was thrown open and the State prisoners in the Fort, which was surrendered without a thought of defence, were released. The Rao had no desire to destroy the authority of Scindia. He re-confirmed in their offices nearly all Scindia's servants, and he did everything compatible with his object (the acknowledgment of the Peshwa as the paramount power in the Mahratta Confederacy) to give his visit a friendly character. The departure or escape of Scindia was to him a most untoward incident. He attempted, through a relative of Scindia's, to negotiate his return, while he also pressed the Baiza Baee to come and take charge of affairs. He wrote to her: " All is well here. Your going from hence was not, to my thinking, right. I have already written to you, but have received no answer. This should not be. I send this letter by Ramjee Chowley Jemdar. Do come and take charge of your seat of Government. It is my intention to take Gwalior, only to have a meeting and go on. This is my purpose. Therefore it is necessary that you should come making no denial." The Baiza Baee sent the letter to Sir Robert Hamilton, who was with Brigadier Smith's force, which was advancing on Gwalior from Sipree by the Jhansi Road.

On the day that Calpee was captured, Sir Hugh Rose detached a pursuing column, (1) commanded by Colonel Robertson, along the Jaloun road to ascertain the real line of the enemy's flight. To overtake them was hopeless as they were not encumbered with baggage, and their Cavalry and Infantry were " in as good as mine were in a bad condition." Sir Robert Hamilton was of opinion that the rebels would move to the north, but Colonel Robertson reported that a great part of their number had made a turn in a westerly direction, and he was certain that they would make for Oudh and cross the Jumna at a ford thirty-five or forty miles to the north-east of Calpee or at a ford to the west of it. A short rest having enabled the European troops to recover a little, Sir Hugh Rose reinforced Lieutenant-Colonel Robertson with one Wing Her Majesty's

---

(1) 2 Troops, 3rd Bombay Light Cavalry.
No. 18 Light Field Battery.
150 Hyderabad Cavalry.
8 Companies 25th Regiment Bombay Native Infantry.

86th Regiment and two Squadrons Her Majesty's 14th Light Dragoons. Then there came two expresses from that officer stating that the Calpee rebels had certainly taken the road to Gwalior. "So little was at that time the great intrigue of Tantia Topee against Scindia's power even suspected that the best authority for intelligence could not bring himself to think that Lieutenant-Colonel Robertson was not mistaken in his information." However, not many hours after the arrival of Lieutenant-Colonel Robertson's last express, Sir Robert Hamilton received similar intelligence, when Sir Hugh Rose sent Brigadier Stuart with a Force (1) to reinforce Robertson and march on Gwalior after the rebels. The news received for the next few days was very uncertain and contradictory. On the 4th of June came the startling intelligence of what had happened at Gwalior. Sir Hugh Rose instantly conceived the gravity of the situation. If Tantia Topee left a portion of his army at Gwalior and marched with the remainder southwards and unfurled the standard of the Peshwa in the Deccan and Southern Mahratta Country, thousands of Mahrattas would flock to it. A land of wild valleys and mountains inhabited by a gallant race would have to be again conquered. The inhabitants of Indore might follow the example of Gwalior, and the task of restoring Central India to British rule would have to be done again. No one, as he said, could foresee the extent of the evil if Gwalior were not promptly wrested from the rebels. His troops were exhausted, the heat was intense, there were no roads and wide rivers had to be crossed Nevertheless, in the face of these difficulties, he resolved to set forth at once, and he immediately telegraphed to the Governor-General that he would be glad to take command of the force ordered to re-capture the city and fortress of Gwalior. Lord Canning thanked him warmly and accepted the offer. Brigadier-General Napier, (2) who had been appointed to succeed Sir Hugh Rose on his taking leave, informed Lord Canning that he would be delighted to serve as second in command. (3)

---

(1) No. 4 Light Field Battery.
    2 Troops Her Majesty's 14th Light Dragoons.
    1 Wing Her Majesty's 71st Regiment.
    1 Wing Her Majesty's 86th Regiment.
    4 Companies 25th Bombay Native Infantry.
    Half a Company Bombay S. and M.
    Two 18-Pounders.
    One 8-inch Howitzer.
(2) Field Marshal Lord Napier of Magdala
(3) Clyde and Strathnairn by Major-General Sir Oliver Tudor Burne, K. C. S. I., pp. 141, 142.

On the 6th of June, Sir Hugh Rose, leaving a small force to garrison Calpee until relieved by Bengal troops, set out with the 1st Troop Bombay Horse Artillery, one Squadron 14th Light Dragoons, one Squadron 3rd Bombay Light Cavalry and Madras Sappers and Miners to overtake Brigadier Stuart's column. To gain on them he had to make forced marches, but he made them at night to avoid the sun. "One day the heat in the shade rose to 130°." The Cavalry constantly slept in their saddles and by the constant lounging and dragging to one side galled their chargers' backs (1). On the night of the third day the Officer Commanding the outlying picket of Her Majesty's 14th Light Dragoons reported to Sir Hugh Rose that his men had fallen from their saddles from exhaustion. "I had the picket relieved by a party of Hyderabad Cavalry."

As the force advanced, the roads became mere tracks cut up by ravines, and it was difficult for the baggage and supplies, carried on bad country carts, to keep up with the troops. "A detachment of the 25th Bombay Native Infantry, who guarded them, were three days without a meal; after a bathe in the Patrooj and a short rest to enable them to make their cakes, these good soldiers were quite ready to go on." On the 11th, Sir Hugh Rose overtook Brigadier Stuart with the 1st Brigade at the smallfort of Indoorkee on the Scinde river. Here he heard from the Commander-in-Chief that Colonel Riddell's movable column of Bengal troops (2) was to escort a large supply of siege guns, mortar and ammunition from Agra to Gwalior for the siege of that fort. He was also informed that Lord Clyde had ordered Brigadier Smith with a Brigade of the Rajpootana Field Force to march from the neighbourhood of Chandaree to Gwalior. Sir Hugh Rose, however, determined by a bold scheme to prevent a scientific siege of the fort, which would be a long difficult task. He hoped that a successful attack on the enemy outside or inside the city would, like Calpee, be followed by its easy capture. The following plan presented itself to his mind, and he proceeded at once to carry it out. He ordered Major Orr, Commanding Hyderabad

---

(1) Recollections of the Campaign in Malwa and Central India, by Assistant Surgeon John Henry Sylvester, p. 175.

(2) The troops were as follows:—
No. 21 Light Field Battery.
320 Bengal Europeans.
200 Sikh Horse.
300 Sikh Infantry.
Siege Artillery.

Contingency, to move from Jhansi to Punear twelve miles from Gwalior, where fifteen years before a British force had routed the Mahrattas. At Punear Major Orr held the Bombay road and was well placed for cutting off the retreat of the rebles. He ordered Brigadier Smith to advance from Sipree by the Jhansi road to Kotah-Ke-Serai, about seven miles to the east of Gwalior. To complete the investment from the south-east and north, he sent instructions to Colonel Riddell to move with the column by the Agra and Gwalior road to the Residency, about seven miles to the north of Gwalior. But the instructions never reached him. Sir Hugh Rose trusted that all the columns of operations would be at their posts by the 19th of June. He himself would advance from the east, because with great trouble he had ascertained that this was the weakest side of Gwalior, and consequently the best for an attack. It was commanded by high hills difficult of access, but when these heights were taken he could drive the enemy from slope to slope till he reached a point from whence he could cannonade the Lushker or New City and, covered by the fire of artillery, storm it. He would cut boldly "in two the enemy's whole line consisting of the old city, above which is the Fort and the Lushker or New City." This point of attack had another advantage. "It enabled me to attack Gwalior almost unhurt by the fire of the Fort." It was a fine daring strategical conception.

On the 12th of June, Sir Hugh Rose's column reached Amean and heard that the Bengal troops had arrived to garrison Calpee and that the weakened 2nd Brigade,(1) which had been left behind, was only seventeen miles in their rear. After having been joined by the 2nd Brigade, Brigadier-General Robert Napier, who at once assumed command of it, pushed forward, and, on the morning of the 16th of June, after a long march, he reached Bahadurpore, about four or five miles from the cantonment on the Morar. The British Commander directed Captain Abbott with his Hyderabad Cavalry to reconnoitre the cantonment, and he announced that the rebels were in force in front of it. Sir Hugh Rose rode forward, himself and staff, and examined closely the enemy's position. He found that the side of the cantonments fronting the British force was occupied by strong bodies of cavalry and that on their right were guns and a large body of infantry. As he surveyed the cantonments with the roofs of the bungalows rising above the bright green trees, a delicate problem arose in his mind. His force had just finished a long and fatiguing

---

(1) The bulk of it remained at Calpee.

march and the sun had been up for some time. It was June and the rains had not burst. Four or five miles' more march in the sun and a combat afterwards would be a great trial of the men's strength. "On the other hand Morar looked inviting with several good buildings not yet burnt; they would be good quarters for a portion of the force; if I delayed the attack until the next day, the enemy were sure to burn them. A prompt attack has always more effect on the rebels than a procrastinated one." And no commander had a greater gift for impromptu plans and unexpected dashes than Hugh Rose. He at once countermanded the order for encamping and hastened to complete his order of battle. The first Brigade under Brigadier Stuart occupied the first line; the second Brigade which mustered only 33 European officers, 9 Native officers and 1,072 Non-commissioned Officers and Rank and File (1) was under Brigadier-General Napier and formed the second line. The first line under the General himself was arranged as follows :— No. 4 Light Field Battery and siege guns in the centre, (2) Her Majesty's 86th on their right; the 25th Bombay Native Infantry on their left; Her Majesty's 13th Light Dragoons on each flank. The second line was disposed as follows :—No. 18 Light Field Battery on the right, supported by Johnston's Hyderabad Horse; in the centre the Madras Sappers and Miners and a wing of Her Majesty's 71st Highland Light Infantry, while on the left was a wing of Her Majesty's 14th Light Dragoons. (3) The Hyderabad Cavalry covered the advance. Sir Hugh Rose requested Napier to watch well the hill and ravines on his left and to advance *in echelon* from the right in support of the 1st Brigade while it took ground diagonally to the right, in order to reach the road which led to the cantonment, and so outflank the enemy's left. As the troops advanced

---

(1) The greater part of the Brigade was at Calpee. On the 16th of June it was composed as follows.—

1st Troop Horse Artillery.
No. Light Field Battery.
14th Light Dragoons.
3rd Light Cavalry (on rearguard).
Madras Sappers and Miners.
71st Highlanders (14 officers, 381 men).
Hyderabad Cavalry.
Hyderabad Infantry (on rearguard).

(2) Sir Hugh Rose writes :— "No. 18 Light Field Battery and the Siege Guns in the centre of the first." But this is an error. The 4th Light Field Battery belonged to the 1st Brigade.

(3) From Brigadier-General R. Napier, C.B., Commanding 2nd Brigade, Central India Field Force, dated Camp Morar, 18th June 1858.

across the level plain the Rebels fell back. But when the 2nd Brigade approached the right of the cantonment, the enemy opened fire upon them from six guns, and Napier directed Lieutenant Harcourt, commanding the No. 18 Light Field Battery, to engage them—" an order which he had barely received when he was summoned to join the 1st Brigade." Sir Hugh Rose was in a critical position. Scindia's agent, who was guiding him to the cantonment road, lost his way, and the 1st Brigade, getting on the edge of broken ground, was taken utterly by surprise by a well directed cross fire from a masked battery in the enemy's centre and guns on their right. Lieutenant Stuart (who commanded the siege pieces) and Lieutenant Harcourt with prompt decision brought their guns into action, and opened a telling fire on the batteries of the enemy. Sir Hugh Rose also brought Captain Lightfoot's Troop 1st Bombay Horse Artillery from the 2nd Brigade against the Rebels' right battery. The Cavalry, owing to the nature of the ground, could not be used. The General, having reinforced his left with the 25th Bombay Native Infantry, advanced with the 86th in skirmishing order. They went over the broken ground, heedless of a heavy cannonade, and took by storm all the cantonment in their front. Then Sir Hugh Rose brought forward the right shoulder of the 86th line of skirmishers and, resting their right on the right bank of the river from which the cantonment takes its name, swept the whole cantonment and occupied it. Abbot, with the Hyderabad Cavalry, got across the nullahs further to the right, and galloped through the cantonment, in the hope of cutting off the enemy's retreat across the stone bridge which spans the river at the back of the cantonment on the road to the city. But he arrived too late. Many had passed over the bridge and they had taken four guns with them. The main body of the rebels had, when driven through the cantonment, joined their comrades who lined the ravines which faced their right.

Whilst Sir Hugh Rose was storming the cantonment, Napier with his Brigade reduced to the Wing of Her Majesty's 71st Highland Light Infantry, the Right Wing of Her Majesty's 14th Dragoons, Madras Sappers and Miners and 100 Horse of the Hyderabad Contingent, continued his advance on the enemy. He saw them retreating in large numbers to their right rear—a tempting and favourable opportunity for Cavalry. But, watching their slow deliberate movement, he became convinced that they were assured of protection by the ground in front of them. He sent his Brigade Major and a few sowars to examine it. They came back and reported a network of ravines lined with infantry.

Napier ordered Colonel Campbell, commanding the Wing of the 71st Regiment, to throw it forward in skirmishing order supported by the 14th Dragoons. The brakes and hollows so screened the sepoys that none could be seen and they gave no sign of life. When the skirmishers on the right, under Major Rich, approached the edge of a deep nullah, the insurgents suddenly opened on them a very heavy fire. Rich moved his skirmishers rapidly forward to dislodge them. " Lieutenant Neaveled with ardent courage the charge and fell when close to the nullah, mortally wounded, sincerely regretted by his brave regiment and his General." In an instant the Highlanders rushed down the ravine and it was taken after a fierce and dogged struggle. Then, pushing on, they took the ravines in rear by storm. (1) The whole of the rebels in them were killed, " after a desperate resistance which cost the 71st, I regret to say, besides Lieutenant Neave several brave soldiers killed and wounded ... In the advanced nullah alone seventy rebels lay dead, belonging to Scindia's faithless Guards and wearing English accoutrements and breast-plates, on which was engraved ' 1st Brigade Infantry '. (2)" Meanwhile, Colonel Campbell took two companies of the 71st under Lieutenant Scott and cleared some ravines on his left and front. He was then directed to clear the top of a hill, where a party of rebels held a temple and some strong ground. " This duty was thoroughly effected and thirty of the enemy left dead on the field. " (3)

The front being now quite clear of the enemy and the success of the day having been completed, Napier withdrew his troops to the shelter of the cantonments. The troops pitched their tents " on what was formerly the well-cared-for gardens of the officers of the Contingent, and what was still covered by flowers and shrubs, lime, custard apple, and pomegranate trees, and vines." The capture of the cantonments gave

---

(1) " Lieutenant Rose, 25th Bombay Native Infantry, afforded them useful co-operation by skilfully placing a party of his Regiment so as to enfilade these dangerous entrenchments." From Major-General Sir Hugh Rose, Commanding Field Force South of the Nerbudda, to Major-General Sir William Mansfield, K.C.B., Chief of the Staff of the Army in India, dated Poonch, the 13th October 1858.

(2) *Ibid. Ibid. Ibid.*
The B Company of the Madras Engineers (reduced to forty-five men) commanded by Lieutenant Gordon joined in the attack on the ravine. Naque Narrainsawmy, seeing a soldier of the 71st about to be killed by the enemy, fired at one of them, and wounded him, but as he still continued to advance, attacked and killed him with his bayonet. The other two, on seeing him killed, ran away ; and the Naque by his great gallantry saved the life of the British soldier. Military History of the Madras Engineers by Major H. M. Vibart, Volume II, page 345.

(3) Brigadier-General R. Napier's Despatch.

Sir Hugh Rose the command of the line of the Morar River, of the road to Agra, and enabled him to communicate with Brigadier Smith to the left, and the Residency to the right. (1)

On the morning of the 17th, Brigadier Smith reached Kotah-ke-Serai which lies between three and four miles south-east of Gwalior. It consisted of a small fort and native caravansary from whence its name is derived. A small river runs past the fort. "Between it and Gwalior lies a chain of small hills, a mile broad, and through a defile in them ran the Jhansi road, flanked on the west by a canal impassable to guns or horse except by a bridge just burnt by the rebels. (2) Brigadier Smith had been ordered by Sir Hugh Rose to halt at Kotah-ke-Serai and communicate with him. Smith was, however, hampered with a large quantity of baggage and Kotah was not a safe position for a halt. The enemy, who were seen in large masses, seemed determined to attack him, and he thought it best to take the initiative. Placing his baggage in and near the fort of Kotah under as strong a guard as he could afford, he crossed the river with a troop of the 8th Hussars to reconnoitre. When they had ridden about a thousand yards, a masked battery suddenly opened on them and, as they turned to gallop out of range, one or two men and horses dropped. The Brigadier's horse, being slightly wounded in the scuffle, fell and rolled over him, bruising his rider severely on the temple and spraining his wrist." (3) But he was soon in the saddle again and no one knew he had been hurt. He had ascertained that the ground in front was impracticable for cavalry and that about fifteen hundred yards from Kotah-ke-Serai their guns were in position and their line ran all under the hills across the road to Gwalior.

As soon as he returned from reconnoitring, Brigadier Smith ordered the Horse Artillery to advance and they soon silenced the enemy's guns. Then he sent his Infantry across the broken ground. Colonel Raines, commanding Her Majesty's 95th, led his men, covered with two companies in skirmishing order and the 10th Bombay Native Infantry *in echelon* as a reserve to attack the enemy's entrenchments. When within fifty yards of the works he ordered the skirmishers to advance at the double and charge. With a loud cheer they rushed forward, and the works were within their grasp, when a deep ditch with four feet of water and steep banks

---

(1) Sir Hugh Rose's Despatch.
(2) Report on the Affairs of Gwalior, by Major S. Charters Macpherson, dated 20th June 1858.
(3) Campaigning experiences in Rajpootana and Central India, by Mrs. Henry Duberly, p. 128.

stopped them. " It was with difficulty that the men got over in single file, and by the time that the skirmishers had ascended the opposite bank, the entrenchment was completely abandoned. " The skirmishers pushed on through the ravines and swept the hills. Then Raines received orders to proceed up the road with the 10th in reserve. While Raines was pushing across the broken ground and driving the enemy from the hills, Smith was for some time unable to bring his cavalry into action, and as the enemy threatened to attack in large numbers his baggage and rear, he was obliged to send back a large detachment of his slender force. With a squadron of the 8th Hussars and two divisions of Horse Artillery and one troop of the 1st Lancers he entered the mouth of the defile. From the hills on the left the rebels opened fire, but on they rode. The end of the defile on the crest of the hills was reached. Below them lay the wide plain between Gwalior and Morar. Two batteries of six and five guns were near the Phoolbagh palace, commanded by Tantia Topee himself. Two eighteen pounders were in the Campoo to the left and many guns at other points. Smith, who had now come in touch with his infantry, saw from the crest the Gwalior Contingent Cavalry in their red uniforms slowly advancing in skirmishing order up a broad ravine to his right and about a hundred yards in front of him. The 95th with a shout opened fire; the horsemen immediately broke from under it. (1) Smith ordered the squadron of Hussars to charge them. Led by Colonel Hicks and Captain Heneage, they dashed down at full speed, sweeping the enemy before them, and they never drew rein until they had ridden through the enemy's camp in the Phoolbagh two and a half miles away. The Phoolbagh was in their possession, but only for a moment. They could not hold it, for they had far outstripped their support. They returned, bringing with them two guns, " the best proofs of how nobly they had fought and conquered." (2) Officers and men were so completely exhausted and prostrated from heat and the day's work that " they could scarcely sit on their saddles, and were for the moment incapable of further exertion." (3) The 95th now arrived near the guns. " They had been out the whole day without a meal under a burning sun and had marched at 2 A. M. that morning from the previous encampment

---

(1) From Lieutenant-Colonel T. N. Hicks, Commanding Artillery, Central India Field Force, Late Commanding Field Force from Jhansi, to Brigadier M. W. Smith, Commanding Rajpootana Field Force, dated Camp Morar, near Gwalior, 25th June 1858.
(2) Sir Hugh Rose's Despatch
(3) Brigadier M. W. Smith's Report.

ground, a distance of 26 miles. Five officers and eighty one men had been struck down by the sun. The enemy were collecting, both on the front and flanks, and, as his troops were incapable of further exertion, Brigadier Smith " retired the Cavalry by alternative Troops protected by the Artillery during which movements both arms showed the greatest steadiness and entered the ravines under the protection of the Infantry posted there. " He then took up a position for the night, and, sending for his baggage, placed it in a sort of amphitheatre formed by a portion of the hills he occupied. " I guarded both ends of the defile with strong pickets of Infantry, in strong positions formed by the ground, and also threw out strong pickets both Cavalry and Infantry, towards the heights on our right ; the left of our position was defended against any sudden assaults by a steep bank and a canal." A brilliant day's work was done by a jaded column.

Among the slain that day was the Ranee of Jhansi. Many tales have been told how she met her death, but the account given by her servant has the strong feature of truth. It was her custom to lead her troops clad in military attire, a red jacket, trousers, and a white turban on her head, which made it impossible to tell her sex. The Brahminee concubine of her late husband, dressed as a trooper of the Gwalior Contingent, never left her side. They were seated together near the Phoolbagh batteries, drinking sherbet, four hundred of the 5th Irregulars near them, when the alarm was given that the Hussars approached. " Forty or fifty of them came up, and the rebels fled, save about fifteen. The Ranee's horse refused to leap the canal, when she received a shot in the side, and then a cut on the head, but rode off. She soon after fell dead, and was burnt in a garden close by." (1) At the same time the Brahminee concubine received a long sabre cut in front. " She rode into the city, was tended by a Fakeer and the Mahomedan Kotwal there, and, dying in their hands, was reputed and buried as a Mahomedan convert." (2) Thus died the Ranee of Jhansi who, Sir Hugh Rose said, " was the bravest and best military leader of the Rebels." To speak of her, as some have done, as " the Indian Joan of Arc " is indeed a libel on the fair fame of the Maid of Orleans. The Ranee of Jhansi was an ardent, daring, licentious woman, and though we must bestow our tribute of admiration for the indefatigable energy and undaunted bravery she displayed, we cannot

---

(1) Report on the affairs of Gwalior, from the 24th of May to the 20th June 1858, by Major S. Charters Macpherson.

(2) Ibid.   Ibid.   Ibid.

forget she was answerable for a massacre of men, women and children, as revolting and deliberate as that of Cawnpore. The voices crying underneath the sod in the garden outside Jhansi were heard and the dark account demanded.

On the evening of the 17th, Sir Hugh Rose received from Brigadier Smith an account of his action and a request for reinforcements. He at once directed Lieutenant-Colonel Robertson to join him with three troops Light Dragoons, 4 Guns No. 4 Light Field Battery and the 25th Bombay Light Infantry. The next morning the troops which had been left to garrison Calpee reached camp, and on the afternoon of the same day Sir Hugh Rose marched from Morar to Kotah Ke-Serai with the following force :

2 Troops 14th Light Dragoons.
No. 18 Light Field Battery.
Madras Sappers and Miners.
Wing Her Majesty's 71st Highland Light Infantry.
Her Majesty's 86th Regiment.
Wing 5th Hyderabad Infantry.
2 18-pounders and 1 8-inch Howitzer.

He left in Morar a sufficient force under Brigadier-General Napier for its protection, the investment of Gwalior, and the pursuit of the enemy when they retreated from it.

The march to Kotah-ka-Serai, full twenty miles, was most harassing. Of the 86th alone, a hundred men were struck down by the sun and had to be carried in dhoolies ; but their commander tells us that these gallant soldiers were not deterred by sickness from taking part next day in the assault on Gwalior. Having crossed the river Morar, the column bivouacked for the night on some rocky ground not far from Smith's camp. The next morning the General reconnoitred the enemy's position and examined the ground occupied by our troops. He found Smith's position was cramped and commanded by a battery of 9 pounders, which the enemy had erected on a ridge on the highest of the series of heights which rose on the other side of the canal from a narrow plain and were intersected by ravines. "To protect the battery and the position, the enemy had concentrated a numerous force of all arms on the ridge, as well as a large body of Cavalry in rear of it." (1) The General also discovered that " about a mile and a half further back and about the same distance from the left of the road was stationed, in a gorge of the

---

(1) Sir Hugh Rose's despatch.

hills, a large body of the enemy's Infantry with guns. They guarded a road which branched off from the ford southwards to Gwalior." (1) Hugh Rose's rapid resource was to cut off both these bodies from Gwalior. The canal which was deep was the main obstacle. To surmount it he ordered a bridge or dam to be made some way to the left rear of his position. The Company of Madras Sappers and Miners, " whose zeal and intelligence no hardship could abate,"(1) would construct it by sunset. At night he would cross it with a force of all arms, get on the south road, and place himself between Gwalior and the two positions occupied by the enemy. Then he would fall on these posts, while Brigadier Smith's Brigade, concealed by the ravines, would attack their front and left flank. This project, characterised by his usual skill and enterprise, Sir Hugh Rose was unable to execute, owing to the activity of the foe. Their troops, accompanied by artillery, poured forth from Gwalior, and they seemed determined to fall on his left flank which they knew was weak. The position in the pass, occupied as a temporary point without any view to fighting a battle, was false, and Hugh Rose could not risk a serious attack. He therefore determined to change the defensive for the offensive. His plan of battle was soon clear to him. He directed Brigadier Stuart to move with the 86th regiment, supported by the 25th Bombay Native Infantry, to cross the canal, and, crowning the heights on the other side of it, to attack the enemy on their left, whilst at the same time Brigadier Smith, with the 95th, supported by the 10th Bombay Native Infantry, should move from his right front cross the canal in skirmishing order, and advance obliquely under cover of the ground over the shoulder of the hill on which was the Rebels' battery against their left front. (2)

Brigadier Smith crossing the canal ascended steadily, with the 86th under Lieutenant-Colonel Lowth, the heights. The enemy, finding that their left was being turned, retired rapidly towards the battery, closely pressed by the skirmishers of the 86th. Beneath their battery was an entrenchment. But they did not hold it. They retreated across it to their guns. " The gallant skirmishers gave them no time to rally in

---

(1) Sir Hugh Rose's despatch.
(2) Sir Hugh Rose writes " against their left flank."
" This attack on their left at once had the effect of making the enemy desist on his right, and no sooner did they find that their left was turned by the movement than they fell back in haste abandoning their guns."—Calcutta Review, Vol. 41.

the battery, but dashing with a cheer at the parapet crossed it, and took the guns which defended the ridge—three excellent English 9-pounders." Lieutenant-Colonel Raines, coming up with a wing of the 95th, turned the captured guns on the enemy's Cavalry and Infantry which he saw in detached bodies in the plain below. Meanwhile, Lieutenant Roome, in command of the 10th Bombay Native Infantry, who were moving up in support of the 95th and in protection of our right, found himself exposed to a fire of artillery and musketry from the heights on the enemy's extreme left. " Advancing with half of his Regiment in skirmishing order, and leading the remainder in support, he cleared the two nearest heights of the Rebel infantry and charging gallantly took two brass field pieces and three mortars, which were in a plain at the foot of the second height."

The British troops were now in possession of the highest range and Gwalior lay at their feet. "The sight," says Sir Hugh, "was interesting. To our right was the handsome palace of the Phoolbagh, its garden and the old City, surmounted by the Fort, remarkable for its ancient architecture with lines of extensive fortifications round the high and precipitous rock of Gwalior. To our left lay the 'Lushker' or new city, with its spacious houses half hidden by trees." He saw that the slopes descended gradually towards Gwalior, and in the plains below could be discovered the rebels driven from the heights, seeking shelter among the houses and trees outside the city. He had intended to proceed no further that day, and had sent word to Napier to attack Gwalior from Morar in concert with himself the next morning. He now changed his plan. " I felt convinced that I could take Gwalior before sunset," and he at once prepared for a fresh onset. Colonel Owen, with the 18th Bombay Lancers, was directed to descend the hills and occupy the road which led to the grand parade of the Lushker. The 3rd Troop Bombay Horse Artillery with a squadron of 8th Hussars were to cover Sir Hugh Rose's extreme right parallel with the troops attacking Gwalior. No. 4 Light Field Battery with two troops of Her Majesty's 14th Light Dragoons were ordered to cover his advanced line and to answer the enemy's battery in position in front of Gwalior.

All being ready, Sir Hugh Rose gave the word for the general attack, and the Infantry, owing to the formation of the hills, moved forward in irregular line. The 86th forming the left was in advance, the 95th the right was refused. The enemy were attempting to load their two

18-pounders when the General ordered the 9-pounder which he had placed in position opposite them to be fired with shrapnel. "The shrapnel a remarkable one burst just over the 18-pounders into about twenty pieces, killed and disabled some of the gunners and put the rest to flight." The enemy's Infantry and Cavalry began to retire in groups across the grand parade. At that instant the 1st Bombay Lancers issuing from the Pass, charged across the wide plain, cut them down and, continuing their rush, pursued them through the Lushker. In the narrow street, bravely leading his men, fell Lieutenant Mills of the 1st Bombay Lancers, " a very promising and popular young officer." Captain Lock in the pursuit cut down the rebel who shot him. Lieutenant-Colonel Owen, not thinking it advisable to have his troopers involved in street fighting, withdrew them from the town.

The British soldiers raised a loud cheer as the Bombay Lancers swept across the plain and Raines, with two Companies of the 95th, charged down the slope " with his usual spirit " and took the two 18-pounders and two small mortars on the grand parade. They were soon joined by the General. He determined to advance across the plain, force his way if necessary through the Lushker and gain possession of Scindia's palace. Captain Meade, who was well acquainted with the town, volunteered to act as a guide. Remembering the bloody fight which had taken place in the streets of Jhansi, Sir Hugh Rose directed Raines to form four companies of his Regiment for street fighting. Placing himself at their head with Meade by his side, "each officer having his pistol at full-cock in their hand," he marched through a mile of streets and arrived at the open space in front of the palace. The approach to the palace block was surrounded by lofty buildings built of solid masonry with terraced roofs screened by a parapet. To storm them would entail a heavy loss of life. The palace court yard was full of excited soldiery and many desperadoes. Meade volunteered to ride forward alone and to endeavour to obtain the peaceful surrender of the palace. The General assented. The column was halted and Meade rode forward to the entrance of the court-yard.(1) There was no gate, but a heavy beam of wood across the gateway prevented a horseman from passing through it. For some minutes Meade on his horse waited outside the portal. Many muskets were levelled at him. " At length to my great

---

(1) General Sir Richard Meade, by Thomas Henry Thornton, C.S.I.

relief a little wizened Mussulman who was close to the gateway recognised me, and shouted out three or four times, 'This is Meade Sahib,' and hearing this three or four men at last complied with my repeated demand to remove the barrier, and I dashed into the court-yard up to a group of some five or six men whom I had previously noticed as being evidently the leaders of the party." Taking one of them, "a tall powerfull man," by the shoulder, he told them he would save their lives if they obeyed his orders. But there must be no delay as the British troops were ready and eager to storm the palace. They said they would hand it over to their Sovereign, but not to the English. He replied that it must be given up at once or it would be stormed and not a man of them would escape. After some parleying, they consented to retire into the interior of the palace buildings. Then Meade rode back and reported the result to the General, and arrangements were made for the security of the palace. Before sunset the Lushker, or new city, and the old town were occupied with very trifling loss to us, " and to the unbounded gratitude of the people and the high credit of the troops with scarcely an act of plunder."

Meanwhile Brigadier Smith had got into action with the enemy near the Palace of Phoolbagh, which after some stiff fighting he captured. He then pursued a large body of the enemy, who were retiring round the rock of Gwalior towards the Residency, covering their retreat with guns. After a stout resistance " which did credit to the enemy's artillery " the guns were captured, (1) and they pressed hard on the fleeing foe long after black night had fallen, until men and horses could go no further.

On the morning of the 20th, Scindia, who had arrived from Agra two days before, was conducted from the cantonment of Morar by the Agent of the Governor-General to the parade before the Phoolbagh. Here he was received by Sir Hugh Rose and his force with every possible mark of respect. Then the victorious Commander, accompanied by his personal and divisional staff and all the superior officers of the Forces " whose duties allowed them to be present " escorted His Royal Highness to his palace in the Lushker, " with a squadron of Her Majesty's 8th Hussars, and another of Her Majesty's Light Dragoons, most honourable

---

(1) "Brigadier Smith speaks very highly of the steadiness with which Her Majesty's 14th Light Dragoons escorting the 3rd Troop Bombay Horse Artillery stood the enemy's artillery fire, shot and shell, and of the ardour with which they afterwards fell on the guns and the retreating enemy." From Major-General Sir Hugh Rose, Commanding Field Force South of the Nerbudda, to Major Mansfield.

representatives of my force." As the cavalcade passed along the long and handsome street, which leads from the grand parade to the palace, the population of the half-empty, half-closed Lushker, which had recently been despoiled by his faithless soldiery, welcomed the return of their Sovereign and of peace.

A grim tragedy, however, marred the joy of that morning. As the troops were drawn out to receive Scindia, four or five shots were fired at them from the ramparts of the Fort, and as His Highness and the Agent advanced with their *cortège*, one shot struck immediately in front of them. It was a startling surprise, for the General had been informed that the Fort had been vacated during the night. It had been vacated, but thirteen men, four of them contingent sepoys, and nine velaites with two women and a child, after proceeding some miles towards Agra, resolved deliberately to return and die in it. (1) Sir Hugh had ordered the fort to be closely invested. Lieutenant Rose of the 25th Bombay Native Infantry, who had distinguished himself at the hand to hand fighting in the ravines, occupied, with a picket furnished by his regiment, the Kotwal or Police Station near the main gateway. Lieutenant Waller, a brother officer, with a small party of the same corps, held an adjoining post. When Rose heard the firing of the guns and learnt that some Ghazees were still defending the fort, he went to Waller and suggested that they should attack the stronghold and destroy the desperate fanatics. Taking with them a blacksmith, the two pickets, and twenty Pathan police they crept up the winding road until they reached the main gateway which they found closed. It was burst open and, surprising the other gates before they could be shut, they reached an archway on which the fanatics had brought a gun to bear.(2) The Ghazees, having taken post on a bastion, flung over the walls all their gold and silver coin, slew their women and children and swore to die. The gun burst at the third discharge and the attacking party rushed through the archway and made their way, regardless of the bullets sent down upon them, to the top of the wall. (3) On the bastion the fanatics withstood them steadfastly and slaying, were slain. Rose, who was swift

---

(1) Report on Gwalior, dated 20th June 1858, by Major S. Charters Macpherson.
(2) Sir Hugh Rose's Despatch. Malleson states: - " By the time the sixth gate was forced the alarm was given." The five gates of a fortress, if they had been fastened, could hardly have been burst open by a "lusty" or "stalwart" blacksmith.
(3) Report on Gwalior, dated 20th June 1858, by Major S. Charters Macpherson.

to do battle among the foremost, fell mortally wounded, "closing his early career by taking the Fort of Gwalior by force of arms."(1)

At 5-15 A.M. on the 28th of June Brigadier-General R. Napier received orders to pursue the enemy and within an hour and a half after receipt of them, he marched from Morar. Early next day he caught up the enemy at Jowra Alipore, thirty-two miles off. His force consisted of a Troop of Horse Artillery and about 500 Cavalry, 60 of whom were Europeans. (2) The enemy were reported to have 12,000 men and 22 guns. He found them strongly posted with their right resting on Alipore,(3) guns and infantry in the centre and cavalry on both flanks. A rising ground hid the approach of the small British force, and Napier was able to reconnoitre their position in security from a distance of about 1,200 yards. (4) He found the ground was open to the enemy's left "and a careful examination with the telescope left me assured that there was nothing to check the advance of my artillery." He directed Captain Lightfoot to take up a position

---

(1) Sir Hugh Rose's Despatch. - Brigadier C. S. Stuart thus referred to Lieutenant Rose in his Brigade orders :—" Brigadier Stuart has received with the deepest regret a report of the death of Lieutenant Rose, 25th Bombay Native Infantry, who was mortally wounded yesterday on entering the Fort of Gwalior, on duty with his men. The Brigadier feels assured that the whole Brigade unite with him in deploring the death of this gallant officer, whose many sterling qualities none who knew him could fail to appreciate."

Lieutenant Waller received the V. C. for his gallantry and Lieutenant Rose would also have obtained it if he had lived.

(2)

Corps.	European Officers.	Native Officers.	Non-Commissioned Officers and Rank and file.
1st Troop Horse Artillery	4	0	95
14th Light Dragoons	2	0	60
3rd Light Cavalry	7	5	92
Hyderabad Cavalry	2	0	243
Meade's Horse	3	3	174
Total	18	8	664

(3) So Brigadier-General R. Napier spells it. Macpherson writes "Joura-Allapore," Malleson "Jaura-Alipur," Holmes "Joora-Alipur."

(4) From Brigadier-General R. Napier, Commanding 2nd Brigade, Central India Field Force, to the Assistant Adjutant General, Central India Field Force, dated Camp Jowra-Alipore, 21st June 1858.

about 600 yards from the enemy's left and enfilade their line, " and to act afterwards as circumstances might dictate." In their column of march the little force was soon again in movement. Abbott's Hyderabad Cavalry were in advance, then came Lightfoot's troop of Bombay Horse Artillery, supported by Captain Prettyjohn's Troop of 14th Light Dragoons, and two Troops 320 Light Cavalry under Lieutenant Dick, with a detachment of Meade's Horse under Lieutenant Burton in reserve. When the troops came into view of the enemy, after turning the shoulder of the rising ground, the whole were advanced at a gallop and as soon as the Artillery had reached the flank of the enemy's position, the line was formed to the left, and the guns opened on the enemy at a distance of 600 yards." (1) After a few rounds, nine guns which were in action under a clump of trees were silenced and the enemy showed signs of abandoning them. Lightfoot quickly limbered up, and advancing at a gallop he and Abbott with the Hyderabad Cavalry charged at the same moment into the battery. " You cannot imagine," writes one who was present, " the dash of the artillery; it was wonderful. We could scarcely keep up with them." Instantaneously Napier, placing himself at the head of his 600 cavalry, gave the order to charge and they swept through the enemy's batteries and camp and past the villages into the open, driving before them and cutting down the rebels for several miles. Never was the rout of an army more complete. Besides twenty-five guns a considerable quantity of ammunition and elephants, tents, carts and baggage fell into the hands of the victors. Many a brave deed was done that day. Napier brings to the notice of Sir Hugh Rose the conduct of Private Novell of Her Majesty's 14th Dragoons who charged alone into a village under a very heavy fire, "for which act of gallantry I beg to recommend him for the Victoria Cross." Six of his Indian comrades were specially recommended by their Commander for the Order of Merit for great gallantry displayed on the field.

Thus, with a daring feat of arms, closed the Central Indian Campaign, which has a high title to be regarded as one of the great achievements recorded in the annals of war. Lord Canning, when he heard of the capture of Gwalior, issued the following proclamation :—" The Right Honourable the Governor-General has the highest gratification in announcing that the town and fort of Gwalior were conquered by Major-General Sir Hugh Rose on the 19th instant, after a general action, in

---

(1) From Brigadier-General R. Napier, Commanding 2nd Brigade, Central India Field Force, to the Assistant Adjutant General, Central India Field Force, dated Camp Jowra-Alipore, 21st June 1858.

which the rebels, who had usurped the authority of Maharajah Scindia, were totally defeated. On the 20th of June Maharajah Scindia, attended by the Governor-General's Agent for Central India, and Sir Hugh Rose, and escorted by British troops, was restored to the palace of his ancestors, and was welcomed by his subjects with every mark of loyalty and attachment. It was on the 1st of June that the rebels, aided by the treachery of some of Maharajah Scindia's troops, seized the capital of His Highness's kingdom, and hoped to establish a new Government, under a pretender, in His Highness' territory. Eighteen days had not elapsed before they were compelled to evacuate the town and fort of Gwalior, and to relinquish the authority which they had endeavoured to usurp. The promptitude and success with which the strength of the British Government has been put forth for the restoration of its faithful ally to the capital of his territory, and the continued presence of British troops at Gwalior to support His Highness in the re-establishment of his administration, offer to all a convincing proof that the British Government has the will and the power to be friend to those who, like Maharajah Scindia, do not shrink from their obligations, or hesitate to avow their loyalty. The Right Honourable the Governor-General, in order to mark his appreciation of the Maharajah Scindia's friendship, and his gratification of His Highness' authority in his ancestral dominions, is pleased to direct that a royal salute shall be fired at every principal station in India."

On the 29th of June, Sir Hugh Rose, on account of ill-health, made over the command to Brigadier-General Napier, and in the following order he bade farewell to the troops he had led to victory upon victory :—

"The Major-General commanding, being on the point of resigning the command of the Poonah Division of the Bombay army, (1) on account of ill-health, bids farewell to the Central India Field Forces and, at the same time, expresses the pleasure he feels that he commanded them when they gained one more laurel at Gwalior. The Major-General witnessed with satisfaction how the troops and their gallant companions-in-arms—the Rajpootana Brigade, under General Smith, stormed height after height, and gun after gun, under the fire of a numerous field and siege artillery, taking finally by assault two 18-pounders at Gwalior. Not a man in these forces enjoyed his natural strength or health ; and

---

(1) The Central India Field Force was a branch of the Poonah Division of the army of the Presidency of Bombay.

an Indian sun and months of marching and broken rest, had told on the strongest; but the moment they were told to take Gwalior for their Queen and country they thought of nothing but victory. They gained it, restoring England's brave and true ally to his throne, putting to complete rout the rebel army, killing numbers of them, and taking from them in the field, exclusive of those in the fort, fifty-two pieces of artillery, all their stores and ammunition, and capturing the city and fort of Gwalior, reckoned the strongest in India. The Major-General thanks sincerely Brigadier-General Napier, C.B., Brigadier-General Stuart, C.B., and Brigadier Smith commanding brigades in the field, for the very efficient and able assistance which they gave him, and to which he attributes the success of the day. He bids them and their brave soldiers, once more, a kind farewell. He cannot do so under better aspects than those of the victory of Gwalior."

THE INDIAN MUTINY.

CHAPTER I.

CENTRAL INDIA.—JHANSI.

No. 1336 of 1859.—His Excellency the Governor General in Council is pleased to direct the publication of the following Extract of a letter from the Officiating Adjutant-General of the Army, No. 1094 of the 18th ultimo, and Reports from Major General Sir Hugh Rose, G. C. B., late Commanding Central India Field Force, of the Capture of Rathghur and of the Action at Barodia.

His Excellency in Council in notifying his entire concurrence in the opinion expressed by the Right Hon'ble the Commander-in-Chief, desires to record his high approval of the manner in which these operations were directed. His Excellency in Council offers his cordial thanks to Major-General Sir Hugh Rose, and to all the Officers and men employed on these occasions, and regrets that the mis-carriage of the Reports of these operations should have delayed the public notice of them.

Extract of a letter from the Officiating Adjutant-General of the Army, To the Secretary to the Government of India, Military Department, No. 1094, dated 18th August 1859.

In continuation of my letter, No. 389, of 20th May last, I am now directed to append for submission to His Excellency the Governor General in Council, the accompanying Despatch, No. 1204A, dated 29th June of the present year, from Major-General Sir Hugh Rose, G. C. B., late Commanding Central India Field Force, giving cover to copies of his Reports of the Capture of Rathghur and Action of Barodia.

With reference to the operations described in the Despatches now forwarded, His Lordship desires me to observe that they reflect the highest credit upon the Commander and the Troops engaged, and are characterised by that complete success which marked the whole of Sir Hugh Rose's Campaign in Central India.

From Major-General SIR HUGH ROSE, K.C.B., *Commanding Central India Field Force*, To the Adjutant-General of the Army, *Head-Quarters, Bombay,—Camp Saugor, 7th February 1858.*

My report of the 31st ultimo will have informed you, for the information of His Excellency the Commander-in-Chief, that the Rebels had determined to defend the Fort of Rathghur in order to prevent my Force from relieving Saugor, and putting down rebellion in the Saugor and Bundlecund Districts.

As I approached Rathghur, I received information of the assemblage of Rebels at Odepore in Scindia's Country and in my front; in order to ensure the safety of the Siege Train, which was a day's march in the rear, and not to lose time, I brought it up by a night march to my Force, and adopted precautions against surprise.

In going through a pass over a range of hills, five miles from Rathghur, the Officer Commanding the leading flankers, embarrassed by the thick jungle, took by mistake the right instead of the left road, as ordered, and crossing, in consequence, the River Beena by the upper, the wrong ford, got into a skirmish with the Rebels posted in the suburbs of Rathghur. I had just arrived, with the advanced guard at the encamping ground; to extricate the flankers from a position so unfavorable to Cavalry, I advanced and covered with the Infantry Guns and supports their return to their proper position. In rectifying this mistake, I had gained a good deal of ground to the right front, and a Company of the 24th Native Infantry had taken with spirit one or two houses and gardens; on reconnoitering, I found that they were the commencement of the suburbs, and that to keep all this would compromise my right, and plan of attacking the Fort from the left flank. I therefore ordered the Troops back to their Camp.

The next day I made with Major Boileau, Commanding Engineer, and a small party of the 3rd Europeans and 3rd Light Cavalry, under Captain Forbes, a complete reconnoisance of eighteen miles of the whole Country round the rock of Rathghur.

I ascertained that the rock, 1½ mile in length, covered and surrounded with thick jungle, slopes from the West, where it is precipitous, to the East, where it is accessible. The North front of the Fort was the only one which was habited; the other fronts were merely fortifications. The River Beena runs under its West face.

The reconnoisance confirmed in all essentials the information on which I had formed my plan of attack. I carried it out, by investing the same evening the rock of Rathghur as closely as the great extent, hills, thick jungle, and a difficult River would allow me. But it is impossible, unless with a very much larger Force than my own, to invest completely such ground, because a great part of it is dense jungle, which, hiding all view of the Enemy's motions, enable him, by a feint, to concentrate videttes and pickets on one point, and then pass through the vacuum.

Sir Robert Hamilton had the goodness to place at my disposal 600 or 700 Troops of all Arms of the Regiment of Bhopall; and I had requested their Commander to invest the South-West of the Fort, as being nearest to their Country, and to take the village of Puttan, which they did with alacrity after firing a few shots.

The next day as soon as the Officers Commanding the Artillery and Engineers had reported that they were ready for the Siege, I attacked the Fort from the left, at the South-West end of the rock, under cover of a feint from the right, against the Town, from which all possible advantage was to be derived.

Both succeeded.

Leaving a Troop of the 3rd Light Cavalry at the foot of the slope to cover our rear, accompanied by Captain Forbes, Commanding the 3rd Light Cavalry, who is always as zealous as he is useful, I mounted, with the Troops in the margin, under the Command of Lieutenant-Colonel Liddell, the slope, two Companies of the 3rd Europeans skirmishing and covering the breadth of the rock, two Companies supporting and the rest in reserve we made our way through thick jungle, and reached, without being discovered, the edge of the open ground in front of the East curtain of the Fort, which Major Boileau had selected for the breaching Batteries.

Lieutenant-Colonel Liddell, Commanding 3rd Bombay European Regiment, Detachment of Siege Train under Lieutenant Mallock, two 18-pounders, 16 men Bombay Artillery.
Two 5½-inch Mortars, 10 men Bombay Artillery, 90 Madras Sappers and Miners, two 6-pounder Guns Artillery.
Hyderabad Contingent, one Troop 3rd Light Cavalry under Captain Forbes.

I directed a road to be cut immediately by the Sappers and Miners from the foot of the slope to this Battery: our left to open a communication down the South of the rock with the Troop of the 3rd Cavalry, investing the South of the rock, our right to open a communication down the North side of the rock with the Camp, and Rifle pits to be made at night in front of our attack, enfilading, as much as possible, the Enemy's line of defences.

The Enemy having perceived our position, commenced rather a sharp fire on it from their jinjals and small guns in the curtain and bastions which I kept down with the fire of the 6-Pounder of the Hyderabad Contingent, and the 5½ Mortars, the former firing at the loop holes and embrasures, the latter with half charges dropping their shells on the banquette. I beg to mention, for his devotion on this occasion, Quarter Master Thompson, Commanding a half Battery of the Artillery of the Hyderabad Contingent, who has completed thirty-two years of meritorious service. Twice hit, he continued to fight his Guns successfully to the close of the day. I thanked his Battery on the ground.

The two 18-Pounders, with Elephant draught, were brought up the hill at 4 P.M.; the 3rd Europeans dragging them up the steep where the Elephants could not go.

The feint against the Town drove the Enemy out of it into the Fort, and enabled Brigadier Steuart, with the Force in the margin, to take possession of the "Eedgha," a Mussulman place of prayer, opposite the North face commanding the Town and within range of the main gate of the Fort, on this height, and another to the left, he skilfully placed Captain Lightfoot's 9-Pounder Battery, one 8-inch Howitzer and two 8-inch Mortars. These Batteries forming the right or Town attack kept up, night and day, an effective fire on the line of defences and buildings of the Fort.

Four 6-Pounder Guns, Bombay Horse Artillery.
Six 9-Pounder Guns, Bombay Light Field Battery, under Captain Lightfoot.
Fifty Bombay Sappers and Miners.
Detachment of Siege Train.
Two 8-inch Mortars. ⎫ 26 Men
One 8-inch Howit-   ⎬ Bombay
zer.   ⎭ Artillery.
All the Artillery under Lieutenant-Colonel Turnbull. Two Troops of Her Majesty's 14th Light Dragoons under Major Scudamore, 24th Regiment Native Infantry.

On the 27th instant, I changed the 8-inch Howitzer from the right to the left attack, in order to enfilade with its fire the defences and palaces of the North face.

I was constantly between the two attacks which were 2½ miles apart.

From the Town attack I directed a Detachment of the 3rd Europeans, supported by another of the 24th Native Infantry, with two Companies of the 24th Native Infantry in reserve, and under cover of houses and trees and of a heavy fire from the Eedgha Battery to take a low massive tower close to the main gate, Captain Lightfoot being of opinion that a Howitzer might be placed in it which would batter the gate, and strengthen and shorten the cordon of investment. I had a couple of 8-inch shells thrown into the Tower, to drive out the Enemy should they be there when the storming party gallantly led by Captain Lightfoot, who volunteered to accompany it, for which I beg to recommend him to His Excellency, entered the Tower under a heavy fire from the walls by the postern opposite the walls from which it was only fifty yards distant; Captain Lightfoot recommends Private Davies of the 3rd Europeans for his gallantry and intelligence on this occasion.

Captain Lightfoot and Lieutenant Bonus, of the Engineers, having, after a thorough examination of the Tower, reported that the massive construction and nature of its defences prevented their being used for the offensive, I withdrew the Troops from it before daylight.

On the 28th instant at 8, the sand bag batteries of the left attack having been completed, the two 18-Pounders and the 8-inch Howitzer having been brought up to them, commenced their fire against the outer wall of the East curtain of the Fort with such good effect, that it was evident that a practicable breach would be soon made.

.I had just returned to the Camp from the Battery when the Rebels coming in force out of the thick jungle, crossed the River Beena and attacked the Videttes of the right rear of the Camp; another large body of them appeared at the same time on the opposite bank, the two bodies amounting to 1,500 or 2,000 men, many of them Sepoys and valaitees.

I moved rapidly with the outlying picket of Her Majesty's 14th Light Dragoons, who in less than a minute, were in their saddles against the Rebels, ordering two guns, and the rest of the pickets to follow in support: the Enemy who were skirmishing with a picket of the 3rd Light Cavalry, on seeing our approach, fired a discharge of muskets and rockets at us, and ran into a gorge of the Beena and up its rocky banks; I directed Captain Hare, following in my rear, to move by a short line and cut off their retreat.

Brigadier Steuart, whom I had called up, advancing from the Eedgha with a few rounds of Artillery, sent the Rebels on the other side of the River into the jungle, and the whole retreated rapidly to a precipitous ridge above the village of Chunderapore, four miles to the North-West of Rathghur, from whence they had started in the morning.

Captain Hare came up with the rear of the Rebels before they reached the ridge, and cut up several of them.

Captain Hare and Lieutenant Westwacott, attached to the Hyderabad Cavalry, did good service on this occasion, and Lieutenant Moore, of the 3rd Bombay Light Cavalry, who, on account of the few Artillerymen, served a gun with effect, deserves also to be mentioned.

After nightfall, the Rebels made a feeble and unsuccessful attack on the left of the Camp from the Saugor Road. The Rebels, who had come from their fortified Camp Noreonlee and from the Fort of Kooreye, failed completely in their attempt to surprise the Camp and relieve Rathghur—during the whole time of their attack, the breaching Batteries continued their fire. Colonel Turnbull reported that the breach would be practicable for an assault the next day at sunset.

Accounts now came in to me that the Rebels from the Chunderapore ridge had early in the morning attacked, in the difficult pass mentioned in the first part of this Report, a convoy of supplies coming for my force from the West, and had killed Scindia's vakeel who was in charge of it.

The safety of my supplies rendered it necessary that the Enemy should be driven from Chunderapore during night. I was employed in making arrangements for attacking them, which was not easy, as my Force was already engaged in an operation for which, in former times, a Force of four times their strength was considered necessary. However, I was on the point of marching against Chunderapore, when two spies I had sent out during the night, came in and reported that the Enemy had left that place for Baroda.

On visiting the Eedgha, Brigadier Steuart reported to me that about 4 o'clock A.M. the Enemy had attempted to make a sortie from the main gate, which he had driven back with Captain Lightfoot's 9-Pounders. A Bhopall Officer came up and reported that he had cut up twenty-five out of fifty of the Garrison who had attempted to force their way by his patrol. Colonel Liddell reported also, at the same time, that judging from the stillness in the Fort, that its garrison were escaping, he had entered it by the incompleted breach with part of the 3rd Europeans, who, after receiving some shots from the few Rebels still there, had killed them and taken possession of the Fort. The main body fled by an ancient sally port and a hole dug under the parapet to the South-West, from which when I entered the Fort the ropes were hanging, by which they had let themselves down. The reports of all the Officers on duty state that these Rebels, crossing a ford over the Beena to the South-West, under the Bhopall Camp, passed through the Bhopall lines into the jungle, the Bhopall Troops fired a few shots at the fugitives, two or three of their dead baggage animals in this ford showed the track they had taken. The Bhopall Troops have been, and are still so useful to me, that I merely mention this circumstance, which is nothing out of the way amongst Oriental Troops, out of justice to my own Force.

The Garrison stated to be 400 or 500 in number had, although many of them were warlike valaitees and Pathans, despite of their determination that they would hold Rathghur or die, not been able to stand the shelling, or meet the approaching assault. I am glad to say that the investment of the rock prevented the escape, and caused the capture of most of the Chief Rebels and of many of the rest. Mahomed Fazil Khan, a relation of the Regent of Bhopal, and the Military Chief of the Rebels in these Districts, and all his Staff, such as they were, attempted to cross the Beena, but seeing the videttes of Her Majesty's 14th Light Dragoons on the other bank, turned back and hid themselves in a cave under the rock where they were captured. The videttes and pickets round the rock, those of Bhopall included, cut down and took many of the fugitive Garrison during the day. I made over eighty prisoners to Sir Robert Hamilton, of whom twenty-four were executed, and forty-eight more to the Civil Authorities.

Of the Cavalry sent in pursuit of the fugitives, the Hyderabad Irregulars came up with and killed forty of them, this being exclusive of the twenty-five killed by the Bhopall Troops; Lieutenant Westwacott on this occasion again distinguished himself.

At sunset Mahomed Fazil Khan and the Nawab Kamdar Khan, a pensioner of the British Government and a son of the great Pindaree Chief, taken by Sir John Malcolm, were hung over the gate of the Fort in presence of Detachments of my Force, the next day seventeen more, most of them Rebels of note and all part of the Garrison of Rathghur were executed, two of them, brothers of the Pindaree Chief, had taken part in the murder of the British Assistant at Bereiseeah, Kishen Ram, a Secretary of Mahomed Fazil Khan, is stated to have been instrumental in atrocities committed on forty Christians. Wallidad Khan, who admitted on his trial "that he had done all he could and three times urged Fazil Mahomed to go down sword in hand and attack the Camp," a valaitee leader, &c.

The Shazadah of Mundesore was not in the Fort, as was proved by an unopened letter from the Rajah of Banpoor to his address found in the Fort by an Officer of the 3rd Europeans, he had left it the day of our arrival. In this letter, which is curious, the Rajah gives him the title of "King," and deplores that many Native Chiefs do not venerate his

Kingly authority as they ought to do, but have the bad taste to prefer the rule of the " Kafir and infidels."

The Fort was provided with a fine tank cut out of the rock fifty feet deep; and in it were found great stores of salt and grain sufficient for a year's consumption, a few Camels, Cattle and several Horses, two of them belonging to Mahomed Fazil Khan, one with a silver bridle and another to the Shazadah of Mundesore, a mould for casting cannon, and shot, and an immense mass of Native correspondence and English accounts, which I made over to Sir Robert Hamilton, one object was also found which excited indignation, the effigy of the head of a decapitated European female, which it appears these supporters of a change of rule in India carried before their Troops, as fitting emblems of their deeds, notwithstanding this, and all that has passed, far worse than this, the 3rd Europeans, when they entered the Fort, treated the women and numerous children of the Rebels who were left there, with the humanity which was to be expected from their discipline, and their faith. I had enjoined the Troops, for the honor of their Country and the Army, not to harm a woman or a child.

I beg to bring to His Excellency's favorable consideration the zealous and able support which I have received before Rathghur from Brigadier Steuart, Lieutenant-Colonel Turnbull, Commanding the Artillery, and Major Boileau, Commanding the Engineers, and which contributed so materially to the success of the operations against it as well as the discipline, courage and thorough good will of the Troops engaged on them.

Anxious not to lose a day in relieving Saugor, I made continued marches without a halt. The Troops, on account of the difficulties of supply, were, at times twenty-four hours, without rations, and four days on duty before Rathghur without a relief, defending their Camp against a numerous Enemy in a dangerous Country in their flanks and rear, attacking with all their energy and taking, in three days, a Fort strong by nature and art in their front, which Scindia with a Force, of at least four times their strength, besieged for five months.

I shall have the honor to make favorable mention of the services of my Staff in a future Report.

I beg leave to enclose a Return of the Oude Artillery found in the Fort, and of the Casualties in my Force before Rathghur.

The Troops took three large Standards, two of which bore the red extended hand, the device of Mahomedan Rebellion.

I beg to offer my excuses for the length of this Report which is caused by the varied nature of the operations. I cannot conclude it without returning my sincere thanks to His Excellency and to Lord Elphinstone, for having made my Force as complete as circumstances would possibly allow, and for the very great kindness with which you have attended to all my requests on this subject.

Return of Killed and Wounded of the 2nd Brigade, Nerbudda Field Force, during the Siege and Attack of Rathghur.

Corps.	Rank and Names.		Killed.	Wounded.	Remarks.
1st Troops H. Artillery.	Asst. Apthy.	W. Conway	...	1	Wounded dangerously: ball through head.
	Gunner	M. Wallace	...	1	Wounded; ball through right arm.
14th Light Dragoons.	Private	G. Trayleu	1	...	Wounded mortally (since dead).
	Ditto	R. Wycherley	...	1	Wounded in the back of the head.
3rd Bombay Euro. Regt.	Ditto	J. Woolaston	1	...	Wounded mortally (since dead).
	Ditto	J. Daley	...	1	Wounded in the head.
	Ditto	J. Levy	...	1	Ditto in the foot.
	Ditto	W. Coombes	...	1	Ditto in left elbow.
	Ditto	R. Stewart	...	1	Ditto in right thigh.
	Ditto	J. Lister	...	1	Contusion of the foot.
Bombay Sappers and Miners.	Serjeant	F. Sappe	...	1	Wounded in leg.
	Private	Girthaurey	...	1	Slightly wounded in forearm.
Madras Sappers and Miners.	Naique	Keeraswamy	...	1	Slightly wounded in back by ball.
	Lc. ditto	Ramswamy	...	1	Slightly wounded in leg.
	Private	Chavathian	...	1	Slightly wounded in thigh by ball.
	Ditto	Ramswamy	...	1	Severely wounded in left fore-arm by ball.
24th Regt. N. I.	Subadar	Bahoodoor Sing	1	...	Shot through right lung.
1st Cavalry Hyderabad Contingent.	Trooper	Shaik Rymon	...	1	Wounded severely in the leg.
	Ditto	Ramas Khan	...	1	Wounded severely in the thigh.
	Ditto	Hyderally Khan	...	1	Wounded severely in the thigh.
2nd Comdg. Arty.	Quarter Master	Thompson	...	1	Wounded slightly in the ear and chest.
			3	18	

T. C. Coley, *Major*,
Offg. D. A. A. G., P. D. A.

(Sd.) H. H. A. Wood, *Captain*,
Asst. Adjt. Genl., Central India F. F.

Return of Horses Killed and Wounded.

CORPS.	Killed.	Wounded.
1st Troop Horse Artillery	..	1
Her Majesty's 14th Light Dragoons	1	4
1st Cavalry Hyderabad Contingent	1	3
Total	2	8

(Sd.) H. H. A. WOOD, *Captain,*
Asst. Adjt.-Genl., Central India F. F.

MEMO.—Names of Officers and Non-Commissioned Officers mentioned by Sir Hugh Rose extracted as per Adjutant General's Memo:—

Lieutenant-Colonel Turnbull, Artillery.
Major Boileau, Madras Engineers.
Captain Forbes, 3rd Light Cavalry.
 „ Lightfoot, Artillery.
 „ Hare
Lieutenant Westwacott } Hyderabad Contingent.
 „ Moore, 3rd Light Cavalry.
Quarter Master Thompson, Artillery, Hyderabad Contingent.
Private Davies, 3rd European Regiment.

From Major-General SIR HUGH ROSE, K.C.B., *Commanding Central India Field Force,* To Colonel GREEN, C.B., *Adjutant General of the Army.*

I have the honor to state to you, for the information of His Excellency the Commander-in-Chief, that, after the capture of Rathghur, the Rebels who had retired from Chunderapore to Barodia, as mentioned in my Report of the 7th February 1858, concentrated in the latter place, having been re-inforced by such of the Garrison of Rathghur as had escaped, and by Rebels from Koraye and other places in Bundlecund.

2. Barodia, on the left bank of the River Beena, is a strong village with a "gurrie" or small Fort, with dense jungle on each side, about 12 miles from Rathghur, on the road to Koraye a strong Fort 29 miles to the North of Saugor.

3. The object of the Rebels in concentrating at Barodia was to prevent or endanger my advance to Saugor, by re-taking Rathghur or by placing themselves in my rear, on the road from Bhopall to Saugor, to cut off, as they had already attempted to do, the supplies coming to me from the friendly States of Scindia and Bhopall. It was consequently necessary to attack the Enemy and drive them out of Barodia.

Four Guns Horse Artillery.
Four Guns Captain Lightfoot's Battery.
Two 5½ inch Mortars with 15 men of Captain Woolcomb's Battery, under the command of Lieutenant Strutt.
Three Troops, 14th Light Dragoons.
Two Troops, 3rd Bombay Light Cavalry.
Twenty five Men, Madras Sappers and Miners.
Third European Regiment, Detachment Hyderabad Contingent Field Force under Captain Hare.

4. Taking with me the Force stated in the margin, I marched at mid-day, on the 31st ultimo, from Rathghur, leaving Brigadier Steuart with the remainder of my Force to protect Rathghur and the Camp.

5. I moved in the order of march which I always adopt when near the Rebels, as a precaution against their system of surprises; that is, a line of flankers of Her Majesty's 14th Light Dragoons on each side of the road, 50 yards in front of the leading file of the advanced guard, which with a file of Irregulars has charge of the guides, another line of Irregular Cavalry, 150 yards in echelon in front of the outward flanks of the 14th, and should thick jungle border the road, a Company of Infantry in extended order on each side of it to support the flankers of the 14th and the advanced guard. By this means all dangerous ground is searched, surprises are almost impossible, and spies lying concealed at a great distance from the road are frequently seized.

6. As we approached Barodia and the River Beena, we had very thick jungle, long grass, and nullahs on our left. The flankers of the Irregulars suddenly halting, reported that they perceived the Enemy in force in ambuscade on our left. Being with the advanced guard, which was under Lieutenant-Colonel Turnbull, I ordered the two guns of his Troop to open their fire to the left on the Enemy; before they could do so the Enemy opened a Musketry fire on us, killing Lieutenant-Colonel Turnbull's horse, and keeping it up with tenacity, although I re-inforced the division of Horse Artillery with four of Captain Lightfoot's 9-Pounders, firing grape and round shot; it was too close for shrapnell.

7. Lieutenant-Colonel Turnbull, with the Horse Artillery, took ground to the right with the view to enfilade the Enemy, but he could not get a slant at them. However, this movement enabled him to obtain good views of a body of Rebel horsemen, with a red standard

endeavouring to gain a wood to our right and outflank us. I had directed a charge of Cavalry against them, but it could not be executed in consequence of the Staff Officer being unable to find a passage down the high banks of the Beena, two rounds of spherical case burst amongst this batch, they disappeared.

8. I had placed the 3rd Europeans in skirmishing order, in front of the flanks of the guns, their united fire diminished, but did not silence the fire of the Rebels.

9. I therefore charged the Rebels out of their advanced position, with the skirmishers of the 3rd Europeans, who, under Lieutenant-Colonel Liddell, gallantly drove them out of their own treacherous element, thick jungle, and twisting nullahs, and took possession of the bank of the river, commanding the ford to Barodia, which now first became visible; the Rebels had displayed so much obstinacy in defending this position in order to prevent our advance across the Beena to Barodia.

10. Lieutenant-Colonel Liddell, Captain Neville, Royal Engineers, Captain Campbell, 3rd Europeans, Captain Rose, my Aide-de-Camp and * Lieutenant Macdonald, Assistant Quarter Master General, were conspicuous in this advance.

* Lieutenant Macdonald was slightly wounded, and his horse twice wounded.

11. I turned the advantage gained by the 3rd Europeans immediately to account, and sent the Hyderabad Irregular Cavalry supported by the 3rd Bombay Light Cavalry under Captain Forbes to cross the ford covered by the skirmishers, to pass through the jungle to the front and fall on the Enemy in the open which I had learnt was between the jungle and Barodia. I followed with four guns of the Horse Artillery and a Troop of Her Majesty's 14th Light Dragoons in support under Lieutenant-Colonel Turnbull, ordering the rest of my Force to follow with the exception of Captain Hare's Infantry and Guns which remained at the Fort to prevent the rear being cut off.

12. Captain Forbes found the Enemy's flanks, particularly their left, posted in thick jungle, their centre in comparatively open ground; he charged and broke their centre, cutting up thirty or forty of them. The third, and a very strong position, the village of Barodia, now came within sight, Captain Forbes having observed a body of Cavalry retreating leisurely on it attempted to cut them off, but their flight on seeing his intention became so rapid, that he only succeeded in killing eight or ten of them before they got well under the protection of their guns in position at their village and of the matchlock men posted in the dense

jungle, which surrounded three sides of it, and lining the banks of a wet nullah running along the front.

13. Captain Forbes mentioned for their conduct on this occasion, and I beg to recommend to His Excellency the Commander-in-Chief, Subadar Soojut Khan, for having killed, himself, three of the Rebels all of his own caste, Naick Hunut Singh very severely wounded, Naick Babadheen Khan and Trooper Vass, also severely wounded, who attracted the notice of their Officers by engaging singly two or three of the Enemy at the same time.

14. On the day before, when the Camp was attacked, the same faithful Subadar hindered the advance of the Enemy by the able disposition of his picket.

15. If His Excellency were pleased to obtain a reward for these brave Soldiers, it would have a good effect on their Regiment, whose fidelity and courage have never failed.

16. Jemadar Jhurut Hoosanie Khan, 3rd Hyderabad Cavalry, was mortally wounded in courageously attacking singly a knot of the Enemy.

17. Captain Forbes conducted the charge with the same gallantry and intelligence which distinguished him at Kashab.

18. Although the Ford was a bad one, Lieutenant-Colonel Turnbull took his Guns across it rapidly in support of the Cavalry, and when by the strength of the Enemy's position, they were compelled to give up the pursuit, unlimbered in front of the village, and the Enemy's Guns, and opened an effective fire on their position. Captain Lightfoot with the 9-Pounder Battery arrived shortly afterwards.

19. The Enemy answered with guns and rockets, killing at my side, to my great regret, Captain Neville of the Royal Engineers, acting as my Aide-de-Camp: knowing what excellent service he had done as an Engineer Officer before Sebastapool, I had brought him up by forced marches to assist in the reduction of the Forts in this Country ; during the action he was most useful to me, exhibiting to the last the courage and intelligence which had obtained for him so honorable a reputation.

20. Driven from their position by the fire of our guns, the Enemy retreated across a wall and open space into the village and jungle. I directed Captain Lightfoot to correspond to this movement, he took ground to the left with guns and gave them before they reached cover an enfilading and destructive fire, the $5\frac{1}{2}$ inch Mortars threw shell into the small Fort of the village and jungle, to which the Enemy had retired.

21. It was now getting dark, taking two Companies of the 3rd Europeans which had just come up, I crossed the wet nullah, and bringing their right shoulders forward occupied the wall round the village and surrounded it with the skirmishers and a Troop of the 3rd Light Cavalry, Lieutenant-Colonel Liddell afterwards occupied it and the little Fort, but the Enemy, except a few valaitee skirmishers who were killed, had fled to Koraye through the jungle, leaving baggage unpacked and other signs of a precipitate retreat.

22. I was not at all sure that my Camp with the Siege Artillery and numerous stores, left with a small Force at Rathghur, under Brigadier Steuart, might not be attacked during my absence, as it had been before; I therefore halted in the village only for a short time in order to rest the Troops, who had been on duty for the last five days, and marched back the same night to Rathghur, they were marching or engaged fifteen hours.

The Enemy's loss was severe, they themselves state it to be from four to five hundred, which is not surprising as they were exposed to well directed fire for a length of time. Amant Sing, their ablest Military leader, and a nephew of Tajie Mahomed Khan were killed; and the Rajah of Banpore was wounded.

The valaitees and Pathans fought with their accustomed courage, several of them, even when dying, springing from the ground and inflicting mortal wounds with their broad swords.

The good result of the defeat of the Rebels at Barodia exceeded my expectations; not only were my communications with the West and Saugor completely opened, but the Rebels, flying from Barodia to Koraye, left in their panic that place, although it is a Fort, in a strong position, and Krulassa, which is between thirty and forty miles to the North-West of Saugor. Nureeawallee, their fortified Camp, was also abandoned, all these places and the Country about them had been in their hands for the last eight months. The Rebels also left at Koraye their Guns which they had at Barodia.

The Troops behaved at Barodia with discipline and courage, keeping in very bad ground their formation and obeying with eager alacrity any orders which brought them closer to the Enemy. The 3rd Europeans, although very young and now for the first time in the Field, have qualified themselves for a career of honor; and Lieutenant-Colonel Liddell is sure to lead the way.

I am much obliged to Captain Wood, my Assistant Adjutant-

General and my Staff, for the assistance which they gave me on this occasion as well at Rathghur, and I ought to add that the Officers of my Divisional Staff, whose duties are non-combatant, still in their zeal accompany me to the Field. Captain Campbell, Baggage Master, who was hit, was very useful and intelligent in conveying my orders, and Lieutenant Lyster, my Interpreter, of the 72nd Regiment Bengal Native Infantry, was wounded when engaging the nephew of Mahomed Fazil Khan whom he killed.

I have the honour to enclose a list of the Casualties at Barodia, as also a list of Sappers and Miners, whom Major Boileau, Commanding Engineer, wishes to be mentioned for having inspected the ditch and the breach of the Fort of Rathghur.

Return of Killed and Wounded of the Head Quarters Staff and 2nd Brigade, Central India Field Force, during the Action of the Rebels at Barodia on the 31st of January 1858.

Corps.	Rank and Names.		Killed.	Wounded.	Remarks.
Staff	Captain	Neville	1	...	Killed by a round shot.
	Ditto	J. Macdonald	...	1	Sword cut on outer part of right thigh.
	Ditto	E. Campbell	...	1	Contusions of right thigh by spent ball.
	Lieutenant	H. H. Lyster	...	1	Deep sword cut on inner part of right fore-arm.
1st Troop Horse Arty.	Ditto	R. Pittman	...	1	By a round shot in right shoulder.
	Gunner	J. Lee	...	1	By a spent Ball.
3rd European Regiment.	Serjeant	J. O'Connors	...	1	Severely by Gun shot wound in chin.
	Lc. Corporal	H. Currie	...	1	Severely by Gun shot wound in neck.
	Ditto	H. Hobeu	...	1	Severely by Gun shot wound in left arm.
	Private	S. Wright	...	1	Severely by Gun shot wound in left thigh.
	Ditto	H. Wingfield	...	1	Fracture of both legs (by Gun carriage wheel).
3rd Light Cavalry.	Cornet	Daniels	...	1	Slightly in right arm.
	Trooper	Hunmunt Singh	...	1	Ditto ditto.
	Ditto	Francis Vass	...	1	Severely in both arms.
	Ditto	Kalkee Pursad	...	1	Slightly in the back.

Return of Killed and Wounded of the Head-Quarters Staff and 2nd Brigade, Central India Field Force, during the Action of the Rebels at Barodia on the 31st of January 1858—continued.

CORPS.	Rank and Names.		Killed.	Wounded.	REMARKS.
1st Cavalry Hyderabad Contingent.	Lieutenant	K. G. Westwacott	...	1	Slightly in the finger.
	Jemadar	Goolam Hossein Khan.	...	1	Severely in the head.
	Duffadar	Murdan Singh	...	1	Very severely in the thigh (since dead).
	Trooper	Emmomally Khan	...	1	Slightly in the body.
	Ditto	Ally Beg	...	1	Severely in the arm.
	Ditto	Shaik Lyfoolah	...	1	Ditto ditto.
	Ditto	Rymattalah Khan	...	1	Ditto ditto face.
3rd Cavly. H. C.	Jemadar	Ahmed Hoosein Khan.	1	...	
		TOTAL	2	21	

HEAD-QUARTERS C. I. F. F.
A. A. Genl's Office,
Camp Saugor, 8th February 1858.

(Sd.) H. H. A. WOOD, *Captain,*
Asst. Adjt. Genl., C. I. F. F

T. C. COLEY, *Major,*
Offg. D. A. A. G., P. D. A.

Horses.

	Killed.	Wounded.	Missing.
Staff	...	2	...
1st Troop Horse Artillery	1	1	...
14th Light Dragoons	1	...	...
3rd Light Cavalry	1	5	1
No. 18 Light Field Battery	...	1	...
1st Cavalry Hyderabad Contingent	...	3	3
3rd Cavalry Hyderabad Contingent	...	...	1
TOTAL	3	12	5

From H. L. ANDERSON, *Esq.*, *Secretary to Government, Bombay,* To Colonel EDWARD GREEN, *Adjutant General of the Army,*—(*No. 960 of 1858, dated 18th March 1858*).

I am directed by the Right Hon'ble the Governor in Council to acknowledge the receipt of your letter, No. 2133, dated the 9th instant, forwarding a Despatch from Major-General Sir Hugh Rose, Commanding the Central India Field Force, detailing his operations before Rathghur.

In reply, I am desired to inform you, that the Right Hon'ble the Governor in Council has perused with great pleasure, Sir Hugh Rose's Report of these operations by which an important service has been rendered to the State, and that His Lordship in Council has derived gratification from the favorable mention made by Sir Hugh Rose of the services of Brigadier C. Steuart and the following Officers and Private:—

Lieutenant-Colonel Turnbull, Artillery.
Major Boileau, Madras Engineers.
Captain Forbes, 3rd Light Cavalry.
Captain Lightfoot, Artillery.
Captain Hare,
Lieutenant Westwacott, } Hyderabad Contingent.
Lieutenant Moore, 3rd Light Cavalry.
Lieutenant Quarter Master Thompson, Artillery, H. C.
Private Davies, 3rd European Regiment.

From the Adjutant General of the Army, To the Secretary to Government, *Bombay,*—*No. 2376, dated Bombay, 17th March 1858.*

In continuation of my previous communications Nos. 2133 and 2288, dated, respectively, the 9th and 13th instant, I am directed by the Commander-in-Chief to transmit, for submission to the Right Honorable the Governor in Council, the enclosed letter, (without date,) from Major-General Sir Hugh Rose, K.C.B., Commanding Central India Field Force, detailing his proceedings subsequent to the capture of the Fort of Rathghur and Action with the Insurgents near the Town of Barodia.

2. The operations of Sir Hugh Rose in the Field, while they have the cordial approval of the Commander-in-Chief, will doubtless be most satisfactory to His Lordship in Council, as the success which has attended them must have the most beneficial effect in tranquillizing a District which has been so long in the hands of the Rebels.

3. The Lieutenant-General Commanding in Chief has desired me to submit in the margin of this letter, the names of Officers prominently brought to notice by Sir Hugh Rose, and to beg that the Right Honorable the Governor in Council will be pleased to bring their conduct prominently to the notice of the Honorable Court of Directors.

> Lieutenant-Colonel Liddell.
> Captain Campbell.
> } 3rd European Regiment.
>
> Captain Forbes, 3rd Light Cavalry.
>
> Captain Wood.
> Captain Macdonald.
> Captain Rose.
> } Staff.

4. The Major-General will be directed to constitute a Court of Inquiry under the provisions of Act 273, Section XXXIX of Jameson's Code, with the view of ascertaining if the Native Officer and men alluded to in the 13th and 14th paragraphs of his Despatch are entitled to admittance to the distinction of the Order of Merit.

Extract from a letter No. 2527, of date 20th March 1858, from the Adjutant-General of the Army, to the Major-General Commanding Central India Field Force.

His Excellency has perused your Despatch with much satisfaction, and I have been commanded to recommend to the especial notice of Government, the conduct of all the Troops on the occasion (Barodia), also to bring prominently forward the Officers, Non-Commissioned Officers and Private named by you, as having distinguished themselves in action with the Enemy.

I am to convey to you the cordial thanks of the Commander-in-Chief for the very valuable services you are performing; and to request you will notify to the Officers, Non-Commissioned Officers and Soldiers, European and Native, that their gallant and excellent conduct is fully remembered and heartily acknowledged by the Government and the Commander-in-Chief.

Resolution by the Honorable Board, dated 22nd March 1859.

The Right Hon'ble the Governor in Council entirely concurs in the cordial approval of Sir Hugh Rose's operations near the Town of Barodia, and will have great pleasure in bringing his services and those of the Officers mentioned in his Despatch, to the favorable notice of the Government of India and the Honorable the Secret Committee.

Allahabad, the 29th April 1858.

No. 110 of 1858.—The Right Hon'ble the Governor General of India is pleased to direct the publication of the following Letter from the Deputy Adjutant General of the Army, No. 266 A, dated 26th April 1858, forwarding a Despatch from Major-General Sir Hugh Rose, K.C.B., Commanding Central India Field Force, reporting the operations of the 2nd Brigade of the Force subsequent to the capture of the Fort of Garrakota :—

From Major H. W. NORMAN, *Deputy Adjutant-General of the Army*, To the Secretary to the Government of India, *Military Department, with the Governor-General,—No. 266A, dated Head-Quarters Camp, Futtehgurh, 26th April 1858.*

Forwards a Despatch from Major-General Sir Hugh Rose, reporting the operations of the 2nd Brigade of the Central India Field Force, subsequent to the capture of the Fort of Garrakota.

I have the honor, by desire of the Commander-in-Chief, to transmit for submission to the Right Hon'ble the Governor General, a Despatch dated 26th Ultimo, from Major General Sir H. Rose, K.C.B., Commanding Central India Field Force, reporting the operations of the 2nd Brigade of the Force subsequent to the capture of the Fort of Garrakota, embracing the forcing of the pass of Mudinpoor, and capture of the Forts of Serai and Marowra.

2. His Excellency considers that these operations were most skilfully conducted.

From Major-General SIR HUGH ROSE, K.C.B., *Commanding Central India Field Force*, To Major-General MANSFIELD, *Chief of the Staff, Cawnpore,—dated Camp before Jhansie, the 26th March 1858.*

I have the honor to report to you, for the information of His Excellency the Commander-in-Chief, the operations of the 2nd Brigade of the Central India Field Force, under my orders, since the capture of the Fort of Garrakota.

A halt of four days at Saugor was necessary for the repair of my Siege Guns; I therefore marched back to Saugor in two days, leaving Major Boileau, with the Sappers and Miners, at Garrakota, to demolish all he could of its defences.

The Rebels had held a steep and thickly wooded hill, a few miles to the North of Garrakota, which gave them the command of the road to Dumoh; after the fall of Garrakota they then abandoned it, leaving open the communication between Saugor and Dumoh.

My Siege Artillery was ready in four days, on the 18th instant. But want of supplies, caused by the devastation of the Saugor and the neighbouring Districts by the Rebels, and other circumstances, did not allow me to leave Saugor till the 27th Instant.

This delay did away, very much, with the good effects of the speedy fall of Garrakota. The Rebels not seeing any further operations or movements to the front against them, regained courage, and occupied again, in force, the strong positions in the Shaghur and adjoining Districts, such as the Forts of Serai and Marowra, and the difficult passes in the mountainous ridges which separate the Shaghur and Saugor Districts.

These passes are three in number. The pass of Narut, and the Fort of Carnelgurh near Malthone, of Mudinpore, and of Dhamooney.

My object was to reach Jhansie, against which I was ordered to move as quickly as I could; but on my road there, I wished to take up my 1st Brigade, which I had marched from Mhow and Indore to Goonah, for the purpose, as previously stated, of clearing and opening the Grand Trunk Road from Bombay to Agra, in obedience to my instructions.

I anticipated resistance to my advance on Jhansie at the passes, the Forts of Serai, Murowra, and Thal-Behut, at which latter place, it was said that the Rajah of Banpore intended to make his last stand.

It was also affirmed by some, but denied by others, that the Fort of Chundeyree, to the West of the River Betwa, formerly a family possession of the Raja of Banpore, would be defended.

It was necessary that the 1st Brigade, on the West, and the 2nd Brigade on the East of the Betwa, should be concentrated for the attack of Jhansie.

I determined to force these obstacles to the forward movement of my Force, and to the union of my 1st and 2nd Brigade; and accordingly gave orders to Brigadier Stuart, Commanding my 1st Brigade, to move from Goonah Westwards, and take Chundeyree, whilst I forced my way Northwards, and, crossing the Betwa, march with both Brigades against Jhansie.

An operation against the passes was more than usually difficult, on account of the great length of my line of march. For knowing the danger of a want of ammunition, I took with me abundant reserves of it, having besides to take care of a convoy of fifteen days' supplies for my Force and its Camp-Followers.

The pass of Narut was by far the most difficult, and the Enemy having taken it into their head that I must pass through it, had increased its natural difficulties, by barricading the road with abatis, and parapets made of large boulders of rock 15 feet thick; all passage by the sides of the road being made impracticable by the almost precipitous hills, covered with jungle, which came down to the edge of the road. The Rajah of Banpore, who is both enterprizing and courageous, defended this pass with 8 or 10,000 men.

The next most difficult pass was Dhamooney; very little was known about the third, Mudinpore, except that in the Ordnance Map it was described as "good for Guns."

Under these circumstances, I requested Major Orr to reconnoitre these passes, whilst I was detained at Saugor for supplies.

Supplies for my Force having come into Saugor, I marched from that place on the 27th Instant to Rijwass, a central point from which I could move against any one of these passes. Major Orr's Force joined me at Rijwass; with his usual intelligence, he had collected information which made me select the pass of Mudinpore for my point of attack.

In order to deceive the Enemy as to my intention, and prevent the Rajah of Banpore from coming from the pass of Narut to the assistance of the Rajah of Shaghur, who defended Mudinpore, I made a serious feint against Narut by sending Major Scudamore, Commanding H. M.'s 14th Light Dragoons, with the Force stated in the margin,* with their tents and baggage, to the Fort and Town of Malthone, just above the pass of Narut, whilst I made the real attack on the pass of Mudinpore. Having taken the ruined little Fort of Barodia, and left a small Garrison in it, to keep up my communications, I marched, on the 3rd Instant, against the pass of Mudinpore, with the Force stated in the margin.† As the Column approached the pass, the Enemy's skirmishers fired on the Advanced guard, from a ridge of hills on our right, near the village of Noonee. I sent up a party of the Salt Customs under Mr. Bartie, who advancing, drove them back.

At about 800 yards from the entrance of the pass, we saw the Enemy in force

---

* *Major Scudamore's Force.*
2 Troops H. M.'s 14th Light Dragoons.
1 Troop 3rd Light Cavalry.
100 Irregular Cavalry.
One 24-Pounder Howitzer.
3 Bhopal 9-Pounders.
24th Regiment Bombay Native Infantry.

† *Sir H. Rose's Force.*
Advanced Guard.
500 Hydrabad Cavalry.
200 Hydrabad Infantry.
4 Guns Artillery.
1 Company 3rd Bombay Europeans.
Centre.
1 Troop H. M.'s 14th Light Dragoons.
Sappers and Miners.
4 Guns Horse Artillery.
Right Wing 3rd Bombay Europeans.
Three 9-Pr. Guns, Captain Lightfoot's Battery.
Two 5½-Inch Mortars.
One 8-Inch Mortar.
One 8-Inch Howitzer.
Left Wing 3rd Bombay Europeans.
Siege Train.
3rd Bombay Light Cavalry.
Baggage and Convoy.
Rear Guard.
125 Hydrabad Infantry.
1 Howitzer and 1 Gun Horse Artillery.

1 Troop H. M.'s 14th Light Dragoons.
50 Hydrabad Cavalry.

on the hills, on the left of the pass. Major Orr made some good practice at them with round shot, and spherical case.

The pass was formed by a sudden descent of the road into a deep glen, thickly wooded. To the right, further on, the road ran along the side of a lake. The left of the road was lined by rocky and precipitous hills.

The ardour of an excellent Officer induced him, at this time, to make an incautious movement with his Guns to his right front, with the view to pour an enfilading fire into the Enemy. But he had not taken into consideration that this movement brought him to within fifty or sixty yards of the edge of the glen, in which lay concealed some hundred Sepoys, who, before he could unlimber, opened a very heavy fire on his Guns, which he was unable to depress on them. The Sepoys fortunately fired too quick, and too high, and the Officer retired his Guns out of the range of their musketry, with only a few Casualties. The Sepoys hailed this little reverse with shouts. But their success had only brought on their more rapid defeat. For knowing now their exact position, and seeing the necessity of showing them that a calm retreat was only the prelude of a rapid offensive, I advanced 100 of the Hydrabad Contingent Infantry under Captain Sinclare, at double time, and made them charge into the glen, bring their right shoulders forward, and sweep it down towards the road, following this up by a movement of a Company of the 3rd Europeans, against the front of the Sepoys, and of the Salt Customs, from the extreme right, against their rear. To still further discomfit them, I sent a Troop of Her Majesty's 14th Light Dragoons to a knoll, quite in rear of the glen, and commanding a view of the Lake, and the other end of the pass. The Rebels were driven with loss from the glen, and, crossing the road, ascended the hill on its left, for the purpose of joining the large body of Rebels who occupied the hills divided by ravines on the left of the road. The Troop of Horse Artillery would have swept them away with grape, had not the Officer Commanding it mistaken the Rebels, on account of the similarity of dress, for Men of the Salt Customs.

Not giving the Rebels time to breathe, I directed Captain Macdonald, my Assistant Quarter-Master General, to storm the hill, to the left of the road, with two Companies of the 3rd Europeans. Captain Macdonald conducted them ably and gallantly, up the almost precipitous height, and extending the Grenadier Company from the right, and supporting them with the other Company, drove them from the first to the second line of hills. As soon as Lieutenant-Colonel Liddell had come up, with the rest of the 3rd Europeans, I moved him up the hill, in support of his two Companies, directing him to advance, and drive the Enemy successively from all the hills commanding the pass. He performed this movement entirely to my satisfaction.

The glens and hills which protected the pass having been taken, I sent Captain Abbott, with the 4th Hydrabad Cavalry to clear the pass, and drive in the Enemy's front; this he did effectually.

The Enemy, repulsed in flank and front, retired to the village of Mudinpore, in rear of the end of the Lake. The village was fortified by a formidable work, in the shape of a bund of great thickness of earth and solid masonry, which dammed up the Lake. The Enemy had placed the few Guns they had in rear of the bund, and had been firing with them on the 3rd Europeans on the hill.

The pass having been gained, I sent directions to Brigadier Stewart, whom I had halted in rear of the pass, with the Reserve and Siege Train to advance through it, and occupy the head of the Lake. As soon as they had arrived, I opened with the 8-inch Howitzer, and the 9-Pounders in advance of it, a fire on the Rebel Guns.

At this time I received a message from the Officer Commanding the Rear Guard, that the Enemy had fired from the range of hills running to the pass of Narut on him and his long line of baggage. I had all along thought it likely that the Rajah of Banpore might come to the aid of the Rebels at Mudinpore as soon as he discovered that the move of Major Scudamore was a feint, and my attack the real one. I therefore sent a Troop of Her Majesty's 14th Light Dragoons and a Regiment of Hydrabad Cavalry, to cover the Rear Guard.

A few rounds drove the Enemy from their position in rear of the bund, and they retired from Mudinpore, through the jungle, towards the Fort of Serai.

I directed Major Orr to pursue, with the remainder of the Hydrabad Cavalry.

The Cavalry which I had detached with Major Scudamore, and to assist the Rear Guard, rendered the Force available for the pursuit small.

Major Orr, and Captain Abbott under him, pursuing, along the road, through the jungle, came up with the rear of the Rebels, consisting principally of the 52nd Bengal Native Infantry, and killed a good many of them, amongst the number the notorious Mutineer, Lall Turbadio, who, as Havildar Major of the 52nd, was instigator of the Mutiny in that Regiment, and whom they made their Commanding Officer.

I owe my acknowledgments to Major Orr and Captain Abbott for their conduct on this occasion. Captain Pinkney, who accompanied my Force as Political Agent at Jhansie, distinguished himself in the pursuit.

I marched the Force several miles beyond the pass, into an open and level country. The line of baggage was so long that it did not come up till the next day; but owing to the precautions I had taken, it did not sustain the slightest loss.

The results of the success at Mudinpore were as numerous as they were favorable. My Force had got into the rear of the passes, and the Enemy's line of defences, of which they thought so much. The pass of Narut considered by them to be impregnable was turned.

Mudinpore, it is true, was the weakest of the passes; but, on the other hand, it had been defended by the Sepoys of the 52nd and other Regiments, and by 7,000 picked Bundeelas. The Sepoys and the Bundeelas quarrelled, the former declaring that the latter had run away, and left them to fight at the pass; general mistrust, and a panic ensued in the Rebel Camp.

The Fort of Serai, or Soyrage, a fortified Palace of the Rajah of Shaghur, perfect in architecture, now used as an Arsenal for the manufacture of powder and shot, fell the next day into the hands of my Troops. The dyes of the old Saugor Mint, from which the Rebels were making balls, were found here, in quantities.

The day after, I took possession of Marowra, an ancient Fort with a double line of defences, in an important position, on the road from Saugor to Jhansie, and from Shaghur to Malthone.

The Shaghur Territory was attached to the British possessions by Sir Robert Hamilton, and in consequence the British Flag was hoisted on the Fort of Marowra in presence of my Brigade.

The passes of Narut and Dhamooney were abandoned, and Sir Robert Hamilton established a Police Station at Malthone.

In fact, the whole country between Saugor and Jhansie, to the East of the River Betwa, which, since the outbreak of the rebellion, had been in the hands of the Insurgents, was now, with the exception of Thal-Behut, restored to the Government.

I beg leave to recommend to Your Excellency, for their conduct at

CENTRAL INDIA.—JHANSI.

the forcing of the pass of Mudinpore, Lieutenant-Colonel Liddell; Major Scudamore, for the skilful manner in which he conducted the feint against Malthone, which neutralized the Force of the Rajah of Banpore; Major Orr; Captain Abbott; Captain Sinclare; Captain Macdonald, Assistant Quarter-Master General; and Mr. Bartie, Commanding the Salt Customs Police, who had a short time before been strongly recommended for his gallant conduct in attacking the Rebels' position at Dhamooney.

I have the honor to enclose a list of the Casualties in forcing the pass.

Return of Killed and Wounded of the 2nd Brigade, Central India Field Force, and Hyderabad Contingent Field Force, during the Action with the Rebels, on the 3rd March 1858, in the pass of Mudinpore.

Corps.	Rank.	Names.	Remarks.
Artillery 1st Troop	Sergeant	Dickenson	Wounded severely below left knee.
	Horsekeeper	Rowjee	Wounded slightly in right hand.
14th Light Dragoons	Captain	Prettejohn	Contusion by a spent ball.
	Private	Bavry	Wounded in the foot.
	,,	Ball	,, severely in the knee.
3rd Light Cavalry	Trumpeter	Francis	Contusion by a musket ball.
3rd European Regiment.	Private	Bernard Dempsay	Wounded severely by gunshot in the chest (since dead).
	,,	Phillips Connors	Wounded slightly in chest by a spent ball.
	,,	John Steen	Wounded by a gunshot in the scalp.
	,,	James Relly	Wounded slightly in left groin by a spent ball.
1st Cavalry, Hyderabad Contingent.	Trooper	Hossein Khan	Dangerously wounded.
	,,	Mandah Khan	,, ,,

H. H. A. WOOD, *Captain*
Asst. Adjt.-Genl.

Asst. Adjt.-Genl.'s Office,
Camp Jhansie,
he 8th April 1858.

No. 111 of 1858.—The Right Hon'ble the Governor General of India is pleased to publish for general information, the following Despatch from the Deputy Adjutant General of the Army, No. 267, dated 26th April 1858, forwarding a detailed Report from Brigadier-General R. Walpole, Commanding Field Force, of his successful affair with the Rebels near Allahgunge, on the 22nd Instant.

From Major H. W. NORMAN, *Deputy Adjutant General of the Army,* To the Secretary to the Government of India, *Military Department, with the Governor General,*—No. 267, *dated Head-Quarters, Futtehghur, 26th April 1858.*

Forwards a Despatch from Brigadier-General Walpole, regarding his Action at Allahgunge.

I have now the honor, by desire of the Commander-in-Chief, to transmit, for the information of the Right Hon'ble the Governor General, a detailed Report from Brigadier-General R. Walpole, dated 23rd Instant, of his successful affair near Allahgunge on the previous day, when 4 Guns were captured and considerable loss inflicted on the Enemy.

2. The action was one of Horse Artillery and Cavalry, and both these arms appear to His Excellency to have highly distinguished themselves.

From Brigadier-General R. WALPOLE, *Commanding Field Force,* To the Chief of the Staff,—*dated Camp Allahgunge, 23rd April 1858.*

I transmitted yesterday a short account of the defeat of that portion of the Rebel Force which occupied the villages on the left bank of the Ram Gunga, from Allahgunge to Hoolapore. I have now the honor to forward, for the information of His Excellency the Commander-in-Chief, a more detailed Report of that operation.

I marched at daylight on the 22nd instant from Sewajpore, intending to encamp in the neighbourhood of Sirsie, and to proceed to this place the following day. However, on the Advanced Guard approaching Sirsie, the Enemy was discovered in our front. I rode forward to reconnoitre, and ordered up Major Remmington's Troop of Horse Artillery and the Infantry, desiring the heavy Guns to follow, and made the following dispositions. Four Guns of Lieutenant-Colonel Tombs' Troop of Horse Artillery (two being on the Rear Guard), supported by a Squadron of 9th Lancers and 100 Infantry, all which Troops had formed the Advanced Guard, occupied the left. Major Remmington's 9-Pounder Troop was directed to its right, and the main body of the Cavalry, consisting of 9th Lancers and 2nd Punjaub Irregulars, under Brigadier

Hagart, was placed on the extreme right to protect that flank from the numerous Cavalry of the Enemy, and with instructions to sweep round the Enemy's left and rear the moment they retired, with the hope of getting any Guns they might endeavour to save.

I knew, from having occupied the right bank of the Ram Gunga during the winter, that our left was covered by that river, and that from the great bend it takes beyond the villages of Mow and Jerapore, our Cavalry would be useless on our left flank.

We advanced in the above order some distance, crossing the Sende Nuddee, when the Enemy opened fire upon us with their Guns, which were placed in the village of Hoolapoor, upon which they had retired, and where they made their stand. Their fire was rapid and good, the shot plunging among our Artillery, but doing little damage. Lieutenant-Colonel Tombs' Troop advanced rapidly to within six or seven hundred yards of the village and opened upon it; Major Remmington's Troop soon after followed, taking ground to its right. The Guns of these two Troops were so well served that, in about 20 minutes, those of the Enemy appeared to be silenced.

I now perceived the Enemy streaming in large numbers from the rear of the village; our whole line advanced, Lieutenant-Colonel Tombs' Troop on one side of the village, Major Remmington's on the other. On the extreme right, just at this place, there was a thick jungle, which prevented Brigadier Hagart turning their left flank at this point; but Major Remmington's Guns having been ordered to accompany him, the jungle was soon cleared, and he advanced between it and Hoolapoor, and as the Enemy's Guns, which had been withdrawn from that village, were being carried off, three of them were gallantly captured by Captain Wilkinson's Troop of the 9th Lancers, he being supported by Lieutenant Richardes with a Troop of 2nd Punjaub Cavalry, and every man with the Guns was killed. A fourth Gun was taken by the Cavalry during the rout that followed.

We now advanced with an extended front, one Squadron 9th Lancers, Lieutenant-Colonel Tombs' Guns, and the Infantry which had formed the Advanced Guard on the left, Major Remmington's Guns, and the Cavalry under Brigadier Hagart, to the right rather in advance, and swept the whole country, driving the Enemy through the villages of Nebonuggra and Jerapoor, at the latter of which their camp was captured, and then through Chumputteapoor and Saibgunge as far as Allahgunge, where they had a bridge-of-boats protected by a breast-work pierced for Guns. Having secured this Town, and the pursuit having continued for six miles, I considered it advisable to halt, and I sent for my baggage and pitched my Camp.

Nizam Ali Khan, who Commanded, was killed in the Action, and some documents were found in his Tent, one describing the preparations he had made for stopping the advance of the English.

The loss of the Enemy must have amounted in the whole to between five and six hundred, and we captured 4 Guns, the Enemy's Camp, ammunition, stores and grain in large quantities.

Our loss, I am happy to say, was small, very small, considering the results obtained; it consisted of one man killed and six wounded.

I am particularly indebted to Brigadier Hagart for the admirable manner in which he conducted the operations of the Cavalry on the right. I beg also to return my best thanks to Major Brind, Bengal Artillery, for his exertions, and the able manner in which he commanded the Artillery, and to Lieutenant-Colonel Tombs, and Major Remmington, commanding Troops of Horse Artillery, for the excellent management of their Guns which drove the Enemy from their position at Hoolapoor with great loss. Brigadier Hagart speaks in great praise of Captain Coles, Commanding 9th Lancers, and Captain Browne, Commanding 2nd Punjaub Irregular Cavalry. I have on all occasions experienced great assistance from these Officers. The Brigadier also expresses his obligations to Captain Sarel, 17th Lancers, Brigade-Major to the Cavalry Brigade, and to Lieutenant Gore, 7th Hussars, who acted as his Orderly Officer; and Major Brind speaks in high terms of Lieutenant Bunny, Bengal Artillery, his Staff Officer.

I beg to record the assistance I received from my Staff, Captain Barwell, Deputy Assistant Adjutant-General, Captain Carey, Deputy Assistant Quarter-Master General, Captain Warner, Aide-de-Camp, and Lieutenant Ecles, Extra Aide-de-Camp.

The Action was fought with Artillery and Cavalry, and the pursuit was so rapid, there was no chance for the Infantry taking a part in it.

I have learnt to-day that the Enemy who were posted at Jelalabad, on the fugitives reaching that place, and on their hearing of the death of Nizam Ali Khan, evacuated the Fort there the same evening, and have proceeded, it is supposed, towards Bareilly.

Nominal Roll of Killed and Wounded in the Field Force under Command of Brigadier-General R. WALPOLE, *on the 22nd April 1858.*

Corps.	Rank and Names.		Nature of Casualty.
Horse Artillery	Gunner	Patrick Gray	Killed in action.
,,	,,	Jonathan Harris	Wounded dangerously
9th Lancers	Sergeant	Charles May	,, slightly.
,,	Corporal	John Cain	,, ,,
,,	Private	Silas Spillett	,, ,,
2nd Punjaub Cavalry	Sowar	Goolab Sing	,, ,,
,, ,,	,,	Ahmed Shah	,, ,,

(Sd.) C. A. BARWELL, *Capt.*,   (Sd.) R. WALPOLE, *Brigdr.-Genl.*,
Depy. Asst.-Adjt. Genl.,   *Comdg. Field Force.*
Field Force.

CAMP ALLAHGUNGE,
The 23rd April 1858.

Allahabad, the 29th April 1858.

No. 113 *of* 1858.—The Right Hon'ble the Governor General of India is pleased to publish the following account, from Major-General G. Whitlock, Commanding Saugor Field Division, of his engagement with the Rebels at Jheeghun, on the 10th April 1858.

From Major-General G. WHITLOCK, *Commanding Saugor Field Division,* To Major-General MANSFIELD, *Chief of the Staff,—No. 121, dated Camp Logassie, the 12th April 1858.*

I have the honor to report, for the information of His Excellency the Commander-in-Chief of India, that Major Ellis, Political Assistant in Bundlecund, having acquainted me that 2,000 Rebels had collected at Jheeghun, one of their strongholds and the depôt for their plunder, distant about seventeen miles from Chutterpore, I decided on making a night march with the view of surprising them.

The Force marched at 8 P.M., on the 9th Instant, but from the intricacies of the road, and ignorance of the guides, it was still four miles from Jheeghun, at 5 A.M on the following morning. The only chance now of a surprise was by a rapid advance of mounted Troops, and I immediately moved with the A Troop Horse Artillery, two Squadrons of Lancers, and Detachment of Ressalah Hydrabad Contingent. The result was satisfactory; the Rebels, leisurely evacuating their position, were unprepared for our sudden appearance.

The Artillery opened, and the Cavalry, gallantly dashing amongst them, committed much havoc.

A portion of Cavalry and Guns were moved to intercept their flight; this was successful.

Under a fire of matchlocks, and through jungle which had been set on fire to impede pursuit, but unavailing, our Troops came up with the Rebels, and the slaughter was heavy.

To follow further without Infantry (for the jungle was becoming dense) would have been as useless as imprudent, and the Force returned to Camp, leaving 97 Rebels dead on the field, and bringing with them 39 Prisoners.

Dassput, the Rebel Chief, long the terror of the District, narrowly escaped capture; he had just returned from Jhansi.

His two nephews, named Beenijao and Jheet Sing, equally notorious for their villainies, fell into our hands, and with seven other prisoners were hanged in the evening. A large portion of baggage, cattle, grain, matchlock ammunition, and some percussion caps, were found; the latter, with articles of uniform stamped Bengal Artillery, lead me to believe that some of the Mutineers must have been present.

The conduct of all the Troops employed gave me much satisfaction, and I only regretted that the Infantry, after a toilsome and wandering night's march, had not an opportunity of being brought into contact with the Rebels.

The village and stronghold has been completely destroyed under the superintendence of our Field Engineer, and the Thakoor of Logassie has expressed his gratification at such a horde of budmashes being driven from his neighbourhood. Our Casualties were two of the Ressalah wounded, and one Horse missing.

Allahabad, the 20th May 1858.

No. 153 of 1858.—The Right Hon'ble the Governor General is pleased to direct the publication of the following Despatches from Major-General G. C. Whitlock, Commanding Saugor and Nerbudda Field Division, dated 24th and 30th April 1858; the former reporting the particulars of a general action with the Troops of the Nawab of Banda on the 19th April, and the latter bringing to notice the valuable service of Major Ellis, Political Assistant for Bundlekund.

From Major-General G. C. WHITLOCK, *Commanding Saugor Field Division*, To Major-General MANSFIELD, *Chief of the Staff, Bengal,—No. 130, dated Camp Banda, the 24th April 1858.*

I have the honor to report, for the information of His Excellency the Commander-in-Chief of India, that the Force under my Command as per margin, fought a general action with the Troops of the Nawab of Banda, on the 19th Instant.

A. Troop H. A. European	110
E. do. do. Native	116
H. M.'s 12th Lancers	227
1 Squadron Hyd. Cavalry	136
Detachment Royal Artillery	111
Detachment Madras Foot Artillery	75
No. 1 Horse Battery	84
Detachment Sappers and Miners	101
3rd M. Eu. Regiment	538
1st Regiment N. I.	255
Detachment 50th N. I.	156
Total of all arms	1,899

Nawab Ali Bahadoor, determined on opposing my advance on Banda, took up during the 18th Instant a position about 5 miles from the left bank of the river Kane, selected with consummate judgment, and in every respect well adapted for the protection of his capital.

His Artillery commanded the main road on which my Force was moving, enabling him to withdraw his Guns if hard pressed,—broken ground with numerous ravines and nullahs covered his whole front, affording excellent cover to a swarm of skirmishers, who not only knew their value, but most skilfully availed themselves of them, whilst every desired movement on my part on the Enemy's flanks was impeded by ground most difficult for the combined operations of Artillery and Cavalry.

The Enemy, six thousand in number, with three thousand in reserve, were under the personal Command of the Nawab, and principally composed of Mutineers of the three arms, the Infantry with percussion muskets. Videttes on our flanks and front watched our advance, and a near approach to reconnoitre disclosed the Enemy's position, from which a sharp fire of Artillery was opened.

An advanced party under Colonel Apthorp, K.F.S., 3rd Madras Europeans, first encountered their Infantry, and soon found themselves under a heavy fire; every nullah was vigorously disputed, and the judgment and decision with which that Officer conducted his movements, thus avoiding much severe loss, called forth my highest commendations.

It now became necessary to dislodge a Battery on our right flank, which would have swept through our skirmishers, had they further advanced, and no men ever charged more nobly than the Squadron of the 2nd Hydrabad Contingent Cavalry, under their gallant leader Captain Macintire; one Gun was captured, the other in the *melée* escaped for a time, but the object was effected.

The main body of my Force had now come up and I directed its movement to the left, thus co-operating with the Advanced Guard which was hardly pressed. A flanking fire soon relieved them, and the desperate resistance and continued struggle of the Enemy to maintain his ground led to many a hand-to-hand conflict, where the bayonet did great execution.

By the most persevering efforts my Artillery and Cavalry flank[ed] the Enemy, causing heavy loss and capturing 3 Guns, and the gallantry of Her Majesty's 12th Lancers and the Rissalah were most conspicuous on these occasions.

The Horse Artillery and Horse Battery did their work with an alacrity, spirit and precision of fire not to be surpassed, and each man of the Native Troop vied with the European Soldier in his vigorous pursuit of the Enemy.

The 18-Pounders, served by the Royal Artillery, made some excellent practice; it was work of much labor to bring them into position, but it was cheerfully and well executed by Officers and men.

Although the Enemy now began to retire, it was four hours before the firing ceased; they fell back occupying every available ground for opposition and our Guns were in constant employment to dislodge them.

The Nawab at length fled, leaving on the field (from information I have since received), more than a thousand of his Men, eight hundred of whom were amongst the killed; several Men of note were slain, and within a few hours many notorious vagabonds have been hanged.

A Fort commanding the Ford was reported to be occupied by the Enemy, and it was necessary to bring up some heavy Guns previous to advancing; this retarded our movement and enabled the Enemy to cross the river and get so far ahead as to escape further pursuit.

A flag of truce now approached; it was borne by some of the principal inhabitants of the City, who informed me the Nawab had fled, the Town evacuated, and the Mutineers had set fire to their lines. So great indeed was the panic and so sudden, that on occupying the Palace, we found food preparing for the Nawab.

My Troops are now in possession of the Palace and Town, 13 large brass Guns, besides several of small Calibre, a large quantity of Ammunition, much valuable property belonging to the Nawab, some 40,000 Rupees in specie, four Elephants, fifty Camels with other Cattle, and about two thousand Rupees' worth of grain of sorts.

The British Flag was hoisted under a general salute in the presence of the Troops, and the Commissioner is busily employed in establishing order.

The contest was a lengthened one, but Europeans and Natives fought well and manfully against their disciplined Enemy, and merit my warmest praise for their conduct.

It was the first time the 3rd Madras European Regiment were under fire. I noticed their steadiness and good discipline with pride, as well as the gallantry of the Hydrabad Company, who charged and with great slaughter, drove a large party from their stronghold.

Our own loss is extraordinarily small, considering the fire to which the Troops were so long exposed. Amongst the killed I have to lament a promising young Officer, Lieutenant Colbeck, of the 3rd Europeans.

I beg to attach copies of the Reports from Brigadier Miller, Commanding the Artillery, and Major Oakes, Commanding the Cavalry Brigade, and it is most gratifying to me to add my testimony to the distinguished gallantry of those Officers whose names they have brought to notice, and the dashing style in which they led their Guns and Troops into action.

Brigadier Miller, a most able and energetic Officer, disposed of his Artillery with a skill and intelligence most praiseworthy, and I cordially thank him. I regret to add he was severely wounded, and that I am thereby deprived for a time of his valuable services. Major Lavie assumed Command, and I have special satisfaction in recording the steadiness and intelligence with which he conducted his important duties.

Major Oakes displayed the zeal and activity of an excellent Cavalry Officer throughout the day.

Brigadier Carpenter brought his Infantry into action with a steady precision with which I was perfectly satisfied.

Colonel Apthorp's management of the Troops placed at his disposal was what I expected from an Officer of his high character. I beg to annex his Report.

It is a pleasing duty to bring to the special notice of His Excellency the Commander-in-Chief a favor which I beg to solicit at your hands, the name of Captain Macintire, of the Madras Artillery, Commanding a Squadron of the 2nd Hydrabad Contingent Cavalry, always distinguished for his zeal, a Soldier's spirit, and a judgment well fitting him for his Command; his charge on the Enemy's Guns (I had no Infantry at hand for that purpose), was the admiration of all who witnessed the affair, and his Men followed their leader with an order with which his high bearing has inspired them, and I cannot express myself in too high terms of their spirit and their gallantry. Lieutenant Ryall, the Adjutant of the Regiment, accompanied the Troop on its attack, and, with his Commanding Officer, cut down several of the Enemy in hand-to-hand combat.

I received much assistance from my Assistant Adjutant-General, Major R. Hamilton, an able, intelligent and worthy Officer, as well as from my Assistant Quarter-Master General, Captain Lawder: both were by my side during the whole of the action; also Major Mayne, Deputy Judge Advocate General to the Force.

Lieutenant Homan, 50th Regiment Native Infantry, my Aide-de-Camp, was very useful to me.

Major Brett, 3rd Madras European Regiment, an experienced and able Officer, who was attached as Orderly Officer to me during the day, was very active in carrying my orders.

The Officers of the Engineers' Department were with me on the Field, and Major Ludlow, Field Engineer, received the flag of truce.

The Commissariat Department under Lieutenant Barrow, has been admirably conducted for the many months the Force has been marching, and from the excellent system of this able Officer, the Troops were furnished without delay with all their customary supplies at the conclusion of the contest.

I am very much indebted to Major Barrow, Commissary of Ordnance, whose duties have been most arduous, but who has performed them with the utmost efficiency; he was with me throughout the day, and of much service to me.

To Major Abbot, of the Bengal Infantry, who, with the Troops of the Chirkarree Rajah, protected my baggage and a lengthened Siege Train, and brought all safely into Camp, my best thanks are due.

The arrangements of the Medical Department were excellent, and my thanks are due to Superintending Surgeon Davidson, and Field Surgeon Macfarlane.

I enclose a List of Killed and Wounded.

From Colonel E. APTHORP, *Commanding 3rd Madras European Regiment*, To Major-General WHITLOCK, *Commanding Saugor Division,—dated Camp, Banda, the 20th April 1858.*

I beg leave prominently to bring to your notice the gallant conduct of Captain Macintire, and his Squadron of Hydrabad Cavalry, which formed part of the Advanced Guard I had the honor to command in the action which took place yesterday morning.

On approaching within six hundred yards of the Enemy's position, I formed my Troops into line, and placed Captain Macintire's Rissallah on the right. After advancing a short distance, I found that one or two of the Enemy's Guns were posted so as to enfilade the Infantry as they advanced. I therefore ordered Captain Macintire to charge the Guns, which was done in most gallant style. The ground to be got over was most difficult for Cavalry, being intersected with deep nallahs filled with the Enemy's Infantry.

I consider this charge enabled the Infantry to reach the Enemy, who were at least 6,000 strong, with comparatively trifling loss.

The whole of the Guard behaved with the greatest gallantry on this occasion.

From Brigadier W. H. MILLER, *Commanding Artillery Brigade, Saugor Field Force*, To the Assistant Adjutant General, *Saugor Field Division,— No. 50, dated Camp Banda, the 20th April 1858.*

I have the honor to forward herewith a Return of Casualties in the Artillery Brigade under my Command, at the battle of Banda yesterday.

2. It will be observed that these are providentially very small, a subject both of astonishment and congratulation, considering the length of time we were under fire, and the obstinate resistance of the Enemy, whilst defending their first position, where their Artillery was chiefly brought into play against us, and which was both well and rapidly served, although, fortunately for us, their range was generally short, probably owing to the inferiority of their powder.

3. It is a source of no slight gratification to me to bring particularly to the Major-General's notice the admirable conduct of the whole of the Native portion of the Artillery, affording as it did the most ample proof of their attachment to the service, and fidelity to the State. Nothing could be finer than the way in which the Native Troop of Horse Artillery, under Major Brice, emulated the cheerfulness, alacrity and cool courage of the[ir] gallant comrades of the European Troop under Major Mein.

4. It is not very often, I believe, that opportunities offer to Artillerymen of distinguishing themselves in any line other than their own, but some such having presented themselves yesterday, were eagerly laid hold of by Officers and Men. Major Lavie cut down one Gunner, and disarmed another flying from one of the Enemy's Guns taken; Major

Barrow and Lieutenant Hennegan, gallantly supported by Lieutenant Blunt, of Her Majesty's 12th Royal Lancers with a few of his Men, captured another Gun; Serjeant-Major Dinwiddie, F. Troop, and Serjeant Alford, D. Troop Horse Artillery (my Orderly Serjeant), cut down several of the Enemy during the action; and the Major-General himself, I believe, witnessed the daring manner in which a Gunner of the A. Troop Horse Artillery (Michael Carroll, General No. 4054), went in on a Mutineer, who was fighting with the resolution of despair, and had for some time kept several Men, both Europeans and Natives, at bay.

5. I cannot help wishing that Captain Palmer's fine Company of the Royal Artillery had had more opportunity of distinguishing themselves, but the effect on the Enemy of the fire they did open from the 18-Pounders and 8-inch Howitzers, was most marked and did them much credit.

6. The conduct during the action of every Officer and Man under my order, merits my unqualified approval and highest admiration; but I would beg leave to bring more prominently to the favorable notice of Major-General Whitlock, the names of the following Officers, *viz.*:— Major Lavie, Commanding Madras Artillery Division; Major Brice, Commanding F. Troop, and Major Mein, Commanding A. Troop, Madras Horse Artillery; Captain Palmer, Commanding Royal Artillery; Lieutenant Pope, Commanding No. 1 Madras Horse Field Battery; Brevet-Captain Holmes and Lieutenant Hennegan, Commanding Detachments of their respective Troops of Horse Artillery with the advance; Major Barrow, Commissary of Ordnance, and Brevet-Captain Harrison, acting as my Brigade Major, for that excellent Officer Captain Gosling unfortunately laid up at present with small-pox.

7. The zeal, kindness and attention of the different Medical Officers of the Brigade, Doctor Macfarlane, Field Surgeon, Assistant Surgeons Allen and Dunman, of the Madras Horse Artillery, and Assistant Surgeon Webb, of the Royal Artillery, were most conspicuous, and as such well deserve especial mention being made of them.

From Major T. OAKES, *Commanding Cavalry Brigade, Saugor Field Division*, To the Assistant Adjutant-General, *Saugor and Nerbadda Field Force*,—*No. 7, dated Camp Bandah, the 20th April 1858.*

I have the honor to inform you, for the information of the Major-General Commanding the Division, that the Rissallah and a Troop of the 12th Lancers were detached with the Advanced Guard, the remainder of the Brigade forming the main column, when the Enemy's Artillery opened fire, (after crossing the dry bed of a river) I advanced the remainder of the Lancers in Column of Troops, when I saw the Rissallah charging the left flank of the Enemy's position. Owing to the bad ground, which was greatly intersected by deep nullahs, the Lancers had to cross in single files, the Rissallah having been temporarily checked by an unexpected fire of grape and musketry from a nullah 20 yards off; before I could bring the Lancers up to support them, they suffered severely. I immediately formed line, and charged the Enemy, who did not stand, but dispersed all over the country. The Lancers followed them up for about four miles to the river Kane, cutting up about three hundred of them. I then deemed it advisable to re-assemble them, and bring them back to the main column. The Troop of Lancers attached to the Advanced Guard, charged the Enemy's right flank and took a Gun.

When we advanced upon the Enemy's second position, I detached a Troop of Lancers to protect the Artillery on our left flank, and a Troop of the Rissallah, the Artillery on the right flank. When the heights were gained, the 12th Lancers advanced, and took a large brass Gun pursuing the Enemy, who were in full retreat, (here Brigadier Miller was cut down, whose life was saved by Private Thomas Elliss, 12th Lancers, who speared the Rebel). The retreat of the Enemy was covered by some heavy Guns on the left of the Fort.

I then, in concert with the Officer Commanding the European Horse Artillery (the fire of the Enemy being very heavy, and our Guns not being able to tell upon them), deemed it advisable to retire out of range and wait until the heavy Guns and main column came up.

I beg to bring to the favourable notice of the Major-General, Captain Prior, Commanding the 12th Lancers, and Captain Macintire, Commanding the 2nd Hyderabad Irregular Horse who gave me every assistance by strictly carrying out my orders: also my Brigade Major, Lieutenant Roe, 12th Lancers, who afforded me every help in conveying orders with rapidity.

A Nominal Roll of Killed and Wounded is transmitted herewith.

General Return of Killed and Wounded in the Saugor Field Division, under Command of Major-General G. C. WHITLOCK, Commanding Saugor Field Division, on the 19th April 1858.

CORPS.	KILLED. Field Officers.	Captains.	Subalterns.	Native Officers.	Troop Serjt.-Major.	Serjeants.	Trumpeters, Drummers.	Rank and File.	Total.	Eur. Officers' Chargers.	N. Officers' Chargers.	Troop Horses.	WOUNDED. Field Officers.	Captains.	Subalterns.	Native Officers.	Troop Serjt.-Major.	Serjeants.	Trumpeters, Drummers.	Rank and File.	Total.	Eur. Officers' Chargers.	N. Officers' Chargers.	Troop Horses.	Troop Horses Missing.	REMARKS.
Staff	...	...	...	...	...	...	...	...	...	...	...	1	...	...	...	...	...	...	...	...	...	...	...	...	...	
A. Troop Horse Artillery	...	...	...	...	...	...	...	...	...	...	...	...	...	...	...	...	...	...	...	...	...	1	1	...	...	
F. Troop Horse Artillery	...	...	...	...	...	...	...	...	...	...	...	...	...	...	...	...	...	...	...	...	...	1	1	...	...	
No. 1 Horse Battery																										
Royal Artillery																										
Detachment Madras Foot Artillery																										
Left Wing H. M.'s 12th Lancers.	...	...	...	...	...	...	...	1	...	...	...	...	)	...	1	1	1	3	7	...	...	8	1			*3 of the wounded since dead.
Squadron Hyderabad Contingent Cavalry.	...	...	1	...	...	3	4	...	1	4	...	...	1	1	...	2	...	11	15	1	...	6	...			
Detachment Sappers and Miners.																										
3rd Madras European Regiment.	...	...	...	...	...	1	1	...	...	...	...	...	1	...	...	...	1	2	4	...	...					
1st Regt. Madras N. I.	...	...	...	...	...	...	...	...	...	...	...	...	...	...	...	...	...	1	1	...	...					
Detachment 50th Regt. N I.																										
TOTAL	...	...	1	...	...	4	5	1	1	4	...	3	1	3	2	19	29	1	...	9	1					

(Sd.) R. HAMILTON, *Major*,   (Sd.) G. C. WHITLOCK, *Maj.-Genl.*
Assist. Adjt.-Genl., Saugor   *Commanding Saugor*
Field Division.   *Field Division.*

CAMP BANDA,
The 20th April 1858.

From Major-General G. C. WHITLOCK, *Commanding Saugor Field Division*, To Major-General J. MANSFIELD, *Chief of the Staff, Bengal,—No. 135, dated Camp Banda, the 30th April 1858.*

I much regret I omitted to mention, in my Despatch of the 24th Instant, the name of the Political Agent for Bundlecund, Major Ellis, who accompanied the Force from Punnah, and his services have been most useful to me; he was on the Field during the action of the 19th Instant, and it was through his valuable intelligence, I became acquainted with the position of the Rebels.

Allahabad, the 31st May 1858.

No. 174 of 1858.—The Right Hon'ble the Governor General of India is pleased to direct the publication of the following Despatch from the Deputy Adjutant-General of the Army, No. 342 A, dated 23rd May 1858, forwarding a communication from Major-General Sir Hugh Rose, K.C.B., Commanding Central India Field Force, detailing his operations against, and the capture of the fortress and town of Jhansie.

His Lordship entirely concurs with the Commander-in-Chief in the satisfaction His Excellency has expressed at the manner in which this fortress has been captured by Major-General Sir Hugh Rose, and in His Excellency's high estimation of the services of the Major-General, and of the Officers and men under his Command.

From Major H. W. NORMAN, *Deputy Adjutant-General of the Army*, To the Secretary to the Government of India, *Military Department, with the Governor General,—No. 342A, dated Head-Quarters Camp, Shahjehanpore, the 23rd May 1858.*

I have the honor, by direction of the Commander-in-Chief, to enclose, for submission to the Right Honourable the Governor General, copy of a Despatch, dated the 30th Ultimo, from Major-General Sir H. Rose, K.C.B., Commanding Central India Field Force, detailing the operations of the Troops under his Command, against the fortress and town of Jhansie.

Forwards Major-General Sir H. Rose's Despatch on the capture of the fortress and town of Jhansie.

2. His Excellency desires to express his cordial satisfaction with the manner in which the capture of this important place was effected, and his perfect appreciation of the services of Sir H. Rose, and those under his Command, and he begs to recommend all to the favorable consideration of His Lordship, especially those who have been more prominently mentioned by the Major-General.

From *Major General* SIR HUGH ROSE, K.C.B., *Commanding Central India Field Force, to the Chief of the Staff,—dated Camp Mote, the 30th April 1858.*

I have the honor to report to you, for the information of His Excellency the Commander-in-Chief, the operations of my Force against the fortress and fortified city of Jhansie.

On the 20th Ultimo, the 2nd Brigade under my Command arrived at Simra, one day's march from Jhansie. My 1st Brigade had not yet joined me from Chandeerie.

The same day I sent Brigadier Stewart, with the Cavalry and Artillery noted in the margin, to invest Jhansie.

Horse Artillery, 6 Guns.
325 Rank and File.
14th Light Dragoons.
140 Rank and File.
3rd Light Cavalry.
476 Sabres, Hyderabad Cavalry.

The 20th Ultimo was the day which, when at Saugor, I had named for my arrival before Jhansie. I should have reached it some days sooner, only for the delay occasioned by my waiting to see whether the 2nd Brigade would be required to assist in taking Chandeerie. I arrived the following day, the 21st Ultimo, with the remainder of my Brigade before Jhansie.

The picquets of the Cavalry sent on the day before had sabred about 100 armed Men, Bundeelas, endeavouring to enter Jhansie, having been summoned by the Ranee to defend it.

Having no plan, or even correct description of the fortress and city, I had, together with the Officers Commanding the Artillery and Engineers, to make long and repeated reconnoissances, in order to ascertain the Enemy's defences; this delayed, for some days, the commencement of the siege operations.

The great strength of the Fort, natural as well as artificial, and its extent, entitles it to a place amongst fortresses. It stands on an elevated rock, rising out of a plain, and commands the city, and surrounding country; it is built of excellent and most massive masonry. The Fort is difficult to breach, because, composed of granite, its walls vary in thickness from sixteen to twenty feet.

The Fort has extensive and elaborate outworks of the same solid construction, with front and flanking embrasures for Artillery fire, and loop-holes, of which, in some places, there were five tiers, for musketry. Guns placed on the high towers of the Fort commanded the country all around.

One tower called the "white turret" had been raised lately in height by the Rebels, and armed with heavy ordnance.

The fortress is surrounded by the city of Jhansie on all sides, except the West and part of the South face.

The steepness of the rock protects the West, the fortified city wall with bastions springing from the centre of its South face, running South, and ending in a high mound or mamelon, protects by a flanking fire its

South face. The mound was fortified by a strong circular bastion for 5 Guns, round part of which was drawn a ditch 12 feet deep and 15 feet broad of solid masonry. Quantities of men were always at work in the mound.

The city of Jhansie is about 4½ miles in circumference, and is surrounded by a fortified and massive wall, from 6 to 12 feet thick, and varying in height from 18 to 30 feet, with numerous flanking bastions armed as batteries with ordnance, and loop-holes, with a banquette for Infantry.

Outside the walls, the city is girt with wood, except some parts of the East and South fronts: on the former is a picturesque lake and water palace; to the South are the ruined Cantonments and residences of the English. Temples with their gardens,—one the Jokun Bagh, the scene of the massacre of our lamented country-men—and two rocky ridges, the Eastmost called "Kapoo Tekri," both important positions, facing and threatening the South face of the city wall and Fort.

I established seven flying Camps of Cavalry, as an investing Force round Jhansie, giving to Major Scudamore half a Troop of Horse Artillery, and later to Major Gall two 9-Pounders. These Camps detached to the front outposts and videttes, which watched and prevented all issue from the city, day and night; each Camp, on any attempt being made to force its line, was to call on the others for help. I gave directions also that the road from the city should be obstructed by trenches and abattis.

The attack of Jhansie offered serious difficulties. There were no means of breaching the Fort, except from the South, but the South was flanked by the fortified City wall and mound just described.

The rocky ridge was excellent for a breaching battery, except that it was too far off, 640 yards, and that the fire from it would have been oblique.

The mound enfiladed two walls of the city, and commanded the whole of the South quarter of it, including the Palace.

It was evident that the capture of the mound was the first most important operation, because its occupation ensured, in all probability, that of the South of the city, and of the Palace, affording also the means of constructing, by approaches, an advanced breaching battery.

The desideratum, therefore, was to concentrate a heavy fire on the mound, and on the South of the City, in order to drive the Enemy out of them, and facilitate their capture, to breach the wall close to the mound, and to dismantle the Enemy's defences which protected the mound and opposed an attack. This was effected—Firstly, by occupying and placing batteries on a rocky knoll, the right attack, which I had found in my reconnoissance to the south of the Lake opposite the Aorcha gate and South-east wall of the town, which took in reverse the mound, and two walls running from it; Secondly, on the rocky ridge the left attack.

These batteries could not be completed till the arrival of the 1st. Brigade with its siege Guns on the 25th Ultimo.

In the meantime, the right attack opened fire, from an 8-inch Howitzer, and two 8-inch Mortars, on the rear of the mound and the South of the City, with the exception of the Palace, which I wished to preserve for the use of the Troops.

A remarkable feature in the defence was, that the Enemy had no works or posts outside the City. Sir Robert Hamilton estimated the number of the Garrison at 10,000 Bundeelas and velaities,* and 1,500 Sepoys, of whom 400 were Cavalry, and the number of Guns in the City and Fort, at 30 or 40.

The fire of the right attack on the first day of the opening of the fire, the 28th Ultimo, cleared the mound of the workmen and the Enemy. The mortars, in consequence of information I had received, shelled and set on fire long rows of hay-ricks in the South of the City, which created an almost general conflagration in that quarter.

The Enemy had been firing actively from the white turret, the tree tower battery in the Fort, and the wheel tower, Saugor and Lutchmen-gate batteries in the town. About mid day their fire ceased almost completely, but re-commenced the next day with increased vigour.

The Chief of the Rebel Artillery was a first-rate Artillery-man; he had under him two Companies of Golundauze. The manner in which the Rebels served their Guns, repaired their defences, and re-opened fire from batteries and Guns repeatedly shut up, was remarkable. From some batteries they returned shot for shot. The women were seen working in the batteries and carrying ammunition. The garden battery was fought under the black flag of the Fakeers.

Everything indicated a general and determined resistance; this was not surprizing, as the inhabitants, from the Ranee downwards, were,

---

* Bundeelas, Natives of Bundelkhand. Velaities are Afghans or any people from the North, such as Persians, etc., etc.

more or less, concerned in the murder and plunder of the English. There was hardly a house in Jhansie which did not contain some article of English plunder, and, politically speaking, the Rebel confederacy knew well that if Jhansie, the richest Hindoo city, and most important fortress in Central India, fell, the cause of the insurgents in this part of India fell also.

To silence the City wall batteries to the South, and cannonade more effectually the town, two 24-Pounder Guns were placed in battery between the 8-inch Howitzer and the two 8-inch Mortars, and opened fire on the 25th Ultimo. They produced a good effect, but not to the extent of silencing the town batteries. Unfortunately on this day the 8-inch Howitzer was disabled by the breaking of its trunnion.

On the 24th Ultimo, I caused the rocky ridge, the left attack, to be occupied by a strong picquet under Captain Hare, with two 5½-inch Mortars, which played on the mound and the houses adjacent to it.

On the 25th Ultimo the Siege Train of the 1st Brigade having arrived, batteries were constructed and opened fire, from the 26th to the 29th Ultimo, on the rocky ridge, as follows, forming the left attack.

Two 18-Pounders to dismantle the defences of the Fort.

Two 10-inch Mortars to destroy the Fort.

Two 8-inch Mortars and one 8-inch Howitzer to act on the mound and adjacent wall and City.

One 18-Pounder to breach the wall near the bastion of the mound, which was thus exposed to a vertical and horizontal fire on its right face and left rear, the 18-Pounders were changed from travelling to garrison carriages.

In order to prevent delay and confusion, I gave names to all the Enemy's batteries in the town, as well as in the Fort; they were 13 in number.

The fire of the two 18-Pounders was so efficient, that towards sunset the parapets of the white turret, the black tower, and the tree tower, which faced our attack, were nearly destroyed.

The two 10-inch Mortars created great havoc in the Fort, and having pointed out to Lieutenant Pettman, Bombay Horse Artillery, the position of a powder magazine respecting which I had information, he blew it up in the third shot, keeping up a well directed fire on the Fort, for which good service I beg to recommend him to His Excellency.

The breaching Gun, so solid was the wall, and so hard the masonry, did not produce the result contemplated on the first or even on the second day, but on the 30th the breach was practicable. The Enemy retrenched the breach with a double row of palisades filled with earth, on which I ordered every description of fire, including red-hot shot, to be directed upon it, and the result was a considerable portion of the stockade was destroyed by fire.

Riflemen to fire at the parapets and the embrasures, and loop-holes were placed in all the batteries, with sand-bag loop-holes, and posts of Riflemen were distributed in the temples and garden of the East and South sides of the city. I occupied also the Jokun Bagh nearly opposite the mound with a picquet of Rifles. The Riflemen caused numerous casualties amongst the Rebels in the town as well as in the parapets.

Two of the Enemy's defences, which annoyed the left attack the most, were the wheel tower on the South, and the garden battery on a rock in rear of the West wall of the city. To silence the former, a new battery, called the Kahoo Tehree or East battery, was established on a ridge to the East of the rocky ridge, with two $5\frac{1}{2}$-inch Mortars, which not proving sufficient, I substituted for them two 8-inch Mortars and a 9-Pounder. I afterwards added a 24-Pounder Howitzer to enfilade the wall running Eastwards from the mound.

Before the sand-bag battery could be made for the 9-Pounder, acting Bombardier Brenna, of Captain Ommaney's Company, Royal Artillery, quite a lad, commanded and pointed the 9-Pounder in the open, and silenced the Enemy's Gun in battery in the bastion, destroying besides its defences. I praised him for his good service on the ground, and promoted him.

The two 8-inch Mortars, and occasionally the two 10-inch Mortars of the left attack, answered the garden battery, shelling also the Nia Bustie, and five wells where the Sepoys had taken up their quarters on account of the good water.

After the capture of Jhansie we had proof of havoc caused by the shelling and cannonade in the Fort and city. Beside the damage done to the houses and buildings, the Rebels acknowledge to have lost from sixty to seventy men a day killed.

Our batteries had by the 30th dismantled the defences of the Fort and city, or disabled their Guns. It is true that the Rebels had made on the white turret an excellent parapet of large sand-bags, which they kept always wet, and still ran up fresh in lieu of disabled Guns: but their best Guns had been disabled, and their best Artillery-men killed; their fire was therefore no longer serious. However, the obstinate defence of the Enemy, the breach, and the extent fired on, had caused a great consumption of ammunition, so much so, that it was evident there would not be sufficient to multiply breaches in the town wall, or to establish a main breach in the South double wall of the Fort.

Under these circumstances, the Officer Commanding the Artillery and Engineers, called to my notice the necessity of having recourse to escalade, to which I gave my consent, requiring however that the breach should form an important and principal point of attack. Both of these Officers entertained a mistrust of the breach, thinking that it was mined, or not practicable.

Knowing the risk which generally attends escalades, I had recourse to every means in my power for facilitating an entry by the breach. In order to widen it, and destroy still more effectually the retrenchment and stockade which the Enemy had constructed in rear of the breach, I kept up a fire day and night on it from the 18-Pounder, and the 8-inch Howitzer, and with the view to prevent the Enemy working, and to render the mound too hot for them, I shelled it and the adjoining houses day and night from the Mortar batteries in the centre and left attacks. Lieutenant Strutt, Bombay Artillery, made excellent practice, throwing the shells on the spots occupied by the guards of the city walls.

I had made arrangements on the 30th for storming, but the general action on the 1st Instant, with the so called Army of the Peshwa, which advanced across the Betwa to relieve it, caused the assault to be deferred.

With the view to acquire rapid information respecting the Enemy's movements, I established a telegraph on a hill commanding Jhansie and the surrounding country. It was of great use, telegraphing the Ranee's flight, the approach of the Enemy from the Betwa, etc.

On the 2nd instant, Major Boileau reported to me that he had made all the necessary preparations for the escalade, and that a 24-Pounder Howitzer had been placed in battery in front of the Jokun Bagh for the purpose of enfilading, and clearing during the night the wall from the mound to the Fort, and the rocket bastion which is on it.

I issued a division order for the assault of the defences of the city wall, of which a copy, with a plan of attack, was furnished to the Officers in Command.

I have the honor to enclose copies of reports from Brigadier Stuart, Commanding my 1st Brigade, and Brigadier Steuart, Commanding my

2nd Brigade, of the operations of their respective Columns against Jhansie.

The left attack, ably and gallantly conducted by Brigadier Stuart, succeeded perfectly, its right Column passing without loss or difficulty through the breach, which turned out as well as I thought it would, and the left effecting, with some casualties, the escalade of the rocket bastion. Colonel Louth, Commanding Her Majesty's 86th Regiment, acted with cool judgment, and I witnessed with lively pleasure the devotion and gallantry of his Regiment.

The 3rd Europeans, under Lieutenant-Colonel Liddell, did their duty, as they always have done; but they could not control adverse circumstances, arising from bad ladders, and a mistake in the road, they returned to the assault with alacrity, and fought their way through the town manfully.

I beg leave to support earnestly the recommendations of Officers contained in these Reports of the Brigadiers, particularly of Captain Darby, wounded, Lieutenant Dartnell, severely wounded in three places, who led the assault of the rocket bastion, and Lieutenant Fox, severely wounded. It will be a gratification also to the relatives of Lieutenants Micklejohn and Dick, of the Bombay Engineers, to know that these two young Officers had gained my esteem by the intelligence and coolness which they evinced as Engineer Officers during the siege. I should have recommended both for promotion, if they had not died in their country's cause, for conspicuous gallantry in leading the way up two scaling ladders.

The 86th on the road to the Palace from the mound sustained many casualties from their left flank being exposed, as they passed through an open space, to a flanking musketry fire from an outwork of the Fort, and from houses, and the Palace itself to their front. I directed loopholes for Riflemen to be made through houses which brought a fire to bear on the outwork of the Fort, a large house to be occupied close to the Palace, and covered communication to be made to the mound.

The skirmishers of the Regiment penetrated gallantly into the Palace. The few men who still held it made an obstinate resistance, setting fire to trains of Gun-powder, from which several of the 86th received fatal injuries.

Having received no reports from the right attack, composed of the 3rd Europeans and Hyderabad Contingent, I made my way to them in the South-east quarter of the City. I found them engaged with the

Enemy, and making their way to the Palace; the Rebels were firing at them from the houses, which the Troops were breaking open, and clearing of their defenders.

I found Lieutenant-Colonel Turnbull, Commanding the Artillery here, wounded mortally, I deeply regret to say, by a musket shot from a house.

He had followed me through the breach into the streets, and having received directions from me to bring Guns into the city to batter houses in which Rebels held out, he had gone round by the right to the East quarter of the City to fix the road by which they were to enter. The Auba gate was the best for Guns, but it was so barricaded by masses of stones, that it could not be opened for several hours.

In the despatches I have recorded the excellent service performed by Lieutenant-Colonel Turnbull, particularly in the general action of the Betwa, always exposing himself to the fire of the Enemy in order to choose the best positions for his Guns. This devoted Officer was as useful to me as Commandant of Artillery as Captain of a Troop of Horse Artillery.

His premature fall prevented his receiving the reward which was his due. I can now only earnestly recommend that his numerous family may inherit their father's claims on his country.

The right and left attacks being now concentrated in the Palace, I gained possession of a large portion of the City by advancing the 3rd Europeans to the North-East, and occupying the Burrahgong-gate, on which I rested their right flank, forming an oblique line from the gate to the Palace with the 3rd Europeans and the 86th in the Palace. The two Regiments occupying with picquets commanding houses to their front. This line was a prolongation of the second line leading from the mound under the front to the Palace. This done, it was necessary to clear the large portion of the City in rear of this oblique line of the numerous armed Rebels who remained in the houses, and who were firing on the Troops. This was not effected without bloody, often hand-to-hand, combats; one of the most remarkable of them was between detachments of Her Majesty's 85th Regiment and 3rd Europeans, and thirty or forty Velaitie Sowars, the body-guard of the Ranee in the Palace Stables under the fire of the Fort. The Sowars, full of Opium, defended their Stables, firing with matchlocks and pistols from the windows and loop-holes, and cutting with their tulwars, and from behind the doors. When driven in they retreated behind their houses, still firing or fighting with their swords in both hands till they were shot or bayoneted struggling even when dying on the ground to strike again. A party of them remained in a room off the stables which was on fire till they were half burnt; their clothes in flames, they rushed out hacking at their assailants, and guarding their heads with their shields.

Captain Rose, my Aide-de-Camp, saved the life of a man of the 86th, who was down, by bayoneting his assailant.

All the Sowars were killed, but not without several casualties on our side. The gallant Soldiers captured in the quarters of the Sowars the Ranee's standards, three standards of the body-guard, three kettle-drums and horses, and an English Union Jack of silk, which Sir Robert Hamilton tells me Lord William Bentinck had given the grandfather of the husband of the Ranee, with the permission to have it carried before him as a reward for his fidelity, a privilege granted to no other Indian Prince. I granted the Soldiers their request to hoist on the Palace the flag of their country which they had so bravely won. Captain Sandwith, who was wounded, commanded with spirit the Europeans on this occasion, and Serjeant Brown, of the Commissariat Department, was the first to dash boldly into the stables.

Numerous incidents marked the desperate feeling which animated the defenders. A retainer of the Ranee tried to blow up himself and his wife; failing in the attempt, he endeavoured to cut her to pieces and then killed himself. Two Vilaities, attacked by the videttes, threw a woman who was with them into a well, and then jumped down it themselves.

Whilst engaged in the town, I received a report from the Officer Commanding one of the Hyderabad Cavalry Flying Camps, that a large body of the Enemy, flying from the town, had tried to force his picquet; that a few had succeeded, but that the main body from 350 to 500 strong, had been driven back, and had occupied a high and rocky hill to the west of the Fort; that he had surrounded the hill with Cavalry till reinforcements were sent. I immediately ordered out from the Camps of the two Brigades, the available Troops of all arms against the Hill. The enclosed Report from Major Gall shows how satisfactorily these Rebels were disposed of. Lieutenant Park was killed whilst gallantly leading on a party of the 24th Bombay Native Infantry along the ridge of the hill. The Ranee's father, Mamoo Sahib, was amongst the Rebels; he was wounded on the hill, and captured some days afterwards and hanged at the Jokun Bagh.

After having cleared the quarter of the town in our possession o the Enemy, I had intended attacking the remainder of it, but deferred doing so till the next day on Brigadier Steuart's representation that the men were too much exhausted for any further operations that day.

Towards sunset it was telegraphed from the observatory that the Enemy were approaching from the East. I had therefore to re-occupy with all the force I could collect the field of action of the Betwa, the devoted Troops marching to a fresh combat after thirteen hours' fighting in a burning sun with as much spirit as if they had not been engaged at all.

The alarm proved to be a false one, Troops from Tehree having been mistaken for the Enemy.

The next day Brigadier Stuart and myself occupied the rest of the City by a combined movement, assisted by Major Gall, who spiritedly scaled the bastion at the Onow-gate from his Flying Camp, and capturing the Gun that was there, threw it down the rampart.

The following morning, a wounded Mahratta retainer of the Ranee was sent in to me from Captain Abbott's Flying Camp. He stated that the Ranee, accompanied by 300 Vilaities and 25 Sowars, fled that night from the Fort; that after leaving it, they had been headed back by one of the picquets where the Ranee and her party separated, she herself taking to the right with a few Sowars in the direction of her intended flight to Bandiri. The observatory also telegraphed "Enemy escaping to the North-East." I immediately sent off strong detachments of Her Majesty's 14th Light Dragoons, 3rd Light Cavalry and Hyderabad Cavalry to pursue, with Guns to support them, as it was said that Tantia Topee had sent a Force to meet her. I also sent Brigadier Steuart, with Cavalry, to watch the forts of the Betwa.

In the meantime detachments of the 86th and 3rd Europeans took possession of the fortress.

In sight of Bandiri, 21 miles from Jhansie, the Cavalry came in sight of the Irregular Horse, sent to meet the Ranee, which separated probably with the view to mislead her pursuers as to her real course. Lieutenant Dowker, Hyderabad Cavalry, was sent by Captain Forbes through the town of Bandiri, whilst he with the 3rd Light Cavalry and 14th Light Dragoons, passed it by the left. In the town, Lieutenant Dowker saw traces of the Ranee's hasty flight, and her tent in which was an unfinished breakfast; on the other side of the town he came up with and cut up forty of the Enemy consisting of Rohillas and Bengal Irregular Cavalry. Lieutenant Dowker was gaining fast on the Ranee, who with four attendants, was seen escaping on a grey horse, when he was dismounted by a severe wound, and obliged to give up the pursuit.

From the time the troops took the Palace, the Rebels lost heart and began to leave the town and fort. Nothing could prove more the efficiency of the investment than the number of them cut up by the picquets of the Flying Camps; the woods, gardens and roads round the towns were strewed with the corpses of fugitive Rebels. The Ranee's flight was the signal for a general retreat. Early in the morning, I caused the outskirts of the City to be scoured with Cavalry and Infantry; it will give some idea of the destruction of insurgents which ensued when a party of the 14th Dragoons alone killed two hundred in one patrol. The Rebels, who were chiefly Vilaities and Pathans, generally sold their lives as dearly as they could, fighting to the last with their usual dexterity and firmness. A band of 40 of these desperadoes barricaded themselves in a spacious house with a court yard, vaults, etc.; before they were aware of its strength, it was attacked by a detachment of Hyderabad Infantry under Captain Hare, with the loss of Captain Sinclair, of whose conduct it is my duty again to make honorable mention. Reinforcements and several pieces of siege Artillery were brought up by Major Orr, who commanded the attack against the house, but even when it had been breached and knocked to pieces, the Rebels continued to resist in the ruined passages and vaults. They were all as usual destroyed, but not without several casualties on our part. Major Orr expresses his obligations to Captains Woolcombe and Douglas, of the Bombay and Bengal Artillery, Lieutenant Lewis, and Ensign Fowler, of Her Majesty's 86th Regiment, the first very severely wounded, who led the men, and also Lieutenant Simpson, 23rd Regiment Bengal Native Infantry, wounded.

Captain Abbott, Hyderabad Cavalry, speaks highly of the gallantry with which Lieutenant Dun and detachments of the 1st and 4th Hyderabad Cavalry stormed, dismounted, a house and garden held obstinately by the fugitives, and he recommends, as I beg to do also, the Officers whose names follow for promotion and for the Order of Merit for gallantry in the field.

RECOMMENDED FOR PROMOTION.

1st Cavalry Hyderabad Contingent.

Ressaidar Allaoodeen Khan, 3rd Troop.
Jemadar Mahomedeen Khan, wounded.

Troopers.

Kurreem Ali Khan, wounded.
Tegmal Sing, wounded.
Meer Amyed Ali.
Train Singo.

4th Cavalry Hyderabad Contingent.

Jemadar Hunooman Sing, wounded.
Duffadar Himmunt Khan.

Troopers.

Bugwan Sing.
Khan Mahomed Khan, wounded.
Khairoolah Khan.
Tahool Khan,
and Syed Sharief, 2nd Cavalry, doing duty with 4th Cavalry.

RECOMMENDED FOR THE ORDER OF MERIT.

1st Cavalry Hyderabad Contingent.

Ressaldar Allaoodeen Khan, 3rd Troop.
Jemadar Mahomedeen Khan, 3rd Troop, Wounded.

4th Cavalry Hyderabad Contingent.

Jemadar Hunooman Sing, wounded.

It was not till Jhansie was taken, that its great strength was known.

There was only one part of the fortress, the South curtain, which was considered practicable for breaching. But when inside, we saw this was a mistake, there being at some distance in rear of the curtain a massive wall 15 or 20 feet thick, and immediately in rear of this a deep tank cut out of the live rock.

I beg leave to bring to the favorable notice of the Commander-in-Chief, the conduct of the Troops under my Command in the siege, investment, and capture of Jhansie.

They had to contend against an Enemy more than double their numbers, behind formidable fortifications, who defended themselves afterwards from house to house, in a spacious city, often under the fire of the Fort afterwards in suburbs, and in very difficult ground, outside the walls. The investing Cavalry force were day and night for 17 days on arduous duty, the men not taking their clothes off, the horses saddled and bridled up at night. The nature of the defence and the strictness of the investment, gave rise to continued and fierce combats; for the Rebels having no hope, sought to sell their lives as dearly as they could. But the discipline and gallant spirit of the Troops enabled them to overcome difficulties and opposition of every sort, to take the fortified city of Jhansie by storm, subduing the strongest fortress in Central India, and killing 5,000 of its Rebel garrison.

According to the first reports which I received, only 3,000 Rebels were killed, but those received since the withdrawal of the seven Flying Camps, make the loss of the Enemy amount to above 5,000 killed. Native accounts received by Brigadier Wheler at Saugor, make the loss of Rebels to amount to more than 5,000.

I beg to recommend to His Excellency, for gallant and good service in investing the fortress and City of Jhansie, Major Scudamore, Her Majesty's 14th Light Dragoons, the Senior Officer in Command of the Flying Camps; Major Gall, Her Majesty's 14th Light Dragoons; Major Forbes, C.B., Commanding 3rd Bombay Light Cavalry; Captain Abbott, and Lieutenant Dowe, Hyderabad Cavalry.

The Commander-in-Chief will learn with pleasure that the Troops, under my Command, treated with great humanity the women and children of Jhansie; neither the desperate resistance of the Rebels nor the recollections of Jhansie of last year, could make them forget that, in an English Soldier's eyes, women and children are spared; so far from hunting, the Troops were seen sharing their rations with them. I gave orders also that the destitute women and children of Jhansie should be fed out of the prize grain.

I have the honor to enclose a List of the Guns and Ordnance Stores, captured in the city and Fort of Jhansie, and of the Casualties of the force during the siege. I regret much that our loss should have been so considerable, but it was caused in a great measure by the strict investment, which proved so fatal to the Enemy, and loss of my force is out of all proportion smaller than that of the Enemy.

They lost 50 to my one killed, not counting the wounded on our side.

I beg leave to state the obligations I am under to the following Officers for the services which they have rendered to me, during the Siege Operations and capture of Jhansie.

Brigadier Stuart, Commanding 1st Brigade; Brigadier Steuart, C.B., Commanding 2nd Brigade; Lieutenant-Colonel Louth, Commanding Her Majesty's 86th Regiment; Lieutenant-Colonel Liddell, Commanding 3rd Bombay European Regiment; Major Scudamore, Commanding Her Majesty's 14th Light Dragoons; Major Orr, Commanding Hyderabad Field Force; Major Forbes, C.B., Commanding 3rd Bombay Light Cavalry; Major Robertson, Commanding 25th Regiment Bombay Native Infantry; Captain Lightfoot, Commanding Battery Bombay Artillery; Captain Woolcombe, Commanding Battery Bombay Artillery; Captain Fenwick, Commanding Company Royal Engineers; Captain Hare, Commanding 5th Regiment, Hyderabad Infantry; Captain Brown, Commanding Company Madras Sappers and Miners; Lieutenant Goodfellow, Commanding Company Bombay Sappers and Miners; Lieutenant Lowry, Commanding Battery Royal Artillery.

General Staff.

Captain Wood, Assistant Adjutant-General; Captain Macdonald, Assistant Quarter-Master General; Major Boileau, Commanding Engineers; Captain Ommaney, Commanding Artillery; Lieutenant Haggard, Commissary of Ordnance; Doctor Arnott, Superintending Surgeon; Doctor Vaughan, Staff Surgeon; Captain Rose, Aide-de-Camp; Lieutenant Lyste, Interpreter.

I have much gratification in bringing to the notice of His Excellency, the Officers mentioned in the Brigade Despatches:—

First Brigade.

Major Stuart, Her Majesty's 86th Regiment; Lieutenant Dartnell, Her Majesty's 86th Regiment; Lieutenant Fowler, Her Majesty's 86th Regiment; Lieutenant Jerome, Her Majesty's 86th Regiment; Lieutenant Webber, Royal Engineers; Ensign Sewell, Her Majesty's 86th Regiment.

Brigade Staff.

Captain Coley, Major of Brigade; Captain Bacon, Deputy Assistant Quarter-Master General.

Second Brigade.

Captain Sandwith, 3rd Bombay European Regiment; Captain Robinson, 3rd Bombay European Regiment; Lieutenant Fox, Madras Sappers and Miners; Lieutenant Bonus, Bombay Engineers; Lieutenant Goodfellow, Bombay Engineers; Lieutenant Park, 3rd Bombay European Regiment; Ensign Newport, 3rd Bombay European Regiment.

Brigade Staff.

Captain Todd, Major of Brigade; Captain Leckie, Deputy Assistant Quarter-Master General.

From Brigadier C. S. STUART, *Commanding 1st Brigade, Central India Field Force,* To the Assistant Adjutant-General, *Central India Field Force,*—No. 101, dated Camp Jhansie, the 13th April 1858.

In compliance with Field Force Orders, No. 7, of yesterday's date, I have the honor to trans[mit] herewith a Return of Casualties in the 1st Brigade, Central India Field Force, during the siege and storm of Jhansie, and with reference to the latter, beg to place on record the part taken in it by the Brigade under my Command.

2. As directed in Field Force Orders, dated 2nd April, the assaulting Column of the 1st Brigade was formed up at day-break of the 3rd April, ready to move on the two points of attack which had been indicated, *viz.*, the breach at the mound, and the rocket tower, and the low curtain immediately to the right of it. Lieutenant-Colonel Lowth, Her Majesty's 86th Regiment, Commanded the former, Major Stuart, Her Majesty's 86th Regiment, the latter, attack. On the signal being given, both parties moved steadily to the point under a smart fire from the Enemy. Captain Darby, Her Majesty's 86th Regiment, led the stormers up the breach in the most gallant manner, and the Enemy were driven before them at all points, while at the same time Major Stuart's attack by escalade at the rocket tower succeeded admirably, though hotly opposed. On gaining the town, Lieutenant-Colonel Lowth, with great judgment, moved part of his men to his right, and thus took the Enemy in flank and rear, when they were meeting the right attack of the 2nd Brigade with great vigour. All the Troops then of the 1st Brigade concentrated in the Ranee's Palace, which was taken possession of by Lieutenant-Colonel Lowth and his men in the most gallant manner. As the

Major-General himself was witness of greater part of the operations at this, and at a subsequent period, I do not enter into further details.

I beg, in conclusion, to bring to the notice of the Major-General, the excellent and gallant behaviour of both Officers and Men, of the 1st Brigade on this occasion: the energy and judgment displayed by Lieutenant-Colonel Lowth, Her Majesty's 86th Regiment, proved of the greatest service, and much contributed to the success of our attack. Major Stuart, Her Majesty's 86th Regiment, carried out the duties confided to him in the most satisfactory manner, and led the escalading party with the greatest gallantry; he was assisted by Lieutenant Dartnell, and Ensigns Sewell and Fowler, of Her Majesty's 86th Regiment, who were all wounded, the first two Officers severely; also by Lieutenant Webber, Royal Engineers, Commanding the ladder party of the Royal Sappers, who most ably performed their duty. On this occasion Lieutenant Dartnell greatly distinguished himself, as also Serjeant Alleyn Wolfe, and Private Roger Mathews, both of Her Majesty's 86th Regiment: the conduct of Lieutenant Jerome, and Private Burns, Her Majesty's 86th Regiment, has also been brought to my notice: under a murderous fire they carried off Ensign Sewell who had fallen severely wounded, and who would otherwise have been cut up. I lament to say that Surgeon Stock, Her Majesty's 86th Regiment, was killed near the Palace whilst most nobly and courageously attending the wounded under a hot fire. I beg also to record an act of daring on the part of Havildar Shaick Dawood, Light Company, 25th Regiment Native Infantry, brought to my notice by Captain Little, Commanding that Regiment. After an entrance had been effected into the city, a number of Rebels were found to have taken refuge in the recesses of a large well, the only approach to which was by narrow and steep stairs having a sharp turning, at which one resolute man could have kept off any number: whilst measures were being arranged for seizing these Rebels, Havildar Shaick Dawood volunteered to capture them, so fixing his bayonet he boldly descended the well, and being followed by others, brought up thirteen of the Enemy.

From Brigadier C. STEUART, C.B., *Commanding 2nd Brigade, Central India Field Force,* To the Assistant Adjutant General, *Central India Field Force,*—No. 236, *dated Camp, Jhansie, the 29th April 1858.*

In obedience to orders received through you, the Brigade under my Command moved in two Columns on the morning of the 3rd of April to the assault of the town of Jhansie.

The left Column led by Captain Robison, 3rd Bombay European Regiment, the right by Lieutenant-Colonel Liddell, advanced with great steadiness through a very heavy fire of musketry and wall pieces towards the ladders, on reaching which they were assailed with rockets, earthen pots filled with powder, and in fact every sort of missile.

On arrival at the temple, where the reserve of which I was in Command was to take up its position, Major Boileau, Madras Engineers, came to me and reported that the ladders were without protection, and requested me to give him some Europeans to protect them. I therefore gave him the hundred men of the 3rd Bombay European Regiment that were with the reserve; Lieutenants Meiklejohn and Dick, of the Bombay Engineers, led the way up the ladders of the right Column, both of whom were wounded, the latter severely. The ladders were found in some instances too short, in others too weak, breaking under the Men, who were withdrawn from the heavy fire to which they were thus unnecessarily exposed, and the movement was made with great precision and coolness.

Shortly after this, Captain Robison, 3rd Bombay European Regiment, was informed by Captain Barby, Executive Engineer, that some of the 86th Regiment had entered by the breach to his left, and he doubled some of his party round to that point, at which he effected an entry and cleared the ramparts so as to enable the remainder to mount the ladders unopposed. Lieutenant-Colonel Liddell, on finding his ladders of no use, ordered Lieutenant Goodfellow, of the Bombay Engineers, to try a bag of powder at a postern, but from being built up inside no entry could be effected; however by this time Captain Robison had made good his lodgement, and was followed by the right Column, when all proceeded towards the Palace, which, as the Major-General is aware, was taken after a desperate resistance.

Both Columns behaved with great coolness and gallantry, and I trust I may be pardoned for bringing their leaders to the notice of the Major-General; as also Captain Sandwith, and Lieutenant Park, 3rd Bombay European Regiment; Lieutenant Goodfellow, Bombay Engineers, and also Privates Few and Whirlpool, 3rd Bombay European Regiment, of whom Lieutenant-Colonel Liddell speaks in the highest terms. Captain Robison's conduct in doubling round with some of his men to the breach, speaks for itself; but he has brought to my notice Corporal Hard, Privates Roger and Archibald, all of the Grenadier Company, and Private Drummond, No. 1, and Private Doran, No. 3 Company, of the

CENTRAL INDIA.—JHANSI.   57

3rd Bombay European Regiment, all of whom fought most gallantly at the head of the ladders till they gave way. Ensign Newport and Private Gillman, of No. 1 Company, 3rd Bombay European Regiment, assisted by Corporal Hard, of the Grenadiers, carried off the body of Lieutenant Fox, of the Madras Sappers and Miners, through the hottest of the fire, after Captain Robison had ordered the Troops to retire; Lieutenant Bonus, Bombay Engineers, has also been specially brought to my notice for the gallant manner in which he led up and maintained his position on the ladders, until disabled and knocked over by the blow of a stone.

Captain Todd, Brigade Major, and Captain Leckie, Deputy Assistant Quarter-Master General of the 2nd Brigade, on this, as on every previous opportunity, have afforded me every assistance, and it is only to the circumstance of all former operations in which they have been engaged, being conducted so entirely under the Major-General, as to render any special report from me unnecessary, that I have failed in earlier bringing my sense of their worth to his notice; a circumstance which I feel sure will not act to their detriment.

Return of Casualties of the Central India Field Force and Hyderabad Contingent Field Force, during the Siege storm of Jhansie, exclusive of those Killed and Wounded on the 1st April at the action of the Betwa.

Corps.	Rank.	Names.	Remarks.
1st Brigade.			
4—2 Artillery	Lieutenant	G. Simpson	Severely wounded.
	Gunner	J. Ponton	,,
21st Company Royal Engineers	Assistant Surgeon	John Cruickshank	,,
	Corporal	Nathaniel Johns	Slightly.
	Sapper	Hempell Ramsey	Severely.
	,,	George Moore	Slightly.
	,,	James Smith	Severely.
	,,	Robert McLay	,,
Her Majesty's 86th Regiment.	Captain	Charles Darby	,,
	Lieutenant	J. G. Dartnell	,,
	,,	W. R. M. Holroyd	,,
	Ensign	S. W. Sewall	,,
	Surgeon	Thomas Stock	Killed.
	Serjeant	Thomas Pickaring	Severely wounded.
	,,	Dennis Connors	,,
	Corporal	Francis Geeaves	,,
	,,	James Murphy	Dangerously.
	Private	C. Sullivan	Mortally, since dead.
	,,	John McRanee	Killed.
	,,	James Leeson	,,

Return of Casualties of the Central India Field Force and Hyderabad Contingent Field Force, during the Siege storm of Jhansie, exclusive of those Killed and Wounded on the 1st April at the action of the Betwa—continued.

Corps.	Rank.	Names.	REMARKS.
	1st Brigade—contd.		
	Private	Wm. White	Killed.
	,,	John Mara	,,
	,,	Thomas Doran	,,
	,,	M. Feeney	,,
	,,	James Nolin	Dangerously burnt, died 9th April.
	,,	James Murphy	Severely wounded.
	,,	Wm. Wheelaham	Severely.
	,,	James McGunness	,,
	,,	Henry Keenan	Severely burnt.
	,,	Edward Hogan	,, wounded.
	,,	John Turner	Severely, since d 8th April.
	,,	Wm. Davis	Severely burnt.
	,,	John Burgin	,, wounded.
	,,	John Lyons	Severely.
	,,	Stephens Brady	,,
	,,	Peter Murphy	Dangerously.
	,,	Richard Ward	,, burnt, died 9th April.
	,,	William Gould	Slightly wounded.
	,,	Peter Naven	Slightly.
	,,	Wm. Kirwin	Severely.
	,,	John Brennen	,,
	,,	George Leethen	,,
	,,	John Ryan	,,
	,,	Thomas Connell	,,
	,,	George Frash	Slightly.
	,,	Robert Oram	Severely.
Her Majesty's 86th Regiment.	,,	George Swany	,,
	,,	Patrick Roach	,,
	,,	Henry McMullen	,,
	,,	Peter Conroy	Dangerously.
	,,	William Youart	Severely.
	,,	Arthur O'Neil	,,
	,,	Timothy O'Connor	,,
	,,	Robert Beggs	Slightly.
	,,	Abraham Kerr	Dangerously burnt, died 7th April.
	,,	Henry Webb	,,
	,,	Thomas Prendegrast	Slightly wounded.
	,,	Peter Cawfield	Severely.
	,,	John Moriarty	,,
	,,	James Waldren	Slightly.
	,,	Richard Batly	Severely.
	,,	James Pearson	Slightly.
	,,	Thomas Mullvibill	,,
	,,	John MacEvoy	Severely.
	,,	John Hannon	,,
	,,	John Byrne	,,
	,,	Thomas Murphy	Severely burnt.
	Lieutenant	R. F Lewis	Dangerously.
	Ensign	George Fowler	Slightly.
	Private	Patrick Conway	Severely.
	,,	Daniel Geraghty	,,
	,,	Edward Nevin	Dangerously.
	,,	Michael Moran	Mortally, since dead, 7th April.
	,,	Hugh Owens	Severely.
	,,	Roger Matthews	,,

CENTRAL INDIA.—JHANSI.

Return of Casualties of the Central India Field Force and Hyderabad Contingent Field Force, during the Siege storm of Jhansie, exclusive of those Killed and Wounded on the 1st April at the action of the Betwa—continued.

Corps.	Rank.	Names.	Remarks.
	One man blown up by Gunpowder, name not known.		
	Lieutenant	J. J. Fenwick	Slightly wounded.
	Private	Bhannoo Patkur	Contusion slightly.
	,,	Goorbuccus Chowbay	,,
	Subadar	Kesson Sing	Slightly.
	Jemadar	Roghooje Powar	,,
	Naick	Pandoo Mengia	Killed.
	,,	Mungul Pursad	Severely wounded.
	Lance Naick	Durgam Sing	Mortally.
	Private	Seetal Coonby	Killed.
	,,	Ugber Sing	,,
	,,	Pursad Moorie	,,
	,,	Ittoo Sowrah	Severely wounded.
	,,	Bappoo Mohitta	Dangerously.
25th Regiment Bombay Native Infantry.	,,	Pandoo Juddoum	Severely.
	,,	Baboo Bagwa	Slightly.
	,,	Rambuccus	Severely burnt.
	,,	Poorun Moochee	Severely wounded.
	,,	Kunie Moorie	Dangerously.
	,,	Ramdeen Lodh	Slightly.
	,,	Ajodia Persad	Dangerously.
	,,	Buldeen Doobay	Severely
	,,	Atnaram	Slightly.
	,,	Chuttoo Gudria	Severely.
	,,	Juggunath Panday	Slightly.
	,,	Dhrum Sing	,,
	,,	Laumon Ghoy	Dangerously.
	,,	Essoo Jugdalay	,,
	,,	Mam Sookh	Slightly.
	,,	Buktawar Khan	Killed.
	,,	Moona Catchee	Slightly.
	2nd Brigade.		
1st Troop Horse Artillery.	Lieutenant-Colonel	Sydney Turnbull	Dangerously wounded, died 4th April.
H. M.'s 14th Light Dragoons.	Serjeant	Frederick Cooper	Severely.
	Corporal	Edward Smith	Slightly.
	Private	John Hoey	,,
	Lieutenant	F. R. Fox	Very dangerously.
	Jemadar	Ally Khan	Slightly.
	Naick	Coopoomoetoog	,,
	Private	Chennion	,,
	,,	Poorun	,,
Company Madras Sappers and Miners.	,,	Mamekun	} Killed.
	,,	Narradoo	
	,,	Armoogam	Dangerously, died 10th April.
	,,	Lutchmanen	Slightly.
	,,	Appasawarry	Severely.
	,,	Vanketsowarry	,,
	,,	Veeraswammy	,,
	,,	Mohamed Cussen	Survived about 5 hours.
	1st Lieutenant	W. G. D. Dick	} Killed in action.
	Private	Sew Goo Kaum	
Bombay Sappers and Miners.	2nd Lieutenant	J. Bonus	Slightly wounded.
	Naick	Ramdeen Ahier	Severely.
	Private	Dyaram Powa	,,
	,,	Bhomoroo Lingoo	Slightly.
	,,	Sudnee	,,
	,,	Oomagee	Right arm taken off by round shot.

THE INDIAN MUTINY.

Return of Casualties of the Central India Field Force and Hyderabad Contingent Field Force, during the Siege storm of Jhansie, exclusive of those Killed and Wounded on the 1st April at the action of the Betwa—continued.

Corps.	Rank.	Names.	Remarks.
		2nd *Brigade*—contd.	
	Corporal	Alexander Anderson	⎫
	Private	James McLaren	⎪
	,,	Wm. Burnham	⎪
	,,	James Grady	⎬ Killed in action.
	,,	Patrick McKenna	⎪
	,,	Myles Bryan	⎪
	,,	Patrick Maye	⎭
	Captain	Sandwith	Slightly wounded.
	Assistant Surgeon	Miller	Severely.
	Color Serjeant	Robert Steavens	Slightly.
	Serjeant	John Walsh	,,
	Corporal	James Groves	,,
	,,	John Stuart	,,
	,,	Robert Hard	,,
	,,	James Geddard	Severely.
	Private	Wm. Wheeler	Gun shot wound, survived two hours.
	,,	Charles Gaton	Dangerously, died 8th April.
	,,	Wm. Hutchinson	,,
	,,	Wm. Tollen	Slightly.
	,,	Patrick Connelly	Severely.
	,,	George Allen	,,
	,,	W. Falgey	,,
3rd Bombay European Regiment.	,,	W. Burder	Slightly.
	,,	M. Cohill	,,
	,,	John Shean	Severely.
	,,	Patrick Farrell	,,
	,,	Charles Smith	Slightly.
	,,	John Haley	,,
	,,	James Bafter	Severely.
	,,	Wm. Mould	,,
	,,	Patrick O'Hallaren	Slightly.
	,,	John Smith	Severely.
	,,	Robert Kennelly	,,
	,,	James Hulston	,,
	,,	Patrick Williams	,,
	,,	William Wilkinson	,,
	,,	Timothy Deegan	,,
	,,	Michael Fitzgerald	,,
	,,	Patrick McDermot	Slightly.
	,,	George Baker	Severely, died 9th April.
	,,	Wm. Cop	Dangerously, died 5th April.
	,,	Thomas Laird	Severely burnt, since dead.
	,,	Samuel Lyle	Severely.
	,,	Michael McBride	,,
	,,	John Harrison	Survived 18 hours.
	,,	Thomas Smith	Severely.
	,,	George Mitchell	,,
	,,	Richard Henn	,,
	,,	John Sinclair	Slightly.
	,,	Rodger Archibald	,,
	,,	Wm. Bingham	,,
	,,	Patrick Doran	,,
	,,	George Booth	Severely.
	,,	John Claran	,,

CENTRAL INDIA.—JHANSI.   61

Return of Casualties of the Central India Field Force and Hyderabad Contingent Field Force, during the Siege storm of Jhansie, exclusive of those Killed and Wounded on the 1st April at the action of the Betwa—continued.

Corps.	Rank.	Names.	Remarks.
24th Regiment Bombay N. I.	Lieutenant	A. A. Park	Killed in action.
	Havildar	Seetal Pursad	,,
	Private	Luxamon Tumulkhan	,,
	,,	Bheewa Amchurakur	,,
	Subadar	Samajee Alrajee	Severely.
	Havildar	Ramdeen	,,
	Private	Tockuondeo Sookul	Died of his wounds.
	,,	Ramjee Sabday	Severely.
	,,	Tooka Ram	,,
	,,	Soobanee Ragura	,,
	,,	Ramjee Yadow	,,
	,,	Kisson Sing	Killed, 5th April.
	,,	Lochun Bahallia	Slightly.
	,,	Mohun Sing	,,
	,,	Balda Misser	,,

Hyderabad Contingent Field Force.

Corps.	Rank.	Names.	Remarks.
1st Cavalry	Trooper	Binda Sing	Slightly wounded.
	,,	Toolja Ram	,,
	,,	Nussur Nulla Khan	,,
	Captain Commanding	H. D. Abbott	Contusion from musket ball.
	Jemadar	Mohomed Deen Khan	Severely wounded.
	Duffadar	Lall Khan	Slightly.
	Lieutenant	H. C. Dowker	Severely.
	Trooper	Kumerali Khan	Slightly.
	,,	Jymal Sing	Severely.
	,,	Meah Khan	,,
	,,	Meer Hussein Ali	Killed.
4th Cavalry	Captain Commanding	W. Murray	Contusion from a musket ball.
	Jemadar	Unooman Sing	Dangerously wounded.
	Duffadar	Runjeet Khan	Killed.
	Trooper	Ummeer Sing	,,
	,,	Meer Hyder	,,
	,,	Khyre Mohomed Khan	Severely wounded.
	Trumpet Major	Mirza Soorab Beg	,,
	Trooper	Ahmed Khan	Slightly.
	,,	Meer Ukbur Ali	Severely.
	,,	Sheik Wuzzeer Ali	,,
1st Company Artillery.	Jemadar	Syud Noor Ali	Dangerously.
	Golandauz	Pertheepal Sing	Severely.
2nd Company Artillery.	Subadar	Doowkul Khan	Killed.
	Havildar	Ramdual	,,
	Golundauz	Kissoon	Severely wounded.
Left Wing 3rd Infantry.	Sepoy	Bucktaoor	Killed.
	,,	Ramdeen	Severely wounded.
	,,	Sheik Chand	,,
	,,	Mohomed Rumzan	,,
	,,	Beechary	Slightly.
	,,	Bindah	Severely.
	,,	Hunnoman	Slightly.
	,,	Rampursaud	Killed.
	,,	Naghojee	Dangerously, died 6th April.
	Captain	John Sinclair	Dangerously wounded, died soon after admission.
	Naick	Lutchmon	Severely, died soon after.

Return of Casualties of the Central India Field Force and Hyderabad Contingent Field Force, during the Siege storm of Jhansie, exclusive of those Killed and Wounded on the 1st April at the action of the Betwa—concluded.

Corps.	Rank.	Names.	Remarks.

Hyderabad Contingent Field Force—contd.

Left Wing 3rd Infantry.	Sepoy	Jokoo Sing	Severely, died soon after.
	,,	Sheik Baboo	,, ,,
	Jemadar	Gunga Sing	Severely wounded.
	Lance Naick	Balla Pursaud	Dangerously.
	Sepoy	Chandica	Severely.
	,,	Mohun	,,
	,,	Ramdyal	Slightly.
	Lance Naick	Chobay Laul	,,
5th Infantry	Serjeant Major	Dixon	Severely.
	Sepoy	Khaim Khan	Killed.
	,,	Hummuth Khan	Severely wounded.
	Subadar	Hoossein Bux	Dangerously.
	Havildar	Ram Deen	Slightly.
	Sepoy	Heera Laul	Severely.
	,,	Bisson	Dangerously.
	,,	Gummaee	Slightly wounded.

ABSTRACT.

Corps.	Killed.	Wounded.	Remarks.
1st Brigade.			
4—2 Artillery	0	2	
21st Company Royal Engineers	0	6	
Her Majesty's 86th Regiment	8	60	6 since dead.
25th Regiment Bombay N. I.	5	25	1 since dead.
Total	13	93	
2nd Brigade.			
1st Troop Horse Artillery	0	1	Since dead.
Her Majesty's 14th Light Dragoons.	0	3	1 Horse killed.
Bombay Company Madras Sappers and Miners	2	11	2 since dead
Detachment Bombay Sappers and Miners.	2	6	1 ,, ,,
3rd European Regiment	7	47	5 ,, ,,
24th Regiment Native Infantry	5	10	1 ,, ,,
Total	16	78	} 3 Horses wounded of the 3rd Light Cavalry.
Hyderabad Contingent Field Force	9	44	5 since dead } 16 Horses killed, died and missing.
Grand Total	33	137	

(Sd.) H. H. A. WOOD, *Captain,*
Asst. Adjt.-Genl.,
Central India Field Force.

Camp Jhansie,
The 16th April 1858.

CENTRAL INDIA.—JHANSI.

Return of Ordnance captured in the Town of Jhansie, on the 3rd April 1858, by the Force under Command of Major-General Sir Hugh Rose, k.c.b.

No.	Nature of Ordnance.	Calibre.	Length. Feet.	Length. Inch.	Manufacture.	Remarks.
1	Brass Gun	10 Pr.	3	4		
2	Do. do.	7 do.	3	11		
3	Do. do.	6 do.	3	0		
4	Do. do.	6 do.	4	3	Native.	
5	Do. do.	3 do.	2	10		
6	Do. do.	3 do.	3	1½		
7	Do. do.	2 do.	3	6		
8	Brass Howitzer	3 do.	0	6		
9	Iron Gun	12 do.	9	1	Europe.	
10	Do. do.	9 do.	1	6	Native.	
11	Do. do.	9 do.	8	9	Europe.	
12	Do. do.	4 do.	5	5		
13	Do. do.	3 do.	3	6		
14	Do. do.	3 do.	7	4		
15	Do. do.	3 do.	4	1		
16	Do. do.	2 do.	5	4½		
17	Do. do.	1 do.	2	0		
18	Do. do.	1 do.	0	10		
19	Brass do.	½ do.	1	3	Native.	
20	Do. do.	½ do.	1	4		
21	Do. do.	½ do.	1	3		
22	Iron do.	½ do.	1	0		
23	Do. do.	½ do.	1	7		
24	Do. do.	½ do.	1	1		
25	Do. do.	½ do.	1	9½		
26	Do. do.	½ do.	1	10½		

(Sd.) Thos. T. HAGGARD, *Lieut.*,
Commissary of Ordnance,
Central India Field Force.

Camp Jhansie,
The 8th April 1858.

Return of Ordnance captured in the Fort of Jhansie, by the Force under Command of Major-General Sir Hugh Rose, k.c.b., *on the 5th April 1858.*

No.	Nature of Ordnance.	Calibre.	Length. Feet.	Length. Inch.	Weight. Cwt.	Weight. Qrs.	Weight. lbs.	Remarks.
1	Iron Gun	68 Pr.	16	0	42	0	0	
2	Do. do.	9 do.	7	10	12	0	0	
3	Do. do.	6 do.	8	0	10	0	0	
4	Do. do.	6 do.	6	6	8	0	0	Of Native manufacture.
5	Do. do.	4 do.	6	10	5	0	0	
6	Do. do.	2½ do.	4	6	5	0	0	
7	Do. do.	1 do.	3	0	2	2	0	
8	Do. do.	½ do.	2	8	3	0	0	
9	Brass do.	5 do.	6	0	10	0	0	

(Sd.) Thos. T. HAGGARD, *Lieut.*,
Commissary of Ordnance,
Central India Field Force.

Camp Jhansie,
The 9th April 1858.

Allahabad, the 30th July 1858.

No. 324 of 1858.—The Right Hon'ble the Governor General is pleased to direct the publication of the following letter, from the Adjutant General of the Army, No. 617, dated the 29th July 1858, forwarding a Despatch from Major-General Sir Hugh Rose, K.C.B., late Commanding the Central India Field Force, reporting the details of his successful Action with the Enemy at Koonch, on the 7th May 1858, and which report was received by the Government in the Military Department, on the 29th Instant :—

From Lieutenant-Colonel W. MAYHEW, *Adjutant General of the Army,* To the Secretary to the Government of India, *Military Department, with the Governor-General,—No. 617, dated Head-Quarters, Allahabad, the 29th July 1858.*

I have the honor, by direction of His Excellency the Commander-in-Chief, to forward for the information of the Right Hon'ble the Governor General a Report from Major-General Sir H. Rose, K.C.B., late Commanding the Central India Field Force, of the successful operations of his Force, dated the 14th May last, but which only reached Army Head-Quarters on the 24th Instant.

From Major-General SIR HUGH ROSE, K.C.B., *Commanding Central India Field Force,* To Major-General SIR WILLIAM MANSFIELD, K.C.B., *Chief of the Staff,—dated Camp Goolowlee, 24th May 1858.*

I have the honor to report to you, for the information of His Excellency the Commander-in-Chief, that the approach of Brigadier Smith's Brigade from Rajpootana to Goonah, having secured Jhansi from attack by Kotah and Bundlecund Rebels, I re-called Lieutenant-Colonel Lowth, Commanding H. M.'s 86th Regiment, whom I had detached with a Column to watch the road from Jhansi to Goonah, and I marched with the 1st Brigade of my Force from Jhansi on the 25th Ultimo on Calpee.

I was still without the Wing of the 3rd Bombay Light Cavalry, which I had sent to Goonah, to re-inforce the Right Wing of H. M.'s 71st Highland Light Infantry, on their march to join me, as encumbered with a very large convoy of treasure, and all sorts of stores, they had to cross the Sind River at a very difficult ghat; and I was not certain that they might not be exposed to a treacherous attack from the late Chandairee Garrison, and other Bundelas, who, as already reported, had made an incursion on the Jhansi and Goonah road, acting it was clear in concert with the Kotah Rebels, to the North of the Indore and Goonah road.

I left at Jhansi for its garrison the Force forming part of the 2nd Brigade detailed in the margin. I left there also Brigadier Steuart, with the remainder of his Brigade, with orders to bring up to me the 71st Regiment and two Troops of the 3rd Bombay Light Cavalry.

<blockquote>
Head-Quarters Wing 3rd European Regiment.
8 Companies 24th Bombay Native Infantry.
100 Hyderabad Cavalry.
3 Guns, late Bhopal Artillery.
½ Company Bombay Sappers and Miners.
</blockquote>

I joined Major Gall's Force at Pooch, 16 miles from Koonch, on the 1st of May. I had the honor to report, on the 17th instant, the movements of this Officer's Moveable Column, as well as those of Major Orr's Field Force.

I received information from Sir Robert Hamilton and Major Gall, whom I had detached along the road from Jhansi to Calpee, with a flying Column to watch the Enemy, and obtain information of their movements, that the Sepoy Garrison of Calpee, of all arms, re-inforced by five hundred Velaities under the Ranee of Jhansi, Cavalry from Kotah, and Guns and Troops from disaffected Rajahs, the whole under the Command of Tantia Topee, had occupied Koonch, and thrown up entrenchments which they had armed to defend the roads to the town from Jhansi, and that they were determined to make a vigorous opposition at Koonch to my advance against Calpee. All the accounts agreed that the Rebels were strong in Cavalry, Mutineers of Bengal Regular and Irregular Cavalry.

Koonch is an open town; but it is difficult to attack, because it is surrounded by woods, gardens, and temples, with high walls round them, every one of which is a defence.

I had directed Major Orr, to do his utmost to prevent the Rajahs of Banpore and Shagur, and any body of Rebels crossing the Betwa, and doubling back southwards. The two Rajahs for the purpose of carrying out this very manœuvre, separated from the Rebels at Koonch, and drove the Troops of the Rajah Goorserai, who held Kotra, commanding a ford across the Betwa, to the South bank of the river.

Major Orr crossed the Betwa, engaged the Rajahs, drove them from their position at Kotra, and took one of their Guns; but he states that it was impossible to cut off the retreat of the Rajahs, who, whilst Major Orr was attacking one part of their force, retired precipitately with the remainder some distance down the river, where they crossed at a ford and took the road Southwards, carriage and supplies being furnished them by the treacherous Rajah of Jignee. Major Orr, by my direction, marched to Koonch.

As nothing puts the Rebels out so much as turning their flank, or defences; and as the excessive heat of the day rendered it advisable that I should not undertake a long operation against Koonch, much less a siege, I made a flank march with my whole Force to the North-West; my left, the 1st Brigade, resting its left flank on the village of Nagupoora; my centre, the 2nd Brigade, under Brigadier Steuart, was in the village of Chomair; my right, Major Orr's Force, in front of the village of Oomree.

This position threatened seriously the Enemy's line of retreat from Koonch to Calpee; and it exposed the North-West of the Town, which was not protected by entrenchments, to attack.

I gave the order that as soon as the three Columns had taken up the positions which I have mentioned, they were to advance against the Town, and each effect a lodgment in it.

When we came within sight of Koonch, we perceived videttes and strong picquets of the Enemy's Cavalry outside the wood. They conformed to our flank movement, and posted themselves nearly opposite to Nagupoora.

A few rounds of shrapnel from Captain Lightfoot's Guns emptied some of their saddles, and they disappeared into the wood. The Rebel Infantry now showed in force behind a long wall to our front, and in the wood to the left of it.

I had marched the 1st Brigade a distance of 14 miles from Loharee that morning, for the purpose of surprising the Enemy by the flank movement, and not giving them time to alter their plan of defence. To rest and refresh the men, I ordered their dinners to be cooked for them, and in the meantime battered the wall with the two 18-pounders and the 8-inch howitzer.

The half Troop of Horse Artillery advancing diagonally to their left, shelled the Infantry to the left of the wall; the Enemy in return shelled the Troop and the Siege Guns from a battery to our right. Two of our Guns were turned on the battery, and soon silenced it.

Lieutenant-Colonel Gall, Her Majesty's 14th Light Dragoons, galloped gallantly into the wood to reconnoitre. The Enemy, although he was in easy musket range of them, did not fire at him, because the shelling from the Horse Artillery had caused confusion in their ranks; he ascertained that the Infantry to the left had retreated further into the wood having in their rear, a large body of Cavalry, that the siege Guns had driven the Enemy from the cover of the wall, but that some way in rear of it was posted a large body of Infantry with elephants.

I determined to drive the Enemy out of the wood, gardens and temples, which surround Koonch, and then to storm the town, including a dilapidated mud Fort on a rising ground, a strong position, which was opposite to the right of the 1st Brigade.

Once in possession of this position in the Town, the Enemy on our left and in our front would be cut off from the rest of their force, in the entrenchments on our right, which would be forced to retreat to the plain on the other side of the Town, pressed by the 2nd Brigade and Major Orr's Force, the 1st Brigade passing through the Town, and pressing the Enemy with whom they had been engaged.

I effected this operation by throwing the Left Wing of Her Majesty's 86th Regiment under Major Steuart, and the whole of the 25th Bombay Native Infantry, under Lieutenant-Colonel Robertson, into skirmishing order, the 86th on the left, the 25th on the right, their flanks supported by the half Troop Horse Artillery, and a troop of Her Majesty's 14th Light Dragoons, and Captain Ommaney's Battery, and two Troops of Her Majesty's 14th Dragoons. I left Captain Woolcombe's Battery, one troop 14th Light Dragoons, and the Right Wing 86th Regiment, in a second line in reserve under the Command of Lieutenant-Colonel Lowth. The rapidity and precision with which this formation was simultaneously made, must have surprised the Sepoys. The 25th Skirmishers charged into the wood, temples, and walled gardens, and occupied them under a fire of Musketry and Artillery from the Battery on our right, which re-opened its fire, and after the Guns of the Royal Artillery under Captain Field had effectually cannonaded the houses in the streets of Koonch in their front, took them also.

I expressed to Lieutenant-Colonel Robertson and the 25th on the ground, my approbation of the gallantry with which they had gained this important position.

The 86th Regiment covered by the three Horse Artillery Guns, under Captain Lightfoot, who throughout the day, made the most of their arm, and the Troop 14th Light Dragoons, made a circuit to their left, took all the obstacles to their front, and then bringing their left shoulders forward, advanced, despite of Artillery and Musketry fire, through the whole North part of the town, and took the Fort. The manner in which the 86th, ably led by Major Steuart, performed this movement, which completed the cutting of the Enemy's line in two, adds another claim to the obligations I owe this Regiment for their very distinguished conduct on all occasions in the field.

Just as the 86th and myself with the 25th were about to enter the Town, Brigadier Steuart, Commanding the 1st Brigade, observed that a large number of Rebel Infantry, strongly posted in cultivated ground, threatened the right of the line of attack of his Brigade. He moved up Captain Field's Battery with Captains Thompson's and Gordon's Troops of Her Majesty's 14th Light Dragoons, and a Troop of the 3rd Regiment Hyderabad Cavalry to dislodge them. The Enemy held the position obstinately, and it was not until a portion of the Infantry of the 2nd Brigade moved down on them from another direction, that they retreated, when Captain Gordon, whom I beg to recommend to His Excellency for his conduct on this occasion, with his Troop and the Cavalry above-mentioned, charged and broke the mass, cutting up several of them; topes of trees favoured the escape of the remainder.

The 2nd Brigade, under Brigadier Steuart, owing to some misconception on his part, did not effect a lodgment in the Town, but moving round the South of it, their Artillery and Cavalry joined in the pursuit.

I have the honor to enclose a copy of Major Orr's Report, which shows that he did his utmost to carry out my orders.

The Enemy's line of defence being now cut in two, and their right completely turned, they retired in masses from Koonch, to the extensive plains intersected by heavy ploughed land, stretching towards Orai and Calpee, forming an irregular and very long line, five or six deep in some places covered by skirmishers at close distances, who at intervals were in groups of small masses, a mode of skirmishing peculiar to Indians; these groups act as a sort of bastions to the line of skirmishers.

The 1st Brigade made their way through the town, as quickly as its narrow and winding streets would allow them, and searched the plains in pursuit of the Enemy.

But the Infantry had already suffered so much during the morning's sun, twelve men of the weak Wing of Her Majesty's 71st having died from sunstroke, that it would have been a heartless and imprudent sacrifice of invaluable Infantry, to pursue with that arm. They were therefore halted, as well as the Infantry of the Second Brigade, and

Major Orr's Force, which had advanced through the wood, round the Town to the plains.

The Cavalry of both Brigades, and of Major Orr's Force (except a party which I had left to watch the Jaloun road and my rear), one Troop of Horse Artillery, Captain Field's Guns, and the four Guns of No. 18 Light Field Battery, went in pursuit.

If, on the one hand, the Enemy had retired from Koonch with too great precipitation, on the other, it is fair to say that they commenced their retreat across the plain with resolution and intelligence. The line of skirmishers fought well to protect the retreat of the main body, observing the rules of Light Infantry drill. When charged, they threw aside their muskets, and fought desperately with their swords.

The pursuit was commenced by Captains McMahon's Squadron and Blyth's Troop of Her Majesty's Light Dragoons charging, the first the right, and the latter the left of the Enemy's skirmishers.

A piece of very heavy plough caused a check in the pace, under a heavy fire of Captain McMahon's Squadron; but the heavy ground was not broad, the Squadron got through it, Captain McMahon leading the way, and cut to pieces the Enemy, who fought fiercely to the last. Captain McMahon received three sabre-wounds, but he continued the pursuit to the last. I beg to recommend him for his gallant conduct and his unvarying zeal and attention to his duties.

On the centre, the Horse Artillery opened a hot fire on, and the Cavalry charged the skirmishers. The Enemy now threw back the extreme right of their skirmishers so as to enfilade our line of pursuit. I directed Captain Prettyjohn to form line to the left, charge, and cut off the enfilading skirmishers, which he did effectually. This Officer, on the horses of his own Troop being knocked up, placed himself with well-timed zeal, at the head of a Troop with fresh horses which was without an Officer, and continued the pursuit with them to the end. I beg to submit his name to the favorable consideration of His Excellency, as well as the names of Captain Blyth, Her Majesty's 14th Light Dragoons, and Captain Abbott, Commanding 3rd Regiment Hyderabad Cavalry, who each very gallantly charged and captured a gun from the retreating Enemy under a heavy fire.

In the course of the pursuit, more Guns and ammunition were captured by the Cavalry.

Captain Field, with the four 9-pounder Guns of Captain Ommaney's Battery of Royal Artillery, notwithstanding the heavy plough he had frequently to go over, and the weight of his Guns, continued to turn them to good account, and kept up well with them to the close of the pursuit.

The greater part of the Enemy's line of skirmishers being killed, the remainder driven in, and the Rebel Artillery captured, the main body, the first line got into confusion, lost their nerve, and crowded into the road to Calpee, a long and helpless Column of runaways. The Horse Artillery and Cavalry were now so beat by sun and fatigue, that they were reduced to a walk; the Guns were only able to rake the Column in its depth with round shot and shell, but could not approach sufficiently close to give it grape. The Cavalry on their part had only strength to reach the numerous stragglers, who could not keep up with the Enemy's main body. On reaching some wood and broken ground, about a village, seven or eight miles from Koonch, profiting by this cover, they sought safety from attack by breaking into scattered flight across the country.

The scorching rays of the sun and the pace at which they retreated, told even on the sepoys; several fell dead on the road, struck by apoplexy; many exhausted, threw away their arms, whilst others, to quench their thirst, rushed to the wells, regardless if our Cavalry were upon them.

But the sun, fatigue, and scarcity of water told still more on my Artillery and Cavalry, a great part of whom were Europeans, and had been marching, or engaged for sixteen hours. The Commanding Officers of Artillery and Cavalry having, on our arrival at the village, reported to me that they were not longer able to pursue, I halted, and having watered the horses as well as I could, marched them back at sunset to Koonch.

The Enemy must have lost about five or six hundred men in the action and pursuit; and according to their own account, the 52nd Regiment Bengal Native Infantry, or "Henry ki Pultun,"* which covered the retreat, was nearly destroyed. Nine Guns and quantities of good English ammunition and stores, furnished to the late Gwalior Contingent, were taken.

The defeat at Koonch gave rise to animosities and mistrust in the Rebel Army. The Infantry Sepoys accused their brother Mutineers of the Cavalry with having pusillanimously abandoned them, and all three arms brought the same charge against their General, Tantia Topee, who had disappeared at Koonch as rapidly as he had done at the Betwa,

---

* Hindree-ka-Pultan.

leaving to its fate, at the most critical moment, the Force which he had called into existence under the pompous title of the "Army of the Peishwa."

The Vilaities also were charged with not having exhibited, at Koonch, the stern courage on which they pride themselves; they were accused with having left the field too soon; and their excuse that they had felt it their duty to escort the Ranee of Jhansi to a place of safety, was not held to be a Military one. It was said that the destruction of Vilaities at Jhansi had made their countrymen less anxious than usual to try the fate of war.

These various causes created confusion in the councils of the Calpee mutineers, my immediate advance towards that fortress made matters worse; a panic seized the Sepoys in Calpee, as well as those retreating towards it; they commenced to take different lines of retreat: and I was assured, and on good authority, that at one time there were only eleven Sepoys in the town and fort.

The unexpected arrival of the Nawab of Banda, with a large Force of good Sepoy Cavalry mutineers, some Guns and Infantry, and his energetic exertions, backed up by those of the Ranee of Jhansi, produced one of those sudden changes from despair to confidence, which mark the Indian character.

Their leaders again exhorted the Sepoys, as I learnt from an intercepted letter, "to hold to the last, Calpee their only arsenal, and to win their right to Paradise by exterminating the Infidel English." The Rebels returned to Calpee and its environs, re-occupying the strong positions in the labyrinth of ravines, which surround it and the entrenchments, which they had thrown up and armed to arrest my advance a few miles in front of the Chowrani (eighty-four) temples, which are two or three miles from Calpee. They had already cut deep trenches across the road near the entrenchments, and in several other places, which were serious obstacles, because the ravines on each side of the road rendered it very difficult to turn them. When driven out of the entrenchments, the Rebels could fall back on the eighty-four Temples, built, as well as the walls round them, of most solid masonry; the outwork of ravines afforded them a third; the town of Calpee a fourth; another chain of ravines between the Town and the Fort, a fifth; and finally, the Fort, a sixth and last line of defence.

The Fort of Calpee is wretched as a fortification, but as a position it is unusually strong, being protected on all sides by ravines; to its front by five lines of defence, and to its rear by the Jumna, from which rises the precipitous rock on which it stands.

Besides the Officers previously mentioned in this Despatch, I beg leave to bring to Your Excellency's favourable notice, two Officers, who have lately joined my Force, Colonel Wetherall, Chief of the Staff, and Captain Cockburn, of Her Majesty's 43rd Regiment, my acting Aide-de-Camp; Colonel Wetherall at Koonch, and since he joined my Force, has given me all the assistance which was to be expected from his coolness, valuable experience, and excellent judgment.

Sickness had deprived me of the services of some of my Staff, amongst others of that of Captain Macdonald, Assistant Quarter-Master General, who, although unable to stand from illness, would, with the never-failing devotion which characterizes him, have taken part in the combat if I had not ordered him back to his bed, but Captain H. H. A. Wood, Assistant Adjutant-General, and Captain Cockburn, made up amply for the deficiency by their intelligence and unwearied zeal, under fire.

Lieutenant Baigree, Acting Deputy Assistant Quarter-Master General, and Lieutenant Lyster, 72nd (late Bengal Native Infantry), my Interpreter, deserve also to be specially mentioned; the former was severely wounded by a sword-cut which all but severed two fingers from his hand; notwithstanding he gallantly continued during the action to discharge his duties with as much efficiency as before. I had sent Lieutenant Lyster with an order to the Cavalry to charge; on his way, he came across a group of some thirty Sepoys, skirmishers; single-handed, he charged in view of the pursuing Force, cut his way through and broke them; his Horse was severely wounded. This is the second time I have had the honor to mention this Officer for gallant conduct in the Field.

The exertions of Dr. Arnott, Superintending Surgeon, to take care of the Sick and Wounded, and to supply the Field and other Hospitals with Medical comfort and requisites, are as unwearied as they are successful.

I ought before now to have mentioned the conduct of Dr. Vaughan, Staff Surgeon, at the pass of Muddenpore, where, on account of the paucity of Officers, he gallantly led a party of the Hyderabad Contingent Infantry, who cleared a difficult position of the Enemy.

The great heat of the sun and the numerous Casualties caused unfortunately by it, called into play all the zeal and devotion of the

Medical Department of my Force, showing how eagerly the members of it go into danger when duty calls them there.

Dr. Stack, of Her Majesty's 86th Regiment, was killed in the streets of Jhansi, in giving his first cares to a wounded man in the conflict.

Brigadier Steuart, C.B., Commanding 1st Brigade, reports that his best thanks are due to the Officers of his Staff, Captain Fenwick, Field Engineer; Captain Coley, Major of Brigade; Captain Bacon, Deputy Assistant Quarter-Master General; Lieutenant Henry, Deputy Assistant Commissary-General; and Staff Surgeon Mackenzie; also to Captain Lightfoot, Commanding 1st Troop Horse Artillery; Major Gall, Commanding Left, Her Majesty's 14th Light Dragoons; Captain Abbott, Commanding 3rd Regiment, Hyderabad Cavalry; Captain Field, Commanding No. 6 Field Battery, Royal Artillery; Lieutenant Strutt, Commanding No. 4 Light Field Battery, Bombay Artillery; Lieutenant Edwards, Assistant Field Engineer; and Lieutenant Gosset, Commanding 21st Company Royal Engineers; Lieutenant-Colonel Lowth, Commanding 86th Regiment, and Major Robertson, Commanding 25th Regiment Bombay Native Infantry.

Brigadier Steuart, C.B., Commanding 2nd Brigade, mentions that his Staff, Captain Todd, Major of Brigade, and Captain Leckie, Deputy Assistant Quarter-Master General, afforded him every assistance.

I beg also to bring to His Excellency's notice the Officers mentioned in Major Orr's Despatch.

Enclosed are the Returns of Killed and Wounded, and of the Guns and Ordnance Stores captured in the Action.

From Major W. A. ORR, *Commanding Field Force, Hyderabad Contingent, serving in Central India*, To Colonel WETHERALL, C.B., *Chief of the Staff, C.I.F.F.*,—No. 147, dated Camp Etowra, *14th May 1858*.

1st Cavalry H. C. 182 Sabres. Lieutenant Dowker, Commanding.
4th Cavalry H. C. 137 Sabres. Captain Murray, Commanding.
1st Co. Arty. 2 6-Pr. Guns.
2nd ,,   ,, 3 6-Pr. Guns.
4th ,,   ,, { 2 12-Pr. Howitzers. 2 ¼-inch Mortars. } Captain Douglas, Comdg.
Left Wing 3rd Infantry 333 Bayonets, Lieutenant Macquoid, Commanding.
5th Infantry 241 Bayonets, Captain Hare, Commanding.

I have the honor to forward the subjoined Report, for submission to the Major-General Commanding, of the part taken by the Field Force, Hyderabad Contingent, under my Command as per margin, in the Action at Koonch, fought with the Rebel Forces under Tantea Topee on the 7th Instant.

2. I received during the night of the 6th, the instructions transmitted to me by you, directing me to move from my encampment at Aite towards my left flank, and proceeding by Bassoop and Sunnow, along my Force by its left, with the right of the 2nd Brigade which I should find resting on the village of Oomree. I marched during the night, and early the next morning, (the 7th) opened a communication with Brigadier Steuart, Commanding 2nd Brigade. From Sunnow, I advanced to Purrayta, took possession of the small village of Daree, about ¼ of a mile in my front, and occupied it with a strong picquet of Cavalry and Infantry.

3. About 8 o'Clock, the Enemy appeared in force on my right flank, a large body of Cavalry supported by Infantry moving steadily down towards Daree, apparently advancing with much determination, and having opened a fire from a Battery mounting two or three Guns, one of them of considerable calibre. I moved forward my line, and a few rounds from the Guns forced the Enemy back to their original position.

4. Having received the Major-General's orders to take ground to the left, I moved in that direction to the front of the village of Oomree, from which I advanced direct upon Koonch. In my immediate front were some gardens and walled enclosures, held in force by the Enemy, and from which a heavy fire was directed upon our line. The Artillery under Captain Douglas advanced, and its fire having silenced that of the Rebels, I ordered the gardens and enclosures to be seized by the Infantry. This was very gallantly effected by a Detachment of the 5th Infantry, consisting of two Companies under Command of Lieutenant Partridge, 23rd Bengal Native Infantry, doing duty 5th Infantry Hyderabad Contingent, a very promising young Officer, and the Enemy were very quickly driven out. At the same time, I directed the whole of the Cavalry under Command of Captain Murray and Lieutenant Dowker, to move to the right and charge the Enemy's Horsemen, who had all this time been threatening our flank. This service was promptly and effectually performed, the Horsemen being driven quite off the field at this point and forced back within the line of their supports of Infantry, occupying several deep ravines and broken ground, and from the shelter of which a heavy fire was directed. The Enemy's Guns at the same time opened with round shot and shrapnell. The Cavalry were subsequently joined by one Squadron of Her Majesty's 14th Light Dragoons, and two Horse Artillery Guns, the whole commanded by Major Scudamore, and they retained possession of the

ground they had gained until the general advance, when they also followed the Enemy in pursuit.

5. The Artillery had meanwhile advanced so far as to bring it completely within range of the Enemy's Guns from two Batteries, and they were thus enabled to open upon it a double fire of round shot, shell and shrapnell from the effects of which several Casualties occurred. The Rebel Infantry also being strongly re-inforced, again suddenly came forward with a rush in great numbers, and forced back the Detachment holding the garden. I was about to advance once more at this point, when I learnt that the Major-General with the 1st Brigade, had forced the Enemy's positions, and was in possession of the Fort and Town. The whole force now advanced, the Enemy was driven from the enclosures he held, and joining in the retreat of his main body, proceeded in the direction of the Orri road. I moved forward with the Cavalry portion of the Force under my Command, and joined with Her Majesty's 14th Dragoons, the Horse Artillery, and Horse Field Battery in the pursuit, which continued for about eight miles, cutting up a great many of the fugitive Rebels, consisting almost entirely of Sepoys of the Mutineer Corps of the Gwalior Contingent and Bengal Army. The great start obtained by the Enemy before the fact of their retreating became known; the extraordinary great heat of the day, and the utter want of water, and the exhaustion of both men and horses from these two causes, all combined to make the loss to the Enemy heavy, though it was less so than it would otherwise have proved. The Force returned to Camp at 8 P.M. having been since 2 A.M. under arms, and in the saddle.

6. My best thanks are due to the under-mentioned Officers for the gallant, zealous, and efficient aid they afforded me throughout the day and at all other times, and I beg to bring their names to the favorable notice of the Major-General:—

Captain Douglas, Bengal Artillery, Commanding Artillery Field Force, Hyderabad Contingent.

Captain G. Hare, Commanding 5th Infantry, Hyderabad Contingent.

„ W. Murray, „ 4th Cavalry „

Lieutenant H. C. Dowker, „ 1st „ „

„ R. K. Macquoid, Adjutant, 5th Infantry, Commanding Left Wing, 3rd Infantry, Hyderabad Contingent.

Lieutenant E. W. Dun, 2nd in Command, 4th Cavalry, Hyderabad Contingent.

Lieutenant H. Fraser, Adjutant, 4th Cavalry and Staff Officer Field Force Hyderabad Contingent.

Lieutenant Westmacott, 23rd Bengal Native Infantry, doing duty 4th Cavalry Hyderabad Contingent.

Lieutenant Johnson, Adjutant, 1st Cavalry, Hyderabad Contingent.

" Partridge, 23rd Bengal Native Infantry, doing duty 5th Infantry, Hyderabad Contingent.

Surgeon J. H. Orr, 4th Cavalry, Hyderabad Contingent, and Senior Surgeon Field Force.

Assistant Surgeon Sanderson, 1st Cavalry, Hyderabad Contingent.

" " Burn, 5th Infantry, " "

7. I beg to forward Casualty Rolls both in Men and Horses.

Nominal Roll of Officers and Men of the Central India Field Force, Killed, Wounded, and Sun-struck in the Action with the Insurgents at Koonch, on the 7th May 1858.

Corps.	Rank.	Names.	Date.	Remarks.
1st Brigade.				
Staff.	Lieutenant	Baigree, Dy. Asst. Qr. Mr. Gl.	7th May 1858	Severely wounded.
	Line Serjeant	Charles H. Wilson	Ditto	Killed.
21st Company Royal Engineers.	Color Serjeant	Charles Hawkins	Ditto	Died of Sun-stroke.
Left Wing, H.M.'S. 14th L. Dragoons.	S. S. Major	Samuel Whitaker	Ditto	Severely wounded.
	Private	Charles Hutchins	Ditto	Slightly.
	"	W. H. Haffernan	Ditto	"
	"	Thomas Hoey	Ditto	"
	"	John Henton	Ditto	"
	"	John Wilbraham	Ditto	Vertigo.
3rd Cavy., Contingent.	Bargeer	Hymut Khan	Ditto	Mortally, since dead.
	"	Syud Khan	Ditto	Fractured severely.
H.M.'s 86th Regiment.	Private	Daniel Rielly	Ditto	Severely wounded.
	"	James Kearn	Ditto	Died of Sun-stroke.
	"	Patrick McInerney	Ditto	Ditto.
	"	Michael McNally	Ditto	Ditto.
25th B. Native Infantry.	Lieutenant	P. P. P. Fenwick	Ditto	Sun-stroke.
	Private	Ramchunder Mohothoy	Ditto	Ditto.

CENTRAL INDIA.—JHANSI. 77

Nominal Roll of Officers and Men of the Central India Field Force, Killed, Wounded, and Sun-struck in the Action with the Insurgents at Koonch, on the 7th May 1858—continued.

Corps.	Rank.	Names.	Date.	Remarks.
Her Majesty's 14th Light Dragoons.	**2nd Brigade.** Private	William Crook	7th May 1858	} Killed in action.
	,,	George Lawrence	Ditto	
	,,	F. G. Topley	Ditto	
	,,	James Steadman	Ditto	
	Captain	W. McMahon	Ditto	Wounded severely by sword-cut in right hand and leg.
	Private	Peter Ward	Ditto	Ditto sword-cut in right shoulder.
	,,	William Gray	Ditto	Contusion of right eye, legs and loins.
	,,	Frederick Maytum	Ditto	Wounded severely, gun-shot wound of the chest.
	,,	Samuel Smith	Ditto	Ditto gun-shot wound in the neck.
	,,	Dennis Tounsend	Ditto	Ditto gun-shot wound in the neck.
	,,	Henry Jeffries	Ditto	Slightly sword-cut on back of right hand.
	,,	Hugh Cunningham	Ditto	Wounded severely, bayonet-wound through left hip.
	,,	William Mitchell	Ditto	Contusion of loins and legs.
	,,	William C. Barnes	Ditto	Contusion of left wrist.
	,,	Peter Pennells	Ditto	Wounded slightly sword-cut on right hand.
	,,	John E. Fitzpatrick	Ditto	Contusion of right hand and thigh.
	,,	Henry Pearce	Ditto	Wounded slightly, sword-cut on right elbow.
	,,	William Hopton	Ditto	Contusion of right eye.
	Captain	A. Need	Ditto	Sun-stroke.
	Lieutenant	W. H. T. C. Travers	Ditto	Ditto.
	Regtl. Serjt. Major	——— Holloway	Ditto	Ditto, Died 16th May 1858.
	Pay Mr. Serjt.	R. Sexton	Ditto	Ditto.
	Serjeant Major	J. Fisher	Ditto	Ditto.
	Serjeant	Stephen Sweeny	Ditto	Ditto.
	Corporal	George Ribbons	Ditto	Ditto.
	Trumpeter	William Hearndon	Ditto	Ditto, Died 13th May 1858.
	Private	William Smith	Ditto	Ditto.
	,,	George Stent	Ditto	Ditto.
	,,	Thomas Cremore	Ditto	Ditto.
	,,	George Wood	Ditto	Ditto.
	,,	James Turner	Ditto	Ditto.
	,,	George Abraham	Ditto	Ditto.
	,,	George Hunter	Ditto	Ditto.
	,,	John O'Neil	Ditto	Ditto.
	,,	Frederick Matty	Ditto	Ditto.
	,,	Thomas Crow	Ditto	Ditto.

78   THE INDIAN MUTINY.

Nominal Roll of Officers and Men of the Central India Field Force, Killed, Wounded, and Sun-struck in the Action with the Insurgents at Koonch, on the 7th May 1858—concluded.

Corps.	Rank.	Names.	Date.	Remarks.
Her Majesty's 71st Regt, Highland Light Infantry.	Private	William Sharp	7th May 1848	Slightly wounded in leg by a spent ball.
	Color Serjeant	Robert Banks	Ditto	Sun-stroke.
	Serjeant	Alexander Ross	Ditto	Ditto.
	Color Serjeant	Stephen McGill	Ditto	Ditto.
	Corporal	Andrew McKay	Ditto	Ditto.
	Private	Hugh Graffin	Ditto	Ditto.
	,,	Peter McKinnon	Ditto	Ditto.
	,,	David Millar	Ditto	Ditto. } Died on the 7th May 1858.
	,,	John Mitchell	Ditto	Ditto.
	,,	William Rutherford	Ditto	Ditto.
	,,	Alexander Stuart	Ditto	Ditto.
	,,	Adam Forbes	Ditto	Ditto. Died on the 8th May 1858.
	,,	Alexander Canneross	Ditto	Ditto.
	,,	William Ferguson	Ditto	Ditto.
	,,	John Dunsmore	Ditto	Ditto.
	,,	William Kirly	Ditto	Ditto.
	,,	Archibald Kirkup	Ditto	Ditto.
	,,	John McPherson	Ditto	Ditto.
	,,	Edward Redstone	Ditto	Ditto.
	,,	William Steel	Ditto	Ditto.
3rd B. Eurpn. Regt.	Private	Robert Hudson	Ditto	Wounded severely, gun-shot wound.
	,,	Francis Doherty	Ditto	Slightly, contused wounds.
	Corporal	John Drayson	Ditto	
24th Regt. Bombay N. I.	Subadar	Sumsagee Israel	Ditto	Sun-stroke.
	Private	Rheman Khan	Ditto	Ditto.

ABSTRACT.

Corps.	War Casualties.					Sun-stroke.		Horse.		
	Officers Killed.	Officers Wounded.	Rank and File Killed.	Rank and File Wounded.		Officers.	Rank and File.	Killed.	Wounded.	Missing.
1st Brigade.										
Staff	...	...	1	...		...	...	...	...	...
Royal Engineers	...	...	...	...		...	1	...	...	...
Left Wing, Her Majesty's 14th Light Dragoons	...	...	...	5		...	...	...	...	...
3rd Cavalry, Hyderabad Contingent	...	...	...	2		...	...	...	...	...
Her Majesty's 86th Regiment	...	...	...	1		...	3	...	...	...
25th Regiment Bombay Native Infantry	...	...	...	...		...	2	...	...	...
2nd Brigade.										
Her Majesty's 14th Light Dragoons	...	1	4	13		2	16	3	6	4
71st Highland Light Infantry	...	...	...	1		...	19	...	,,	...
3rd European Regiment	...	...	...	2		...	1	...	...	...
24th Bombay Native Infantry	...	...	...	...		1	1	...	...	...
Total	...	1	5	24		3	43	3	6	4

H. H. A. WOOD, *Captain,*
Assistant Adjutant General,
Central India Field Force.

CENTRAL INDIA.—JHANSI. 79

Nominal Return of Officers and Men of the Field Force Hyderabad Contingent, Killed, Wounded, and Sun-struck in the Action with the Enemy at Koonch, on the 7th May 1858.

Corps.	Rank.	Name.	Date.		Remarks.
1st Cavalry	Rissaldar	Zoolicar Ali Beg	May	7th	Contusion.
	Russaidar	Sufdar Ali Beg	,,	,,	Killed.
	Duffadar	Gunnace Sing	,,	,,	Severely wounded.
	Trooper	Nannoo Sing	,,	,,	Slightly.
	,,	Dhan Sing	,,	,,	,,
	,,	Widut Sing	,,	,,	Severely.
	,,	Nujoo Khan	,,	,,	,,
	,,	Lall Sing	,,	,,	,,
	,,	Bachoo Sing	,,	,,	Contusion.
4th Cavalry.	Duffadar	Meer Golom Hoosain	,,	,,	Slightly.
	Trooper	Shaik Jumla Mahomed	,,	,,	Killed.
	,,	Shitah Khan	,,	,,	Slightly.
	,,	Mirza Hymud Beg	,,	,,	Severely.
	,,	Sudun Khan	,,	,,	Slightly.
	,,	Golam Ali Khan	,,	,,	,,
1st Co. Arty.	Gun Lascar	Nursoo	,,	,,	Severely.
	,,	Rajumah	,,	,,	Killed.
	Maistry	Tackeerah	,,	,,	Slightly.
2nd Co. Arty.	Jemadar	Chobee Sing	,,	,,	,,
5th Infy.	Sepoy	Takoor Sing	,,	,,	Severely.
	,,	Darrah Sing	,,	,,	,,
	,,	Bunkut	,,	,,	Slightly.
	,,	Takoor	,,	,,	,,
	,,	Ittoojee	,,	,,	Severely.

ABSTRACT.

Corps.	War Casualties.				Sun-stroke.	
	Officers Killed.	Officers Wounded.	Rank and File Killed.	Rank and File Wounded.	Officers.	Rank and File.
Field Force Hyderabad Contingent.						
1st Cavalry	1	1	...	7	...	...
4th Cavalry	...	...	1	5	...	...
1st Company Artillery	...	...	1	2	...	...
2nd Company Artillery	...	1	...	...	...	...
5th Infantry	...	...	...	5	...	...
Total	1	2	2	19	...	...

H. H. A. WOOD, *Captain,*
Assistant Adjutant General, C.I.F.F.

ORDNANCE DEPARTMENT.
CENTRAL INDIA FIELD FORCE.

Return of Ordnance captured from the Rebels by the Force under Command of Major-General SIR HUGH ROSE, K.C.B., *in an engagement at Koonch on the 7th May 1858, and in the subsequent pursuit.*

No.	Description.	Calibre.	Manufacture.	Length. Feet.	Length. Inches.	Remarks.
1	Brass Gun	3 Pr.	Native	3	10	
2	Ditto	1½ „		4	2½	
3	Ditto	3 „		4	6	
4	Ditto	2½ „		4	8	
5	Ditto	3 „		3	9	
6	Ditto	2 „		0	0	Burst in Action.
7	Iron Gun	12 „		5	3	
8	Ditto	½ „		3	0	
9	Ditto	½ „		1	6	

THOS. J. HAGGARD, *Lieut., Bombay Artillery,*
Commissary of Ordnance,
Central India Field Force.

CAMP SUNDEE;
10th May 1858.

Return of Ordnance Stores, captured from the Rebels at Koonch by the Force under Command of Major-General SIR HUGH ROSE, K.C.B., *on the 7th May 1858.*

No.	Names of Stores.	Quantity.		Remarks.
1	Ball Ammunition for small arms	11,800	All of European manufacture.	Also a quantity of Native made round shot, grape and powder, this last was expended in destroying the Fort at Hurdowi.
2	Caps, Percussion	3,100		
3	Portfires	114		
4	Powder, Ordnance, in Barrels, lbs.	200		
5	Ditto in Cartridges	850		
6	Shot, solid, 9-Pounder	410		
7	Ditto, 6-Pounder	49		

THOS. J. HAGGARD, *Lieut., Bombay Artillery,*
Commissary of Ordnance,
Central India Field Force.

CAMP ORAI,
5.

CHAPTER II.

CALPEE.

No. 272 of 1859.—His Excellency the Governor General in Council is pleased to direct the publication of the following letter from the Deputy Adjutant General of the Army, No. 11, of the 2nd instant, forwarding a Despatch from Major-General Sir Hugh Rose, K.C.B., detailing the operations attending the capture of Culpee, on the 24th May 1858. This report was only received by Government in the Military Department on the 8th ultimo.

In publishing it the Governor General in Council desires to take the opportunity of thanking Sir Hugh Rose, and the Officers and men engaged in the operations, for the complete success with which these were attended.

From Major H. W. NORMAN, *Deputy Adjutant-General of the Army, Head-Quarters Camp, Lucknow,* To the Secretary to the Government of India, *Military Department,—No. 11, dated 2nd February 1859.*

In continuation of my letter dated the 19th ultimo, No. 3, I have now the honor, by desire of His Excellency the Commander-in-Chief, to forward for submission to His Excellency the Viceroy and Governor General in Council, a Despatch from Major-General Sir H. Rose, K.C.B., detailing the operations attending the capture of Culpee, dated the 22nd June last, but which has only now reached Head-Quarters.

From Major-General SIR HUGH ROSE, K.C.B., *Commanding F. D. A. and Field Forces,* To Major-General SIR WM. M. MANSFIELD, K.C.B., *Chief of the Staff of the Army in India,—Dated Gwalior, 22nd June 1858.*

In reporting to you, for the information of the Commander-in-Chief in India, my operations against Culpee, it is my duty, in justice to the unvarying devotion and discipline of the Troops under my Command, to state the new and very serious difficulties which beset them after leaving Jhansi. They had to contend, not only against the Rebel Army, fighting as usual with all the advantages on their side of very superior numbers, and knowledge of the ground, but they had to encounter also a new antagonist, a Bengal Sun, at its maximum of heat. This formidable ally of the Rebel cause was more dangerous than the Rebels themselves; its summer blaze made havoc amongst Troops, especially Europeans, who already exhausted by months of over-fatigue, and want of sleep, by continued night-watchings and night-marches, were often exposed to its rays, manœuvring or fighting as at Konch, from sunrise to sunset.

At Konch, the Thermometer was 115°; before Culpee 118° in the shade, and on the march to Gwalior, it burst in an Officer's tent at 130°.

Her Majesty's 71st Highland Light Infantry, less inured than any other Corps, to Sun, because just arrived in India, suffered the most from it. Besides the twelve men, of a weak Wing of this Regiment, killed in their ranks by the Sun, at Konch, a great many more had to go into the Field Hospital, sick from sun-stroke; and the whole Wing was more or less affected by it.

The number of Officers and men in the sick list, all of whom had to be carried, on the march, in Dhoolies, increased with each day's operations, and in proportion as I was deprived of fighting men, the difficulties of taking care of the sick, and transporting them in continued marches increased. Whilst my Force suffered so much from sun-stroke, they were deprived in a great measure of its antidote, water. Between Jhansi and Culpee, we found no streams; all was well water; the wells, which are neither numerous nor abundant, being of extraordinary depth, as we approached the Jumna, which increased the difficulties of obtaining water.

Forage also was as scant as water.

The scarcity of these two essentials hurt the efficiency of the Cavalry and the Transport, at the very time that they were both urgently required—the first against the Rebel Cavalry, whose numbers and organization made them unusually enterprizing; and the latter, for the numerous and daily-increasing sick.

The scarcity of water had another disadvantage; it prevented concentration of my Force, when the strength of the enemy, and my difficulties rendered it necessary for a rapid advance against Culpee.

The Enfield Rifles had made up a good deal for my inferiority in numbers; that advantage, however, no longer now existed. The heat and other causes had had such an effect on the ammunition of the Rifles, that their loading becoming difficult, and their fire uncertain, the men lost confidence in their aims.

The above were some of the Military disadvantages of my position. They were increased by Political causes.

The inhabitants of the valley of the Jumna were the most disaffected my Force had yet met with. They had been under Rebel rule, and had never felt the influence of British Power since the commencement of the insurrection. Every village had its one or two Mahratta Pundits, who had made a most successful propaganda in favour of Nana Sahib as Peishwa. The villagers did good service to the Rebels, by betraying to them our Dâks and movements, as well as some carts, when their drivers, on account of the exhausted state of their cattle, could not keep their place in the Column, or sought water at a distance from the road.

The Rebels had another great source of strength. They fought their best because they were defending Culpee, their best fortified stronghold in Central and Western India and only Arsenal full of warlike stores and ammunition. Culpee, on the right bank of the Jumna, in the hands of the Rebels, prevented the concentration of the British Armies of the West, with those of the East of India; exposed to attack, from the line of the Jumna, the Army engaged in operations against the insurgents in the Doab, the line of the Ganges; Oudh; and Rohilcund; and so long as Culpee was Rebel, so long had it the enemy in their power to say that the East and West of India might be British, but that the pivot of its centre was theirs.

Whilst so many drawbacks weakened me, the enemy, physically speaking, was unusually strong. They were under three leaders of considerable influence, Rao Sahib, a nephew of Nana Sahib, the Nawab of Banda, and the Ranee of Jhansi. The high descent of the Ranee, her unbounded liberality to her Troops and retainers, and her fortitude which no reverses could shake, rendered her an influential and dangerous adversary. The Rebel Army was composed of the Gwalior Contingent, the finest men, best drilled and organized, Native Troops of all arms in India; other mutinous Bengal Infantry Regiments, such as the 52nd; Rebel Cavalry from Kotah; and a chosen band of Valaitees, the whole reinforced by the Force of all Arms of the Nawab of Banda, comprising a great deal of mutinous Bengal Cavalry, of which the 5th Irregulars, dressed in their red uniforms, formed a part. All the Sepoy Regiments kept up, carefully, their English equipment and organization; the words of command for drill, grand rounds, &c., were given, as we could hear, at night, in English.

The numerous difficulties of my situation above recited, were rendered more grave by a series of accidents which occurred in the 2nd Brigade, over which I had no control, and which embarrassed my operations.

I wished to follow up the enemy and attack him, as rapidly as possible, whilst still suffering under his reverse at Konch. For this purpose I marched from Konch, immediately after the action with the 1st Brigade, directing the 2nd Brigade to follow me, at one day's interval, on account of the scarcity of water and forage on the line of march.

A result of this advance was my occupation of the village and strong Fort of Hurdowi, one march from Konch, which the enemy had abandoned in their retreat, and the surrender of its Chief, one of the most influential adherents of Nana Sahib.

But a further rapid movement to the front was prevented by Brigadier Stewart's reporting to me from Konch, that he had been unable to march from that place, as I had directed, in consequence of a storm of rain having rendered the tents too heavy for Transport. The Brigade was delayed three days at Konch.

Other tactical plans of mine were frustrated by similar obstacles.

My original instructions were to take Culpee. I was subsequently directed to make my appearance on some point of the right bank of the Jumna, to effect a communication with Lieutenant-Colonel Maxwell, Commanding a Column of the Bengal Army, who was ordered to cooperate with me against Culpee from the left bank of the Jumna, for the purpose of receiving from him a supply of ammunition for the Siege of Culpee, to make good the large amount which my Force had expended in the Sieges of Chanderey and Jhansi.

I had written to Colonel Maxwell that I would be on the Jumna, a few miles below Culpee, on the 14th of May: this letter never reached him. The communications with this Officer, and the left bank of the Jumna were hazardous, and were only effected by Spies, in disguise, who conveyed our letters in the heels or soles of their sandals, or in quills in their mouths.

The information which I had collected on the road, and a reconnoisance made by Lieutenant-Colonel Gall, H. M. 14th Light Dragoons, with his usual skill, confirmed all I had the honor to state in my report of the action at Konch as to the enemy's elaborate lines of defences for the protection of Culpee on the main road from Konch to that Fortress.

I could not have concentrated a force, on account of the want of water, against these defences. I determined, therefore, to turn them, to break off to the right, from the high road from Oraye to Culpee, march to the Jumna, to the village of Golowlee, about 6 miles below Culpee, effect a communication from thence with Lieutenant-Colonel Maxwell, and then, my right resting on the Jumna, and covered by the flank fire of Colonel Maxwell's Batteries and Riflemen from the other bank of the Jumna, advance up its right bank, against Culpee. The Fort of Culpee, and the part of the Town, facing my advance, to be well shelled before the attack.

The Jumna is fordable at Golowlee; it stands in the Nullahs running down to the Jumna, just outside the dangerous labyrinth of ravines which surround Culpee.

My march to Golowlee was, with the exception of a few bad and unbridged Nullahs, over a table land, from which, during the Monsoon, the waters shed into the ravines.

To mislead the enemy, and mask this movement, I directed the 2nd Brigade to close up to Oraye from Konch, and following the high road to Culpee, take up a position at the village of Banda. This plan was foiled by the Brigade's losing its way, and instead of going to Banda, making a double march, and following me to Sucalee. Their long exposure to the Sun, in this protracted march, caused a great many casualties, and the general prostration of the Brigade; Brigadier Stewart, and the whole of his Staff, forming part of the Sick List.

It was important to keep the appointment I had made with Colonel Maxwell to be on the Jumna, on the 14th instant. But the 2nd Brigade could not, on account of its sickness, co-operate with me; and it would have been hazardous to go too far away from it, weak as it was, especially as the enemy, aware, as I learnt, of the sickness in my Camp, and of our difficulties, had concentrated all their Cavalry, with Infantry and guns, from their bivouacs in the villages round Culpee, for the purpose of unceasingly harassing my force, in its separated state, by making attacks feigned and real; falling on parties going for water, wood, grass, &c.; part of their tactics being to force my Troops to be exposed, at the hottest time of the day, in large numbers to the sun, which they knew was fatal to Europeans.

In giving assistance to my 2nd Brigade, I had to be careful that I did not reduce the 1st by too much exposure to Sun, to the same state of inefficiency.

To meet all these obligations and difficulties, I delayed one day at Etowa to give a rest to the 2nd Brigade at Sucalee, and detaching all my carriage, for the sick, to their assistance, and calling off the attention of the enemy from them, by a diversion in an opposite direction,

Lieutenant-Colonel Campbell, who had succeeded Brigadier Stewart in the Command of the 2nd Brigade, brought it up to the 1st, on the night of the 14th instant, without molestation.

A few hours afterwards, I marched with the 1st Brigade, and Major Orr's Force for Golowlee, which I reached with no other opposition than an attack on the baggage by the Rebel Cavalry, concealed in a ravine; they were put to flight by a Troop of the 14th, which in anticipation of an ambuscade, I had sent to reinforce the rear guard. In this march we crossed the high road from Jullalpoor to Culpee. I directed Major Orr to drive in a strong picket of the enemy of all Arms, posted on this road between us and Culpee; halt afterwards on the road; cover the march of my rear guard to Golowlee; and then encamp at the village of Tehree, near the road, for the purpose of watching it, keeping up my communication with the 2nd Brigade, and assisting it, in its march, during the night of the 15th to Diapoora, a village near Tehree.

On my arrival at Golowlee, I despatched two of the Hyderabad Cavalry across the Jumna to Lieutenant-Colonel Maxwell, who was about thirty miles off on the other side of it, requesting him to move up to the River immediately.

I also ordered two Pontoon rafts, which I had brought with great trouble from Poona, to be floated, by sun-set, on the Jumna, for communication with Lieutenant-Colonel Maxwell, and transport of the ammunition for my Force. The Rebels had destroyed or taken to Culpee all the boats on the river.

One of the most important of my instructions was now carried out. My Force had marched from Bombay to the Jumna, and had effected an union with the Bengal army; the immediate result of which was a combined operation of Bengal and Bombay Troops against Culpee.

The advanced guard and centre of the 2nd Brigade reached Diapoora, on the morning of the 15th without opposition, but its rear guard, under Major Forbes, which I had strongly reinforced had hardly

No. 1 Enclosure. Major Forbes' Report. left Etowa, when it was vigorously attacked by about 1,000 or 1,200 Cavalry, besides Infantry, and Guns. The enclosed Report from Major Forbes shows how successfully he repulsed, aided by Major Orr, the enemy, with loss; and brought, safely, the long and helpless line of baggage, over difficult ground, to the Camp at Diapoora. I beg to mention, specially, Major Forbes for this good service. Having received at Golowlee a report that Major Forbes was hard-pressed, and hearing a heavy cannonade in his direction, I marched with the Troops, detailed in the margin, to his assistance. The urgency of the case alone made me undertake this operation, as I foresaw that the suffocating heat of the sun must strike down a large portion of my Force. I galloped on, and found that Major Forbes had reached Diapoora; but that the enemy, baffled in their attempt to cut off the rear guard, had taken ground to the left, and reinforced by three or four Battalions from Culpee, who were now swarming out of the ravines, was preparing, firing heavily to storm the village of Mutha, which Lieutenant-Colonel Campbell had judiciously occupied from Diapoora, for which I beg to make special mention of him. For if the enemy were in possession of Mutha, the Camp at Diapoora would no longer have been tenable. A large body of Cavalry, deployed across the road from Etowa to Muttra, were approaching in support of the Infantry. The Officer Commanding in Mutha, felt himself so hard-pressed that he had given orders for evacuating it. The enemy were pressing forwards. I immediately gave orders to the Troops who were retiring, to re-occupy the village, and hold it at any price, ordering up in their support, at a trot, the ½ Troop Horse Artillery, and the ½ of No. 4 Light Field Battery, a Troop of the 14th and the 3rd Hyderabad Cavalry, with two Companies of Hyderabad Infantry, and the 25th Bombay Native Infantry.

Margin:
½ Troop B. H. A.
1 Troop 14th Lt. Dragoons.
1 Troop Hyd. Cavly.
3 Guns No. 4 L. F. B.
38th and 25th Regt. N. I.

Captain Lightfoot placed the Artillery skilfully, on the left of Mutha, the accurate fire of their shrapnel and round shot broke the Rebel Cavalry, and drove them from their position in support of the Infantry, who still held the deep and twisting ravines in front of Mutha. I directed Captain Douglas, Bengal Artillery, Commanding Artillery Hyderabad Contingent, to post four 6-pounders on the right of Mutha, and burst shrapnel just over the heads of the Rebels in the ravines; this he did with his usual skill and devotion, under a heavy fire of the enemy's Riflemen so effectually, that the Rebels who were suffering from the admirable fire of Her Majesty's 71st, who still had some of the better sort of ammunition, retired from their ambuscades, the main body down the ravines, a few across country to Culpee, the 71st making killing practice at the latter, at 700 or 800 yards. I did not pursue, because fresh exertion in the sun, and in most difficult ground, would have been fatal to men, the greater part of whom had been marching all night, and engaged all day in fearful heat. My game was a waiting one, and I abstained carefully from playing that of my adversary, which was to disorganize and prostrate my Force by continued exposure to sun. I never yielded an inch to the enemy's attacks; but, on the other hand, husbanded the strength and health of my men for one great combat for Culpee. As it was, the intense heat made havoc amongst my Troops, Officers as well as men. Upwards of 200 out of less than 400 men of the 25th Bombay Native Infantry fell out of the ranks on the line of march, struck by sun. This gallant Regiment suffered as much as Europeans from sun, the constitutions of the men having been weakened by scurvy. Captain Wood, Assistant Adjutant General, fell, struck, it was feared mortally, by sun-stroke; he recovered partially, and with the unyielding resolution which characterized the conduct of the Force, resumed his duties under fire. Having provided for the protection of Mutha, I returned with the detachments of the 1st Brigade to Golowlee.

The enemy, the same day, in order either to prevent me from giving support to the 2nd Brigade, or hoping to beat the 1st Brigade weakened by the reinforcements which I took from it, reinforced strongly their lines of out-posts in the ravines, and supporting them with guns, and masses, at a distance, menaced and kept up a heavy fire on my position at Golowlee, from the Jumna to the village of Tehree, against which latter place they advanced with a thick chain of skirmishers.

Brigadier Stuart, Commanding the 1st Brigade, at Golowlee, and Captain Hare, Commanding at Tehree, met the attack with vigor; the former answered the enemy's cannonade so effectually with his mortars and guns, that they retired. Captain Hare repulsed the enemy's advance and following them up took a tope of trees in advance of his position, in which they had concentrated a force. I beg to make special mention of both these Officers for their conduct on this occasion.

The enemy having shown signs of fortifying a high ridge opposite my right front, about half way between Golowlee and Culpee, I had a Battery of two 8-inch Mortars constructed in front of my right, which shelled with good effect the ridge and the ravines near it.

The next day, the 17th instant, after noon, the enemy again attacked the 2nd Brigade at Diapoora, and was repulsed, with loss as it appears by an extract of a Report from Lieutenant-Colonel Campbell enclosed.

No. 2 Enclosure.
Lieut.-Col. Campbell's Report.

Colonel Maxwell, leaving his column of the strength, as detailed in the margin, to march to a position opposite Culpee, came on to me at Golowlee, when I communicated to him my plan of attack, and gave him the requisite directions. Part of his column had been detached from him, but was expected back.

I have already had the honor to state the outline of my plan of attack. Its details were as follows:

Colonel Maxwell was to construct, on the opposite bank of the Jumna, Mortar Batteries; one to shell, vigorously, the "Fort of Culpee" and blow up, if possible, the powder magazines in it, destroying also the defences of the Fort facing my position at Golowlee; another to shell the part of the Town fronting the same way, so as to prevent the enemy from holding these localities in force, when I attacked them; another Mortar Battery to be placed lower down the Jumna and opposite the village of Rehree. Rehree stands on the edge of the small sandy plain bordered by the Jumna, which is situated between the belt of ravines and Culpee. The enemy had a force and a Battery in Rehree for the purpose of sweeping off my right column of attack, when it debouched from the ravines against Culpee, and preventing its occupying the "Sandy Plain" which was an important point for me, because, once in possession of it, my right flank resting on the Jumna, I could bring up all my Artillery through the pass through the ravines, and concentrate from the "Sandy Plain" a vertical and horizontal fire, on the part of Culpee which I wished to attack. I wished Rehree, the ravines and ground about it, to be destroyed, and made untenable by fire from the opposite bank.

These Batteries were to shell their "objectifs" for 16 or 20 hours before, and during the advance against Culpee.

Riflemen and Field Guns were to be stationed opposite the "Sandy Plain" on the other, the left bank of the Jumna and clear its right bank, and the "Sandy Plain" of the enemy.

I hoped to beat the Rebel Army in one decisive action. I felt certain that if I routed them, they would not, with the fate of "Jhansi" and "Sohaie" before their eyes, have the heart to shut themselves up in the Fort and become the victims of an investment. At the same time, it was evident that to take by storm, such tremendous ground, if well defended, as the ravines surrounding Culpee, every yard of which was a dangerous obstacle and an ambush, was no ordinary operation, particularly under the various difficulties of my situation, previously enumerated.

Whilst, with my right, the 1st Brigade, I attacked Culpee by its left, I intended to make a strong feint against the right of the enemy to be converted into a real attack, if feasible, with my left, the 2nd Brigade, along the Julalpoor and Culpee Road, Major Orr's Force in Tehree keeping up the communication between the two Brigades, and assisting both as required.

Fresh difficulties compelled me to modify this plan. Some few days must elapse before the Mortar Batteries on the left, the opposite bank of the Jumna, could be ready. The wells of the villages where the Hyderabad Field Force, and the 2nd Brigade were stationed, began to fail. The sick from sun-stroke could not have the water which was necessary for their treatment; Troop horses and baggage animals died from drought. My left, the 2nd Brigade, was exposed, sickly as it was, to constant attack. Concentration and abundance of water were the only remedies for these fresh embarrassments. On the morning of the 19th I brought the 2nd Brigade and Hyderabad Field Force from Diapoora and Tehree, to my Camp on the Jumna.

The enemy continued their tactics of harassing unceasingly my Troops, and forcing them into the sun; large bodies of Cavalry hanging on my position, retiring when attacked, but ready to fall on escorts, which I was obliged to send to a distance for forage, the want of which was the cause of serious losses. Out of 36 men of the 14th Light Dragoons, forming part of one forage escort, seventeen were brought back to the Camp in dhoolies after only two hours' exposure to sun.

This prostration of more than half a body of men by sun, after two hours' mere marching, and a similar amount of sun-sickness in the 25th Bombay Native Infantry, on the march to Mutha, give a correct estimate of the sanitary state of my Force before Culpee; that state was dangerous. The prostration of the whole Force had become a matter of arithmetical calculation. So many hours' sun laid low so many men. I had, weakened by every sort of difficulty, to conquer the greatest stake in the campaign, against the greatest odds; half of my Troops sickly; every man of them ailing, to say nothing of a very numerous and daily increasing Sick List, crowded into tents, where the Thermometer stood 118° in the shade. To compare small things to great, myself and my Force were suffering under two evils, which have overcome the greatest Armies, under the most successful Generals, sickness and climate.

This view of the case was borne out by an official letter which I received at this time from Dr. Arnott, Superintending Surgeon, a Gentleman, who is distinguished by his cool and correct judgment.

The object of Dr. Arnott's letter was to make known to me the critical state of the health of the Central India Field Force. Dr. Arnott showed that the great proportion of it, Officers as well as men, beginning with my personal and divisional Staff were ill; that the health of all was so weakened by the continual hardship and over-fatigues of an arduous campaign, that it was fast succumbing under Sun; finally, that if the operations against Culpee were to be protracted, the whole Force might be prostrated.

I knew this and a good deal more. I knew that from the commencement my Force had been engaged in operations on a scale, for which, according to Military Rules, and in former times in India, three or four times their number were considered necessary.

In a quiet Garrison to be on guard every other day is held to be too much for a Soldier's health; but my men, for months had been making the strongest physical exertions, with broken sleep, or no sleep at all, watching the camp in unknown and hostile districts, against surprize, half the night, and marching the other half to avoid sun; then often all day, without a rest, fighting, or on the rear guard, or on reconnoissances, or escorts, under a burning sun. The fewness of numbers of my Force did not allow of the Reliefs which according to the rules of the Service, are considered indispensable, even in Peace.

In my long march, from the West to the Centre of India, the hardships of the service were not lightened by good roads. On the contrary, country tracks and unbridged nullahs, with very few exceptions, were my communications. The consequence of this was that one deep Nullah, often, detaining the baggage, guns, and rear guard for hours, the Transport and Troops employed were exposed to all the bad effects of a protracted march in Sun. Bad roads and an unorganized system of transport and supply, were also the cause that the rations, notwithstanding best endeavours of the Commissariat, were at times in arrears, and that the Troops, on those occasions performed hard duties, or fought all day on insufficient nourishment.

The evil of the numerical strength of the Force being far too small for the extent of its operations (the Government was unable to complete it to the strength intended, on account of the necessities of the times), was increased subsequently by that strength being constantly diminished by casualties in the field, and by a large and daily-increasing Sick List. The details of Recruits who joined me, did not make good these vacancies; and it became necessary to weaken, still more, my Field Force, at a time when every man of it was urgently required, by leaving a Garrison at Jhansi, consisting of a Wing of the 3rd Europeans; six Companies of the 24th Bombay Native Infantry; half a Battery of 9-pounders, and a proportionate amount of Cavalry, under Lieutenant-Colonel Liddell, one of my best superior Officers.

I beg leave to apologize for the length of these details. But it is right that His Excellency the Commander-in-Chief should know the reasons in their fullest extent, which compelled me to reinforce myself with part of Lieutenant-Colonel Maxwell's Force; that His Excellency should know also, what the Troops, whom I had the honor to command, bore for the cause of their Queen and Country, and how they bore it. I have the satisfaction to report that these noble Soldiers, whose successes were never chequered by a reverse, with a discipline which was as enduring as their courage, never proffered one complaint. They fell in their ranks struck down by Sun, and exhausted by fatigue; but they would not increase the anxieties of their General, or belie their devotion by a complaint. No matter how great their exhaustion, or how deep their short sleep, they always sprung to my call to arms, with the heartiest good will. To think of yielding or retreating would have been ignominy.

All felt that physical strength might fail, but that the spirit and discipline of British Soldiers never could. They were often too ill to march, but their devotion made them fight. It is almost superfluous to add that Troops animated by so high a sense of duty were sober, orderly, and most respectful to their Officers. There was less crime in my Camp than in Garrison.

When I speak of springing to their arms, I ought to make special mention of Her Majesty's 14th Light Dragoons, for the admirable order and celerity with which their in-lying and out-lying picquets mounted on the frequent occasions when I turned them out, on alarms, or sudden attacks of the enemy. Their videttes and patrols also were always watchful and intelligent.

My first, and most important instructions were to take Culpee. There were two ways of doing so, either by one decisive action, or a protracted operation.

In either case, I required reinforcements. The fight for Culpee was sure to be an obstinate, perhaps a desperate struggle. I should have compromised the whole spirit of my most important instructions, and the success of the British cause in India, if I had attempted that struggle with a Force, whose health was such as I have described it, and had neglected to reinforce it with a portion of the gallant Troops, who fresh and unimpaired in vigour, were only separated from me by the Jumna.

A check before Culpee in the advanced state of the hot season, and the rains close at hand, would have resuscitated rebellion throughout India, compromised the safety of Cawnpore, exposed to a flank, or rear attack the extensive line of operations of His Excellency the Commander-in-Chief in India, and lit the torch of rebellion in the Deccan, and the Southern Mahrattas, full of ill-disposed Arabs and Rohillas, and partizans, of Nana Sahib as Peishwa.

Under the influence of these important considerations, I directed Lieutenant-Colonel Maxwell to send across the Jumna, to my Camp the reinforcements detailed in the enclosed Report from that officer; they arrived at my Head Quarters at Golowlee on the night of the 20th instant.

No. 3 Enclosure.
Lieutenant-Colonel Maxwell's Report.

The Agent of the Governor-General for Central India, who, in his official capacity, accompanied my Force, was of opinion that the peculiar circumstances justified my bringing the reinforcements across the Jumna. I was relieved, therefore, from any political objection to the step. The result proved its necessity. A day or two after the arrival of the reinforcements in my Camp, the Camel Corps, the principal reinforcement, saved, by their timely aid, my right, the key of my position, from a disaster, in a desperate and general attack on it, on the 23rd of May; and that success was followed by a conquering advance of my whole line from the Jumna to my extreme left; the total rout of the enemy, and the capture, next day, of Culpee, with all its Artillery and rich Arsenal.

* 682 Camel Corps.
2 Companies 88th Regiment.
124 Seikh Battalion.

On the morning of the 20th I made a reconnoissance on the left bank of the Jumna, and selected a position for a Battery of 8-inch Mortars, at the village of Russulpoor, to batter the village of Rehree, &c., as already stated.

On the 22nd instant this Battery was ready, as well as one of four

---

* This number includes, I believe, the Guns.

10-inch Mortars opposite the Fort, and another of two 8-inch Mortars, opposite the Town and Cutcherry, in which latter place Rao Sahib, the Nawab of Banda, and the Ranee of Jhansi were reported to be stationed with a large body of Infantry and Guns. A Division of 9-pounder guns, and a Company of Her Majesty's 88th were stationed at Russulpoor against Rehree, and the "Sandy Plain" on the opposite bank.

The enemy were now exposed to my attack of their left flank from Golowlee and to a cross vertical and horizontal fire, into the same flank and their rear from the other side of the Jumna.

I had hardly returned to Camp, on the 20th, before the enemy again advanced, covered by a very thick chain of skirmishers, through the ravines and attacked with much determination my right flank. The pickets were immediately reinforced by four Companies of the 86th, two Companies of the 25th Bombay Native Infantry, and three 9-pounders.

The reinforcements had not joined me; and the Mortar Batteries on the other side of the Jumna were not ready to cover my advance; the heat was at its maximum; and I had fixed the 23rd instant for the general attack of the enemy's positions and of Culpee. I did not therefore play the game of my adversary by allowing myself to be drawn into a general action under disadvantageous circumstances, but directed the pickets merely to maintain their ground, which they did steadily and gallantly, under the able command of Major Stewart, Her Majesty's 86th Regiment, until the enemy were beat back.

The casualties in this day's partial affair were four Officers and forty Rank and File. Lieutenant Jerome, 86th, severely wounded, and Lieutenant Forbes, 25th Bombay Native Infantry, struck down by sun, led their Companies with the same high Military spirit for which they have been specially mentioned on former occasions.

On the 21st instant, I received information that the Rebel Army intended to make a general attack on my position, at Golowlee at 8 A.M., the next day; that they had sworn a religious oath on the waters of the Jumna, a sacred River, that they would drive my Force into the Jumna and destroy it, or die, and that afterwards, they would move Southwards against General Whitlock; that large quantities of opium had been issued to the Troops for the purpose of making them fight desperately.

The positions occupied by my force were as follows:—

The right flank, facing the left of Culpee, rested on the ravines running down to the Jumna; in these ravines stood the villages of Soorowlee and Golowlee. Both these villages were connected and held by strong pickets and prevented my right being turned.

Half of the 1st Brigade, my right flank, was encamped perpendicularly to the Jumna, facing the belt of ravines, and the left front of Culpee, on the table land, immediately outside the belt.

The remainder of the 1st Brigade facing the continuation of the belt of ravines, which took a sweep outward, and the 2nd Brigade and Hyderabad Field Force, facing the table land or plain stretching from Golowlee across the road from Culpee to Jullalpoor, were thrown back "en potence." This ground was adapted to the movements of Artillery and Cavalry.

My whole front was well guarded by strong out-posts with advanced sentries in the ravines and pickets.

On the morning of 22nd I made the following disposition of my Troops to resist the expected attack.

The pickets on the right front of Her Majesty's 86th Regiment and 3rd Europeans were reinforced by the remainder of the 86th in skirmishing order; their right resting on the Jumna. In support were three guns of No. 4 Light Field Battery, one Troop Her Majesty's 14th Light Dragoons, a Troop of the 3rd Bombay Light Cavalry and four Companies of the 25th Bombay Native Infantry, the whole under the command of Brigadier Stuart.

The pickets of the right centre were supported by the other half of No. 4 Light Field Battery, the remainder of the 25th Bombay Native Infantry, with the 21st Company Royal Engineers, the whole under Lieutenant-Colonel Robertson.

My left centre, facing the plain and the village of Tehree, was guarded by No. 1 Bombay Troop Horse Artillery, supported by two Troops Her Majesty's 14th Light Dragoons.

The Siege Guns, two 18-pounders, one 24-pounder and two 8-inch Howitzers, each of their flanks guarded by detachments of the 3rd Europeans, formed the centre, supported by the Wing of Her Majesty's 71st, one squadron of the 14th, a Troop of the 3rd Light Cavalry, and Captain Field's Royal Artillery, 9-pounders.

The left was formed by the Camel Corps and No. 18 Light Field Battery, supported by a detachment of the Sikh Corps, the Hyderabad Field Force covering my extreme left.

Two Companies Her Majesty's 88th whose strength, although they had only been two or three days in my Camp, was already much weakened by sun casualties, and four Companies of the 25th Bombay Native Infantry, were left in the Camp for its protection.

Shortly after 8 o' clock A.M., on the 22nd of May, the enemy who continued their tactics of forcing my Troops to fight in the heat of the day were reported, by continued messages from my videttes and outposts, to be advancing in great force from Culpee and its environs towards the belt of ravines on my right, and along the Jullalpoor and Culpee Road against my left.

Their left manœuvred so skilfully that they got under cover of broken ground into the ravines, without being perceived on the right; and Brigadier Stuart reported to me as I was posting the Siege Guns, that my right was no longer threatened.

The enemy's right, consisting of 1,300 or 1,400 Cavalry, supported by several Battalions of Infantry, and Horse Artillery 9-pounders, continuing their advance along the Jullalpoor Road, brought their left shoulders up, when opposite the village of Tehree, in front of my centre, from whence they re-inforced strongly their pickets in the ravines opposite my right centre, and deploying their guns and cavalry to the right menaced to out-flank and turn my right. I still felt the conviction that the enemy's real object of attack was my right; and that this ostentatious display of force against my left and the perfect stillness in the deep ravines on my right, were ruses to mislead me and induce me to weaken my right, by sending reinforcements from it to my left, when they would have attacked with all their energy my right, endeavoured to take the Mortar Battery and the Camp, their right falling at the same time on my left and cutting me off in combination with their left, from the Jumna.

Whilst therefore I protected my left against a feint, which might become a serious attack, I did not take a man away from my right, and endeavored to catch the enemy in their own trap. I reinforced the pickets, on the left, in the first instance, with a squadron of the 14th Light Dragoons under Lieutenant-Colonel Gall, and the 3rd Hyderabad Cavalry under Captain Abbott, and afterwards directed these Troops to retire slowly before the enemy, obliquely across my front, in order to conceal my heavy guns, and draw the Rebel Cavalry into their fire. Captain Abbott was directed, after having completed this movement, to place his Regiment perpendicularly to my front, in order to be able to charge, with all his Horse, the right flank of the advancing Cavalry. The manœuvre succeeded partially; the Rebel Horse were enticed into the fire of the Siege Guns, which caused confusion and numerous casualties amongst them, killing, amongst others, the Commanding Officer of the 5th Bengal Irregulars. But the mutinous Cavalry adhered to their system of never allowing the British Cavalry to close with them, and kept carefully out of the way of the Hyderabad Horse.

To discover the enemy, who, I felt assured, were concealed in the ravines in front of my right, I had ordered a Company of the 3rd Europeans to be pushed some hundred yards forward in front of my outposts, into this network of ambushes. The 3rd Europeans, after advancing some distance, found the Rebel host crouched in their lair, and started them from it. In an instant, a serious and general engagement began along the whole line from the Jumna to the village of Tehree; the belt of ravines in front of my position, becoming enveloped in smoke and fire, the Sepoys rose out of their hiding places in thick chains of skirmishers, advancing and firing heavily, followed by large supports and columns *en masse* at a distance. All my guns opened on the advance of the Rebels; and the supports closed up to their threatened fronts.

I was watching the determined attack on the centre of my position, from the left of the village of Tehree, and at the same time their movements towards my right and left when I heard a slackening of our fire on the right, I instantly sent an enquiry to Brigadier Stuart, whether he would wish to be reinforced by half of the Camel Corps; he replied that he should be very glad to have them; directly afterwards, Brigadier Stuart's fire became fainter and fainter, and that of the enemy heavier. I understood that my right, the key of my whole position, was in danger, and instantly proceeded myself to its assistance with the whole of the Camel Corps at their best pace. On the way, I met an orderly coming to me at full speed, from Brigadier Stuart, asking for further reinforcements; I knew that they were required, for the enemy's fire now came from within our position. The Camel Corps, under Major Ross, having reached the foot of the rising ground, on which were the Mortar Battery and the three 9-pounders, and dismounted, went up the rise in line at the double, in perfect order.

The situation of Brigadier Stuart's position was very critical. Volleys of musketry, which killed or wounded every horse of my Staff but one, were coming over the crest of the rising ground from the Sepoy Troops, who had debouched, and were debouching, in great numbers from the gallies [gullies] leading into the ravines, and were advancing rapidly, firing heavily with yells of triumph, their faces distorted by opium and fury, across a small piece of level ground against the Mortar Battery and Guns, to which they were close. The guns had ceased firing. Brigadier Stuart was on foot at the guns ordering the few Artillerymen, who served them, to draw swords and defend their guns, his lines of defence had been driven in, the men having been struck down to the ground by sun-stroke, where they lay, and the fire of the rest rendered insufficient by the defective ammunition of their Rifles. Without halting on the crest I charged down it with the Camel Corps, the dense lines of the mutineers who were ten times superior to us in number, the gallant Soldiers of Her Majesty's Rifle Brigade and Her Majesty's 80th Regiment giving one of those cheers which all over the world have been the heralds of British successes. The rebels wavered, turned and fled, pursued by the Camel Corps, with all their energy, through the ravines, where numbers of them were bayonetted or killed by musketry fire.

I ordered up rapidly the half of No. 4 Light Field Battery, from the Mortar Battery, to the front, to a Knoll in the ravines, from whence they fired grape at the nearest Rebels, and round shot at the more distant masses which, following the example of their front line, had also made a precipitate retreat.

The men of the Camel Corps fell so fast and thick, struck by sun in their violent pursuit of the Enemy, up and down the steep sides of the rocky ravines, which reflected back the burning rays, that the whole of them would have been prostrated, if I had not called them off, which I did after they had driven the enemy over, and taken the commanding ridge between my position and Culpee.

In this, as well as in the previous operations, since Konch, sun-stroke caused sudden death, delirium, and hysterical fits of crying and laughing.

The very important service rendered on this occasion by Major Ross, Commanding the Camel Corps, requires that I should make special mention of the ability and resolute gallantry with which he led his brave Corps. This very promising Officer is perfectly qualified to turn to the best account all the vast advantages of fleet or mounted Infantry.

Lieutenant Buckley, of the same Corps, attracted my attention by the spirit with which his party attacked and bayonetted Rebels; for which I beg to mention him specially.

Lieutenant-Colonel Louth, Commanding on the extreme right, on the Jumna, relieved from pressure by the success of the Camel Corps, and reinforced by one of its Companies, moved forward through the ravines, and by a skilful manœuvre cut off and surrounded a considerable body of Rebel Sepoys, who had advanced too far. Part were killed on the bank of the Jumna, the rest were driven into the river, where they were shot or drowned. I beg to mention specially Lieutenant-Colonel Louth for the good service he did on this occasion : he is a good and gallant Officer, who always leads his Regiment to success. He is well seconded by his admirable Soldiers, whom I cannot eulogize more highly than by saying that they do credit to Ireland.

The enemy simultaneously with their attack on my right had advanced with equal vigor against my right centre, guarded by part of the 25th Bombay Native Infantry, who, despite a most gallant resistance were driven back by overpowering numbers, which afforded an opportunity to Lieutenant Edwards, Commanding the 21st Company of Royal Engineers, which I had placed in support of the 25th, to charge with his Company, most successfully, the very superior force of the Rebels, routing them with loss and pursuing them till out of reach. I beg to mention, specially, Lieutenant Edwards for his prompt resolution on this occasion ; he is an enterprizing and promising Officer. The 21st Company fight as well in the field, as they work in the trenches, and are worthy of their distinguished Corps.

The remainder of the 25th guarding my left centre. under Lieutenant-Colonel Robertson, held their ground stedfastly; the Rebel Sepoys advancing close up to the 25th firing, halted and addressed them bitter reproaches, couched in the most revolting language, for their unshaken fidelity to the English. The 25th answered the malediction of the mutineers in a manner worthy of their reputation and English discipline, a volley, a cheer, and a charge with the bayonet. Lieutenant-Colonel Robertson, of whose gallantry and ability I have had so many proofs, and his devoted Regiment whose loyalty and discipline have so often conquered treason and insubordination, deserve to be specially mentioned for their distinguished conduct on this occasion.

My whole line was now advancing and driving the enemy from their positions. I have already spoken of the triumphant advance of the right and right centre. The left centre was equally successful under Lieutenant-Colonel Robertson, who, following up his spirited charge, dashed through the ravines with the 25th after the Rebels, came up with the rear of them, near the village of Tehree, bayonetted them and continued the pursuit beyond the village, till his men, unable to go any longer, fell exhausted.

The whole of my Infantry on the left now brought their left shoulders forward, and covered by Captain Lightfoot's Troop of Horse Artillery, three Guns of No. 4 Light Field Battery, and the whole of the Cavalry, I had reinforced the Cavalry on the left with all the Cavalry from the right, made a converging attack on the enemy's right and the village of Tehree. The enemy broke and fled, pursued for some miles by the Horse Artillery and Cavalry. Their exhaustion and ground broken by ravines stopped the pursuit which cost the enemy dear. The Rebels were so completely beaten and disheartened that broken parties of them did not retire on Culpee, but were seen flying across the ravines in a Westerly direction towards Jaloun.

Colonel Wetherall, whose state of health qualified him for the sick list, although his devotion like that of so many more of the Force kept him out of it, was struck by sun in the pursuit three or four miles from Camp, and brought back to it on a litter.

The complete defeat and serious loss which the enemy had sustained this day, despite their having displayed tactics and an energy of attack, which I had not previously witnessed in them, convinced me that an immediate advance to Culpee, which I had some days back fixed for the next day, the 23rd instant, would with the prestige of this day's victory make me master of it at once. I therefore only gave the Troops the time which was indispensable for their rest after the long day's combat in the sun, and dividing my Force into two columns of attack, marched the next morning long before break of day against Culpee, according to my original plan of attack; one Column, the right, under Brigadier Stuart, through the ravines, their right resting on the Jumna; the other, the left Column, under myself, along the Jullalpoor and Culpee Road.

I left my numerous sick, Parks, and baggage, in Camp, which was struck, under Captain Hare.

The Mortar Batteries on the other side of the Jumna had, according to my orders, opened their fire the day before, the 22nd; and during the fight, I was glad to see the shells dropping, with great precision, into the Fort, the Town, and all about the village of Rehree.

When my column had marched from Camp, across the plain, in front of my left and reached the Jullalpoor and Culpee Road, I brought their left shoulders forward, and taking the road for the direction of my centre, covered my advance against Culpee with the Camel Corps under Major Ross, supported by the Hyderabad Cavalry.

From the road I despatched a Staff Officer, with a party of Cavalry, to effect a communication with Brigadier Stuart's left.

My column descended into deep ravines, and mounted their steep banks, formidable, almost impregnable positions, which the enemy had totally abandoned panic-struck by the previous day's defeat.

Faint firing on the right announced faint opposition to the advance of Brigadier Stuart, of whose report of this and the previous day's operations a copy is enclosed.

<small>No. 4 Enclosure.
Brigadier Stuart's Report.</small>

After marching some distance along the road, the enemy opened a fire on our advance from a secret Battery, in a ravine at a great distance and elevation. Major Ross made a rapid flank march across the ravines to cut it off. But a few rounds from Captain Ommaney's Royal Artillery Guns, which he had brought rapidly up considerably in advance of the column, caused the Battery to make off through the ravines. All of their guns were afterwards taken by the pursuing Cavalry.

Shortly afterwards, I got into communication with the right of Brigadier Stuart's Brigade, and by 10 o'clock A.M. both my Brigades were masters of the Fort and Town of Culpee.

My prediction had come to pass that the Rebels would make one desperate struggle for Culpee outside its walls; and that if they were defeated, they would not make a stand within them. The hard-fought fight of the day before on the banks of the Jumna had given us Culpee.

Whilst my Force was involved in the labyrinth of ravines, the enemy could be observed moving off to the North-West from Culpee, in large bodies, with Elephants.

Once clear of the ravines, I instantly directed Lieutenant-Colonel, then Major, Gall, Her Majesty's 14th Light Dragoons, to pursue the enemy as closely, and as far as he could, with Horse Artillery and Cavalry. I have the honor to enclose a copy of this Officer's report of his very successful pursuit of the enemy, for which I beg to mention him specially.

<small>No. 5 Enclosure.
Major Gall's Report.</small>

His column took the whole of the guns with which their main body retreated from Culpee, and six caparisoned elephants. The Hyderabad Cavalry and scouts brought in more guns, which detached parties of the Rebels had abandoned in their wild flight; so that every piece of Field Artillery, which the enemy had, was taken.

The pursuing Cavalry, made great havoc of the Rebel Sepoys, the Sind Valaitees, and the mercenaries of the Nawab of Banda, till neither horse nor man could go further.

The Rebels, broken completely by Lieutenant-Colonel Gall's column, fied in the utmost disorder, in twos and threes across country, throwing away their arms and accoutrements, and even their clothes, to enable them to run faster. This low and altered state of *morale* of the Rebels must be attributed to the loss of their last hope, Culpee, after their great effort to overthrow its assailants; to their continued defeats, without one success; and lastly, to the dejection which ensued in the excitement caused by the large quantities of opium which they had swallowed for the purpose of quickening their resolution, in the action of the day before.

Besides the captured guns above mentioned, all the Artillery in the Fort, including a fine English 18-pounder gun, fell into our hands, as well as twenty-seven silk embroidered Standards of the Gwalior Contingent, bearing Scindiah's device, a cross and a serpent round it; and one of the Kotah Contingent, also three cannon and mortar foundries, which had been constructed in the Town and Fort; a very complete and extensive subterraneous Arsenal, containing 60,000 pounds of English powder; every description of warlike stores and ammunition; numerous boxes of new and old English muskets; quantities of English shot and shell, of which there were also piles outside the Arsenal in the Fort; engineering tools of every description; boxes of brass shells of native manufacture of the same sort as those frequently used against us; topographical and surveying instruments; quantities of English stationery, &c., &c. The brass shells cause a worse wound than the iron, but do not burst into so many pieces as they do.

The Commissary of Ordnance estimates the value of this Arsenal at £20 or £30,000.

From information furnished by Lieutenant-Colonel Gall, it was clear that the principal part of the Rebels had retreated by the Jaloun Road; and Sir Robert Hamilton was of opinion that they would make to the North for the Sheer Ghat, a ford across the Jumna, or another ford higher up the River. Colonel Riddell, with a moveable column was guarding the former ford. It was of vital importance to make a fresh pursuit of the enemy, in order, either to catch him between Colonel Riddell's and my fire, to meet him if he turned, or to ascertain the real line of his flight. Notwithstanding therefore the exhausted state of my Force, I detached without delay, Lieutenant Colonel Robertson with a pursuing column, of which the strength is detailed in the margin, along the Jaloun Road. To overtake the enemy was hopeless, because, *firstly* they had a start, and were not encumbered, like our Troops, with baggage, tents, and Commissariat or even the usual kit of Rebels, which they had thrown away; *secondly*, their Cavalry and Infantry were in as good, as mine were in bad condition; *thirdly*, my European Cavalry, riding eighteen stone could not catch Indian Cavalry riding ten or at most eleven stone.

1 Troop 14th Light Dragoons.
1 Squadron 3rd B. Light Cavalry.
No. 18 Light Field Battery.
160 Hyderabad Cavalry.
25th Regiment B. Native Infantry.

The Rebels had also adopted a mode of retreat which facilitated escape. They separated, and in ones and twos, took short cuts across country, meeting at a distant and given point.

The operations of the pursuing column, which again called into action Lieutenant-Colonel Robertson's energy and intelligence, will be detailed in my Report of the operations against Gwalior.

Besides the Officers specially mentioned in this Report, and in the Reports of the Officers under my orders, all of which I beg fully to confirm for distinct acts of distinguished conduct before Culpee, I beg leave to enclose two lists of other Officers, specially mentioned, or mentioned for generally important, or useful service under most trying circumstances, in the operations before Culpee.

No. 6 Enclosure.
List of Special Mentions.
No. 7 Enclosure.
List of Mentions.

The conduct of the Central India Field Force in the general action of the Jumna, was characterized by the ardent and unyielding courage, the devotion and exemplary discipline, which they had shown throughout the Campaign. And all of us witnessed, with admiration, the skill and noble courage with which the Troops of the Bengal Army, under Lieutenant-Colonel Maxwell, fought by our side, and contributed so largely to the success of the operations. I beg most respectfully to recommend these gallant Soldiers, those of the Bengal, as well as those of the Bombay Army, one and all, to the most favorable consideration of His Excellency the Commander-in-Chief. They had to contend, under a deadly sun, and in most difficult ground, with a desperate foe, greatly their superior in numbers. They fought till they dropped or conquered. The Fort and Town of Culpee exhibited proofs of the high service of Captains Blunt and Turnbull, of the Bengal Artillery and

Engineers, and of their Officers and men stationed in the Batteries on the other side of the Jumna. The shells had fallen almost as I could have wished, and caused a destruction, which no doubt influenced a good deal the Rebels in their determination to abandon the Fort and Town.

I have the honour to enclose Returns of the Casualties of the Forces engaged in the operations before Culpee, and of the enemy's Ordnance captured in the Fort of Culpee, and in the pursuit of the Rebel Army.

No. 8 Enclosure.
No. 9 Enclosure.

I was placed by the Commander-in-Chief in India, during His Excellency's absence in Rohilcund, under the direct orders of the Governor General; and it is a grateful duty to me to state that my Force and myself are under the greatest obligations to His Lordship for the liberal and excellent arrangements which he caused to be made for furnishing us with supplies; and for the practical sympathy which led His Lordship, overwhelmed as he must have been by important affairs, to give immediate attention to all my applications in favor of the Troops, even for the smallest items of medical comforts.

I am equally indebted to Lord Elphinstone and the Bombay Government and His Excellency Sir Henry Somerset, for doing all that was possible to render my Column efficient, from the time it started till it was hundreds of miles distant from Bombay; proofs of their constant and efficacious care for the welfare of the Force, reaching it on the banks of the Jumna.

The Bombay and Indore Bullock Train, which Lord Elphinstone created and organized with laudable promptitude, shortened the great distance between my original base, Bombay and Central India, and assisted my operations essentially. I beg to make special mention of Major Kane, 15th Regiment Bombay Native Infantry, Director of the Train, for the great energy and intelligence with which he developed and turned to the best account the resources of this newly-raised Military Transport.

Sir Robert Hamilton, Agent of the Governor General for Central India, who, in his official capacity, accompanied my Force throughout the Campaign, rendered very important service in obtaining supplies for the Troops and intelligence for myself, respecting the plans and movements of the enemy. Sir Robert Hamilton, whose knowledge of the roads and country is very great, gave me the first news as to the formation of the so-called Peishwa's Army, intended to establish the Peishwa's

Rule in the ancient Peishwahcate, and of their rapid and determined advance against me to relieve Jhansi. Sir Robert Hamilton showed great sympathy for the sick and wounded, and spared no trouble to alleviate, by all the means in his power, their sufferings.

So much of the success of the operations is due to the portion of the Hyderabad Contingent which formed part of my Force, that I ought not to fail to express my best thanks to Colonel Davidson, Resident at Hyderabad, for the proof of confidence which he placed in me by putting at my disposal, Troops whose organization in the three Arms, light equipment, knowledge of the Indian language and country, combined with their high Military qualities, enabled them to act as the wings of my operations.

I am much indebted for their good will and assistance to Major Rickards, Political Agent for Bhopal, who was wounded when spiritedly accompanying the charge of Captain Need, of Her Majesty's 14th Light Dragoons at the Betwa; Major Western, Deputy Commissioner of the Saugor District; Captain Keatinge, Officiating Political Agent for Western Malwa, dangerously wounded when very gallantly leading the storming party at Chundaree, having previously reconnoitred the ground and the breach; Captain Pinkney, Commissioner of the Jhansi and Jaloun Districts, specially mentioned by me for gallantry in the pursuit after the storming of the Mudunpoor Passes, his horse killed; Captain Ternan, Deputy Commissioner of Jaloun, and Captain Maclean, Deputy Commissioner of Jhansi.

Sir Robert Hamilton and these Officers of the Civil Service were, at different times, voluntarily under fire. On these occasions their bearing was that of English gentlemen. I venture to hope that, under these circumstances, the Commander-in-Chief in India may be pleased to bring to the notice of the Governor General and Viceroy my favorable opinion of the conduct of these gentlemen.

Brigadiers Sage and Wheler, Commanding at different times at Saugor; Captain Ogilvie, Assistant Commissary General, and Captain Nicholl, Commissary of Ordnance, all of the Bengal Service, were of very great assistance to the Force in giving me elephants, two 6-pounder guns, with which I completed the 1st Troop Bombay Horse Artillery, other warlike stores, all they had, and supplies.

I hope that His Excellency, the Commander-in-Chief in India will do me the favor to represent to the Governor General the great obligations I am under to the Ranee of Bhopal. Her Highness displayed the very best feeling towards the English and British interests; she did so courageously, in the worst times, when the Natives in her part of the World, thought that Rebellion must triumph. Her Highness gave me two 9-pounder guns, and a 24-pounder howitzer, with the Gunners belonging to them, very good Artillerymen, when I marched through Bhopal, which enabled me to complete No. 18 Light Field Battery. Her Highness was indefatigable in obtaining supplies for my Force, when it was very much in want of them.

So great and varied were the difficulties with which the Central India Field Force had to contend, all of which I have not thought it necessary to detail, that having stated so fully the obligations I am under to human aid, I should not do justice to my own feelings, nor I am sure to those of the generous spirits whom I led, were I not to say how large a share of our gratitude for preservation and success is due to the signal mercy of Heaven.

I beg to apologize for the length of this Report; it would have been more convenient for me to have written a short one. But justice to the Troops would not allow me to curtail the details of either their deeds or of their sufferings.

In excuse of the very tardy arrival of this Report, for which I am solely to blame, and for which I beg to offer my respectful apologies to the Commander-in-Chief in India, I must adduce a circumstance to which I should not otherwise have alluded. I had three attacks of sun during the assault and capture of Konch; one in the action at Mutha and a fifth in the general action of the Jumna. As the remedies to enable me to rise again, ride and retain the Command in the Field, which I never left, were necessarily strong, and as my determination to exercise the Command, till Culpee was taken, did not allow of my taking the rest, or following the treatment necessary for the cure of sun-sickness, and as the heat of the sun increased instead of diminishing, and the duties of the Command daily became more onerous, all my Staff sick, or ailing, my health and strength suffered so much, that all I could do with great difficulty was to command; and that I was totally unable, although I attempted it, to compose Despatches, which were to describe the remarkable operations before Culpee, and do justice to the signal merits of the Troops engaged.

Before marching against Gwalior, I had a very strong Medical Certificate in my possession, recommending my immediate departure from Central India; a sense of duty made me remain in it, and command the expedition against Gwalior. On the march to that place the heat rose to 130° in the shade. The same cause, as before, prevented me from making reports of the operations, except in telegrams. After the taking of Gwalior, I made forced marches to reach quickly the good climate of the Deccan. The papers relating to the Culpee and Gwalior operations were unfortunately left with my heavy baggage, which on account of the heavy rain, great distance, and want of roads, the whole country being a swamp, did not arrive at Poona till after the Monsoon.

These were the causes of the delay in transmitting Culpee and Gwalior Reports. I most sincerely regret that anything should have retarded the publication of the records of so much heroism. But I trust that the very detailed lists already transmitted of the Officers and men who distinguished themselves before Culpee and Gwalior, and in the Campaign generally, and which I drew up with the utmost care, and the most anxious solicitude, that the merits of each individual should be fully known and perfectly appreciated, will palliate the evil of delay.

From Major FORBES, C. B., *Commanding Rear Guard*, To Captain TODD, *Brigade Major, 2nd Brigade, Central India Field Force, dated Camp near Deopore, 16th May 1858.*

I have the honor to report, for the information of the Brigadier Commanding the 2nd Brigade, the arrival in Camp of the Rear Guard, having been closely followed up from within a mile of our last encampment at Etora by 4,000 to 5,000 of the Rebel Army, of which 1,000 to 1,200 were Cavalry.

Her Majesty's 14th Dragoons, 42 Sabres, under Lieutenant Beamish.
Royal Artillery, 2 guns, under Lieutenant Lowry.
3rd Bombay Light Cavalry, 170 Sabres, under Lieutenant Dick.
3rd Europeans, 93, under Lieutenant Mackintosh.
24th Native Infantry, 113, under Lieutenant Estridge.
Cavalry Hyderabad Contingent, 200, Captain Murray.

2. As the Brigadier is aware a broad and deep ravine only passable for Carts by one narrow road intersects the route, about a mile from Etora.

3. It was when halted here on account of the baggage that I first saw the Rebels approaching from the Culpee direction towards my left flank. They took up a position on my left rear and rear, occupying the village of Etora, and from their strength, particularly in Cavalry, it was throughout apparent that our bold front alone saved the Rear Guard from being driven in, and the consequent loss of the guns, owing to the only line of retreat being choked up by carts.

4. During the two hours or more we were halted here, the enemy's Cavalry made several advances, one or two at a rapid pace, but deceived, I imagine, by the perfect steadiness of the Troops into supposing that a larger force was concealed in the broken ground in our rear, they did not close, and as soon as the road was clear I withdrew, first the guns and Infantry to a position on this side the ravine, then the Troop of Her Majesty's 14th Dragoons, and lastly the remainder of the Cavalry at a walk, until concealed from the enemy by the nature of the ground, then at a gallop.

5. As I expected, this retrograde movement brought the enemy on us, and before the Cavalry had had time to form on the right and left of the guns, he had occupied the position we had given up.

6. This further advance in force was, however, for some time checked by the Rifles of the 3rd Europeans, and the excellent practice of the two guns of the Royal Artillery, and time given for the baggage to get on a considerable distance.

7. For the first three miles of the remainder of our march, we were almost surrounded by the Rebel Cavalry, and fired into by their Artillery, but alternately halting and retiring, we succeeded in preventing any of the baggage from falling into their hands.

8. If any baggage was lost, it could not have been on the road by which I marched, and to have divided the Rear Guard or even extended it more than was done, would have been its destruction, followed by the loss of the greater portion of the ammunition, stores and baggage of the Brigade.

9. I herewith enclose a list of Casualties during the day.

10. I would beg to bring to your notice the Officers named in the margin of this Report, and in an especial manner Lieutenant Lowry, to the precision of whose fire and the manner in which he handled his two guns do I chiefly attribute our being able to keep in check so large a body of Cavalry.

11. Lieutenant Bonns, Bombay Engineers, and Veterinary Surgeon Lamb, 3rd Light Cavalry, were most useful to me in getting on the baggage and in conveying orders. Mr. Lamb rode into Camp at my request to report the presence of the enemy and returned at very considerable risk of being cut off.

(Signed) J. FORBES, *Major,*
3rd Bombay Light Cavalry,
Commanding Rear Guard.

From Lieutenant-Colonel CAMPBELL, *Commanding 2nd Brigade, Central India Field Force,* To the Chief of the Staff, *Central India Field Force,—No. 3 of 1858, dated Camp Deopore, 18th May 1858.*

I have the honor to report for the information of the Major-General Commanding Central India Field Force, that a large body of upwards of 1,200 of the enemy's Cavalry with 3 guns moved suddenly out yesterday at 2 P.M. from the rear of a large village situated about two *coss* on our left flank. The plain intervening is not intersected by nullahs, and they were soon after reported to be advancing with an evident intention of attacking our Camp.

2. The small village of Muttra which forms out [? our] left point of Appir was then occupied by two Companies of the 71st Highland Light Infantry and two guns belonging to the Bombay Light Battery No. 18, with a support from the 24th Native Infantry, immediately reinforced this post with the whole of the 71st and the remaining two guns of No. 18 Battery and giving orders for the 14th Light Dragoons and two guns of the Royal Artillery to follow, proceeded at once to meet the enemy, taking with me the 3rd Light Cavalry and the half Battery whom I met on their way to Muttra.

3. I found that the enemy were advancing rapidly in line about one and a half mile from us, with their line so far extended as to threaten our left rear, to this point I directed our advance and soon after coming within range the enemy halted. This enabled the 14th Light Dragoons under Major Scudamore and the two guns of the Royal Artillery to take up a position connecting our line with Muttra.

4. A heavy fire commenced on both sides, the enemy firing remarkably well and sending two or three round shot into the ranks of the 3rd Light Cavalry, but the superior fire of the Royal Artillery and No. 18 Battery effectually stopped all further advance on their part.

5. An attack on Muttra now attracted my attention, but to withdraw any of my guns would also have drawn the enemy again upon us. Major Orr, Commanding Hyderabad Contingent, however, most opportunely appeared and galloping down with him ascertained that a very strong body of the Rebel Infantry had been repulsed by the 71st Highland Light Infantry under Majors Rich and Loftus. The loss of the enemy has since been ascertained to have been very great, but having had time during the morning (since yesterday's attack) to loophole the houses, the fire of the enemy was harmless.

6. The precautions for protecting the right of the Camp were not unnecessary for another Column of Infantry and two heavy guns came

down from Culpee and sent several shot right through the Camp without however much damage. Captain Field, Royal Artillery, most ably kept these at a distance supported by the 3rd European Regiment and the remainder of the 24th Native Infantry.

7. Foiled on all sides and it being now sun-set, the enemy slowly retired, taking with them dead and wounded in the nullahs.

From Lieutenant-Colonel G. V. MAXWELL, C. B., Her Majesty's 88th Regiment, Commanding Moveable Column, Cawnpore District, To Colonel E. R. WETHERALL, C.B., Chief of the Staff, Central India Field Force, dated Camp before Culpee, May 24th, 1858.

I arrived here on the morning of 18th instant, with the force as per margin, and broke ground the same night. On the following morning we had three 10-inch Mortars in position opposite to the Fort of Culpee, and a fourth on the next day.

4 Guns, Major Blunt's Battery.
266 Towana Horse.
578 of H. M.'s 88th Regiment.
682 Camel Corps.
458 Sikh Police Corps.
4 10-inch Mortars.
4 8-inch Mortars.

2. On the morning of the 19th, I received an urgent requisition from Sir Hugh Rose for a Wing of Her Majesty's 88th Regiment, a Wing of the Sikh Police Battalion, and the whole of the Camel Corps, to join his force on the opposite side of the Jumna; the demand for this amount of Troops from my column was made upon the supposition that a patrol of three Companies of the 88th Regiment, 200 of the Sikh Battalion, and 100 of the Towana Horse and 2 guns which I had sent to Sherghur, had rejoined me, but as that patrol had not returned, and I had no reason to expect it back for some time, I did not consider myself justified in complying to the full extent with Sir Hugh's request, and I sent across the Jumna on the night of the 20th, two Companies of the 88th, the whole of the Camel Corps, and 124 of the Sikh Infantry, informing Sir Hugh that as soon as I could hear of the approach of the patrol I would send the remainder of the men asked for by him.

3. By Sir Hugh Rose's orders, I sent on the morning of the 21st two 8-inch mortars and two field guns, with a Company of the 88th Regiment to Russoolpoor, a village about 3 miles below Culpee on the left bank of the Jumna, and opposite to the village of Rebree, where the enemy had a battery which commanded the road by which Sir Hugh purposed advancing on Culpee.

4. During the night of the 21st, two 8-inch mortars were put into position in the village of Diloule opposite the Kutcherry and Town of Culpee.

5. Under instructions from Major-General Sir Hugh Rose, the three above-mentioned Mortar Batteries opened fire at noon on Saturday, the 22nd. The well-directed fire of the mortars and guns from the Russoolpoor Battery, under Lieutenant Hare, of the Bengal Artillery, soon cleared the village of Rehree, and the Rebels withdrew what guns they had there. The practice of Major Blunt's four 10-inch Mortar Battery was beautifully accurate, and that from Captain Turnbull's at Diloule was most effective and well sustained until the occupation of the town by Sir Hugh Rose's force.

6. The river Jumna being between my force and the enemy, the Infantry and Cavalry under my command had not the opportunity of giving that active co-operation to Sir Hugh Rose that I could have wished, but they performed their picquet and battery duties much to my satisfaction, the Enfield Rifles of the 88th Regiment annoyed the enemy very much and prevented them having the free use of the river in front of the town.

7. The chief credit of the operations of my column on the left Bank of the Jumna is due to two Officers, *viz.*, Major Blunt, of the Bengal Artillery, and Captain Turnbull, of the Bengal Engineers. I believe the merits of Major Blunt are already known to His Excellency the Commander-in-Chief, but I beg to express my acknowledgments of the valuable services Major Blunt has afforded me since he joined my column in February last; he has been indefatigable, active and zealous for the good of the service, not confining himself to the mere routine of his own branch of it, but he has given me on all occasions his advice which his knowledge of the country and professional acquirements rendered so valuable to me. Of Captain Turnbull, of the Bengal Engineers, I cannot speak too highly. Not only was he most persevering in making the batteries, exposing himself all day to the overpowering heat of the sun, but when he had finished his duty as an Engineer, he then became an Artilleryman and worked the Mortar Battery at Diloule. It will be a subject of much gratification to me if the expression of my thanks of these Officers were productive of the appreciation of their services by His Excellency the Commander-in-Chief.

It is due to Lieutenant G. L. Fraser, of the late 23rd Native Infantry Regiment, that I should speak most favourably of the way he has performed his duties as Staff Officer to the Column: he has been most zealous and hard working.

I beg to enclose a Report from Major Blunt, also one from Captain

Turnbull, and the usual Casualty Return which I am very glad to say is very trivial.

Return of Casualties of the Moveable Column under the Command of Lieutenant-Colonel G. V. MAXWELL, C.B., from 18th to 23rd instant inclusive.

DETAIL.	KILLED.			WOUNDED.			MISSING.			REMARKS.
REGIMENTS.	Serjeants and Havildars.	Rank and File.	Total.	Serjeants and Havildars.	Rank and File.	Total.	Serjeants and Havildars.	Rank and File.	Total.	Horses.
3rd Bengal Artillery and No. 17 Light Field Battery	...	...	...	1	...	...	...	...	...	...
Towana Horse	...	...	...	...	1	...	1	...	...	...
Total	...	...	...	1	1	...	1	...	...	...

List of Men Wounded.

REGIMENT.	RANK AND NAMES.	REMARKS.
3rd Bengal Artillery and No. 17 Light Field Battery.	Serjeant John Doolin	Slightly wounded.
Towana Horse	Sowar Gowhar Khan	Severely wounded.

(Sd.) G. VAUGHAN MAXWELL, *Lieut.-Colonel, 88th, Commanding Moveable Column.*

G. L. FRASER, *Lieutenant, Detachment Staff, Lieutenant-Colonel Maxwell's Moveable Column.*

CAMP CHOWRA;
24th May 1858.

From Brigadier STUART, C. B., *Commanding 1st Brigade, Central India F. F.*, To the Assistant Adjutant General, *Central India Field Force,--No. 128 of 1858, dated Camp Culpee, 29th May 1858.*

I have the honor to report that about 9 A.M., of the 22nd May, the 1st Brigade Central India Field Force got under arms in compliance with instructions from the Major-General Commanding, and in consequence of the enemy threatening the right and front of our Camp near the village of Golowlee in force, I myself proceeded to the Mortar Battery on the right, the picquet at which consisting of one Company 3rd European Regiment, also the picquet on the bank of the Jumna, composed of one Company Her Majesty's 86th Regiment, which guarded our extreme right flank, had, by the orders of the Major-General, been reinforced by nearly the whole of Her Majesty's 86th

Regiment which, thrown into skirmishing order, covered almost the whole of our position to the right. The Major-General also directed half of No. 4 Light Field Battery to move down to the Mortar Battery, and fire was immediately opened on the enemy, who were advancing in great numbers, and with much spirit over ground most favorable to them, as it was thickly intersected in every direction by nullahs and ravines close up to our position. Finding that the enemy were commencing to outflank the left of our line of skirmishers, I sent for three Companies of the 25th Regiment Native Infantry which, when extended, made all secure in that direction; the action now became general throughout the whole line, but the advance of the enemy was checked, though most obstinately persevered in on the extreme right, where Lieutenant-Colonel Lowth, Her Majesty's 86th Regiment, was Commanding; matters thus continued until about noon, when the enemy made a most determined assault on the Mortar Battery and position held by the guns, taking advantage of our line of skirmishers being weakened by many men having been compelled to fall to the rear from the effects of the sun, which as felt by all was most overpowering as also from their Rifles having become leaded. At this juncture I could only muster a handful of men to defend the Mortar Battery and guns, and the enemy were steadily pushing on when the timely arrival of two Companies of the Rifle Brigade, which in reply to my call for aid, the Major-General himself brought up, and led against the enemy, caused them to retire precipitately, and they made no further stand. About this time also I had been compelled to reinforce my right with a Company of Her Majesty's 80th Regiment, and my left with the 21st Company Royal Engineers, as the determination shown by the enemy was so great, and the distress occasioned by the excessive heat of the day so paralysed the men that they could scarcely hold their ground; simultaneously however with the repulse in the centre, the enemy were driven back on both flanks and our whole line, pushing on, completely routed them. In compliance with the Major-General's instructions, I checked the pursuit of the enemy beyond a certain point. It was however persevered in on the right by Lieutenant-Colonel Lowth, Her Majesty's 86th Regiment, further than was intended: having reinforced the original picquets, I directed that the remainder of the Troops should return to their tents. Nothing further occurred this day.

2. Of the operations of the 1st Troop Horse Artillery, Left Wing Her Majesty's 14th Light Dragoons, 3rd Regiment Cavalry, Hyderabad

Contingent, half of No. 4 Light Field Battery, Madras Sappers and Miners, and Wing 25th Regiment Native Infantry, on the 22nd May, I make no mention, as they were not serving under my direction, and I understand Majors Gall and Robertson, who were in Command of these Troops, have sent in their reports.

3. On the 23rd May at half past 3 o'clock A.M. the 1st Brigade consisting of the Troops named in the margin, in compliance with instructions received, advanced on Culpee, line was formed in skirmishing order, the right resting on the right bank of the Jumna, and the left extending Westward to the utmost extent permitted by the number of Infantry at my disposal: the cart road leading to Culpee nearly bisected the line. I accordingly entrusted the general superintendence of the Troops on the right of this road to Lieutenant-Colonel Lowth, Her Majesty's 86th Regiment, and that of the Troops on the left of it to Lieutenant-Colonel Campbell, Her Majesty's 71st Regiment, who had joined me under instructions from the Major-General. The Brigade advanced steadily, meeting with no opposition till the village of Rehree was reached, when the men of Her Majesty's 86th Regiment, who were moving on it, received a volley, but charging in with a cheer drove the enemy out of it at once, and put them to flight, the Brigade continued to advance till the position indicated by the Major-General was reached and secured. I then sent for the Guns and Cavalry, having as the Major-General is aware on account of the nature of the ground over which we marched, been obliged to leave both in the rear, until our new position had been gained, the Brigade now remained halted until a junction was effected with the Column under the personal Command of the Major-General, when having received orders to enter the Town of Culpee, I did so with all my Infantry, and finding it deserted bivouacked the men in the most suitable manner I could, till I was ordered to march into Camp at about 5 o'clock, P. M.: the remainder of the 1st Brigade were serving immediately under the Major-General on this day. I do not therefore report their proceedings, Major Gall, Her Majesty's 14th Light Dragoons, has intimated to me, that he was in Command of

Margin:
H. M.'s 14th Light Dragoons, 40 Sabres.
Regt. Cavalry Hyderabad Contingent, 50 Sabres.
No. 4 Light Field Battery.
No. 18 Light Field Battery.
21st Company R. E., 84 Rank and File.
Wing H. M.'s 71st Regt., 210 Rank and File.
H. M.'s 86th Regt., 520 Rank and File.
Dett. H. M.'s 88th Regt., 85 Rank and File.
Wing 3rd Eu. Regt., 190 Rank and File.
Seikh Infantry, 200 Rank and File.

the pursuing Cavalry on this occasion, and that he has sent in his report to the Chief of the Staff.

4. In conclusion it gives me the greatest pleasure to state that the Troops of the 1st Brigade on this occasion as at Koonch displayed a determined fortitude which nothing could overcome: in the action of the 22nd May they were exposed to a fiercely burning sun from 9 A.M. to 2 P.M., and though as I have mentioned they were much distressed by the same, yet every man struggled to get to the front until fairly beaten down. I am much indebted to the Officers of my Staff; Captain Fenwick, Field Engineer; Captain Colly, Major of Brigade; Captain Bacon, Deputy Assistant Quarter Master General, and Lieutenant Henry, Sub-Assistant Commissary General, for their gallantry, zeal, and indefatigable exertions during these operations; also to Surgeon Mackenzie, Staff Surgeon, who on this occasion was, as I have ever found him, most unremitting in his exertions in his Department. Captain Colly, my Brigade Major, has served with this Brigade since it was first organized in June last, and during the eventful year that has passed has shown great gallantry in the field and untiring zeal and application in the performance of his various duties, which he has conducted much to my satisfaction. I therefore most earnestly beg to bring the services of this meritorious Officer to the favourable notice of the Major-General Commanding. I beg also to place on record how ably I was seconded in the operations herein detailed by Lieutenant-Colonel Lowth, Her Majesty's 86th Regiment, an Officer of great energy and judgment, most conspicuous also on every occasion for his gallantry. Lieutenant-Colonel Lowth reports to me that Major Stuart, Captain Lepper, Ensign Keane, and Assistant Surgeon Barry all did good service, and that Captain Lepper and Dr. Barry left sick beds to join their Regiment in the field. I had also occasion to remark the excellent conduct of Ensign Trueman who commanded the picquet of the 3rd European Regiment at the Mortar Battery on the 22nd instant. This Officer though very young in the Service, behaved with great steadiness and gallantry. The Wing 25th Regiment Native Infantry, employed under me on the 22nd instant, greatly distinguished themselves: they were hotly engaged the whole morning and fought most stoutly: the conduct of Serjeant Major Graham on whom devolved the Command of the half Battery No. 4 Light Field Battery when Lieutenant Strutt was directed to proceed with the remainder of his guns to another part of the field, deserves great praise for; when the

crisis I have alluded to was at hand, I found him prepared to meet it with the utmost steadiness.

P.S.—I have already transmitted a Casualty Return.

From Major GALL, *Commanding Left Wing, 14th Light Dragoons,* To the Chief of the Staff, *Central India Field Force, Culpee, dated Camp Culpee, 25th May 1858.*

I have the honor to report, for the information of the Major-General Commanding the Central India Field Force, that on the 23rd instant, when directed by your order to pursue the enemy supposed to be retiring from Culpee by the Gwalior or Jaloun Road with the Troops as per margin, I immediately proceeded to assemble the force placed under my Command on the road indicated to me which proved to be the high road from Culpee to Jhansi. This however diverges to Jaloun about three miles as near as I can recollect from Culpee.

14th Dragoons 4 Troops, in all 153 Sabres.
6 Guns Horse Artillery, 3rd Regiment Hyderabad Contingent Cavalry.
Subsequently increased by 1st Troop 14th Dragoons (48 Sabres).
50 Sabres 1st Regiment Hyderabad Contingent Cavalry.

Captain Lightfoot reporting his horses to be suffering greatly from want of water, an order was issued to water them before commencing the pursuit.

Whilst they were drinking, Captain Abbott informed me that a large Mussulman tomb about half a mile up the Jhansi Road was occupied by 300 of the enemy, and we at once proceeding thither made preparations for surrounding it with our Cavalry, and as we moved towards it Lieutenant Dowker, of the 1st Regiment Hyderabad Contingent, joined me with 50 Sabres.

The building was found to be unoccupied, but at the same time the enemy was descried retiring in great numbers over the plain beyond it to our right front and a pursuit which soon brought me to the point where the roads from Jhansi and Jaloun to Culpee unite, was commenced. Here I left Captain Need who had accompanied me thus far with his Squadron, to bring up the Horse Artillery I had sent back for.

Lieutenant Dowker I detached a little to my right and accompanied by Captains Abbott and Barrett at the head of their respective Detachments, I charged through the enemy's retiring line and dispersed it, the Rebels were cut up in all directions with the loss of two guns which they abandoned to Lieutenant **Dowker** on the right. The Dragoons in the centre sabred a great many of the fugitive Sepoys who, firing wildly and completely panic-stricken by the suddenness and rapidity of our advance, fell an easy prey to their pursuers, in some instances casting away their arms, in others suffering themselves to be followed into ravines where they were slain. Four elephants were soon after captured as the pursuit continued.

On the left, ahead of all, Captain Abbott charged along the road to Jaloun, and to the right and left of it, capturing on his way a 9-pounder gun which the paralysed enemy though loaded and placed in position did not fire, but abandoned after several of them had been cut down round about it, a few Casualties, as per margin, occurred in Captain Abbott's Regiment.

2 Men wounded.
1 Horse killed.
1 Lost.
3 Wounded.

Trooper Sher Ali, of the 3rd Regiment Hyderabad Contingent, has been specially recommended to the favorable consideration of the Major-General by his Commanding Officer. He lost his hand during the pursuit by a musket shot, also Trooper Mahomed Khan 6th Troop, also Trooper Nuttoo Khan, of the 6th Troop, as well as the following Native Officers : Shah Mirza Beg Bahadoor, Ressaldar Major of the Regiment; Ressaldar Major Mustijab Khan, Ressaldar Major Ahmed Buksh Khan and Ressaldar Major Mahommed Hoossein Khan.

Beyond the village of Hurkhoopoora, about a hundred of the enemy's *red* Cavalry crossed our front, from the left, accompanied by some Infantry, and entered a village about half a mile to our front ; as it appeared that they were disposed to make a stand here, and my Cavalry being thrown into some disorder by the pursuit, I sounded the assembly and reformed my line with the intention of attacking them, but before this could be done, they had fled, and in the exhausted state of the men and horses further pursuit for the moment was out of the question. I therefore halted and proceeded to water my horses at a well to my left rear. Between two and three hundred of the Rebels had been sabred, without any Casualties on our side beyond those specified. On my left the sound of Captain Lightfoot's guns had been heard as we approached by the Jhansi Road, preceded by Captain Need who extending to the right and left of the road, charged the rear of an Infantry Column of whom he cut down nearly two hundred, while Captain Lightoot plied them with shot and shell.

Captains Need and Lightfoot captured three pieces of Ordnance during this advance, continued by the former to the 8th mile stone on the Jhansi Road.

After watering, I joined the Horse Artillery on the Jhansi Road and proposed advancing, but the exhausted state of the Horse Artillery horses and indeed of our men generally, would not admit of this, and I gave orders for the return of the Force to Camp at Culpee, which we reached after having been upwards of thirteen hours on the saddle.

A considerable body, some hundreds of the Rebels went off early to my right, in a Northerly direction, descending into ravines where it would have been very difficult to follow them with Cavalry (amongst them were a great many women and children); this body I did not pursue.

I cannot speak too highly of Captain Abbott's conduct during the pursuit, which on the left he led well in advance at the head of his Regiment, animating it by an example it nobly followed.

The very weak Squadron of Dragoons that I had with me was ably led by Captain Barrett, whose good conduct whilst serving under my immediate Command I have already had occasion to bring to the notice of the Brigadier, Commanding 1st Brigade Central India Field Force, for favorable recommendation to the Major-General. Captain Barrett's men did great execution amongst the Rebels, and the Sowars of the 1st Cavalry Hyderabad Contingent led by Lieutenant Dowker emulated them.

To all the Troops, all the Officers, Non-Commissioned Officers and Men placed under my Command, my best thanks are given for the energy and fortitude displayed by them. Surgeon Stewart, 14th Dragoons, I have to thank for his attention to those who fell sick during the pursuit carried on through the hottest part of the day. My thanks are also due to Assistant Surgeons Lofthouse and Lumsdaine, Lieutenant and Adjutant Gills, Left Wing 14th Dragoons, as on many previous occasions distinguished himself in several personal encounters with armed Sepoys.

I specially recommend Captains Abbott, Barrett and Need, and Lieutenant Dowker, to the notice of the Major-General. Acting Regimental Serjeant Major Clark and Private Winton, B. Troop 14th Dragoons, behaved with great gallantry. The captures were as per margin.

5 Guns.
1 Gingall on Wheels.
2 Artillery Waggons filled with Ammunition.
1 Native Tumbril.
20 Boxes of Ammunition.
6 Elephants.
8 Camels.
42 Bullock Draughts.
3 Hackeries.
1 Spring Cart.

List of Officers and men of the Central India Field Force specially mentioned for important or good service in the operations before Culpee, from 17th to 23rd May 1858.

Colonel Wetherall, C.B., Chief of the Staff. Important service during the operations as a very active and intelligent Chief of the Staff, although very ill and suffering from climate. Gallant conduct in the charge of the Camel Corps. Horse wounded.

Captain Wood, Assistant Adjutant-General. Useful service and zeal during the operations.

Captain Cockburn, Her Majesty's 43rd Regiment, Aide-de-Camp. Useful service and zeal during the operations; and gallant conduct in the charge of the Camel Corps. Horse wounded.

Lieutenant Luard, late 1st Bengal Native Cavalry, Acting Aide-de-Camp. Useful service and zeal during the operations.

Lieutenant Baigrie, 3rd Bombay Europeans, Acting Assistant Quarter-Master General; useful service and great devotion in continuing to discharge his duties during the whole of the operations, although badly wounded. Gallant conduct in the charge of the Camel Corps. Horse killed.

Lieutenant Lyster, Interpreter, late 72nd Bengal Native Infantry. General useful service during the operations.

Lieutenant Gordon, Assistant Commissary General. Zeal and intelligence in supplying the Force under most difficult circumstances.

Dr. Arnott, Superintending Surgeon, expresses his approval of the Medical Officers of the Force under his orders in the following terms, and I beg to confirm his approval;—

" To the distinguished skill and ability of Field Surgeon Ritchie, is due the eminent success of the Depôt Hospital at Jhansi, in which every capital operation has completely succeeded, and among 200 European and 100 Native Sick and Wounded the Casualties have been far below the average. To the indefatigable zeal of Drs. Ritchie and Naylor, and their attention to that enormous charge, must be ascribed in a great measure such extraordinary success. Dr. Stewart, Her Majesty's 14th Light Dragoons, unfortunately was not present at Jhansi, but his duties, since the 7th of May, have been onerous in the extreme, and the zeal with which he has devoted himself to them, merits every praise. The exposure and fatigue so cheerfully undergone by Dr. Dees in his duties with the 3rd Cavalry, and his unceasing attention to his duties, are gratefully remembered. Dr. Mackenzie, 3rd Hyderabad Cavalry, has been most active and his exertions at the storming of Jhansi in carrying on the duties of Dr. Stack, when shot dead, were most useful, and the saving of much suffering among the wounded of Her Majesty's 86th Regiment. Dr. Vaughan in undertaking to conduct the duties of Field Surgeon, in addition to his own, only evinced that zeal for the service of which we had already ample proof. His duties since the Force left Jhansi have been of the most arduous and trying description, but they have on all occasions been most cheerfully and ably performed."

"These Officers I would beg to recommend to your most favorable notice, though my warmest thanks are due to all for the cordial and steady support and co-operation they have on all occasions afforded me."

Reverend Mr. Schwabbe, Protestant Chaplain. Unwearied zeal in the execution of his duties and most praiseworthy attention to the sick and wounded, went home on sick certificate, dangerously ill from sun sickness.

Reverend Mr. Strickland, Roman Catholic Chaplain. Unwearied zeal in the execution of his duties and most praiseworthy attention to the sick and wounded.

Lieutenant-Colonel Maxwell, Commanding Flying Column, on the left Bank of the Jumna. Important service during the operations, particularly in shelling and firing very efficiently on the Fort and Town of Culpee and the enemy's position.

Dr. Arnott, M.D., Superintending Surgeon. Great zeal and ability in the discharge of his difficult and important duties as Chief Medical Officer to the Force. Great zeal in riding back in extreme heat, voluntarily from Culpee the day of our arrival, the whole way to the Camp of Golowlee, and bringing back from there all the sick to Culpee, thus performing a triple march in one day.

Ensign Mackintosh, 3rd Bombay Europeans. Posting his men advantageously, and beating back the enemy by the good fire of the Detachment of this Regiment on the 17th of May.

Captain Douglas, Bengal Artillery. Gallantly and skilfully placing his guns at Muttra, under a heavy musketry fire, and clearing the ravines of Rebels, on the 17th May.

Captain Todd, Brigade Major of 2nd Brigade. Giving very useful assistance on the 17th May to Lieutenant-Colonel Campbell, Commanding 2nd Brigade in the Field, although very ill and in the sick report.

Major Orr, Commanding Hyderabad Field Force. Efficient aid to the 2nd Brigade at Diapoora, on the 18th May.

Majors Rich and Loftus, skilfully loopholing the houses, and driving back the enemy with great loss when they attacked Muttra on the 18th May.

Major Stuart, Her Majesty's 86th Regiment. Skilful disposition of the picquets and re-inforcement, and in repulsing the determined attack of the enemy on the 20th May.

Lieutenant Jerome, Her Majesty's 86th Regiment, severely wounded. Most gallantly and successfully leading his Company against the enemy on the 20th May.

Captain Lepper, Her Majesty's 86th Regiment. Skilfully directing the different Companies of skirmishers against the attack of the enemy on the 20th May.

Lieutenant Forbes, 25th Bombay Native Infantry (Partial Sunstroke). Gallantly and successfully leading his Company against the enemy on the 20th May.

Captain Lightfoot, Commanding 1st Troop Bombay Horse Artillery. Good service in the pursuit on the 22nd May.

Serjeant Major Graham, Commanding half No. 4 Light Field Battery. Bravery and skill in Commanding his guns, when attacked in position on the right, and afterwards when his guns advanced in pursuit on the 22nd May.

Assistant Surgeon Barry and Captain Lepper, Her Majesty's 86th Regiment. Having left their beds, being in the sick report, to join their Regiment in the field on the 22nd of May.

Ensign Trueman, 3rd Bombay Europeans. Great steadiness and gallantry on the 22nd May when in command of the picquets of his Regiment at the Mortar Battery when attacked.

Brigadier Stuart. Ably commanding the advance of the Right Wing, and bringing up the Artillery and Baggage rapidly through the difficult ravines on the 23rd May.

Captain Ommanney, Royal Artillery, Commanding Artillery. Good service, in covering the advance, and silencing the enemy's guns, with the Battery Royal Artillery on the 23rd May.

Serjeant Judgson, Hyderabad Artillery. Excellent conduct under Captain Turnbull, Bengal Engineers, in the Mortar Battery on the left bank of the Jumna.

Gunner Farrell, Royal Artillery. Excellent conduct under Captain Turnbull, Bengal Engineers, in the Mortar Battery on the left bank of the Jumna.

List of Officers mentioned for useful service during the operations before Culpee, from 17th to 23rd May 1858.

Captain Lightfoot, Commanding 1st Troop Bombay Horse Artillery. Placing skilfully his guns at Muttra on 7th May.

Major Stuart and Ensign Keane, Her Majesty's 86th Regiment. For having on the 22nd instant rendered good service in the Field.

Lieutenant Haggard, Commissary of Ordnance. Causing on the 22nd May casualties and disorder by the fire of his siege guns in the enemy's Cavalry.

Captain Hare, Commanding 5th Regiment, Hyderabad Contingent. Useful service when left in charge of the Camp on the 22nd May.

Lieutenant Macquoid, Adjutant of the 5th Hyderabad Infantry. Useful service and constant zeal under Captain Hare on the 22nd May and other occasions.

Captain Abbott, Commanding 3rd Cavalry, Hyderabad Contingent. Guarding well on the 22nd May the outposts on the left, and executing skilfully and successfully a retrograde movement to draw on the enemy into the fire of our siege guns.

Major Ross, Commanding Camel Corps. Useful conduct in covering the advance of the Left Column against Culpee on the 23rd of May.

HUGH ROSE,
Comdg. F. D. A. and Field Forces.

Casualty Return of the Central India Field Force, from the 15th instant to the termination of the operations against Culpee, dated 27th May 1858.

Corps.	Rank.	Names.	Date.	Remarks.
Left Wing Her M.'s 14th Lt. Dragoons.	Troop. Serjt. Major Private ,, ,, ,, ,, ,,	Edwin Elis D. H. G. Austin F. George H. Hopper J. Meller Roland Smart Joseph Thwaites Alexander Viner	May 22nd ,, 24th ,, ,, ,, ,, ,, ,, ,, 20th ,, 22nd ,, 24th	Died from sun-stroke. Ditto. Ditto. Ditto. Ditto. Ditto. Ditto. Ditto.
1st Troop B.H.A.	Gunner ,,	Francis Hurat John Cathcart	,, 22nd ,, ,,	Ditto. Ditto.

CALPEE.

Casualty Return of the Central India Field Force, from the 15th instant to the termination of the operations against Culpee, dated 27th May 1858—contd.

Corps.	Rank.	Names.	Date.	Remarks.
	Troop.			
4-2 Bombay Artillery.	Gunner	Henry Cox	May 22nd	Killed in action.
	Bombardier	William Harris	,, ,,	Ditto.
	Driver	Marwattee	,, ,,	Wounded slightly.
	Gunner	John Maynalian	,, ,,	Wounded.
2nd Co. Rl. Engineers.	Bugler	William Leathed	,, 15th	Died from sun-stroke.
Her M.'s 86th Regiment.	Lieutenant	H. E. Jerome	,, ,,	Wounded.
	Serjeant	Hugh Burns	,, ,,	Ditto.
		Richard Foley	,, ,,	Ditto.
		James Barnes	,, ,,	Ditto.
		Michael Byrnes	,, ,,	Wounded, since dead.
		Robert Barker	,, ,,	Died of *Coup-de-soleil*.
		George Burrowclough	,, ,,	Ditto.
		Cornelius Corcoran		Wounded.
		Timothy Foley		Died of *Coup-de-soleil*.
		Samuel Grier		Ditto.
		Patrick McEllenen		Wounded.
		Thomas Madden		Ditto, since dead.
		John Martin		Ditto.
		Dennis Morrissy		Wounded.
		John Nicholas		Ditto.
		Patrick Shaughnessy		Ditto.
		John Wall		Ditto.
25th Regiment, Bombay Native Infantry.	Naique	Futtay Khan		Killed in action.
	Private	Shew Churn Sing		Ditto.
	,,	Takoor Aheer		Ditto.
	,,	Essoo Pehakul		Ditto.
	,,	Puray Doobay		Ditto.
	,,	Gunput Silkay		Ditto.
	,,	Baywa Poway		Ditto.
	,,	Rama Mooray		Ditto.
	,,	Babboo Morgoot		Ditto.
	,,	Luxumon Powar		Wounded.
	,,	Gooman Sing		Ditto.
	,,	Esram Rao Moray		Ditto.
	,,	Chandee Aheer		Ditto.
	,,	Sunker Argoonhotry		Ditto.
	,,	Essoo Purrah		Ditto.
	,,	Custwajee Moosuker		Ditto.
	,,	Ordiel Tewary		Ditto.
	,,	Dhonda Sita		Ditto.
	,,	Beharry Culwar		Ditto.
3rd Regiment Hyderabad Cavalry.	Duffadar	Chand Khan	May 23rd	Wounded slightly.
	Trooper	Shair Ali	,, ,,	Ditto severely.
	,,	Missar Ali Beg	,, 22nd	Dangerously, since dead.
	2nd Brigade.			
No. 6 Field Battery Royal Artillery.	Trumpeter	Thomas Gomes	May 16th	
	Gunner	David Howell	,, ,,	Died from *Ictus Solis*.
	,,	James Wharton	,, ,,	
	,,	Thomas Holland	,, 22nd	
H. M.'s 14th Light Dragoons.	Regl. Serj. Maj.	H. Holloway	,, 16th	
	Private	J. J. Cowles	,, 29th	Ditto.
	,,	Hugh Sudden	,, 20th	
	,,	James King	,, 23rd	

*Casualty Return of the Central India Field Force, from the 15th instant to the termination of the operations against Culpee, dated 27th May 1858—*contd.

Corps.	Rank.	Names.	Date.	Remarks.
	Troop.			
3rd Regiment Light Cavalry.	Trooper " " "	Emaum Bux Surroop Sing Wooree Sing Juan Carlos	May 16th " " " " " "	} Killed in action. Wounded severely by round shot in abdomen.
H. M.'s 71st Highland Light Infantry.	Trumpeter Trooper Serjeant Private " " "	Mark Fernandez Bugger Sing Alexander Rose James Anderson W. Fergusson T. Johnston J. Livingstone	" 17th " " " 22nd " 17th " 21st " " " 22nd	Killed in action. Grazed by round shot in right leg. } Died of *Ictus Solis*.
3rd Bombay European Regiment.	" " " " " "	Peter Brown James Madden William Tootle John Reynolds John Hastings Patrick Doyle Michael Cosgrove	" 16th " " " 21st " 23rd " " " 16th " 23rd	Killed in action. } Died of *Ictus Solis*. Gun shot wound (since dead).
Detachment 24th Regt. Bombay Native Infantry.	" " " " " " " "	Lalla Mooljie Gurradhur Pandy Bhowaree Bhoghur Shaik Raj Bup Narrain Salvee Bulwuntee Gurconna Chunmebur Mhadomulla. Ajudia Nawoo	" 16th " " " " " " " " " " " " " 20th	} Killed in action. Wounded severely by gun shot wound in right leg. Wounded slightly by gun shot wound in arm. " " in chest. Contusion.
		Camel Corps attached to 2nd Brigade.		
Camel Corps.	Color Serjt. Private ,	Worall T. Wood James Jones	May 23rd " " " "	} Severe contusion. Dangerous.

Casualty Return of the Central India Field Force, from the 15th instant to the termination of the operations against Culpee, dated 27th May 1858—concld.

Corps.	Rank.	Names.	Date.	Remarks.
		Hyderabad Contingent Field Force.		
1st Cavalry	Trooper	Peer Khan	May 17th	Killed.
	,,	Mahomed Emaum	,, 15th	Severely wounded.
4th Cavalry	,,	Ram Deen	,, 16th	Killed.
	,,	Mahomed Khan	,, ,,	Ditto.
	Duffadar	Dumma Khan	,, 17th	Slightly wounded.
	,,	Goolam Nubbick	,, 23rd	Severely ,,
	Jemadar	Chotay Khan	,, ,,	Killed.
Left Wing 3rd Infantry.	Qr. Mr. Serjt.	C. J. Moore	,, 15th	Sun-stroke, died.
	Subadar	Bhyjoo Sing	,, 20th	Do. severely.
	Sepoy	Jankee	,, ,,	Do. slightly.
	,,	Dulloo	,, ,,	Do. ,,
	,,	Luchmean	,, ,,	Do. ,,
	,,	Kurreem Khan	,, ,,	Do. ,,
	,,	Syud Jaffer	,, ,,	Do. ,,
	,,	Shaik Cammoo	,, ,,	Do. ,,
	,,	Liddajee	,, ,,	Do. ,,
	,,	Rajahme	,, ,,	Do. ,,
	,,	Shaik Balla	,: ,,	Do. ,,
	Havildar	Lutchmon	,, ,,	Do. ,,
	Sepoy	Cullian	,, 17th	Severely wounded.
	,,	Babboo Sing	,, ,,	Slightly.
5th Infantry	Naique	Duljeet Sing	,, 20th	Sun-stroke, severely.
	Havildar	Seetul Pandy	,, ,,	Do. slightly.
	Sepoy	Ramdyal	,, ,,	Do. ,,
	,,	Narrain	,, ,,	Do. severely.
	,,	Tackoor	,, ,,	Do. died.

ABSTRACT.

Corps.	Killed.	Wounded.	Missing.	Died from Exhaustion.	Sunstroke.	Remarks.
1st Brigade.						
Her Majesty's 14th Light Dragoons.	0	0	0	0	8	
1st Troop Bombay Horse Artillery.	0	0	0	0	2	
4-2 Artillery	2	2	0	0	0	
21st Company Royal Engineers.	0	0	0	0	1	
Her Majesty's 86th Regiment.	0	*3	0	0	0	*Since dead (2) two.
25th Regiment Bombay Native Infantry.	9	10	0	0	0	
3rd Regiment Cavalry Hyderabad Contingent.	0	†3	0	0	0	†One since dead.

ABSTRACT—concld.

Corps.	Killed.	Wounded.	Missing.	Died from Exhaustion.	Sun-stroke.	REMARKS.
2nd Brigade.						
No. 6 Field Battery Royal Artillery.	0	0	0	0	4	
Her Majesty's 14th Dragoons	0	0	0	0	4	
3rd Bombay Light Cavalry	4	2	0	0	0	
Her Majesty's 71st Highlanders.	0	0	0	0	5	
3rd Bombay European Regiment.	1	*1	0	0	5	*Since dead.
Detachment, 24th Regiment Bombay Native Infantry.	4	4	0	0	0	
Camel Corps attached to 2nd Brigade.	0	3	0	0	0	
Hyderabad Contingent Field Force.	4	5	0	0	†17	†2 Since dead.
Total	24	43	0	0	46	

H. H. A. WOOD, *Captain,*
Assistant Adjutant-General, Central India Field Force.

CAMP CULPEE;
The 27th May 1858.

SUPPLEMENTARY.

Return of Horses of the Central India Field Force, Killed and Wounded from the 15th instant to the termination of the operations against Culpee.

Corps.	Killed.	Wounded.	Missing.	Died from exhaustion.	Sun-stroke.
Divisional Staff.					
Major General Commanding	...	1	...	...	...
Colonel Wetherall, Chief of the Staff.	...	1	...	...	...
Captain Cockburn, A. D. C.	...	1	...	...	...
Lieutenant Lyster, A. D. C.	...	1	...	...	...
Lieutenant Baigrie, Assistant Quarter-Master General.	1	...	...	...	...
2nd Brigade.					
No. 6 Field Battery Royal Artillery.	1	...0	...	2	...
Her Majesty's 14th Dragoons	2	...	...	2	2
3rd Bombay Light Cavalry	4	3	2	...	...
Total	8	7	2	4	2

H. H. A. WOOD, *Captain,*
Assistant Adjutant-General, Central India Field Force.

CAMP CULPEE;
May 1858.

ORDNANCE DEPARTMENT.
CENTRAL INDIA FIELD FORCE.

Return of Ordnance captured in the Fort of Culpee, and in the pursuit of the Rebel Army on the 23rd May 1858 by the Force under Command of Major-General Sir Hugh Rose, K.C.B.

No.	Nature of Ordnance.	Manufacture.	Length Feet.	Length Inches.	Calibre.	Remarks.
1	Iron Gun	English.	8	8	18 pr.	On English Carriage, with Limber and Elephants. With Ammunition Waggons.
2	Brass Guns		5	8·7	9 pr.	
3	Ditto		5	8·7	9 pr.	
4	Ditto Mortar		1	6·5	5½ inch.	
5	Brass Howitzer		2	0	9 inch.	
6	Ditto Gun	Native.	4	3·1	6 pr.	
7	Ditto ditto		5	8½	6 pr.	
8	Ditto ditto		4	1	3 pr.	
9	Ditto ditto		2	10½	3 pr.	
10	Ditto ditto		4	2	3 pr.	
11	Ditto ditto		4	0	2 pr.	
12	Ditto ditto		3	1	1 pr.	
13	Ditto ditto		1	8	½ pr.	
14	Iron ditto		2	1·7	12 pr.	2, 3, 7, 8, 15, 16, 17, and 23 taken in the pursuit. The rest in the Fort.
15	Ditto ditto		3	0	1 pr.	
16	Ditto ditto		3	7	½ pr.	
17	Ditto ditto		4	0	½ pr.	
18	Ditto ditto		2	0	¼ pr.	
19	Ditto ditto		2	7	¼ pr.	
20	Ditto ditto		2	3	¼ pr.	
21	Ditto ditto		2	10	½ pr.	
22	Ditto ditto		2	2	½ pr.	
23	Ditto ditto		5	10	3 pr.	

THOMAS T. HAGGARD,
Lieutenant, Bombay Artillery,
Commissary of Ordnance, Central India Field Force.

CAMP CULPEE;
The 28th May 1858.

CHAPTER III.

GWALIOR DESPATCHES.

Fort William, 22nd February, 1859.

No. 231 of 1859.—The Right Hon'ble the Governor General of India in Council is pleased to direct the publication of the following letter from the Deputy Adjutant-General of the Army, No. 3, of the 19th January 1859, forwarding a Despatch from Major-General Sir Hugh Rose, K.C.B., reporting the Capture of Gwalior.

This report was received by the Government in the Military Department on the 25th January 1859.

His Excellency in Council very highly appreciates the services rendered by Sir Hugh Rose and the Troops under his Command, as described in these Papers.

The vigorous and successful operations of the Central Indian Field Force in June last had a widely spread effect in pacifying the Provinces, not only of Central India, but of the North-Western Government; and the Governor General in Council cordially thanks Major-General Sir H. Rose, and the officers and men of that distinguished Force for all that was then accomplished by them.

It will be satisfactory to the Governor General to bring these Papers to the notice of Her Majesty's Government.

R. J. H. BIRCH, *Major-General,*
Secy. to the Govt. of India.

From Major H. W. NORMAN, *Deputy Adjutant General of the Army*, To the Secretary to the Government, *Military Department, No. 3, dated Allahabad, 19th January 1859.*

I have the honor, by desire of the Commander-in-Chief, to enclose, for submission to His Excellency the Right Hon'ble the Governor General, a Despatch, dated 13th October last, received only this day, from Major-General Sir Hugh Rose, K.C.B., reporting the capture of Gwalior.

2. It gives Lord Clyde much pleasure to acknowledge the great and distinguished service rendered upon this occasion by Sir Hugh Rose and the Troops under his Command.

From Major-General SIR HUGH ROSE, *Commanding Field Forces, South of the Nerbudda*, To Major-General SIR WILLIAM MANSFIELD, K.C.B., *Chief of the Staff of the Army in India, dated Poonah, the 13th October 1858.*

I have the honor to report to you, for the information of the Commander-in-Chief in India, the operations against Gwalior of the Central India Field Force and other Troops, placed under my command by His Excellency.

After the capture of Calpee, the first reports made to me by Lieutenant-Colonel Robertson, Commanding the Column of pursuit, were to the effect that the scattered parties of the routed Rebel Army, without guns, tents, etc., were making, in the utmost disorder, for the Sheer Ghat *via* Jaloun, a ford across the Jumna, 35 or 40 miles to the North-east of Calpee. Subsequent accounts from the same officer stated that a great part of the Rebels had, after leaving Jaloun, made a turn in a more Westerly direction, which was contrary to the one Sir Robert Hamilton felt persuaded the Rebels would follow; he was certain that they would make for Oude and cross the Jumna at the Sheer Ghat; or the ford to the West of it, near Juggurmanpore.

2 Troops 3rd Bom. Lt. Cavalry.
150 Hydrabad Cavalry.
No. 18 Light Field Battery.
8 Companies 25th Bombay N. I.

In this uncertainty Lieutenant-Colonel Robertson, with good judgment, took up a position with the pursuing Column, which enabled him not to be the dupe of a feigned move to draw him off the real chase, but to follow the Rebels by the shortest line, should they move Westwards or Northwards.

1 Wing Her Majesty's 86th Regiment.
2 Squadrons Her Majesty's 14th Light Dragoons.

A short rest having enabled my European Troops to recover a little, I reinforced Lieutenant-Colonel Robertson with the Troops detailed in the margin.

Subsequent reports from Lieutenant-Colonel Robertson stated that he had reason to think, that all the rebels had decidedly taken a Westerly direction, and that they had been reinforced by 800 Oude Cavalry under Ruheem Ali Nurut, of Bareilly.

Lieutenant-Colonel Robertson followed the line to the West taken by the rebels, from Jaloun towards the Pohooj and Scinde Rivers, and got into communication with the Raja of Rampura, to the West of the Pohooj, a faithful friend of the English; Lieutenant-Colonel Robertson's intelligence and knowledge of the Natives, and their language, enabled him to obtain some very valuable information from this person; and that Officer reported to me, in two expresses, that the Calpee rebels had certainly taken the road to Gwalior.

So little was at that time the great intrigue of Tantia Topee against Scindiah's power even suspected, that the best authority for intelligence could not bring himself to think that Lieutenant-Colonel Robertson was not mistaken in his information. However, not many hours after the arrival of Lieutenant-Colonel Robertson's last express, Sir Robert Hamilton received similar intelligence; when I instantly ordered off Brigadier Stuart, with the Force detailed in the margin, to reinforce Lieutenant-Colonel Robertson, and march on Gwalior after the Rebels.

No. 4 Light Field Battery.
2 Troops Her Majesty's 14th Light Dragoons.
1 Wing Her Majesty's 71st Regiment.
1 Wing Her Majesty's 86th Regiment.
4 Companies 25th Bombay Native Infantry.
½ a Company Bombay S. & M.
Two 18-Pounders.
One 8-Inch Howitzer.

Before the taking of Calpee, in compliance with instructions from the Governor-General and the Commander-in-Chief in India, conveyed to me through Sir Robert Hamilton, that after the taking of that place, and the breaking up of the Central India Field Force, part of it should be sent to Gwalior, and the rest to Jhansi, as Garrisons for those places, I had submitted to His Lordship the details of the distribution of Troops for the two services.

The news received for the next few days was very uncertain and contradictory. An express letter from Scindiah's Agent at Gwalior removed apprehensions for his safety, and that of his Government; it stated that the Rebels, who were in a destitute condition, had, being still several miles from Gwalior, implored Scindiah's favor and protection in language and with a demeanour the reverse of hostile.

Subsequent accounts from Lieutenant-Colonel Robertson, which were confirmed by Sir Robert Hamilton, conveyed the news which created a sensation throughout India, only equalled by that which was caused by the first mutinies. The Rebel Army had attacked Scindiah at Bahadurpoor, 9 miles from Gwalior; his Troops of all Arms, with the exception of a few of his Body Guard, had treacherously gone over, the Artillery in mass, to the enemy. His Highness himself, after bravely doing his best to make his Troops do their duty, had been forced by the fire of his own Artillery, and the combined attacks of his Troops, and of the Rebel Army, to fly to Agra, which he reached with difficulty, accompanied only by one or two attendants; the Rebels had entered Gwalior, taken Scindiah's Treasury and Jewels, the latter said to be of fabulous value; the Garrison of the Fort of Gwalior, considered to be one of the strongest, if not the strongest, Fortress in India, had, after a mock resistance, opened its gates to the Rebels; finally, from 50 to 60 fine guns, comprising Horse, Field and Siege Artillery, had fallen, as well as an Arsenal with abundance of Warlike Stores into the hands of the enemy. In short, the Rebels, who had fled, in the most disorderly flight and helpless state from Calpee, were now completely set up with abundance of money, a capital park of Artillery, plenty of material, and Scindiah's Army, as their allies.

Gwalior itself, without the Fort, was a prize of no ordinary value, comprising the Old City, and the "Lushker," that is, the ancient Mahratta Camp, converted into a handsome and flourishing City, both together containing a population of 170,000 souls.

But other circumstances combined to render the loss of Gwalior the most serious event which had occurred since the revolt.

Scindiah, the Maharajah or Prince of Gwalior, is our very faithful ally; and with one exception he is the most powerful of the independent Princes of India. The centrical and geographical position of the Gwalior States, and their extent, give their Rulers great political and Military power over the whole of India. The main artery of communication and the electric line from Bombay to Central India, Agra, and the North-Western Provinces, traverse for hundreds of miles Scindiah's dominions.

Scindiah's Troops, who went over to the Rebels, were the best organized and drilled of all the Native Levies.

To render this state of things still more embarrassing, Gwalior fell into Rebel hands at the most unfavourable time of the year for Military operations—on the eve of the great rains, and when the heat of summer was at its maximum.

No one, therefore, could foresee the extent of evil if Gwalior were not promptly wrested from the Rebels; if Tantia Topee, with the immense acquisition of political influence and Military strength which the possession of that place gave the Rebel cause, had time to re-organize the Calpee Army, which he could easily do, with the resources of Gwalior at his disposal. The worst forebodings would have come to pass, if Tantia Topee, leaving either the Calpee or the Gwalior Army at Gwalior, for its defence, marched with the other Southwards and unfurled the standard of the Peshwa in the Deccan and Southern Mahrattas. These Districts, and the West of India generally, were very much denuded of Troops; and the attachment of the inhabitants of the ancient Peishwarate to their former Government is too well known to admit of a doubt as to what course they would have pursued, if Tantia Topee had appeared amongst them with a large Army.

The inhabitants of Indore had given so many proofs of unfavourable feeling, that there was reason to fear that they would, if the opportunity offered, follow the example of Gwalior.

It was of vital importance that Troops should reach Gwalior before the rains set in; *firstly*, because I had no pontoons for Siege Artillery; and to have transported the Siege Guns across the Scinde and Pohooj Rivers, swollen to a great height by the rains, would have been most difficult if not impossible. '*Secondly*, the siege of the Fort or City of Gwalior, protracted by the difficulties consequent on the monsoons, would have had the worst effect on our Military prestige and the state of affairs.

The Governor General expressed a wish that not an hour should be lost in reaching Gwalior. I, therefore, leaving by order Captain Ommaney's Royal Artillery Battery of four 9-pounders, belonging to the 2nd Brigade Central India Field Force, as part of the permanent garrison of Calpee, and one troop 3rd Bombay Light Cavalry, 21st Company Royal Engineers, a Wing of the 3rd Bombay Europeans, and 400 of the 24th Bombay Native Infantry to garrison Calpee until relieved by Bengal Troops, marched with the Troops detailed in the margin from Calpee on the 6th of June and followed Brigadier Stuart's column, by forced marches, on the road to Gwalior by Jaloun, marching by night to avoid the sun.

Margin: 1st Troop Bombay Horse Artillery. 1 Squadron 14th Light Dragoons. 1 Squadron 3rd Bombay Light Cavalry. Madras Sappers and Miners.

One day the heat in the shade rose to 130°.

The Officer Commanding the outlying picquet of Her Majesty's 14th Light Dragoons, having reported to me, on the night of the third day, that his men had fallen from their saddles from exhaustion, I had the picquet relieved by a party of Hydrabad Cavalry.

Owing to the difficulties of the baggage on very bad carts crossing one very deep nullah, and the rapid advance of my column, a Detachment of the 25th Bombay Native Infantry, who guarded them, were three days without a meal; after a bathe in the Pohooj, and a short rest to enable them to make their cakes, these good Soldiers were quite ready to march on.

I caught up Brigadier Stuart's column at the Fort of Indoorkee on the Scinde river.

I received His Excellency the Commander-in-Chief's instructions that I was reinforced for the operations against Gwalior, as follows:

Colonel Riddell's moveable column of Bengal Troops, of the strength detailed in the margin, was to escort a large supply of Siege Guns, mortars and ammunition, from Agra to Gwalior for the siege of that place.

No. 21 Light Field Battery.
3rd Bengal Europeans.
200 Sikh Horse.
300 Sikh Infantry.
Siege Artillery.

Brigadier Smith, with a brigade of the Rajpootana Field Force, was to march from the neighbourhood of Chandaree to Gwalior.

The Hydrabad Contingent, after their hard service, had received permission and orders to return home; almost all of these Troops had commenced their return to the Deccan, and some of them were far advanced on their road. With a good feeling, which cannot be sufficiently praised, all of the Contingent which had formed part of the Central India Field Force, instantly countermarched and moved against Gwalior on the wish being intimated to the Officers Commanding their separate bodies, that they should perform this fresh act of good service for the Government.

When the crisis occurred at Gwalior, part of the Central India Field Force were garrisoning Calpee, part had marched to Gwalior, and part had been left as a garrison at Jhansi.

His Excellency the Commander-in-Chief in India was pleased to direct my attention to preventing the move of the Rebels Southwards from Gwalior to the Deccan.

His Excellency was pleased to express his entire approbation of my having selected Agra as the base of my operations, in consequence of the communication between that place and Gwalior being the shortest and the best. But even this communication was rendered imperfect by the passage of a very difficult ford across the Chumbul.

My plan of attack of Gwalior was as follows—To invest it as much as its great extent would allow, and then to attack it by its weakest side; the investing Troops cutting off the escape of the Rebels.

I hoped that a successful attack of the enemy, outside or inside the City, would, like Calpee, be followed by the capture of the Fort.

In order to invest Gwalior from the South, I directed Major Orr, Commanding Hydrabad Contingent, to move from Jhansi to Punear on the road from Gwalior to Seepree. Major Orr's force was too weak to attack Gwalior from that quarter, but he was perfectly placed for cutting off the retreat of the Rebels to the South, assisted as he would be, by the other investing Corps.

Information as to the enemy's position is the surest guarantee of success; I had no plan of Gwalior or its environs. With great trouble

I had ascertained that the weakest side of Gwalior, and consequently the best for an attack, was the East, as it was girt by high hills on that side, the summits of which were difficult, it is true, of access; but that, on the other hand, slopes which descended gradually from these summits towards and close to the " Lushker," would enable me, after taking the heights, to drive the enemy down from slope to slope, from the lowest of which I could cannonade the " Lushker," and covered by the fire of Artillery storm the new Town, that is the " Lushker," thus cutting in two the enemy's whole line, consisting of the old city, above which is the Fort, and the " Lushker," or new City.

This point of attack had another advantage. It enabled me to attack Gwalior almost unhurt by the fire of the Fort.

I directed Brigadier Smith, with the Rajpootanah Field Force, to move from Seepree to Kotah-ka-Serai, about seven miles to the East of Gwalior.

I myself, with Brigadier Stuart's column, and the small one I had brought from Calpee, marched against the Morar Cantonments, which were said to be occupied in force by the enemy. These Cantonments for the Troops stationed at Gwalior are about five miles from that city, on the river Morar. They had only been partially burnt by the Rebels; and Scindiah's Government had been at much trouble and expense to repair the old buildings and construct others for the force which was to be the garrison of Gwalior.

Once in possession of the Morar Cantonments, I could establish there my hospital, parks, etc. Divested of these incumbrances, and leaving a force in the Morar Cantonments, which could protect it, and at the same time form part of the investment of Gwalior and pursue when required, I was free to join Brigadier Smith at Kotah-ka-Serai and with his force and my own, attack Gwalior.

To complete the investment which, roughly speaking, was to enclose Gwalior from the South-East and North, I sent instructions to Colonel Riddell to move with his column by the Agra and Gwalior road to the Residency, about seven miles to the North of Gwalior. Colonel Riddell, by extending his force from the Residency down the West side of Gwalior, invested it from that side.

I had the honor to report that all the columns of operations would, I trusted, be at their posts by the 19th of June.

On the 16th of June I arrived at Bahadurpoor, about four or five miles from the Morar Cantonments.

I directed Captain Abbott, with his Cavalry, to reconnoitre Morar; he reported that the Rebels were in force in front of it. I reconnoitred their position myself closely; and found that the side of the Cantonments fronting us, was occupied by strong bodies of Cavalry, and that on their right were guns and a good deal of Infantry.

My force had had a long and fatiguing march, and the sun had been up for some time. Four or five miles' more march in sun, and a combat afterwards, would be a great trial for the men's strength. On the other hand, Morar looked inviting with several good buildings not yet burnt; they would be good quarters for a portion of [the] force; if I delayed the attack until the next day, the enemy were sure to burn them. A prompt attack has always more effect on the Rebels, than a procrastinated one.

I therefore countermanded the order for encamping and made the following arrangements to attack the enemy.

I formed my force in two lines; the first line consisting of the 1st Brigade, under Brigadier Stuart, the second line, under Brigadier-General Napier, in support of the first, consisting of only a small part of the 2nd Brigade as the rest of it was at Calpee.

Captain Abbott, Hydrabad Cavalry, covered the advance.

I requested Brigadier-General Napier to watch well hills on my left and rear, in which the enemy were supposed to be; and to advance *in echelon* from the right, which enabled him, his left refused to guard my left rear, on the outward flank of which I left baggage and incumbrances.

I also sent patrols of Cavalry far away into the hills on my left and rear to search them.

Sir Robert Hamilton, who has a remarkable acquaintance with the ground and localities of Central India, had warned me to take care of the ground on the proper right, and in front of Morar, as it was full of ravines and treacherous ground.

Both lines advanced: No. 18 Light Field Battery, and the Siege Guns in the centre of the first; Her Majesty's 86th Regiment on their right; the 25th Bombay Native Infantry on their left; Her Majesty's 14th Light Dragoons on each flank.

To march to our position in order of battle, we had gone over the ground on which, a short time before, Scindiah had been attacked and routed by his faithless Troops and the Calpee Rebels. It was strewed with dead horses.

My plan was to mask the dangerous ground to my left, towards which the enemy evidently wished to draw me; to outflank the enemy's left, double it up, and cut off their retreat from the road over the bridge in rear of the Cantonments leading to Gwalior.

My first line advanced in line across the plain between Morar and Bahadurpoor dressing by their centre with the regularity of a parade movement. The enemy retired from their position in front of Morar into the Cantonments.

No. 1 Enclosure.
Brigadier General Napier's Report.

I have the honor to enclose a copy of Brigadier General Napier's Report of the operations of his Brigade, and to confirm fully all his recommendations of the Officers under his command.

Under the guidance of Scindiah's Agent, I took ground diagonally to the right in order to get on the road which led to the Cantonments and which enabled me to turn the enemy's left; but he missed the road; in the mean time we had got on the edge of broken ground; a masked Battery in the enemy's centre, concealed by trees, and the guns on their right opened a cross fire on us, causing some Casualties amongst Captain Abbott's Hydradad Cavalry, who showed admirable steadiness.

I directed the Siege Guns under Lieutenant Strutt, B.A., and No. 18 Light Field Battery, under Lieutenant Harcourt, Bombay Artillery, to be placed in position obliquely to my front, which enabled them to open a telling fire diagonally to their left on the enemy's Batteries. I beg to mention specially Lieutenants Strutt and Harcourt, for the prompt steadiness with which they brought their guns into action on difficult ground, and for the efficiency of their fire.

The Rebel Artillery caused some Casualties amongst the horses of these guns.

The lay of the ground favouring the Rebels' right Battery, I brought to my left, Captain Lightfoot's 1st Troop Bombay Horse Artillery against it from the 2nd line.

Nullahs and broken ground prevented the advance of Captain Abbott's Cavalry, whom I placed under cover; and of Her Majesty's 14th Light Dragoons under Captain Thompson, on the right, who reinforced my left.

The enemy's Cavalry, of whom the 5th Irregulars formed part, showed in force in position in our front along the road through the Cantonments.

I reinforced my left, now near the dangerous ground on the enemy's right, with the 25th Bombay Native Infantry, and advanced across bad ground. Her Majesty's 86th Regiment firing, whom I had thrown into skirmishing order, and took by storm under a cannonade of the enemy's right Battery, all the Morar Cantonments in our front. The Rebels retired at a gallop.

I brought forward the right shoulders of the 86th line of skirmishers and resting their right on the right bank of the Morar swept the whole Cantonments and occupied them.

Captain Abbott, whose horse was killed under him by a round shot, in the meantime had contrived to get across the nullahs further to the right, and wheeling to his left, galloped through the Cantonments, and joined in the pursuit of the enemy, who retired from their right.

But the delay in his advance, caused by the very difficult ground, prevented his arriving in time, to cut off the retreat of the enemy across the bridge.

The Rebels withdrew their batteries, crippled by the fire of Captain Lightfoot's, Lieutenants Strutt's and Harcourt's guns, as soon as they saw their left compromised by the successful advances of the 86th.

My left, which had been refused, conformed to the right, and changed position to the left, fronting the nullahs on the enemy's right, which it had now approached.

The advanced nullah and others in rear of it were lined with Rebel Sepoys, who gave no sign, until my left approached them, when they opened on it a very heavy fire, on which Major Rich, Her Majesty's 71st Highland Light Infantry, moved his skirmishers rapidly forward to dislodge them. Lieutenant Neave led with ardent courage the charge, and fell, when close to the nullah, mortally wounded, sincerely regretted by his brave Regiment and his General.

The 71st very gallantly took the nullah and others in rear by storm; Lieutenant Rose, 25th Bombay Native Infantry, afforded them useful co-operation by skilfully placing a party of his Regiment so as to enfilade these dangerous entrenchments. The whole of the Rebels in them were killed, after a desperate resistance, which cost the 71st, I regret to say, besides Lieutenant Neave, several brave Soldiers killed and wounded; Serjeant McGill, killed; Serjeant Wilson, wounded dangerously; Corporal Leslie, killed; two Privates killed and six wounded, of the whole of whom I make special mention. In the advanced nullah alone seventy Rebels lay dead, belonging to Scindiah's faithless Guards and wearing English accoutrements and breast-plates, on which was engraved "1st Brigade Infantry."

Her Majesty's 71st Regiment proved, on this as well as on every other occasion, whilst under my orders, that they will maintain by their courage and discipline the historical renown, of which they bear so many honoured records on their colours.

When a Wing of the Regiment was prostrated by sun-sickness after the action at Koonch, the only complaint I heard in the field hospitals from these gallant young Soldiers was that they could not rise and fight.

The success of the day was completed by the destruction of the Rebels in the nullahs, and a most successful pursuit of the Rebels by Captain Thompson, with a Wing of Her Majesty's 14th Light Dragoons. These Rebels had been turned by Captain Abbott's advance from the ford of the river, across which and the bridge the main body had retreated; Captain Thompson caught them in the plains, before they could reach the hills to which they were hurrying, and made a great slaughter of them. I beg to mention specially Captain Thompson, Her Majesty's 14th Light Dragoons, for the very good service which he did on this occasion.

In making special mention of Captain Lightfoot for his good services this day, I beg to state how very much indebted I am to the Officers and Men of his, the 1st or "Eagle" Troop Bombay Horse Artillery, for their excellent and gallant conduct throughout the Campaign. In my actions, I made very liberal use of the Troop, in pouring an unexpected or flank fire into the enemy. On all these occasions, the 1st Troop was worthy of its former fame, and proved that no Arm of the service is more dangerous to its foes than fleet Artillery.

I beg to make special mention of Brigadier-General Napier for the very important assistance which he afforded me in the action of the 16th of June.

I beg to bring to His Excellency's notice the good spirit and gallantry which the Troops displayed in the rapid and successful operation against the Morar Cantonments. Their march from Calpee was a very trying one. In consequence of the great heat in the tents by day, the men could not get the rest which they lost by marching at night to avoid sun.

Notwithstanding a long march to Bahadurpoor, the troops ceased their preparations for encamping and marched, fasting, with the utmost alacrity and steadiness against Morar, going five miles and taking it in two hours, under a heavy and well-directed cannonade, and a resolute resistance on the left. The capture of Morar had good results. It was the first defeat which the combined forces of the Calpee and Gwalior Rebels had sustained.

Morar, the Military Station and an outwork of Gwalior, was an important strategical point. It gave me the command of the line of the Morar River, of the road to Agra, and enabled me to communicate with Brigadier Smith to the left, and the Residency to the right.

The Rebels were surprized by my rapid march from Calpee; they intended to make a determined stand at Morar, and had commenced storing it with supplies, which fell into our hands. They had not time to burn the houses, still standing since the mutiny, nor the temporary sheds prepared by Scindiah, all of which were turned to good account.

I got immediately into communication with Brigadier Smith at "Kotah-ka-Serai," and reconnoitred Gwalior.

I have the honor to enclose Brigadier Smith's report of his operations from "Kotah-ka-Serai." I beg fully to confirm his recommendation of the Officers under his command, and to draw His Excellency's attention particularly to the great gallantry and devotion displayed by Her Majesty's 8th Hussars, in the brilliant charge which they made through the enemy's Camp; of which one most important result was the death of the Ranee of Jhansi; who, although a lady, was the bravest and best Military leader of the Rebels. The enemy's guns which the 8th Hussars brought back out of the Rebel Camp into their own, were the best proofs of how nobly they had fought and conquered.

No. 2 Enclosure. Brigadier Smith's Report.

Brigadier Smith having asked for reinforcements, I directed Lieutenant-Colonel Robertson to join him with the Force detailed in the margin.

3 Troops 14th Light Dragoons.
4 Guns No. 4 Light Field Battery.
25th Bombay Native Infantry.

My reconnoissance of Gwalior satisfied me that the information on which I had decided to attack it was good. If I had attacked it from Morar, I should have had to cross the plain between Morar and Gwalior, under the fire of the Fort, and of masked and formidable batteries, established in strong houses and gardens on the banks of the old canal, and a dry river in front of the Phool Bagh Palace.

I could not leave "Morar" so close to Gwalior without adequate protection. The arrival of the Troops, which had been left to garrison Calpee on the morning of the 18th of June, enabled me, leaving my incumbrances, to march from Morar on the afternoon of the same day for "Kotah-ka-Serai," with the force detailed in the margin.

2 Troops 14th Light Dragoons.
No. 18 Light Field Battery.
Madras Sappers and Miners.
Wing H. M.'s 71st Highland Light Infantry.
H. M.'s 86th Regiment.
Wing 5th Hyderabad Infantry.
2 18-pounders and 1 8-inch Howitzer.

1st Troop Bombay Horse Artillery.
3 Troops 14th Light Dragoons.
3 Troops 3rd Light Cavalry.
50 1st Hydrabad Cavalry.
3rd Hydrabad Cavalry.
2 Squadrons Meade's Horse.
21st Company Royal Engineers.
Wing 3rd Bombay Europeans.
4 Companies 24th Bombay Native Infantry.
3 Guns Hydrabad Artillery.

leaving in Morar the force also detailed in the margin, under Brigadier-General Napier, for its protection, the investment of "Gwalior," and the pursuit of the enemy, when they retreated from it.

The march to "Kotah-ka-Serai," about 20 miles, was very harassing; 100 men of Her Majesty's 86th Regiment alone were compelled, by sun-sickness, to fall out and go into dhoolies. These same men the next day, unmindful of their illness, fell in with their Companies, and took part in the assault of Gwalior, which corroborates what I said in a previous report, that the spirit of the Soldiers often made them fight when they were too weak to march.

My column bivouacked on the left bank of the river Morar, and during the night I communicated with Brigadier Smith and Colonel Hicks, Commanding Artillery, Central India Field Force.

Brigadier Smith reported to me that, in consequence of the enemy occupying in great numbers the hills opposite "Kotah-ka-Serai" on the other side of the river Morar, and pressing on him, he had advanced from his position at "Kotah-ka-Serai," and following the road from that place to Gwalior, by the ford across the river, had attacked and driven the enemy from the hills, on his right front, and occupied the road, which led through a pass, about two miles in length, through the hills, and to the left or South side of a very deep and dry old canal cut out of the rock, which led from the ford close by the left of the road through the pass, to the foot of the rock or Fort of Gwalior.

The enemy retained possession of the hills to the left of the pass and canal.

To the left of the road and canal in the pass rose from a narrow plain a succession of slopes, intersected by ravines; a ridge ran along the top of the slopes, on which the enemy had placed a Battery of 9-pounders. To protect the Battery and position, the enemy had concentrated a numerous force of all Arms on the ridge, as well as a large body of Cavalry in rear of it.

About a mile and a half further back, and about the same distance from the left of the road, was stationed, in a gorge of the hills, a large body of the enemy's Infantry, with guns. They guarded a road which branched off from the ford Southwards through the hills to Gwalior.

Brigadier Smith's position in the hills was weak and cramped. His left and rear were threatened by the two bodies just described. The Camp baggage and guns were in the pass, into which came shots from the enemy's Battery on the ridge.

It was clear that the enemy must be driven from both positions, the one on the ridge and the other in the gorge, before I advanced on Gwalior.

The enemy by occupying positions on the hills so far from and unsupported by Gwalior had exposed himself to be cut off. The impediment to my doing so was the deep canal, impracticable for Cavalry and Infantry; on this obstacle the enemy probably relied for protection. To remove it I directed the Company of Madras Sappers and Miners to make a bridge some way, to the left rear of our position across the canal. The bridge or dam was to be ready by sun-set. I made the plan to cross over this bridge during the night, with a force of all arms, get on the south road to Gwalior through the hills above-mentioned, place myself between Gwalior and the enemy's two positions; fall on them a little before day-break, when Her Majesty's 86th and 95th Regiments supported by the rest of Brigadier Smith's brigade, were concealed by the ravines, to attack their front and turn their left flank.

I beg to make special mention of Major the Hon'ble E. C. H. Massey, 95th Regiment; Captain Bolton, Deputy Assistant Quarter-Master General, Rajpootana Field Force, and Lieutenant Harris, of the 3rd Troop Bombay Horse Artillery, for the assistance which their intelligence and knowledge of the ground enabled them to give me in making the reconnoissance and plan.

Lieutenant Haggart, Commissary of Ordnance, by my desire, had, during the night, moved the two 18-pounders and 8-inch Howitzer, from our bivouac, up to the top of a steep height, which was to the right of the road and canal and opposite the ridge. I selected a point at the extremity of a spur of this height towards Gwalior as a position for these guns, from whence they commanded the plain below the entrance to the pass, and were enabled to fire on the enemy's Battery on the ridge.

The enemy's Battery opened a fire on the Siege pieces as they were being taken into position, wounding two draught elephants and causing, subsequently, some casualties in the Battery, after it had opened its fire under Lieutenant Haggart's orders.

The enemy set on fire with their Guns some monster hay ricks, which were close to the canal, in the narrow plain, in order that our outposts might not be covered by them.

The carriage of 8-inch howitzer had been so shaken by hundreds of miles' marching, that its charge was reduced a pound below the regulation, in order to save the carriage: this irregular charge rendered its fire much less certain. The want of sights on the 18-pounders affected the accuracy of their fire in field-firing.

Colonel Hicks suggested to me the withdrawal of the Siege guns as they did not appear to damage the enemy; whereas they had our range. I thought that it would be better that the Battery should cease firing gradually, when the enemy would probably do the same, than that it should be withdrawn. This was done, and the enemy's Battery ceased to fire.

Before the Batteries had begun to diminish their firing, I had gone to our Battery to inspect it and to watch an advance of the enemy's Infantry, in skirmishing order, from the ridge and a spur of it to the left, against our chain of outposts and left, which rested on the canal.

Soon afterwards, a large body of Troops was seen debouching from Gwalior; and my videttes reported that fresh guns were ascending the heights to reinforce the Battery on the ridge, which was good news as the more guns the Rebels brought up to the heights the more were we likely to take next morning.

I reinforced the sentries and pickets on our left on the line of the canal, and ordered the Troops in Camp to be ready to turn out.

The enemy's skirmishers and my line guarding the canal became engaged. At this time I received an express from Sir Robert Hamilton, telling me that he had received information that the Sepoys and Valaitees had agreed to attack me to-day.

The enemy seemed inclined not to confine their advance to an affair of outposts, but to be determined to attack my left flank, which they knew was weak.

The Central India Field Force was the worse for last night's harassing march, and a bad bivouac on rock. The Company of Madras Sappers and Miners, whose zeal and intelligence no hardships can abate, would have completed the bridge across the canal by sun-set; and I anticipated the best results from availing myself of it for the purpose of cutting off during the night the enemy's numerous force of all Arms on the hills.

I would, therefore, have preferred not engaging the enemy before the time determined on.

On the other hand, the position in the narrow pass was so false that it became necessary to free it from the risk of a serious attack, and to change the defensive for the offensive.

I therefore directed Brigadier Stuart, with Her Majesty's 86th Regiment who were encamped between the pass and the river "Morar," to move from my left rear, supported by the 25th Bombay Native Infantry across the canal, crown the heights on the other side of it, and attack the enemy in their left flank, by which means they would mask the fire of the Battery.

As a diversion in favor of Brigadier Stuart's attack, I directed Brigadier Smith to move Lieutenant-Colonel Raines with Her Majesty's 95th Regiment, from the left of my right front, across the canal in skirmishing order, over the shoulder of the hill, on which was the Rebels' Battery, against the enemy's left flank. This oblique movement, and the lay of the ground prevented the 95th suffering seriously from the guns of the Battery.

I further directed Brigadier Smith to move up the 10th Bombay Native Infantry from the right of my right front across the canal, to support the advance of the 95th and to cover my right.

I ordered up also the 3rd Troop Bombay Horse Artillery to the entrance of the pass towards "Gwalior," supported by a squadron of Her Majesty's 8th Hussars.

I disposed the rest of my force in support of the attacking columns, and for the defence of the Camp from the rear.

Brigadier Smith crossing the canal ascended steadily with Her Majesty's 86th Regiment, under Lieutenant-Colonel Louth, the heights. The enemy taken in flank, retired rapidly from the attack of our left flank towards the Battery. The skirmishers of the 86th, with their usual ardour, pressed the Rebel Infantry so hard that they did not make a stand even under their guns, but retreated across the entrenchment, in the rear of which they were in position. The gallant skirmishers gave them no time to rally in the Battery, but dashing with a cheer at the parapet crossed it, and took the guns which defended the ridge—three excellent English 9-pounders.

The 86th, leaving a party with the captured guns, passed on after the enemy's Cavalry and Infantry, who fled, part towards Gwalior, part to the hills to the South.

Lieutenant-Colonel Raines coming up with a wing of the 95th to the entrenchments, with good judgment turned the captured guns on the enemy's Cavalry and Infantry, which he saw in detached bodies in the plain below at a distance of 1,000 yards, as well as on the body which had retired to our left.

Lieutenant-Colonel Raines placed Lieutenant Brockman of the 86th, with some men of his Regiment, in command of one gun; and Lieutenant Budgeon and Lieutenant and Adjutant Sexton, of the 95th, with men of their Regiment, who had been instructed in the gun exercise, in command of the two other guns. These guns thus manned by Infantry made excellent practice, and although sometimes short, the shot ricocheted amongst the enemy. Four Rebel Batteries in front of "Gwalior" now opened a hot fire of shot and shell on our advanced lines.

Lieutenant-Colonel Raines reports that Lieutenant Read, 10th Bombay Native Infantry, rendered him great assistance in firing and pointing the enemy's Artillery.

The 10th Bombay Native Infantry, under the command of Lieutenant Roome, crossed the pass and the canal, and passing by the hay stacks, which were now one burning mass, and moving up, as ordered, in support of the 95th, and in protection of my right, found himself exposed to a fire of Artillery and Musketry, from the heights on the enemy's extreme left. Advancing with half of his Regiment in skirmishing order, and leaving the remainder in support, he cleared the two nearest heights of the Rebel Infantry, and charging gallantly, took two brass field pieces and three mortars, which were in a plain at the foot of the second height.

My Troops were now in possession of the highest range of heights to the East of Gwalior which we saw at our feet. The sight was interesting. To our right was the handsome palace of the Phool Bagh, its gardens, and the old City, surmounted by the Fort, remarkable for its ancient architecture, with lines of extensive fortifications round the high and precipitous rock of Gwalior. To our left lay the "Lushker" or new City, with its spacious houses half hidden by trees.

The ground corresponded exactly with the accounts of it which I had collected: the slopes descended gradually towards Gwalior; the lowest one commanding the grand parade of the "Lushker," which was almost out of fire of the Fort and afforded an entrance into the City.

I felt convinced that I could take Gwalior before sun-set.

I determined to make a general advance against all the positions which the enemy occupied for the defence of Gwalior, extending from beyond the palace of the Phool Bagh on their right, to the extensive Barracks on the left of the grand parade of the " Lushker," and then take the " Lushker" by assault.

For this purpose, I ordered the 3rd Troop Bombay Horse Artillery with a squadron of the 8th Hussars, to follow the road which led out of the pass, and advance, covering my extreme right parallel with the Troops attacking Gwalior.

Lieutenant-Colonel Owen, with the 1st Bombay Lancers, had been moved to the heights, to cover the captured guns; the rapidity and dexterity with which they got over very difficult ground does the Regiment and their Commander much credit. I now ordered them to descend the heights to the rear, get into the road which led through the hills to the South, and occupy the entrance to it, which led to the grand parade, for the purpose of assisting in the attack of that important point and of the " Lushker."

I left a sufficient force of all arms for the protection of my Camp, which was exposed.

I had some time before ordered up No. 4 Light Field Battery with two Troops of Her Majesty's 14th Light Dragoons to the heights to cover my advanced line, and to answer the enemy's Batteries in position in front of Gwalior. The hilly and difficult nature of the ground, particularly the deep canal which the guns had to traverse, prevented their arrival.

The advanced line was irregular, as it followed the formation of the hills. The 86th formed the left which was in advance; the 95th, the right, was refused.

The left of the 86th, who pursued, across a deep ravine to the range of hills to the South, the body of the enemy who retreated to the left, had returned and rested their left on a hamlet situate on the crest of the range which commanded Gwalior. The enemy immediately brought a Battery of two 18-pounders in front of the grand parade to bear on the hamlet, and firing from a great elevation sent round shot into it in rapid succession and with accurate aim.

Skirmishers of the 86th had descended the hill towards the Barracks, and were advancing against the enemy, who had made a stand in houses amongst trees at the foot of the hill. Lieutenant-Colonel Raines with good judgment detached Captain Smith's Company of the 95th in support of them.

I moved the 86th from the hamlet lower down the hill, extending them at large intervals from the left to the right. This new position of the 86th rendered the fire of the 18-pounders harmless and gave more support to the skirmishers, who soon gave a good account of the enemy in the houses.

In front of, and between the two hills occupied by the 86th and 95th, was the last slope, a spur of the hill on which were the 86th commanding the rows of Barracks and the grand parade of the "Lushker," to which the enemy, pressed by our advance, had now withdrawn the two 18-pounders.

I occupied the left of this slope with a Wing of the 25th Bombay Native Infantry, which I brought up from the second line, leaving the other Wing in support. I moved a party of the 95th down to the right of the slope under Major Vialls, who judiciously took possession of a strong powder magazine, surrounded by a wall at the further end of it.

Lieutenant Roome, with the 10th Regiment Bombay Native Infantry on the right, after he had captured the guns and field pieces, took with much spirit a strong building used as an Arsenal on his right, from which the enemy had poured a galling fire on his Regiment, and occupied a trench at the bottom of the hill on which was the Arsenal, from which the 10th kept up a heavy fire on the enemy, who had retreated to a position in front of Gwalior.

Lieutenant-Colonel Raines, leaving a Company of the 95th to guard the captured guns, which kept up an effective fire on the enemy, joined with the rest of his Regiment, and reinforced Major Vialls on the lowest slope.

Lieutenant-Colonel Raines perceived a large body of the enemy's Cavalry in the vicinity of the two 18-pounders now placed in Battery, who he believed were posted there for the purpose of making a dash at the British Troops, should they attempt to take the guns. He therefore halted and waited for orders and reinforcements, placing two Companies of the 95th in skirmishing order, lying down along the crest of the hill, a part of the 10th Bombay Native Infantry being in rear as supports. The enemy now took courage to come out, and fired the 18-pounders with grape and canister at our position, on which Lieutenant-Colonel Raines detached some skirmishers of the 95th to covered ground to his front, who kept up with their Enfelds such an effective fire on the 18-pounders and the Cavalry, that after firing eight rounds, the enemy was obliged to cease firing, and retire behind the buildings of the grand parade.

Lieutenant Knatchbull, and seven or eight men of No. 1 Company of the 95th Regiment, dragged a small howitzer and its tumbril, captured by the 10th Bombay Native Infantry, up the slope, and opened fire with it on the enemy behind the buildings.

The Officer Commanding No. 4 Light Field Battery, by following the road through the pass beyond its entrance, had found a passage, a very difficult one, across the canal; but on taking them up a bridle road which led to the heights, a gun upset and delayed very inopportunely the arrival of this Artillery on the heights. Lieutenant Goldsworthy, of Her Majesty's 8th Hussars, who acted as my Aide-de-Camp during the day, and whose activity and intelligence were most useful to me, at last brought up one 9-pounder to the heights.

The enemy were firing with much vivacity, but little effect, from the Batteries on the right, and the captured guns were answering them.

Large bodies of the enemy's Infantry and Cavalry were marching out of Gwalior, by all its issues, and moving towards us, but not in order or with resolution as if to attack, or take up a position of defence.

Besides storming the grand parade, from which I could enter the "Lushker" and pass by the main street to Scindiah's palace, I directed Brigadier Smith, with No. 3 Bombay Troop Horse Artillery and a squadron of Her Majesty's 14th Light Dragoons, to be ready to attack the enemy's positions at the Phool Bagh and beyond it. This attack protected the right of the Troops attacking the grand parade, and turned at the same time the enemy's left.

The 1st Bombay Lancers were to debouch from the entrance of the road on which I had placed them, charge the enemy on the grand parade, and assist the 95th in taking it.

The 10th Bombay Native Infantry were to support these Regiments.

One 9-pounder, the only piece of Artillery which, on account of the ground, had been able to reach the heights, was to cover from the lowest slope the advance of the 1st Lancers and of the 95th and to clear the grand parade.

The 86th were to remain in their position on the left of the heights, cover my left, and if necessary assist the Camp.

One Wing of the 25th Bombay Native Infantry was to attack the Barracks and cover the left of the 95th attacking the grand parade. The other was to be in support on the slopes.

Two Troops of the 14th Light Dragoons were in support of the lower slopes.

All being ready, I gave the word for the general attack of Gwalior.

I had placed the 9-pounder in position, opposite the two 18-pounders. I directed it to be fired with shrapnel at the enemy, who were attempting to load them. The shrapnel, a remarkable one, burst just over the 18-pounders into about twenty pieces, killed and disabled some of the gunners, and put the rest to flight. Parties of the enemy's Cavalry and Infantry on the grand parade began to retire.

An animated war scene " ensued."

The 1st Lancers, under Lieutenant-Colonel Owen, the 1st squadron led by Lieutenant Heath, that in support by Captain Loch, issuing from the road, charged most gallantly, in sight of the British Troops, descending the slopes of the heights of Gwalior into the grand parade, and clearing all the right of it, pursued, carried away by their ardour, the enemy's infantry into the " Lushker," Captain Loch leading and Lieutenant Heath supporting this second charge, in which, I much regret to say, fell in the streets, shot through the heart, Lieutenant Mills of the 1st Lancers, bravely leading his men—a very promising and popular young officer; Captain Loch in the pursuit cut down the rebel who shot him.

Lieutenant-Colonel Raines, with two Companies of the 95th, charged down the slope with his usual spirit and took the two 18-pounders and two small mortars, on the grand parade.

After going down the slope, and pointing out to Brigadier Smith the position which he was to attack, I joined Lieutenant-Colonel Raines on the grand parade, and went with him against the Town, with the intention of forcing our way, if necessary, to the Palace, the possession of which would give us the "Lushker." As I did not know whether the enemy might not, as at Jhansi, defend the streets and houses, I directed Lieutenant-Colonel Raines to form four Companies of his Regiment for street-fighting, and to leave the remainder of them in reserve on the grand parade.

Lieutenant Roome, with the 10th Bombay Native Infantry, on the general advance being ordered, moved to the front skirmishing through the buildings to the right of the grand parade, and killed many of the enemy who stood there; those who escaped were afterwards cut up by the 1st Bombay Lancers.

The Fort kept up a constant fire during our advance, but as I foresaw, our position masked us from it.

Shortly after entering the Lushker we met the 1st Lancers returning with Lieutenant Mills just killed, Lieutenant-Colonel Owens not thinking it advisable that his Regiment as Cavalry should be involved in street-fighting, with the large number of the enemy who were in the Town.

The enemy's Cavalry and Infantry retreated before us through the Town so rapidly, that we could not even get a sight of them, although we advanced by more streets than one with the view to cut them off. The Rebel Cavalry, as usual, availing themselves of their horses, headed the retreat instead of covering it. After marching for more than a mile through the streets we reached the Scindiah's palace.

I detached Patrols in every direction to clear the streets; before sunset the whole of the "Lushker" or new City was completely in our hands. I also directed the old Town and Fort to be occupied immediately, Scindiah's Agent, who made his appearance on our entering the palace, having informed me that the enemy had evacuated the Fort.

I appointed Lieutenant-Colonel Robertson to be Commandant of Gwalior, and to occupy it with his Regiment.

Brigadier Smith got into action with the enemy near the palace of the Phool Bagh, which he took, killing numbers of the enemy. He then pursued a large body of the enemy who were retiring round the rock of Gwalior towards the Residency, covering their retreat with Horse Artillery guns. After a stout resistance, which did credit to the enemy's Artillery, Brigadier Smith, who did good service on this occasion, as well as throughout the day, captured the guns and killed numbers of the retreating Rebels. Brigadier Smith speaks very highly of the steadiness with which Her Majesty's 14th Light Dragoons, escorting the 3rd Troop Bombay Horse Artillery, stood the enemy's Artillery fire, shot and shell, and of the ardour with which they afterwards fell on the guns and the retreating enemy. Brigadier Smith, who was directed by me to pursue with all his vigor the enemy retreating by the Residency, inflicted much loss on them and captured more guns; he continued the pursuit until long after night, and until his men and horses were unable to move on.

The Officer directed to occupy the old City and Fort of Gwalior reported that the enemy still held the Fort, and had fired on him when he approached it.

The information therefore of Scindiah's Agent that the Fort was evacuated was incorrect.

As it was now night, I directed the Fort to be invested as closely as possible from the old City, and the Lushker; and the Officer

Commanding the Cavalry at the Phool Bagh, to complete the rest of the investment.

The next morning, the enemy again fired from the Fort on the Troops. Lieutenant Rose, 25th Bombay Native Infantry, Lieutenant Waller and a party of the 25th under his orders, with some of Scindiah's Police, burst open the main gate-way of the Fort, and surprizing the other gates before the Garrison, a party of fanatical Artillerymen, Mussulmans, could shut them, reached an archway on which the Rebels brought a gun to bear; Lieutenant Rose and his party got through the archway unscathed by the fire of the guns, and then engaged in a desperate and hand-to-hand combat with the rebels, who defended the narrow street leading into the Fort. But the determined gallantry of Lieutenant Rose, and of the Soldiers of the 25th aided by Lieutenant Waller, who climbed with a few of his men on the roof of a house and shot the gunners, carried all before them; they took the Fort and killed every man in it. But the gallant leader, Lieutenant Rose, who has been twice specially mentioned by me for good and gallant conduct, fell in the Fort, mortally wounded, closing his early career by taking the Fort of Gwalior by force of arms.

Tantia Topee's character is a singular anomaly; he gives proof of a great moral courage in undertaking the execution of the daring and important plans which he forms, but his nerve fails him in the combat which is to decide their success. Thus he planned the successful conspiracy to overthrow Scindiah's power. But as at "Koonch" and "Betwa," his flight was too early to be excusable, and too precipitate to be dignified.

Abandoning the defence of Gwalior, whilst his troops were still fighting, Tantia Topee, with a considerable body of Cavalry and Infantry attempted to retreat Southwards by the road from Gwalior to Puniar and Goonah; but learning that Puniar was occupied by Major Orr's force, he went to the Residency, where the rest of the Rebel Army joined him in their retreat from Gwalior.

The Residency was to have been occupied by Colonel Riddell, but reports from that Officer showed that the difficulty of crossing the ford across the river "Chumbul," at Dhalpoor, where he had arrived on his road from Agra to Gwalior, rendered it impossible that his Force could reach the Residency in time to invest Gwalior; a part of his Force, two squadrons of Meade's Horse, arrived at Morar the day I left it for "Kotah-ka-Serai," as an escort to Scindiah. I left the two squadrons there to reinforce Brigadier-General Napier for the defence of Morar, and the pursuit. Captain Meade volunteered to accompany me as acting Aide-de-Camp; his zeal and knowledge of the country rendered him of great use to me during the operation.

I sent an express to Brigadier-General Napier, at the Morar Cantonments, requesting him to pursue the enemy as far and as closely as he could.

<small>No. 3 Enclosure.
Brigadier General Napier's Report.</small>

The enclosed report from that Officer shows how gallantly and successfully he and his Troops carried out that very important service. Twenty-five pieces of Artillery were the fruits of his most able pursuit and the total dispersion of the enemy.

I wrote to Sir Robert Hamilton, informing him of the capture of Gwalior, and took the liberty to suggest, with the expressions of my sincere respect and esteem for the Prince of Gwalior, that the sooner His Highness returned to his Capital the better.

The next morning His Highness arrived at Gwalior with Sir Robert Hamilton, Major Macpherson and his retinue. I received Scindiah with every possible mark of respect, and accompanied by all the superior Officers of the Forces, whose duties allowed them to be present, and all my personal and Divisional Staff, had the honor of escorting His Highness to his palace in the "Lushker" with a squadron of Her Majesty's 8th Hussars, and another of Her Majesty's 14th Light Dragoons, most honorable representatives of my Force. Our road lay through the long and handsome street which leads from the grand parade to the palace, which was lined by crowds of inhabitants who greeted Scindiah with enthusiastic acclamations.

British Officers and Soldiers, as well as myself, were rejoiced to see that in restoring to his rights the brave and faithful ally of our Government and Country, we had also given back to his people a Ruler who to all appearance had won their affections.

Scindiah is not a man of words, or professions: but it is due to him to say that he has been unceasing in his endeavours to prove how deep his gratitude is to the Supreme Government of India for their most prompt, energetic, and successful efforts in his favor, and to the Troops who executed their orders in this respect. His Highness is always asking how he can prove those feelings to the Troops. To a communication that His Highness wished to present the Forces with six months' batta, I replied that I was extremely obliged to His Highness, but that it was quite impossible that we could accept pecuniary remuneration from a foreign Prince; that we had only performed a grateful duty, and were abundantly rewarded by having been useful to a Prince, who had so bravely and so truly stood by our Government, and their cause; His Highness, afterwards, expressed the wish to give a medal for "Gwalior" to the Troops engaged. I beg, without dilating on this matter, to leave it in the hands of His Excellency the Commander-in-Chief in India, merely observing that my only wish is, that the Officers and men should, if it be deemed right, have the permission to wear the medal; and that as regards myself, I would most willingly give up all claim to the decoration, if for the sake of precedent, or any other cause, my doing so would facilitate their obtaining it.

I have the honour to enclose:—

No. 4 Enclosure. Return of Casualties. (1) A return of the casualties in the operations before "Gwalior."

(2) A list of Officers and Soldiers specially mentioned, and mentioned,
No. 5 Enclosure. List of Mentions. besides those specially mentioned in my report, for their conduct on the same occasion.

No. 6 Enclosure. Return of Ordnance. (3) A return of the Ordnance captured before and in Gwalior on the 19th instant.

I venture to recommend most earnestly all the Troops engaged in the "Gwalior" operations, the Central India Field Force, as well as Brigadier Smith's brigade of the Rajpootana Field Force to His Lordship's most favorable consideration. It is not for me to describe the importance of the service which they performed. I am convinced that it is fully and generously appreciated by the exalted authorities, whose high attributions and experience constitute them the judges of what would have been the state of India, if Gwalior had remained for any length of time, or, worse still, permanently, in the hands of the Rebels.

But as the Commander of the Troops engaged, it is my duty to say that, although a most arduous campaign had impaired the health and strength of every man of my Force, their discipline, devotion and courage remained unvarying and unshaken, enabling them to make a very rapid march in summer heat to Gwalior, fight and gain two actions on the road, one at the Morar Cantonments, the other at Kotah-ka-Serai; arrive at their posts, from great distances and by bad roads, before Gwalior before the day appointed, the 19th of June; and on that same day, carry by assault all the enemy's positions on strong heights, and in most difficult ground, taking one Battery after another, twenty-seven pieces of Artillery in the action; twenty-five in the pursuit; besides the guns in the Fort; the old City; the new City; and finally the Rock of Gwalior held to be one of the most important and strongest Fortresses in India.

I marched on the 6th of June from Calpee for Gwalior, and on the 19th of the same month the Gwalior States were restored to their Prince.

His Lordship having been pleased to permit me on account of my health to give over the command to Brigadier General Napier, I did so on the 29th of June.

From Brigadier General R. NAPIER, C.B., *Commanding 2nd Brigade, Central India Field Force*, To the Assistant Adjutant General, *Central India Field Force,—dated Camp Morar, 18th June 1858.*

On the 16th instant, the 2nd Brigade, composed as per margin, when in sight of the Cantonments of Morar was ordered by the Major-General Commanding the Central India Field Force to advance *in echelon from the right*, in support of the left of the 1st Brigade.

Corps.	European Officers.	Native Officers.	N. C. O. and R. and File.	REMARKS.
1st Troop H. Artillery	4	0	85	In the 1st Brigade.
No. 18 Lt. Fd. Battery	1	0	49	Ditto.
14th Light Dragoons	10	0	259	
3rd Light Cavalry	7	6	136	On Rear Guard.
Madras Sappers and Miners	1	2	42	
71st Highlanders	14	0	381	
Hyderabad Cavalry	1	0	100	
,, Infantry	0	0	0	On Rear Guard.
,, Artillery	0	0	0	Ditto.
Towana Horse	0	1	20	
TOTAL	38	9	1,072	

The Force was disposed as follows:—No. 18 Light Field Battery on the right, supported by Johnstone's Hyderabad Horse; in the centre, the Madras Sappers and Miners, and Wing of Her Majesty's 71st Highland Light Infantry, while on the left was a Wing of Her Majesty's 14th Light Dragoons.

On approaching the right of the Cantonment, the enemy opened upon us from six guns, and I directed Lieutenant Harcourt, Commanding No. 18 Light Field Battery, to engage them—an order which he had barely received when he was summoned to join the 1st Brigade.

My Brigade being then reduced to the Wing of Her Majesty's 71st Highland Light Infantry, the Right Wing of Her Majesty's 14th

Light Dragoons, Madras Sappers and Miners, and 100 Horse of the Hyderabad Contingent, continued to advance on the enemy, who were retreating in large numbers, towards their right rear. At one moment there appeared a favorable opportunity to charge them with Cavalry, but the deliberation with which they moved led me to suspect that they were assured that they were protected by the ground in front of them, and I sent my Brigade-Major, Lieutenant Maclachlin, and some Towana Sowars to examine it. The result showed that the ground was completely intersected with ravines, lined with the enemy's Infantry. I therefore directed Colonel Campbell, Commanding the Wing of the 71st Regiment, to throw it forward in skirmishing order, supported by the 14th Light Dragoons, which was executed with great spirit by Major Rich on the right, who cleared the ravines on his front, leaving them filled with the enemy's dead, and relieving the Horse Artillery from much annoyance from their musketry.

I regret to say that this service was not performed without the loss of a very promising young Officer of Her Majesty's 71st, Lientenant Neave, who was shot whilst gallantly leading his men to the ravines.

Colonel Campbell took two Companies of the 71st under Lieutenant Scott and cleared some ravines on his left and front, killing every man of the enemy that held them; after which he was directed to clear the top of a hill, where a party of Rebels held a Temple and some strong ground. This duty was thoroughly effected, and thirty of the enemy left dead on the hill.

Whilst this was going on a Troop of Her Majesty's 14th Light Dragoons passed round the base of the hill, and cut up all the enemy who attempted to escape from it.

The protection of the left of the Force and the rear being placed under my especial charge by the Major-General, I moved the remainder of the 14th Dragoons and Johnstone's Hyderabad Horse towards the left to cover the rear, and to intercept the enemy's Cavalry, who showed some disposition to move in that direction; but on observing our Cavalry they rapidly disappeared through the hills to south of Gwalior.

The front being now quite clear of the enemy, I withdrew my Brigade to the shelter of the Cantonments, leaving, by the Major-General's order, the Hyderabad Cavalry to watch the flank and rear, until the whole of the baggage should come up. Towards sun-set I withdrew them to a village on the left of the Cantoments, where they were quartered for the night.

The conduct of the whole of the Troops under my Command was excellent. Their perfect steadiness while under the fire of the enemy's Batteries and the gallantry with which they advanced to clear the ravine were deserving of the Major-General's warm commendation.

The 71st dashed into the ravines and encountered the enemy hand-to-hand; the nature of the wounds received was evidence of the desperate resistance made by the Rebels, who were almost entirely composed of Scindiah's mutinous Sepoys.

I beg particularly to recommend to the Major-General's notice Colonel Campbell, Commanding Her Majesty's 71st, for the Soldier-like way in which his Regiment was brought into action; also Major Rich, Her Majesty's 71st, for the spirited manner in which he cleared the ravines in his front. Also Lieutenant Scott, 71st, Commanding the party which scoured the ravines on the left, and cleared the hill occupied by the enemy, which was of considerable height and difficult of access. The enemy held a very strong position on the top of the hill in the Temple, with rocks and broken ground to its rear. Also Major Scudamore, commanding the Right Wing of Her Majesty's 14th Dragoons, which was skilfully handled and ready for every call for its services. His skirmishers attacked and destroyed many of the enemy in the ravines.

Lieutenant Gowan, with his Troop, most efficiently cut off the enemy's retreat from the hill, and destroyed many of them.

Lieutenant Gordon, of the Madras Sappers, kept pace with the 71st and joined in the attack on the ravines.

Also Lieutenant Johnstone and the Hyderabad Cavalry, whose conduct gave me very great satisfaction; they continued exposed to the fierce heat of the day, without food or shelter, for many hours after the rest of the troops had withdrawn to the Cantonments.

The attention of the Medical Officers to the wounded was, as I have always seen it, most exemplary.

I beg particularly to recommend to the Major-General my Acting Brigade-Major, Lieutenant Maclachlin, Adjutant of the Bombay Artillery, whose services were placed at my disposal. His activity, zeal, and intelligence have assured me that he is a most valuable Officer.

Also Lieutenant Bonus, of the Engineers, Acting Assistant Quarter-Master General of the 2nd Brigade, who rendered most zealous and efficient assistance.

The 1st Troop Horse Artillery and No. 18 Light Field Battery having been withdrawn from my Brigade early in the day, I am unable to say anything in regard to their services, which were rendered under the Major-General's own observation.

Jemadar Ishan Khan, with 20 Sowars of Towana Horse, made himself very useful to me.

I beg to enclose a return of killed and wounded.

From Brigadier M. W. SMITH, *Commanding Brigade, Rajpootana Field Force,—No. 25, dated Camp before Gwalior, 25th June 1858.*

I have the honor to report, for the information of Major-General Roberts, Commanding Rajpootana Field Force, that on the morning of the 17th instant, I marched by Major-General Sir H. Rose's order from Antree through the pass to Kotah-ka-Serai, which lies between three and four miles South-east of Gwalior.

I had reconnoitred the pass the evening before, and occupied the difficult points by strong pickets and posts, so that had there been any enemy I should have been prepared.

I met with no opposition whatever, and reached Kotah-ka-Serai at 7½ A.M. Upon my arrival I saw the enemy occupying the heights in front, and between me and Gwalior.

I had orders from Sir Hugh Rose to halt at Kotah-ka-Serai and communicate with him, but as the enemy appeared determined to attack me, and being also hampered with a large quantity of baggage, and Kotah-ka-Serai not being a secure position, I thought it best to take the initiative. I therefore collected my baggage in and near the fort of Kotah-ka-Serai, placing it under a Troop of Her Majesty's 8th Hussars, and a squadron of Lancers, and as strong a guard of Infantry as I could afford. I reconnoitred the ground in front, and found it to be most difficult, intersected with nullahs and impracticable for Cavalry. About 1,500 yards from Kotah-ka-Serai, their guns were in position, and their line ran all under the hills across the road to Gwalior.

This I ascertained by advancing with my reconnoitring party to within about 4 or 500 yards, when they opened so heavy a fire upon us that we were obliged to retire, not however before I had made myself acquainted with the nature of the ground, and thus enabled myself to avoid being intangled in the nullahs above mentioned.

I advanced the Horse Artillery and soon silenced their guns; after three or four rounds they began to retire, and I sent my Infantry across the broken ground giving the command of that branch to Lieutenant-Colonel Raines, Commanding Her Majesty's 95th (the senior Infantry Officer present), with orders to follow up the enemy as far as he thought advisable. I have called upon Lieutenant-Colonel Raines to furnish me with a report, which I enclose, as I consider it gives a detailed and accurate account of the proceedings of the Infantry part of the Force from the time I gave him the order to advance up to the time of occupying the heights above Gwalior. I have only to add that I cannot speak too highly of the steady and Soldier-like conduct of both Officers and men of the 10th Native Infantry, who have given me the most prompt and ready assistance upon all occasions, and of Officers and men of the 95th Regiment, who though exhausted from fatigue and want of food, stormed the heights under a burning sun and a heavy fire.

In consequence of threatening movements of the enemy, as well as the unprotected position of the baggage, I was obliged to send back (to reinforce the Troops already left at Kotah-ka-Serai) one Troop of Her Majesty's 8th Hussars, one Division Horse Artillery and two Companies 10th Native Infantry.

From the nature of the ground already described, I was unable for some time to bring my Cavalry into action, and merely retained them as support and escort to the Troop Horse Artillery under Lieutenant-Colonel Blake, but having advanced to the head of the pass, partially occupied the heights above the plain near the Phool Bagh and placed Infantry to guard the entrance of the defile, and protect a retreat, I thought I might venture to advance with a Squadron of the 8th Hussars, and the two divisions of Horse Artillery remaining at my disposal, and one troop of the 1st Lancers, sending back for the remaining troop of the 1st Lancers as a support.

I then ordered the Squadron of Hussars to charge to the front, which they did most gallantly, passing right through the enemy's Camp, carrying everything before them.

Upon the return of the Squadron both Officers and men were so completely exhausted and prostrated from heat, fatigue, and great exertion they could scarcely sit on their saddles and were for the moment incapable of further exertion. This was a critical moment, as the enemy were collecting both on the front and flanks, but the 95th had arrived near the guns, and the 8th Hussars, in spite of their fatigue, formed to their front in line, and in order to show a greater front I formed them in single ranks. In the mean time the remaining Troop of the 1st Lancers had arrived to support, as second line. I then retired the Cavalry by alternative Troops, protected by the Artillery, during which movement both arms showed the greatest steadiness and entered the ravines, under the protection of the Infantry posted there. I then took up a position for the night on the heights, sending for my baggage and placing it in tolerable security, in a sort of amphitheatre formed by a portion of the hills we occupied. I guarded both ends of the defile with strong pickets of Infantry, in strong positions formed by the ground, and also threw out strong pickets, both Cavalry and Infantry, towards the heights on our right; the left of our position was defended against any sudden assaults by a steep bank and a canal.

Having now finished my first day's proceedings, I have only to add the names of some Officers, who gave me most valuable assistance.

Lieutenant-Colonel Hicks, Commanding details, who was most energetic and always in the front, both in reconnoitring and in the charge, and it was at his suggestion that I ordered the charge of the Squadron of the 8th Hussars through the enemy's Camp, which although venturous, succeeded well with the enemy we had to deal with.

Captain Sir John Hill, acting as my Brigade Major who, in spite of the intense heat and great fatigue, was always at my side, ready to give me assistance and carry out my instructions: also Captain Bolton, Acting Quarter-Master General to the Brigade, who in addition to the performance of his own peculiar duties, which, under the circumstances, were arduous and trying in the extreme, gave me most efficient assistance. Lieutenant Williams, Sub-Assistant Commissary General attached to the Brigade, who is always most active, energetic and indefatigable in the discharge of his duties, but on this occasion, when the obtaining of any supplies were most difficult, in fact, next to impossible, he never spared himself in endeavouring to overcome difficulties.

Captain MacMullen, 23rd Bengal Infantry, who volunteered to act as my Aide-de-Camp and gave me most valuable and efficient assistance.

Cornet Goldsworthy, Her Majesty's 8th Hussars, who also acted as my Aide-de-Camp, gave me most valuable assistance in carrying my orders under a burning sun, and over very difficult ground, and once at a most critical moment, *viz.*, when I required Cavalry support upon the return of the Squadron of Her Majesty's 8th Hussars from their charge.

P. S.—I am much indebted to Officers Commanding Regiments, for their services to me during the day.

Extracts from Notes received from Brigadier M. W. SMITH, *subsequent to the receipt of his Report, dated 25th June, detailing the operations of his Brigade on the 17th June 1858.*

"Two Companies of the 10th Native Infantry advanced with the two Companies of the 95th Regiment, to attack the enemy's entrenchments on the 17th June."

"Colonel DeSalis wishes to mention the zeal and intelligence evinced by Major Chetwode when in command of a detached portion of the 8th Hussars on the _____ June."

"Lieutenant Jenkins, 8th Hussars, was also employed by me in conveying orders to bring up supports, which he executed to my satisfaction."

"While the Infantry skirmishers were feeling their way through the pass leading to Gwalior, their progress was checked for a time by the fire of two or three guns which the enemy had brought into the pass. Lieutenant-Colonel Blake therefore proposed taking a division of his guns into the heights on our right, which was accordingly done, and the result was most successful. By firing at low elevations, round shot and shrapnel were dropped on the enemy's guns near, obliging them to retire precipitately to another position, and by thus advancing and coming into action on every occasion of their making a stand, they were at length fairly driven out of the pass, which was then made clear for the advance of our force."

From Lieutenant-Colonel T. N. HICKS, *Commanding Artillery, Central India Field Force, Late Commanding Field Force from Jhansi,* To Brigadier M. W. SMITH, *Commanding Rajpootana Field Force,—dated Camp Morar, near Gwalior, 25th June 1858.*

As commanding the Field Force from Jhansi, in conjunction with your division, I have the honor to bring to your notice the good service done by Troops which you did me the honor to place under my command on the evening of the 17th, on my personal report to you that a body of the enemy were collected at the gorge of the pass leading to the plain in the direction of the Phool Bagh.

2. Captain Forster and Lieutenant Morris, with a Company of the 95th Regiment, crowned the hill on each side, and with a shout opened fire: the horsemen immediately broke from under the hill: the Hussars led by myself and Captain Heneage charged with one Squadron, overcame and slew numbers, captured two guns, and continued the charge

right through the Phool Bagh Cantonment, leaving bungalows and camp equipage in our possession.

3. But we had advanced too far without any support, and on its arrival it was I believe reported that the Hussars were not fit for a second immediate attack. Captain Heneage was certainly quite black in the face and unable to speak, although on his horse. It was a gallant charge, and I am sure you will with pleasure report to the Major-General Commanding Central India Field Force the soldier-like conduct and good service done by Heneage, Forster and Morris with their men.

4. Since the capture of Gwalior, it is well known that in this charge the Queen of Jhansi, disguised as a man, was killed by a Hussar, and the tree is shown where she was burnt.

From Lieutenant-Colonel J. A. R. RAINES, *Her Majesty's 95th Regiment, Commanding the Infantry,* To Brigadier M. W. SMITH, *Commanding the Column of the assault on the enemy's entrenched position before Kotah-ka-Serai and subsequent capture of the heights in rear, near Gualior, dated 18th June 1858.*

10th Regiment Native Infantry.
1 Man severely wounded.
1 „ slightly „

Her Majesty's 95th Regiment.
List of Casualties by the Action on the 17th June.
Lieutenant I. N. Crealock, slightly wounded.
Private William Hall, dangerously, since dead.
 „ Robert Dutton, severely.
 „ James Suttle „
 „ John Bird „
 „ James Shan, slightly.

Agreeably to your order received about 8 o'clock A.M., on the banks of the stream, near Kotah-ka-Serai, I proceeded with two Companies of the 95th Regiment in skirmishing order to attack the Rebel entrenchments with supports, and the 10th Regiment Native Infantry *in echelon* as a reserve. On nearing their breast-work they opened a brisk fire of musketry on both Corps along the line accompanied with round shot and shell as fast as they could load their guns. Seeing our approach many of them commenced to retire from their left, when the skirmishers from the 95th opened fire on them.

When within 50 yards of their works I ordered the skirmishers to advance at the double and charge, and on reaching their works I discovered their Infantry retiring up the ravines towards the left and right, and taking away the guns to our left. Here we were stopped by a deep ditch with four feet of water and the banks were so steep, that it was with difficulty that the men got over in single file, and by the time that the skirmishers had ascended the opposite bank, the entrenchment was completely abandoned, but we still found a small body, evidently their rear, extended, firing and retiring through the ravines and up the hills in disorder. The skirmishers with the greatest eagerness pushed on, and succeeded in shooting several of them.

On gaining the heights in rear of the encampment, during which time a Company of the 95th had swept round the base of the hill to the left, I observed that the enemy had guns, about 800 or 1,000 yards in front, on another hill about the same height, with Infantry and a large proportion of Cavalry. I sounded the halt and assembly, on which a fire of shrapnel was opened on the men. I then noticed on my immediate right, about 500 yards off, and which I afterwards ascertained was the road to Gwalior, about 100 of the Gwalior Contingent Cavalry, protected from our fire by a high embankment, and as I anticipated that they would endeavour to turn my right flank by a charge and thus cut me off from my reserve, I ordered the retire on the entrenchments, opening at the same time on them a sharp fire from the Enfields, and having our rear covered by a Company of the 10th Regiment in skirmishing order.

On reaching the entrenchment I found that Major Vialls, who commanded the reserve, was attacking the Gwalior Contingent Cavalry above alluded to, with two Companies of 95th, keeping them in check and preventing them from advancing down the road, where they had brought a couple of 9-pounder guns to bear on us. In the meantime another gun of heavy metal, judging from the distance of its range (1,200 yards), was brought into position on a high hill to our extreme left front, when immediately afterwards two guns of the Bombay Artillery were placed to silence the fire which considerably annoyed us.

Soon after this I received your orders to proceed up the road with the 10th in reserve, and on our advancing, the Gwalior Contingent Cavalry as well as the guns retired. After advancing along the road for about a mile (with a deep nullah and a high embankment on our left, and the two Companies in skirmishing order in front and covering the ridges to our right), and until the skirmishers had entered on the plain of the Phool Bagh, large bodies of the enemy's Cavalry were observed as if preparing for a charge, and in such force, as to imperil the safety of the skirmishers. However (after being halted for an hour) I ordered the support up a hill, on cresting which I observed the Gwalior Cavalry in their red uniforms slowly advancing in skirmishing order up a broad ravine to our right, and about 200 yards in front of us.

M

I immediately caused file-firing in line to be opened on them, and on discovering our position they instantly retired with the utmost precipitation, when you, Sir, directed the splendid charge of the 8th Hussars in pursuit. I immediately proceeded to support and follow them to within a quarter of a mile of the Cantonments, when by your orders I halted. A portion of the 10th Native Infantry during the advance supported the 95th, and a Company from each Corps was left to guard the narrow passes as we advanced.

During the halt and whilst the Cavalry were engaged in sweeping through the Cantonments, the enemy brought two guns into position on our left, one on our right, and two from the Fort opened, fired on the 95th and a division of the Horse Artillery immediately and close to us.

Having remained here for about half an hour you directed us to retire and take up a position on the heights in front of Gwalior for the night. We reached them about 7 P.M.

I have the greatest pleasure in bearing witness to the extreme endurance (specially of the 95th) and gallant conduct of both Corps. They had been out the whole day without a meal under a burning sun, and had marched at 2 A.M. that morning from the previous encampment ground, a distance of 10 miles, and although the list of casualties in my Regiment actually occurring from the enemy's fire (and which with that of the 10th is copied in the margin) presents a small proportion of 1 man killed and 1 Officer and 4 men wounded, I regret to say that 84 cases of *coup-de-soleil* occurred, 1 of which proved fatal on that day, exclusive of 5 Officers dangerously, but not fatally, attacked.

In conclusion, I beg respectfully to bring to your notice the valuable assistance I received from Major Vialls, Major Massey, and Lieutenant and Adjutant Sexton, who acted as my Staff Officer during the day, also from Lieutenant Crealock who so ably headed his Company, and assisted in the reconnoissance previous to the attack, and from Captain Pelley, Commanding the 10th, who with his men greatly contributed and assisted towards our success in the action.

From Brigadier-General R. NAPIER, C.B., *Commanding 2nd Brigade, Central India Field Force*, To the Assistant Adjutant-General, *Central India Field Force, dated Camp Jowra-Alipore, 21st June, 1858.*

I have to report that I received at 5¼ A.M., on the 20th June, orders to pursue the enemy, with the details shown in the margin, which marched within an hour and a half after receipt of orders. The Fort which had been reported in our possession, opened upon us, as we came within range, and obliged us to make a detour to reach the Residency.

Corps.	European Officers.	Native Officers.	N. C. O. & Rank and File.
1st Troop Horse Artillery	4	0	95
14th Light Dragoons	2	0	60
3rd Light Cavalry	7	5	92
Hydrabad Cavalry	2	0	243
Meade's Horse	3	3	174
TOTAL	18	8	664

We arrived late in the evening at Sumowlee, having marched about 25 miles.

The enemy were reported to have 12,000 men and 22 guns, and to have marched from Sumowlee to Jowra-Alipore, in the forenoon.

We were too tired to go beyond Sumowlee, the heat of the sun having been terrific: so we rested until 4 o'clock A.M., on the 22nd, then advanced on Jowra-Alipore, where we found the enemy strongly posted with their right resting on Alipore, guns and infantry in the centre, and Cavalry on both flanks.

A rising ground hid our approach, and enabled me to reconnoitre their position, in security, from a distance of 1,200 yards. They opened several guns on the reconnoitring party, disclosing the position of their Artillery which I had not previously been able to discover.

The ground was open to the enemy's left, and a careful examination with the telescope left me assured, that there was nothing to check the advance of my Artillery.

I directed Captain Lightfoot to take up a position, about 600 yards from the enemy's left flank, and enfilade their line; and to act afterwards as circumstances might dictate.

Our column of march was the most convenient formation for attack: Abbott's Hydrabad Cavalry in advance; Lightfoot's Troop of Horse Artillery, supported by Captain Prettijohn's Troop of 14th Light Dragoons and two Troops 3rd Light Cavalry, under Lieutenant Dick, with a Detachment of Meade's Horse under Lieutenant Burlton in reserve. When the Troops came into view of the enemy after turning the shoulder of the rising ground, the whole were advanced at a gallop, and as soon as the Artillery had reached the flank of the enemy's position, the line was formed to the left, and the guns opened on the enemy at a distance of 600 yards.

After a few rounds the enemy's guns were silenced and a rapid thinning and wavering of their ranks took place. Captain Lightfoot limbered up, and advanced at a gallop; and Captain Abbott with his Hydrabad Cavalry charged at the same moment.

The movement was instantaneously followed by the rest of the Cavalry, and the whole of the little force swept through the enemy's Batteries and Camp, and past the villages into the open plain, driving before them, and cutting down the Rebels for several miles. Detachments of the Cavalry charged a body of the fugitives on the right, and cut up many of them.

Wherever there was a body of the enemy collected in front, Lightfoot's guns opened and dispersed them. A party of their Cavalry made a move to our left rear, as if to cut off the baggage, but on perceiving a body of the Hydrabad Cavalry, left to cover the road to the rear, and being themselves threatened by a party of the 3rd Light Cavalry from our left, they retreated rapidly out of sight.

We had now advanced about six miles from our first point of attack; the enemy were dispersed in every direction throwing away their Arms; 25 guns had been captured, and were lying broadcast over the plain; men and horses were exhausted and it was necessary to retrace our steps.

The villages in our rear were still full of the enemy, who were cutting up our Camp followers, and firing on all who passed within range; two guns and a party of Abbott's Cavalry were sent to clear them out, which was effected by the fire of the guns, and by parties of dismounted Cavalry, with their swords and carbines.

Besides the guns, a considerable quantity of ammunition and elephants, tents, carts, and baggage fell into our hands.

Never was the rout of an army more complete. It is difficult to estimate the number of the enemy killed, but I believe between 3 and 400. The villagers say 500, but the escape of many was facilitated by the villages into which our Cavalry could not follow them.

It is with great pleasure that I bring to your notice the excellent conduct of the Troops of all arms under my command. Nothing could excel their cheerful endurance of the fatigue, and the intense heat of the march.

Their good discipline has only been equalled by the courage with which they charged such a superior force.

Many occasions arose when it was necessary for detached parties to act against the enemy's Infantry, and they were invariably met with the promptest gallantry. Captain Barrett's Troop of the 14th Light Dragoons arrived after the close of the action, and a party dismounted, and turned twenty of the enemy out of a garden, killing every man.

Private Novell, of Her Majesty's 14th Light Dragoons, charged alone into the village, and killed one of the emeny under a very heavy fire, for which act of gallantry I beg to recommend him for the "Victoria Cross."

Dr. Mackenzie, of the 3rd Hydrabad Cavalry, being interrupted in his attendance on the wounded, by the fire of a party of the enemy from behind a wall and ditch, called on Subadar Soojab Khan, 3rd Bombay Light Cavalry, to dislodge them. Their position was a difficult one, but the Subadar, with one half his party with slung carbines, and the other with drawn swords, gallantly led the charge and succeeded in dislodging them, and killing every man.

I beg to recommend him for promotion to the "Order of Merit."

Trumpeter Charles Sappery, of Meade's Horse, killed a standard bearer, and captured a standard. Naib Russaldar Kurreeni Sing, 1st Troop, killed five of the enemy; Jemadar Jurtub Sing, Wordie Major, and Sowar Mahomed Bux (wounded) displayed great gallantry and slew many of the enemy. I beg to recommend these men for the "Order of Merit."

The way in which the Troops were led into action excited my admiration; more especially the superb manner in which Captain Lightfoot took up his position on the flank of the enemy, and the dash with which he followed them when broken.

Captain Abbott, Commanding Hydrabad Cavalry, distinguished himself highly, by his activity and intelligence generally, and the gallantry of his charge on the enemy's Batteries.

Those experienced Officers, Captain Prettijohn, Her Majesty's 14th Light Dragoons, and Lieutenant Dick, 3rd Light Cavalry, were charged with the duty of supporting the guns, which they performed to my entire satisfaction.

Lieutenant Burlton, of Meade's Horse, had the honor of leading the Detachment of the Corps for the first time into action, and acquitted himself creditably.

To Surgeon Stewart, of Her Majesty's 14th Light Dragoons, and the Medical Officers of the Force, I am much indebted for the attention to the sick and wounded.

It remains for me now to recommend most earnestly to your favorable notice my Staff Officers, Captain Todd, Brigade-Major, and Lieutenant Maclachlin, Acting Assistant Quarter-Master General. I cannot speak too highly of their zeal and gallantry.

I beg to be pardoned if I have dwelt at too great length on the services performed by the men and officers of the Force. The disproportion of the enemy's number to ours seemed very great,* certainly not less than four thousand men were drawn up in line with a formidable Artillery to oppose us; and though the action was brief, many things occurred during a very short time, and the circumstances were such as to call for the exertions of every individual of the Force.

I beg to enclose a return of killed and wounded, and of ordnance captured.

I also opened a letter from Captain Abbott, Commanding 3rd Hydrabad Cavalry, bringing to notice several men of his Regiment for distinguished conduct, and I beg most strongly to second his recommendation that they may receive the Order of "British India."

Return of Killed and Wounded in the Pursuing Column under Command of Brigadier-General R. Napier, C.B., in the Action at Jowra-Alipore, on the 21st June, 1858.

Corps.	Rank and Names.	Killed and Wounded.	Remarks.	Horses. Killed.	Horses. Wounded.	Horses. Missing.	Remarks.
1st Troop Horse Artillery.	Syce Dooga.	Killed.	...	1	...	...	
1st Troop Horse Artillery.	„ Gennoo						
3rd Troop Horse Artillery.	Gunner Dennis Burns.		Died of Sunstroke	...	...	...	
14th Light Dragoons.	Private George Staple.	Wounded	Severe sword cut, left urial.				
H. C. Cavalry.	Bargeer Miaz Meer Khan.	Killed.	...	1	2	1	

* "The disposition of the enemy seemed very great" in original.

GWALIOR.

Return of Killed and Wounded in the Pursuing Column under Command of Brigadier-General R. Napier, C B, in the Action at Jowra-Alipore, on the 21st June, 1858—continued.

Corps.	Rank and Names.	Killed and Wounded.	Remarks.	Horses. Killed.	Horses. Wounded.	Horses. Missing.	Remarks.
H. C. Cavalry	Duffadar Mahomed Bux.	⎫	Slightly in face, sword cut.				
Ditto	Sowar Mahomed Bux.	⎪	Slightly in face, sword cut.				
Ditto	Sowar Chokutta	⎪	Slightly both arms, and right hand.				
Meade's Horse	Sowar Gholam Ali	⎬ Wounded	Severely, left ear and cheek divided.				
Ditto	Sowar Nawal Khan	⎪	Slightly on both hands, finger amputated.				
Ditto	Sowar Jumal Oodeen.	⎪	Slightly grazed by gun-wheel.	...	2	...	
Ditto	Sowar Chain Singh	⎭	Slightly on two fingers.				
3rd Light Cavalry.	...	...	Nil.				

R. NAPIER, *Brig.-Genl.,*
Commanding Pursuing Column.

CAMP JOWRA-ALIPORE;
21st June, 1858.

ABSTRACT.

Corps.	European. Killed.	European. Wounded.	Natives. Killed.	Natives. Wounded.	Horses. Killed.	Horses. Wounded.	Horses. Missing.
1st Troop Horse Artillery.	...	...	2	...	1	...	...
3rd Troop Horse Artillery.	1	...	...	...	...	...	...
14th Light Dragoons	...	1	...	...	...	...	...
H. C. Cavalry	..	...	1	...	1	2	1
3rd Light Cavalry	...	...	...	...	...	...	...
Meade's Horse	...	...	...	7	...	2	...
Total	1	1	3	7	2	4	1

R. NAPIER, *Brig.-Genl.*
Commanding Pursuing Column.

CENTRAL INDIA FIELD FORCE—ORDNANCE DEPARTMENT.

Return of Ordnance captured from the Rebels by a portion of the Central India Field Force under Command of Brigadier-General Napier, C.B., on the 21st June, 1858.

No.	Description.	Manufacture.	Calibre.	Length Feet.	Length Inches.	Remarks.
1	Brass Gun	Native	12 Pdrs.	3	8	
	Ditto	English	9 „	5	9	
	Ditto	Native	6 „	6	10	
	Ditto	} English {	6 „	5	0	
5	Ditto		6 „	5	0	
	Ditto	Native	6 „	4	10½	
	Ditto	Ditto	6 „	4	10½	
	Ditto	Ditto	6 „	4	10½	
	Ditto	Ditto	6 „	4	10½	
10	Ditto	Ditto	6 „	4	10½	
	Ditto	Ditto	6 „	4	10½	
	Ditto	Ditto	6 „	4	10½	
	Ditto	Ditto	6 „	4	6	
15	Ditto	Ditto	6 „	4	2	
	Ditto	Ditto	6 „	4	2	
	Ditto	Ditto	6 „	4	2	
	Ditto	Ditto	6 „	4	2	
	Ditto	Ditto	6 „	4	2	
20	Ditto	Ditto	6 „	4	2	
	Ditto	Ditto	6 „	4	1½	
	Ditto	Ditto	3 „	2	6	
	Ditto	Ditto	2 „	2	0	
	Brass Howitzer	Ditto	18 „	2	8½	
	Ditto	English	12 „	3	9	
26	Iron Gun	Native	½ „	3	1½	

THOMAS J. HAGGARD, *Lieut., Bombay Artillery,*
Commissary of Ordnance, Central Field Force.

GWALIOR;
28th June, 1858.

From Captain H. D. ABBOTT, *Commanding 3rd Cavalry, Hydrabad Contingent, to Captain* TODD, *Major of Brigade, 2nd Brigade, Central India Field Force — dated Camp Poharee, 25th June, 1858.*

In continuation of my letter No. 72, of the 23rd instant, I have the honor to forward a list of men of the 3rd Regiment Cavalry Hydrabad Contingent, and respectfully beg the Brigadier General will be pleased to recommend them for the "Order of British India." This will give to Privates an increase of pay of 4 Rupees monthly and a decoration. I feel sure the men will fully appreciate this, and that it will be an incentive to their comrades to obtain the same by gallant conduct in the Field.

List of Men of the 3rd Regiment Cavalry, Hydrabad Contingent.

1st Troop.

Trooper	Nutteh Khan.
,,	Sadoolla Khan.
,,	Mahomed Khan.
,,	Jaffer Khan.
,,	Mytab Khan.
,,	Suadut Khan.

4th Troop.

Trooper	Sallow Khan.
,,	Noor Khan.
,,	Shaikh Meeran.
,,	Shaikh Oomur "Commanding Officer's Orderly."
,,	Jaffer Ali Beg.

5th Troop.

Duffadar	Shaik Gholam Nubbi.
Trooper	Shaikh Mahomed.
,,	Budroodean Khan.
,,	Abdul Kureem Khan.
,,	Shaik Kubeeroodean.
,,	Davi Sing.

6th Troop.

Duffadar	Nahar Khan.
Trooper	Allahdad Khan.
,,	Syeed Oosman.
,,	Nutteh Khan.
,,	Myboob Khan.

1st Cavalry H. C.

Jemadar	Alleef Khan.
Duffadar	Gunga Sing.
Trooper	Mookorim Khan.

H. D. ABBOTT, *Captain,*
Commanding 3rd Cavalry, Hydrabad Contingent.

R. NAPIER, *Brigadier-General,*
Commanding 2nd Brigade, Central India Field Force.

Return of Killed and Wounded of the Central India Field Force during the operations before Gwalior.

Rank.	Names.	Killed.	Wounded.	Remarks.

1st Brigade, Central India Field Force.

4th Company 2nd Battalion Artillery.

Rank	Name	K	W	Remarks
Gunner	Gaffey Peter	0	1	Slightly.
Driver	Seetul	0	1	Since dead.
,,	Bhiva	1	0	

Her Majesty's 14th Light Dragoons.

Rank	Name	K	W	Remarks
Lance Corporal	James Badder	0	1	Slightly.
Private	Thomas Davis	0	1	,,
,,	Edwin Overing	0	1	Severely.
,,	James Williams	0	1	,,

25th Regiment Native Infantry.

Rank	Name	K	W	Remarks
Lieutenant	W. Rose	0	1	Mortally, since dead.
Havildar	Buldee Sing	0	1	Dangerously.
Naique	Doorga Sing	0	1	Slightly.
Private	Ramlall Tewarry	0	1	Sword cut.
,,	Mattadeen Moraye	0	1	Dangerously.
,,	Seeumber Ahire	0	1	,,
,,	Chota Sing	0	1	Severely.
,,	Goonajee Gowra	0	1	Slightly.
,,	Mahadoo Gowlee	0	1	,,

3rd Regiment Cavalry, Hyderabad Contingent.

Rank	Name	K	W	Remarks
Trooper	Maddoo Khan	1	0	
,,	Hussan Khan	1	0	
,,	Issery Sing	0	1	Dangerously.
,,	Shaik Kubbeer Odeen	0	1	Slightly.
,,	Nujmoodeen Khan	0	1	,,

2nd Brigade Central India Field Force.

71st Highland Light Infantry.

Rank	Name	K	W	Remarks
Lieutenant	Wyndham Neave	1	0	
Serjeant	William Sheddon	1	0	Sun-stroke.
,,	Hugh McGill	1	0	
,,	James Wilson	0	1	Dangerously.
Corporal	Thomas Leslie	1	0	
Private	Daniel Brown	1	0	
,,	David Kinniburgh	1	0	
,,	Allen Anderson	0	1	Slightly.
,,	James Cromar	0	1	,,
,,	Bernald Daly	0	1	Dangerously.
,,	Donald Fergusson	0	1	Slightly.
,,	Samuel Nicolson	0	1	Severely.
,,	William Watson	0	1	,,

GWALIOR.

Return of Killed and Wounded of the Central India Field Force during the operations before Gwalior—continued.

Rank.	Names.	Killed.	Wounded.	Remarks.
\multicolumn{5}{c}{Brigadier Smith's Brigade, Rajpootana Field Force.}				
\multicolumn{5}{c}{*3rd Troop Horse Artillery.*}				
Serjeant	T. H. Law	0	1	Contusion in abdomen.
Corporal	W. Craggs	0	1	Severely, right leg amputated.
Gunner	Thomas Currie	0	1	Slightly.
,,	Steven Shorten	0	1	,,
\multicolumn{5}{c}{*Artillery.*}				
Gunner	John Field	0	1	Severely.
,,	John Henessey	0	1	,, since dead.
,,	Patrick Connors	1	0	
\multicolumn{5}{c}{*Her Majesty's 8th Hussars.*}				
Lieutenant	J. Reilly	1	0	Sun-stroke.
,,	R. W. Jenkins	0	1	Slightly.
Assistant Surgeon	H. Sherlock	0	1	,,
Serjeant	Joseph Ward	0	1	Severely.
,,	J. Lynch	1	0	
Corporal	Thomas Smith	1	0	
Private	Edward Berry	0	1	Severely, since dead.
,,	John Bowler	1	0	
,,	James Cave	0	1	Slightly.
,,	Thomas Cox	1	0	
,,	Alfred Jackson	1	0	
,,	James Lindsay	1	0	
,,	Michael Kelly	0	1	Slightly.
,,	John Pearson	0	1	,,
,,	George Tuft	1	0	Sun-stroke.
,,	George Hollis	0	1	Severely.
\multicolumn{5}{c}{*1st Native Light Cavalry (Lancers).*}				
Captain	W. W. Anderson	0	1	Slightly.
Cornet	W. Mills	1	0	Musket ball through the spine.
Naique	Shook Lall	0	1	Severely.
Trooper	Shaikh Kyrastee	0	1	Slightly.
,,	Maun Singh	0	1	,,
,,	Shaikh Sillar Bux	0	1	Severely.
,,	Shaikh Noor Mahomed	0	1	,,
\multicolumn{5}{c}{*Her Majesty's 95th Regiment.*}				
Lieutenant-Colonel	J. A. R. Raines	0	1	Slightly.
Lieutenant	J. W. Crealock	0	1	,,
,,	J. M. Sexton	0	1	Severely.
Corporal	Joseph Hunt	0	1	Slightly.
Lance Corporal	Michael Hogan	0	1	Severely.
Private	William Hall	0	1	Dangerously, since dead.
,,	Robert Dutton	0	1	Severely.
,,	James Suttle	0	1	,,

Return of Killed and Wounded of the Central India Field Force during the operations before Gwalior—concluded.

Her Majesty's 95th Regiment—contd.

Rank.	Names.	Killed.	Wounded.	Remarks.
Private	John Bird	0	1	Severely
,,	James Swan	0	1	Slightly.
,,	Henry Robinson	0	1	,,
,,	Thomas Johnson	0	1	,,
,,	Joseph Shan	1	0	Round shot.
,,	Hugh Nelson	0	1	Dangerously, left leg amputated.
,,	William Pike	0	1	Severely.
,,	Joseph McCartney	0	1	Slightly.
,,	Edward Rodden	0	1	,,

10th Regiment Native Infantry.

Rank.	Names.	Killed.	Wounded.	Remarks.
Naique	Hunoman Dhobe	0	1	Slightly.
Private	Thakoor Pursaud	0	1	Severely.
,,	Ittoo Pendicker	0	1	,,
,,	Babajee Kuddon	0	1	Slightly.
Fifer	Davee	0	1	Severely.
Bheestee	Sewa Juddoo	0	1	Slightly.

Total Killed   Europeans 17   Natives 4.
Total Wounded   Europeans 44   Natives 22.
Grand Total { Killed 21 / Wounded 66—87

Died of Wounds since the Action, 4 Europeans and 1 Native.

H. H. A. WOOD, *Captain,*
Assist. Adjt. General, Central India Field Force.

List of Officers and Soldiers of the Central India Field Force and Brigadier Smith's Brigade of the Rajpootana Field Force, the whole under the Command of Major-General Sir Hugh Rose, K.C.B., specially mentioned, and mentioned for gallant and good service in the operations before Gwalior, from the 16th to the 19th of June 1858, both days inclusive.

Captain Cockburn, Her Majesty's 43rd Regiment, Acting Aide-de-Camp, "mention." For good service during the operations.

Lieutenant Lyster, Interpreter, "mention." For good service during the operations.

Captain Wood, Assistant Adjutant General, "mention." For good service during the operations.

Captain Ashburner, Deputy Judge Advocate General, "special mention." Voluntarily attending me on almost all occasions under fire, and very useful in carrying orders correctly and with intelligence.

Captain Gordon, Assistant Commissary General, "special mention." Supplying the Forces well on all occasions under very great difficulties; and always doing his utmost to lend me animals from his Department when required on any important service, for transport of Troops or Guns.

Captain Scott, Pay Master of the Force, "special mention." Voluntarily attending me on almost all occasions under fire, and very useful in carrying orders correctly and with intelligence.

Captain Campbell, Baggage Master, "special mention." Voluntarily attending me on almost all occasions under fire, and very useful in carrying orders correctly and with intelligence.

Lieutenant Clerk, of the Commissariat Department, "mention." Efficient performance of his duty in difficult circumstances.

Having already recorded the excellent services of the Medical Department under Dr. Arnott, it is not necessary to say more than that they continued to render under difficulties the same good service to the end.

Central India Field Force.

Brigadier Stuart, Commanding 1st Brigade, "special mention." Important service in leading ably and gallantly his Brigade, when they took the heights above Gwalior.

Lieutenant-Colonel Lowth, 86th Regiment, "special mention." Gallantly and ably commanding his Regiment, who took by storm the heights on the left and the Guns in the enemy's entrenchments.

Lieutenant-Colonel Robertson, 25th Bombay Native Infantry, "5th special mention." Good service in supporting rapidly and effectually with his Regiment the advanced lines of attack and afterwards taking ably and gallantly a good position to the front.

Lieutenant Brockman, Her Majesty's 86th Regiment, "mention." Ably serving the captured Guns.

Lieutenant Rose, 25th Bombay Native Infantry (killed), "special mention." Very gallant conduct in taking with a small party of his Regiment, by storm, the Fort of Gwalior from a band of fanatics.

Lieutenant Waller, 25th Bombay Native Infantry, "special mention." Gallant conduct on the same occasion.

Brigadier Smith's Brigade, Rajpootana Field Force.

Brigadier Smith, Commanding Brigade Rajpootana Field Force, "2nd special mention." Good service in attacking with a Division of

Lieutenant-Colonel Blake's Horse Artillery Guns, supported by a Troop of Her Majesty's 8th Hussars, and 14th Light Dragoons, the extreme left of the enemy, taking guns and the palace of the Phool Bagh.

Lieutenant-Colonel Raines, Her Majesty's 95th Regiment, "2nd special mention." Gallantly and ably commanding Her Majesty's 95th Regiment when they took the heights on the right above Gwalior and captured two pieces of Artillery. Good service in turning the guns captured on the enemy, and taking by assault two 18-pounders on the Grand Parade of Gwalior.

Lieutenant-Colonel Owen, Commanding 1st Bombay Lancers, "special mention." Ably and gallantly leading his Regiment over very difficult ground, in very good order, up to the top of the heights of Gwalior, to cover the Troops serving the captured guns, and afterwards clearing by a gallant charge the Grand Parade of Gwalior of the enemy.

Lieutenant-Colonel Blake, Commanding 3rd Troop Bombay Horse Artillery, " special mention." Good service on the same occasion with Brigadier Smith.

Major Vialls, Her Majesty's 95th Regiment, "special mention." Good service for taking the extreme right of a spur of the last and lowest height above Gwalior.

Captain Loch and Lieutenant Heath, both 1st Bombay Lancers, "special mention." Gallant conduct on the same occasion as Lieutenant-Colonel Owen; Captain Loch cut down the Rebel who shot Lieutenant Mills.

Captain Meade, Commanding Meade's Horse "special mention." Good service acting on my Staff, and giving me important local information.

Lieutenant Roome, Commanding 10th Bombay Native Infantry, "special mention." Gallantly and ably taking a position from the enemy and two field-pieces.

Lieutenant Mills (killed), " special mention." Gallant conduct on the same occasion as Lieutenant-Colonel Owen.

Lieutenant Goldsworthy, Her Majesty's 8th Hussars, "special mention." Able assistance in bringing up the Cavalry and Guns on very difficult ground.

Lieutenant Budgen and Lieutenant and Adjutant Sexton, Her Majesty's 95th Regiment, "mention." Ably serving the captured guns.

Lieutenant Knatchbull, Her Majesty's 95th Regiment, "mention." For with some men of his Company removing a Howitzer, and turning it on the enemy.

Lieutenant Read, 10th Bombay Native Infantry, "mention." Ably serving a captured gun.

Doctor Clark, Her Majesty's 95th Regiment, "mention." Attendance on sick and wounded.

Privates P. Murphy, Loix Dempsey, and Colville, Her Majesty's 95th Regiment, "mention." Ably serving captured guns.

Color Havildar Gunnoo Powar.
Havildar Rumzad Khan.
Private Bhow Seerka.
" Gonajee Goura (wounded).
" Metadeen Moray do.
" Sen Ammee Aheer do.
" Chota Sing do.

} 25th Bombay Native Infantry, "special mention." For gallant conduct in the storming of the Fort of Gwalior.

Special Mentions of Officers who distinguished themselves in previous operations of the Central India Field Force, but of whose service no written record was addressed to me, but whose statements as to their services are perfectly correct.

Lieutenant Fox, Madras Sappers and Miners, "special mention." Gallant conduct in killing eight men with his own hand in the general action of the "Betwa."

Lieutenant Arbuthnot, Royal Artillery, "special mention." For being the Officer, who gallantly accompanied voluntarily Lieutenant-Colonel Gall, when he reconnoitred closely the enemy's position, under a heavy fire, at Koonch.

Lieutenant Frazer, Staff Officer of the Hyderabad Contingent, "special mention." Gallantly killing three of the enemy at the General Action of the "Betwa," and unwearied zeal and good service during the whole of the Campaign of the Central India Field Force.

Lieutenant Shakespeare, 2nd Madras Cavalry, "special mention." Gallant and good service when voluntarily acting as my Aide-de-Camp in actions with the enemy.

HUGH ROSE, *Major-General, Commanding.*

Action at Kotah-ka-Serai on the 17th of June, under Brigadier Smith, Commanding Brigade Rajpootanah Field Force.

Brigadier Smith, "special mention." Good service in conducting the operations.

Lieutenant-Colonel Hicks, Commanding Bombay Artillery, "special mention." Very gallant conduct in leading a most gallant charge of the Squadron Her Majesty's 8th Hussars mentioned below.

Captain Heneage, Her Majesty's 8th Hussars, "special mention." Leading a daring and very gallant charge of a Squadron of his Regiment through the enemy's Camp and Battery of field-pieces and bringing back two of the enemy's field-pieces under a cross fire.

Captain Poore, Her Majesty's 8th Hussars, "special mention." Very gallant conduct on the same occasion, and unyielding resolution in remaining in the saddle under a burning sun several hours, and so ill as to be fit for the sick report, bringing himself, the other Officers although being disabled by sickness, the brave Squadron in good order to his Camp, under a heavy and cross fire from the enemy's Guns.

Lieutenant Reilly (killed by sun-stroke) and Lieutenant and Adjutant Harding, both of the 8th Hussars, "special mention." Good conduct on the same occasion.

Lieutenant-Colonel Raines, Commanding Her Majesty's 95th Regiment, "special mention." Good service in assisting to take and hold the position of Kotah-ka-Serai.

Major Vialls, Her Majesty's 95th Regiment, Major Massey, and Lieutenant and Adjutant Sexton, "mention." Good service on the same occasion.

Captain Pelley, Commanding 10th Bombay Native Infantry, "mention." Good service on the same occasion.

Captain Forster, Her Majesty's 95th Regiment, "special mention." Good service in supporting with gallantry and ability the charge of the 8th Hussars.

Captain Sir T. Hill, Acting Brigade-Major, Captain McMullen, late 23rd Bengal Native Infantry, and Cornet Goldsworthy, Her Majesty's 8th Hussars, "special mention." For the valuable and efficient assistance they gave on the same occasion.

Lieutenant Maurice, Her Majesty's 95th Regiment, "special mention." Good service on the same occasion.

Lieutenant Williams, Sub-Assistant Commissary General, "special mention." Great energy and good service in obtaining supplies, when it was most difficult to do so.

Captain Anderson, 1st Bombay Lancers, "mention." Wounded in the arm by a musket ball, good service on the same day.

Assistant Surgeon Sherlock, Her Majesty's 8th Hussars, severely wounded by a spent ball, "special mention." For rendering great assistance in bringing in the wounded under fire.

HUGH ROSE, *Major-General,*
Commanding.

P.S.—Brigadier Smith requests that Major Chetwode, Her Majesty's 8th Hussars, may be mentioned for good service on the 17th June 1858.

HUGH ROSE, *Major-General,*
Commanding.

CENTRAL INDIA FIELD FORCE. ORDNANCE DEPARTMENT.

Return of Ordnance captured by the Force under Command of Major-General Sir Hugh Rose, K.C.B., Commanding Central India Field Force, at Gwalior, on the 19th instant.

Camp Gwalior, 24th June 1858.

No.	Description.	Manufacture.	Calibre.	Length Feet.	Length Inches.	Remarks.
1	Brass Guns.	Native.	32 pr.	9	1	Captured on the 19th instant, on the heights and in and about the Town.
	Ditto.		12 pr.	8	6	
	Ditto.		9 pr.	5	9	
	Ditto.		9 pr.	5	9	
5	Ditto.	English.	9 pr.	5	9	
	Ditto.		6 pr.	5	0	
	Ditto.		6 pr.	5	0	
	Ditto.		6 pr.	5	0	
	Ditto.		6 pr.	4	10½	
10	Ditto.		6 pr.	4	10	
	Ditto.		6 pr.	4	10	
	Ditto.		6 pr.	4	10	
	Ditto.		6 pr.	2	8	
	Ditto.		3 pr.	3	4	
15	Ditto.		3 pr.	3	1	
	Ditto.		3 pr.	2	10½	
	Ditto.		2 pr.	3	6	
	Ditto.		1 pr.	2	10	
	Ditto.		½ pr.	1	7½	
20	Brass Howitzer.	Native.	6 pr.	1	4	
	Brass Mortar.		15 ins.	2	5	
	Ditto.		8 ins.	1	11½	
	Ditto.		2½ ins.	0	8½	
	Iron Gun.		3 pr.	4	8½	
25	Ditto.		3 pr	4	0	
	Ditto.		1½ pr.	3	3	
	Ditto.		1½ pr.	3	1	
	Brass Gun.		24 pr.	8	8½	Found in the Fort on the 20th instant, burst in halves.
	Iron Gun.		18 pr.	3	10	
30	Ditto.		6 pr.	7	0	
	Ditto.		6 pr.	4	10	
32	Ditto.		6 pr.	6	10	

THOMAS T. HAGGARD,
Lieutenant, Bombay Artillery,
Commissary of Ordnance, Central India Field Force.

APPENDIX A.

Mutiny at Jhansie.

Captain P. G. Scot's Report.

Some days before it occurred, Captain Dunlop commanding the left wing of the 12th Native Infantry, and the station of Jhansie too, sent over to Major Kirke letters from Major Skene, the Superintendent, and Captain Gordon, Deputy Superintendent of Jhansie, informing him that they had learnt from separate sources that one Luckmun Rao, the servant of the Ranee of Jhansie, was doing his best to induce the men of the 12th to mutiny. It was not known whether the Ranee authorised these proceedings. Subsequent letters from the same authority informed Captain Dunlop that spies or agents of sedition found great difficulty on entering his lines. Captain Dunlop, I believe, had not time to send more. He never seemed to think that there was any danger to be apprehended from the 14th Irregulars. At Nowgong and Jhansie, they let the infantry begin the mutiny. I believe the reason was solely that they wished to conceal the character of the movement, *viz.*, its being a Mahomedan one. They were the most blood-thirsty when the mutiny did break out.

I have learned the following particulars from three natives who were at Jhansie at the time of the mutiny. One of them was in the fort of the city of Jhansie with the party who defended it. The three told their tales separately at Nowgong, Muhoba, and Banda; and as they agree very nearly, I think the information is correct.

Only the 7th company, 12th Native Infantry, mutinied on the 4th of June. It marched into the Star Fort headed by a havildar, Goorbuccus, a very likely man. Captain Dunlop paraded the rest of the 12th and the cavalry, and they said they would stand by him. Next day, June 6th, he was busy at the quarter-guard of the 12th, preparing shells (a thing he was likely to do). He was returning from the post office where he had posted some letters, and was on or near the 12th Native Infantry parade, when men of the 12th attacked and killed him and Ensign Taylor.

I hope I may be permitted to mention here that Lieutenant Ewart who passed through Cawnpore in the end of May on his way to

Nowgong, to join the 12th, was personally told by General Sir H. M. Wheeler to tell Captain Dunlop that he had reported of him to the Adjutant General, that "he was a man for the present crisis."

The sowars there severely wounded with pistols or carbines Lieutenant Campbell of the 15th Native Infantry, the only officer present with the 14th Irregulars. He escaped to the city fort pursued by sowars, some of whom were wounded by the officers inside it. Lieutenant Turnbull of the artillery employed in the revenue survey failed to reach the fort. I suppose he was on foot; he took refuge in a tree, he was seen to climb it, and was shot down. Lieutenant Burgess of the revenue survey department and some of his English and Eurasian subordinates had been living for some time in the city fort. On the evening of the 4th of June he was joined by Major Skene, his wife (and I believe two children); Captain Gordon, Madras Native Infantry; Dr. McEgan, 12th Native Infantry, and his wife; Lieutenant Powys, 6th Native Infantry, canal department, and his wife and child; two ladies from Orai, relatives or guests to Captain Browne; and the English and Eurasian employés in the civil and canal department and salt excise. They employed their time until they were attacked on the 7th in getting provisions and ammunition, and fire-arms into the fort; they piled stones behind the gates to prevent their being opened. They appear to have made great havoc among the assailants with rifles and guns, only one of their number being killed by those outside—Captain Gordon; he was shot through the head when he exposed himself at the parapet. A native who was in the fort said he was kneeling over pulling up a bucket, some syce in the lower inclosure had filled with wheat. A native who was in the city at the time said he was firing at the assailants, but both agreed that he (Captain Gordon) was shot in the head when exposing himself at the parapet; they all agreed that Lieutenant Powys was killed by Mussulmans inside the fort. The native who was inside the fort says that Lieutenant Powys was found by Captain Burgess and others lying bleeding from a wound in the neck, and was able to say that four men beside him had attacked him; the four were immediately put to death, one was a ressaldar (?) moonshee, another a jemadar, and two chaprassis: all four were employed in the revenue survey; the informant who was in the city said that Lieutenant Powys saw a khitmutgar of Captain Burgess attempt to pull down the stones that closed the fort gates and shot him, that this man's brother cut Lieutenant Powys down with his tulwar, and was instantly shot down by Lieutenant Burgess.

The party at last were induced to open the gates relying on the most solemn promises made to Major Skene that the lives of all would be spared; they all walked out save Lieutenant Powys who was alive, but unable to move; his wife was torn from him, and, with the rest of the Christians, was beheaded in a garden near or in the city. Women and children were alike killed; the men are said to have pleaded hard for the lives of these last. The informant who was inside the fortress says that quarter master Sergeant John Newton, of the 12th Native Infantry, and his wife and four little children were alone spared, and taken with the rebels when they left Jhansie; he was a dark East Indian; he was received in September or October last from 3rd Europeans.

The Ranee's troops joined in the attack, so I believe did the men of the salt excise. A Mr. Stewart of that department made his way from near Jhansie disguised as a Hindoo; he joined our party on the 14th June, and at Kubrai he disappeared preferring to make his way alone as a native; his colour and knowledge of the language made this somewhat easy. I regret to say I have not since heard of him; he left us in the dark of evening without a word; he stated that in consequence of the mutiny he had received orders to come to Jhansie fort with all his men, and had moved along the salt boundary towards Jhansie, collecting his men as he went; but finding they mutinied, he had to flee for his life; he was told ere he fled that the heads of some murdered officers were being carried about the villages around Jhansie, and were then being exhibited in a village he was close by.

Lieutenant Ryves was in command with the only native officer, jemadar Lall Mahomed, and sixty men of the left wing, 12th Native Infantry, and forty sowars of the 14th Irregulars. I was told at Muhoba, by a man from Jhansie, that Lieutenant Ryves had been seen riding towards Lullutpore. I have no doubt that he escaped.

In conclusion I beg to say that this report is made from memory; I had no documents or papers to refer to. All books, papers, etc., that we left at our quarters at Nowgong must have perished in the flames; no trace of them was to be seen when I visited cantonments on the 12th and 13th June, and I think I can safely state that no records of the 12th Regiment, Native Infantry, exist safe, save such papers as have been forwarded to the brigade, and other offices. Descriptive rolls of many of the mutineers must exist in the collector's office. Of the young men of four or five years' service or less, only three, I think, joined the officers after the mutiny broke out.

Appendix A

The following account of the Jhansie massacre is from a written deposition of one present :—

For some time since, the gentlemen were in the habit of passing the nights in the fort, and spending the days at their bungalows. Captain Burgess and his establishment had their tents pitched within the fort, and everything was being put in readiness to retreat into it as soon as there should be occasion to do so, which occurred on the evening of the 4th of June. Some few effected their escape from the place altogether; one gentleman (name unknown) reached Burwa Saugor, when meeting with a native surveyor of the canal establishment, Saheb Rai, he gave him his watch and horse, and procuring a Hindoostanee dress, escaped on foot. He was scarcely out of sight, when two sowars, who were hotly pursuing him, arrived there, and recognizing the horse, took Saheb Rai and the Thanadar prisoners back to Jhansie, where they were still when last heard of. Lieutenant Turnbull was not so fortunate; not having been able to gain the fort, he climbed a large tree; he had, however, been seen, and was shot on the tree. From the evening of the 4th, until noon of the 8th, the gentlemen in the fort kept good their position, the ladies assisting them in cooking for them, sending them refreshments, casting bullets, etc. They were fifty-five in number altogether (Europeans), inclusive of the ladies and children, and they began to get very much straitened for want of provisions. Behind all the gates, they had piled high heaps of stones to strengthen them, and kept up so good a defence, that one of the cannon which had been brought too near the gates, was abandoned; and it was only by fixing ropes to it in the night that the mutineers were able to regain possession of it. Lieutenant Powys was the first person killed in the fort. The way he met his death was this: two men, brothers, in Captain Burgess' employ, one was his jemadar, declared that he would go out. They were told they would be shot down if they attempted it, but they said they might as well be shot as stay there to be starved, and accordingly commenced undoing the fastenings. One was shot immediately. The other turned on Lieutenant Powys who happened to be near him, and cut him down with his tulwar. This one was directly shot by Captain Burgess. The only other person killed inside the fort was Captain Burgess himself who received a bullet in his head, after having, I am told, killed no less than twenty-five with his own hand. All the natives spoke of his great skill as a marksman. The mutineers at last having forced the Ranee to assist them with guns and elephants, succeeded in effecting an entrance at one of the gates, and they promised the gentlemen that if they laid down their arms and gave themselves up quietly, their lives would be spared. The gentlemen unfortunately listened to their words and came out. They were tied in a long line between some trees, and, after a short consultation, had their heads struck off. Such ladies as had children had to see them cut in halves before their own turn came. The sowars, it appears, bore the principal part in all these atrocities. This took place on the afternoon of the 8th of June.

Written deposition of a native of Bengal.

I am a native of Bengal and was attached to the writers' establishment of the Jhansie Customs Collector's office.

On the 5th of June last at about 3 P.M., while we were in attendance at the office, we were alarmed by the report of musketry fired in the direction of the magazine; instantly two peons and a duffadar of the Customs establishment, who had been sent by Mr. Carshore to pay in 1,500 rupees of the Customs collections in the Deputy Commissioner's treasury, returned to our office panic-stricken, and stated that they had been informed by certain sepoys that the revenue treasury was in imminent danger of being plundered by a gang of robbers. Our office was ordered to be closed directly, and the peons on the establishment were called in to hold themselves in readiness within the office compound for any contingency which might occur. Mr. Wilton was next seen dashing in from the military lines, and urging Mr. Carshore to fly from the place with his family, intimating at the same time that the regiments had mutinied and all was over. Accompanied by Mr. Wilton, Mr. Carshore drove with his family in a buggy to the dâk bungalow where they arrived in safety. Myself and other amlahs then quitted the office compound, leaving the peons in charge of the office, and took our stand on an adjoining road to witness what was going on. Seeing nothing where we stood, we determined to cut into the town by striking across the parade ground, but we had not advanced many steps in our intended direction, before we were accosted by a sepoy from a distance to the effect that we should keep ourselves out of the way, as some men of the 12th Native Infantry had broken into open mutiny and taken possession of the magazine. We, however, pushed on regardless of consequences, till we came up to a spot where the officers of the 14th Irregular Cavalry with a party of sowars belonging to that regiment were haranguing the men of the 12th Native Infantry, who had not already mutinied, to continue true to their colours, and we then cut into the town. On our way, however, we observed a party of sepoys running towards the cutcherries of Messrs. Skene and Gordon intent upon mischief; but as those officers and all other Christian residents with the exception of officers attached to the regiments had been timely escorted by a party of the 14th Irregular Cavalry into the fort, the sepoys were in this instance foiled in their attempt to massacre the Christian population of Jhansie. When all the Christian residents, with the aforesaid exception, had taken shelter in the fort, the town gates were closed by order of Captain Skene who had directed that no one should be permitted to enter the town except with the privity of the head of the police.

I heard the following morning that fifty-two men of the 12th Native Infantry had mutinied the previous day, and were in possession of the magazine and treasury. The remaining troops in the station passed the first day and night of the outbreak in a state of passive mutiny, regardless of the exhortations of their European officers, who commanded them to attack and take the mutineers, and endeavoured, though unsuccessfully, by kind words as well as by threats, to persuade the mutineers to return to their duty.

The fifty-two men of the 12th Native Infantry had the previous afternoon raised the standard of revolt near the magazine, and invited all men of the 'deen' to flock to their standard, offering to remunerate each man for his services at the rate of twelve rupees per month. They kept their post at the magazine and round their white flag till noon of the 6th, when they were joined by the remaining troops in the station, *viz.*, by the remainder of the 12th Native Infantry and the whole wing of the 14th Irregular Cavalry. These first fell upon their European officers, who had not for one moment forsaken their men; Lieutenant Campbell was first attacked, but though wounded, he kept his seat on his fleet charger which enabled him by overleaping a gate to escape into the fort without further injury. Lieutenants Dunlop and Taylor, however, were unable to escape, and consequently fell victims to the fury of their men. Two havildars and a sepoy hid the latter under a charpoy, but to no purpose. The mutineers next broke up into parties and proceeded to set fire to the bungalows and to liberate the convicts from jail. A party consisting of fifty sowars and 300 sepoys then approached the town with two guns and a number of Customs and Police chaprassis, led by the jail daroga, in their train—and the doors of the Orcha gate were thrown open to them to the cry of 'deen ka chyr.' The Ranee placed guards at her gate and shut herself up in her palace. Captain Gordon sent a message to the Ranee soliciting her assistance at this crisis, but this was refused, as the mutineers threatened to put her to death and to set fire to her palace in case of her compliance with Captain Gordon's request. The Ranee's guards then joined the mutineers.

The rebels next proceeded towards the fort with the intention of storming it, but were kept at a respectful distance by the gallantry of the European inmates, who shot a number of the former with their muskets. Baffled in their attempt, the besiegers retired for the day after placing guards of sowars and Mussulman chaprassis of the Customs and Police departments over the gates.

The night passed quietly; the following morning Messrs. Andrews, Purcell, and Scott issued from the fort, disguised as Mussulmans, with the intention of seeing the Ranee and obtaining her aid, but the feint being discovered, the gentlemen were taken to the palace of the Ranee, who did not even condescend to honour them with an interview, but ordered them to be carried before the mutinous ressaldar for orders. Her words were to the effect: "She had no concern with the English swine." This was a signal of death. The three gentlemen were then dragged out of the palace; Mr. Andrews was killed before the very gates of the Ranee's residence by Jharoo Comar's son, supposed to be a personal enemy of his, and the other two were despatched beyond the walls of the town. In the afternoon a second attempt was made to surprise the fort by breaking open a gate, but the besieged succeeded in repelling the invaders who retreated after stationing guards at the gateway as they had done the preceding day.

On the third day of the outbreak commenced an indiscriminate plunder of the property of Europeans, Bengalees, and other amlahs in the town. The Bengalees were specially singled out for vengeance because one of them, the post office writer, had concealed one Mr. Fleming in his house, and the mutineers had succeeded in tracing him out, and murdering him in the Baboo's house. The following morning a general search was made for Bengalees, and myself and two others of the Customs establishment fell into the hands of the ruffians and were hauled up in presence of the ressaldar who ordered us to be kept in confinement until the fort should surrender.

After we had been secured, a fresh attempt was made upon the fort, and the Ranee was threatened with instant assassination, provided she refused to side with the rebels. She accordingly consented and supplied them with a reinforcement of 1,000 men and two heavy guns which she had ordered to be dug out of the earth. They had been buried three years ago. Thus strengthened they commenced a brisk cannonade upon the fort, but failed to make any impression upon it, as not a single brick of the fort was injured by the balls which struck against the battlements. The fire of musketry from the fort, however, did a good deal of execution, and the besieged might have been able to hold out much longer, had they not been betrayed by certain native servants who had been received into the fort for the performance of menial offices. Captain Gordon received this day a gun-shot wound of which he immediately expired. Then a kherkie or secret door was treacherously thrown open by the natives within. Captain Powys shot and killed one of the traitors, but was shot dead in return by the brother of the man he had slain. The handful of Europeans in the fort were now for a moment paralysed—they knew not how to overcome such odds from within and without. They, however, mustered courage, and when they observed that a rush was made from outside through the passage, they all ascended the terrace of a high building in the fort, and thence kept firing upon the enemy below. The latter then proposed a parley, promising to allow the Europeans to quit the fort unmolested provided they surrendered themselves and their arms to them. This the Europeans consented to, but no sooner did they leave the fort unarmed than they were seized by the rabble and conveyed to Jokhun Bagh, where they were separated into three lines, one comprising all adult males, another all adult females, and a third all the children. Then commenced the horrid massacre, the daroga of the jail first raising his sword and killing Captain Skene. Then all hands were raised and an indiscriminate slaughter took place, the males were despatched first, the females next, and the murder of children closed the brutal scene.

Poor Captain Skene before he received the finishing stroke exclaimed to a sepoy who was standing beside him "that it was idle for the mutineers to hope that England would be denuded of all her bold sons by the destruction of the handful of men that were now at their mercy," and poor Mr. Carshore's eldest son before he was murdered begged in Hindee that his life might be spared as he hoped that the vengeance of the mutineers had been satisfied by the blood of his father and mother.

When the above cruel business had been gone through, myself and the other Bengalee prisoners were set free under a promise of not keeping up any correspondence with Europeans.

Subjoined is a list of the Europeans who were massacred at Jhansie, viz. :—

Captain Skene and family; Lieutenant Gordon, Deputy Commissioner; Captain Burgess, Revenue Surveyor; Lieutenant Powys and family; Doctor McEgan and family; Captain Dunlop, 12th Native Infantry; Sergeant Kailly, Engineers; Ensign Taylor; Lieutenant Turnbull, Revenue Surveyor; Lieutenant Campbell, 14th Irregular Cavalry; Mr. W. S. Carshore, Collector of Customs, with family; Mr. T. Andrews, P. S. A.; Mr. R. Andrews, Deputy Collector, and family; Mr. Wilton, Customs Patrol, and family; Mrs. Browne and her daughter; Mr. Scott and family; Messrs. Purcell, both brothers; Messrs. Crawford, both brothers; Messrs. Elliot, brothers, and mother; Mr. Fleming; and many other Christians (names unknown).

Abstract translation of the statement of Sahibood-deen, khansamah of Major Skene, dated 23rd March 1858.

I have been in Major Skene's service for the last three years. On the 5th of June, about 3 P.M., muskets were fired near the magazine, and a loud cry was raised that the dacoits had attacked the station. Major Skene came to his house from his cutcherry, and placing his wife and children and Miss Brown in the carriage of Captain Burgess, who had come to see him, sent them all to the fort with Captain Burgess. In the meantime he ordered his carriage, which being brought to him, he drove to the Jokhun Bagh, where Mr. Gordon met him. He was also taken into the carriage. Both these gentlemen went to the fort. I remained at the bungalow. I had sent the mussalchee and khitmutgar to the fort. At 7 P.M. having dressed dinner, I and the cook went to the fort. All the officers that were present dined together. During the night I remained in the fort. Ahmed Hossein, tahsildar of Jhansie, the next morning came to see Major Skene in the fort. I told him to send us coals, wood, fowls, and eggs. He did so. He also sent some men, seven or eight in number, with sweetmeats; breakfast was then served. Memsahib and Mr. Gordon asked for tiffin without delay. There was no khitmutgar present, all had gone to the bungalow. I, Dildar chaprassi, and Captain Brown's khitmutgar assisted in serving the tiffin, which being done, the superintendent ordered me to remove all the silver from the fort to Akheychund treasurer, but to keep as much as was required. I obeyed his orders and packed up all the things in two boxes, which I, in company with Mungul Khan and Khodabux, chaprassis, took to the house of the treasurer. While I was leaving the fort, Mr. Gordon called me back, and impressed upon me the necessity of making some arrangement that they might be put to no trouble for their meals. I went to the treasurer, gave him the two boxes, told him to examine the contents, which he refused to do, stating that there was no need for that. I locked up the boxes, keeping the keys in my possession. I went towards the bungalow, taking with me some rice, potatoes, two sheep, and four geese. Gholam Mahomed chaprassi was with me. On reaching Ashan Allee Sheristadar's house we heard a loud noise and firing of guns. It was about 2 o'clock. Near the city gateway, we saw that the Adjutant was galloping hard, and two sowars were following him. The Adjutant dismounted and went into the city through the wicket. The sowars took his horse and pelting and kicking us told us that we were going to feed the officers. We were arrested and taken to the kotee. Our houses were plundered. The sowars and the sepoys went to the jail and liberated the prisoners, who set fire to the bungalow of — Andrews. A few sowars, prisoners, jail burkundauzes, and men from the town, both Hindoos and Mahomedans, commenced plundering the house of the superintendent. I and Bissram Sirdar taking advantage of this opportunity ran to the garden. Busis Allee, jail daroga, made his burkundauzes carry two boxes from the superintendent's bungalow to his house. The same day some other boxes were carried off by Moroo Bulwant *alias* Mama Sahib, Ranee's father; Goolzar Khan, jail burkundauze, took three bullocks and one cow. This man with his followers came to the garden, asked the gardener where we lay concealed. He pointed out our hiding place. Goolzar Khan caught me; his two men drew swords and pointed their muskets towards us asking where was Major Skene's treasure. I told him that the money was always kept in the treasury, which was plundered. They then took all I had on my body. The sirdar was then plundered of all his wife's ornaments that he had with him at the time. I was then set free; I remained in the same garden. On the morning of the 7th of June I went towards the fort with two bottles of milk and four loaves of bread. I remained outside the fort near a hay rick. Mr. Gordon, who was walking on the fort wall, saw me. Major Skene also came to the same spot; they dropped a rope to which I tied the loaves and the bottles of milk. I at the same time informed him that the house was plundered. I was told that I could not get access to the fort, but that I should try if I could furnish them with provision in the same way. While returning from the fort I was arrested by Choonee, a relative of Jharoo Koar, and some other men from the town whom I can recognize, but whose names I do not know, and was taken to Mama Sahib, because I had supplied the officers with food. Mama Sahib ordered his men to take me to Jemadar Lall Bahadoor and the ressaldar to be murdered or to be blown from a gun. The jemadar and the ressaldar first ordered me to be shot, then they recalled their order and kept me confined. The next morning it was reported that some force was advancing upon Jhansie. All got under arms. I escaped to the town and saw that the Karukbijlee gun had been put in order by the Ranee's order to be used against the officers, and that the town people, mutinous sepoys, and Ranee's servants were firing. Thakoors were also passing up and down. About 4 or 5 P.M. it was reported that the officers were coming down from the fort. I also went to the gateway. When my master with memsahib and other officers came down, I saluted him and could not help weeping. The sowars and sepoys pelted us with stones and obliged us to separate. All the officers went to one side and their servants joined me. The mutinous sepoys and Ranee's men took the officers to the Jokhun Bagh, and all the servants, including myself, were sent to the pultun. The ladies and officers were murdered near the garden. All the people of the town were with the sepoys. After perpetrating this inhuman deed, Bukish Ally, the jail daroga, sowar, sepoys, and the Ranee went to the pultun to the ressaldar. Bukish Ally observed that he had killed the burra sahib with one stroke. Then the subadar, the ressaldar, and the Ranee's men came to the parade ground, and ordered that the prisoners should be set free. We were in consequence liberated. The next morning I went to the garden of Jokhun Bagh, and saw that the bodies of the officers, ladies, and children were lying unburied, without clothes. The third day I was told that the bodies were buried in a pit, but by whom is not exactly known; when I had gone to see the dead bodies, I wrapped memsahib in a piece of cloth which was tied to my head. One day before the murder of the officers it was proclaimed in the town by the beat of drum that "the country belonged to the king, the Ranee held the rule, and that the officers will be killed to-morrow." After the murder no proclamation was issued.

March 25.—The Ranee opened her own mint. Mahomed Sanah, doctor, told me that the officers were not willing to come down from the fort, but when they were assured by him that they would not be killed, they came down.

Nijim Hossein, revenue tahsildar, and Ahmud Hossein, tahsildar of Jhansie, were also put in confinement by the ressaldar. On seeing me they began weeping. When the mutineers left Jhansie, I went to the treasurer and asked him where he had kept the silver and jewellery. He said that all was taken by the rebels. On my observing that how could they know that such things were kept in such a place, that although maltreated, I had not given them any clue, how had he given them these things without asking me. The treasurer did not speak to me upon this point before I had asked him. I know nothing regarding the promissory notes possessed by Major Skene, but Madarbux, khitmutgar, stated to me that Major Skene had told him that Akheychund had his money, which was to be laid out in supporting his wife and children, whom he wished to place under the charge of the said khitmutgar and myself. I had heard that Madarbux had gone to Saugor, but I am not sure where he is at present. I saw Akhey Mull going to the cutcherry of the Ranee, and heard that he took service with her and became her treasurer.

Statement of Mrs. Mutlow.

4th June, about three o'clock in the evening, I ordered my ayah to get water ready to bathe my little boy, so she put everything ready and came to me. I took my child and undressed him to bathe, so I heard the sepoys were making a noise. I sent my ayah out to see. She told me the sepoys were running up to the magazine with their guns. As soon as I heard that, I took my boy quite naked to Mrs. Newton's house. Mr. and Mrs. Newton took their children to the dâk bungalow. I was not able to keep up with them; I turned back to the post office, so the Baboo gave me a chair to sit down, and ordered his chaprassi to fan me. When I came to my senses he sent his chaprassi with me to my bungalow. As soon as I came to my place I sent my servant to the office to see where were Mr. M. Mutlow and brother. He saw no one there; he turned back and told me that everyone went up to the fort, and the sepoys were firing their guns at everyone they saw, so no one was killed that day, and I was still in my house with my child. Mr. A. Skene heard of me; he sent his two servants and chaprassis to take me up to the fort, so I got in the fort about six o'clock in the evening, and met with my husband and brother-in-law there and remained in Mrs. Blythe's room that night and the next morning. Mr. A. Skene and

APPENDIX A   xiii

Mr. Gordon went to the Ranee, and got about fifty or sixty guns, and some powder and shot and balls, and she sent about fifty of her own sepoys in the fort to assist us; and about 12 o'clock during the day they killed those gentlemen who were with them, and commenced burning the bungalows and speared Mr. Taylor belonging to the cavalry. So he galloped his horse and came to the fort. When the Ranee heard of it she got all her sepoys down from the fort. The Ranee and her sepoys joined with the regiment, so we changed our clothes that night and wanted to get out of the fort, but was not able; the sowars were around the fort, so we kept there Friday night, Saturday, and Sunday. Monday, about eight o'clock in the morning, Mr. Gordon was shot, that regiment subadar wrote to Captain Skene to come out of the fort, saying, " We will not kill any of you—we will send you all to your own country;" so Captain Skene wrote to the Ranee to tell the sepoys to take their oath and to sign her name on the letter. All the Hindoos took their oath, " If any of us touch your people just as we eat beef ;" and those Mussulmans took their oath, "if any of us touch you just as we eat pork;" and the Ranee signed her name on the top of the letter, and it was given to Captain Skene. As soon as he read the note everyone was agreed to it; some of us changed our dress, some were with their own dress. As we came out of the fort the sepoys came and put their guard around them. I was out of the guard with my ayah; they did not take notice of me. I told my ayah to take me to her house; she said they would kill her; she brought and left me in the Jokhun Bagh, where a Hindoo grave is made like a house. I remained there about a month. I gave my earring to that gardener to get something for me to eat; he brought *chunna* flour and made *rotie*, so I lived on *mowah* and *chunna* for some time, and Dowlutram came from Saugor and heard of me; he came to me that very evening, and prepared everything for me, and saved me from those sowars who came from Saugor. From the month of July this man gave me to eat; he used to get me wheat and rice, ghee, and when not able to go to the bazar, he used to give me ready money, and he gave me a female to do every business for me, and used to give her a rupee per month and four annas for house rent every month; and I sent Dowlutram twice to Saugor; he was caught twice on the road; those letters came to Jhansie to the Ranee, and she was looking out for me and Dowlutram. So Dowlutram hid himself and me and two children. It was the Ranee's order if anyone caught us going out of the town that she would give 100 rupees as a present in those days. Guneshee Lall used to write me to come out of Jhansie. I was very glad to leave the place, but there was a sentry on every gate. No one could go out without the Ranee's order, and no one was so brave as that to get an order for me to take me out. Guneshee Lall wrote to me to go to a Seth's place, that he would take me out with his family. As soon as I saw his letter, I was very glad and sent Dowlutram to go to the person and ask him if he would take me with his family. Dowlutram went and asked him, he was not willing; said he would be found out if he do so. So I tried my best to come out of Jhansie, but was not able to get out on account of the doors. I suffered a great deal in this Jhansie, lost my husband and brother-in-law, and all my property, and turned as a beggar, only to save my two children. Now its master's will to do some good for me and two children. I have no one in this world just now, except master. I have one sister in Rangoon in the 84th regiment, Mrs. Susan Leary, and one sister was in Nagode in the 3rd Native Infantry, Mrs. Agnes W. Karard. But I don't know where they are now. My father-in-law and mother-in-law is in Vellore, Queen's pensioner, Mr. Mark Mutlow.

The original was written down by the deponent herself.

APPENDIX B.

MUTINY AT NOWGONG.

Captain Scot's statement.

I have the honour to report that the force at Nowgong, in Bundelcund, mutinied on the 10th ultimo, and compelled their officers and all who stood by them to quit the station.

Major H. Kirke, 12th Regiment, Native Infantry, commanded the station at the time. His death on the 19th idem left me senior survivor of the officers at the station, and it has thus become my duty to make this report.

As there is too much reason to fear that reports that Major Kirke made prior to the mutiny cannot have got further than, or even so far, as Cawnpore, it seems proper that I should relate what passed at Nowgong, and was entered in the reports I suppose to have perished.

The cartridge question had been settled at Nowgong. The infantry men there and at Jhansie were ashamed at the mention of it; the burning of empty bungalows had long been over when on the 23rd of May, a sepoy of the 12th Native Infantry, then Major Kirke's orderly, rushed into the house, and told him that he had just got away from a party of twenty or so Poorbeas and Bundelas, who had asked him to point out the officers' mess-house to them; they appeared to be disappointed in the non-appearance of an accomplice to guide them. The sepoy said he had consented, and making an excuse that he was hungry, got away, promising to return. Major Kirke, with his adjutant and his son, and one or two armed sepoys, went to the spot indicated, after directing the ressaldar commanding the right wing, 14th Irregulars, to surround it with sowars and prevent the escape of anyone. Only three men were found; one ran off and rather than stop or make a reply beyond saying he was a sepoy, let himself be fired at three times; two other men hiding in a hollow tree, let the party pass, and then darted off towards the artillery lines; sowars and infantry at once searched the station and found no one. Doubt was, a day or two afterwards, thrown on the sepoy's statement by the men of the 12th Native Infantry, and especially by those at Jhansie; and the senior ressaldar of the 14th next day expressed doubts to me, but Major Kirke did not give up his belief in the man, having warned him of some plot, though he seemed to think the sepoy had not revealed the facts of it. The ressaldar disobeyed orders as if to let the man escape. The sentry at the artillery lines falsely denied any men having passed near him and some time afterwards when four men of the company were convicted of exciting others to mutiny, it was observed (and that after their conviction and discharge) that this sentry was one of the four; materials for firing bungalows were found on the spot by myself two hours after when search was made, and with them there was a peculiar stick slightly burnt at one end as if from being used to stir burning thatch. These circumstances indicated that some mischief was afoot. Whether the sepoy did not dare to tell the truth, and made up the story to put the officers on their guard, or the story was entirely untrue, it was thoroughly believed at the time that Bundelas and others outside cantonments meditated the assassination of the British officers, and the men of the 12th manifested an affection for them that was most gratifying. It was felt that some one of the men of the 12th had caused the bungalows to be set on fire in April; the men were then plainly told that there could be no doubt upon this point, and also that it seemed as clear that the man was not known to more than one or two of his comrades. The display of feeling by the mass of the sepoys that thus accidentally took place was re-assuring, and it bound them strongly to their officers. In proof that the men felt that the fires were lit by one of themselves, I think it well to mention that when I came upon the materials for firing bungalows, two sepoys eagerly examined a piece of cloth that was among them, and said that the dhoby's mark had been torn away; other sepoys who next day saw the cloth, did and said the same.

Next night Major Kirke planted two guns under an artillery sergeant on a long, straight road that traverses the road of cantonments, which is crossed by many fine roads leading to all the lines and into the bazars. A strong guard was close to the guns; I was posted there, and had an officer under me. Two guns were posted on the left point of the 12th Native Infantry lines on the parade; they commanded a road leading out of cantonments. The remaining two guns of the battery were at the gun shed between the infantry and cavalry lines; Second Lieutenant S. Townsend commanding the battery, and the only European officer present with it, was with these guns; a strong guard with a European officer was posted beside him. There were fears felt of the cavalry taking the guns; they furnished a number of pickets all round the station. This duty kept many of the men divided, and at a distance. Suspicion had fallen on the ressaldar commanding the cavalry and his men; he had informed Major Kirke on the 23rd, the day of the alarm, that his corps had learnt by letters from Delhi that every Christian there had been murdered. He appeared to wonder at the little the Europeans knew of affairs in Delhi, and that his men and himself were in communication with the place. His neglect or disobedience of orders, a few hours after, was very suspicious; and from that night the men and officers, by their demeanour, awoke strong distrust in our minds, even the sick in the hospital were most insolent to the doctors until a few days before the mutiny, when they put on another tone—it may be—to lull suspicion.

The 23rd of May fell a few days before the Eed; and the news of the massacre of the Christians at Delhi roused a fanatic feeling, which may have given place, in the lapse of days, to a feeling that their pay and earthly prospects were not to be despised. They seemed so ripe for revolt that when Major Kirke saw that there was no danger of a foe from outside the cantonments, he kept up the arrangements I have described, as they put it out of the power of the sowars to effect anything against the infantry and artillery, who were staunch. The whole of the guns could in a few minutes be brought to bear on the cavalry lines, and the road to Jhansie, which the cavalry were likely to take if they mutinied, as the left wing of the corps was there. Another equally strong reason was that no one suspected that the arrangements had respect to any foe but outsiders.

A letter from Captain Gordon, Deputy Superintendent of Jhansie, had informed Major Kirke that 400 Bundelcund men had been discharged from the late 34th Regiment, Native Infantry, and it was thought very likely that they would, on their return, try to get up an assault on the treasure chest. The number was overrated, and the men could not have got near Nowgong by that time; this was not clear at first, and the men were not told afterwards that it was clear to us that the disbanded 34th were far off. The cavalry obeyed all orders, but their faces betrayed an exultation about the revolt that was conclusive. No signs of distress were shown them; officers visited their pickets, and during the day went to the lines and talked with the native officers; they were received with freezing politeness.

The 12th Native Infantry men and the artillery liked the arrangements very much; they were greatly gratified by the confidence in them shown by the officers who slept amongst them. It gave the officers

B

opportunities of conversing with the men; there can be no doubt that it knit the two to each other. The arrangement had the great advantage of working well, and therefore, in such critical times, it was thought the best policy to keep it up. Major-General Sir Hugh Wheeler, commanding the division, when Major Kirke reported to him that he was maintaining it, and that the men were well disposed and pleased, replied that the report was highly satisfactory. This, of course, was a paramount argument in its favour. All went on quietly till about the 30th of May, on which day the pay havildar of the artillery came to Second Lieutenant Townsend, about 5 P.M., and reported that he had awoke from sleep during the day and heard men of the company plotting mutiny around him, and that some Seikhs of the 12th Native Infantry were with them; this was instantly reported to Major Kirke. Next morning it was learnt from many sowars that mutiny had been openly plotted the day before in the artillery lines; and it was said, by men likely to speak truths, that the only thing that prevented an outbreak was the determination of the men of the 12th to have nothing to do with it. This havildar in the morning spoke out more fully; a private employed as steward or store-keeper to the battery confirmed his evidence, and so did the subadar Birjnath, a very fine old man, who had just been invalided after fifty years' service.

Major Kirke had made all the invalided native officers remain at their old posts and do duty; and they were most willing and useful, with the exception of subadar Doorgah Singh and jemadar Lall Mahomed of the 12th Native Infantry, who afterwards joined the mutineers. Doorgah Singh then took a prominent part, I believe.

The above-named men agreed in their evidence that mutiny had been openly plotted in the company by a strong party, to which the senior men were opposed. The strongest abuse had been applied to the old subadar, and the havildar had been told he would be shot, because they were faithful to Government. Four men were named by the subadar as the worst of the mutineers; they were sent for quietly with other men who could be trusted. They were told that as they were ill-pleased with the Company's service, they were discharged from it. They were paid up; a guard was ready and they were sent off at once to Chutterpore, to be kept there till further orders, from access to any one, lest they should work some mischief in the lines if merely told to go home.

The havildar, who commanded this escort, said that he had been greatly apprehensive of an attempt being made by the sowars to rescue the men. The men then had no idea that we distrusted the sowars.

The men who even after the mutiny stuck to their officers (this havildar was one) testified surprise when I told them that guns had been posted so as to provide against a rise of the sowars. The major thought that if a court-martial were held on the four accused, the delay might lead to an *émeute,* while a sudden blow at the root of the evil would do good. Only one man of the 12th, a Hindoo, was named as sharing in the plot; he was a well-behaved, quiet man. I believe that the Seikhs of the 12th were taking an open share in the plot, and that the artillery did not dare to denounce them. The officers put great trust in the Seikhs, the Poorbeas were well aware of this, and it made the Seikhs formidable to them. This man was believed to be innocent; his protestations were believed and he was not punished. I believe that the dismissal of the four men had a good effect on the artillery company; it intimidated the ill-affected, and it undoubtedly encouraged the faithful portion. Major Kirke from that night had the whole of the guns of the battery brought in front of the quarter-guard of the 12th Native Infantry. I think that the men of the company felt affronted and humiliated by this measure. I observed that the old subadar two days after the discharge of the men gave up keeping pistols about him, and I felt that it showed that he thought the men were to be trusted. Major Kirke promoted to the rank of havildar the steward Seetaram, and wrote a strong letter to General Wheeler recommending the havildar for promotion, as a reward for their fidelity. Things went on quietly after this, and the sowars' altered demeanour led me to think they were perhaps wronged by our suspicions on the 4th of June; the men of the 12th following the example of the 70th Native Infantry sent word to their company officers that they were anxious to serve against the rebels. Four out of the companies of the wing had done so when at 11 o'clock A.M. a letter brought by express was put into Major Kirke's hand; it was from Captain Dunlop, 12th Native Infantry, commanding at Jhansie; it had been dashed off in great haste and ran thus:—

To the Officer Commanding at Nowgong.

Jhansie, June 4, 1857, 4 P.M.

"Sir,—The artillery and infantry have broken into mutiny and we have entered the Star Fort. No one has been hurt as yet. Look out for stragglers."

APPENDIX B

Major Kirke at once sent for the native officers of the 12th Native Infantry, said he had received the petition from the various companies (the 5th had by this time been received), and that he was much pleased and would report the loyalty of the wing to the Governor-General. The native officers were allowed to say what they pleased about their fidelity, etc., and then the news from Jhansie was communicated. They were much dismayed and sincerely distressed. They set to work at once and drew up a letter to the left wing at Jhansie, telling them of the right wing's offer to serve against the rebels; that they had done very wrong in mutinying, and should at once undo what they had done. The letter was at once despatched by an express.

The ressaldar commanding the irregulars was present on this occasion; he had come to speak to Major Kirke about a letter (dated the 3rd instant) he had just received from his commanding officer at Jhansie, Lieutenant Campbell, desiring him to give up the names of some sowars that he had reported to Major Kirke as using mutinous language.

The truth was this: several sowars were said by a drummer of the 12th Native Infantry to have told him in the sudder bazar that they would make crow's meat of him. The ressaldar appears to have been aware of such words having been used, and for some object or other stated to Major Kirke that his younger men would be likely to talk foolishly in the bazar, and he therefore begged that they might be forbidden the bazar after a certain hour. Lieutenant Campbell must have heard something about this, and thereon wrote the ressaldar the above letter the day before the mutiny. The ressaldar's object in coming was to say that he had never accused any of his men of having actually used mutinous language. He was very indignant about it.

The ressaldar was much discomposed at the Jhansie news; he was a grey-headed man, whose constitution was delicate, and to him it was of consequence to keep his rank and pay; the fanatical feelings the Eed festival raises in a Mahomedan had had time to cool, and he appeared now anxious to conciliate. A parade was ordered at once, and the native officers dismissed with injunctions not to say anything to the men about Jhansie until the revolt was announced on parade.

The right wing, 12th Native Infantry, when asked if they would stand by the colours, rushed forward to them as one man, and were enthusiastic in their expressions of fidelity. The artillery company embraced their guns with expressions of devotion. The men of the 14th said at once that they would be true to Government. They expressed no enthusiasm.

APPENDIX B

The officers were much gratified at the men's reply, and word of it was sent to Jhansie.

That day (the 5th June) two parties of the 14th Irregulars, consisting of forty sowars, each under a native officer, were despatched to Jhansie and Lullutpore, at the requisition of the superintendent of Jhansie, under authority from the Lieutenant-Governor at Agra. The Jhansie party was required to relieve one of like strength under the command of Lieutenant Ryves, 12th Native Infantry. On the 7th of June a report was received from the native officer commanding the Jhansie party to the effect that he had halted at Mowraneepore (thirty miles from Nowgong) on hearing that all the Europeans at Jhansie were murdered. The same sowars brought a letter from the tessildar at Mowraneepore saying the same, and mentioning that a naick and four sepoys of the right wing, 12th Native Infantry, were there with some magazine stores. They had left Nowgong on the 30th May, with muskets, ammunition, and buff-belts from Allahabad, for the deputy superintendent at Jhansie. The news of the mutiny had caused them to turn back when about ten miles from Jhansie.

Major Kirke sent out written orders to the native officers that if the cavalry had mutinied at Jhansie he should return, but if not, he should push on.

The ressaldar of the 14th seemed very uneasy at this news, and when we said that no word had come of the 14th mutinying, he said he much feared they would, as they had very few officers, European or native, and many of the men were very young. He seemed far from anxious now that a mutiny should take place.

In the afternoon of the 9th the shepherd of the left wing mess came in and said that Captain Dunlop and Ensign Taylor had been killed on the parade ground at Jhansie on the 5th by the men of the 12th Native Infantry. The 12th men at Nowgong seemed horrified at the news, most certainly many of them were sincerely so, and that night the men of the artillery volunteered to serve against the rebels. The men seemed to be well affected, but the bazar people seemed to be very anxious to send away their women and children, which Major Kirke would not allow them to do. We were informed that murmurs were going about that the treasury was being emptied in small sums, and that it was to be made over at once to the Gurawlee Rajah. Both tales were without foundation, but they were alarming indications that the agent of the general rebellion, who had got the bungalows lighted, and stories set afloat about cartridges, and bone-dust *atta* was as determined as ever to effect his intention, and that some men aided him. On the 10th a letter in English came from Twearry Hossein, the tessildar of Mowraneepore, saying that he had heard of the murder of every European at Jhansie, that he had received a purwannah to the effect that the Ranee of Jhansie was seated on the guddee, and that he was to carry on business as hitherto. He added that he meant to leave the place at once, and I know that he did so.

The mails that had been sent towards Jhansie on the 5th and subsequent days came back in one bag in the afternoon. The runners had feared to enter the station.

At sunset the mutiny broke out. Up to that moment the men of the 12th had showed the greatest good-will, attachment, and respect to their officers; I have been ten years with the men and never before did I see them show so much good feeling as they had at all times done since the 23rd May, when the alarm arose that a massacre of the officers was meditated. I believe that in the majority of the men sincerity and fidelity existed, and that many who mutinied did so under intimidation, and from an infatuated feeling that mutiny was a matter of destiny at present, Benares Brahmins having predicted it.

The artillery company had been cheerful and well disposed until the guns had been brought before our quarter-guard.

The driver company were unruly for a few days in May, while an impression was abroad that the infantry would not fire cartridges, but they quieted down the moment the infantry fired, and they remained so. The artillery sergeant told me of this feeling, which went to this length, that the men paid little attention to his orders and were very elated. Lieutenant Townsend told me that the sergeant had reported this state of things to him; he appeared to be sure that it was a true report.

The mutiny broke out thus:—

At sunset of the 10th the guards paraded, a number of the men began to load, and three Seikhs at the same time stepped to the front. One of them, Kana by name and sepoy of No. 1 Company, shot the Havildar Major (Abeem-aun-Sing of No. 4 Company, acting as Havildar Major) through the head; he fell dead and did not move. The Seikhs then made a rush at the guns; they were drawn upon the parade ground as usual. The artillery sergeant made some resistance; he says no one aided him, and he fled and gave information. The sergeant major, 12th, was fired at, and a sepoy, Dursun Sing of No. 3 Company, pushed the barrel aside; he was one of those who stuck to the officers to the last and Major Kirke said that he would recommend him for the Order of Merit.

The sergeant major fled to the mess-house. I was told afterwards by sepoys who remained faithful that the quarter-guard loaded or began to do so to fire on the mutineers, but were stopped by a jemadar, Mobaruck Ally, who asked him why they loaded without order. This jemadar, a few minutes afterwards, joined the mutineers, and was first (report says) in command of the wing.

The first use the mutineers made of the guns was to load one with grape, and fire it into a tent that officers occupied close to the quarter-guard. They then seized the treasure tumbrils, and placed them in the midst of the guns; the treasure tumbrils were at the quarter-guard.

Ensign Franks happened to be at the lines at the time; he saw the guns seized, and immediately went to Major Kirke's to report. All the other officers were at the mess; the shots in the lines gave them the alarm. Second Lieutenant Townsend was the first to reach the lines; his guns were by that time in the mutineers' hands. Lieutenant Ewart, 12th Native Infantry, and myself were the next. Before mounting I went to the top of the mess-house to have an idea of what was going on.

When I reached the magazine I found that four sentries were mounted. One of them, a Seikh, seemed not at all surprised at what was going on (being in the plot of course); a few sepoys were leaving the lines by a road that crosses the centre of them, and others were hanging about the magazine in a panic-stricken state. I could not induce them to advance on the guns. I hoped to collect men in such numbers that they would make a dash on them: and getting hold of a bugle I blew the assembly repeatedly, but no one came. The mutineers just before I did so fired grape from a gun over the lines, and this struck terror into the men. As none would advance, I entered the lines by the cross road and some came on with me, others joined me from their huts, but none would go against the mutineers: indeed myself and Mr. Ewart had great difficulty in making our way forward as the men held our horses by the bridles, and, as far as they could, prevented our proceeding. I had ordered the magazine to be opened that I might get a bugle out, and I was told that the sentries would not let the magazine be opened. I perceived, too, that of the men around me some were in the plot, and wished to save Mr. Ewart and myself. The jemadar Mobaruck Ally gave me a most meaning warning look, and waved his hand as a sign that I had better go. It was clear that I could effect nothing, so I went back to the mess, ordering Lieutenant Ewart to come with me. Major Kirke and the officers with him tried to induce the sepoys that were there (about 100) to attack the mutineers, but they all fell back, and the attempt had been given up by the time I came back.

A party of the mutineers had now come almost in front of the mess house with one gun. The major seeing this ordered us to leave the cantonments, and we began to retire; the sowar orderlies then galloped off to their lines. When we had proceeded about 300 yards a round shot and a round of grape or canister were fired at us; as we were hidden from sight, the aim was incorrect, and no one was hurt. Mrs. Mawe, wife of the doctor, Mr. Smalley, the band-master, and his wife had joined us at the mess, no ladies were left behind, and we pushed on. The major directed us to take the road to Chutterpore, but Dr. Mawe, who was leading in a buggy, took the Gurrowlee road, which crosses the other at right angles. It was most providential that this mistake was made, as it led to the sowars, when their thirst for plunder was somewhat appeased, going out to Gurrowlee in quest of us. When it was dark, and we were hidden from cantonments by a hill, we turned towards Chutterpore, meaning to get on the metalled (*sic*) road that leads to it, through the town of Mhow; providentially again our intentions were accidentally defeated. We had kept too much to our right, and found impassable ground between us and this road; we, therefore, took the road to the Gora lake, and on arrival there, we found a Bhoondela boatman, a servant of the adjutant, 12th Native Infanrty, Lieutenant Jackson, who took us by a country road to Chutterpore, which we reached at daybreak in safety.

Had the sowars attacked us on the way, I do not think the thirty sepoys who were with us would have been of any use, they were so panic-stricken, and that the party would have been cut up. The bungalows were surrounded by the mutineers the moment we left, they took what they pleased, let no one else take anything, and then burned the bungalows, guarding them till no one dare enter; they then plundered the bungalows, and plunder being over, they sent parties in quest of us. I believe the sowars reproached the infantry for not having killed us all, they ranged the country for us, and seizing our servants threatened their lives under a supposition that they knew what road we had taken; they, too, supposed we had gone to Gurrowlee, some were able to say that the people at Mhow assured them we had not gone to Chutterpore.

The serai at Chutterpore was given up to us, and at first we were well treated. The Ranee meant well, but some of the chief officers were Mahomedans, and seemed to sympathize with the rebels. They told us that a message had come from Nowgong that the troops had risen for "deen," and that the Ranee must not shelter us. Fifty sowars, they said, were a *coss* off, and had brought the message; I believe that none came beyond Mhow, eleven miles off.

One man, a sepoy, named Toorab Khan, grenadier company, 12th Native Infantry, rode out to Chutterpore, and ascertained that we were there; the horse belonged to Lieutenant Becher. A week before this sepoy was reported by the naick of his guard for having been absent for several hours during the night; his excuse was that he left the guard for a few minutes, and fell down senseless. Major Kirke would not punish him.

At 2 or 3 P.M. of the 11th we heard guns firing at Nowgong. The rebels were firing a salute ere marching. During the night some sepoys came to join us, and caused an alarm that the rebels were approaching. A large force, I believe, turned out to oppose them. I was asleep, and did not know of this till morning. I mention this to show that the Ranee was determined to defend us.

By the night of the 12th June there were with us four native officers (three were Brahmins and one a Mahomedan), five havildars, and seventy-eight sepoys of the 12th Native Infantry; only one was a Mahomedan. A number of the Christian bandsmen and their wives had come also; of the artillery only a Christian bugler and a private had come; none came afterwards. Two sepoys of the 12th afterwards joined at Muhoba on the 15th; one had been plundering, and he was made over to the civil authority. No sowar joined the officer.

On the 12th Major Kirke sent me to Nowgong to see what state it was in, and to do what might be necessary and possible. Second Lieutenant Townsend of the artillery accompanied me at his own wish. We met a number of people after 9 P.M., carrying towards Mhow wood they had plundered from houses in cantonments.

We found that all the thatched bungalows had been burnt; three pucka houses were standing, two of them very small ones. Of the public buildings only one had been burned, the bungalow of the sergeant-major of the 12th Native Infantry. The magazine of the 12th Native Infantry had been blown up. The men of the 12th had set fire to their lines, but very few huts were burned—they were tiled. The artillery and cavalry lines were uninjured; so were the bazars of the 12th and the cavalry. A large portion of the main street of the sudder bazar was burned down. One house was still burning; I had no means of putting the fire out. A guard from Chutterpore was in the station for its protection. They were guarding some grain in the sudder bazar, meaning, I believe, to keep it, and they allowed hundreds of villagers to plunder the houses of wood.

I feared they have allowed the public buildings to be deprived of all their wood-work, and the huts to be stripped of their roofs for the timber. They could easily have prevented plunder, for Lieutenant Townsend and myself cleared the station by firing a few shot so as not to hurt anyone. I gave the official in charge of this station particular orders that villagers were to be intimidated, and, if that failed, shot down to prevent plunder. He and others at Nowgong thought our rule was over, and the station the Ranee's for the future, and my orders were listened to, but not carried out.

I found a sepoy (a Brahmin) in one hospital in the last stage of sickness, left there to starve or to be killed by dogs, and an old bed-ridden woman, mother of an invalided naick and grandmother of a sepoy musician, who had left her uncared for to march with the rebels. I entrusted them to the moofedar of the cantonments who resides in the village, Bellaree, close at hand, and gave his servant money for their food. This man, Ramgopal Dilchit, and his head servant, Lala Doma, were well disposed towards our Government, and did their best to give us information of the doings of the mutineers. On the day of the mutiny he sent us word that the forty sowars on their way back from Mowraneepore to Nowgong had been out at Alipore (a large place ten miles from Nowgong), that they were going back to murder all the Europeans. The Moonshee of the 12th told me, when he joined us at Chutterpore, that the native officer who brought their party back said all he could in the presence of the Moonshee and the native doctor of the 12th Native Infantry, in the dwelling of the senior ressaldar of the irregulars, to cause a mutiny, stating that the Rajah of Alipore had prepared a feast, for the force, expecting it to mutiny, and march to Jhansie. I forget the native officer's name, I may find it out some day. I mention the circumstance that it may not be forgotten against him. He was a tall old man, very thin-faced. Major Kirke took no notice of the information beyond mentioning it to myself and some of the officers.

The head-quarters of the regiment marched from Chutterpore on the night of the 12th, and reached Muhoba on the morning of the 15th.

Major Kirke left the party during the first march, and went to Logassee where I met him on the night of the 13th. The Rajah was very kind and hospitable to us. Next morning we left under an escort furnished by the Ranee of Nyagong. We left it—a place called Koolpeeha on the borders of the Chirkaree country—and at daybreak of the 15th reached Chirkaree. The Rajah in fear of the rebels was most unwilling to receive us, and hid us from sight. In the course of a day he heard of the dâk from Agra having reached Muhoba, and then he seemed better disposed. In the evening, he no longer dreaded publicity, and sent us in a carriage to Muhoba.

Mr. Carne, the deputy collector, was there, but his district was so disturbed that he had made arrangements for the Rajah of Chirkaree taking charge of it.

On the 16th news came in of the mutiny at Banda and at Hameerpore. One party therefore marched on the night of the 17th for Kallinger in Mirzapore or Chunar, instead of Allahabad, as before intended. The guide took the party out of the way to a village, Jeyroho in the Jalan territory. A pass between two hills was pointed out as the one we were to proceed by; some armed men were in it and on the hills. The men in the village, too, were all provided with *lathies*. We thought they were afraid of us, and assured them we had no hostile intentions. As matchlock men were guarding the only village we had passed on the way, and the whole country seemed alarmed, we thought that no danger against us led to the men being on the hills: indeed, it was thought they were seeking their own safety.

The sun was up, so the party halted under some trees, some distance from the pass. About noon, the men in the pass sent us a message demanding money. The men were ordered to be ready to force the pass at 4 P.M., and they seemed well pleased with the orders. But in less than an hour two of the native officers came to urge that the money should be paid. It was determined after much consideration that we must yield to the native officers and men, and let them have their own way in the matter. They were most obedient and showed more anxiety to please us than I ever before saw them show, but we felt that we could not coerce them and could not defend the large number of women and children without their aid; indeed, it was too great for the number of sepoys we had, for on the march it was found utterly impossible to prevent the line of carts lengthening out to more than a mile. The country seemed ready for rapine, and the freebooters would have had little difficulty in collecting any number of men from the villages on our road.

Mr. Carne, the deputy collector, was with us; the Rajah of Chirkaree had refused to shelter him, and he was of opinion that the escort of the party to Kallinger should be purchased as offered. The men accordingly paid down 300 rupees to the head of the party who called himself Pran Singh, and applied to the officers for 400 rupees to make up the advance agreed on. It was given out that the whole was paid to Pran Singh.

Next morning before daybreak, as the party was getting ready to move on without Pran Singh (who had not appeared), the camp was fired into from a tree between it and the pass, where some men were gathered. The sepoys immediately began to fire wildly, and after a few minutes they all retreated, save ten or twelve who held their ground with Lieutenant Ewart, Lieutenant Townsend, and myself.

Major Kirke and the officers went after the retreating men, trying in vain to bring them back and restore order. They moved away at a quick pace. Lieutenant Townsend was shot in the heart in the course of a quarter of an hour; he died instantly. He was firing when hit. He was a very gallant young officer of less than three years' service. He had for more than a year held the sole charge of his battery; and I am sure that were Major Kirke now alive he would bestow great praise on him for the excellent condition his battery was in.

The whole party, women and children, were by this time a good distance from camp. I therefore followed them; the dacoits' fire was nearly over, but the main party were gone. We moved slowly away keeping the attacking party at a distance by turning on them frequently When we reached the Chutterpore territory the pursuit ceased, but a village fired on the main party, and they moved on as fast as before. The women and children, all on foot, could not keep up or get rest. I remained in the rear with two havildars, and four or five sepoys, and had great difficulty in getting the women and children brought on, and in keeping the men back from them; I had no means of helping them on, but my own two horses which I gave up to them, and in spite of all my efforts, several dropped out of sight. I am much distressed to have to state that before two o'clock Major Kirke, the sergeant-major lascar, and Mrs. Smalley, the wife of the band-master, all died of sun-stroke or apoplexy; Major Kirke was with the main party when he died, and he alone was buried, the sepoys helping with their bayonets to dig his grave, which is on the outskirts of the town of Karee Puhuree, midway between Muhoba and Kubrai. Major Kirke was failing ere the mutiny took place; and the privations and distress of mind that the mutiny caused him greatly impaired his mental powers; and on the 16th of June at Muhoba he told me to act for him, and leave him to sign papers. I did so, referring everything of consequence to his final decision. At the firing of the dacoits around him, and while trying to rally the men and lead them on, he was himself again while the excitement lasted. I am told the men went on after the major's death, and stopped at a well till I joined them.

We entered Kubrai at 3 P.M. The men gave out that they were rebels, taking us to the Banda Nawab to be killed by the king of Delhi's order; they feared to escort us otherwise. The city people were taken in by the ruse, and obeyed the sepoys' requisition for food for us and our horses. People came in crowds to see us, but they did not insult us. A "Nana Sahib" was usurping authority at Kubrai; perhaps the man spoken of under this title was agent of the Nana of Bithoor. When it was dark and the city people all gone, the men told us that our ruse was discovered, that the Moonshee and a Mahomedan native officer had taken all the Christian drummers to the city, and that the sepoy we had imprisoned at Muhoba was in the town, and had told upon us, and they could protect us no further, and we must take our way by ourselves; this was said sadly and respectfully. We left at Kubrai, a writer, P. Johnson, who preferred to remain, and a Mrs. Tierney (a wife of some sergeant that she had deserted for our sergeant-major) and her two children, as she had no chance of her life with us, and I had good hopes she would not be injured at Kubrai. The sergeant of artillery was likewise left behind; he had been drunk during the day. When I passed Muhoba he went back and entered a deserted police chowkee to sleep there. I heard it said that he had come up just before we started; I never saw him and he made no attempt to join us. Mr. Carne left us at Muhoba and went to Chowkaree. The rajah received him. I have seen a letter from him dated the 29th of June.

The party that moved on consisted of Lieutenants Ewart, Barber, Jackson, Remington, and Franks; Dr. Mawe, 12th Native Infantry, and Mrs. Mawe and child; Mr. Harvey Kirke, eldest son of Major Kirke; Mr. Smalley and child; and Sergeant Kirchoff and his wife. This man was employed at Jaitpore, near Nowgong, in the canal department, under Lieutenant Powys; he joined us at Muhoba. We had only nine horses amongst us. We moved along the Banda road past villagers all on the look-out for an attack.

Next morning, the 20th June, we were attacked by villagers, whose number increased every moment. They were joined by two armed horsemen and some footmen from the road, and it seemed likely to go very hard with us. Mrs. Kirchoff had fallen off her horse, and we were all crippled for action by having some one behind us or a child before. While I was doing my best my horse was struck with a spear and instantly set off at full gallop. He was a runaway by habit. I had only the single bridle; the curb had fallen off while I had Mrs. Mawe's child before me and Mr. Smalley behind, and I could not stop the animal until it reached a nullah it could not leap. Lieutenant Franks was with me, a loose horse had attacked him and his mare, and after chasing him round, the combatants compelled him to go straight off. Lieutenant Remington had followed us. None of the party we had left were in sight. I feared that all had been killed save one or two who might have ridden off; we therefore moved on as fast as my lame horse could go. We were next day (the 21st) surrounded when resting in a mangoe tope and taken to the Nawab of Banda, who treated us very well for sixteen days, when under orders from Major Ellis, the Political Agent for Bundelcund, he sent us to Nagode. We stayed two days at Adzighur, and were very kindly treated by the Ranee. We reached Nagode on the 12th instant.

I have learnt that the villagers who attacked us on the 20th, drew off on Lieutenant Jackson shooting the man who speared my horse. Mrs. Kirchoff's horse having run off she was placed behind Lieutenant Jackson and tied to him; he carried her thus till the 24th when he reached Adzighur. The party then pushed on and crossed the Cane above Banda. They halted at a nullah for a short time, but some villagers threatening them, they mounted and rode off. Dr. and Mrs. Mawe here fell off their horse; he had been suffering terribly for some time, and he died in half an hour. The villagers plundered him and his wife before he died and then left them. In an hour or two more villagers came down and searched Mrs. Mawe for plunder, and then made her walk barefooted three miles to the village Makkoopore. Early in the morning of the 22nd June they sent her off in a doolie to Banda. She was met on the way by a palkee the Nawab had sent out when he heard of her being in their village. The Nawab had sent orders to all the villagers round not to injure Europeans. Mrs. Mawe reached Banda in an hour or two's time; she had suffered terribly from the sun and fatigue. I regret to say that Lieutenant J. H. Barber died on the 20th, an hour or two after Dr. and Mrs. Mawe were left behind. He fell from his horse as if shot. Lieutenant Ewart died on the 22nd, also of sunstroke. Mr. Harvey Kirke went to a village to get him some water, though he was insensible; he came with a troop of villagers yelling at his heels like devils, and the party were obliged to push on. They were shortly after this drinking at a village and observed a signal given by one of the villagers; Sergeant Kirchoff was too slow in mounting, and he was stunned with blows and left for dead. Lieutenant Jackson, Mr. Harvey Kirke, and Mrs. Kirchoff were able to get away. They were well treated when they entered the Adzighur territory, and after resting some days were sent on to Nagode which they reached on the 29th June.

I am glad to say that Sergeant Kirchoff came to himself after the villagers had left him for dead, got up and reached a village in Adzighur territory where he was kindly treated. He was sent on direct to Nagode and arrived here on the 24th or 25th June. He and his wife have gone on to Mirzapore; so have Mrs. Mawe and her child. Lieutenant Jackson is at Rewah employed as second-in-command of a force being raised there. Lieutenant Remington, Ensign Franks, and myself are here, detained by Major Hampton commanding. Mr. Smalley, the 12th Native Infantry band-master, is also here; his child died on the road.

We all found the villagers in the British territory most hostile. One man sheltered myself and party on the 20th, and gave us food. I have reported his conduct to the collector of Banda, and a sepoy of the 50th Native Infantry, named Rabuccus, ran after Lieutenant Jackson a long way, to say he had a strong party at his village, and said he would protect him as long as he chose to remain here.

Ere I left Banda, fourteen drummers of the 12th Native Infantry and our artillery bugler with their families (forty-one persons in all) reached Banda. The Nawab gave the strictest orders in the city that if anyone molested them he would blow him from a gun, he also gave the drummers some money. I have written to him to request him to advance them money (which I should be responsible for), as this is the rainy season, and there are no tents for the men and their families. I think it better to let them remain under their Nawab's protection. Four of the bandsmen are missing and one man remained at Nowgong; I saw him there on the 13th, and ordered him to go with some men of ours to Muhoba. He disobeyed me.

The widow of a drummer long deceased, and her three children, I have not been able to learn anything about. I think they went to Jhansie with the rebels. She was of native extraction, but a Christian. It is said that the wife of Mr. Langdale died of the sun or otherwise on the road, and I fear another very old woman must have died too, on the 19th June; they had great difficulty in walking : the one from being very fat, the other from her great age. I fear very much they are dead.

The drum major at Banda informed me that he had left at Muntuoo (a large place between Kubrai and Banda) Sergeant Raite, of the artillery; Mr. Langdale, a writer; P. Johnson, a writer; and Mrs. Tierney and her two children. The zemindar was very kind to them. I have written to the Nawab of Banda to send for them, if they be not at Banda, and to advance them money.

I have now accounted for all the Christians who were at Nowgong when the mutiny broke out.

I heard it said that one Christian drummer was killed by a sowar near Nowgong. There is one that I had not seen since the mutiny, and I have set him down as killed. He is an African, George Dick by name; but I have heard from a khitmutgar that he saw an African at Banda, so I hope the man has escaped. I have put him down as missing. No other Christian at Nowgong was killed, thank God, by the mutineers. I know that three of the four Christian drummers that I have put down as missing were not left behind; they left us on the 19th, seeking, I suppose, some way of their own to escape by.

Only one native was killed at Nowgong by the mutineers, the acting Havildar Major Aheemâun Sing of No. 4 Company ; Subadar Doolar Tewarry, invalided from the 12th Native Infantry, was wounded in the abdomen by a bullet on the 19th June. I hear that he died a day or two after at Muhoba of his wound. Two sepoys were likewise wounded by the matchlock men on the 19th June, one was a Seikh, Kaun Sing, the other's name is Saligram Sing, Grenadier Company. Roderick, an artillery bugler, was wounded on the same occasion. The sepoys left at Kubrai went on to Banda ; after leaving that place I know not where they went. I saw jemadar Emam Bux there the day I entered the city, namely, the 21st of June.

The Government treasure that fell into the mutineers' hands at Nowgong amounted to 1,21,494 rupees as nearly as I can recollect.

The colours of the native infantry were taken.

I know not what stores there were in the artillery magazines—it was entirely emptied.

I rather think that the annual practice supply had been received from Allahabad.

The 12th got in the magazine at Nowgong and Jhansie 1,256 pounds of gunpowder for musketry, besides some barrels of coarse powder for cannon that was in the Jhansie magazine (the quantity is unknown to me); 360,000 small percussion caps; 130,000 ball cartridges; 20,000 blank cartridges; about 10,000 carbine and ball cartridges, the 6th Light Cavalry left, though muskets were in store beyond the complement of the corps.

Besides the bullocks of the battery, there were 66 commissariat ones at Nowgong.

Rewah, August 16th, 1857.

SIR,—As the senior survivor of the force recently stationed at Nowgong, in Bundelcund, I deem it my duty, Second-Lieutenant Townsend being killed, to report to you the excellent conduct of the invalid subahdar, Byjnath, of No. 4 Company, 9th Battalion Artillery, and also of Pay-Havildar Sirdar Khan, and private Seetaram (steward of the stores), likewise of that company, previous to the mutiny of the troops on the 10th of June. Some days before that date mutiny was being openly plotted in the lines of the company; these three men opposed the disaffected and were threatened with death; they reported and gave evidence in the matter that led to the mutiny then hatching being put a stop to for the time. Major Kirke at once promoted Seetaram to the rank of Havildar, and notified in station orders, that he had strongly recommended Sirdar Khan to Major General Sir H. M. Wheeler for promotion to the rank of subahdar. The Major wished him to supersede the existing jemadar, as useless a man as could be found; he took advantage of the circumstance of his wife having died a day or two before, to keep out of the men's way at a time when he must have well known mutiny was being plotted, and his constant presence necessary. The report made by the three named above made no difference; he feared to do his duty, and it was essential that he should be superseded.

Some days after this, news came to Nowgong on the 5th of June, that the wing of the 12th Native Infantry, and the Artillery, at Jhansie, had mutinied the day before. The troops at Nowgong were at once paraded in undress; the right wing at its own lines; the Artillery Company half-way between its lines and those of the 12th; the wing of the Irregulars in their lines. The 12th and Artillery were then separately asked if they would stand by the Government; when it came to the turn of the Artillery Company, the old subahdar expressed at once his loyalty to Government with a boldness and enthusiasm that did him high honour. It was a fine sight to see that old man of fifty years' service, struggling with the difficulty of weakened lungs and organs of speech time had impaired, to proclaim loudly a loyalty most of those about him had no great sympathy with; they, however, followed his example, and seized hold of the Queen's colour of the 12th, which was at hand, and said they would be loyal; on their return to their lines, they embraced their guns, and were enthusiastic about their loyalty. During their absence from the guns, Seetaram stood beside them with spikes and a hammer ready to spike them in case of the company mutinying. When the mutiny broke out, the whole battery was on the 12th Native Infantry parade, according to an order issued, when the report of the mutiny in the company was made: the 20th Native Infantry pickets or guards were being marched off, when the Sikhs dashed to the front, loading; many men, say thirty or forty, loaded too. They then killed their Havildar-Major, and rushed on the guns; the sergeant, Raite by name, drew his sword, and was fired at; I think one of the artillerymen interceded to save him. I cannot discover that they did anything to save the guns; indeed, in about a minute's time, they fired grape at tents on parade that the officers slept in, and subsequently two rounds more at the officers.

The old subahdar, I am glad to say, escaped, and I hear that he was met at Kubrai, or Mahoba, by a nephew, and that he reached home. He is a noble old man; and I am sure that all who were at Nowgong, from the time mutinies began in the army, would say that he deserves some distinction, such as admission into the Order of Merit. After being invalided, he most willingly remained with the company, knowing well the danger there was of a mutiny taking place. I am sure he would have been most unwilling to go had he been allowed to do so. He did every thing that lay in his power to avert a mutiny; and Major Kirke, commanding at Nowgong, thought most highly of him. I have heard that Seetaram and Sirdar Khan were caught by the men of their company, and would have been killed but for the interference of some rebels of the 12th, who said the guns could not be worked without them. I have also heard that Seetaram made his escape, and that Sirdar Khan was taken from Nowgong, tied on a charpoy, by the mutineers. The guns were captured at Futtehpore, and Sirdar Khan may have been killed on that occasion; but should he, or Seetaram, or Byjnath, ever turn up alive, I trust the facts I have related may be of service to them. Second-Lieutenant Townsend wrote to the Adjutant of the battalion when at Mahoba, on the 17th June, reporting the mutiny. The only members of the company then with him were Sergeant Raite, Naik Kundhya, and Bugler Roderick: no others joined Lieutenant Townsend after the mutiny.

I some days ago reported to Government the death of Lieutenant Townsend, on the 19th of June. The party who had followed the officer from Nowgong marched from Mahoba on the night of the 17th idem; on their way to Callingur, their guide led them into a trap. He brought them a little way off the road to a village (Seuroho) in the Salone district. The men in the village were ready in great numbers, grouped about the place, with long thick *lathies* in their hands; others were seen in the hills. It was thought they feared an attack from our party, and some pains were taken to assure them we had no hostile intention. We encamped a quarter of a mile from the village, at a long shot from the hills, and rested all the 18th. Next morning, as we were preparing just before daybreak to move off, the camp was fired into by matchlockmen. The sepoys, numbering from eighty to ninety men, replied for a few minutes with a wild fire, as they could scarce see an assailant; and at length ten or twelve fell back, and could not be got to advance. Lieutenant Townsend waited, with Lieutenant Ewart, myself, and two or three sepoys, at a tree, firing at any men we could see. He showed the most perfect courage amid the confusion and the fire, which was brisk: and I regret very greatly to say that he was shot through the heart, and died in about half a minute, merely exclaiming, "O God, I am hit!" The main body was far off, in a hopeless and rapid retreat, that the officer was vainly trying to stop or to slacken: and I had to leave this brave young man's body where it fell. I brought away his sword, and gave it to a sepoy or havildar; but that night the men said they could not protect their officers any longer, and the latter had to ride for their lives: I thus lost the sword, I regret to say, but I secured Lieutenant Townsend's horse.

I was station staff officer at Nowgong, and the second officer there; and I think it my duty to say, that were Major Kirke, who commanded, alive, he would bestow high praise on Lieutenant Townsend for the order his battery was in, and for his attention to his duties. I think he was a most promising young officer. I was at Nowgong all the time he was there, about two years. Sergeant Raite had, when I last heard of him, left a village called Muntuvo (where he had been most kindly treated from about June 20th to July 20th) for Banda. The Nawab of the latter place sent for him at my request. I except that he and Roderick, the bugler, and his mother, who were kept for a long time at Banda, have by this time reached Nagode. The Naik Kundhya arrived there on the 7th or 8th instant; he and his wife were plundered on passing Mahoba on June 19th. They stayed there a day or two, and then moved on and reached Banda, where they stayed some time. I sent the naik back to bring his wife, along with the Christians of the 12th Native Infantry band that were at Banda, to Nagode. He was very likely to meet them on the way.

Lieutenant Townsend and his battery received, at Nowgong, pay for April. He received a hundred rupees on the march from Nowgong. Sergeant Raite most probably received an advance of pay for May, on June 12th and 18th. I have requested the Nawab of Banda to give him twenty rupees, and I do not doubt his having received them. Drummer Roderick probably received some pay on June 12th and 18th. The Nawab of Banda paid him, at my request, fifteen rupees in July. Roderick was shot on June 19th. A bullet hit his head, but did not do much damage. I have been at Nagode for some time, and am leaving it. I reported in writing to the station staff, that the sergeant, naik, and drummer would soon arrive. I gave him all the information I could about them.

I have, &c.,

P. G. SCOT, CAPTAIN,
2nd Regiment.

P S.—I forgot to mention above that Kundhya Sing told me on August 8th, that he had been paid in full for May. I then gave him twelve rupees for June. The advances given to the above-named— Lieutenant Townsend, Sergeant Raite, Roderick, and Kundhya Sing— were obtained from rajahs, on Major Kirke's receipts, and must be recovered from their pay for Government. I am proceeding to Allahabad. Believing Lieutenant Townsend's father to be dead, I have written to Mrs. Townsend, inclosing the letter to Captain J. H. Barber, Leadenhall Street, requesting him to do his utmost to discover her correct address.

APPENDIX C.

Brigadier Ramsay to the Agent to the Governor-General for Central India, Gwalior, May 30, 1857.

I have the honor to report for your information the following circumstances which have occurred here during the last four days.

On the evening of the 26th instant, Major Macpherson, Political Agent, mentioned to me that he had been informed by His Highness that the men of the Contingent were not to be trusted, that they had insulted the Dewan on his entering into cantonments, and that the latter was so much afraid of personal violence from them that he returned to the Luskur by a bye-road, and on horseback, instead of in a carriage, in which he had come, to avoid observation.

On the following morning, Major Macpherson called on me and said that His Highness had stated that the whole of the Contingent troops were all wrong and disaffected, that they had all sworn on the Ganges water and Koran to stand by each other, and that an outbreak was so imminent that His Highness urged the ladies being sent at once to the Residency for protection; and that officers could, on the outbreak showing itself, at once mount their horses and ride off. Major Macpherson also expressed a wish that the guard of the Contingent on duty at the Residency should be at once withdrawn, as he had no longer any confidence in them, and that he would apply to His Highness for a party of his troops to take their place. He added that he himself was considered by the troops to be the cause of the movement of the grenadiers from the station to Etawah, which had interfered with their schemes, and that he had thus become the object of their vengeance.

I must here mention that, a few days previous to this, a report was spread, both in the Luskur and in the cantonments, that a large quantity of *atta* and *sukur* had arrived for sale at extraordinary low prices, that both were impregnated with bone dust, and were being sold for the express purposes of destroying the men's caste and making them Christians. The Dewan made full enquiries into this and found that the whole was a malicious rumour doubtless spread to excite mutiny and rebellion, and Major Macpherson stated that the circumstance of the Dewan's having exposed this trick, had brought down on him also the animosity of the traitors.

Although Major Macpherson was most anxious that the ladies should be at once sent away from the station, I considered their removal, unless imperatively necessary, so fraught with evil that in the absence of some proof of disaffection I determined to say nothing on the subject.

Major Macpherson that evening quitted cantonments and returned to the Residency, and the Contingent details on duty there came back in obedience to the order, of which an extract is appended. I think it here important to mention that the wish of the Political Agent to withdraw their guard and remove the ladies for the reasons assigned by him as above, was the same day known in cantonments, and was repeated to me. This information must have emanated from the Luskur.

The following morning a private servant (a Mussulman) of my own, informed me, while out riding with me, that the sowars of the 1st Cavalry in the lines and of His Highness's ressallah were talking of nothing but going to Delhi, and that I should be on the look-out.

About 3 P.M. that day, a lance-duffadar of the 1st Cavalry came to Captain Meade, the Brigade Major, and asked him if he had heard of anything that was going on. Captain Meade replied in the negative and seeing that the man had something important to communicate examined him privately and at once brought him to me.

The duffadar's statement was to the following effect : that the troops in cantonments were all to break out into open mutiny, on a bugle sounding at 11 o'clock that night ; that the lines and bungalows were to be fired and the officers massacred, that the treasury in cantonment was to be seized, and the whole force to proceed towards Delhi. This man had hardly completed his statement when a sowar of the same regiment (Captain Alexander's darogah) arrived at my house and expressed a wish to see me on urgent business. Before admitting him I carefully concealed the first informer. His statement was to the same purport as the other's, and he most strongly insisted on the determination of the mutineers to murder the officers.

These two reports apparently confirming the information I had received from Major Macpherson the previous day, and coupled with the result of enquiries which Captain Meade and myself privately instituted as to what was going on in the lines, determined me on sending away the ladies to the Residency in the evening, which, though done as quietly as possible, of course became immediately generally known.

Having ascertained that a rumour had been circulated in the lines that all confidence in the men of the Contingent had been lost by the

Political Agent and the officers of the station, and that the treasure (amounting to Rs. 60,000), then in the custody of the 4th Infantry, was in consequence to be taken from them that evening, and made over to a party of Luskur troops for removal to the Gunja Inli at the palace, and that this distrust, coupled with the withdrawal of the guard from the Residency, and the departure of the Political Agent from cantonments, had greatly incensed the men, I determined in order to restore confidence and avert if possible a fatal outbreak, to increase the guard of the 4th Regiment over the treasury (with a view to lead the men to think that I feared danger from without, and not from the troops themselves), and having been assured by Major Blake, commanding 2nd Infantry, and Captain Hawkins, commanding No. 1 Light Field Battery, that it was impossible the whole of their men could be implicated without the slightest symptoms having come to their knowledge, and having great confidence in these officers, we resolved to pass the night in the lines, telling the native officers and men on arrival that reports of a proposed outbreak had been made to me, that I considered it had been set on foot by malicious persons, that I did not credit it, and to show them that I had full confidence in their loyalty and good conduct, that I and all the officers would sleep in the lines and commit ourselves to their care for the night. We also gave them all to understand that in consequence of this determination we considered it unsafe to have the ladies to sleep alone at some distance in thatched bungalows exposed to risk by fire from any of the miscreants always ready to take advantage of a night disturbance, and that they had therefore been sent out for safety to the Residency.

Not the slightest disturbance took place during the night.

Next morning (yesterday) in consequence of a telegraphic message from Major Macpherson to Mr. Colvin sent by the former for my perusal, in which His Honor was informed that Scindia declared that the whole of the Contingent was wrong, that he distrusted his own troops and required the immediate return of his body-guard from Agra; that the ladies of the cantonment had been forced to seek refuge in the palace whence he was preparing to forward them under escort of a body of horse to Agra; and that the body-guard would meet them for this purpose at Dholepore; I took on myself to report to Mr. Colvin that we had slept in the lines the previous night, that all was quiet and confidence increasing, and that I considered Scindia was disposed to enhance his own services at the expense of the Contingent.

I learnt in the morning with great surprise that the ladies had, without any communication either with myself or their husbands, been removed from the Residency to the palace. This step appeared to me and the officers so fraught with mischief not only here, but over the whole country, that at my suggestion several officers wrote to their wives immediately to return to cantonments. Captain Meade was also informed by his pay office treasurer, a respectable banker, whose *kothe* is in the Luskur, that it was generally reported that the ladies had been seized by His Highness and imprisoned in the palace.

I also wrote to Major Macpherson that I apprehended no outbreak, and that I thought the ladies should return. Two ladies, Mrs. Meade and Mrs. Murray, in opposition to the most urgent solicitations of Major Macpherson, returned to cantonments late in the afternoon, and the news of their having done so immediately spread through the station, and had the most beneficial effect on the men generally, who it was reported to me had been greatly hurt at the distrust implied by their leaving the cantonments. Many enquiries were made of the other officers whose wives and children had not returned, and voluntary offers of protection and even of rescue were made to their officers by many other men.

We again passed last night in the lines, and received every possible kindness and attention from the men, and the night passed perfectly quiet with the exception of some little anxiety at hearing a few shots in the direction of the Luskur, and a rumour which arrived about 11 o'clock, that a portion of the Maharajah's troops were under arms with the intention of proceeding to Delhi. There subsequently appeared to be no grounds for this assertion.

I am happy to say that the rest of the ladies returned to cantonments this morning, and I consider that the excitement caused by the above occurrences has, so far as this cantonment is concerned, subsided.

I have refrained from reporting by telegraph these occurrences as they happened, as I consider it preferable to give you a detail of all the events by letter, and trust you will approve of my desire to avoid unnecessary alarm, and also of the steps I have taken throughout this anxious business.

I take this opportunity of recording the very valuable assistance I have received from Majors Blake and Sheriff and Captains Hawkins and Stewart on this occasion, and I am convinced that their influence with, and knowledge of, their men have been of very great importance in enabling them to withstand any temptations to which they have been exposed.

That an attempt was made by some evil-disposed persons to wean the men of their officers and destroy the confidence of the latter in the former, I have no doubt from the industrious circulation of reports that the 1st cavalry and grenadier regiments had risen on and destroyed their officers (excepting Major Hennessy, whom they had let go), and from the extreme anxiety evinced by one of my informers under pretence of interest in my preservation that I should not trust the brigade, but be prepared for flight.

The conduct of the officers during the last three days merits the highest approbation. The coolness and zeal displayed by all deserve my warmest thanks, and I feel confident that, but for the very able aid afforded by them throughout the business, the pernicious influence exercised by evil-disposed persons might have been crowned with success.

I take this opportunity of acquainting you that I have received most satisfactory reports of the grenadier regiment from Major Hennessy, and of the other corps of the Contingent at out-stations from their respective commandants. Major Hennessy's report, though in a private form, was considered at this crisis so important, that Major Macpherson requested to be permitted to forward it to the Lieutenant-Governor.

APPENDIX D.

Mutiny at Mhow.

*Brevet Major Cooper to the Officiating Adjutant-General, Bengal Army.
Head Quarters, Mhow, 9th July 1857.*

It is with feelings of extreme pain that I fulfil the duty of reporting for the information of His Excellency the Commander-in-Chief the circumstances of the mutiny of the sepoys of the 23rd Regiment, Native Infantry, and the murder by their hands of Brevet Colonel Platt, commanding the regiment, and of Lieutenant and Brevet Captain and Adjutant Fagan.

On the 1st July, 1857, Colonel Platt received about half-past 10 A.M. a pencil note from Lieutenant-Colonel Durand, Agent for the Governor-General in Central India, at Indore, stating that the Residency at that place was attacked by Holkar's troops. Subsequent information came that Lieutenant-Colonel Durand had been overpowered, and that he, with several officers and ladies, had been obliged to fly for their lives from Indore, accompanied by a few faithful troops only.

About noon, Colonel Platt despatched the two flank companies of the 23rd Regiment, Native Infantry, under command of Captain Trowers, and accompanied by Lieutenant Westmacott, down the road to Bombay, with orders to bring back into cantonments at all hazards two 9-pounder brass guns belonging to the Maharajah, which had passed through Mhow two hours previously. With the assistance of a troop of 1st Light Cavalry under Captain Brooks, who overtook the guns, and brought them to a standstill till the infantry came up, this duty was satisfactorily performed, and the guns brought back into the fort at Mhow, about 3 P.M.; no casualties having occurred in the detachment.

Meanwhile Colonel Platt was taking every precaution for the defence of the cantonments, expecting an attack from Holkar's troops, and placing full reliance on the loyalty and attachment of his regiment. The ladies and children with the European battery of artillery were ordered into the fortified square, and the officers of the 23rd Native Infantry were ordered to proceed at dusk to their men's lines, and remain there all night ready at any moment to turn out and repel any attack. At about a quarter past 10 P.M. several of them were sitting together talking in front of the lines of the grenadier company, when a shot was heard from the cavalry lines on the left followed by several others. Immediately afterwards the fusillade commenced in the rear of the lines of the grenadier company, 23rd Native Infantry, and was rapidly taken up from right to left all along the lines of huts. The men were evidently firing on their officers, who, supposing the lines were attacked by Holkar's troops, went towards their respective cavalry lines and the quarter-guard to turn out the men to repel the attack. It soon, however, became evident what was the true state of the case, and finding they could do nothing, and as the parade ground was literally whistling with bullets fired from the lines at them, the officers made their escape to the fort; there they found Colonel Platt, who had not as yet been down to the lines, and whom it was difficult to persuade of the fact of the regiment having mutinied, so confident was he of their loyalty.

However, the men of the regiment on duty at the fort gate were immediately disarmed and turned out by the artillery, and four guns of the horse battery were immediately got ready and went down to the sepoy lines. Colonel Platt, however, without waiting, ordered Captain Fagan, his adjutant to accompany him, and the two rode down together to the lines of the 23rd Native Infantry. They were never seen alive again; all night after the return of the four guns they were anxiously expected; but it now appears that they were shot down by the men by a volley whilst Colonel Platt was in the act of haranguing them, and before the guns had time to come up. Their bodies as well as those of their horses were found next morning lying on the parade ground in front of the bells-of-arms, literally riddled with bullets. Colonel Platt had also been fearfully gashed by the cut of a tulwar across the mouth and the back of the head. The two guns under Captain Hungerford of artillery opened on the lines with grape and canister, and speedily cleared them of their occupants. The men all rushed out of cantonments, not even waiting to take their property with them, and with the cavalry went off to Indore, not, however, before they had managed to burn down the regiment mess-house and the bungalows of several other officers.

Since then small parties have occasionally returned, or have been hanging about the neighbouring villages, from which the guns drove them out on the following day.

The remainder of the officers with their families are safe in the fort at Mhow, and the officers have all placed themselves under the orders of

Captain Hungerford, commanding the fort, and act as volunteers for night duties and sentries on the walls, and to accompany the guns mounted as a covering party whenever they have occasion to move out. They, with myself, await the orders of His Excellency the Commander-in-Chief as to our future disposal; but as yet the disturbed state of the country will not admit of our leaving the fort. Of the men of the regiment, only the drum major, a Musalman, and five Christian drummers have remained with their officers. Two sepoys preserved the life of Lieutenant Simpson, who was on picket duty with them on the night of the mutiny, and brought him safely into the fort next morning; but though I promised these men promotion to havildar, they have since gone and joined their comrades. The colours of the regiment have been carried away as well as the arms, except a certain number recovered; returns of which shall be hereafter furnished. The regiment magazine has been blown up by Captain Hungerford's orders. We are now in a dangerous position, in a weak fort, utterly untenable against an enemy with guns for any length of time, with only a handful of Europeans, in the midst of a country risen all around; but we trust to be able to hold our own until such time as assistance, so much needed, may reach us.

The Secretary to Government, Bengal.
Mhow Fort, 17th July 1857.

Sir,—Details of the occurrences at Indore and Mhow, written hurriedly, have been sent at different times to the Bombay Government, for transmission to you. I beg now to send a more connected account for your information.

1. When the news of the mutiny at Meerut and Delhi reached Mhow, I requested permission from the commanding officer, Colonel Platt, to place a guard from my European company of artillery at the fort gateway, instead of the guard of the 23rd Regiment, Native Infantry. The fort contained many heavy guns, much ammunition, and valuable stores of various kinds, which, falling into the hands of mutineers, would have much strengthened them. Colonel Platt considered that the change of guards would show a want of confidence in his own men, and would not permit it; but I was authorised to dismount and disable the heavy guns.

2. On the news of the Neemuch mutiny reaching Mhow, I wrote to the commanding officer a letter dated June 6th, 1857. My guns were

then in their sheds, 200 yards from the barracks, and the men could not have turned out in battery under half an hour. A portion of my letter is as follows :—

"One hundred men, placing themselves in front of the gun-sheds armed, would deprive the company of its means of offence and defence.

"Precautionary measures have been taken, in almost all stations of the army, to prevent an outbreak of the native troops, although the latter were perfectly loyal. The commanding officer appears to think that precautions taken here may lead to the result it is desirous to avoid. With my battery at command, and guarded from sudden seizure, I believe that I could quell and crush any disturbance that might arise at Mhow from the native troops; and I request, therefore, that I may be permitted to take such precautions (by having my battery drawn out on open ground, where it can easily be manned) as may render my guns ready for action when required. Should the commanding officer deem any precautions inadvisable, such as I have suggested, and should it be my misfortune, in the event of any disturbance occurring, to meet with difficulty in arming and turning out my battery, I trust that this letter will be convincing proof that I have used every endeavour to avoid such a result."

3. I was directed, in reply to this letter, to draw out my battery in front of the gun-sheds on Monday morning, the 8th June (two days after the above letter was written); but instead of waiting until Monday morning, an opportunity offered for turning out on the 3th. The horses were harnessed, guns turned out, and the battery and company made ready for service at a moment's notice.

4. On the 8th June I received a letter from Colonel Durand, Acting Resident at Indore, which contained the following :— "You and your men cannot be too much on the alert. Your readiness with your horses the day the Neemuch news reached cantonments prevented a rise."

5. From the 6th June to the end of the month my battery was parked in front of the barracks; the horses stood harnessed every night; the men were warned never to be distant from the barracks; and, in the event of any rise at Mhow, the battery could have turned out to crush it in less than a quarter of an hour, night or day.

6. Many applications were made to the commanding officer for some precautions to be taken for the safety of the wives and families of officers and men; but Colonel Platt placed such implicit confidence in his men, that nothing was done beyond placing a guard of sipahies of the 23rd Regiment, Native Infantry, every night, over the houses of the officers of that regiment.

7. On the morning of the 1st July, about half-past 8 or 9, guns were heard firing in the direction of Indore; at 11 A.M. Colonel Platt called

at my house with a note from Colonel Durand. Colonel Durand wrote :—

"Send the European battery as sharp as you can. We are attacked by Holkar."

I rode down to the barracks and turned out the battery; no escort was ordered to accompany the battery for its defence; two men were therefore told off for each gun and waggon, and mounted on the limber boxes armed with muskets. The battery was trotted to Mhow, half-way to Indore. There a sowar rode up to me with a note in pencil from Colonel Travers, commanding the Bhopal Contingent, saying, " We are retreating on Simrole, on the Mundlaysir road from Indore."

The sowar added that Colonel Durand and the officers and ladies from the Residency were with Colonel Travers, that Colonel Durand had not retired on Mhow, as Mhow was in Holkar's territories, and would be attacked by Holkar's troops either that night or the following morning. There being no road to Simrole which I could follow, the battery was brought back to Mhow as quickly as possible.

8. Colonel Platt met me on re-entering cantonments. I gave him Colonel Travers' note, and told him what the sowar had said, requesting permission at the same time to take my battery into the fort, as the fort could be defended for any length of time. Colonel Platt would not hear of it. At the artillery barracks all the wives and families of officers and men had taken refuge. The barracks could not be well defended, from their extent and position. I urged repeatedly on Colonel Platt, during the afternoon, the advisability of defending the fort; but only at the very last moment could he be persuaded to allow me to enter it. At half-past 6 P.M. Colonel Platt rode down to the artillery barracks, and told me to enter the fort. He had strengthened the guard at the gateway to fifty men from his own regiment.

9. I afterwards learnt that, about 6 P.M., sipahies had been sent round to all the cantonment guards, to warn them, and the guards at officers' houses, that there would be a rise of the whole of the troops that night.

10. At dusk, the mess-house of the 23rd Regiment, Native Infantry, was observed to be on fire; and before 10 P.M. several other houses were in flames. About 10 P.M. shots were heard in the direction of the cavalry and infantry lines; and immediately afterwards several officers of both corps ran into the fort, stating that both regiments were in open mutiny, and that they had been fired upon both by troopers and sipahies. I ordered the guard within the fort to be disarmed, and their muskets

were taken from them. Colonel Platt rode into the fort about 10 P.M. and ordered me to turn out my battery. There was a little delay in doing this, from the horses being knocked up, and from several of the drivers having already deserted; and before we were ready, Colonel Platt, accompanied by his adjutant (Captain Fagan), rode out of the fort. We followed them in about ten minutes, but did not see them again. On advancing up the infantry parade (the lines being more than half a mile from the fort) we were several times fired upon, but saw no one. The infantry parade ground was illuminated by the blazing bungalows, but the huts of the men were in darkness. When opposite the centre of the infantry lines I halted, expecting to be joined by Colonel Platt or his adjutant. My staff sergeant, bugler, and myself rode up to the bells-of-arms, but no one could be seen. Whilst thus halted the battery was again fired upon. I unlimbered, and fired several rounds of grape and round shot into the lines. There was some groaning and noise, but nothing visible; and in a few minutes everything was perfectly quiet.

11. I was told the next day that, on my opening fire, the whole of the cavalry, in regular files, had left their lines in a hard trot, and taken the road to Indore. The infantry who were in their lines took flight at the second round of grape, and running out by the rear of their lines, fled in the greatest disorder across country towards Indore. The next day their lines were found full of their clothes, cooking vessels, etc., and many muskets, coats, etc., were found scattered for a great distance all over the country.

12. Colonel Platt and Captain Fagan, I learnt, had ridden straight to the quarter-guard of the regiment, and whilst the Colonel was there speaking to the men, the guard fired a volley at the unfortunate officers and they fell riddled with balls. A party of troopers was told off to murder Major Harris of the 1st Light Cavalry who waylaid him near the cavalry mess. A volley was fired which killed his horse; and Major Harris, in attempting to escape, was shot and cut down by his own men.

13. In mentioning the deaths of these officers, I cannot help expressing my deep sorrow at the infatuation which possessed Colonel Platt with regard to his own men. Nothing could persuade him to believe that they could act as their comrades all over the country have acted. Numerous circumstances occurred before the regiment mutinied which should have warned him against over-confidence; but, when reported, they were all thought to be exaggerated, and he would not

believe that his men could show signs of disaffection. So blindly confident was he of their fidelity that, at 9 o'clock on the night the mutiny took place, he commenced a note to Colonel Durand in these words:—
" All right ; both cavalry and infantry very ' khoosh ' and willing."
Whilst writing he was interrupted, and called away to be shot down by the very men regarding whom he was so lamentably mistaken.

14. Several of the officers had very narrow escapes ; the cavalry more particularly, as their lines were furthest from the fort, and they had to run the gauntlet of the sipahies after escaping from their own men. Captain Brooks, Lieutenants Martin and Chapman ran on foot, pursued by troopers, to within a few hundred yards of the fort, and were drawn into the fort over the walls of one of the bastions. Had the ladies remained in their own houses, instead of taking refuge in the fort, the massacre would probably have been as dreadful as at Indore.

15. On the morning of the 2nd July we became acquainted with the lamentable deaths of the three officers before mentioned. All the officers who had escaped voluntarily offered their services to me as commanding the only troops in the fort, to be put on any duties I might think necessary. They were all armed and horsed, and divided into two divisions, with all the other Europeans in the fort (road sergeants, clerks, etc.), and placed under the command of Captain Brooks, 1st Light Cavalry, and Captain Trower, 23rd Regiment, Native Infantry, to act as flanking parties to the guns when necessary to move out of the fort, and to assist in sentry duties at night. Parties of artillerymen were employed, the first thing in the morning, to throw up entrenchments before the northern gate of the fort, to mount the heavy guns and howitzers on their carriages, and to place light guns on the four corner bastions. Men hard at work all day. Mr. Postance, the Deputy-Commissary of Ordnance, employed in making up ammunition for the heavy guns ; and Mr. Madras, the Commissariat Officer, in laying in stores of all descriptions for men and horses. During the night, the whole of the driver company, with the exception of five men, all the lascars, all the syces but eight, and the whole of the grass-cutters, deserted. All the artificers but three also made their escape from the fort. A detachment, consisting of two guns, ridden by gunners (Europeans) and escorted by volunteers, was sent out under Captain Brooks to search for the bodies of the missing officers. Their bodies were brought in before noon, much mutilated ; and they were buried in the afternoon, in the south-east bastion of the fort. (Report sent in, marked A.)

16. *3rd July.*—Proclaimed martial law this morning throughout the station of Mhow. Parties of troopers and sipahies having been reported as still in their lines and harbouring in the villages in the vicinity, I moved out two guns, escorted by volunteers. We first marched through the Sudder Bazar, recovered a large quantity of muskets from the Kotwallee, and disarmed those men not belonging to the police. Then went to the cavalry lines. Several troopers were seen skulking about the lines, and two cavalry horses saddled broke out of a neighbouring village, and galloped past the guns. The troopers were driven out and followed by several officers: they ran down to the nullah in rear of their lines, and then turned and fired. Corporal Potter, of the artillery, cut one man down. Fired the village in rear of the cavalry lines from whence the horses broke out; fired another village in rear of the infantry lines in which, and in the lines, several sipahies were seen. As many more were supposed to be hidden in the houses, fired several round shot into the lines. Wrote this day to the Maharajah (letter B) as it was reported to me that Holkar's troops, accompanied by the mutineers from Mhow, meant to attack the fort. By the evening of the 3rd July two light guns were mounted on each of the four corner bastions of the fort. A heavy battery of one 10-inch howitzer, one 8-inch howitzer, one 24-pounder, one 18-pounder, and two 12-pounders were formed and armed outside the northern gate of the fort. Small arms and ammunition were placed in the bastions, and every preparation made to repulse any attack made by Holkar or any portion of his army.' Men and officers worked unceasingly and uncomplainingly. By this evening, too, Mr. Madras had laid in stores for a fortnight.

17. As the magazines of the cavalry and infantry regiments were full of ammunition, and might fall into the hands of enemies, a party was turned out on the 4th under Captain Brooks, 1st Light Cavalry, the guns under Lieutenant Mallock, Artillery, to blow them both up; both magazines were blown up successfully. A hole was blown through the southern curtain of the fort, and preparations made to arm another battery for the protection of that side of the fort. (Report sent in to the Adjutant-General of the Bombay Army, marked C.)

18. On the morning of the 5th another heavy battery of four 18-pounders was placed in position to protect the southern face of the fort. About 10 A.M. two of Holkar's principal men, his Minister, the Bhao Rao Ramchunder, and his Buxee Khooman Sing, accompanied by Captain Fenwick, an East Indian in the service of the Maharajah, came

to the fort with a letter from the Maharajah (marked C 2). They stated that the Maharajah had been quite unable to control his mutinous troops, expressed on his part deep regret at the occurrences at Indore, a detailed account of which was handed to me by Captain Fenwick. They offered also to send over the remaining treasure from the Residency to Mhow, and were prepared to carry out any measures I might advise for opening up communication through and tranquillising the country. The Minister also stated that the mutinous troops from Mhow and Indore had marched the preceding evening towards Dewass, having carried off with them nine (9) lacs of rupees from the Residency treasury, and having seized at Indore every horse, bullock, camel, and cart that they could find for the transport of their baggage. They had taken also with them nine guns belonging to the Maharajah. By evening of the 5th Mr. Madras had laid in stores of all kinds for one month. The station was perfectly quiet; the inhabitants of the bazars carrying on business as usual; burning and thieving in bungalows put a stop to; and night alarms at an end. On the night of the 5th thirteen elephants were sent in by Holkar for the use of General Woodburn's column, and forwarded at once to Mundlaysir.

10. On the morning of the 6th July a general court-martial was assembled for the trial of a gun lascar of my company for mutiny and desertion. The prisoner was sentenced to fifty lashes, but the punishment was commuted to dismissal. The troops from Indore who accompanied the mutineers from Mhow, not being allowed to share in the treasure, returned to Indore last night, and, having received some assistance from Holkar, marched immediately in pursuit to try and recover the treasure.

20. An express was sent on the morning of the 7th to Colonel Durand. Captain Hutchinson, an assistant to the Resident, was reported on the morning of this day to have been taken prisoner by the Amjheera Rajah. Captain Elliot was written to by the Durbar on the subject, and the correspondence is annexed (marked D). The Maharajah was written to this day; and a request made that he would follow up and attack the mutineers from Mhow and Indore (letter marked E). Another gun lascar was brought in this morning, tried by court-martial for mutiny and desertion, sentenced to death, and hanged by my orders in front of the northern gate of the fort at 6 P.M. Whilst the execution was taking place the whole of the treasure remaining in the Resdency treasury, sent in by the Maharajah, arrived in the fort, and

Captain Elliot was ordered to receive charge of it. The amount of treasure is R4,16,690, besides nearly 23½ lacs in Company's paper. The country round Mhow perfectly tranquil.

21. On the morning of the 8th a letter (No. 428) was forwarded to the Secretary, Bombay Government, detailing what had occurred, forwarding correspondence with the Durbar, and reporting receipt of treasure. A memorandum was also forwarded of the persons murdered at Indore (this letter is attached). On the 8th July a correspondence took place with the Durbar regarding the Malwah Contingent, and it will be found attached to letter 431. A telegraph message was received this day from the Governor of Bombay (attached, marked F).

22. On the 9th two messages were despatched to Bombay regarding the troops marching on Mundlaysir under Captain Orr (marked G). Two prisoners, sipahies, of the 23rd Regiment, Native Infantry, (Mahomedans), were sent in by the Maharajah of Indore. They were tried by drum-head court-martial on arrival at Mhow, sentenced to death, and hanged in front of the northern gate of the fort. Much excitement had prevailed amongst the Maharajah's troops on his giving over these prisoners, and an anonymous letter was found in his Durbar hall, accusing him of not being a Hindoo, and being under the influence of ministers who were Christians.

23. Letter No. 431 (attached) written to Secretary, Bombay Government, on the 10th. Everything perfectly tranquil at Mhow and its neighbourhood. Telegraph message received from Bombay regarding Captain Orr's detachment (marked H).

24. Oomed Sing and Gunesh Shastree came in from the Maharajah, to say that the latter was in great alarm about the two columns advancing from Bombay: he feared that his actions had been misconstrued, and an erroneous impression of them conveyed to Government. It was with great difficulty that they had prevented the Maharajah from starting immediately for Bombay to offer in person an explanation of the disturbances at Indore. Wrote to the Maharajah a letter (annexed, marked I). Breastworks were completed in front of both heavy batteries this day, and the fort so much strengthened that it would take a native army to attack it.

25. On the 12th an express was again forwarded to Colonel Durand (marked K). On the 13th the telegraph wire was brought into the fort at Mhow, an office established, and communication opened with Bombay. Dâk communications to Bombay, and all places to the southward, open;

also to Neemuch; but the road to Sehore and Saugor has been and continues closed from the 27th ultimo. The Durbar report that their troops are still mutinous and excited, and they look with anxiety for the arrival of European troops, to enable them to disarm the disaffected. On the 13th a telegraph message was received from Lord Elphinstone, for delivery to Holkar (marked L), and an answer returned on the 14th (marked M). A report also was forwarded to Bombay on the 14th.

26. I have, in the foregoing, brought up my report of everything that has taken place at Mhow to this date (15th July). Troops are marching to our relief, whom we expect to see on the 26th instant. Colonel Durand has been written to, and may probably return to Mhow immediately. The country is perfectly quiet, the Maharajah of Indore most anxious for opportunities to prove his friendship and fidelity to the Government. This fort is strengthened and provisioned in such manner as to enable us to hold it for any length of time against any native force; trade and business are carried on as usual in the towns in Holkar's States. The Maharajah's tributaries having discovered the mistake they first fell into, of thinking Holkar inimical to the British, have suppressed all disorders in their own districts, and are willing to assist in maintaining order. Some of the Maharajah's troops alone show a bad spirit, and are still mutinous and disaffected; but they will, I think, be restrained from any further excess, and on the arrival of European troops the Maharajah will at once disarm and punish them.

The Company's rupee has fallen to a discount of one rupee per cent. at Indore, and three per cent. at Oojein.

27. In closing this report I trust that, should the Government deem that our duty at Mhow has been performed to its satisfaction, I may state how much I have been indebted to the untiring exertions of officers and men for everything that has been done. At this trying season the non-commissioned officers and men of my company, under the orders of Lieutenant Mallock, have worked cheerfully and laboriously night and day, in mounting heavy guns, throwing up entrenchments, and other duties, and have shown throughout a willing and ready spirit, which no praise of mine can do justice to. The officers of the 23rd Regiment, Native Infantry, and 1st Light Cavalry, and other volunteers under Captain Brooks and Captain Trower, have always been ready to turn out at any moment for duties which they have never before been accustomed to, and have taken regular sentry duties every night since our occupation of the fort, to enable the artillerymen to get some sleep after their

heavy duties in the day. Mr. Madras, the commissariat Officer, has worked most efficiently in laying in stores of every description for the artillery, Europeans who have taken refuge in the fort, horses and cattle, for six months ; and the fact that six months' supplies have been laid in in little more than a week will speak for itself. Mr. Conductor Postance, too, has been unwearied in his exertions in making up ammunition, and other duties, which have occupied every moment of his time, and which he has fulfilled to my entire satisfaction. To Captain Elliot I am deeply indebted for support and assistance ; his knowledge of the country has enabled him to aid me with advice in many matters of which I should otherwise have remained ignorant. Besides supporting me in my communications with Holkar's Durbar, he has readily taken upon himself a share of all the duties the other officers have been employed in.

28. I trust it is needless to repeat what I have said so often regarding the fidelity of the Maharajah of Indore ; — his actions will best prove his feelings. The anxiety he laboured under, lest his conduct should be misconstrued, has been dissipated since the receipt of the message from the Right Honourable the Governor of Bombay ; and yesterday I received the annexed letter (marked N) from the Minister on this subject.

29. Having been left alone at Mhow, without any political officer to consult, I trust, if I have acted in an irregular manner, by assuming political authority to communicate with Holkar, the advantage which has been gained in keeping the country tranquil, and restoring the confidence of the Maharajah in the friendship of the Government, may form my excuse for the informality. I have acted with a zealous desire to serve Government, and trust my actions may not meet with disapproval.

I have the honour to be,
Sir,
Your obedient servant,
T. HUNGERFORD, CAPTAIN,
Commanding at Mhow.

A.
No. 422.
The Brigade Major, Saugor.

Mhow Fortified Square, 2nd July 1857.

SIR,—I have the honour to report, for the information of the Brigadier commanding at Saugor :—

1. That yesterday morning, at 11 o'clock, Colonel Platt, commanding the station, called at my house with a note from Colonel Durand, Acting

Resident at Indore, in which Colonel Durand requested that my battery might be sent over to Indore instantly, as he was attacked by Holkar.

2. I accordingly marched from Mhow at about half-past 11. My battery trotted to Rhow, half-way to Indore, when a sowar rode up to me with a note from Colonel Travers, commanding Bhopal Contingent, stating that he was retreating on Simrole, on the road to Mundlaysir. The sowar stated that Colonel Travers was accompanied by Colonel Durand and by all the Europeans who had been resident at Indore.

3. To reach Simrole there was nothing but a " cutcha " narrow road cut up with ruts, along which my battery, in the blown state of the horses, could not have travelled a mile. I therefore determined on returning to Mhow, more especially as from circumstances which have lately occurred here, I had strong suspicions that the native troops would mutiny as soon as Holkar's conduct had become known.

4. On returning to Mhow I met Colonel Platt on entering the station. I gave him the note received from Colonel Travers, explained the reasons for which I had not proceeded to Indore, and requested his permission to enter the fortified square at once. I told him, if he would permit me to enter the fort, and that I could be secure of two days' non-interference to mount the heavy guns I formerly dismounted, lay in stores, water, etc., that I would guarantee the safety of the fort against any attacks for a month.

5. Colonel Platt was unfortunately so secure in the fidelity of his own regiment, and of the wing of the 1st Light Cavalry stationed at Mhow, that my request was refused ; and it was only after great entreaty, and pointing out to the commanding officer that the lives of every European in the station were at hazard, that he gave me permission to enter the fort with my company and guns at half-past 6 P.M. last evening. The whole of the European ladies and families at Mhow took refuge in the fort at the same time.

6. At 9 P.M. last night, it was reported that an agent from Holkar had arrived to communicate with Colonel Platt, and had been stopped by the cavalry picket stationed on the Indore road. Whether this agent misled the troops or not, I am ignorant.

7. At 10 P.M. several musket shots were heard in the direction of the cavalry and infantry lines, and shortly afterwards nearly all the officers of the 23rd Regiment and wing Light Cavalry, ran into the fort, and reported that they had run the gauntlet of their respective

regiments, having all of them been fired upon, though fortunately none were hit.

8. Almost immediately afterwards Colonel Platt rode into the fort, and ordered me to turn out my battery. The night was dark, my horses were much knocked up; but, in about half an hour, the horses were traced to, and we moved out and advanced to the infantry lines. Colonel Platt and his adjutant (Captain Fagan) preceded me about a quarter of an hour; but from the moment I left the fort I did not see them. On nearing the infantry lines my battery was fired upon; and before reaching the cavalry lines, several shots having been fired, I halted and fired several rounds of round shot into the lines of the 23rd Regiment, Native Infantry. No person was visible, but much noise was heard, and I think some men must have been killed.

9. By this time several officers' bungalows were in a blaze; and as no persons were visible in any direction, and it was too dark for the battery to be in the least serviceable, I returned to the fort.

10. Unfortunately we learnt afterwards that the mutiny of the troops had been accompanied by great treachery and violence. Colonel Platt and his adjutant, I grieve to report, were shot down by the quarter-guard of the 23rd Regiment, and Major Harris was cut down and shot by the men of his own guard. I sent out a detachment to bring in the bodies this morning, which have been recovered, much mutilated.

11. Every precaution is being taken now for the protection of the fort. I have laid in, and am laying in, stores of all descriptions for men and horses. All my bullocks have been carried off by the bullock drivers, but we have still some bullocks, though not sufficient to move my extra wagons. We are threatened with an attack from Holkar, probably accompanied by the troops which have mutinied; but I hope to hold the fort until relieved; and as the Brigadier commanding at Saugor may perhaps be able to communicate with Colonel Woodburn, if he will hurry that officer in his advance on Mhow, it may perhaps save us if attacked by an overpowering force. The fort is very weak; but we shall do our best to hold out until reinforced.

I have, &c.,

T. HUNGERFORD, CAPTAIN,

Commanding at Mhow.

B.

To His Highness the Maharajah of Indore.
Mhow Fortified Square, July 3rd, 1857.

RAJAH SAHEB,—You must be as well aware as myself of the occurrences at Mhow. After the disturbance at Indore, the native troops at Mhow mutinied, cut down their commanding officers, and marched upon Indore yesterday morning.

I understand, from many natives, that you have given food to the mutinous troops. I have heard also, but do not know whether to believe, that you have lent them guns and offered them irregular cavalry, as assistance. These reports are probably very much exaggerated; I do not believe them. You owe so much to the British, and can be so utterly ruined by showing enmity towards them, that I do not believe you can be so blind to your own interests as to afford aid and show friendship to the enemies of the British Government. Let me understand, therefore, from yourself what your wishes are. From your not throwing obstacles in the way of the mutinous troops passing through your territory, and not punishing them, as a power friendly to the British would do, many may suppose that you are not so much the friend of the British Raj as I believe you to be. Write, therefore, and let me understand your intentions. I am prepared for everything, alone and without assistance; but with the assistance I very shortly expect, I can act in a manner that you will find, I fear, very injurious to your interests; and if you will take my advice, you will write to me at once, and let me know what I am to think of the reports which have reached me.

Your obedient servant,

T. HUNGERFORD, CAPTAIN,
Commanding at Mhow.

C.

No. 425.

To the Adjutant-General, Bombay Army.
Mhow, 4th July, 1857.

SIR,—I request you will be good enough to communicate to the Adjutant-General, Bengal Army, the following:—

1. I forwarded, on the morning of the 2nd instant, an electric

APPENDIX D lvii

telegraph message to the Agent at Ackberpore, requesting that officer to report to the Bombay Government, and to Colonel Woodburn, commanding a field force, our position at Mhow, in the hope that reinforcements would be hurried on for our relief.

2. At 10 P.M., on the 1st current, a mutiny took place at this station of the native troops, consisting of the 23rd Regiment, Native Infantry, and wing 1st Light Cavalry. Colonel Platt, commanding the station and 23rd Regiment, Captain Fagan, the adjutant of that regiment, and Major Harris, commanding 1st Light Cavalry, were cut down by the mutineers. These officers were blindly confident of the fidelity of their troops, though repeatedly warned that the men were not staunch; and no precautionary measures for the safety of the station, I regret to say, were taken until the very last moment. At half-past 6 P.M., on the 1st current only, could I prevail on the commanding officer to allow me to occupy the Fort of Mhow, the only place where Europeans could take refuge in the event of a rise of the native troops.

3. At 11 A.M., on the morning of the 1st, Colonel Platt had called on me with a letter from Colonel Durand, Acting Resident at Indore, begging that the battery under my command might be sent to Indore instantly. I marched my battery, therefore, at once on Indore; but, on getting half-way, was met by a sowar with a note from Colonel Travers, commanding the Bhopal Contingent, stating that he was retreating on the Mundlaysir road. As it was impossible to know where Colonel Travers might be, and he was accompanied by Colonel Durand and the other British residents of Indore, I returned to Mhow.

4. On the commencement of the mutiny, I turned out my battery. Colonel Platt and his adjutant preceded me to the parade ground, and were shot down before our arrival. On arriving in the lines we were fired upon; but the lines were nearly deserted, and the men had marched *en masse* to Indore.*

5. From the blown state of my horses in the morning, and the darkness of the night, which prevented our seeing anything, it was impossible to follow the mutineers; and as I had no covering party of any description, I returned to the fort, after having fired several rounds of round shot into the lines.

7. During the last three days we have laid in ample store of provisions for some time, and are prepared to hold this position until relieved.

* It was subsequently ascertained that the men were all in the lines, but fled precipitately as soon as we opened fire upon the huts.

We are threatened by an attack from the Rajah of Indore or the mutineers, and are anxious and quite ready to meet them; but, as sudden retribution should reach the scoundrels who have shown such treachery and ingratitude to their benefactors, I trust that Colonel Woodburn may be ordered to hurry on a portion of his Dragoons, by the aid of whom we can amply avenge ourselves for what has been done.

7. Yesterday and to-day I have turned out a portion of my battery, accompanied by flanking parties of officers, to destroy the villages surrounding Mhow, in which many of the mutineers have taken refuge, and from whence they have turned out to burn and pillage the houses in the cantonments. Several villages have been burnt, much property recovered, and some sipahies and troopers destroyed.

I have, etc.,

T. HUNGERFORD, Captain,
Commanding at Mhow.

C 2.

To Captain Hungerford, Commanding at Mhow.

My dear Sir,—I have just received your letter, No. 424, dated 3rd instant. The accounts you seem to have received of my assistance to the enemies of the British Government are, as you supposed, not only exaggerated, but entirely false. No one in the world regrets more than I do the most heartrending catastrophe which befell at Indore and at Mhow. My troops, probably under the influence of the Mhow mutineers, mutinied openly on the morning of the 1st instant; and the very companies and guns that were sent to protect the Residency picked up a general quarrel with some one, and began at once to fire upon the Residency house. The mischief done was great; many lives were lost. No companies of the Contingent, etc., assisted the British officers; but it is cheering to hear that Colonel Durand, Mr. Shakespear and family, and others went away quite safe. The rascals then plundered the whole Residency.

The next morning the Mhow troops, after committing similar brutalities, arrived here; the whole town was in a panic. A greater part of my troops were in open mutiny, and what remained could not be trusted. The Mahomedans raised a standard of "Deen," and the disorder was complete. Under these sad circumstances the mutineers exacted their own terms. They not only demanded the heads of a few Europeans whom I had concealed in my own palace, but also of a few officers of the court who were supposed to be in the British interest. They prepared to plunder and destroy all, if I myself did not come out. I had no alternative left but to offer them my own person, but I would not allow the poor Europeans to be touched before being killed myself. After plundering the British treasury, and the carriage from the town, and taking with them all the guns which had gone over to them in a state of mutiny, all the mutineers of this place and Mhow have marched off last night in a body towards Dewass.

The tale is a painful one, and will be described to you in detail by Rao Ramchunder and Bukshee Khooman Sing, who are bearers of this to you. I have not, even in a dream, ever deviated from the path of friendship and allegiance to the British Government. I know their sense of justice and honour will make them pause before they suspect even for a moment, a friendly chief, who is so sensible of the obligations he owes to them, and is ready to do anything for them; but there are catastrophes in this world which cannot be controlled, and the one that has happened is one of the kind.

Yours sincerely,
(Signed) TOOKAJEE RAO HOLKAR.

D.

Indore, 7th July 1857, 11 P.M.

MY DEAR SIR,—His Highness the Maharajah has learnt with great regret the astounding account of Captain and Mrs. Hutchinson and parties' detention at Amjheera. He looks upon Mrs. Hutchinson as his sister, and the whole family as his own relations; and though not crediting that the Rajah of Amjheera could be so blind to his own interest he has, however, lost no time in ordering Bukshee Khooman Sing, with three companies of infantry, two guns, and 200 sowars, towards Amjheera, with orders to blow up the town, and bring in the Rajah dead or alive, should he have proceeded to any extremities with the party. Amjheera, it must be recollected, is not a tributary to Holkar, but to Scindia; but in this emergency His Highness thinks hesitation as to his being a foreign state inadmissible.

His Highness has, however, been informed by the Amjheera Vakeel, on the strength of a letter dated Amjheera, the 5th instant, that Mrs. and Captain Hutchinson and party have safely reached Jhabooa, and are quite well there. He has, therefore, started a runner to Jhabooa, to ascertain the truth of the thing; and as the column detached under Bukshee Khooman Sing shall be at Beitwa to-morrow, His Highness wishes to know whether at this crisis it will be any responsibility for Holkar's army to enter a foreign state, and to proceed to extremities should the emergency require it.

His Highness is overjoyed to hear of the safety of Colonel Durand and party at Sehore, and shall be obliged by your writing to him his best compliments. Pray let me know soon your opinion on the Amjheera subject, and oblige me.

I am, Sir,

Yours very truly,

(Signed)   RAMCHUNDER RAO.

By His Highness' order.

To Rao Ramchunder Rao Saheb, Indore.
Mhow, 8th July 1857.

DEAR SIR,—Your letter just received, dated the 7th instant, and written by order of His Highness the Maharajah, has given me much pleasure; and I hasten, through you, to thank the Maharajah for the promptitude he has displayed in taking upon himself, if necessary, the deliverance of British subjects from enemies, and the punishment of such offenders. Such a proof of friendship is most gratifying, and will be the best proof to evil-disposed persons that the good-will and friendship that exist between the two Governments will remain unchangeable for ever.

I am desired by Captain Hungerford to express his entire concurrence with the view taken by His Highness of this matter, with whom he thinks that in such an emergency as the present no hesitation as to the offending state being a foreign state is admissible; but Captain Hungerford is further of opinion that, having marched to the borders of such offending state, an inquiry as to the truth of the report should be made, and, if true, followed by a formal demand for the kidnapped prisoners previous to entering the same; and if not complied with, you might then proceed to extremities, with the assurance from Captain Hungerford that the British Government will not fail to support you and accept the responsibility, should it be found necessary to compel the Amjheera Rajah to restore these officers, ladies, and children to liberty; and I also fully concur in this opinion.

I trust the assurances of the Amjheera Vakeel are correct, and that Captain Hutchinson and party have safely reached Jhabooa, and this intelligence may be confirmed by the return of the runner you have despatched to make inquiry; but you will allow that the testimony offered us, as to the act of violence having been committed by people from Amjheera, was deserving of a certain amount of credit.

If Moonshee Dhurm Narain could be spared to come here, he would be of great assistance in facilitating correspondence between us, as he could afford Captain Hungerford and myself much information as to the proper forms to be observed, and we should find his knowledge of official matters of much assistance to us.

I have, etc.,
A. ELLIOT,
*Assistant Government
Superintendent in Malwah.*

E.

To The Maharajah of Indore.
Mhow, July 7th, 1857.

MAHARAJAH,—A Sahookar has just brought me intelligence that your troops which misbehaved have returned to Indore; that they are much enraged with the mutineers from Mhow, and have either gone or are going on the road to Dewass, for the purpose of attacking them and recovering the treasure which has been carried off from Indore.

I understand also that you have made arrangements with the Rajah of Dewass and others to intercept and attack our mutinous troops simultaneously, and that it is your wish to destroy them, and that for this purpose you have assisted your troops with guns.

I trust that the above reports are correct. Your friendly feelings towards our Government cannot be better shown than by your punishing with the utmost severity the men who have been faithless to their salt. By acting in this manner it will be proved to the Government that the events at Indore have occurred contrary to your wishes; and by your taking the earliest opportunity of using your troops in a manner which will be beneficial to the interests of the British Government, you will prove that their former actions were not influenced by yourself.

Allow me to know whether the above reports are correct, as it will give me the greatest pleasure to report to Government how faithfully you wish to execute the duties that your friendship towards them lays upon you.

I shall feel obliged by your allowing Gunesh Shastree to come over and stay at Mhow for a short time, as there are many matters I wish to consult you upon, and he will be a better medium of communicating with your Highness than any other.

I have, etc.,

T. HUNGERFORD, Captain,
Commanding at Mhow.

To Captain Hungerford, Commanding at Mhow.

Sir,—I am commanded by His Highness the Maharajah Saheb to acknowledge the receipt of your letter of yesterday's date, and to inform you, in reply, that a few of those troops who were supposed to have mixed up with the mutineers have returned, and measures will at a proper time be taken to ascertain the extent of their guilt.

His Highness had ordered an attack to be made on the Mhow and Indore mutineers as soon as the safety of the town was secured by their march from before it. The Komisdar of Teerana has now, according to orders, assembled about 1,100 men, together with two guns, and was to attack them at or near Rajwas; an attacking column has also been in pursuit of a few stragglers towards Jamere; a third column, to the strength of 350 horse, was sent on yesterday; and a fourth column, of two guns of horse artillery, 100 sipahies, and 50 horse, has been despatched from Indore yesterday. Letters have also been addressed to Scindia's authorities at Shahjeanpore and Oojein, as well as to the Rajahs of Dewass and Nur-ingur, to send succour, copies of which are enclosed for your information; and the result of these operations shall soon be made known.

Circular orders are also issued, offering a reward of Rs. 5,000 for any one bringing Saadut Khan, the ringleader's head, Rs. 500 for that of Bunsgopal, and Rs. 500 for that of Mahomed Ali, and smaller rewards of Rs. 150 for the head of each officer and man amongst them respectively.

Gunesh Ramchunder, an intelligent man, has been directed to wait on you as Vakeel at Mhow, and though Gunesh Shastree, having so much to do on his hands at this place, cannot be spared for a constant attendant at Mhow; he has, however, been directed to be going to and fro, and will wait on you every second day, or as occasion may require.

No means shall be spared on the Durbar's part to prove its usual sincerity and loyalty to the British Government; and His Highness rests assured they will find in him as staunch a friend as he hopes he has always proved to be.

Yours, etc.,
(Signed) RAMCHUNDER RAO.

July 8th, 1857.

Letter 428.
Mhow, July 8th, 1857.

SIR,—Not having heard anything from Colonel Durand, and having received no authentic intelligence of his whereabouts, I beg to continue my report to the Bombay Government, as the nearest authorities, and beg that a copy of my letter may be forwarded to the Supreme Government.

1. My last letter forwarded was dated the 5th, and contained copies of letter to the Maharajah and his reply. I omitted to state therein that I had blown up the magazines in the cavalry and infantry lines which were full of ammunition, and which, being distant upwards of one mile from the fort, I feared might fall into the hands of enemies.

2. On the 3rd July I proclaimed martial law throughout Mhow; and having suggested the advisability of such a step to the Maharajah of Indore, he has done the same throughout his territory.

3. By the evening of the 3rd a heavy battery was mounted and in position, in front of the north gate of the fort. The north battery consists of one 10-inch howitzer, one 8-inch, one 24-pounder, one 18-pounder, and two 12-pounders. The south battery, of four 18-pounders, was armed on the morning of the 5th. Ammunition for all these pieces, to the extent of twenty rounds per gun, has been made up by the deputy commissary of ordnance; supplies of all descriptions are laid in for one month: two light guns are also mounted on each of the four corner bastions of the fort, and small arms placed in the bastions, and every preparation made to resist any attack that might be made upon us.

4. On the night of the 4th the mutineers from Mhow, accompanied by some troops of the Maharajah, marched from Indore towards Dewass,

having carried off nine lacs of treasure from the Indore treasury. The two parties quarrelled with each other, and Holkar's troops returned to Indore on the 6th current. No portion of the treasure had been made over to them, I believe: and they were so enraged that they requested permission to follow up the Mhow mutineers and recover the treasure from them.

5. Thinking that an attack on the mutineers by the Rajah's troops would be advantageous in every way, I wrote the accompanying letter to the Maharajah (marked E *ante*), and forward his reply.

6. The accompanying letters were received yesterday from the Bhao Ramchunder Rao, and Captain Fenwick, an individual in the service of the Rajah.

7. Yesterday evening also the remainder of the treasure from Indore was sent here by the Rajah, consisting of four or five lacs of rupees in cash, and twenty-four lacs in Government notes, which I have ordered Captain Elliot, Assistant Thuggee Superintendent, now in the Mhow Fort, to take charge of.

8. A naik of my lascar company was brought in prisoner yesterday morning, who had deserted and joined the mutineers; and, having been tried by court-martial and condemned to death, was hanged in front of the fort yesterday by my orders.

9. The country around Mhow appears to be in a settled state, and I am doing what I can to keep communication open both by dâk and electric telegraph. The electric telegraph wire has been cut near Indore, but a signaller is now bringing in the wires to this fort; and as instruments will be here in the course of to-morrow, I hope soon to be able to communicate more rapidly any intelligence it may be necessary to send, than by letter dâk.

I have, etc.,
T. HUNGERFORD, Captain,
Commanding at Mhow.

The Secretary to Government, Bombay.

F.
From Lord Elphinstone, to Captain Hungerford.
Telegraph message, July 8th, 1857.

I have received your message of the 2nd. Captain Orr, with 3rd Nizam's Cavalry, is on his way to Mundlaysir, and will endeavour to communicate with you and assist you. I hope you will be able to send away in safety the ladies, women, and children under his escort. Unforeseen difficulties have prevented the advance of General Woodburn's force. A second column is now being despatched for your relief, comprising European infantry and cavalry, and a half troop of horse artillery. It will be pushed on as fast as possible; but it will be at least three weeks before it can reach you, as the infantry are going from Bombay. If you can hold out at Mhow for a month, I think you should remain until relieved; but if you are unable to do this, you must fall back on Mundlaysir, covered by Orr's horse and any of the Bhopal Sikhs or Bheels who may be at hand. Send the names of the ladies and officers at Mundlaysir, and inform me what they intend doing.

G.
To Lord Elphinstone, from Captain Hungerford.
Telegraph message, July 9th.

I request that your Lordship will not send any native troops for our relief. We will hold our own as long as we can. Hurry the European troops; cavalry, if possible. Holkar has shown by his actions that he is friendly to our Government; but he has been forced against his own inclinations to give way in some degree to his own mutinous troops and mutineers from Mhow. The whole of the mutineers have marched from Indore towards Delhi; but Holkar's troops are still doubtful, and we are threatened with an attack by the Mehidpore Contingent. The whole country is in such a state of excitement that I think any native troops will certainly be turned from their fidelity to Government; whereas the arrival of a European force at Mhow would tend immediately to establish tranquillity throughout Malwah, and would prove to Holkar that the Government are ready to assist him in his endeavours to quiet the country. A column to assist us should be sent to Mhow as quickly as possible, as it will tend more to tranquillize the country than anything else. I have nobody here but my own company of artillery and the officers who escaped from the 23rd Regiment, Native Infantry, and wing 1st Light Cavalry, and have been obliged to assume political authority to communicate with the Maharajah of Indore.

The Europeans—Captain and Mrs. Keatinge, Mr. Theobald, Mr. and Mrs. Naher and children, and a surgeon—have quitted Mundlaysir, in consequence of a dispute amongst some native officers, and have taken refuge in a small fort at Parnasa in Nimaur. Captain Keatinge talks of returning to Mundlaysir when things are quiet.

Pray telegraph strength of the column approaching, that supplies may be got ready on their line of march; also the route they will come by.

From Captain Hungerford, to Lord Elphinstone.
Telegraph message, July 9th.

The advance of Captain Orr's column has been reported, but it has not yet reached the Nerbudda. I have written to Captain Orr to carry out his orders concerning Mundlaysir, but not to advance to Mhow.

Malwah is in such an excited state, that no native troops can come here without injury. Holkar's troops have already joined in one mutiny, and have only just returned to a very slight degree of subordination; the arrival of fresh native troops would probably lead to renewed intrigue, and might cause incalculable mischief.

I beg, therefore, of your Lordship to allow only European troops to advance on Mhow. We are safe; and a few European troops would tranquillize the whole country.

APPENDIX E.

Brigadier Stewart, Commanding Malwa Field Force, to the Adjutant-General of the Bombay Army, Camp Mundesore, November 27th, 1857.

Sir,—With reference to my telegrams of the 25th and 26th instant, I have now the honour to forward the reports and to communicate for the information of His Excellency the Commander-in-Chief, full particulars of the successful operations in which the Malwa field force and the field force, Hyderabad Contingent, under command of Major Orr, were engaged on the 21st, 22nd, 23rd, and 24th instant against the rebel enemy in the vicinity of Mundesore.

2. On the morning of the 21st November, the force, accompanied by the field force, Hyderabad Contingent, which, as I have already reported, is co-operating with me under command of Major Orr, arrived within three miles and-a-half of Mundesore about 9 A.M., and as I had no good information as to the roads or the country in the immediate vicinity of the town, neither as to the fords of the river Sowna, which it was necessary to cross before reaching the town, I determined upon encamping until a good reconnaissance had been effected. The rebel enemy at Mundesore, hearing of our approach, had posted pickets entirely covering the country over which we were advancing and, observing our pickets thrown out, they mustered in some force outside the walls of the town, and appeared inclined to attack. I, however, contented myself with reinforcing the pickets, and leaving the whole charge of the front to Major Robertson, 25th Regiment Native Infantry, the field officer of the day, returned to camp. About 3 o'clock P.M. I received intimation from him that the enemy were advancing in force, and threatening both our flanks and centre at the same time. I accordingly moved out to meet them; they advanced steadily, with banners flying, and appeared in great numbers. On approaching our right front, however, they were most gallantly charged by Lieutenant Dew, Her Majesty's 14th Light Dragoons, who, with some of his men, occupied that ground as a picket. Major Orr, commanding 3rd Regiment Cavalry, Hyderabad Contingent, supported Lieutenant Dew, and the enemy were driven back with great loss, and before our guns, which had quickly moved up, could open upon them, the attack on our centre was repulsed by a few rounds of our Artillery, whilst that on the left was successfully met by the field force under Major Orr. The enemy having been thus driven back at all

points, were pursued for some distance, in fact, until they nearly reached the walls of the town, and nothing further occurred that day.

3. Having received intelligence from the Governor General's Agent that the portion of the rebel army before Neemuch, amounting to about 5,000, would probably raise the siege of that place, and endeavour to effect a junction with their head-quarters at Mundesore, I determined to frustrate this by intercepting them. Accordingly, early on the morning of the 22nd instant, I moved forward my force in order of battle, our advance was unopposed, and on my left flank reaching the village of Kulgipore, I made a flank movement to the left, as previously determined on, leaving the advance guard to cover it, and to reinforce the rear guard, as we crossed the Bakri ford of the river Sowna, about 1,400 yards to the south-west of the town of Mundesore. Thus secured, the movement was safely effected, opposed only by a slight and ineffective fire from a gun on one of the south-west bastions of the town. I then encamped facing the west of the town, my flanks well protected by the two branches of the river, and my line running at right angles to the right of Sir Thomas Hislop's camp in 1817. Just previous to the camp being marked out, it was reported that Cavalry were seen on the left, and Major Orr taking the 1st Cavalry, Hyderabad Contingent, under Captain Abbott, and 4th Cavalry, Hyderabad Contingent, under Captain Murray, saw about 300 horse, supposed to be under Heera Sing, endeavouring to draw them off in a north-westerly direction, but keeping at too great a distance to allow of being attacked. Reinforcements of Cavalry were sent for, and whilst the left wing, Her Majesty's 14th Light Dragoons, under Captain Gall, and 3rd Cavalry, Hyderabad Contingent, under Lieutenant Clerk, were moving up, intelligence was brought to Major Orr that Heera Sing's baggage had just left the village of Goraria, on the Neemuch road, the object of Heera Sing's party, to draw our Cavalry away from his baggage, thus being apparent. Her Majesty's 14th Light Dragoons, the 1st Cavalry, Hyderabad Contingent, and the 4th Cavalry, Hyderabad Contingent, galloped off in pursuit, the 3rd Cavalry, Hyderabad Contingent, remaining as a reserve. They caught up the enemy about two miles south of Peeplia, and, after cutting up about 200 of them, halted at a nullah, a mile to the south of that village. On perceiving it strongly occupied by the enemy's infantry, who showed many standards, they then returned to camp.

4. Feeling assured that the infantry seen in Peeplia formed the advance guard of the enemy, I moved at 8 o'clock A.M. on the 23rd

instant by my left, and crossed the northern branch of the river Sowna I then halted my column, and collected all my baggage on the reverse flank, then moving on to my proposed camp on the Neemuch and Mundesore Road, ready to oppose the enemy either from one or the other direction. On coming on to the ground, the enemy appeared in great force to the north; so, ordering my baggage to be collected on a strong mound, I strongly reinforced my rear-guard, and proceeded to meet them. After a short advance, I formed line to my front, facing northward, and found the enemy occupying a very strong position, with their right in and beyond the village of Goraria, their right centre covered by a date nullah and lines of date trees, their battery of six guns on a rising ground, with a large mud hut protecting their gunners, and their left stretched along the ridge running east from the village. My line advanced, covered by skirmishers; the enemy's infantry, with banners flying (many of them green), moved down to meet us through the intermediate fields of high jowarry, and their guns opened fire. I immediately halted my line, and replied to the fire with Captains Hungerford's and Woolcombe's batteries, at a range of about 900 yards. After a few rounds I again advanced the line, and permitted Captain Hungerford to move his half battery to a position on our right front, from which he could enfilade the enemy. After an advance of about 300 yards, our line was again halted and firing resumed, that from both batteries being very effective. A most gallant charge was then made on the enemy's guns by the escort of Her Majesty's 14th Light Dragoons, attached to Captain Hungerford, under Lieutenant Martin, who found, however, that the position was still very strongly held by the enemy's infantry, and was compelled to retire, he himself being very severely wounded. Captain Hungerford's half battery was again advanced to within 100 yards, and after a round or two of grape, the guns were at once again charged and captured, the enemy flying in great numbers into the village to their right. The 3rd Regiment of Cavalry, Hyderabad Contingent, under Major S. Orr, was just at this moment rapidly advanced to our right front, and having been wheeled to the left, it swept down upon them in their retreat, and killed great numbers. Our line then changed front about the eighth of a circle, right thrown forward, and moved steadily on the village, which evidently held great numbers of the enemy. Their skirmishers disputed our advance, but were soon driven back. Having halted within about 300 yards of the village, our Artillery opened upon it with shot and shell, after which I directed the Infantry to advance and carry it.

The men of the 86th and 25th Regiments dashed forward in the most gallant manner, and, having entered the village, commenced to drive all before them. They soon met, however, with very warm opposition, the enemy having taken possession in great force of many houses, from which a most harassing fire was kept upon our men. Under these circumstances, and as, moreover, I could get no satisfactory accounts of what was passing in my rear which I knew from the firing I heard, as also from the pressing applications I had received for reinforcements had been warmly engaged, I recalled the Infantry, and posted strong pickets all round the village, and moved the remainder of the men a short distance off to where the baggage had been passed up from the rear. I then learnt that, during the afternoon, when we were hotly engaged in the front, a strong body of the enemy from Mundesore attacked our rear, and endeavoured to carry off the siege train, baggage, etc. They were, however, most gallantly repulsed on every occasion. In one of these attacks, I regret to say that Lieutenant Redmayne, Her Majesty's 14th Light Dragoons, was killed, whilst most bravely leading his men against the enemy. Notwithstanding the many attempts made by the enemy to press upon and harass our rear, it gives me great satisfaction to be able to state that not a particle of baggage was lost, nor a follower injured, on this occasion. Lieutenant Leith, commanding a squadron 14th Light Dragoons, appears to have done good service, as also Lieutenant Fenwick, 25th Regiment, Native Infantry, in charge of the baggage, gunner Maitland of the Bengal Artillery and gunner Thomson of the Bombay Artillery also distinguished themselves by assisting to work the heavy guns most effectively against the enemy.

5. On the 24th instant I arranged with Captain Hungerford, Commandant of Artillery, that the village of Goraria in which the rebels had taken refuge, should be well shelled and again assaulted by the Infantry. Accordingly, I moved up to it about noon, and found that the enemy were as I had left them the preceding evening, excepting that a few had attempted to escape, nearly all of whom were killed. After a heavy fire of three hours' duration, the detachment of Her Majesty's 86th Regiment, under command of Major Keane, and the 25th Regiment, Native Infantry, under Major Robertson, again stormed the village and carried it, killing great numbers of the enemy; they themselves also suffering severely. At sunset I withdrew the troops, intend-

ing to move against the fort of Mundesore the next day. Early, however, on the morning of the 25th instant, intelligence reached me that the enemy had, during the night, completely evacuated Mundesore, and were scattered in flight throughout the country, in various directions, having lost, it is computed, about 1,500 of their number during our operations against them. I accordingly removed my camp to Mundesore, and am now engaged in dismantling the forts, destroying the guns, etc., before leaving this neighbourhood.

6. By the successful operations of the Malwa field force, and field force Hyderabad Contingent, in the vicinity of Mundesore, the Neemuch garrison has been relieved from the assault with which it was threatened. The insurgent rebels have been dispersed from their stronghold in which, for months past, they have been daily collecting all those disaffected to our rule; and peace and order will now, it is to be hoped, be re-established in these districts.

7. I must now, in conclusion, place on record my grateful acknowledgments to Colonel Durand, Officiating Agent to the Governor General for Central India, for his cordial assistance to me on all occasions. He was present in the field throughout the operations, and gave me the benefit of his advice, which proved of great service to me. Major Orr, commanding field force, Hyderabad Contingent, most ably co-operated with me on all occasions, and to him and all under his command I am very much indebted; to Major Boileau, Field Engineer, and his assistants, Lieutenant Prendergast (severely wounded), and Gordon; to Captain Mayne, Intelligence Department, to Captain Coley, Major of Brigade, to Lieutenant Macdonald, Deputy Assistant Quartermaster-General, to Lieutenant Thain, Sub-Assistant Commissary-General, and to Surgeon Mackenzie, Staff Surgeon, my warmest thanks are due. The assistance rendered me by these officers left me nothing to wish for. A perusal of the report made by Captain Gall, commanding left wing of Her Majesty's 14th Light Dragoons, will convey to His Excellency the Commander-in-Chief some idea of the good service performed by all ranks under his command. I most fully concur in Captain Gall's report, and beg to commend to the consideration of His Excellency all the officers and men mentioned by him. Of Captain Gall himself, I must in justice add that a more able, zealous, and hard-working officer I have never met with, nor one more worthy of distinction. Of Major Orr, 3rd Regiment Cavalry, Hyderabad Contingent and the officers and men under his command, I have already had reason to send the most favour-

able report to the Resident at Hyderabad. On this last occasion, nothing could surpass the bravery shown by all ranks of this regiment; Major Orr himself is, I consider, a first-rate cavalry officer; his daring courage is admired by all, and in every affair in which he is engaged his personal combats are most prominent features. To Captain Hungerford, Commandant of Artillery, Malwa field force, and to Captain Woolcombe, commanding No. 4 light field battery, and the officers and men under their command, my best thanks are due. I do not think Artillery practice could have been better, and there can be but little doubt that the successful issue of operations is much to be attributed to their assistance. Of the conduct of Captain Brown, and the officers and men of the B Company, Madras Sappers and Miners, I have much pleasure in speaking in the highest terms; whether as Sappers or as Infantry, they have distinguished themselves on every occasion; they have undergone an incredible amount of hard labour, during our late march with a siege train over a country without roads, nor must I omit to mention that they accompanied the storming parties into the village of Goraria, and proved of the greatest service. My best thanks are also due to Major Keane and the officers and men of the detachment, Her Majesty's 86th Regiment. The gallantry of all ranks was most conspicuous, and on both occasions that the village was assaulted the coolness and daring of the officers and men, at whose head Major Keane placed himself, elicited the praise of all. My despatch from Dhar will have made His Excellency the Commander-in-Chief aware of the very high opinion I held of Major Robertson and the officers and men of the 25th Regiment, Native Infantry. During the late operations nothing could have been finer than the behaviour of all in this regiment. Major Robertson distinguished himself on the 21st instant as field officer of the day, in the disposition of the pickets, which duty I entirely confided to him, and by the skilful manner in which he met the attack made upon him in force on the afternoon of that day. During the succeeding days, Major Robertson rendered me the greatest assistance; the manner in which he led his regiment on two occasions to storm the village of Goraria is beyond all praise, and I consider that the admirable conduct of the 25th Regiment of Native Infantry fully attests the worth of this officer, who will, I hope, meet with some mark of distinction. In the praise conveyed to Captain Little, 25th Regiment, Native Infantry, by his commanding officer, I quite concur, and trust that His Excellency may be able to grant some mark of favour to this deserving officer. In the two attacks on the village of Goraria, I could see no difference between the conduct of the men of the 25th Regiment, Native Infantry, and their comrades of Her Majesty's 86th Regiment—the same daring and gallantry characterised both. Their list of casualties will shew how warmly they were engaged, and I trust His Excellency will recognise the merits of this Regiment. Before closing this despatch, I beg to report on the admirable conduct of Assistant Surgeon Butler, of the Artillery, who during the engagement of the 23rd instant, though suffering severely from sickness, left his doolie, and was engaged in the most active manner during the whole day in assisting to administer comfort to the wounded. The conduct of this officer has been brought to my notice by the staff-surgeon of the force, and will, I trust, meet with some reward.

I have, etc.,

(Signed) C. S. STUART.

Major Orr, to the Deputy Assistant Quartermaster-General. Camp near Mundesore, November 25th, 1857.

Sir,—I have the honour to forward, for submission to the Brigadier commanding Malwa field force, a report of the part taken by the field force, Hyderabad Contingent, under my command during the operations near Mundesore, commencing from the 21st instant.

2. On the forenoon of that date, after making arrangements for the safety of my camp, I directed a village on the extreme left to be occupied and held by a party of cavalry and infantry as its possession appeared of importance. About 2 o'clock P.M. it was reported that the village was threatened. On reaching the spot I found a strong body of the enemy, horse and foot, moving out into the open country, and advancing with much boldness. I directed reinforcements and guns to be brought up at once; but before these could arrive the enemy had succeeded in forcing back the picket and occupying the village. On being joined by the guns and infantry, with the 1st and 4th regiments of Cavalry, Hyderabad Contingent, the artillery, assisted by two guns of the Bombay (Captain Woolcombe's) battery, under command of Lieutenant Strutt, opened a very well-directed and effective fire, which cleared the village and forced back the insurgents. It was again occupied by our troops, the enemy retiring slowly and in considerable force towards

Mundesore. My orders being explicit on the subject of not forcing a general engagement, I contented myself with retaining possession of the village.

3. On the morning of the 22nd, the force, by a flank movement, crossed the river, encamped on the west side of the town of Mundesore. Whilst making a reconnaissance with Captain MacDonald, Deputy Assistant Quartermaster-General, two bodies of the enemy were observed moving away. These consisted principally of horsemen. One got away too rapidly for pursuit, but the other was followed by the troops, as per margin,* and, after a hard gallop of some five or six miles, overtaken and severely punished, a great many being cut down by Her Majesty's 14th Light Dragoons and Contingent Cavalry. The pursuit was stayed by our finding a large body of the enemy drawn up in our front, in a strong position, in a village, against which cavalry could not act.

4. On the enemy being observed in strength to the left of the village of Goraria, whilst the column was *en route*, on the morning of the 23rd, I received the directions of the Brigadier commanding to deploy with my force to support the general attack, and to conform my movements to those of the column. These directions were implicitly carried out; the cavalry was held ready wherever it might be necessary to act, and to prevent any attempt on the left flank, a detachment of two companies of the 3rd Infantry, Hyderabad Contingent, under command of Captain Sinclair, with two guns of the 1st Company Artillery, was ordered to reinforce the rear-guard; the remainder of the infantry and two guns of the 4th Company, Artillery, under Captain J. deC. Sinclair, assisted by two guns of Captain Woolcombe's battery, under command of Lieutenant Keating, Bombay Artillery, advanced in line with the column, and aided in the general operations. The fire of the guns was most effective and good, throwing shot and shell with much precision into the enemy's ranks. On the capture of the guns and the advance of the cavalry on the right, I brought forward the cavalry on the left flank also, which was completely cleared of flying parties of the insurgents. Having received orders further to reinforce the rear-guard by two more guns, I considered I should be best carrying out the views of the Brigadier, and conducing to the success of the day's operations if I moved down the whole cavalry to the rear, which had been reported to be hard pressed.

---

* One squadron, Her Majesty's 14th Light Dragoons, Major Gall commanding; two troops, 1st Cavalry, Hyderabad Contingent, Captain Abbott commanding; two troops, 4th Cavalry, Hyderabad Contingent, Captain Murray commanding.

This was rapidly effected; I found the enemy had advanced to a position about 800 yards distant from the rear-guard, that they were in force and that it was necessary they should be dislodged as soon as possible, their number and boldness increasing. I accordingly directed the line to move forward, and, after a short advance, the guns opened and drove back the enemy, they answering our fire from matchlocks. After a second advance I ordered the cavalry as per margin,* to charge and clear the front. They rapidly advanced upon a large body of retreating footmen, but, unfortunately, the nature of the ground being broken, and full of large graval pits, from which a close and sharp matchlock fire was opened, prevented the attack being as effective as otherwise it would have been. A good many insurgents, however, were cut up, and those in the pits were afterwards shot down on the infantry coming up.

5. I deeply regret to have to report that in this charge fell Lieutenant Redmayne, Her Majesty's 14th Light Dragoons, whilst gallantly leading on his men, he was mortally wounded. His gallantry and daring courage were conspicuous to all, and I trust I may be permitted to say that in him Her Majesty's service has lost an officer of high promise.

6. In the operations against the village of Goraria, on the 24th instant, this force also took part, and a detachment of infantry under Captain Sinclair, 3rd Regiment, joined the stormers, and shared in the assault upon the village.

7. I beg to bring to the favourable notice of the Brigadier commanding the Malwa field force the conduct of the entire force under my command. My best thanks are due to Lieutenant Hastings Fraser, 4th Cavalry, my staff officer, for his zealous exertions in the performance of the numerous duties which devolved upon him, as well as for his prompt and ready aid at all times; to Captain Abbott, commanding 1st Cavalry; Captain Murray, commanding 4th Cavalry; Captain Sinclair, commanding left wing, 3rd Infantry; Captain J. de C. Sinclair, commanding Artillery; and Lieutenant Johnson, Adjutant, 1st Cavalry; to Surgeon Orr, 4th Cavalry, and Senior Surgeon, field force, Hyderabad Contingent, my best ackowledgments are due for the assistance he afforded me in the field during the entire operations for his care and attention to the wounded, and the arrangements made by him for their comfort.

---

* One squadron, Her Majesty's 14th Light Dragoons, Lieutenant Leith commanding; 1st Cavalry, Hyderabad Contingent, Captain Abbott commanding; 4th Cavalry, Hyderabad Contingent, Captain Murray commanding.

8. I beg to forward a nominal return of the killed and wounded during the four days' operations.*

I have, etc.,

(Signed) W. A. ORR, *Major,*
Commanding Field Force, Hyderabad Contingent.

Nominal Roll of Officers of the Malwa Field Force killed and wounded in the engagement with the insurgents before and in the vicinity of Mundesore, from the 21st to the 24th November 1857.

Staff.—Lieutenant H. Prendergast, Madras Engineers, severely wounded.

Her Majesty's Left Wing, 14th Light Dragoons.—Lieutenant James Leith, slightly wounded; Lieutenant L. Gowan, slightly wounded; Lieutenant C. Martin, severely wounded; Lieutenant W. L. Redmayne, killed.

Twenty-fifth Regiment, Bombay Native Infantry.—Major G. H. Robertson, slightly wounded; Lieutenant Charles Jameson, severely wounded; Lieutenant John Foster Forbes, slightly wounded, Lieutenant D. B. Young, slightly wounded.

I have, etc.,

(Signed) W. A. ORR, *Major,*
Commanding Field Force, Hyderabad Contingent.

Two killed, 11 wounded of the 3rd and 5th Infantry; horses, 12 wounded.

APPENDIX E   lxxvii

Numerical Returns of Officers and Men of the Malwa Field Force, and Field Force, Hyderabad Contingent, killed and wounded in the engagement with the insurgents before and in the vicinity of Mundesore, from the 21st to the 24th November 1857.

Europeans.	KILLED.										WOUNDED.									
	Major.	Lieutenant.	Sergeant-Major.	Troop Sergeant-Major.	Sergeant.	Farrier Sergeant.	Corporal.	Gunner.	Trooper.	Privates.	Major.	Lieutenants.	Sergeant-Major.	Troop Sergeant-Major.	Sergeant.	Farrier Sergeant.	Corporal.	Gunner.	Troopers.	Privates.
Staff	...	...	...	...	...	...	...	...	...	...	...	1	...	...	...	...	...	...	...	...
Bengal Artillery	...	...	...	...	...	...	...	...	...	...	...	...	...	...	...	1	1	...	...	...
Bombay Artillery	...	...	...	...	...	...	...	...	...	...	...	...	...	...	...	...	...	1	...	...
Her Majesty's Left Wing 14th Light Dragoons.	...	1	...	...	...	...	...	...	...	...	...	3	1	1	...	...	...	...	5	...
Her Majesty's 86th Regiment	...	...	...	...	...	...	...	...	...	2	1	...	...	...	1	...	...	...	...	8
25th Bombay Native Infantry	...	...	...	...	...	...	...	...	...	...	...	3	...	...	...	...	...	...	...	...

Abstract of wounded, since dead.

Her Majesty's 86th Regiment—1 Sergeant.   25th Bombay Native Infantry—3 privates.

APPENDIX E

Numerical Return of Officers and Men of the Malwa Field Force, and Field Force, Hyderabad Contingent, killed and wounded in the engagement with the insurgents before and in the vicinity of Mundesore, from the 21st to the 24th November 1857.

Natives.

	Killed.									Wounded.								
	Subadar.	Havildar.	Duffadar.	Naick.	Trooper.	Sepoys.	Trumpeter.	Bugler.	Syce.	Driver.	Subadar.	Havildar.	Duffadars.	Naicks.	Troopers.	Sepoys.	Trumpeter.	Buglers.	Syces.	Drivers.
Bengal Artillery	...	...	...	...	...	...	...	...	...	...	...	...	...	...	...	...	...	...	2	...
Bombay Artillery	...	...	...	...	...	...	...	...	...	...	...	...	...	...	...	...	...	...	...	2
3rd Cavalry, Hyderabad Contingent	...	...	...	...	1	...	...	...	...	...	...	...	4	...	4	...	1	...	...	...
25th Bombay Native Infantry	...	...	...	...	...	3	...	...	...	...	...	...	...	7	...	21	...	...	...	...
3rd Infantry, Hyderabad Contingent	...	...	...	1	...	1	...	...	...	...	1	...	...	...	...	6	...	...	...	...
5th Infantry, Hyderabad Contingent	...	...	...	...	...	...	...	...	...	...	...	1	...	...	...	...	...	4	...	...

lxxviii

Appendix E

(Confidential.)

Major General Mansfield to Major General Rose, dated Head-Quarters, Cawnpore, 11th February 1858.

Sir,—I have the honour, by desire of the Commander-in-Chief, to call your attention to the defence of Jhansi.

You are probably aware that it is of great importance that Jhansi should be reduced with as little delay as possible; but if the defence be strong, and if there be a very large assemblage of insurgents in that city, it may be doubted whether you have a force sufficient to undertake the siege.

His Excellency observes that you have not, at the very outside, more than 1,500 of British infantry.

Sir Colin Campbell, therefore, considers that before undertaking this operation you should have made quite certain from intelligence to be derived from Sir R. Hamilton, or other quarters, that a serious opposition, to overcome which your force is unequal, is not likely to be encountered at Jhansi, as a check might have very disagreeable consequences.

If, after weighing all these circumstances, you should be of opinion that the siege cannot prudently be undertaken, your march may be directed in two divisions, *viz.*, one on Calpee on the Jumna through Chirkaree, and the other on Banda from each of which places you would report for the information of the Commander-in-Chief.

I have, etc.,

(Signed) **W. R. MANSFIELD**, *Major General, Chief of the Staff.*

Lord Canning, to Sir R. Hamilton, dated Allahabad, 11th February 1858.

Dear Sir Robert,—If the Nerbudda Field Force proceeds to Jhansi, and if the Ranee should fall into its hands, she must be tried, not by a Court Martial, but by a Commission appointed for the purpose.

Sir H. Rose will be directed to hand her over to you, and you must put together the best Commission which your material will allow.

If for any reason it should not be possible to deal with her at once, and if there should be difficulty in keeping her in custody in or near Jhansi, she may be sent here. But it is very desirable that the preliminary inquiry into her conduct, which will decide whether there be grounds for a trial, should be completed before she arrives here. She must not come here with any doubt as to whether she deserves to be tried or not. I hope, however, you will be able to finish her trial on the spot; what may be done with her after trial will depend upon the sentence.

I say "if" the Nerbudda force proceeds to Jhansi, because Sir H. Rose will receive authority to pass by that place in the event of his having any doubt as to his being strong enough to deal with it. In that case the Nerbudda Field Force should be directed upon Calpee or Banda (one or both) and operations against Jhansi be suspended until additional strength can be sent from this side. Nothing would be more embarrassing and even dangerous than that the Nerbudda column should sit down before Jhansi, or any other place in that direction, and find itself unable to achieve its purpose without aid from this quarter.

I therefore wish that Sir H. Rose should not consider himself under any obligation to attempt the reduction of Jhansi against the probability of success; and he will receive instructions from the Commander-in-Chief in this sense.

He is too weak in European infantry to run such risks.

I see you have brought away Captain Keatinge. Was there any risk in leaving him where he was? and would not his remaining have tended to keep Western Malwa straight?

(Signed) CANNING.

To Major General Whitlock, Commanding Movable Column, Camp Dumoh, Military Department, Allahabad, 13th March 1858.

Sir,—From intelligence which has reached the Right Honourable the Governor General from Chirkaree, it cannot be doubted that the fort of that place has, by this time, fallen into the hands of the insurgents, who were laying siege to it, and who were already masters of the town, part of which was burnt.

Punnah also and Rewah are threatened.

It is of urgent importance that support should be given to the loyal chiefs of Bundelcund as soon as possible, and as no troops can be moved into the Bundelcund States from this side of the Jumna, the Governor

General directs me to request that you will proceed at once, with the column under your command, in the direction of Punnah, Chirkaree, or such other point as you may judge expedient, with the object of supporting the chiefs who may be threatened by the insurgents, and freeing them from the danger to which they are now exposed.

You will use your discretion as to having a garrison at Dumoh, or elsewhere, in the Saugor territory, but you are requested to bear in mind that the Governor General wishes the relief of the well-affected Bundelcund chiefs to be considered as the paramount object for the present.

It is necessary that you should communicate your movements to Major General Sir H. Rose, in order that he may be able to shape his own course, so as to combine with yours in giving confidence and support to the chiefs.

Sir H. Rose will receive instructions to this effect.

I have, etc.,

(Signed) R. J. H. BIRCH, *Colonel,*
Secretary to Government of India,
Military Department, with the Governor General.

Copy forwarded for the information and guidance of Major General Sir H. Rose, K.C.B., Commanding Central India Field Force.

By order,

(Signed) R. J. H. BIRCH, *Colonel,*
Secretary to Government of India,
Military Department, with the Governor General.

From Major General Sir Hugh Rose, K.C.B., Commanding Central India Field Force, to Colonel Birch, Secretary to the Government of India, Military Department; dated Camp Sirrus, on the left bank of the River Betwa, 19th March 1858.

Sir,—I have the honour to acknowledge the receipt, this day, for my information and guidance, of a copy of your letter of the 15th instant, to Major General Whitlock, containing the Right Honourable the Governor General's instructions to that officer respecting his advance with the column under his command, in the direction of Punnah, Chirkaree, or such other points as he may judge expedient, for the purpose of supporting the well-affected chiefs who may be threatened by the insurgents, and freeing them from the danger to which they are now exposed.

I have the honour to say that I shall pay the strictest attention to these instructions, and be careful to shape my own course so as to give, in combination with Major General Whitlock, confidence and support to these chiefs.

I may, I hope, be permitted to say that I have received, with sincere pleasure, these instructions; strategically and politically speaking, they are calculated to produce the best effect in this part of India; and they develop and complete a plan of operations, which Sir Robert Hamilton and myself had agreed yesterday that it would be advantageous to carry out after the reduction of Jhansi, for the relief of the chiefs in question, and the defeat of the rebel army concentrated at Chirkaree and Nowgong, whose numbers Sir Robert Hamilton says amount to 60,000 men, according to the last reports received.

Both Sir Robert Hamilton and myself had always felt the strongest wish to assist the Chirkaree chiefs who had supported the English Government with so much devotion. But the reports from Mr. Carne, which represented his position at Chirkaree as quite desperate on the 1st of March, when my force could not possibly have reached that place till three weeks or a month later, precluded all hope of relieving him.

The plan I have mentioned, that is, a march against the rebels at Chirkaree, or in that direction, has, under existing circumstances, advantages over a direct march to Calpee from Jhansi.

If I marched straight to Calpee, I leave sincere and influential supporters of the British Government—the Rajah of Chirkaree, the Ranee of Bigaroo and Tehree, and others—to be overrun by masses of rebels; and I should have the so-called army of the Peishwa on my right flank, and closing in, as I advanced, on my rear. It is evident that it is more advantageous to attack the Peishwa's army separately, and Calpee separately, than to place myself between their two fires.

The round I should have to make to relieve Chirkaree would not delay me much as to my arrival at Calpee, and the defeat of the rebels will leave friends instead of enemies in my rear.

The arrival of Major General Whitlock, on my right flank, and his co-operation with me, is a most important improvement on the plan just mentioned and I may add, that nothing will tend more to cause, effectually, the permanent pacification of the Saugor district than an advance of Major General Whitlock's force in the direction pointed out by the Governor General.

I have, etc.,

(Signed) H. ROSE, *Major General.*

From Major General Whitlock, to Major General Sir Hugh Rose, K.C.B., Commanding Central India Field Force, dated Head-quarters, Camp beyond Jhansi, Assistant Quartermaster General's Office, Camp at Dumoh, 19th March 1858.

Sir,—I have the honour to enclose, for your information, the accompanying copy of a letter received from the Secretary to Government of India, Military Department, with the Governor General.

2. In consequence of these instructions, I returned to Dumoh, and placed myself on the high road to Punnah, on which place I shall move the moment my details of artillery, cavalry, and infantry join me from detached duty, which I hope will be on the morrow.

3. I have communicated with Major Ellis, and of course, must be guided in my future operations by such information as I receive from that officer.

4. In the meantime you shall be kept regularly acquainted with my movements, and I beg the favour of hearing what arrangements you purpose making to carry out the wishes of the Governor General that our plans may be combined.

I have, etc.,

(Signed) G. C. WHITLOCK, *Major General, Commanding Saugor Field Division.*

From Major General Sir H. Rose, K.C.B., Commanding Central India Field Force, to Major General Whitlock, Commanding Saugor Field Division; dated Sirrus Ghat, two marches from Jhansi, 19th March 1858.

Sir,—I have the honour to state to you that I received this day the copy of a letter, dated 15th instant, from Colonel Birch, Secretary to Government of India, Military Department, and with reference to it to say that I shall be most happy to combine my future movements with yours in giving confidence and support to the Chirkaree and other loyal Bundelcund chiefs, and, as the best means of doing so, to attack, in combination with your force, the numerous rebels who are besieging him at Chirkaree, and who are concentrating at Nowgong.

I should feel extremely obliged to you if you would have the goodness to acquaint me with your future movements.

I march from here to-morrow, intending to arrive before Jhansi on the 20th instant, when I shall commence its attack without any delay. Sir R. Hamilton tells me that its garrison consists of 1,500 Sepoys and 1,000 Bundelas. Immediately after its capture I shall proceed with my two brigades to carry out, in combination with yourself, the operations pointed out by the Governor General, crossing the river Betwa.

The greatest concentration of rebels appears to be at Nowgong and Chirkaree; the former have assumed the title of the army of the Peishwa.

Brigadier Stuart, commanding my first brigade, reports to me that on the 17th instant he stormed the fort of Chandaree at 5 A.M. that day; there were about 50 dead bodies found about the fort, but the jungly and mountainous nature of the country enabled the garrison to escape.

Brigadier Stuart will join me before Jhansi immediately.

I have, etc.,

(Signed) H. ROSE, *Major General,*
Commanding Central India Field Force.

From Sir R. Hamilton, Agent for the Governor General in Central India, to G. F. Edmonstone, Esq., Secretary to the Government of India, Foreign Department, dated March 1858.

Sir,—I have the honour to acknowledge the receipt, at 1 P.M. this day, of your Despatch, No. 273, dated 13th March, and to state that I immediately communicated its contents to Major General Sir Hugh Rose.

To enable the Governor General to form a correct opinion on the position of this brigade, it is necessary for me to enter into the following details :—

It, the second brigade, is to-day within 10 miles of Jhansi. The whole of its cavalry under Brigadier Stuart, will have invested the fort and town before sunset, and Major Boileau, the Chief Engineer, will have made reconnaissance, with a view to fix the site of our batteries on the arrival of the remainder of the brigade before Jhansi early to-morrow morning. The garrison of Jhansi are aware of, and prepared for, our approach, so that any cessation of the operations would now be looked on as a retreat, the moral effect of which would be hazardous, if not actually most fatal.

Moreover, the first brigade has been detained at Chandaree, and could only move this morning to join this, to effect which will take at least five long marches.

Their junction with this brigade is essential to any forward movement, even supposing Sir Hugh Rose were now to refuse Jhansi, and draw off to proceed to succour Punnah, and the loyal chiefs in Bundelcund.

Again, it is important that our communications with Goonah and Saugor, from whence our reinforcements and our supplies must come, be secured, and that nothing be left in our rear which would require to be watched.

If Sir Hugh Rose were now to turn off, he must pass almost within range of the guns of the fort to reach the Burwa Saugor road, the ford of which must be taken, for his force to cross that difficult and unbridged river, the Betwa; but this advance would entirely cut off his communications with his first brigade, and place Jhansi, with its 1,500 mutineers, town and fort, and 1,000 Bundelas, not only in his rear, but between the two brigades, and entirely cut off his communication with Goonah and Saugor, and consequently with his reinforcements and supplies.

Further, Chirkaree is, by the nearest route, eight marches, but that place could not be reached in eight days by his brigade, with its large siege train. Supposing it were to move to-morrow morning, probably not before the 31st of this month, it would be some days longer in reaching Punnah, whilst General Whitlock's force should reach Punnah in eight marches from Dumoh, or by the 24th or 25th, if they march from Punnah to Chatterpore, would be four marches more, and thence to Chirkaree is about 50 miles.

There is then every reason, and the hope, that Punnah and Rewah will both be relieved by Major General Whitlock's force before Sir Hugh Rose could arrive there, supposing he went at once, and direct, and met with no opposition or delay.

Already has the pressure on Jhansi caused the Ranee to call in all her troops who were attacking Oorcha and Mhow and it has also forced her to send and ask assistance from Tantia Topee, which, if complied with, must cramp his operations to some extent, and relieve, in some degree, our loyal chiefs in that quarter, whom the advance of General Whitlock will effectively protect.

Under these circumstances now existing here, and the above statement of facts, I hope the Governor General will consider that it would not be politic to suspend operations before Jhansi, but rather to urge them on vigorously, until the first brigade arrives from Chandaree, when Sir Hugh Rose will be able to form a flying column, which can move rapidly towards Begawur, Chutterpore, and elsewhere, to succour the loyal states between Tehree and Punnah, by routes along which heavy artillery could not travel.

I may add that in the opinion of the vakeels in camp, the fall of Jhansi is likely to have a very great effect on the rebels and mutineers now infesting Bundelcund, and the advance of Sir Hugh Rose's force, after its capture, will be the more effective, and greatly accelerate the rout and destruction of the rebels.

In conclusion, I beg to state that Sir Hugh Rose desires me to express his entire concurrence in the views and reasonings above expressed, and his hope that they will be considered sufficient to allow of a slight delay in giving effect to His Lordship's wishes.

(Signed) W. R. HAMILTON.

General Whitlock was at Dumoh on the 16th March, and should on that or the next day have received the Government order.

From the Secretary to the Government of India, with the Governor General, to the Agent to the Governor General, Central India, dated Allahabad, 30th April 1858.

Sir,—The Right Honourable the Governor General has had under consideration your letter, No. 118, dated 20th instant, explaining the reasons which have prevented execution of the orders communicated in the letter of this office, dated 13th instant, by which it was directed that the freeing of the loyal Rajahs of Chirkaree, Punnah, and Rewah, from the danger which threatens them, should be considered paramount to the operations against Jhansi.

2. In reply, I am desired by His Lordship to inform you that under the circumstances represented, and with advertence to the fact of Sir Hugh Rose's force having been already committed before Jhansi, the decision taken in respect of the prior reduction of that place was unquestionably right, and is therefore entirely approved.

I have, etc.,
(Signed) G. F. EDMONSTONE,
Secretary to the Government of India with the Governor General.

No. 718 of 1858.
Forwarded to Major General Sir H. Rose, K.C.B., for information.

(Signed) R. HAMILTON,
Agent to Governor General for Central India.

INDORE RESIDENCY;
10th April 1858.

Sir Robert W. C. Hamilton, to G. A. Hamilton, Esq., Avoncliffe, Stratford-on-Avon, 20th March 1862.

Sir,—I shall be obliged by your doing me the honour to submit the accompanying memorandum to Viscount Palmerston and the Lords of Her Majesty's Treasury.

I have, etc.,
(Signed) ROBERT W. C. HAMILTON.

Memorandum of Sir Robert W. C. Hamilton, 20th March 1862.

I have for the first time to-day seen the memorial of the prize agents to the Madras Army, addressed to Lord Palmerston and the Lords Commissioners of Her Majesty's Treasury, and consider it a duty I owe to the troops who formed the army that operated in Central India or south of the Jumna, to state some facts and circumstances hitherto unknown to them or to any one not in direct communication and confidential correspondence with the Governor General of India and the authorities.

I have abstained from all connexion with any parties; I have avoided all correspondence, and preserved a complete silence, because I considered that holding the high appointment I did, in connexion with the Central Indian field force, and having the entire and sole conduct of all political matters with the princes and chiefs in or through whose territories any portion of the army employed in that service moved, I should not be justified in opening my mouth or in writing a line without the sanction of the Government under whom I served. Having received the sanction of the Secretary of State for India, I shall state facts which may serve to guide the judgment which may be come to on the questions raised in the memorial above alluded to.

For a period of ten years I held the appointment of Resident at Indore, and for a greater part of that time Agent for the Governor General in Central India. Before the mutiny broke out, I had sole control over the states of Gwalior, Holkar, Rewah, Bundelcund, and all the intermediate petty states.

The boundaries of my authority were the Jumna, along the Gwalior frontier, the districts of Humeerpore, Banda, Allahabad, and Mirzapore, along the Rewah frontier the line of the Chumbul, towards Rajpootana, the Goozerat frontier, the Salpoora range of hills, and the Taptee, towards Candeish, and the Nerbudda, with the Saugor territory.

A glance at a map will at once show the extent of my political superintendence before the mutiny, and when the operations after the mutiny began, the whole of the Saugor and Nerbudda territory were likewise placed under me, so that the Nagpore and Hyderabad states became the boundary.

It is important to bear this extent of country in mind, because within it is the whole sphere of Sir Hugh Rose's as well as Sir G. Whitlock's operations; neither of these commanders had any political authority. I was with Sir Hugh Rose, and my assistant, Major Ellis, with General Whitlock throughout the entire operations, and we were in daily and constant inter-communication, both in respect to intelligence, supplies, carriage, cash, and other requisites for the troops.

I was in England on leave of absence when the outbreak at Meerut took place, and hearing from the late Sir James Melvill that some of the

Appendix E

Court of Directors rather wished that I would return, I at once wrote officially (though I had not been six weeks at home), and asked permission to return to my appointment in Central India. My request was at once complied with, but I was directed to remain until further intelligence was received by the expected mail. I was afterwards directed to proceed to Calcutta, to the Governor General, and I reached Calcutta shortly after Sir Colin Campbell, now Lord Clyde.

In Calcutta I was called on to state what I considered necessary to restore tranquillity in Central India. I drew up a memorandum, which I gave to the Governor General, and was directed to wait on the Commander-in-Chief on the subject. I did so. The Commander-in-Chief, Lord Clyde, with his chief of staff, Sir William Mansfield, went over the whole plan, with the map on the table, which was that, by a combined operation, the whole of the country between Jubbulpore and Indore, Mhow, as a base, and the Jumna, should be swept by the forces to be employed, Calpee and Banda being the two points on which they were to act. I was asked by the Commander-in-Chief to say by what date we might reach these two points on the south bank of the Jumna. I replied, if there were no delay in collecting the force, by the 1st May. I had traversed every state and almost every mile of the routes, and knew where opposition was likely to be met.

The Commander-in-Chief made one alteration in the plan I had submitted, which was the junction of the two brigades of the Mhow or Indore column at Goonah, instead of at Supree, previous to their advance on Jhansi. At this time no commander, neither General Rose nor General Whitlock, had been named; the base of operations had been fixed at Mhow, Indore and Jubbulpore; the Indore or Mhow column was to be formed into two brigades, one to move by Sehore, Bhopal relieve Saugor, if the Jubbulpore column had not, then pass by the valley of the Betwah to Jhansi, and so to Calpee; the other brigade of the Indore or Mhow force was to march by the Agra and Bombay road, to clear and open that line of communication,* and form a junction with the main column at Goonah, previous to advance on Jhansi. Bombay was to furnish troops for this column.

The Jubbulpore column was to be composed of Madras troops, to relieve Saugor, and clear the line of communication with Allahabad and Mirzapore, passing across Bundelcund to Banda.

---

* Between Agra and Bombay, by which the whole English or European correspondence passes.

I left Calcutta with this plan, and to reach the Jumna by 1st May was the great object I had in view, having swept the country.

I do not enter into the details of the route or marches at present, because I wish to state facts, to prove that Sir G. Whitlock only carried out a plan which he did not originate, and from which he was not at liberty to diverge, that the base of operations was settled and determined before even he was nominated to the command. This remark is equally applicable to Sir Hugh Rose, who had to carry out a plan with Mhow (Indore) as his base: both were employed in a combined operation, the one having Banda, the other Calpee, as the terminus.

In consequence of the Jubbulpore (Sir G. Whitlock's) column not being able to reach Saugor, Sir Hugh Rose, or the first brigade of his column, after the siege and capture of Ratghur, relieved Saugor, and then had to move on Gurrakoteh, a strong fort occupied by the Shaghur Rajah, with the mutineer sepoys, the 52nd N. I., and other sepoys of native infantry regiments. Having taken Garrakotta (*sic*), the brigade returned to Saugor, from whence, after awaiting the approach of General Whitlock's column from Jubbulpore, the brigade moved on the line to Jhansi, leaving a detachment of dragoons and infantry at Saugor for its protection until General Whitlock should arrive; the brigade had to force the pass of Muddenpore, where there was a very sharp affair; after this Banpore was occupied; Shaghur also by a detachment, and the valley of the Betwah cleared, but the rebels moved into Chandarie. The second brigade moved from Mhow (Indore) and reached Goonah, from whence it turned to Chandarie, which fort was gallantly stormed and captured on the 17th March; the first brigade being at hand at Tal Bate, in case of need as support.

After the capture of Chandarie, the two brigades joined the march before Jhansi was reached. The cavalry of the 1st Brigade, Her Majesty's 14th Dragoons, Bombay 2nd, and Nizam Horse were sent on to invest Jhansi. As the infantry were about to follow, an express arrived with a despatch to me from Lord Canning, desiring that I would move on Chirkaree, to relieve the Rajah, who was besieged by Tantia Topee and the Gwalior Contingent in his fort, General Whitlock's force not being within reach. There came also a despatch from the Commander-in-Chief, Lord Clyde, to Sir Hugh Rose, ordering him to proceed to Chirkaree, to save the loyal Rajah of that state.

Sir Hugh Rose considered the order of the Commander-in-Chief imparative; there was not anything left to my discretion in my letter from the Governor General; it was clear to me that it would be a great political mistake to draw off from Jhansi, which our cavalry were investing and our force within 14 miles; moreover, supposing the force moved on Chirkaree, it was not possible to march the 80 miles before the rebels had carried the fort, the Rajah having no provisions, and having lost the outworks, according to my intelligence, I therefore took on myself the responsibility of proceeding with our operations against Jhansi, trusting to that course as the most effective to draw Tantia Topee from Chirkaree, and so I wrote to the Governor General. Sir Hugh Rose, therefore, continued the attack, and Tantia Topee with his whole force came to raise the siege, and the battle of the Betwa occurred on the Thursday before Good Friday; in this very severe fight he lost all his guns but two, and fled to Calpee with the remnant of his force.

Had General Whitlock been up, he must have relieved Chirkaree, who was on his line of march to Banda, but when he arrived " the Peishwa Army ", under Tantia Topee, had not only left, but had been beaten and dispersed; those of the Nawab of Banda had fled to Banda, whilst his chief enemy had gone away to oppose Sir Hugh Rose. The town of Jhansi was stormed and taken on the Saturday, and the fort occupied on Easter Monday.

Up to this point, from the above facts, it must be admitted that the operations of Generals Rose and Whitlock were combined and one; that which one could not perform, the other was required to do, both were acting in concert on one plan, and the Commander-in-Chief of India had settled that plan.

I must here state I possessed the orders of the Governor General as to the disposal of the Nana Sahib, the Rao Sahib, Tantia Topee, the Nawab of Banda, the Rajahs of Banpore and Shaghur, and the Ranee of Jhansi, in the event of any of them falling into the hands of any of the troops. I had applied for specific orders to prevent delay, and the official correspondence is no doubt in the India Office. Major Ellis, my assistant, with Sir G. Whitlock, had his instructions from me, reported to me, and acted under my orders; he sent copies of his letters direct to the Governor General to save delay, owing to the post being interrupted.

In consequence of a large body of rebels having escaped from Koteh (which had fallen to General Roberts' force) and fled towards Calpee, passing between Jhansi and Gwalior, Sir H. Rose was compelled to remain at Jhansi until our rear was clear and safe, and Brigadier Smith, of General Roberts' force, occupied Goonah. This delay allowed Tantia

Topee to collect his force at Koonch, so as to oppose Sir H. Rose's advance on Calpee; this led to a severe action at Koonch, from whence the rebels fled to Calpee. The morning the force arrived in sight of Calpee, the Nawab of Banda with 2,000 horse, with many followers, entered Calpee, having been defeated at Banda by Sir G. Whitlock on the 19th April.

Whilst Calpee was invested, I wrote and requested the officer commanding on the left bank of the Jumna (I think Major Middleton) opposite to Humeerpore, to occupy Humeerpore, which I had heard had been evacuated, and thus to secure our communication with Banda.

Calpee was attacked and occupied on the Queen's birthday (May 24), the Rao Sahib, the Rance of Jhansi, and Nawab of Banda, then fled towards Gwalior, whither Tantia Topee had gone.

By the assistance rendered by the troops on the left bank of the Jumna, the battery there erected by order of Lord Clyde, the operations against Calpee were materially assisted. The sun was annihilating Sir Hugh Rose's Europeans, and it became a mere question of figures how many days would suffice for the force to cease. On two occasions, if not on three, Sir Hugh Rose's column had disposed of General Whitlock's enemy: first at Garrakottah after it had occupied Saugor; then at the Betwah, when Tantia Topee and the whole of the Peishwa army left General Whitlock's line, *en route* at Chirkaree to raise the siege of Jhansi, thereby leaving him an open way to Banda; then at Calpee where the Nawab of Banda and his force fled after their defeat at Banda, and never returned into Bundelcund; stripping Kerwee of the means of defence and of a force or a body of men to resist.

After the fall of Calpee, I applied to the Governor General to move up a part of General Whitlock's force to Calpee to enable me to move on Gwalior, which had suddenly fallen into Tantia's power, and was occupied by the Rao Sahib. Sir Hugh Rose had tendered his resignation before the crisis at Gwalior was known. I was again instructed to do everything to recover Gwalior, and I moved at once with as many troops as could be got together under the command of Brigadier, now Sir C. Steuart.

Sir Hugh Rose followed and caught us up, as did Sir R. Napier; from the 29th May until 19th June not an European had a night in bed. Gwalior fell on the 18th June; the Ranee of Jhansi was shot and burnt. The Nawab of Banda fled, and subsequently gave himself up to Sir Michael, by whom he was sent to me, and Tantia Topee was hunted down, caught, and hung by my orders, under the instructions above alluded to, without any reference for authority. Between the fall of Calpee and the capture of Gwalior, Sir George Whitlock moved into and occupied Kirwee from Banda, unopposed.

I do not add more, for fear this has been too long already, but I shall forward this through Lord Clyde to be laid before the Lords of the Treasury, as I trust the facts stated will go to show that the Madras column did not "effect its operations from its own base", unsupported or unsustained "by any other force or division;" and that General Whitlock did not act on his own plan, but in co-operation with one general plan, and that his movements were influenced by the plans and achievements of others.

To conclude, I am prepared to reply to any inquiries that may be made by any competent authority, but I shall not enter into any correspondence, or even keep a copy of this memorandum.

In justice to Brigadier Smith, and the portion of General Roberts' Rajpootana Force, I must add that they moved up and joined the force before Gwalior, rendering most important aid, and doing very gallant service, during the operations resulting in the capture of Gwalior, which was only 18 days in the possession of the rebels.

(Signed) R. N. C. HAMILTON,
Late Agent, Governor General in Central India.

AVONCLIFFE, STRATFORD-ON-AVON;
   20th March 1862.

APPENDIX F.

General Orders by the Right Hon'ble the Governor General of India.

Military Department,

Allahabad, the 30th June 1858.

No. 243 of 1858.—The Right Hon'ble the Governor General is pleased to direct the publication of the following letter, from the Assistant Adjutant General of the Army, No. 408 A., dated the 9th June 1858, enclosing a Despatch from Major-General Sir Hugh Rose, K.C.B., Commanding Central India Field Force, reporting the details of an action with the Rebel Army under Tantia Topee near Jhansie, during the siege of that fortress.

The Governor General cordially concurs with His Excellency the Commander-in-Chief, in the unqualified approbation he has expressed of the conduct of the Officers and Men concerned in this action, and in his admiration of the brilliant charge made by Captain Need, at the head of a Troop of Her Majesty's 14th Light Dragoons:—

No. 408 A.

From

THE ASST. ADJT. GENL OF THE ARMY,

To

THE SECRETARY TO THE GOVT. OF INDIA,

Military Department, with the Governor General.

Adjt. Genl.'s Office, Camp Poora, 9th June 1858.

SIR,

I am desired by the Commander-in-Chief to forward, for submission to the Right Hon'ble the Governor General, the enclosed copy of a Despatch, dated 30th April last (which has only now reached Head Quarters), from Major General Sir H. Rose, K.C.B., Commanding Central India Field Force, reporting the details of an action fought on the 1st idem with the Rebel Army under Tantia Topee on the River Betwa near Jhansie.

2. The operations of the troops engaged upon this occasion appear to His Excellency to have been conducted with the highest skill and

vigor; and the behaviour of all concerned merits his unqualified satisfaction.

3. Sir Colin Campbell cannot, however, refrain from drawing His Lordship's attention to the gallant and successful charge made by a Troop, Her Majesty's 14th Light Dragoons, under Captain Need; and, indeed, to the services of all those especially named by the Major-General and Brigadier Stuart.

I have the honor to be,

SIR,

Your most obedient Servant,

D. M. STEWART, MAJOR,

Asst. Adjt. Genl. of the Army.

FROM

MAJOR GENL. SIR HUGH ROSE, K.C.B.,

Comdg. Central India Field Force.

To

THE CHIEF OF THE STAFF.

Dated Camp Pooch, 30th April 1858.

SIR,

I have the honor to report to you, for the information of His Excellency the Commander-in-Chief, that on the 1st of April, the Force under my orders fought a general action with the so-called army of the Peishwa, which attempted to relieve Jhansie while I was besieging it, and gained a complete victory over it, pursuing him two miles beyond the River Betwa, taking 18 guns, of which one was an 18-pounder, one an 8-inch Mortar, two 12-Pounders, and two English 9-pounders, and killing upwards of 1,500 rebels.

For some time past, Sir Robert Hamilton had given me information that Tantia Toopee, a relative and the Agent of Nanna Sahib, had been collecting and organizing a large body of troops in the neighbourhood of Mhow and Nowgong in Bundlekund, which was called "the army of the Peishwa," and displayed the standard of that abolished authority.

After the fall of Chirkaree, this army was reinforced by the numerous rebel troops, sepoys from Calpee, and Bundeelas, who had besieged and taken it. Towards the end of last month, I received constantly reports that this Force, estimated at 20 or 25,000 men with 20 or 30 Guns, was advancing against me. On the 30th ultimo, Sir Robert Hamilton informed me, that its main body had arrived at Burra Saugor, about three miles from the Betwa, would cross that river during the night, and attack me next morning.

In the hope of forcing the Enemy to engage with the river in his rear, I left the park and heavy baggage of the 2nd Brigade, with which I was, with the 1st Brigade, and marched at 9 P.M., on the 30th ultimo, from Jhansie to the village of Bupoba, six miles from Jhansie, which commands the two fords at Rajpore and Kolwur, by which the Enemy coming from Burra Saugor, must cross the Betwa.

At Bupoba I received reports from the two outposts which I had sent to watch the fords, that they had seen and heard nothing of the Enemy. The next morning they made a similar report.

I came to the conclusion that the Enemy would not cross the river whilst I was so close to it, and that nothing would be more likely to encourage them to do so than a retrograde movement on my part, which they would construe into a retreat.

I returned, therefore, to camp, leaving the outposts to watch the fords. I was not mistaken: that same day the Enemy crossed the upper ford, the Rajpore, in great numbers, preceded by an advanced Guard of Vilaities, and took up, after sunset, a position in order of battle, opposite the rear of the camp of the 2nd Brigade.

At sunset, the Enemy lit an immense bonfire on a rising ground on this side of the Betwa, as a signal to Jhansie of their arrival: it was answered by salvos from all the batteries of the Fort and City, and shouts of joy from their defenders.

It was evident that the Enemy sought a battle with my force: this self-confidence was explained afterwards by prisoners, who stated that Tantia Topee had been informed by his spies that nearly all my force was scattered and engaged in the siege and investment, and that he could easily destroy the few who guarded the Camp.

The fact is that Jhansie had proved so strong, and the ground to be watched by Cavalry was so extensive, that my force had actually enough on its hands. But I relied on the spirit of British soldiers, which rises with difficulties, and resolved, whilst I fought a general action with the Enemy, not to relax either the siege or the investment.

APPENDIX F

The details in the margin show how weak I was when compared with the Enemy. My first Brigade had only a little more than 200 European Infantry, my second Brigade about the same. On the first news of the approach of the Enemy, I had sent Major Orr with a party of his Cavalry along the road to the Betwa to watch their movements.

Artillery.
16 Light Field Guns.
Non-Commd. Rank and File.
14th Dragoons . . 243
Hyderabad Cavalry . . 207
H. M.'s 86th Regt. . . 208
3rd European Regt. . . 226
24th Regt. N. I. . . 298
25th Regt. N. I. . . 0
Siege Guns . . . 3

I drew up my force across the road from the Betwa, half a mile from my Camp. On the right flank of my first line, the 2nd Brigade, I placed Lieutenant Clark's Hyderabad Horse, a Troop 14th Light Dragoons, and 4 Guns Horse Artillery in the centre, detachments of the 24th Regiment Bombay Native Infantry and 3rd Europeans, 3 heavy Guns and Detachments Hyderabad Infantry on the left flank, Captain Lightfoot's Battery and two Troops 14th Light Dragoons.

The second line was in contiguous columns at quarter distance; a weak Troop 14th Light Dragoons on the right, and Hyderabad Cavalry on the left flank; in the centre Her Majesty's 86th Regiment, Captain Woolcombe's Battery of 6, and Captain Ommaney's Battery of 9-Pounders, and Detachments 25th Regiment Bombay Native Infantry.

I threw out strong picquets and lines of videttes of the 14th Light Dragoons and Hyderabad Cavalry well to my front and flanks. The Vilaitie outposts called out during the night, that they were very numerous, that we were very few, that in the morning they would finish us, etc.

In consequence of the lateness of the Enemy's advance, and the distance of my first Brigade, my force was not in position till long after dark. The silent regularity with which it was effected, did credit to their discipline. Both ourselves and the Enemy slept on our arms, opposite each other.

A little after midnight, one of the Hyderabad Cavalry, left at the lower, the Kolwar, ford, came in as hard as he could, and reported that the Enemy were crossing in great numbers. I thought it probable that they would make this move, of which the object was to turn my left flank, and force their way along the Burra Gong road, through Major Scudamore's flying Camp into Jhansie. I had therefore ordered the outpost at the Kolwar ford to watch it with the utmost vigilance.

I detached Brigadier Stuart at once with the 1st Brigade along the Burra Gong road, to the village of the same name, about 8 miles from Jhansie, close to the river Betwa, from whence he could oppose and outflank the Enemy, who had crossed by the ford above Burra Gong.

The accompanying copy of a Report from Brigadier Stuart shows how well he executed my instructions, and how much he contributed to the success of the day. I beg to record my acknowledgments of the good service he did, and to second warmly his recommendation of the Officers and Men of his gallant Brigade.

The departure of the 1st Brigade left me without a second line; I was therefore obliged to withdraw the Detachments of the 24th Native Infantry from the 1st, and make a second line of them.

The best way with Indians for making up for numerical inferiority is a determined attack on their weak point. I had, therefore, intended to commence the attack at daylight, advance in line, pour into the Rebels the fire of all my Guns, and then turn and double up their left flank. But the Enemy, before daybreak, covered by a cloud of skirmishers, advanced against me.

My picquets and videttes retired steadily, closing to each flank, in order that I might open upon them the fire of my guns, and then turn his left flank from my right. Before my line was uncovered, the Enemy took ground to his right. I conformed, to prevent his outflanking my left, but very cautiously, lest he should draw me away too much to the left, and then fall on my right flank. This was probably his intention; for a body of Horse was seen towards my right. I halted and fronted; the Enemy did the same, and instantly opened a very heavy Artillery Musket and matchlock fire on my line from the whole of his front to which my Batteries answered steadily.

The Enemy had taken up an excellent position, a little in rear of a rising ground, which made it difficult to bring in effective fire on him. I ordered my front line of Infantry to lie down, the Troop of Horse Artillery to take ground diagonally to the right, and enfilade the Enemy's left flank. In this movement, a round shot broke the wheel of a Horse Artillery Gun.

Captain Lightfoot took up an advanced position to his left front, which made the fire of his Battery much more efficacious.

Whilst the Enemy were suffering from the fire of the Troop and Battery, I directed Captain Prettijohn, 14th Light Dragoons, to charge with his Troops, supported by Captain MacMahon, 14th Light Dragoons, the Enemy's right flank, and I charged myself their left with Captain Need's Troop, 14th Light Dragoons, supported by a strong Troop of Hyderabad Cavalry.

Both attacks succeeded, throwing the whole of the Enemy's first line into confusion, and forcing them to retire. I beg to do justice to Captain Need's Troop; they charged with steady gallantry the left, composed of the Rebels' best Troops, Vilaities and Sepoys, who throwing themselves back on a right, and resting the flanks of their new line, four or five deep, on two rocky knolls, received the charge with a heavy fire of musketry. We broke through this dense line, which flung itself amongst the rocks, and bringing our right shoulders forward, took the front line in reverse and routed it. I believe I may say that what Captain Need's Troop did on this occasion was equal to breaking a square of Infantry, and the result was most successful because the charge turned the Enemy's position and decided in a great measure the fate of the day.

I have the honour to recommend to His Excellency's favorable consideration Captain Need and his devoted Troop, and Lieutenant Leith* who saved Captain Need's life, for which I have ventured to recommend him for the Victoria Cross.

The Enemy's right gave way before the Squadron of the 14th Light Dragoons, under Captain Prettijohn, reached them; he pursued and cut up several of them.

In order to follow up rapidly this success, I ordered a general advance of the whole line, when the retreat of the Rebels became a rout.

I moved forward the whole of the Artillery and Cavalry in pursuit, the Horse Artillery following the road to the Betwa, from which it had enfiladed the Enemy's position, the field Battery going across country.

We soon came up with 6 Guns, and their ammunition waggons, which we left for the Infantry, and passed on to the main body of the Rebels, broken into knots, and scattered in every direction.

Serious combats occurred between the pursuing Cavalry and the fugitives, who, singly, or standing back to back, always took up, like

---

* Lieutenant James Leith, of the 14th Light Dragoons, received the Victoria Cross, on the 24th December 1858, for "conspicuous bravery at Betwah, on the 1st of April 1858, in having charged alone and rescued Captain Need of the same regiment, when surrounded by a large number of rebel infantry." *The Victoria Cross*, pp. 35 and 66.

most Indians, the best position the ground admitted, and fought with the desperation which I have described on other occasions. One body wedged themselves so dexterously into the banks of a nullah, that neither Musketry nor Artillery fire would destroy them. Lieutenant Armstrong, of the 3rd Bombay European Regiment, coming up with a few skirmishers dashed at them, and bayonetted them all, but not without some loss. This Officer is Post Master of the Force, but his zeal always leads him into action, where he does good service on those occasions which require bold decision.

The pursuit had now penetrated, and cleared away the first line. A cloud of dust about a mile-and-a-half to our right, pointed out the line of retreat of another large body, the second line of the Rebels, which, by a singular arrangement of the Rebel General, Tantia Topee, must have been three miles in rear of his first line.

The whole Force again went in immediate pursuit, and came up with the skirmishers in rocky and difficult ground, covering the retreat of the 2nd line: driven in, they closed to their right, and uncovered the main body which cannonaded the Troops in pursuit with an 18-Pounder and 8-inch Mortar and other Guns. Colonel Turnbull answered with a few rounds, which told. Captain Lightfoot who had come up, thinking that he could bring his Guns to ground, from which he could enfilade the Enemy's left, I directed him to join the Hyderabad Cavalry, and a Troop of the 14th Light Dragoons, whom I had sent to turn their left flank and take, if possible, their Guns.

The Enemy did not wait for this attack, but retired with precipitation by the high road to the Rajpore ford.

Neither the Jungle which was set on fire to stop the pursuit, nor difficult ground, could check the ardour of the pursuing Troops, who saw within their reach the great prize, the Enemy's heavy Artillery. Once on the road, Guns and Cavalry galloped without a check, till they came within gunshot of the village of Rajpore, where the Enemy made their last and third stand.

The Troop and Battery, advantageously placed on two rising grounds crossed their fire on the Enemy, who rapidly left this, but kept up a heavy fire of musketry, and with a 12-Pounder from the opposite bank of the river; the 12-Pounder hit by a round shot, retired disabled.

I ordered two Troops of the 14th Light Dragoons, and Hyderabad Cavalry, across the Betwa.

On going down the road to the river, we saw the stream crowded with the Enemy's Artillery, Ordnance Park, and quantities of Stores, the 18-Pounder and the 8-inch Mortar, drawn by two elephants, ammunition waggons, and carts full of ammunition, of the Gwalior Contingent.

The Enemy kept up a heavy fire on us as we crossed the ford, and ascended the steep road leading up the opposite bank. The 14th Light Dragoons and Hyderabad Cavalry gallantly surmounted all opposition, and sabred the Rebels who still held their ground.

I detached parties in pursuit of the numerous fugitives who took across country; another body followed the road, and captured, a mile and-a-half from the Betwa, the disabled 12-Pounder, being the 18th and last Gun of the Rebel Army. Two standards were also captured.

The Infantry, who had followed in skirmishing order to prevent the escape of any of the Enemy, gave proof of their zeal, by the rapidity with which they marched up to the front.

Horses and Men being completely exhausted by incessant marching and fighting during the last forty-eight hours, and being now nine miles from Jhansie, I marched the troops back to Camp.

I beg leave to bring to the favourable notice of the Commander-in-Chief the conduct of the Force under my Command, which, without relaxing, in the least, the arduous siege and investment of a very strong fort and fortified city, garrisoned by 10,000 desperate men, fought, with the few numbers left in Camp, a grand action with a relieving Army; beat and pursued them nine miles, killing 1,500 of them, and taking from them all their Artillery, Stores, and Ammunition.

The Officers whom circumstances called prominently into action, and who, profiting by the opportunity, did valuable service, were,—Brigadier Stuart, Commanding 1st Brigade, and the Officers whom he mentions; Lieutenant-Colonel Turnbull, Bombay Horse Artillery; Captain Lightfoot, Bombay Artillery; Captain Need, 14th Light Dragoons; Lieutenant Leith, 14th Light Dragoons; Lieutenant Armstrong, 3rd Bombay European Regiment; and Lieutenant Prendergast, Madras Sappers and Miners, who, on various occasions, under my eye, has distinguished himself by his merit and gallantry, as devoted as they were unostentatious.

Sergeant Gardener, 14th Light Dragoons, attacked and killed a Cavalry Soldier, as well as two armed men on foot; his gallant conduct at Dhar had been previously honorably mentioned. The conduct of the men of the 14th Light Dragoons, was so uniformly good, that their

Commanding Officer finds it difficult to bring any particular case of good conduct to my notice.

I am much indebted for their zeal and assistance to me during the action; to Major Orr, Commanding Hyderabad Contingent Field Force; Captain Prettijohn, Commanding 14th Light Dragoons; Captain Hare, Commanding Regiment, Hyderabad Force; and Lieutenant Haggard, Commissary of Ordnance, in Command of the Siege Train; also to my Staff, Captain MacDonald, Assistant Quarter Master General; Captain Wood, Assistant Adjutant General; Captain Rose, my Aide-de-Camp; and Lieutenant Lyster, 72nd Bengal Native Infantry, my Interpreter.

I have, etc.,
(Signed) HUGH ROSE, *Major-Genl.*,
Comdg. Central India Field Force.

No. 93,

From—BRIGADIER C. S. STUART, *Comdg. 1st Brigade,*
Central India Field Force,
To—The ASSISTANT ADJUTANT GENERAL,
Central India Field Force.
Dated Camp Jhansie, 6th April 1858.

SIR,

For the information of the Major-General Commanding Central India Field Force, I have the honor to report the proceedings of the 1st Brigade, Central India Field Force, strength as per margin, on the morning of the 1st April last.

Left Wing, Her Majesty's 14th Light Dragoons, 40 Rank and File, under command of Lieutenant Giles.

Two Troops, Hyderabad Cavalry; one of 1st Regiment, one of 3rd Regiment, both commanded by Lieutenant Johnstone, 107 Sabres.

Two Guns, Captain Ommaney's Battery.

Captain Woolcombe's Battery.

Her Majesty's 86th Regiment, under Command of Lieutenant-Colonel Lowth, 208 Rank and File.

25th Regiment Native Infantry, under Major Robertson.

2. In compliance with the instruction conveyed to me by the Major-General, I marched my Brigade from its position, as support to the 2nd Brigade, about one o'clock A. M. on the 1st instant, and proceeded by the Calpee road to another ford of the Betwa river, by which the Rebels were expected to pass; the village of Boregaum, about half a mile from the ford in question, was reached about daybreak, when I heard heavy firing from the direction of the 2nd

Brigade; accordingly I halted the column, and pushed on the Cavalry to the ford, with orders to reconnoitre and return with all despatch; in a very short time I received information that none of the Enemy were to be seen or heard of in the vicinity of the river, so I counter-marched my force, and proceeded to rejoin the 2nd Brigade as quickly as possible. After about an hour's march some fugitive Rebels were observed on our left front. I sent Detachment, Her Majesty's 14th Light Dragoons, in pursuit, and many of them were cut up. The Brigade was now approaching the village of Kooshabore, and I found that a large body of the Enemy, upwards of two thousand in number, and consisting of Artillery, Cavalry, and Infantry, were prepared to oppose our progress, having placed some Guns in position in and about the village. I immediately threw all my infantry into skirmishing order, placing my Cavalry on either flank and moving my Guns on the main road until within about 600 yards of the Enemy's position; fire was then opened by the Artillery with most excellent effect; the Enemy were soon shaken, and the moment our Guns ceased firing, the skirmishers of Her Majesty's 86th Regiment, and 25th Regiment, Native Infantry, dashed forward, carried the village at the point of the bayonet, capturing all the Enemy's Artillery consisting of six pieces, together with supply of ammunition, etc. The line then steadily advanced, driving the Enemy over some difficult ground in rear of the village, until a second village was reached on the outskirts of which the Enemy made another stand. From this the men of Her Majesty's 86th Regiment immediately dislodged them, and they retired in good order, leaving a strong Rear Guard to cover their retreat, which was effected in so compact a manner, that though the small body of Her Majesty's 14th Light Dragoons, and the Squadron of the Cavalry Hyderabad Contingent, charged them as opportunity offered, they could do little more than cut up stragglers. The ground over which the Enemy were now passing was, I regret to say, of such a nature, that I could only with the greatest difficulty bring up my Artillery, otherwise their loss would have been more severe; about 250 of their number were, I compute, killed. In addition to their guns and ammunition, two elephants and some camels were captured. Had not the Troop of my Brigade been in such an exhausted state from the exertions of the previous thirty-six hours, during which, as the Major-General is aware, they were under arms, or marching with but little intermission, I should have continued the pursuit; I felt, however, that as the Enemy were rapidly moving off from the vicinity of Jhansie, nothing further could be done, so returned to camp.

3. I have now, in conclusion, the pleasure of placing on record how much I was indebted on the occasion to the Officers of my Staff, to Commanding Officers of Regiments, and to all Officers and Men under their Command; all ranks, both European and Native, were called upon to exert themselves to the utmost, and they responded to the call most nobly. Lieutenant and Adjutant Cochrane, Her Majesty's 86th Regiment, behaved in the most gallant manner during this engagement; he was ever to the front, and had three horses shot under him. I beg to support the recommendation of Lieutenant-Colonel Lowth, Her Majesty's 86th Regiment, that some mark of distinction may be awarded to this deserving Officer. Lieutenant Mills, 25th Regiment, Native Infantry, also did good service in surrounding and destroying, with a small number of his men, some Rebels who had taken up a difficult position amongst rocks. The conduct of Ressaidar Allahodeen Khan, of the 1st, and Ressaidar Secunder Ali Beg, of the 3rd Cavalry, Hyderabad Contingent, was also marked by great bravery; the latter Officer, I regret to say, has received two very severe and dangerous wounds.

4. I have already transmitted a Casualty Roll of the Men who suffered in this engagement, and I beg to report that all the guns and ammunition taken from the Enemy have been made over to the Commissary of Ordnance, Central India Field Force.

I have, etc.,

(Signed) C. S. STUART, *Brigr.,*
Comdg. 1st Brigade, C. I. F. F.

APPENDIX F   cv

Return of Ordnance captured by the Force under Command of Major-General Sir Hugh Rose, K.C.B., on the 1st April 1858, in an engagement with the Rebels on the Betwa.

No.	Nature of Ordnance.	Register No.	Cast. When.	Cast. Where.	Cast. By whom.	Length. Feet.	Length. Inches.	Weight. Cwt.	Weight. Qrs.	Weight. lbs.	Calibre.	Remarks.
1	Iron Gun	114	...	Low Moor	G. Hutchinson	9	0	42	2	9	18-Pr.	⎫ Europe manufacture, as also their carriages.
2	Brass Gun	80	1829	Fort William	S. Timbrell	5	8	8	3	22	9 ,,	⎬
3	,,	42	1828	,,	,,	5	8	8	3	19	9 ,,	⎭
4	Iron Gun	...	...	...	...	6	0	7	0	0	3 ,,	
5	,,	...	...	...	...	2	6¼	0	2	0	⅜-inch	
6	Brass Howitzer	...	...	...	...	2	4	9	2	0	9-inch	
7	Brass Gun	...	...	...	...	2	11	5	0	0	12-Pr.	⎫
8	,,	...	...	...	...	2	13	7	2	0	9 ,,	⎪
9	,,	...	...	...	...	4	4¼	9	1	0	9 ,,	⎪ Country manufacture,
10	,,	...	...	...	...	3	5¼	6	2	0	6 ,,	⎬ as also their carriages and limbers.
11	,,	...	...	...	...	5	0	5	0	0	4 ,,	⎪
12	,,	...	...	...	...	5	10	7	2	0	3 ,,	⎪
13	,,	...	...	...	...	3	9	4	0	0	3 ,,	⎭
14	,,	...	...	...	...	4	7½	6	0	0	3 ,,	
15	,,	...	...	...	...	3	6	5	0	0	2 ,,	
16	,,	...	...	...	...	2	9½	3	0	0	1 ,,	
17	,,	...	...	...	...	2	10½	3	0	0	1 ,,	
18	,,	...	...	...	...	3	10	2	2	0	1 ,,	

(Signed) THOS. J. HAGGARD, *Lieutenant,*
Commissary of Ordnance,
Central India Field Force.

APPENDIX F

Return of Ordnance Stores captured by the Force under Command of Major-General Sir Hugh Rose, K.C.B., on the 1st April 1858, in an engagement with the Rebels on the Betwa.

No.	Names of Stores.	Quantity.	Remarks.
1	Carriages, Ammn., with Limber, 9-Pounder, R. P.	2	
2	Cartouches, leather, Field Ordnance	16	
3	Fuzes, filled, Shrapnel, 5½-inch	79	
4	,, ,, common, 8-inch	55	
5	Portfires	42	
6	Shell, Shrapnel fd. and fixed, 24-Pounder	20	
7	,, ,, ,, 12 ,,	8	English pattern and make.
8	,, ,, ,, 8-inch	4	
9	Shells, common, loose, 8 ,,	75	
10	Shot, case gun, 18-Pounder	63	
11	,, ,, ,, 9 ,,	29	
12	,, ,, Howitzer, 8-inch	25	
13	,, solid, loose, 18-Pounder	130	
14	,, ,, ,, 9 ,,	274	
15	Powder, Native manufacture, Hs.	2,800	
16	Shot of Native ,,	...	
17	Shot, case and Grape	112	Country pattern and make.
18	Shot, solid country, of sizes	1,000	
19	Tumbrils, Ammunition	3	

(Signed) THOS. J. HAGGARD, *Lieutenant,*
Commissary of Ordnance,
Central India Field Force.

APPENDIX F cvii

Return of Killed and Wounded of the Central India Field Force, during the engagement with the Enemy, on the 1st April 1858, on the Betwa.

Corps.	Rank.	Names.	Date.	REMARKS.
		1st Brigade.		
H. M.'s 14th Light Dragoons.	Regt. Sergt. Major	Thomas Clark		Slightly wounded.
	Sergeant	John Myers		Ditto.
	Private	Thomas Ransem		Killed.
	Ditto	Walter Roberts		Severely wounded.
	Ditto	Cornelius Gray		Ditto.
	Ditto	—— Leonard		Slightly wounded.
3rd Cavalry Hyderabad Contingent.	Lieut. Commanding	Henry Clark		Severely ,,
	Ressaidar	See Kundar Ali Beg.		Dangerously ,,
	Duffadar	Mir Muksood Ali		Killed.
	Silladar	Ashum Ali Khan		Ditto.
	Bargeer	Mukun Khan		Dangerously wounded.
	Ditto	Mir Imdad Ali		Severely ,,
H. M.s' 86th Regiment.	Sergeant	William Cairns	1st April	Dangerously ,,
	Private	Thomas Vahay		Severely ,,
25th Regiment, Bombay N. I.	Private	Bhannoo Patkur		Killed.
	Ditto	Goolab Minia		Ditto.
	Ditto	Burmadin Awasty		Wounded mortally (since dead).
	Ditto	Ramchunder Manay		Severely wounded.
	Ditto	Gunpatrao Sindah		Slightly ,,
		2nd Brigade.		
1st Troop, Horse Arty.	Lieutenant-Colonel	S. Turnbull		Contusion of right shoulder caused by musket ball.
	Qr. Mr. Sergeant	Richard Hiles		Dangerously wounded.
	Sergeant	William Bright		Mortally wounded (since dead).
	Gunner	James Kelly		Contusion of head and leg.
	Ditto	Edward Boston		Musket shot in right hand.
2nd Company, Reserve Artillery.	Captain	J. G. Lightfoot		Sword cut in right hand.

Appendix F

Return of Killed and Wounded of the Central India Field Force, during the engagement with the Enemy, on the 1st April 1858, on the Betwa—continued.

Corps.	Rank.	Names.	Date.	Remarks.
		2nd Brigade—contd.		
	Lance Sergeant	William Crosby		⎫
	Private	Robert Barker		⎬ Killed in action.
	Ditto	John Leigh		⎪
	Ditto	William Watkin		⎭
	Sergeant	Thomas Bowen		Slightly.
	Ditto	William Parkins		Severely.
	Private	Joseph Williams		Ditto.
	Ditto	James Elton		Slightly.
	Ditto	James Parton		Ditto.
	Ditto	George Robinson		Ditto.
	Ditto	John Waite		Dangerously.
H. M.'s 14th Light Dragoons.	Ditto	Elijah Clegg	1st April.	Severely.
	Ditto	Francis Jones		Ditto.
	Ditto	Samuel Smith		Slightly.
	Ditto	John Ridler		Severely.
	Ditto	Abraham Smith		Slightly.
	Ditto	John Byott		Dangerously.
	Ditto	Richard Baker		Ditto.
	Ditto	Charles Smith		Slightly.
	Ditto	William Pearce		Ditto.
	Ditto	William Best		Ditto.
	Ditto	John Price		Severely.
	Ditto	A. Williams		Slightly.
	Corporal	Michael Hennessy		Right leg shattered by round shot.
3rd Bombay European Regiment.	Ditto	William Amos		⎫ Killed in action.
	Private	James Watson		⎭
	Ditto	Patrick Mehan		Dangerously.
	Sergeant	James Laine		Slightly.

Appendix F

Return of Killed and Wounded of the Central India Field Force, during the engagement with the Enemy, on the 1st April 1858, on the Betwa—concluded.

Corps.	Rank.	Names.	Date.	Remarks.
		2nd Brigade—contd.		
4th Regiment, Bombay N. I.	Private	Awswairey		Killed by round shot.
	Ditto	Ram Sing		Wounded in right hand by round shot.
	Ditto	Peer Buccus		
	Ditto	Lall Sing		
	Ditto	Balgoving Now		
	Ditto	Luxumon Narwakur.		Severely burnt by explosion of Tumbril.
	Ditto	Kundoo Jadow		
	Ditto	Kalka Pursad		
	Ditto	Hirnac Essuar		
1st Cavalry, Hyderabad Contingent.	Trooper	Abdool Rymon Khan.		Slightly wounded.
	Ditto	Ali Khan		Ditto.
	Ditto	Sheik Mahomed Yacoob.	1st April.	Killed.
	Ditto	Kamta Sing		Severely wounded
	Ditto	Ussud Ali Khan		Slightly.
4th Cavalry, Hyderabad Contingent.	Jemadar	Syud Noor Ali		Ditto.
	Trooper	Fyze Oola Khan		Ditto.
	Ditto	Mahomed Ibrahim Khan.		Killed.
	Ditto	Shab Baz Khan		Ditto.
Left Wing, 3rd Infantry.	Sepoy	Lutchmun		Dangerously burnt
	Bheestie	Sheik Banbun		Slightly
	Sepoy	Ramdeen		Ditto.
	Ditto	Kahdeedeen		Slightly wounded.
5th Infantry, Hyderabad Contingent.	Lance Naick	Gunnace Singh		Ditto.
	Sepoy	Rugoonath Sing		Dangerously burnt (since dead).
	Bheestie	Shah Ahmed		Severely burnt.
	Ditto	Sheik Boodun		Ditto.
	Ditto	Raj Ahmed		Severely.
	Ditto	Sheik Yacoob		Slightly wounded.

APPENDIX F

ABSTRACT.

Corps.	Killed.	Wounded.	Remarks.
Her Majesty's 14th Light Dragoons.	1	5	} 1st Brigade.
3rd Cavalry, Hyderabad Contingent	2	4	
25th Regiment, Bombay Native Infantry.	2	*3	1 since dead
1st Troop, Horse Artillery	0	*5	* Ditto
Her Majesty's 14th Light Dragoons	4	19	} 2nd Brigade.
2nd Company, Reserve Artillery	0	1	
3rd Bombay European Regiment	2	*3	*1 since dead
Her Majesty's 86th Regiment	0	2	1st Brigade.
24th Regiment, Bombay Native Infantry.	1	8	
1st Cavalry, Hyderabad Contingent	1	4	
4th ,, ,, ,,	2	2	} 2nd Brigade.
3rd Infantry, ,, ,,	0	4	
5th ,, ,, ,,	0	6	*1 since dead
Total	15	66	

Return of Horses Killed and Wounded during the Action, on the 1st April 1858.

Corps.	Killed.	Wounded.	Remarks.
1st Troop, Horse Artillery	2	0	
Her Majesty's 14th Light Dragoons.	11	16	
Total	13	16	

(Signed) H. H. A. WOOD, *Captain,*
Asst. Adjt. Genl., Central India Field Force.

(True copies.)
D. M. STEWART, *Major,*
Assistant Adjutant General of the Army.

APPENDIX F

Allahabad, the 1st July 1858.

No. 244 of 1858.—The Right Hon'ble the Governor General is pleased to publish the following despatch from Major-General Sir Hugh Rose, K.C.B., Commanding Central India Field Force, bringing to notice the names of certain Officers inadvertently omitted in his Despatch, published in G. O. G. G. No. 174, dated 31st May last, detailing the operations against, and the capture of, Fort and Town of Jhansie :—

FROM
    MAJOR-GENL. SIR HUGH ROSE, K.C.B.,
        Comdg. Central India Field Force,

To
    THE CHIEF OF THE STAFF.

Dated Camp Soopowlie, 14th June 1858.

SIR,

In my Despatch, detailing the operations against, and the capture of, the Fort and Town of Jhansie, the names of several Officers of the Force under my Command were inadvertently omitted, whose services I should have acknowledged; I have now the honor to request you to bring them to the notice of His Excellency the Commander-in-Chief.

The name of Captain Abbott, Commanding 3rd Hyderabad Cavalry, although mentioned more than once in the Despatch, is omitted in the list of Officers in Command of Corps. Captain Abbott, at the commencement of operations, was placed by me in Command of the whole of the Cavalry of the Hyderabad Contingent, engaged in the investment of the Fort and Town.

The name of Captain Montriou, Commanding 24th Regiment, Bombay Native Infantry, was also omitted in the same list.

Captain Scott, Military Pay Master, Captain Ashburner, Deputy Judge Advocate General, and Captain Gordon, Assistant Commissary General to the Force, have each, in their several Departments, performed their duties to my entire satisfaction. To the two first I have been indebted more than once for assistance volunteered in the Field.

I have, etc.,
(Signed)   HUGH ROSE, *Major-Genl.,*
    Comdg. Central India Field Force.

Appendix F

(True copy.)

Forwarded, by direction of His Excellency the Commander-in-Chief, to the Secretary to the Government of India, Military Department, for submission to the Right Hon'ble the Governor General.

(Signed) W. MAYHEW, *Lieut.-Col.,*
Adjutant General of the Army.

Head Quarters;
Allahabad, 28th June 1858.

APPENDIX G.

No. 160 of 1859.

From

    THE MAJOR-GENERAL,
        Commanding Northern Division of the Army,

To

    THE CHIEF OF THE STAFF,
        Army Head-Quarters, Allahabad.

        Head-Quarters, Northern Division of the Army,
        Dated Camp Ahmedabad, 23rd April 1859.

SIR,

In obedience to the orders of His Excellency the Commander-in-Chief conveyed to me in a letter from the Adjutant-General of this Army, No. 2344, of the 18th ultimo, copy of which is hereto attached, I have the honour to forward the accompanying letter No. 27, of the 15th January last, and its accompaniments, for the favourable notice of the Right Honourable the Commander-in-Chief in India.

2. The delay in forwarding Brigadier Smith's Report, which I much regret, has been caused by its having only now been received back from Army Head-Quarters, where in the first instance it was forwarded.

        I have, etc.,

        (Signed) H. S. ROBERTS, *Major-General,*
        Commanding Northern Division of the Army.

No. 27 of 1859.

From

    BRIGADIER M. W. SMITH,
        Commanding Brigade, P. F. F.,

To

    THE ASSISTANT ADJUTANT-GENERAL,
        Rajpootana Field Force.

        Dated Camp Omra, 15th January 1859.

SIR,

I have the honour to forward duplicate of latter portion of copy of my Report of operations before Gwalior on 17th of June 1868, the original of which appears to have mis-carried and only a copy of the first part of my Report seems to have reached the Major-General, then in Command of the Rajpootana Field Force, of which this Brigade formed a detached portion.

I was not aware of the mis-carriage of this latter portion of my Report, until I saw the publication of the first portion, or should have earlier forwarded a duplicate, as the services of a portion of this Brigade are mentioned in this latter portion of my Report, which I am most anxious to bring to the notice of the Major-General.

I also take this opportunity of supplying a few omissions, which I regret to say occurred in my first Report.

I have, etc.,
(Signed) M. W. SMITH, *Brigadier*,
Commanding Brigade, P. F. F.

No. 44 of 1858.

From

BRIGADIER M. W. SMITH,
Commanding Brigade, Malwa Division.

To

THE ADJUTANT-GENERAL,
Poona Division, Poona.

Dated Camp Sepree, 25th July 1858.

SIR,

In accordance with the wishes of Major-General Sir Hugh Rose, K.C.B., conveyed to me in your note dated Pachesi, 11th July, that I should furnish an official Statement of all the circumstances of the charge made by a Squadron of the 8th Hussars on the 17th of June, and evidence should be officially recorded.

I have the honour to state that on the afternoon of the 17th June, the Enemy having been driven from the heights, we advanced through the Pass which runs by the large canal or nullah in the direction of Gwalior; some two or three hundred of the Enemy's Cavalry being formed in front of Gwalior, I advanced with a Squadron of the 8th Hussars, under Captain Heneage, and a Division of Guns under Lieutenant Le Cocq, Bombay Artillery, into the open ground beyond the Pass, leaving orders that a Company of the 10th Regiment, Native Infantry, and a Division of Guns under an escort of Gunners, should secure the mouth of the Pass, and a Squadron of the 1st Bombay Lancers should move up in the open ground in support.

The Squadron of the 8th Hussars advanced out of the Pass in file, and formed line at a gallop after advancing about three hundred yards; I ordered the Squadron to charge. The Squadron then charged, broke the Enemy, and pursuing them closely entered their own Camp along with them. The Camp was soon cleared and the 8th followed the fugitives, now increased by large numbers of panic-stricken Infantry, from the Camp into the ground beyond, and never stopped until all who remained had taken shelter in the outskirts of the town itself.

In so doing the 8th took five Guns, cutting down the Gunners. The Ranee of Jhansi also lost her life in the *mêlée*; all this took place under a heavy fire from the Guns of the Fort, and from several Field Guns in position round the town, and from which was opened a converging fire upon the Squadron.

During the charge, Colonel Raines, of Her Majesty's 95th Regiment, brought up a portion of his Regiment and took up a position on the left flank of Lieutenant Le Cocq's Division of Guns, I having sent him an order to that effect by Cornet Goldsworthy, 8th Hussars.

I shall next record the statement of Captain Heneage who commanded the Squadron, and also some evidences collected by him as to further particulars and details.

Statement and evidences collected by Captain Heneage.

Captain Heneage's Squadron of 8th Hussars was ordered by Brigadier Smith to attack some 2 or 300 of the Enemy's Cavalry who were threatening our Guns. They advanced out of the Pass in file and formed line at a gallop. After advancing some 300 yards they were ordered to charge, which they did, and were upon the Enemy in a moment, many of whom were cut down and the rest fled towards the town; the ground here being very rough and intersected with small nullahs, about one-third of the Squadron was obliged to diverge to the right under Lieutenant Harding, the remainder under Captain Heneage, with Captain Poore and Lieutenant Reiley, going a little to the left and continuing the attack, came shortly into the midst of the Enemy's camp, where they took

3 Guns, cutting down the Gunners and completely clearing the Camp of the Enemy's Troops under a continuous fire from the Guns in the Fort, and small Field Guns on the right and left. After passing through the Camp and crossing the road from Gwalior to Moorar, the Squadron came upon a large force of the Enemy's Cavalry and Infantry in a disorganized mass who were trying to escape from the Camp into the Fort. Many of them made a stand, but the 8th slackened their pace and dashing into the midst of them, cut them down by scores, the Ranee of Jhansi being amongst the slain; two Guns were taken here.

The whole of the ground over which the charge had been made being now completely cleared of the enemy, Captain Heneage withdrew his Squadron at an easy pace, and was shortly joined by the Detachment under Lieutenant Harding, which had charged through the right of the Camp, cutting down many of the Enemy's Gunners and Infantry, and had taken four Guns. Lieutenant Harding was shot at by a dismounted Sowar, who missed him, but the shot struck his charger in the eye and completely destroyed it. He was attacked at the same time by two of the Enemy's Infantry, whom he cut down and killed.

Captain Heneage then halted and re-formed his Squadron in front of the supports of Artillery, Cavalry, and Infantry, which had meanwhile come up, and was then ordered by Brigadier Smith to form his men in single rank in order to show a larger front.

The Squadron of the 8th being then formed in single rank on the right flank of Artillery and Infantry, the Squadron of Lancers in second line, he again advanced in order to secure the enemy's Guns; after that Captain Heneage was obliged to relinquish the Command of the Squadron, in consequence of the heat of the sun and great exhaustion. Captain Poore assumed the Command and remained with the Squadron until the Guns were brought away.

Colonel Hicks of the Bombay Artillery charged with the Squadron through the Camp; Lieutenant Reiley, upon the return of the Squadron from the charge, was obliged to dismount from his horse and died almost immediately from the effects of the sun and exhaustion. Assistant Surgeon Sheilock charged with the Squadron and was wounded by a musket ball in the shoulder; he was ready and active in affording his assistance when required.

Cornet Goldsworthy was on my left and in front of the Squadron when preparing to charge, and was about to charge with them, when I, in consequence of the very great necessity of having support up quick, ordered him to go back and bring up the Horse Artillery and Infantry to a spot which I had pointed out to him, which he did; this officer gave me much assistance both on the 17th and 19th in carrying my orders and other matters.

Several of the Enemy's Guns remained in our possession after the charge, but from the want of horses and the exhaustion of the men, only two could be got away, and it was only through the exertion and skill of Lieutenant Le Cocq and the men of his Division (the right Division of the 3rd Troop under the personal superintendence of Lieutenant-Colonel Blake) that this could be effected.

One of the Enemy's Gun had a limber and a pair of wheel horses, the broken harness was lashed up in the best way circumstances would admit of, and a leading pair of our own horses hooked in the Gun was sent to the rear, the wheel horses were got to move with great difficulty, being completely done up and one severely wounded.

The other Gun had no limber, but Colonel Blake having taken back one of his own Guns to the entrance of the Pass, left the Gun within it, and sending back the limber, the enemy's was hooked on it and brought to the entrance of the Pass, when our Gun was lashed to the muzzle and thus drawn off.

These operations were conducted with great coolness and steadiness under four cross-fires from the Fort and Guns in different directions on the place.

This being effected, and seeing the enemy collecting upon our flanks and having too small a force at my disposal to warrant my advancing further or to enable me to hold my position if I had done so, we retired across the Plain by alternate Squadrons, and re-entering the Pass took up a position for the night, as stated in my former Report of the operations during the seventeenth.

I have, etc.,
(Signed) M. W. SMITH, *Brigadier*,
Commanding Brigade M. D.

(True copy.)
(Signed) W. L. GOLDSWORTHY, *Cornet*,
Acting Brigade Major, R. F. B.

APPENDIX G

From

    Lieutenant-Colonel T. R. Raines,
        Her Majesty's 95th Regiment,

To

    Brigadier M. W. Smith,
        Commanding Brigade M. D.
        Dated Camp Godowlie, 12th November 1858.

Sir,

With reference to my Report to you on the taking of Gwalior on the 19th June last, I beg to correct an impression I was then under that the Guns alluded to in the 5th paragraph were found by the 10th Native Infantry *abandoned*, the words should have been "captured from the Enemy by the 10th Native Infantry," which I was not cognizant of when I addressed you on the proceedings of that day.

I am informed by Lieutenant Sexton, to whose charge I gave one of the captured Guns, which was afterwards turned on the Rebels and alluded to in the 3rd paragraph of the same Report, that he received great assistance from Lieutenant Read, 10th Native Infantry, who made some good practice in pointing and firing the said Gun. I therefore beg to bring Lieutenant Read's name to your favourable notice.

        I have, etc.,
        (Signed) T. R. RAINES, *Lieutenant-Colonel,*
        Her Majesty's 95th Regiment.

While the Infantry skirmishers were feeling their way through the Pass leading to Gwalior, their progress was checked for a time by the fire of two or three Guns, which the enemy had brought into the Pass. Lieutenant-Colonel Blake therefore proposed taking a Division of his Guns on to the heights on our right, which was accordingly done and the result was most successful; by firing at low elevation round shot and shrapnel were dropped on the Enemy's Guns near, obliging them to retire precipitately to another position, and by thus advancing and coming into action on every occasion of their making a stand they were at length fairly driven out of the Pass, which was thus made clear for the advance of our force.

Appendix G

Extract from letter from Colonel Blake, Commanding 3rd Troop, Horse Artillery, dated 12th November 1858.

"In that part of your Report of bringing away the two captured Guns, you mention that it was done "under four cross-fires." I think it would be well to mention the number of from 16 to 18 Guns."

Colonel De Salis wishes to mention the zeal and intelligence evinced by Major Chetwode, when in command of a detached portion of the 8th Hussars, on the 17th June.

Lieutenant Jenkins, 8th Hussars, was on one occasion employed by me in carrying orders to bring up supports which he executed to my satisfaction.

(Signed) M. W. SMITH, *Brigadier,*
Commanding Brigade M. D.

INDEX

(*N.B.—Each sub-reference is terminated by a semi-colon or a period. A page-number standing alone indicates a distinct mention of the main subject. Roman numerals refer to the Appendixes.*)

A

Abbot, Maj. (Beng. Inf.)
Mtd. in desp.—p. 34.

Abbott, Capt. (Hyderabad Contingent Cavalry.)
Clears Pass of Mudinpore—p. 23.
Pursues rebels, *ib.*
Mtd. in desp.—pp. 24, 25.
Cmdg. Flying Camp before Jhansi—p. 49.
Recommends officers for promotion—p. 50.
Mtd. in desp. (Jhansi)—p. 52.
Wd. at Jhansi—p. 61.
Captures gun (Koonch)—p. 69.
Mtd. in desp.—p. 73.
At Calpee—p. 96.
In pursuit of rebels—p. 116.
Captures gun—p. 117.
Mtd. in desp. (Calpee)—p. 118.
Mtd. in desp. (May 22, 1858)—p. 122.
Reconnoitres Morar—p. 135.
At Morar—p. 136.
His horse kld.—p. 137.
Turns retreating rebels—p. 138.
At Jowra-Alipore—p. 164.
Mtd. in desp.—p. 165.
Notices men for distinguished conduct—p. 166.
Desp. from—pp. 168, 169.
At Mundesore—lxviii.
In pursuit of rebels—lxxiv.
Mtd. in desp.—lxxv.
At Jhansi—cxi.

Abdool Rymon Khan, Tpr. (1st Cav., H. C.)
Wd. (the Betwa)—cix.

Abdul Kureem Khan, Tpr. (3rd Cav., H. C.)
Recmd. for "Order of British India",—p. 169.

Aheem-Aun-Sing, Acting Havildar Major.
Shot by mutineer—xxii.

Abraham, George, Pte. (H. M. 14th Lt. Dragns.)
S.-s. (Koonch)—p. 77.

Ackberpore.
Agent at—lvii.

Adzighur
Rance of, treats Eng. fugitives well—xxx, xxxi.

Agra.
Scindiah flees to—p. 130 ; 133.
Road to—p. 139.

Aheemaun Sing, Havildar Maj.
Kld. at Nowgong—xxxii.

Ahmed Buksh, Ressaldar-Maj. (Cav. H. C.)
Mtd. in desp. (Calpee)—p. 117.

Ahmed Hoosein Khan, Jem. (3rd Cav., H. C.)
Kld. at Barodia—p. 16.

Ahmed Khan, Tpr. (4th Cav., H. C.)
Wd. at Jhansi—p. 61.

Ahmed Shah, Sowar (2nd Punj. Cav.)
Wd. near Allahgunge—p. 29.

Ahmud Hossein, Tahsildar.
ix, xii.

Aite.
Hyd. Contgt. encamped at—p. 74.

Ajodia Persad, Pte. (25th B. N. I.)
Wd. at Jhansi—p. 59.

Ajudia Nawoo, Pte. (24th B. N. I.)
Wd. at Calpee—p. 124.

Akheychund.
Treasurer at Jhansi—ix.
Alleged to hold Maj. Skene's property—xii.

Akhey Mull.
Alleged Treasurer of Ranee of Jhansi—p. xii.

Alford, Sgt. (H. A.)
Mtd. in desp.—p. 36.

Ali Bahadoor, Nawab.
Opposes British near Banda—p. 31.
Flight of—p. 32.

Ali Khan, Nizam.
Kld. at Allahgunge—p. 28.

Ali Khan, Tpr. (1st Cav., H. C.)
Wd. (the Betwa)—cix.

Alipore.
Rebels at—p. 163.
Situation of—xxvi.
Rajah of—ib.
Rebels reported at—ib.

Allahdad Khan, Tpr. (3rd Cav., H. C.)
Recmd. for "Order of British India"—p. 169.

Allahgunge.
Brigr. Walpole's Report on action—p. 26—29.
Losses of rebels at—p. 28.
British Casualties—p. 29.

Allaoodeen Khan, Ressaldar (1st Cav., H. C.)
Recmd. for promotion and "Order of Merit"—pp. 50–51.
Mtd. in desp. (Betwa)—civ.

Alleef Khan, Jemadar (1st Cav., H. C.)
Recmd. for "Order of British India"—p. 169.

Allen, Asst. Surg. (Madras H. A.)
Mtd. in desp.—p. 36.

Allen, George, Pte. (3rd B. E. R.).
Wd. at Jhansi—p. 60.

Ally Beg. Tpr., (1st Cav., H. C.)
Wd. at Barodia—p. 16.

Ally Khan, Jemadar, (Madras S. M.)
Wd. at Jhansi—p. 59.

Amant Sing.
Kld. at Barodia—p. 14.

Amjheera.
Rajah of—1.
Detention of English at—lix.
Vakeel of—lx, lxi.

Amos, William, Corp. (3rd B. E. R.)
Kld. (the Betwa)—cviii.

Anderson, Allen, Pte. (H. M. 71st Highland Lt. Inf.)
Wd. at Gwalior—p. 170.

Anderson, Alex., Corp. (3rd B. E. R.)
Kld. at Jhansi—p. 60.

Anderson, H. L.
Sec. to Govt. Bombay—p. 17.

Anderson, James, Pte. (H. M. 71st Reg.)
Died s.-s. at Calpee—p. 124.

Anderson, W. W., Capt. (1st Nat. Lt. Cav.).
Wd. at Gwalior—p. 171.
Mtd. in desp.—p. 176.

Andrews, R,
And family, murdered at Jhansi—vii, ix ; x.

ntree.
Brigr. Smith marches from—p. 156.

orcha Gate.
(Jhansi)—p. 42.

Appasawarry, Pte. (Madras S. M.)
Wd. at Jhansi—p. 59.

Apthorp, E., Col., K.F.S. (3rd Madr. Eur. Reg.)
Leads advance at Banda—p. 31.
Mtd. in desp.— 33.
Cmdg. Advanced Guard—pp. 34—35.

Arabs.
Disaffected—p. 93

Arbuthnot, Lt. (R. A.)
" Special mention "—p. 175.

Archibald, Pte. (3rd B. E. R.)
Mtd. in desp. (Jhansi) —p. 56.

Archibald, Rodger, Pte. (B. E. R.)
Wd. at Jhansi—p. 60.

Armoogam, Pte. (Mad. S. M.)
Mortally wd. at Jhansi—p. 59.

Armstrong, Lt. (3rd B. E. R.)
At the Betwa—c.
Mtd. in desp.—ci.

Army of the Peshwa.
So-called—p. 45.

Arnott, Dr. (Suptdg. Surg.)
Mtd. in desp. (Jhansi)—p. 53.
Mtd. in desp. (Koonch)—p. 72.
His report on the health of the C.I.F.F. —p. 91.
Mtd. in desp. (Calpee)—p. 120.
Mtd. in desp. (Gwalior)—p. 173.

Artillery.
See *Regiments.*

Ashan Allee Sheristadar.
x.

Ashburner, Capt. (Dep. Judge Adv. Gen.)
" Special mention," (Gwalior.)—p. 172.
Mtd. in desp. (Jhansi)—cxi.

Ashum Ali Khan, Silladar (3rd Cav., H. C.)
Kld., R. Betwa—cvii.

Atnaram, Pte. (25th B. N. I.)
Wd. at Jhansi—p. 59.

Auba Gate.
at Jhansi, barricaded—p. 47.

Austin, D. H. G., Pte. (H. M. 14th Dragns.)
Died s.-s., Calpee—p. 122.

Awswairey, Pte. (4th B. N. I.)
Kld. (the Betwa)—cix.

B

Babadheen Khan, Naick.
Wd. at Barodia ; mtd. in desp.—p. 13.

Babajee Kuddon, Pte. (10th N. I.)
Wd. at Gwalior—p. 172.

Babboo Morgoot, Pte. (25th B. N. I.).
Kld. at Calpee—p. 123.

Babboo Sing, Sepoy (5th Inf., H. C.).
Wd. at Calpee—p. 125.

Baboo Bagwa, P, (25th B. N. I.).
Wd. at Jhansi—p. 59.

Bachoo Sing, Tpr. (1st Cav., H. C.).
Wd. at Koonch—p. 79.

Bacon, Capt. (D.A.Q.M.G.)
Mtd. in desp. (Jhansi)—p. 53.
Mtd. in desp. (Koonch)—p. 73.
Mtd. in desp. (Calpee)—p. 115.

Badder, James, Lc.-Corp. (H. M. 14th Lt. Dragns.)
Wd. (Gwalior)—p. 170.

Bafter, James, Pte. (3rd B. E. R.).
Wd. at Jhansi—p. 60.

Bahadurpore.
Defeat of Scindiah at—pp. 130, 135.
Position of—p. 134 ; 136¦; 138.

Bahoodoor Sing, Subadar, (24th N. I.)
Kld. at Rathghur—p. 9.

Baigree, Lt. (3rd B. E. R., acting D. A. Q. M. G.)
Wd., mtd. in desp. (Koonch)—pp. 72, 76.
Mtd. in desp. (Calpee)—p. 119.
Horse kld.—p. 126.

Baker, George, Pte. (3rd B. E. R.).
Mortally wd. at Jhansi—p. 60.

Baker, Richard, Pte. (H. M. 14th Lt. Dragns.)
Wd. (the Betwa),—cviii.

Bakri.
Ford at - lxviii.

Balda Misser, Pte. (24th B. N. I.)
Wd. at Jhansi—p. 61.

Balgoving Now, Pte. (4th B. N. I.)
Severely burnt (the Betwa)—cix.

Ball, Pte. (14th Lt. Dragns.)
Wd. at Mudinpore—p. 25.

Balla Pursaud, Lc. Naick (5th Inf., H. C.)
Wd. at Jhansi—p. 62.

Banda.
General action of, Maj.-Gen. Whitlock's Report—pp. 31—4.
Occupied by British — p. 32.
Gallantry of Hyderabad Cavalry at—p. 34—5.
Village of—p. 85.
Mutiny at—xxvii.
Suggested attack on—lxxx.
Ditto —lxxxix.
Camp,—pp. 31, 34, 35, 36.

Banda, Nawab of.
Joins the rebels—p. 71.
At Calpee—pp. 83, 94.
His mercenaries cut up—p. 102.
xxix.
Succours English fugitives—xxx, xxxi.
Capt. Scot writes to—xxxii.
Pays British soldier—xxxvi.
Orders as to disposal of—xci.
Defeat of—xcii.

Bandiri.
Ranee of Jhansi intended flight to—p. 49.
Position of - *ib*.

Banks, Robt., Col. Sgt. (H. M. 71st Highland Lt. Inf.)
s.—s. (Koonch)—p. 78.

Banpore.
Occupied—xc.

Banpoor, Raja of.
Letter from, to Shazadah of Mundesore —p. 7.
Wd. at Barodia—p. 14.
Aids rebels—p. 65.
Orders as to disposal of—xci.

Bappoo Mohitta, Pte. (25th B. N. I.)
Wd. at Jhansi—p. 59.

Barber, J. H., Lt.
At Muhoba—xxix.
Death of—xxxi, xxxvi.

Bareilly.
Ruheem Ali Nurut, of—p. 129.

Barker, Robert, Pte. (H. M. 14th Lt. Dragns.).
Kl. (the Betwa)—cviii.

Barker, Robert, Pte. (H. M. 86th Reg.)
Died s.-s., Calpee—p. 123.

Barnes, James, Pte. (H. M. 86th Reg.)
Wd. at Calpee—p. 123.

Barnes, Wm. C., Pte. (H. M. 14th Lt. Dragns.)
Wd. at Koonch—p. 77.

Barodia.
Rebels escape from Chunderapore to—pp. 6, 10.
Situation of —*ib*.
Rebels concentrate at—p. 11.
Difficulty of approach to—*ib*.
Rebels driven from jungle—p. 12.
British guns cross the ford—p. 13.
Position shelled—*ib*.
Village and fort occupied—pp. 14, 21.
Losses of the rebels—*ib*.
Result of defeat of rebels—*ib*.
British casualties at—pp. 15, 16.

Barrett, Capt. (H. M. 14th Dragns.)
In pursuit of rebels—p. 116.
Mtd. in desp. (Calpee)—p. 118.

Barrow, Lt. (Commst. Dept.)
Mtd. in desp.—p. 34.

Barrow, Maj. (Commissary of Ordnance)
Mtd. in desp.—pp. 34, 36.

Bartie, Mr.
Leads party against rebels—p. 21.
Mtd. in desp.—p. 25.

Barry, Asst. Surg. (H. M. 86th Reg.)
Mtd. in desp. (Calpee)—p. 115.
(May 22, 1858)—p. 121.

Barwell, C. A., Capt. (Dep. Asst. Adjt. Gen.)
Mtd. in desp.—p. 28 ; 29.

Bassoop.
Hyd. Contgt. at—p. 74.

Batly, Richard, Pte. (H. M. 86th Reg.)
Wd. at Jhansi—p. 58.

Bavry, Pte. (14th Lt. Dragns.).
Wd. at Mudinpore—p. 25.

Baywa Poway, Pte. (25th B. N. I.)
Kld. at Calpee—p. 123.

Beamish, Lt. (H. M. 14th Lt. Dragns.)
At Diapoora—p. 107.

Becher, Lt.
His horse used by mutineers—xxv.

Beechary, Sepoy (3rd Inf., H. C.)
Wd. at Jhansi—p. 61.

Beena.
River, fords of, near Rathghur—pp. 2, 5, 6, 11, 12.

Beenija.
(Mutineer), hanged—p. 30.

Begawur.
lxxxvi.

Beggs, Robt., Pte. (H. M. 86th Reg.)
Wd. at Jhansi—p. 58.

Beharry Culwar, Pte. (25th B. N. I.)
Wd. at Calpee—p. 123.

Bellaree.
Village near Nowgong—xxvi.

Bengal Army.
Troops of, eulogised by Sir H. Rose—p. 103.

Bereiseeah.
British Asst. at, murdered—p. 7.

Berry, Edward, Pte. (H. M. 8th Hussars.)
Mortally wd. at Gwalior—p. 171.

Betwa, River.
Maj. Orr crosses—p. 65.
Rebels under Tantia Topee, at—xciv.
Sir H. Rose's Report on action—xcv.
Enemy cross the river—xcvi.
Sir H. Rose's forces at—xcvii.
Enemy open fire—xcviii.
Charge of British—xcix.
Retreat, and pursuit, of rebels—xcix, ci.

Betwa—*contd.*
Rajpore ford—c.
Brig. Stuart's Report on action—cii—civ·
Rebel losses—ciii.
Casualties at—cvii—cx.

Best, William, Pte. (H. M. 14th Lt. Dragns.)
Wd., the Betwa—cviii.

Bhao Rao Ramchunder.
Arrives at Mhow—xlix.
Letter from—lxii.

Bhannoo Patkur, Pte. (25th B. N. I.)
Wd. at Jhansi - p. 59 ; Kld. (Betwa),— cvii.

Bheewa Amchurakur, Pte. (24th B. N. I.)
Kld. at Jhansi,—p. 61.

Bhiva, Driver (4th Co. 2nd Batt. Arty.)
Wd. at Gwalior—p. 170.

Bhomoroo Lingoo, Pte. (Bombay S. M.)
Wd. at Jhansi—p. 59.

Bhopal.
Regt. of, see *Regiments.*
Road from, to Saugor—p. 11.
Ranee of, Sir H. Rose's obligations to—p. 105-106.

Bhow Seerka, Pte. (25th B. N. I.)
"Special mention," (Gwalior)—p. 175.

Bhowaree Bhoghur, Pte. (24th B. N. I.)
Kld. at Calpee—p. 124.

Bhyjoo Sing, Subadar (3rd Inf., H. C.)
s.-s., Calpee—p. 125.

Bigaroo and Tehree.
Loyalty of Ranee of - lxxxii ; loyal states near—lxxxvi.

Binda Sing, Tpr. (1st Cav., H. C.)
Wd. at Jhansi—p. 61.

Bindah, Sepoy (3rd Inf., H. C.)
Wd. at Jhansi— p. 61.

Bingham, William, Pte. (3rd B. E. R.).
Wd. at Jhansi—p. 60.

Bird, John, Pte. (H. M. 95th Reg.)
Wd. (Kotah-ka-Serai)—p. 160.
Wd. at Gwalior—p. 172.

Birch, R. J. H., Maj.-Gen.
(Sec. to Govt. of India)—p. 128.
(Col.)—lxxxi.

Birjnath, Subadar.
Loyal native at Nowgong—xviii, xxxiii—xxxiv.

Bisson, Sepoy (5th Inf., H. C.).
Wd. at Jhansi—p. 62.

Bissram Sirdar.
At Jhansi—x.

Bithoor.
Nana of—xxix.

Blake, Lt. Col. (cmdg. 3rd Tp. Bombay H. A.)
At Kotah-ka-Serai—p. 157
Drives rebel artillery from pass—p. 159.
" Special mention " (Gwalior)—p. 174.
At Gwalior—cxvii.
Extract from letter of—cxix.

Blake, Maj. (2nd N. I.).
Good influence over his men in mutiny at Gwalior—xxxix—xl.

Blunt, Capt. (Beng. Arty.)
Mtd. in desp. (Calpee)—p. 103.
(Maj.) mtd. in desp. (Jumna)—p. 111.

Blunt, Lt. (H. M. 12th Roy. Lancers.)
Mtd. in desp.—p. 36.

Blyth, Capt. (H. M. 14th Dragns.).
At Koonch—p. 69.
Mtd. in desp.—*ib.*

Blythe, Mrs.
At Jhansi—xii.

Boileau, Maj., (Field Engineer)
Assists in reconnaissance of Rathghur—p. 2.
Selects position for batteries—p. 3.
Mtd. in desp.—pp. 8, 17 ; 15.
Demolishes defences at Garrakota—p. 19.
Reports readiness for escalade at Jhansi—p. 45.
Mtd. in desp. (Jhansi)—p. 53.
At Jhansi— p. 56.
Mtd. in desp. (Mundesore)—lxxi ; lxxxv.

Bolton, Capt. (D. A. Q. M. G.)
Mtd. in desp. (Gwalior)—p. 141.
(Kotah-ka-Serai) – p. 158.

Bombay Army.
Troops of, eulogised by Sir H. Rose—p. 103.

Bone dust.
Alleged use of, at Gwalior, to destroy caste—xxxvii.

Bentinck, Lord Wm.
Gives Union Jack to grandfather of husband of Ranee of Jhansi—p. 48.

Bonus, J., Lt. (Bombay Engineers.)
At Rathghur—p. 5.
Mtd. in desp. (Jhansi)—pp. 54, 57.
Wd.—p. 59.
Mtd. in desp. (Etora)—p. 108.
Acting Asst. Q. M. G., mtd. in desp. (Gwalior)—p. 155.

Booth, George, Pte. (3rd B. E. R.)
Wd. at Jhansi—p. 60.

Boregaum.
Situation of—cii.

Boston, Edward, Gnr. (1st Tp. H. A.)
Wd. (the Betwa)—cvii.

Bowen, Thomas, Sgt. (H. M. 14th Lt. Dragns.)
Wd. (the Betwa)—cviii.

Bowler, John, Pte. (H. M. 8th Hussars.)
Wd. at Gwalior—p. 171.

Brady, Stephens, Pte. (H. M. 86th Reg.)
Wd. at Jhansi—p. 58.

Brahmins.
At Benares predict mutiny—xxii.

Brennen, John, Pte. (H. M. 86th Reg.)
Wd. at Jhansi—p. 58.

Brenna, Acting Bombardier (R. A.)
Praised for good service and promoted on the ground—p. 44.

Brett, Maj. (3rd Madr. Eur. Reg.)
Mtd. in desp.—p. 34.

Brice, Maj.
Leads Native Horse Arty. at Banda—p. 35.
Mtd. in desp.—p. 36.

Bright, William, Sgt. (1st Tp., H. A.).
Mortally wd. (the Betwa)—cvii.

Brind, Maj. (Beng. Arty.)
Mtd. in desp.—p. 28.

Brockman, Lt. (H. M. 86th Reg.)
Cmds. gun at Gwalior—p. 144.
Mtd. in desp.—p. 173.

Brooks, Capt., (1st Lt. Cav.)
Intercepts guns taken from Mhow—xlii.
Narrow escape of—xlviii.
Brings in bodies of murdered officers—xlviii.
Blows up magazine—xlix ; lii.
Volunteers under—lii.

Brown, Capt. (Cmdg. Co. Madr. S. M.)
Mtd. in desp. (Jhansi)—p. 53.
Mtd. in desp. (Mundesore)—lxii.

Brown, Miss
At Jhansi—ix.

Brown, Sgt. (Commst. Dept.)
Mtd. in desp. (Jhansi)—p. 48.

Brown, Daniel, Pte. (H. M. 71st Highland Lt. Inf.)
Kld. (Gwalior)—170.

Brown, Peter, Pte. (3rd B. E. R.).
Kld. at Calpee—p. 124.

Browne, Capt. (Cmdg. 2nd Punj. Irr. Cav.)
Mtd. in desp.—p. 28.

Brown(e), Capt.
At Jhansi—ii ; ix.

Browne, Mrs., and daughter.
Murdered at Jhansi—ix.

Bryan, Myles, Pte. (3rd B. E. R.).
Kld. at Jhansi—p. 60.

Buckley, Lt. (Camel Corps.)
Mtd. in desp. (Calpee)—p. 98.

Bucktaoor, Sepoy (3rd Inf., H. C.)
Kld. at Jhansi—p. 61.

Budgeon, or Budgen, Lt. (H. M. 95th Reg.)
Cmds. gun at Gwalior, 144 ; mtd. in desp. (Gwalior)—p. 174.

Budroodean Khan, Tpr. (3rd Cav., H. C.)
Recmd. for "Order of British India" —p. 169.

Bugger Sing, Tpr.
Kld. at Calpee—p. 124.

Bugwan Sing, Tpr. (4th Cav., H. C.)
Recmd. for promotion—p. 51.

Bukish Ally.
Mutineer—xi.

Bukshee Khooman Sing.
Brings letter to Mhow from Holkar— lix.
Holkar's alleged orders to him,—lix—lx.

Buktawar Khan, Pte. (25th B. N. I.)
Kld. at Jhansi—p. 59.

Buldee Sing, Havildar, (25th B. N. I.)
Wd. (Gwalior)—p. 170.

Buldeen Doobay, Pte. (25th B. N. I.)
Wd. at Jhansi—p. 59.

Bullock Train.
Organized by Ld. Elphinstone—p, 104.

Bulwuntee Gurconna, Pte. (24th B. N. I.)
Wd. at Calpee—p. 124.

Bundeelas.
At Mudinpore—p. 24 ; 40.
The term explained—p. 42 ; 64 ; lxxxiv ; xcv.

Bundelcund.
p. 2 ; rebels from—pp. 10, 64.
Natives of, in 34th N. I., xvii ;
Loyal chiefs of—lxxx ; lxxxv ; lxxxvi ; lxxxviii ; xcv.

Bunkut, Sepoy (5th Inf., H. C.)
Wd. at Koonch—p. 79.

Bunny, Lt. (Beng. Arty.)
Mtd. in desp. —p. 28.

Bunsgopal.
Mutineer, reward for his head—lxii.

Bupoba.
Sir H. Rose at—xcvi.
Situation of—*ib*.

Burder, W., Pte. (3rd B. E. R.)
Wd. at Jhansi—p. 60.

Burgess, Lt. (Rev. Surveyor)
Kills 25 mutineers at Jhansi—iv.
Killed—iv, ix.

Burgin, John, Pte. (H. M. 86th Reg.).
Wd. at Jhansi—p. 58.

Burmadin Awasty, Pte. (25th B. N. I.)
Mortally wd., the Betwa,—cvii.

Burlton, Lt. (Meade's Horse)
At Jowra—Alipore—p. 163.
Mtd. in desp.—p. 165.

Burn, Asst. Surg. (5th Inf., H. C.)
Mtd. in desp. (Koonch)—p. 76.

Burnham, Wm., Pte. (3rd B. E. R.)
Kld. at Jhansi—p. 60.

Burns, Pte. (H. M. 86th Reg.).
Mtd. in desp. (Jhansi)—p. 55.

Burns, Dennis, Gnr. (3rd Tp. H. A.)
Died s.-s. (Jowra-Alipore)—p. 166.

Burns, Hugh, Sgt. (H. M. 86th Reg.)
Wd. at Calpee—p. 123.

Burra Gong.
Road to Jhansi, from—xcvii.
Village of—xcviii.

Burra Saugor.
"Army of Peishwa" at—xcvi.

Burrahgong Gate.
At Jhansi—p. 47.

Burrowclough, George, Pte. (H. M. 86th Reg.).
Died s.-s. Calpee—p. 123.

Burwa.
Road from, to Saugor—lxxxv.

Burwa Saugor.
Fugitive from Jhansi reaches—iv.

Busis Allee.
See *Bukish Ally.*

Butler, Asst. Surg. (Arty.).
Mtd. in desp. (Mundesore)—lxxiii.

Byott, John, Pte. (H. M. 14th Lt. Dragns.).
Wd., (the Betwa)—cviii.

Byrne, John, Pte. (H. M. 86th Reg.).
Wd. at Jhansi—p. 58.

Byrnes, Michael, Pte. (H. M. 86th Reg.).
Mortally wd. at Calpee—p. 123.

C

Cain, John, Corp. (9th Lancers.)
Wd. near Allahgunge—p. 29.

Cairns, W., Sgt. (H. M. 86th Reg.).
Wd., R. Betwa—cvii.

Callingur.
p. xxxv.

Calpee.
Its strong position—p. 71.
Its high importance to the rebels—p. 83.
Its external lines of defence—p. 84.
Rebels concentrate in villages around—p. 85.
Bengal and Bombay troops co-operate against—p. 86.
Sir H. Rose's plan of attack—pp. 89—90.
Prostration of British from sickness—p. 90.
Bad roads near C.—p. 91.
Spirit and discipline of British before C.—p. 92.
Sir H. Rose reinforced—p. 93 ; 110.
Sir H. Rose's dispositions—pp. 94—95.
Rebel advance from C.—p. 96.
Determined attack by rebels.—p .97.
Attack repulsed—p. 98.
General advance of British—pp. 99—114.
Flight of rebels towards Jaloun—p. 100.
British pass through the ravines—p. 101.
Pursuit of rebels by Maj. Gall—pp. 101, 116-117.
Capture of the Fort, and arsenal—p. 102.
Pursuit of rebels by Lt.-Col. Robertson—p. 103.
Sir H. Rose's reflections on the operations—p. 106— 107.
Casualties before C.—pp. 112, 122—26.

Campbell, Sir Colin.
p. lxxxix. See also, *Clyde, Lord.*

Campbell, Capt. (3rd B. E. R).
Mtd. in desp. (Barodia)—pp. 12, 14, 18.

Campbell, E., Capt. (Baggage Master)
Mtd. in desp. (Barodia)—p. 15.
Wd.—*ib.*
"Special mention " (Gwalior)—p. 173.

Campbell, Lt. (15th N. I.)
With 14th Irr. Cav., mortally wd. by Mutineers—ii, vi, ix.
A letter from—xx.

Campbell, Lt.-Col.
Succeeds Brigr. Steuart—p. 86.
" Special mention "—p. 87 ; 88.
His report on Diapoora and Muttra—pp. 109—110 ; 114.

Campbell, Col. (H. M. 71st Reg.)
In pursuit of rebels—p. 154.
Mtd. in desp. (Gwalior)—p. 155.

Candeish.
lxxxviii

Cane, R.
Eng. fugitives cross—xxx.

Canneross, Alex., Pte. (H. M. 71st Reg.)
s.-s. (Koonch)—p. 78.

Canning, Lord.
Letter to Sir R. Hamilton, with reference to the Nerbudda F. F.—lxxix.
(See also *Governor General.*)

Carey, Capt. (D. A. Q. M. G.)
Mtd. in desp.—p. 28.

Carne, Mr.
Deputy Collector at Muhoba—xxvii, xxviii.
Proceeds to Chowkaree—xxix.
Reports his position there—xxxii.

Carnelgurh.
Fort of—p. 20.

Carpenter, Brigr.
Mtd. in desp.—p. 33.

Carroll, Michael, Gnr. (H. A.)
Mtd. in desp.—p. 36.

Carshore, W. S.
Attempts escape—v.
Murdered with his family at Jhansi—pp. viii, ix.

Casualties, Returns of.
At Rathghur—pp. 9—10.
At Barodia, (Jan. 31, 1858)—pp. 15-16.
At Pass of Mudinpore, (Mar. 3, 1858)—p. 25.
Under Brigr.-Gen. R. Walpole (Ap. 22, 1858)—p. 29.
Under Maj.-Gen. G. C. Whitlock (Ap. 19, 1858)—p. 38.
During siege storm of Jhansi—pp. 57—62.
At Koonch, (May 7, 1858)—pp. 76—79.
Under Lt.-Col. G. V. Maxwell, (May 18—23, 1858)—p. 112.
During operations against Calpee, (May 15—24, 1858)—pp. 122—126.
In action at Jowra-Alipore, (June 21, 1858)—pp. 166—167.
During operations before Gwalior—pp. 170—172.
Near Mundesore, (Nov. 21—24, 1857)—lxxvii—lxxviii.
On the Betwa, (Ap. 1, 1858)—cvii—cx.

Cathcart, John, Gnr. (1st Tp., B. H. A.)
Died s.-s., Calpee—p. 122.

Cavalry.
See *Regiments.*

Cave, James, Pte. (H. M. 8th Hussars).
Wd. at Gwalior—p. 171.

Cawfield, Peter, Pte. (H. M. 86th Reg.)
Wd. at Jhansi—p. 58.

Chain Sing, Sowar (Meade's Horse.)
Wd. (Jowra-Alipore)—p. 167.

Chandaree.
1st Brig. at—p. 40.
Garrison of—p. 64.
Siege of—p. 84.
Brigr. Smith marches from—p. 133.
Fort of, stormed by Brigr. Stuart—lxxxiv ; lxxxv ; lxxxvi ; xc.

Chand Khan, Duffadar, (3rd Cav., H. C.)
Wd. at Calpee—p. 123.

Chandee Aheer, Pte. (25th B. N. I.)
Wd. at Calpee—p. 123.

Chanderey.
See *Chandaree*.

Chandica, Sepoy (5th Inf., H. C.)
Wd. at Jhansi—p. 62.

Chapman, Lt.
Narrow escape of, at Mhow, xlviii.

Chavathian, Pte. (Madras S. M.)
Wd. at Rathghur—p. 9.

Chennion, Pte. (Madras S. M.)
Wd. at Jhansi—p. 59.

Chetwode, Major (H. M. 8th Hussars).
Mtd. in desp.—p. 159.
Ditto. (June 17, 1858)—p. 177.
Ditto.—cxix.

Chirkaree.
lxxix.
Supposed fall of—lxxxi.
Great rebel army at—lxxxii; lxxxiv.
Situation of—lxxxv; xci; xcii;
Fall of—p. xcv.

Chirkaree, Rajah of.
His men protect baggage at Banda—p. 34.
His fear of rebels—xxvii;
Refuses shelter to Mr. Carne—xxviii.
Sincere supporter of British—lxxxiii.
Besieged by rebels—lxxviv.
Loyal—lxxxvii.

Chobay Laul, Lc. Naick (5th Inf., H. C.).
Wd. at Jhansi—p. 62.

Chobee Sing, Jemadar (2nd Co. Arty., H. C.).
Wd. at Koonch—p. 79.

Chokutta, Sowar (Cav., H. C.)
Wd. (Jowra-Alipore)—p. 167.

Chomair.
2nd Brig. at—p. 66.

Choonee, (a native)
xi.

Chota Sing, Pte. (25th B. N. I.)
Wd., (Gwalior)—p. 170.
"Special mention"—p. 175.

Chotay Khan, Jemadar, (4th Cav., H. C.),
Kld. at Calpee—p. 125.

Chowra, Camp.,
Lt.-Col. Maxwell at—p. 112.

Chowrani, Temples.
p. 71.

Chumbal, R.
Difficult ford of—pp, 133; 150.

Chumputeeapoor.
Mutineers driven from—p. 27.

Chunar.
p. xxvii.

Chunderapore.
Situation of—pp. 5; 6.
Evacuated by rebels—*ib.*

Chundaree.
See Chandaree.

Chundeyree, Fort of.
Formerly owned by Rajah of Banpore—p. 20.

Chunmebur Mhadomulla, Pte. (24th B. N. I.)
Wd. at Calpee—p. 124.

Chutterpore.
Near Jheeghun—p. 29.
Mutineers sent to, from Nowgong-xviii.
Fugitives reach—xxiv; xxv.
Fugitives at—xxvi.
Territory of, hostile—xxviii.
Situation of—lxxxv; lxxxvi.

Chutterpore, Ranee of.
Well disposed to English—xxv.

Chuttoo Gudria, Pte. (25th B. N. I.)
Wd. at Jhansi—p. 59.

Claran, John, Pte. (3rd B. E. R.)
Wd. at Jhansi—p. 60.

Clark, Acting Reg. Sgt.-Maj. (H. M. 14th Dragns.)
Mtd. in desp. (Calpee)—p. 118.

Clark, Dr. (H. M. 95th Reg.).
Mtd. in desp. (Gwalior)—p. 175.

Clark, Thos., Reg. Sgt.-Maj. (H. M. 14th Lt. Dragns).
Wd., R. Betwa, cvii.

Clerk, Henry, Lt., (Cmdg. 3rd Cav., H. C.)
At Mundesore, lxviii; xcvii.
Wd. (Betwa), cvii.

Clegg, Elijah, Pte. (H. M. 14th Lt. Dragns.)
Wd. (the Betwa), cviii.

Clerk, Lt. (Commst. Dept.).
Mtd. in desp. (Gwalior)—p. 173.

Clyde, Lord.
Acknowledges services of Sir H. Rose and Troops—p. 128 ; lxxxix, xcii.

Cochrane, Lt. and Adj. (H. M. 86th Reg.)
Mtd. in desp. (the Betwa) — civ.
Three horses shot under him—*ib.*

Cockburn, Capt. (Staff,
Mtd. in desp. (Koonch) —p. 72.
His horse wd.—p. 126.

Cockburn, (Capt. H. M. 43rd Reg.)
Mtd. in desp. (Calpee)—p. 119.
Mtd. in desp. (Gwalior)—p. 172.

Code, Jameson's.
Court of Inquiry
under—p. 18.

Cohill, M., Pte. (3rd B. E. R.)
Wd. at Jhansi—p. 60.

Colbeck, Lt. (3rd Madr. Eur. Reg.).
Kld. at Banda—p. 33.

Coles, Capt. (Cmdg. 9th Lancers.)
Mtd. in desp.—p. 28.

Coley, Capt. (Maj. of Brig.)
Mtd. in desp. (Jhansi)—p. 53.
Mtd. in desp. (Koonch)—p. 73.
Ditto, (Calpee)—p. 115.
Ditto, (Mundesore)—lxxi.

Coley, T. C., Maj. (Offg. D. A. A. G.).
p. 9 ; 16.

Colville, Pte. (H. M. 95th Reg).
Mtd. in desp. (Gwalior) —p. 175.

Colvin, Mr.
Informed of threatened mutiny at Gwalior—xxxix.

Connell, Thos., Pte. (H. M. 86th, Reg.)
Wd. at Jhansi—p. 58

Connolly, Patrick, Pte. (3rd B. E. R.)
Wd. at Jhansi—p. 60.

Connors, Dennis, Sgt. (H. M. 86th Reg.)
Wd. at Jhansi—p. 57.

Connors, Patrick, Gnr. (Arty.)
Wd. at Gwalior—p. 171.

Connors, Phillips, Pte. (3rd B. E. R.)
Wd. at Mudinpore—p. 25.

Conroy, Peter, Pte. (H. M. 86th Reg.)
Wd. at Jhansi—p. 58.

Conway, Patrick, Pte. (H. M. 86th Reg.)
Wd. at Jhansi—p. 58.

Conway, W., Asst. Apthy, (1st Tp., H. A.)
Wd. at Rathghur—p. 9.

Coombes, W., Pte. (3rd B. E. R.).
Wd. at Rathghur—p. 9.

Cooper, Bvt.-Maj.
Sends report of Mutiny at Mhow to Officiating Adjt.-Gen.—xlii.

Cooper, Frederick, Sgt. (H. M. 14th Lt. Dragns.)
Wd. at Jhansi—p. 59.

Coopoomoetoog, Naick (Madras S. M.)
Wd. at Jhansi—p. 59.

Cop, William, Pte. (3rd B. E. R.).
Mortally wd. at Jhansi—p. 60.

Corcoran, Cornelius, Pte. (H. M. 86th Reg.)
Wd. at Calpee—p. 123.

Cosgrove, Michael, Pte. (3rd B. E. R.)
Mortally wd. at Calpee—p. 124.

Cowles, J. J., Pte. (H. M. 14th Lt. Dragns.)
Died s.-s., Calpee—p. 123.

Cox, Henry, Gnr. (Bombay Arty.).
Kld. at Calpee—p. 123.

Cox, Thos., Pte. (H. M. 8th Hussars.)
Wd. at Gwalior—p. 171.

Craggs, W., Corp. (3rd Tp. H. A.)
Wd. at Gwalior—p. 171.

Crawford, Messrs., (two brothers.)
Murdered at Jhansi—ix.

Crealock, I. N., Lt. (H. M. 95th Reg.)
Wd. (Kotah-ka-Serai)—p. 160.
Mtd. in desp.—p. 162.
Wd. at Gwalior—p. 171.

Cremore, Thomas, Pte. (H. M. 14th Lt. Dragns.)
s.-s. (Koonch)—p. 77.

Cromar, James, Pte. (H. M. 71st Highland Lt. Inf.)
Wd. at Gwalior—p. 170.

Crook, Wm., Pte. (H. M. 14th Lt. Dragns.)
Kld. at Koonch—p. 77.

Crosby, William, Lc.-Sgt. (H. M. 14th Lt. Dragns.).
Kld. (the Betwa)—cviii.

Crow, Thos., Pte. (H. M. 14th Lt. Dragns.)
s.-s. (Koonch)—p. 77.

Cruickshank, John, Asst. Surg. (21st Coy. R. E.)
Wd. at Jhansi—p. 57.

Cullian, Sepoy (5th Inf. H. C.).
Wd. at Calpee—p. 125.

Culpee.
See *Calpee*.

Cunningham, Henry, Pte. (H. M. 14th Lt. Dragns.)
Wd. at Koonch—p. 77.

Currie, H., Lc.-Corp. (3rd B. E. R.)
Wd. at Barodia—p. 15.

Currie, Thos., Gnr. (3rd Tp. H. A.).
Wd. at Gwalior—p. 171.

Custwajee Moosuker, Pte. (25th B. N. I.).
Wd. at Calpee—p. 123.

D

Daley, J., Pte. (3rd B. E. R.)
Wd. at Rathghur—p. 9.

Daly, Bernald, Pte. (H. M., 71st Highland Lt. Inf.)
Wd. at Gwalior—p. 170.

Daniels, Cornet, (3rd Lt. Cav.)
Wd. at Barodia—p. 15.

Darby, Charles, Capt. (H. M. 86th Regt.)
Mtd. in desp., wd.(Jhansi)—p. 46.
Leads storming party—p. 54; 57.

Daree.
Hyd. Contgt. occupy—p. 74.

Darrah Sing, Sepoy (5th Inf., H.C.)
Wd. at Koonch—p. 79.

Dartnell, J. G., Lt. (H. M. 86th Reg.)
Leads assault on bastion at Jhansi—p. 46.
Mtd. in desp. (Jhansi)—p. 53; 55.
Wd.—p. 57.

Dassput, Rebel Chief.
Escape of—p. 30.
His nephews hanged—*ib.*

Davee, Fifer (10th N. I.)
Wd. at Gwalior—p. 172.

Davi Sing, Tpr. (3rd Cav., H. C.)
Recmd. for "Order of British India"—p. 169.

Davidson, Col. (Resdt. at Hyderabad.)
Thanked by Sir H. Rose—p. 105.

Davidson, Suptdg. Surg.
Mtd. in desp—p. 34.

Davies, Pte. (3rd B. E. R.)
Mtd. in desp. (Rathghur)—p. 5; 17.

Davis, Thos., Pte. (H. M., 14th Lt. Dragns.)
Wd. (Gwalior)—p. 170.

Davis, Wm., Pte. (H. M. 86th Reg.)
Wd. at Jhansi—p. 58.

Deccan.
Sir H. Rose makes forced marches to—p. 107.
Denuded of troops—p. 131.

Deegan, Timothy, Pte. (3rd B. E. R.)
Wd. at Jhansi—p. 60.

Dees, Dr.
Mtd. in desp. (Calpee)—p. 119.

Dempsay, Bernard, Pte. (3rd B. E. R.)
Wd. at Mudinpore—p. 25.

Dempsey, Loix, Pte. (H. M. 95th Reg.)
Mtd. in desp. (Gwalior)—p. 175.

Deopore.
See *Diapoora.*

De Salis, Col.
Notices services of Maj. Chetwode—p. 159.

Despatches.
See *Letters and Despatches.*

Dew, Lt.
Leads charge at Mundesore—lxvii.

Dewass.
Mutineers march towards—p. 1; lix; lxi; lxiii.
Rajah of, his arrangements with Holkar—lxi; lxiii.

Dhalpoor.
Ford at—p. 150.

Dhamooney.
Pass of—p. 20; 21.
Abandoned—p. 24.

Dhan Sing Tpr. (1st Cav., H. C.)
Wd. at. Koonch—p. 79.

Dhar.
Brigr. Stuart's despatch from, alluded to—lxxii; ci.

Dhonda Sita, Pte. (25th B. N. I.)
Wd. at Calpee—p. 123.

Dhrum Sing, Pte. (25th B. N. I.)
Wd. at Jhansi—p. 59.

Dhurm Narain.
Moonshee, his presence requested at Mhow—lxi.

Diapoora.
  Situation|of—p. 86.
  2nd Brig. reaches—*ib*, 87.
  Attacked—p. 88 ; 90.

Dick, George.
  Uncertain fate of—p. xxxii.

Dick, Lt., (3rd Lt. Cav.)
  At Diapoora—p. 107.
  At Jowra-Alipore—p. 163.
  Mtd. in desp.—p. 165.

Dick, W. G. D., 1st Lt. (Bombay S. M.)
  Mtd. in desp. (Jhansi)—p. 46.
  Leads escalade—p. 56.
  Wd.—*ib*;
  Kld.—p. 59.

Dickenson, Sgt. (Arty.)
  Wd. at Mudinpore—p. 25.

Dildar.
  Chaprassi—p. ix.

Diloule.
  British battery at—p. 110—111.

Dinwiddie, Sgt.-Maj. (H. A.)
  Mtd. in desp.—p. 36.

Dixon, Sgt.-Maj. (5th Inf., H. C.).
  Wd. at Jhansi—p. 62.

Doab, The.
  p. 83.

Doherty, Francis, Pte. (3rd B. E. R.).
  Wd. at Koonch—p. 78.

Dooga, Syce (1st Tp., H. A.).
  Kld. (Jowra-Alipore)—p. 166.

Doolar Tewarry, Subadar.
  Mortally wd. at Nowgong—xxxii.

Doolin, John, Sgt. (3rd Beng. Arty. and No. 17 Lt. Field Batt.).
  Wd.—p. 112.

Doorga Sing, Naique, (25th B. N. I.)
  Wd. (Gwalior)—p. 170.

Doorgah Sing, Subadar (12th N. I.)
  Joins mutineers—p. xviii.

Doowkul Khan, Subadar (2nd Co. Arty., H. C.).
  Kld. at Jhansi—p. 61.

Doran, Patrick, Pte. (3rd B. E. R.)
  Mtd. in desp.—p. 56.
  Wd. at Jhansi—p. 60.

Doran, Thos., Pte. (H. M. 86th Reg.)
  Kld. at Jhansi—p. 58.

Douglas, Capt. (B. A.), Cmdg. Arty. F. F., H. C.
  Mentioned in desp. (Jhansi)—p. 50.
  At Koonch—p. 73; 74.
  Mtd. in desp. (Koonch)—p. 75.
  His services at Mutha—p. 87.
  Mtd. in desp. (Calpee)—p. 120.

Dowe, Lt. (Cav., H. C.)
  Mtd. in desp. (Jhansi)—p. 52.

Dowker, H. C., Lt. (1st Cav., H. C.)
  Sent to Bandiri—p. 49.
  His pursuit of the Ranee—p. 50.
  Wd.—*ib*.
  At Jhansi—p. 61.
  Cmdg. 1st Cav., H. C., at Koonch—pp. 73, 74.
  Mtd. in desp.—p. 75; 116; 117.
  Ditto. (Calpee)—p. 118.

Dowlutram.
  Saves Mrs. Mutlow's life—xiii.

Doyle, Patrick, Pte. (3rd B. E. R.)
  Died s.-s., Calpee—p. 124.

Drayson, John, Corp. (24th B. N. I.)
  Wd. at Koonch—p. 78.

Drummond, Pte. (1st Co., 3rd B. E. R.)
  Mtd. in desp., (Jhansi)—p. 56.

Duljeet Sing, Naick (5th Inf., H. C.)
  s.-s., Calpee—125.

Dulloo, Sepoy (3rd Inf., H. C.)
s.-s., Calpee—p. 125.

Dumma Khan, Duffadar, (4th Cav., H. C.).
Wd. at Calpee—125.

Dumoh.
Situation of—p. 19.
Maj.-Gen. Whiltlock at—lxxxiii ; lxxxvi.
Camp, lxxx, lxxxv.

Dun, E. W., Lt. (4th Cav., H. C.)
Mtd. in desp. (Jhansi)—p. 50.
Mtd. in desp. (Koonch)—p. 75.

Dunlop, Capt. (12th Nat. Inf.).
Kld. by his men at Jhansi—i.
Gen. Sir H. M. Wheeler's confidence in him—ii.
Details of his murder—vi, ix.
His letter to Maj. Kirke—xix.
His men at Nowgong regret his death—xxi.

Dunman, Asst. Surg. (Madr. H.A.)
Mtd. in desp.—p. 36.

Dunsmore, John, Pte. (H. M. 71st Reg.).
s.-s. (Koonch)—p. 78.

Durand, Lt.-Col., (Agent to Gov.-Genl. for Central India.)
Announces attack by Holkar's men at Indore—xlii.
His flight—*ib*.
Message to Capt. Hungerford—xlv.
And to Col. Platt—xlvi.
Express sent to—l, lii.
Retreats on Simrole—
Safety of—lviii.
At Sehore—x.
Mtd. in desp. (Mundesore)—lxxi.

Durgam Sing, Lance Naick (26th B. N. I.)
Mortally wd. at Jhansi—p. 59.

Dursun Sing.
Loyal Sepoy, commended by Maj. Kirke—xxiii.

Dutton, Robert, Pte. (H. M. 95th Reg.)
Wd. (Kotah-ka-Serai)—p. 160; 171.

Dyaram Powa, Pte. (Bombay S. M.)
Wd. at Jhansi—p. 59.

E

Ecles, Lt.
Mtd. in desp.—p. 28.

Edmonstone, G. F.
Sec. to Govt. of India (For. Dept.)—lxxxiv.

Edwards, Lt. (Asst. Field Engineer.)
Mtd. in desp. (Koonch)—p. 73.

Edwards, Lt., cmdg. 21st Co. R.E.
"Special mention" (Calpee).—p. 99.

Eed Festival.
Its effects on Moslems—xx.

Elephants.
Use of, at Rathghur—p. 4.
Captured from rebels—pp. 101 ; 118.
Sent to Mhow by Scindiah—l.

Elliot, Capt. (Asst. Supdt., Malwa.)
Written to by the Durbar—li.
Takes charge of treasure—li ; lxiv.
His services at Mhow—liii.
Letter from—lx.

Elliot, Messrs.
(Two brothers), and mother, murdered at Jhansi—ix.

Ellis, Edwin, Sgt. (14th Lt. Dragns.)
Died s.-s., Calpee—p. 122.

Ellis, Major, (Political Asst. in Bundelcund.)
Announces presence of rebels at Jeeghun—p. 29.
Despatch mentioning services of—p. 38; xxx; lxxxiii; lxxxviii; xci.

Elliss, Thos., Pte. (12th Lancers.)
Saves Brigr. Miller's life—p. 37;

Elphinstone, Lord.
Sir H. Rose's indebtedness to—pp. 9; 104.

Elton, James, Pte. (H. M. 14th Lt. Dragns.)
Wd. (the Betwa)—cviii.

Emam Bux.
Jemadar, at Banda—xxxii.

Emaum Bux, Tpr. (3rd Bombay Lt. Cav.)
Kld. at Calpee—p. 124.

Emmomally Khan, Tpr., (1st Cav., H. C.)
Wd. at Barodia—p. 16.

Enfield Rifles.
Effect of great heat on the ammunition of—p. 82.
Effective fire of—p. 146.

Esram Rao Moray, Pte. (25th B. N. I.).
Wd. at Calpee—p. 123.

Essoo Purrah, Pte. (25th B. N. I.).
Wd. at Calpee—p. 123.

Essoo Pehakul, Pte. (25th B. N. I.).
Kld. at Calpee—p. 123.

Essoo Jugdalay, Pte. (25th B. N. I.)
Wd. at Jhansi—p. 59.

Estridge, Lt. (24th N. I.).
At Diapoora—p. 107.

Etora.
Second Brigade encamped at—p. 107.
Occupied by rebels—ib.

Etowa.
Sir H. Rose halts at—p. 85.
Repulse of rebels near—pp. 86; 87.

Ewart, Lt., (12th N. I.)
Bears message to Capt. Dunlop—i.
At Nowgong—xxiii; xxiv; xxviii.
At Muhoba—xxix.
Death of—xxxi; xxxv.

F

Fagan, Bvt.-Capt. and Adjt. (23rd N. I.).
Murdered at Mhow—xlii; xlvii; lviii.

Fakeers.
Black flag of, at Jhansi—p. 42.

Falgey, W., Pte. (3rd B. E. R.)
Wd. at Jhansi—p. 60.

Farrell, Gnr. (R. A.).
Mtd. in desp.—p. 122.

Farrell, Patrick, Pte. (3rd B. E. R.).
Wd. at Jhansi—p. 60.

Feeney, M., Pte. (H. M. 86th Reg.)
Kld. at Jhansi—p. 58.

Fenwick, Capt. (Cmdg. Co. R. E.).
Mtd. in desp. (Jhansi)—p. 53.
Mtd. in desp. (Koonch)—p. 73.
Ditto (Calpee)—p. 115.

Fenwick, Capt.
(In Scindiah's service) arrives at Mhow—xlix.
Brings account of occurrences at Indore—l; lxiv.

Fenwick, J. J., Lt. (25th B. N. I.)
Wd. at Jhansi—p. 59.
s.-s. (Koonch)—p. 76.
Mtd. in desp. (Mundesore)—lxx.

Ferguson, William, Pte. (H. M. 71st Reg.).
s.-s. (Koonch)—p. 78.

Fergusson, Donald, Pte. (H. M. 71st Highland Lt. Inf.)
Wd. at Gwalior—p. 170.

Fernandez, Mark, Trumpeter, (H. M. 71st Reg.)
Kld. at Calpee—p. 124.

Few, Pte. (3rd B. E. R.).
Mtd. in desp. (Jhansi)—p. 56.

Field, Capt. (R. A.)
At Koonch—pp. 67; 68; 69-70.
Mtd. in desp. (Koonch)—p. 73.
At Calpee—p. 95.
At Muttra—p. 110.

Field, John, Gnr. (Arty.)
Wd. at Gwalior—p. 171.

Fisher, J., Sgt.-Maj. (H. M. 14th Lt. Dragns.)
s.-s. (Koonch)—p. 77.

Fitzgerald, Michael, Pte. (3rd B. E. R.)
Wd. at Jhansi—p. 60.

Fitzpatrick, John E., Pte. (H. M. 14th Lt. Dragns.)
Wd. at Koonch—p. 77.

Fleming, Mr.
Murdered at Jhansi—vii, ix.

Flying Camps.
At Jhansi—p. 41.

Foley, Richard, Pte. (H. M. 86th Reg.)
Wd. at Calpee—p. 123.

Foloy, Timothy, Pte. (H. M. 86th Reg.)
Died s.-s., Calpee—p. 123.

Forage.
Scarcity of, between Jhansi and Calpee—p. 82.

Forbes, Adam, Pte. (H. M. 71st Reg.).
Died s.-s. (Koonch)—p. 78.

Forbes, J., Capt. (3rd Bom. Lt. Cav.)
Assists in reconnaissance of Rathghur—p. 2.
Mtd. in desp.—p. 3.
Leads cavalry at Barodia—p. 12.
Gallantry of—pp. 13; 17.
Mtd. in desp.—p. 18.
Cmds. cavalry at Bandiri—p. 49.
Mtd. in desp.—pp. 52; 53.
Repulses enemy near Etowa—p. 86.
Mtd. in desp. -ib., 87.
His report on action at Diapoora—pp. 107—108.

Forbes, John Foster, Lt. (25th B. N. I.)
s.-s. (Calpee)—p. 94.
Mtd. in desp. (May 20, 1858)—p. 121.
Wd. at Mundesore—lxxvi.

Forster, Capt. (H. M. 95th Reg.).
Mtd. in desp. (Jhansi)—pp. 159; 160.
"Special mention," (Kotah-ka-Serai)—p. 176.

Fowler, George, Ens. (H. M. 86th Reg.)
Mtd. in desp. (Jhansi)—p. 50; 53; 55.
Wd. at Jhansi—p. 58.

Fox, F. R., Lt. (Madras S. M.)
Wd., mtd. in desp. (Jhansi)—pp. 46; 54.
Wd.—pp. 57, 59.
Kills eight rebels, "special mention,"—p. 175.

Francis, Trumpeter, (3rd Lt. Cav.)
Wd. at Mudinpore—p. 25.

Franks, Ens.
At Nowgong—xxiii.
At Muhoba—xxix; xxx.

Frash, George, Pte. (H. M. 86th Reg.)
Wd. at Jhansi—p. 58.

Fraser, G. L., Lt. (23rd N. I.)
Mtd. in desp. (Jumna)—p. 111; 112.

Fraser, H., Lt. (Adjt. 4th Cav., and Staff off. F. F. H. C.)
Mtd. in desp. (Koonch)—p. 76.
"Special mention"—p. 175.
Mtd. in desp. (Mundesore)—lxxv.

Futteh Khan, Naick, (25th B. N. I.)
Kld. at Calpee—p. 123.

Futtehpore.
Guns at, captured by mutineers—xxxv.

Fyze Oola Khan, Tpr. (4th Cav. H. C.)
Wd. (the Betwa)—cix.

G

Gaffey, Peter, Gnr. (4th Co. 2nd Batt. Art.)
Wd. at Gwalior—p, 170.

Gall, Maj. (H. M. 14th Lt. Dragrs.)
Cmds flying camp before Jhansi—p. 41
Report from, mentioned—p. 48.
Scales bastion at Jhansi—p. 49.
Mtd. in desp. (Jhansi)—p. 52.
At Pooch—p. 65.
Gallantry at Koonch—p. 66.
Mtd. in desp.—p. 73.
Reconnaissance by—p. 84.
At Calpee—p. 96.
In pursuit p 101.
"Special mention"—pp. 101, 102.
114.
His report on pursuit of rebels—pp. 116—118.
lxviii.
Mtd. in desp. (Mundesore)—lxxi; lxxiv.

Gardener, Sgt. (H. M. 14th Lt. Dragns.)
Mtd. in desp. (the Betwa)—ci.
His gallantry at Dhar—*ib.*

Garrakota, Fort of.
Capture of—p. 19 ; 20 ; xc ; xcii.

Gaton, Chas., Pte (3rd B. E. R.)
Mortally wd. at Jhansi—p. 60.

Geddard, James, Corp. (3rd B. E. R.)
Wd. at Jhansi—p. 60.

General orders.
See *Governor General.*

Gennoo, Syce (1st Tp. H. A.)
Kld. (Jowra-Alipore)—p. 166.

George, F., Pte. (H. M. 14th Dragns.)
Died s.-s., Calpee—p. 122.

Geraghty, Daniel, Pte. (H. M. 86th Reg.)
Wd. at Jhansi—p. 58.

Gholam Ali, Sowar (Meade's Horse.)
Wd. (Jowra-Alipore)—p. 167.

Gholam Mahomed.
Chaprassi—x.

Gillman, Pte. (1st Co., 3rd B. E. R.)
Mtd. in desp. (Jhansi)—57.

Gills, Lt. and Adj. (H. M. 14th Dragns.)
Mtd. in desp. (Calpee)—p. 118.
At the Betwa—cii.

Girthaurey, Pte. (Bombay S. M.)
Wd. at Rathghur—p. 9.

Golam Ali Khan Tpr. (4th Cav. H. C.)
Wd. at Koonch—p. 79.

Goldsworthy, W. L., Lt. (H. M. 8th Hussars)
Sir H. Rose's Aide-de-Camp—p. 147.
At Kotah-ka-Serai—p. 158.
"Special mention" (Gwalior)—p. 174.
Ditto —p. 176
At Gwalior—cxv, cxvi, cxvii.

Golowlee.
Situation of—p. 84.
Ford across R. Jumna at—p. 85.
Sir H. Rose arrives at—p. 86.
Rebels attack—pp. 88, 89.
Reinforcements reach—p. 93 ; 94 ; 95, 112.

Golundauze.
Two Cos, of, at Jhansi—p. 42.

Gomes, Thomas, Trumpeter (R. A.
Died s-s., Culpee—123.

Gonajee Goura Pte. (25th B. N. I.)
Wd. "special mention", (Gwalior)—p. 175.

Goodfellow, Lt., (Cmdg. Co. Bom. S. M.)
Mtd. in desp. Jhansi—p. 53; 54; 56.

Goolab Minia, Pte. (25th B. N. I.)
Kld., R. Betwa—cvii.

Goolab Sing, Sowar (2nd Punj. Cav.)
Wd. near Allahgunge—p. 29.

Goolam Hossein Khan, Jemadar (1st Cav., H. C.)
Wd. at Barodia—p. 15.

Goolam Nubbick, Duffadar, (4th Cav., H. C.)
Wd. at Calpee—p. 125.

Goolzar Khan.
Mutineer—x.

Gooman Sing, Pte. (25th B. N. I.)
Wd. at Calpee—p. 123.

Goonah.
Road from Jhansi to—p. 64.
3rd B. Lt. Cav. at—ib.
Road from, to Indore—p. 65.
Road from Gwalior to—p. 150; lxxxv; lxxxix.
Brigr. Smith at—xci.

Goorbuccus, Havildar, (12th N. I.)
Mutineer—p. i.

Goorbuccus Chowbay, Pte. (25th B. N. I.)
Wd. at Jhansi—p. 59.

Goorserai, Rajah.
His troops at Kotra—p.

Gora, Lake.
British fugitives reach—xxiv.

Goraria.
Situation of—lxviii.
Rebel position at—lxix.
Stormed—lxx; lxxiv; lxxv.

Gordon, Capt. (Madr. N. I.)
Dep. Supdt. of Jhansi, warns Maj. Kirke of impending mutiny—i.
Shot by mutineers - ii; viii; ix; x.
His visit to the Ranee—xiii.

Gordon, Capt. (H. M. 14th Lt Dragns.)
At Koonch—p. 68.
Mtd. in desp.—ib.

Gordon, Capt. (Asst. Com. Gen.)
Mtd. in desp. (Calpee)—p. 119.
"Special mention" (Gwalior)—p. 173.

Gordon, Lt. (Madras S. M.)
Mtd. in desp. (Gwalior)—p. 155.
(Mundesore)—lxxi.

Gore, Lt. (7th Lancers)
Mtd. in desp.—p. 28.

Gosling, Capt.
Attacked by small-pox—p. 36.

Goonajee Gowra, Pte. (25th B. N. I.)
Wd. (Gwalior)—p. 170.

Gosset, Lt. (R. E.).
Mtd. in desp. (Koonch)—p. 73.

Gould, Wm., Pte, (H. M. 86th Reg.)
Wd. at Jhansi—p. 58.

Governor General of India in Council, General Orders of:—
(No. 1336 of 1859), directing publication of Sir Hugh Rose's Despatches (Rathghur and Barodia), recording high approval, and offering thanks—p. 1.
Expressing satisfaction at the conduct of operations near Barodia, and thanking officers and men—pp. 18, 19.

Governor General of India in Council, General Orders of :— (*Contd.*)

(No. 110 of 1858), directing publication of Sir Hugh Rose's Despatch of March 26, 1858, (Pass of Mudinpore) and noticing skilful conduct of operations —p. 19.

(No. 111 of 1858), directing publication of Brigr.-Gen. R. Walpole's Despatch of April 23, 1858, (Allahgunge)— p. 26.

(No. 113 of 1858), directing publication of Maj.-Gen. G. Whitlock's Despatch of April 12, 1858, (Jheeghun)—p. 29.

(No. 153 of 1858), directing publication of Maj.-Gen. G. Whitlock's Despatches of April 24 and 30, 1858, (Battle of Banda, etc.)—p. 30.

(No. 174 of 1858), directing publication of Sir H. Rose's Despatch of April 30, 1858, (Jhansi), and expressing satisfaction—p. 39.

(No. 324 of 1858), directing publication of Sir H. Rose's Despatch of May 24, 1858, (Koonch)—p. 64.

No. 272 of 1859, directing publication of Sir H. Rose's Despatch of June 24, 1858, (Calpee), and thanking Sir H. R. and his forces—p. 81.

(No. 231 of 1859), directing publication of Sir H. Rose's Despatch of October 13, 1858, (capture of Gwalior), and cordially thanking Sir H. R. and the C. I. F. F.—p. 128.

Approving Sir H. Rose's decision to reduce Jhansi before relieving loyal Rajahs—lxxxvii.

(No. 243 of 1858), directing publication of Sir H. Rose's Despatch of April 30, 1858, (Battle of the Betwa), and expressing unqualified approbation— p. xciv.

(No. 244 of 1858), supplementary to No. 174 of 1858—p. cxi.

Letter expressing satisfaction at the conduct of operations before Rathghur—p. 17.

Gowhar Khan, Sowar (Towana Horse.)
Wd.—p. 112.

Gowan, L., Lt. (H. M. 14th Lt. Dragns.)
Mtd. in desp. (Gwalior)—p. 155.
Wd. at Mundesore—lxxvi.

Graffin, Hugh, Pte. (H. M. 71st Reg.).
Died s.-s. (Koonch)—p. 78.

Grady, James, Pte. (3rd B. E. R.)
Kld. at Jhansi—p. 60.

Graham, Sgt.-Maj.
Mtd. in desp. (Calpee)—p. 115.
Ditto (May 22, 1858)—p. 121.

Gray, Cornelius, Pte. (H. M. 14th Lt. Dragns.)
Wd., R. Betwa—cvii.

Gray, Patrick, Gnr. (H. A.)
Kld. near Allahgunge—p. 29.

Gray, Wm., Pte. (H. M. 14th Lt. Dragns.)
Wd., at Koonch—p. 77.

Greaves, Francis, Corp. (H. M. 86th Reg.)
Wd. at Jhansi—p. 57.

Green, Edward, Col.
Adjt.-Gen. of the Army—p. 10, 17.

Grier, Samuel, Pte. (H. M. 86th Reg.).
Died s.-s., Calpee—p. 123.

Groves, James, Corp. (3rd B. E. R.).
Wd. at Jhansi—p. 60.

Gummaee, Sepoy (5th Inf., H. C.)
Wd. at Jhansi—p. 62.

Gunesh Ramchunder.
Holkar's Vakeel at Mhow—lxii.

Gunesh Shastree.
Brings Message to Mhow from Holkar—li :
Sent for by Capt. Hungerford—lxii lxiii.

Guneshee Lall.
Assists Mrs. Mutlow—xiv

Gunga Sing, Duffadar, (1st. Cav. H. C.)
Recmd. for "Order of British India"—p. 169.

Gunga Sing, Jemader (5th Inf., H. C.)
Wd. at Jhansi—p. 62.

Gunja Inli.
The, at Gwalior—xxxix.

Gunnace Sing, Duffadar, (1st Cav., H. C.)
Wd. at Koonch—p. 79.

Gunnace Singh, Lc. Naick (5th Hyd. Inf.)
Wd. (the Betwa),—cix.

Gunnoo Powar, Color Havildar, (25th B. N. I.)
"Special mention," (Gwalior)—p. 175.

Gunpatrao Sindah, Pte. (25th B. N. I.)
Wd. (the Betwa),—cvii.

Gunput Silkay, Pte. (25th B. N. I.)
Kld. at Calpee—p. 123.

Gurradhur Pandy, Pte. (24th B. N. I.)
Kld. at Calpee—p. 124.

Gurawlee Rajah.
The, rumour about, at Nowgong,—xxi.

"Gurrie."
Explained—p. 10.

Gurrowlee.
Mutineers proceed to—xxiv.

Gwalior.
British force ordered to march on—p. 130.
G. captured by the rebels—p. 130–1.
Great importance of its recapture—p. 131.
Sir H. Rose proceeds to G. by forced marches—p. 132.
Sir H. Rose's plan of attack,—p. 133.
Situation of G.—p. 134.
Dry canal leading to Fort—p. 140.

Gwalior—(contd.)
Position of British batteries,—p. 141.
Rebels place guns on the heights—p. 142.
The guns captured—p. 143.
View of G. obtained from the heights—p. 144.
Road to the south occupied by British—p. 145.
Arsenal captured—p. 146.
Sir H. Rose's dispositions for general attack—p. 147.
The attack begins—ib.
The Lushker occupied—p. 148.
Phool Bagh palace taken—p. 149.
Gallant capture of the Fort—p. 150.
Scindiah returns to G.—p. 151.
Importance of the operations—p. 152-3.
Casualties at Gwalior—p. 170-2.
Brigr. Ramsey's account of threatened mutiny at—xxxv-xl.

Gwalior Contingent.
Mutineers of—pp. 70 ; 75 ; 83 ; 161 ; xc.

Gwalior States.
The commanding position of—p. 131.

H

Haffernan, W. H., Pte. (H. M. 14th Lt. Dragns.)
Wd. at Koonch—p. 76.

Hagart, Brigr.
Commands Cavalry at Allahgunge—p. 27.
Mtd. in desp.—p. 28.

Haggard, T. J., Lt. (Commissary of Ordnance, C. I. F. F.)
Mtd. in desp. (Jhansi)—p. 53 ; 63.
    Ditto (May 22, 1858)—pp. 122 ; 127.
Before Gwalior—pp. 141 ; 168 ; 177.
Mtd. in desp. (Betwa)—cii ; cv ; cvi.

Haley, John, Pte. (3rd B. E. R.)
Wd. at Jhansi—p. 60.

Hall, William, Pte. (H. M. 95th Reg.)
Mortally wd. (Kotah-ka-Serai)—pp. 160; 171.

Hameerpore.
Mutiny at, reported—xxvii.

Hamilton, Sir Robert W.
Places troops at Sir H. Rose's disposal—p. 3.
Captured rebels handed over to—p. 7.
Papers found at Rathghur handed to—p. 8.
Annexes Shaghur—p. 24.
Establishes police station at Malthone—p. 24.
His estimate of garrison at Jhansi—pp. 42; 48; 65; 102.
Sir H. Rose's indebtedness to—pp. 104—105.
p. 129; 130.
His knowledge of Central India—p. 135.
Information from—p. 142.
With Scindiah—151.
lxxix; lxxxii; lxxxiv.
Memorandum to Lord Palmerston—lxxxvii; xcv.

Hamilton, R., Maj. (Asst. Adjt. Gen., Saugur F. F.)
Mtd. in desp.—p. 34; 38.

Hannon, John, Pte. (H. M. 86th Reg.)
Wd. at Jhansi—p. 58.

Hare, G., Capt. (Cmdg. 5th Inf., H. C.)
In pursuit of rebels (Rathghur)—p. 5.
Mtd. in desp.—*ib.*
At Barodia—p. 11; 12; 17.
Cmds. picquet on ridge at Jhansi—p. 43.
Attacks fortified house—p. 50.
Mtd. in desp. (Jhansi)—p. 53.
(Cmdg. 5th Inf., H. C.) at Koonch—p. 73.
Mtd. in desp.—p. 75.
"Special mention" (Tehree)—p. 88; 100.
Mtd. in desp. (May 22, 1858)—p. 122.
Ditto (Betwa)—cii.

Hare, Lt., (Bengal Arty.)
His services before Calpee—p. 111.

Harcourt, Lt., (Bombay Arty.)
Mtd. in desp. (Morar)—pp. 136; 137.
Cmdg. Artillery—p. 153.

Hard, Robt., Corp. (3rd B. E. R.)
Mtd. in desp. (Jhansi)—pp. 56; 57.
Wd. at Jhansi—p. 60.

Harding, Lt. and Adjt. (H. M. 8th Hussars).
"Special mention," (Kotah-ka-Serai)—p. 176.
At Gwalior—cxv; cxvi.

Harris, Lt., (3rd Tp., Bombay H A.)
Mtd. in desp. (Gwalior)—p. 141.

Harris, Maj. (1st Lt. Cav.)
Murdered by his own men—xlvii; lv; lvii.

Harris, Jonathan, Gnr. (H. A.)
Wd. near Allahgunge—p. 29.

Harris, William, Bombardier, (Bombay Arty).
Kld. at Calpee—p. 123.

Harrison, Bvt.-Capt.
Mtd. in desp.—p. 36.

Harrison, John. Pte. (3rd B. E. R.)
Mortally wd. at Jhansi—p. 60.

Hastings, John, Pte. (3rd B. E. R.)
Died s.-s., Calpee—p. 124.

Hawkins, Capt.(F. A.).
Coolness of, at Gwalior—xxxix—xl.

Hawkins, Chas., Col.-Sgt. (21st Co. R. E.)
Died s.-s., at Koonch—p. 76.

Hearndon, William, Trumpeter (H. M. 14th Lt. Dragns.)
Died s.-s. (Koonch)—p. 77.

Heat, Solar.
(instances of high temperatures)—pp. 66; 72; 75; 81; 82; 85; 88; 90; 98; 103; 106; 107; 113; 115; 132; 138; 163; 164.

Heath, Lt. (1st Bombay Lt. Cav.)
Leads charge at Gwalior—p. 148.
"Special mention"—p. 174.

Heera Laul, Sepoy (5th Inf., H. C.)
Wd. at Jhansi—p. 62.

Heera Sing.
Rebel leader—lxviii.

Heneage, Capt., (H. M. 8th Hussars.)
Leads charge of 8th Hussars—p. 158.
Mtd. in desp —p 159.
"Special mention"—p. 176.
His report on the charge—cxv.

Henessey, John, Gnr. (Arty.)
Mortally wd. at Gwalior—p. 171.

Henn, Richard, Pte. (3rd B. E. R.)
Wd. at Jhansi—p. 60.

Hennegan, Lt., (H. A.)
Mtd. in desp.—p 36.

Hennessy, Major.
Report of, on alleged mutiny at Gwalior—xli.

Hennessy, Michael, Corp. (3rd B. E. R.).
Wd., the Betwa—cviii.

Henry, Lt. (Sub Asst. Com. Gen.)
Mtd. in desp. (Koonch)—p. 73.
Ditto   (Calpee)—p. 115.

"Henry ki Pultan."
Meaning of—p. 70.

Henton, John, Pte. (H. M. 14th Lt. Dragns.)
Wd. at Koonch—p. 76.

Hicks, T. N., Lt. Col. (Cmdg. Arty. C. I. F. F.)
p. 140; 142.
Mtd. in desp. (Kotah-ka-Serai)—p. 158.
Leads charge of 8th Hussars—p. 159.
"Special mention" (Kotah-ka-Serai)—p. 176.
With 8th Hussars at Gwalior—cxvi.

Hiles, Richard, Qr. Mr. Sgt. (1st Tp., H. A.)
Wd. (the Betwa)—cvii.

Hill, Sir John, Capt. (Brig.-Maj.)
Mtd. in desp. (Kotah-ka-Serai)—p. 158.
"Special mention"—176.

Himmunt Khan, Duffadar, (4th Cav., H. C.)
Recmd. for promotion—p. 51.

Hindree-ka-Pultan.
Corruption of—p. 70.

Hirnac Essuar, Pte. (4th B. N. I.)
Severely burnt, (the Betwa)—cix.

Hislop, Sir T.
His camp in 1817—lxviii.

Hoben, H., Lc.-Corp. (3rd E. R.)
Wd. at Barodia—p. 15.

Hoey, John, Pte. (H. M. 14th Lt. Dragns.)
Wd. at Jhansi—p. 59.

Hoey, Thos., Pte. (H. M. 14th Lt. Dragns.)
Wd. at Koonch—p. 76.

Hogan, Edw., Pte. (H. M. 86th Reg.).
Wd. at Jhansi—p. 58.

Hogan, Michael Lc.-Corp. (H. M. 95th Reg.)
Wd. at Gwalior—p. 171.

Holkar, Maharajah of Indore.
Supposed attack by—xlvi ; xlix.
Sends letter of regret to Mhow—l.
Fears he is misunderstood—li.
His loyalty—lii.
Letter to, from Capt. Hungerford—lvi.
Explains occurrences at Indore—lviii—ix
Threatens the Rajah of Amjheera—lix.
Urged to punish mutineers—lxi
Orders attack on rebels—lxii.
His friendliness proved—lxv.

Holland, Thos., Gnr. (R. A.)
Died s.-s., Calpee—p. 123.

Hollis, George, Pte. (H. M. 8th Hussars.)
Wd. at Gwalior—p. 171.

Holloway, H., Reg. Sgt.-Maj. (H. M. 14th Lt. Dragns.)
p. 77.
Died s.-s., Calpee—p. 123

Holmes, Bvt.-Capt. (H. A.)
Mtd. in desp.—p. 36.

Holroyd, W. R. M., Lt. (H. M. 86th Reg.)
Wd. at Jhansi—p. 57.

Homan, Lt. (50th N. I.)
Mtd. in desp.—p. 34.

Hoolapore.
Stand made by rebels at—p. 27.

Hoossein, Bux, Subadar (5th Inf., H. C.)
Wd. at Jhansi—p. 62.

Hopper, F., Pte. (H. M. 14th Dragns.).
Died s.-s., Calpee p. 122.

Hopton, Wm., Pte. (H. M. 14th Lt. Dragns.)
Wd. at Koonch—p. 77.

Horses, Returns of killed and wounded.
At Rathgur—p. 10.
At Barodia—p. 16.
Under Maj. G. C. Whitlock, April 19th, 1858—p. 38.
At Jhansi—p. 62.
At Koonch—p. 78.
At Calpee —p. 126.
At Jowra-Alipore—pp 166-7.
On the Betwa- cx.

Hossein Khan, Tpr. (1st Cav., H. C.)
Wd. at Mudinpore—p. 25.

Howell, David, Gnr. (R. A.)
Died s.-s., Calpee—p. 123.

Howitzers.
At Rathghur—pp. 4 ; 5.
At Barodia —11 ; 21.
At Jhansi—p. 43.

Hudson, Robert, Pte. (3rd|B. E. R.)
Wd. at Koonch— p. 78.

Hulston, James, Pte. (3rd B. E. R.)
Wd. at Jhansi—p. 60.

Humeerpore.
lxxxviii ; xcii.

Hummuth Khan, Sepoy (5th Inf., H. C.)
Wd. at Jhansi—p. 62.

Hungerford, T., Capt.
Turns his guns on the mutineers at Mhow — xliii.
In command of fort - xliv.
His account of mutiny at Mhow—xliv.
Asks leave to turn out his battery—xlv.
Receives letter from Col. Durand (Indore) —xlv.
Appeals to Col. Platt for protection for women and children—xlv.
Ordered to Indore—xlvi ; lvii.
Checked by note from Col. Travers—*ib.*; lvii.
Brings back battery to Mhow—xlvi.

Hungerford, T., Capt.—(contd.)

Urges Col. Platt to defend fort—xlvii, liv.
Disarms the guard of the fort—xlvi.
Is fired at, and replies with grape—xlvii; lv.
Organizes defence of fort—xlviii; lxiii.
Proclaims martial law—xlix; lxiii.
Fires neighbouring villages—*ib.*
Writes to Holkar—*ib.*
Sends report to Adjt.-Gen., Bombay Army—*ib.*
Orders mutineer to be hanged—l.
Trusts his action at Mhow may meet with approval—liii.
Letter to Holkar—lvi.
Letter to Adjt -Gen., Bombay Army—*ib.*
Second letter to Holkar—lxii.
Letter to Secy. to Govt., Bombay—lxiv.
Blows up magazines—xliv; lxiii.
Telegrams from, to Lord Elphinstone—lxv, lxvi.
(Cmdg. Arty. Malwa F. F.), mtd. in desp. (Mundesore)—lxxii.
His battery at Goraria—lxix, lxx.

Hurat, Francis, Gnr. (1st Tp., B. H. A.).

Died s.-s., Calpee—p. 122.

Hurdowi, Fort at.

Blown up with native-made powder—p. 80.
Site occupied—p. 84.
Surrender of its chief—*ib.*

Hunmunt Singh, Tpr. (3rd Lt.-Cav.)

Wd. at Barodia—p. 15.

Hunnoman, Sepoy (3rd Inf., H. C.).

Wd. at Jhansi—p. 61.

Hunoman Dhobe, Naick, (10th N. I.)

Wd. at Gwalior—p. 172.

Hunooman Sing, Jemadar, (4th Cav., H. C.)

Recmd. for promotion and Order of Merit—p. 51.

Hurkhoopoora.

Village of—p. 117.

Hussan Khan, Tpr. (25th B. I. N.).

Kld., (Gwalior)—p. 170.

Hutchins, Chas., Pte. (H. M. 14th Lt. Dragns.)

Wd. at Koonch—p. 76.

Hutchinson, Capt.

Reported taken prisoner—l.

Hutchinson, Wm., Pte. (3rd B. E. R.)

Wd. at Jhansi—p. 60.

Hunt. Joseph, Corp. (H. M. 95th Reg.)

Wd. at Gwalior—p. 171.

Hunter, George, Pte. (H. M. 14th Lt. Dragns.)

S.-s. (Koonch)—p. 77.

Hunut Singh, Naick.

Wd. at Barodia, mtd. in desp.—p. 13.

Hyderabad Contingent.

Sir Hugh Rose's commendation of—p. 105.
Permitted to go home, but return to attack Gwalior—p. 133.
Commended—p. 136.

Hyderally Khan, Tpr. (1st Cav. H. C.).

Wd. at Rathghur—p. 9.

Hymut Khan, Bargeer, (3rd Cav., H. C.)

Mortally wd. at Koonch—p. 76.

I

Indore.
Road from, to Goonah—p. 65.
Disaffection of—p. 132.
Attack on Residency at—p. xlii.
Mutineers from Mhow proceed to—xliii.
Flight of mutineers to—xlvii.
Treasury looted by rebels—l.
Persons murdered at—li.
Value of rupee at—lii ; liv.
Holkar's account of mutiny at—lviii—ix.
Sir R. W. C. Hamilton, Resident at—lxxxviii.

Indoorkee.
On Scinde River—p. 132.

Infantry.
See *Regiments*.

Ishan Khan, Jemadar (Towana Horse.)
Mtd. in desp. (Gwalior)—p. 156.

Issery Khan, Tpr. (3rd Cav., H. C.)
Wd. (Gwalior)—p. 170.

Ittojee, Sepoy (5th Inf., H. C.)
Wd. at Koonch—p. 79.

Ittoo Pendicker, Pte. (10th N. I.)
Wd. at Gwalior—p. 172.

Ittoo, Sowrah, Pte. (25th B. N. I.)
Wd. at Jhansi—p. 59.

J

Jackson, Alfred, Pte. (H. H. 8th Hussars.)
Wd. at Gwalior—p. 171.

Jackson, Lt., (Adjt., 12th N. I.)
xxiv.
At Muhoba—xxix ; xxxi.

Jaffer Ali Beg, Tpr. (3rd Cav., H. C.)
Recmd. for "Order of British India"—p. 169.

Jaffer Khan, Tpr. (3rd Cav., H. C.)
Recmd. for "Order of British India"—p. 169.

Jaitpore, near Nowgong.
xxix.

Jalan territory.
xxvii.

Jamere.
Rebels flee to—lxii.

Jameson, Chas., Lt. (25th B. N. I.)
Wd. at Mundesore—lxxvi.

Jankee, Sepoy. (3rd Inf., H. C.)
S.-s., Culpee—125.

Jaloun.
Road to—pp. 69 ; 100 ; 102 ; 103 ; 116.
Ford across Jumna at—pp. 129 ; 132.

Jeffries, Henry, Pte. (H. M. 14th Lt. Dragns.)
Wd. at Koonch—p. 77.

Jelalabad.
Mutineers evacuate fort at—p. 28.

Jenkins, R. W., Lt. (H. M. 8th Hussars.)
Mtd. in desp.—p. 159.
Wd. at Gwalior—p. 171.
Mtd. in desp.—cxix.

Jerapore, village of.
On Ram Gunga—p. 27.
Rebel camp at, captured—*ib*.

Jerome, H. E., Lt. (H. M. 86th Reg.)
Mtd. in desp., (Jhansi)—p. 53 ; 55.
Wd. at Calpee—p. 94.
Wd., and mtd. in desp. (May 20, 1858)—pp. 121 ; 123.

Jeyroho.
fugitives led to—xxvii.

Jhabooa.
English fugitives reach—lx ; lxi.

Jhansi.
Brigr. Stuart sent to invest—p. 40.
Sir H. Rose arrives before—*ib.*
Reconnaissance made—*ib.*
The Fort and its outworks described—*ib.*
The City and suburbs described—p. 41.
Difficulties of attack—*ib.*
Importance of the "mound"—*ib.*
Position of British batteries—p. 42.
Right attack begins—*ib.*
Number of the garrison—*ib.*
Burning of hay-ricks—*ib.*
Rebel artillery well served—*ib.*
Women in rebel batteries—*ib.*
Inhabitants implicated in murder of British—p. 43.
Importance of capturing the city—*ib.*
Progress of the cannonade—*ib.*
Parapets destroyed—*ib.*
Breach made practicable—p. 44.
Good service of riflemen—*ib.*
Daily loss among rebels—*ib.*
The defences dismantled—*ib.*
Obstinate defence—p. 45.
Escalade ordered—*ib.*
Assault deferred—*ib.*
Approach of the "Army of the Peshwa,"—*ib.*
Telegraph established—*ib.*
Order for assault issued—*ib.*
Success of the left attack—p. 46.
Houses loop-holed—*ib.*
Skirmishers enter Palace—*ib.* ; p. 54.
Progress of the right attack—p. 47.
Burrahgong gate occupied—*ib.*
House-to-house fighting—*ib.*
Combat in the Palace stables—*ib.*
Rebel standards captured—p. 48.
Union Jack hoisted on Palace—*ib.*
Desperation of rebels—*ib.*
Flight of body of rebels—*ib.*
They are intercepted—*ib.*
False alarm of approaching rebel force—p. 49.
The whole city occupied—*ib.*
Flight of the Ranee—*ib.*
Force sent in pursuit—*ib.*

Jhansi—(*contd.*)
Narrow escape of the Ranee—pp. 49-50.
Final destruction of rebels—p. 50.
Desperate defence of a house—*ib.*
Great strength of the fortress—p. 51.
Difficulties of the British task—p. 52.
Losses of rebels—p. 52.
Humanity of British troops—*ib.*
Losses of British—*ib.*
Brigr. Stuart's report (1st Brig.)—pp. 54-55.
Brigr. Stuart's report (2nd Frig.)—pp. 55—57.
Ladders found too short—p. 56.
Desperate resistance at Palace—*ib.*
British garrison of—p. 65.
Party of 14th Irregulars despatched to—xxi.
Mutiny at, account of—i-xiv.

Jhansi Rance of.
Her responsibility for mutiny there—vii ; xi ; xiii ; xxii.
Accounts of her death—pp. 139, 160, xci, cxv, cxvi.
Velaitees under—p. 65.
Supports Nawab of Banda—p. 71.
Her great influence—p. 83.
At Cutcherry of Calpee—p. 95.
Orders as to disposal of—xci.

Jharoo Comar, son of.
Murders Mr. Andrews—vii.

Jharoo Koar, (a native).
xi.

Jheeghun.
Maj-Gen. Whitlock's account of engagement with rebels at, April 10, 1858)—p. 29-30.
Destroyed—p. 30.

Jheet Sing, (Mutineer.)
Hanged—p. 30.

Jhurut Hoosanie Khan, Jemadar. (3rd Hyd. Cav.)
Wd. at Barodia, mtd. in desp.—p. 13.

Jignee, Rajah of.
His treachery—p. 66.

Johns, Nathaniel, Corp. (21st Coy R. E.)
Wd. at Jhansi—p. 57.

Johnson, Lt. (Adjt., 1st Cav., H. C.)
Mtd. in desp. (Koonch)—p. 76.
At Mundesore—lxxxv.

Johnson, P., Writer.
Remains at Kubrai—xxix.
At Muntuoo—xxxii.

Johnson, Thomas, Pte. (H. M., 95th Reg.)
Wd. at Gwalior—p. 172.

Johnston, T., Pte. (H. M., 71st Reg.)
Died s.-s., Calpee—p. 124.

Johnstone, Lt. (Cav., H. C.)
Mtd. in desp. (Gwalior)—p. 165.
At the Betwa—cii.

Jokoo Sing, Sepoy (3rd Inf., H. C.)
Mortally wd. at Jhansi—p. 62.

Jokun Bagh, Jhansi.
Massacre at—p. 41.
Occupied—pp. 44 ; 45.
Mamoo Sahib hanged there—p. 48.
Massacre at—viii; ix; xi.

Jones, Francis, Pte. (H. M. 14th Lt. Dragns.)
Wd. (the Betwa)—cviii.

Jones, James, (Camel Corps.)
Wd at Calpee—p. 124.

Jowra Alipore.
Brigr. Napier's Report on action, at—p. 163.
Rebel losses at—p. 164.
Casualties at—pp. 166-167.
Ordnance captured at—p. 168.

Juan Carlos, Tpr. (3rd Bombay Lt. Cav.)
Wd. at Calpee—p. 124.

Jubbulpore.
lxxxix.

Judgson, Sgt. (Hyd. Art.)
Mtd. in desp.—p. 121.

Juggermanpore.
Situation of—p. 129.

Juggunath Panday, Pte. (25th B. N. I.)
Wd. at Jhansi—p. 59.

Jullalpoor.
Road from, to Calpee—p. 86 ; 90; 95 ; 96 ; 100.

Jumal Oodeen, Sowar (Meade's Horse.)
Wd (Jowra-Alipore) - p. 167.

Jumna, R.
Rebels take oath on waters—p. 94.
General action of the—pp. 97—100
Its effects—p. 101.
Conduct of troops at, eulogised—p. 103.

Jurtub Sing, Jemadar.
Recond for "Order of Merit"—p. 165.

Jymal Sing, Tpr. (1st Cav., H. C.)
Wd. at Jhansi—p. 61.

K

Kahdeedeen, Sepoy (3rd Inf., H. C.)
Wd. (the Betwa)—cix.

Kahoo Tehree.
Battery, at Jhansi—p. 44.

Kailly, Sgt. (Engineers).
Kld by mutineers at Jhansi—ix.

Kalkee Pursad, Tpr. (3rd Lt. Cav.)
Wd. at Barodia—p. 15.

Kalka Pursad, Pte. (4th B. N. I.)
Severely burnt (the Betwa)—cix.

Kallinger.
In Mirzapore—xxvii.

Kamdar Khan, Nawab.
Hanged at Rathghur—p. 7.

Kamta Sing, Tpr. (1st Cav., H. C.)
Wd. (the Betwa)—cix.

Kana, Seikh.
Leader of mutineers—xxii.

Kane, Maj., (15th B. N. I.)
Director of Bullock train, "special mention"—p. 104.

Kane, R.
Rebel position on —p. 31.

Kapoo Tekri.
A ridge at Jhansi—p. 41.

Karard, Agnes W.
Sister to Mrs. Mutlow—xiv.

Karee Puburee.
Maj. Kirke buried near—xxix.
Situation of—*ib*.

Karukbijlee.
Gun at Jhansi—p. xi.

Kashab.
Mentioned—p. 13.

Kaun Sing, Sepoy.
Wd. at Nowgong—xxxii.

Keane, Ens. (H. M. 86th Reg.)
Mtd. in desp. (Calpee)—p. 115.
Ditto (May 22, 1858)—p. 122.

Keane, Maj. (H. M. 86th Reg.)
At Goraria—lxx
Mtd. in desp. (Mundesore)—lxxii.

Kearn, James, Pte. (H. M. 86th Reg.)
Died s-s., (Koonch)—p. 76.

Keating, Lt. (Bombay Arty.)
At Mundesore—lxxiv.

Keatinge, Capt. (Offg. Pol. Agt., W. Malwa)
Wd. at Chundaree—p. 105.

Keatinge, Capt. and Mrs.
Take refuge at Parnasa—lxv.
Capt. K.—lxxx.

Keelan, Henry, Pte. (H. M. 86th Reg.)
Wd. at Jhansi—p. 58.

Keeraswamy, Naique (Madras S. M.).
Wd. at Rathghur—p. 9.

Kelly, James, Gnr. (1st Tp., H. A.)
Wd. (the Betwa)—cvii.

Kelly, Michael, Pte. (H. M. 8th Hussars)
Wd. at Gwalior—p. 171.

Kennelly, Robert, Pte. (3rd B. E. R.)
Wd. at Jhansi—p. 60.

Kerr, Abraham, Pte. (H. M. 86th Reg.)
Fatally wd. at Jhansi—p. 58.

Kerwe.
See *Kirwee*.

Kesson Sing, Subadar (25th B. N. I.)
Wd. at Jhansi—p. 59.

Khaim Khan, Sepoy (5th Inf., H. C.)
Kld. at Jhansi—p. 62.

Khairoolah Khan, Tpr. (4th Cav., H. C.)
Recmd. for promotion—p. 51.

Khan Mahomed Khan, Tpr. (4th Cav., H. C.).
Wd. and recmd. for promotion—p. 51.

Khodabax.
Chaprassi—x.

Khooman Sing, Buxee.
Arrives at Mhow—xlix.

Khyre Mohomed Khan, Tpr. (4th Cav., H. C.
Wd. at Jhansi—p. 61.

Killed and wounded.
Returns of, see *Casualties*.

King, James, Pte. (H. M. 14th Lt. Dragns.)
Died s.-s., Calpee—p. 123.

Kinniburgh, David, Pte. (H. M. 71st Highland Lt. Inf.)
Kld. (Gwalior)—p. 170.

Kirke, H., Maj. (12th B. N. I.)
In command at Nowgong—xv.
Is informed of mutinous outbreak—*ib*.
Places guns to command roads—xvi.
Receives letter from Capt. Gordon—xvii.
Maj.-Gen. Sir H. Wheeler approves his dispositions—xviii.
Is again warned of mutiny—*ib*. xxxiii.
Places guns before quarter-guard of the 12th B. N. I.—xix.
Hears of mutiny at Jhansi—*ib*.
Addresses Native officers—xx.
Refuses to allow Native women and children to leave Nowgong—xxi.
Is informed of seizure of guns by the mutineers—xxiii.
Tries to induce sepoys to attack mutineers—xxiv.
His clemency to a sepoy—xxv.
Sends Capt. Scot to Nowgong—*ib*.
Goes to Logassee—xxvii.
Endeavours to restore order among escort—xxviii.
Dies of sun-stroke—*ib*.
His failing powers before the mutiny—xxix.
Requests Capt. Scot to act for him—*ib*.

Kirchoff, Sgt. and wife.
Among fugitives from Nowgong—xxix; xxx.
Sgt. K. wd.—xxxi.

Kirke, H.
Son of Maj. Kirke—xxix; xxxi.

Kirkup, Archibald, Pte. (H. M. 71st Reg.)
S.-s. (Koonch)—p. 78.

Kirly, William, Pte. (H. M. 71st Reg.)
S.-.s (Koonch)—p. 78.

Kirwee.
xcii. Occupied by Sir G. Whitlock—xciii.

Kirwin, Wm., Pte. (H. M. 86th Reg.).
Wd. at Jhansi—p. 58.

Kishen Ram.
Atrocities of—p. 7.
Executed—*ib*.

Kissoon, Golundauz (2nd Co. Arty., H. C.).
Wd. at Jhansi—p. 61.

Kisson Sing Pte. (24th B. N. I.).
Kld. at Jhansi—61.

Knatchbull, Lt. (H. M. 95th Reg.)
At Gwalior—p. 147.
Mtd. in desp., (Gwalior)—p. 174.

Kolwur.
On the Betwa, rebels cross ford at—xcv; xcvii.

Konch.
See *Koonch*.

Koolpeeha.
Near Chirkaree—p. xxvii.

Koonch.
Sir H. Rose's despatch describing the Action at—p. 64.
Occupied by rebels under Tantia Topee—p. 65.
Difficulties of attacking—p. *ib*.
British arrive within sight of—p. 66.
The environs cleared of rebels—p. 67.
The fort captured—*ib*.
Charge of British Cavalry—p. 68.
1st Brigade enters the town—*ib*.
The retreating rebels pursued—p. 69.
Great heat checks the pursuit—p. 70.
Rebel losses—*ib*.
Maj. Orr's report on the action—p. 73.
The attack on the outskirts—p. 74.
The pursuit—p. 75.
List of casualties at—pp. 76—9.
Rebel ordnance captured at—p. 80.
Sir H. Rose marches from—p. 84.

Kooreye, fort.
  Rebels at—pp 6; 10.

Kooshabore.
  Capture of—ciii.

Koraye.
  Situation of—p. 10.
  Rebels fly to—p. 14.
  Leave their guns at—*ib.*

Kotah.
  Rebels from—pp. 64; 65.
  Cavalry from—p. 83.
  K. Contingent—p. 102.

Kotah-ka-Serai.
  Situation of—pp. 134; 139; 140; 150; 152.
  Brigr. Smith marches to—p. 156.
  Rebels attack—*ib.*
  Troops at, reinforced—p. 157.
  Charge of 8th Hussars at—*ib.*
  Lt.-Col. Raines at—p. 160.

Koteh.
  Escape of rebels from—xci.
  See also, *Kotah.*

Kotra.
  Maj. Orr drives rebels from—p. 65.

Kotwallee.
  At Mhow, Muskets recovered from—xlix

Krulassa.
  Rebels abandon—p. 14.

Kubrai.
  English fugitives reach—xxix.
  Nana Sahib at—*ib.*

Kulgipore.
  Near Mundesore—lxviii.

Kumerali Khan, Tpr. (1st Cav., H. C.)
  Wd. at Jhansi—p. 61.

Kundhya.
  Naik—xxxv.

Kundoo Jadow, Pte. (4th B. N. I.)
  Severely burnt, (the Betwa)—cix.

Kunie Moorie, Pte. (25th B. N. I.)
  Wd. at Jhansi—p. 59.

Kurreem Ali Khan, Tpr. (1st Cav., H. C.)
  Wd. and recmd. for promotion—p. 51.

Kurreem Khan, Sepoy (3rd Inf., H. C.)
  S.-s., Calpee—p. 125.

Kurreeni Sing, Naib Russaldar.
  Recommended for "Order of Merit"—p. 165.

L

Laine, James, Sgt. (3rd B. E. R.)
  Wd., the Betwa—cviii.

Laird, Thomas, Pte. (3rd B. E. R.)
  Mortally wd. at Jhansi—p. 60.

Lala Doma.
  Servant of Moofedar of Bellaree—xxvi.

Lall Khan, Duffadar (1st Cav., R. C.)
  Wd. at Jhansi—p. 61.

Lall Mahomed Jemadar, (12th N. I.)
  Jemadar, (12th N. I.)—iii, xi.
  Joins mutineers—xviii.

Lall Sing, Pte. (4th B. N. I.).
  Severely burnt, (the Betwa)—cix.

Lall Sing, Tpr. (1st Cav., H. C.)
  Wd. at Koonch—p. 79.

Lall Turbardio, (52nd B. N. I.)
  Leader of mutineers, killed—p. 24.

Lalla Mooljie, Pte. (24th B. N. I.)
  Kld. at Calpee—p. 124.

Lamb, Vet.-Surg. (3rd Lt. Cav.)
  Mtd. in desp. (Etora)—p. 108.

Langdale, Mr.
  At Muntuoo—xxxii.

Langdale, Mrs.
  Reported death of—xxxii.

Laumon Ghoy, Pte. (25th B. N. I.)
Wd. at Jhansi—p. 59.

Lavie, Maj. (Cmdg. Madr. Arty.)
Mtd. in desp.—p. 33; 35; 36.

Law, T. H., Sgt. (3rd Tp., H. A.)
Wd. at Gwalior—p. 171.

Lawder, Capt. (A. Q. M. G.)
Mtd. in desp.—p. 34.

Lawrence, George, Pte. (H. M. 4th Lt. Dragns.)
Kld. at Koonch—p. 77.

Leary, Susan.
Sister to Mrs. Mutlow—xiv.

Leathed, William, Bugler, (2nd Co. R. E.)
Died s.-s., Calpce—p. 123.

Leckie, Capt. (D. A. M. G.)
Mtd. in desp. (Jhansi)—pp. 54, 57.
Ditto   (Koonch)—p.

Le Cocq, Lt. (B. A.)
Cmdg. guns at Gwalior—cxiv; cxv; cxvii.

Lee, J., Gnr. (1st Tp. H. A.)
Wd. at Barodia—p. 15.

Leethen, George, Pte. (H. M. 86th Reg.)
Wd. at Jhansi—p. 58.

Leigh, John, Pte. (H. M. 14th Lt. Dragns.)
Kld., the Betwa—cviii.

Leith, James, Lt. (H. M. 14th Lt. Dragns.)
Mtd. in desp.—lxx.
Wd. at Mundesore—lxxv, lxxvi.
Mtd. in desp. (Betwa) xcix.
Awarded Victoria Cross—*ib.*; ci.

Leonard, Pte. (H. M. 14th Lt. Dragns.)
Wd., R. Betwa—cvii.

Lepper, Capt. (H. M. 86th Reg.)
Mtd. in desp.(Calpee)—p. 115.
Ditto (May 20 and May 22, 1858)— p. 121.

Leslie, Corp. (H. M. 71st Reg.)
" Special mention,"(Morar)—p. 137.
Kld.—p. 170,

Letters and Despatches :—
(1) (Extract). From Officiating Adjt.-Gen. of the Army, to Sec. to Govt. of India, Mil. Dept., No. 1094, Aug. 18th, 1859, [enclosing (2) and (3)]. —p. 1.
(2) From Maj.-Gen. Sir H. Rose, to Adjt.-Gen. of the Army, (Camp Saugor, Feb. 7th, 1858), reporting capture of Rath.-ghur.—p. 2.
(3) From Maj.-Gen. Sir H. Rose, to Col. Green, Adjt.-Gen. of the Army, (undated),' reporting action of Barodia,— p. 10.
(4) From H. L. Anderson, Esq., Sec. to Govt., Bombay, to Col. Edw. Green, Adjt.-Gen. of the Army (March 18th, 1858)—p. 17.
(5) From Adjt.-Gen. of the Army, to Sec to Govt., Bombay (March 17th, 1858). —p. 17.
(6) (Extract). From Adjt.-Gen. of the Army, to Maj.-Gen. Cmdg. C. I. F. F. (March 20th 1858)—p. 18.
(7) From Maj. H. W. Norman, Dep. Adjt.-Gen. of the Army, to Sec. to Govt. of India, Mil. Dept., (Futtehgurh, April 26th, 1858), [enclosing (8)]—p. 19.
(8) From Maj.-Gen. Sir H. Rose, Commanding C. I. F. F., to Maj.-Gen. Mansfield, Chief of Staff, Cawnpore, (March 26th, 1858), reporting forcing pass of Mudinpore, etc.—p. 19.
(9) From Maj. H. W. Norman, Dep. Adjt.-Gen. of the Army, to Sec. to Govt. of India, Mil. Dept. (April 26th, 1858). [enclosing (10)]—p. 26.
(10) From Brig.-Gen. R. Walpole, Cmdg. F. F., to Chief of the Staff, (Allahgunge, April 23rd, 1858)—p. 26.

Letters and Despatches—(Contd.)

(11) From Maj.-Gen. G. Whitlock, Cmdg. Saugor Field Div., to Maj.-Gen. Mansfield, Chief of the Staff, reporting engagement at Jheeghun, (April 12th, 1858)—p. 29.

(12) From Maj.-Gen. G. C. Whitlock, Cmdg. Saugor Field Div., to Maj.-Gen. Mansfield, Chief of the Staff, reporting Battle of Banda, (April 24th, 1858)—p. 31.

(13) From Col. E. Apthorp, Cmdg. 3rd Madras Eur. Reg., to Maj.-Gen. Whitlock, (Banda, April 20th, 1858), [enclosing (14) and (15)]—p. 34.

(14) From Brigr. W. H. Miller, Cmdg. Art. Brig., Saugor F. F., to Asst. Adjt. Gen., Saugor Field Div., (Banda, April 20th, 1858)—p. 35.

(15) From Maj. T. Oakes, Cmdg. Cav. Brig., Saugor Field Div., to Asst. Adjt.-Gen., Saugor and Nerbudda F. F., (Banda, April 20th, 1858)—p. 36.

(16) From Maj.-Gen. G. C. Whitlock, Cmdg. Saugor Field Div., to Maj.-Gen. Mansfield, Chief of Staff, (Banda, April 30th, 1858), [addendum to (12)]—p. 38.

(17) From Maj. H. W. Norman, Dep. Adjt.-Gen. of the Army, to Sec. to Govt. of India, Mil. Dept., (Shejehanpore, May 23rd, 1858), [enclosing (18)]—p. 39.

(18) From Maj.-Gen. Sir H. Rose, Cmdg. C. I. F. F., to the Chief of Staff, reporting operations against Jhansi (Camp Mote, April 30th, 1858) [enclosing (19) and (20)]—p. 39.

(19) From Brigr. C. S. Stuart, Cmdg. 1st Brig., C. I. F. F., to Asst. Adjt.-Gen. C. I. F. F., (Camp Jhansi, April 13th, 1858)—p. 54.

(20) From Brigr. C. Steuart, Cmdg. 2nd Brig. C. I. F. F., to Asst. Adjt.-Gen. C. I. F. F., (Camp Jhansi, April 29th, 1858)—p. 55.

Letters and Despatches—(Contd.)

(21) From Lt. Col. Mayhew, Adjt.-Gen. of the Army, to Sec. to Govt. of India, Mil. Dept., (Allahabad, July 29th 1858), [enclosing (22)]—p. 64.

(22) From Maj.-Gen. Sir H. Rose, Cmdg. C. I. F. F., to Sir W. M. Mansfield, Chief of Staff, describing battle of Koonch (Camp Goolowlee, May 24th, 1858), [enclosing (23)]—p. 64.

(23) From Maj. W. A. Orr, Cmdg. F. F., Hyd. Contingent, to Col. Wetherall, Chief of Staff, C. I. F. F., (Camp Etowra, May 14th, 1858)—p. 73.

(24) From Maj. H. W. Norman, Dep. Adjt. Gen. of the Army, to Sec. to Govt. of India, Mil. Dept., (Feb. 2nd, 1859) [enclosing (25)]—p. 81.

(25) From Maj.-Gen. Sir H. Rose, Cmdg. F. D. A. and F. Fs., to Maj.-Gen. Sir W. M. Mansfield, Chief of Staff, describing capture of Calpee, (Gwalior, June 22nd, 1858), [enclosing (26) (27), (28), (29), and (30)]—p. 81.

(26) From Maj. Forbes, Cmdg. Rear Guard, to Capt. Todd, Brig. Maj., 2nd Brig., C. I. F. F., (Camp near Deopore,, May 16th, 1858)—p. 107.

(27) From Lt.-Col. Campbell, Cmdg. 2nd Brig., C. I. F. F., to Chief of Staff, C. I. F. F., (Camp Deopore, May 18th, 1858)—p. 109.

(28) From Lt.-Col. G. V. Maxwell, H. M. 88th Reg., Cmdg. Moveable Col., Cawnpore District, to Col. E. R. Wetherall, Chief of Staff, C. I. F. F. (Camp before Calpee, May 24th, 1858)—p. 110.

(29) From Brigr. Stuart, Cmdg. 1st Brig. C. I. F. F., to Asst. Adjt.-Gen., C. I. F. F., (Camp Calpee, May 29th, 1858)—p. 112.

(30) From Maj. Gall, Cmdg. Left Wing 14th Lt. Dragns., to Chief of Staff C. I. F. F., (Camp Calpee, May 25th, 1858)—p. 116.

Letters and Despatches—(Contd.)

(31) From Maj. H. W. Norman, Dep. Adjt.-Gen. of the Army, to the Sec. to Govt. Mil. Dept., (Allahabad, Jan. 19th, 1859), [enclosing (32)]—p 128.

(32) From Maj.-Gen. Sir H. Rose, Cmdg. F. Fs., South of the Nerbudda, to Maj.-Gen. Sir W. Mansfield, Chief of Staff, reporting capture of Gwalior, (Poonch, Oct. 13th, 1858) [enclosing (33), (34), (38)]—p. 129.

(33) From Brigr.-Gen. R. Napier, Cmdg. 2nd Brig., C. I. F. F., to Asst. Adjt.-Gen., C. I. F. F., (Camp Morar, June 18th, 1858)—p. 153.

(34) From Brigr. M. W. Smith, Cmdg. Brig., Rajpootana F. F., (Camp before Gwalior, June 25th, 1858), [enclosing (37)]—p.156.

(35) Extracts from notes of Brigr. M. W. Smith, received subsequent to receipt of No. 34—p. 159.

(36) From Lt.-Col. T. N. Hicks, Cmdg. Arty., C. I. F. F., to Brigr. M. W. Smith, Cmdg. Rajpootana F. F. (Camp Morar, June 25th, 1858)—p. 159.

(37) From Lt.-Col. J. A. R. Raines, H. M. 95th Reg., Cmdg. Inf., to Brigr. M. W. Smith, (June 18th, 1858)—p. 160.

(38) From Brigr.-Gen. R. Napier, Cmdg. 2nd Brig., C. I. F. F., to Asst. Adjt.-Gen., C. I. F. F., (Jowra-Alipore, June 21st, 1858)—p. 163.

(39) From Capt. H. D. Abbott, Cmdg. 3rd Cav. H. C., to Capt. Todd, Brigr. Maj., 2nd Brig., C. I. F. F., (Poharee, June 25th, 1858)—p. 168.

(40) From Capt. Dunlop, 12th N. I., Cmdg. at Jhansi, to Officer Cmdg. at Nowgong, (Jhansi, June 4th, 1857)—xix.

(41) From Brigr. Ramsay, to Agent to Gov. Gen. for C. I. (Gwalior, May 30th, 1857),—xxxvii.

Letters and Despatches—(Contd.)

(42) From Bvt.-Maj. Cooper, to officiating Adjt.-Gen., (Mhow, July 9th, 1857)—xlii.

(43) From Capt. T. Hungerford, Cmdg. at Mhow, to Sec. to Govt., Bengal (Mhow, July 17th, 1857), [enclosing (44)—(52)],—xliv.

(44) The same, to Brigr.-Maj., Saugor, (Mhow, July 2nd, 1857),—liii.

(45) The same, to the Maharajah of Indore, (Mhow, July 3rd, 1857),—lvi.

(46) The same, to Adjt.-Gen., Bombay Army, (Mhow, July 4th, 1857)—lvi.

(47) Tookajee Rao Holkar, Maharajah of Indore, to Capt. Hungerford—lviii.

(48) From Ramchunder Rao, to Capt. T. Hungerford, (Indore, July 7th, 1857).—lix.

(49) From A. Elliot, Asst. Govt. Supdt. in Malwah, to Rao Ramchunder Rao Saheb, (Mhow, July 8th, 1857)—lx.

(50) From Capt. T. Hungerford, to the Maharajah of Indore, (Mhow, July 7th, 1857),—lxi.

(51) From Ramchunder Rao, to Capt. Hungerford, (July 8th, 1857),—lxii.

(52) From Capt. T. Hungerford, to Sec. to Govt., Bombay, (Mhow, July 8th, 1857)—lxiii.

(53) (Telegram) from Lord Elphinstone to Capt. Hungerford, July 8th, 1857—lxiv.

(54) (Telegram) from Capt. Hungerford, to Lord Elphinstone, (July 9th, 1857)—lxv.

(55) ————————————lxvi.

(56) From Brigr. C. S. Stuart, Cmdg. Malwa F. F., to Adj.-Gen. of Bombay Army, (Mundesore, Nov. 27th, 1857) [enclosing (57)]—lxvii.

(57) From Maj. Orr, Cmdg. F., F. H. C., Dep. Asst. Q. M. G., (Mundesore, Nov. 25th 1857),—lxxiii.

(58) From Maj.-Gen. Mansfield, to Maj.-Gen. Rose, confidential, (Cawnpore, Feb. 11th, 1858),—lxxix.

Letters and Despatches - (Contd.)

(59) From Lord Canning, to Sir R. Hamilton, (Allahabad, Feb. 11th, 1858)—lxxix.

(60) From Col. R. J. H. Birch, Sec. to Govt. of India, Mil. Dept., to Maj.-Gen. Whitlock, Cmdg. Moveable Col., (Allahabad, March 13th, 1858)—lxxx.

(61) From Maj.-Gen. Sir H. Rose, Cmdg. C. I. F. F., to Col. Birch, Sec. to Govt. of India, Mil. Dept., (Camp Sirrus March 19th, 1858)—lxxxi.

(62) From Maj.-Gen. Whitlock, Cmdg. Saugor Field Div., to Maj.-Gen., Sir H. Rose, Cmdg. C. I. F. F., (Dumoh, March 19th, 1858),—lxxxiii.

(63) From Maj.-Gen. Sir H. Rose, Cmdg. C. I. F. F., to Maj.-Gen. Whitlock, Cmdg. Saugor Field Div., (Sirrus Ghat, March 19th, 1858),—lxxxiii.

(64) From Sir R. Hamilton, Agent for the Gov.-Gen. in Central India, to G. F. Edmonstone, Sec to Govt. of India For. Dept., (March 1858),—lxxxiv.

(65) From Sec. to Govt. of India, to Agent to Gov.-Gen., Central India, (Allahabad, April 30th, 1858),l—lxxxvi.

(66) From Sir R. Hamilton to G. A. Hamilton, Esq., enclosing memorandum, (Stratford-on-Avon, March 20th 1862)—lxxxvii.

(67) From Asst. Adjt.-Gen. of the Army (Maj. D. M. Stewart), to Sec. to Govt. of India, Mil. Dept., (Camp Poona, June 9th, 1858), [enclosing (68)],—xciv.

(68) From Maj.-Gen. Sir H. Rose, Cmdg. C. I. F. F., to Chief of Staff, describing Battle of the Betwa, (Camp Pooch, April 30th, 1858)—xcv.

(69) From Brigr. C. S. Stuart, Cmdg. 1st Brig., C. I. F. F., to Asst. Adjt.-Gen., C. I. F. F., (Jhansi, April 6th, 1858) [enclosing (78)],—cii.

Letters and Despatches—(Concld.)

70) From Maj.-Gen. Sir H. Rose, Cmdg. C. I. F. F., to Chief of Staff, (Soopowlie, June 14th 1858)—cxi.

(71) From Maj.-Gen. H. S. Roberts, Cmdg Northern Div. of Army, to Chief of Staff, (Ahmedabad, April 23rd 1859) [enclosing (72)],—cxiii.

(72) From Brigr. M, W. Smith, Cmdg. Brig., P. F. F., to Asst. Adjt.-Gen. Rajpootana F. F., (Omra, Jan. 15th, 1859),—cxiii.

(73) From Brigr. M. W. Smith, Cmdg. Brig., Malwa Div., to Adjt.-Gen. Poona, (Sepree, July 25th, 1858)—cxiv.

(74) From Lt.-Col. T. R. Raines, H. M. 95th Reg., to Brigr. M. W. Smith, Cmdg. Brig. M. D., (Nov. 12th, 1858)—cxviii.

(75) (Extract) Col. Blake, Cmdg. 3rd Tp., H. A., (Nov. 12th, 1858)—cxix.

Levy, J., Pte. (3rd B. E. R.)
Wd. at Rathghur—p. 9.

Lewis, R. F., Lt., (H. M. 86th Reg.)
Mtd. in desp.—p. 50.
Wd. at Jhansi—p. 58.

Liddajee, Sepoy (3rd Inf., H. C.)
S.-s., Calpee—p. 125.

Liddell, Lt. Col., (3rd B. E. R.)
Cmds. Troops at Rathghur—p. 3.
Enters the Fort—p. 6.
Mtd. in desp.—p. 12.
Occupies Barodia—p. 14.
Mtd in desp.—p. 18.
Leads an attack at Mudinpore—p. 23.
Mtd. in desp.—p. 24.
Leads his reg. at (Jhansi)—pp. 46 ; 56.
Mtd. in desp., (Jhansi)—p. 53.
Commands Garrison at Jhansi—p. 92.

Lightfoot, J. G. Capt. (Cmdg. 1st Tp., B. H. A.)
In command of battery at Rathghur—p. 4.
Leads storming party—pp. 5, 6.
Commands battery at Barodia—pp. 11; 13; 17.
Mtd. in desp. (Jhansi)—p. 53.
At Koonch—p. 67.
Mtd. in desp. (Koonch)—p. 73.
At-Mutha—pp. 87; 100; 116; 117.
Captures guns before Calpee—p. 118.
Mtd. in desp. (May 7 and May 22, 1858)—p. 121.
At Morar—pp. 136, 137.
" Special mention "—p. 138.
At Jowra-Alipore—pp. 163, 164.
Mtd. in desp.—p. 165.
His battery at the Betwa—xcvii; xcviii; c.
Mtd. in desp.—ci.
Wd. (Betwa)—cvii.

Lindsay, James, Pte. (H. M. 8th Hussars.)
Wd. at Gwalior—p. 171.

Lister, J., Pte. (3rd B. E. R.)
Wd. at Rathghur—p. 9.

Little, Capt. (25th B. N. I.)
Mtd. in desp. (Mundesore)—lxxii.

Livingstone, J., Pte. (H. M. 71st Reg.)
Died s.-s., Calpee—p. 124.

Loch, Capt. (1st Bombay Lt. Cav.)
Leads charge at Gwalior—p. 148.
" Special mention "—p. 174.

Lochun Bahallia, Pte. (24th B. N. I.)
Wd. at Jhansi—p. 61.

Lofthouse, Asst. Surg.
Mtd. in desp. (Calpee)—p. 118.

Loftus, Maj. (H. M. 71st Reg.)
At Muttra—p. 109.
Mtd. in desp. (May 18th, 1858)—p. 121.

Logassie.
Maj. Kirke at—xxvii.

Logassie, Thakoor of.
Gratified at defeat of rebels—p. 30.

Loharee.
1st Brig. March from—p. 66.

Lowry, Lt. (Cmdg. Bat. R. A.)
Mtd. in desp. (Jhansi)—p. 53.
At Diapoora—p. 107.
Mtd. in desp.—p. 108.

Lowth, Lt.-Col. (H. M. 86th Regt)
His cool judgment at Jhansi—p. 46.
Mtd. in desp.—p. 53.
Leads attack—p. 54.
Mtd. in desp.—p. 55.
Watches road to Goonah—p. 64.
At Koonch—p. 67.
Mtd. in desp.—p. 73.
" Special mention " (Calpee)—p. 99.
In action on the Jumna—pp. 113, 114.
Mtd. in desp.—p. 115.
Occupies heights before Gwalior—p. 143.
" Special mention "—p. 173.
At the Betwa—cii, civ.

Luard, Lt. (Late 1st Ben. N. C.)
Mtd. in desp. (Calpee)—p. 119.

Luchmean, Sepoy, (3rd Inf. H. C.)
S.-s., Calpee—p. 125.

Luckmun Rao.
Incites men to mutiny at Jhansi—i.

Ludlow, Maj.
Field Engineer., receives flag of truce at Banda—p. 34.

Lullutpore.
Party of 14th Irregulars despatched to—xxi.

Lumsdaine, Asst. Surg.
Mtd. in desp. (Calpee)—p. 118.

Lushker.
 (Gwalior), described—p. 130 ; 134 ; 144 ; 145.
 Grand parade—p. 146 ; 147 ; 148.
 Occupied—p. 149.
 Palace in—p. 151.

Lutchmanen, Pte. (Madras S. M.)
 Wd. at Jhansi—p. 59.

Lutchmen Gate.
 (Jhansi)—p. 42.

Lutchmon, Havildar, (5th Inf., H. C.)
 S.-s., Calpee—p. 125.

Lutchmon, Naick, (3rd Inf., H. C.)
 Mortally wd. at Jhansi—p. 61.

Lutchmun, Sepoy, (3rd Inf., H. C.)
 Dangerously burnt, (the Betwa)—cix.

Luxamon Tumulkhan, Pte. (24th B. N. I.)
 Kld. at Jhansi—p. 61.

Luxumon Narwakur, Pte. (4th B. N. I.)
 Severely burnt, (the Betwa) - cix.

Luxumon Powar, Pte. (25th B. N. I.)
 Wd. at Calpee—p. 123.

Lyle, Samuel, Pte. (3rd B. E. R.)
 Wd. at Jhansi—p. 60.

Lynch, J., Sgt. (H. M. 8th Hussars.)
 Wd. at Gwalior—p. 171.

Lyons, John, Pte. (H. M. 86th Reg.)
 Wd. at Jhansi—p. 58.

Lyster, H. H., Lt. (Interpreter, late 72nd B. N. I.)
 Wd. at Barodia—p. 15.
 Mtd. in desp. (Jhansi)—p. 53.
  Ditto (Koonch)—p. 72.
  Ditto (Calpee) —p. 119.
 Horse shot under him—p. 126.
 Mtd. in desp. (Gwalior) —p. 172.
  Ditto (Betwa)—cii.

M

Macdonald, Capt. (Asst. Q. M. G.)
 Mtd. in desp. (Barodia), wd.,—p. 12 ; 18.
 Leads storming party at Mudinpore—p. 22.
 Mtd. in desp.—p. 24.
  Ditto Jhansi—53.
  Ditto (Koonch)—p. 72.
 Mundesore—lxxi, lxxiv.
 Mtd. in desp. (Betwa)—cii.

Macdonald, J., Capt. (Sir H. Rose's Staff.)
 Wd. at Barodia—p. 15.

MacEvoy, John, Pte. (H. M. 86th Reg.)
 Wd. at Jhansi—p. 58.

Macfarlane, Field Surg.
 Mtd. in desp.—p. 34 ; 36.

Macintire, Capt., (2nd Cav., H. C.)
 His gallantry at Banda—p. 31 ; 33.
 Mtd. in desp.—p. 34 ; 35 ; 37.

Mackenzie, Dr. (3rd Cav., Hyd. Congt.)
 Mtd. in desp.—p. 119.
 At Jowra-Alipore—p. 165.

Mackenzie, Surg. (Staff Surg.)
 Mtd. in desp. (Koonch)—p. 73.
  Ditto (Calpee)—p. 115.
 At Mundesore—lxxi.

Mackintosh, Lt. (3rd B. E. R.)
 At Diapoora—p. 107.
 Mtd. in desp. (Calpee)—p. 120.

Maclachlin, Lt. (Adj. Bo. Arty.)
 Acting Brigade Maj.—p. 154.
 Mtd. in desp. (Gwalior)—p. 155.

Maclachlin, Lt., (Acting Asst. Q. M. G.)
 Mtd. in desp.— p. 166.

Maclean, Capt., (Dep. Commr. of Jhansi.)
 Mtd. in desp.—p. 105.

INDEX

McMahon, Capt. (H. M. 14th Dragns.)
Wd., mtd. in desp. (Koonch)—p. 69.

MacMullen, Capt. (23rd Beng. Inf.)
Mtd. in desp. (Kotah-ka-Serai)—p. 158.
" Special mention"—p. 176.

Macpherson, Maj. (Political Agent at Gwalior.)
With Scindiah—p. 151.
Conveys Scindiah's warnings to Brigr. Ramsay—xxxvii.
And to Mr. Colvin—xxxix.
His unfounded apprehensions—xl, xli.

Macquoid, R. K., Lt., (Adjt 5th Inf., H. C.)
Cmdg. 3rd Inf., H. C., at Koonch, —p. 73.
Mtd. in desp.—p. 75.
    Ditto   (May 22nd, 1858)—p. 122.

Madarbux, Khitmutgar.
—xii.

Madden, James, Pte. (3rd B. E R.)
Died s.-s., Calpee—p. 124.

Madden, Thos., Pte. (H. M. 86th Reg.)
Mortally wd. at Calpee—p. 123.

Maddoo Khan, Tpr., (3rd Cav., H. C.)
Kld. (Gwalior)—p. 170.

Madras, Mr. (Commst. Officer.)
At Mhow—xlviii ; xlix—l.
Mtd. in desp.—liii.

Mahadoo Gowlee, Pte., (25th B. N. I.)
Wd. (Gwalior) — p. 170.

Mahoba.
See *Muhoba*.

Mahomed Ali, Mutineer.
Reward offered for his head—lxii.

Mahomed Bux, Duffadar, (Cav., H. C.)
Wd. (Jowra-Alipore)—p. 167.

Mahomed Bux, Sowar (Cav., H. C.)
Wd. (Jowra-Alipore)—p. 167.

Mahomed Bux, Sowar.
Recmd. for " Order of Merit "—p. 165.

Mahomed Emaum, Tpr. (1st Cav., H. C.)
Wd. at Calpee—p. 125.

Mahomed Fazil Khan.
Takes refuge, with his staff, in a cave.— p. 7.
Hanged—*ib*.
Horses of, at Rathghur—p. 8.

Mahomed Fazil Khan, nephew of.
Kld. at Barodia—p. 15.

Mahomed Fazil Khan, Secy. of.
Executed—p. 7.

Mahomed Ibrahim Khan, Tpr. (4th Cav., H. C.)
Kld., (the Betwa)—cix.

Mahomed Khan, Tpr. (Cav., H. C.)
Mtd. in desp. (Calpee)—p. 117.

Mahomed Khan, Tpr. (3rd Cav., H. C.)
Recmd. for " Order of British India "— p. 169.

Mahomed Khan, Tpr. (4th Cav., H. C.)
Kld. at Calpee—p. 125.

Mahomedeen Khan, Jemadar, (1st Cav., H. C.)
Wd., recmd. for promotion and " Order of Merit"— pp. 50-51.

Mahomed Sanah.
His statement regarding massacre at Jhansi—p. xi.

Mahratta Pundits.
Favour Nana Sahib—p. 83.

Mahrattas, Southern.
Ill-disposed population of—p. 93.
Denuded of troops—p. 131.

Maitland, Gnr. (Beng. Arty.)
Mtd. in desp. (Mundesore)—lxx.

Makkoopore.
Village near Banda—xxx.

Mallock, Lt., (Arty.)
Cmdg. Siege Train at Rathghur—p. 3.
In cmd. of guns at Mhow—xlix.
His services at Mhow—lii.

Malcolm, Sir John.
Reminiscence of—p. 7.

Malthone.
Feint against—p. 21.
Police station established at—p. 24.

Malwa.
Field Force—lxvii, lxxi.

Malwa, Western.
p. 105.

Mama Sahib (father of Ranee of Jhansi.)
x, xi.

Mamekun, Pte. (Madras S. M.)
Kld. at Jhansi—p. 59.

Mamoo Sahib.
Father of Ranee of Jhansi, captured and hanged—p. 48.
(See also *Mama S.*)

Mam Sookh, Pte., (25th B. N. I.)
Wd. at Jhansi—p. 59.

Mandah Khan, Tpr. (1st Cav., H. C.)
Wd. at Mudinpore—p. 25.

Mansfield, J., Maj.-Gen.
Chief of Staff, Bengal—p. 38.

Mansfield, Sir W. M.
Chief of Staff of the Army in India—
Despatch to—p. 19.
Ditto   p. 29.
Ditto   pp. 31; 81.
Ditto   p. 129.
Letter from, to Sir H. Rose—lxxix.
Assists Ld. Clyde—lxxxix.

Mara, John, Pte. (H. M. 86th Reg.)
Kld. at Jhansi—p. 58.

Marowra.
Fort of, capture of—pp. 19; 20.
Occupied by Sir H. Rose—p. 24.

Martin, Lt.
Narrow escape of, at Mhow—xlviii.

Martin, C., Lt. (H. M. 14th Lt. Dragns.)
Leads charge at Goraria—lxix.
Wd. at Mundesore—lxxvi.

Martin, John, Pte. (H. M. 86th Reg.)
Mortally wd. at Calpee—p. 123.

Marwattee, Driver, (Bombay Art.)
Wd. at Calpee—p. 123.

Massey, Hon. E. C. H., Maj. (H. M. 95th Reg.)
Mtd. in desp. (Gwalior)—p. 141.
Ditto   p. 162.
At Kotah-ka-Serai—p. 176.

Mathews, Roger, Pte. (H. M. 86th Reg.)
Mtd. in desp. (Jhansi)—p. 55.

Mattadeen Moraye, Pte. (25th B. N. I.)
Wd. (Gwalior)—p. 170.

Matthews, Roger, Pte. (H. M. 86th Reg.)
Wd. at Jhansi—p. 58.
(See also *Mathews*.)

Matty, Fredk., Pte. (H. M. 14th Lt. Dragns.)
S.-s. (Koonch)—p. 77.

Maun Singh, Tpr. (1st Nat. Lt. Cav.)
Wd. at Gwalior—p. 171.

Maurice, Lt. (H. M. 95th Reg.)
"Special mention" (Kotah-ka-serai)—p. 176.

Mawe, Mrs.
—xxiv.
Among fugitives from Nowgong—xxix.
Her treatment by villagers—xxx.

Mawe, Dr.
With fugitives from Nowgong—xxiv, xxix.
Death of—xxx.

Maxwell, G. V., Lt.-Col. (H. M. 88th Reg.)
Cmdg. colmn. of Bengal Army—pp. 84, 85, 86, 88, 89, 92.
Sends reinforcements—p. 93.
Eulogised—p. 103.
His report on action on the Jumna—pp. 110—12.
Mtd. in desp. (Calpee)—p. 120.

May, Charles, Sgt. (9th Lancers.)
Wd. near Allahgunge—p. 29.

Maye, Patrick, Pte. (3rd B. E. R.)
Kld. at Jhansi—p. 60.

Mayhew, W., Lt.-Col.
Adjt.-Gen. of the Army—p. 64, cxii.

Maynalian, John, Gnr. (Bombay Art.)
Wd. at Calpee—p. 123.

Mayne, Maj. (Dep. Judge Adv. Gen.)
Mtd. in desp.—p. 34.

Mayne, Capt. (Intell. Dept.)
Mtd. in desp.—(Mundesore)—lxxi.

Maytum, Fredk., Pte. H. M. 14th Lt. Dragns.)
Wd. at Koonch—p. 77.

McBride, Michael, Pte. (3rd B. E. R.)
Wd. at Jhansi—p. 60.

McCartney, Joseph, Pte. (H. M. 95th Reg.)
Wd. at Gwalior—p. 172.

McDermot, Patrick, Pte. (3rd B. E. R.)
Wd. at Jhansi—p. 60.

McEgan, Dr. (12th N. I.)
Murdered, with his family, at Jhansi—ix.

McEllenen, Patrick, Pte. (H. M. 86th Reg.)
Wd. at Calpee—p. 123.

McGill, Hugh, Sgt. (H. M. 71st Highland Lt. Inf.)
"Special mention"—p. 137.
Kld. (Gwalior)—p. 170.

McGill, Stephen, Col.-Sgt. (H. M. 71st Highland Lt. Inf.)
S.-s. (Koonch)—p. 78.

McGunness, James, Pte. (H. M. 86th Reg.)
Wd. at Jhansi—p. 58.

McInerney, Patrick, Pte. (H. M. 86th Reg.)
Died s.-s. (Koonch)—p. 76.

McKay, Andrew, Corp. (H. M. 71st Highland Lt. Inf.)
Died s.-s. (Koonch)—p. 78.

McKenna, Patrick, Pte. (3rd B. E. R.)
Kld. at Jhansi—p. 60.

McKinnon, Peter, Pte., (H. M. 71st Reg.)
Died s.-s. (Koonch)—p. 78.

McLay, Robt., Sapper (21st Coy. R. E.)
Wd. at Jhansi—p. 57.

McLaren, James, Pte. (3rd B. E. R.)
Kld. at Jhansi—p. 60.

McMahon, W., Capt. (H. M. 14th Lt. Dragns.)
Wd. at Koonch—p. 77.

McNally, Michael, Pte. (H. M. 86th Reg.)
Died s.-s. (Koonch)—p. 76.

McMullen, Henry, Pte. (H. M. 86th Reg.)
Wd. at Jhansi—p. 58.

McPherson, John, Pte., (H. M. 71st Reg.)
S.—s. (Koonch)—p. 78.

Meade, Capt., (Cmdg. Meade's Horse)
Mtd. in desp.—p. 151.
"Special mention." (Gwalior)—p. 174.
Informed of mutiny at Gwalior—xxxviii.

Meade, Mrs.
Bravery of, at Gwalior—xl.

Meah Khan, Tpr. (1st Cav., H. C.)
Wd. at Jhansi—p. 61.

Meer Amyed Ali, Tpr. (1st Cav., H. C.)
Recmd. for promotion— p. 51.

Meer Golam Hosain, Duffadar (4th Cav., H. C.)
Wd. at Koonch—p. 79.

Meer Hussein Khan, Tpr. (1st Cav., H. C.)
Kld. at Jhansi— p. 61.

Meer Hyder, Tpr. (4th Cav., H. C.)
Kld. at Jhansi—p. 61.

Meer Ukbur Ali, Tpr. (4th Cav., H. C.)
Wd. at Jhansi—61.

Meerut.
Outbreak at—lxxxviii.

Mehan, Patrick, Pte. (3rd B: E: R.)
Wd., (the Betwa)—cviii.

Mehidpore.
Contingent from, threaten Mhow—lxv.

Mein, Maj.
Leads Eur. Arty. at Banda—p. 35.
Mtd. in desp.—p. 36.

Meller, J:, Pte. (H. M., 14th Dragns.)
Died s.-s., Calpee—p. 122.

Melvill, Sir James.
—lxxxviii.

Metadeen Moray, Pte. (25th R. N. I.)
Wd., "special mention," (Gwalior—p. 175.

Mhow, (see also *Hungerford, Capt.*)
Guns from Indore pass through—xlii.
Mutiny breaks out—xliii, xlvi, liv, lvii.
English retire to |fort—xliii—iv, xlvi, liv, lvii.
Martial law proclaimed—xlix.
Magazines blown up—xlix.
Mutineers hanged—l, li.
Electric telegraph to Bombay opened—li.
Batteries mounted—lxiii.
Ranee of Jhansi attacks—lxxxvi.
Tantia Topee active near—xcv.

Miaz Meer Khan, Bargeer (Cav., H: C:)
Kld. at Jowra-Alipore—p. 166.

Micklejohn Lt., (Bombay Engineers.)
Mtd. in desp.—p. 46.
Kld. (Jhansi)— *ib.*
Leads escalade at Jhansi—p. 56;
Wd.—*ib.*

Middleton, Maj.
—xcii.

Millar, David, Pte. (H. M. 71st Reg:)
Died s.-s. (Koonch)—p. 78.

Miller, Asst. Surg. (3rd B. E. R.)
Wd. at Jhansi—p. 60.

Miller, W. H., Brigr., (Cmdg. Art. Brig., Saugor F. F.)
Wd. (Banda)—p. 33.
Mtd. in desp.—pp. 33, 35.
Narrow escape of—p. 37.

Miller, W., Cornet, (1st Bombay Lt. Cav.)
Kld. (Gwalior)—pp. 148; 171.
"Special mention"—p. 174.

Mir Imdad Ali, Bargeer, (3rd Hyd. Cav.)
Wd., R. Betwa—cvii.

Mir Muskood Ali, Duffadar, (3rd Hyd. Cav.)
Kld. (R. Betwa)—cvii.

Mirza Hymud Beg, (4th Cav., H. C.)
Wd. at Koonch—p. 79.

Mirzapore.
Eng. fugitives reach—xxxi.

Mirza Soorab Beg, Trumpet Maj., (4th Cav., H. C.)
Wd. at Jhansi—p. 61.

Missar Ali Beg, Tpr., (3rd Hyd. Cav.)
Mortally wd. at Calpee—p. 123.

Mitchell, George, Pte. (3rd B. E. R.)
Wd. at Jhansi—p. 60.

Mitchell, John, Pte., (H. M. 71st Reg.)
Died s.-s. (Koonch)—p. 78.

Mitchell, Wm., Pte., (H. M. 14th Lt. Dragns.)
Wd. at Koonch—p. 77.

Mobaruck Ali.
A leader of mutineers—xxiii.
Warns officers—xxiii—iv.

Mohamed Cussen, Pte., (Madras S. M.)
Wd. at Jhansi—p. 59.

Mohomed Deen Khan, Jemadar, (1st Cav., H. C.)
Wd. at Jhansi—p. 61.

Mohomed Rumzan, Sepoy, (3rd Inf. H., C.)
Wd. at Jhansi—p. 61.

Mohun, Sepoy, (5th Inf., H. C.)
Wd. at Jhansi—p. 62.

Mohun Sing, Pte., (24th B. N. I.)
Wd. at Jhansi—p. 61.

Mookorim Khan, Tpr., (1st Cav., H. C.)
Recmd. for "Order of British India"—p. 169.

Moona Catchee, Pte., (24th B. N. I.)
Wd. at Jhansi—p. 59.

Moore, C. J., Qr. Mast. Sgt., (3rd Inf., H. C.)
Died s.-s., Calpee—p. 125.

Moore, George, Sapper, (21st Coy., R. E.)
Wd. at Jhansi—p. 57.

Moore, Lt., (3rd Bomb. Lt. Cav.)
Mtd. in desp. (Rathghur)—pp. 6; 17.

Mooroo Bulwant.
See *Mama Sahib*.

Montriou, Capt. Cmdg., 24th B. N. I.)
At Jhansi—cxi.

Moran, Michael, Pte. (H. M. 86th Reg.)
Wd. at Jhansi, mortally—p. 58.

Morar Cantonments.
Value of—p. 134.
Attacked by British—pp. 135; 136.
Captured—p. 138.
Results of capture—pp. 139.
Troops left at—pp. 140; 150; 153; 151; 152; 153.

Morar, R.
  British bivouac on—pp. 140 ; 143.

Moriarty, John, Pte., (H. M. 86th Reg.)
  Wd. at Jhansi—p. 58.

Morris, Lt., (H. M. 95th Reg.)
  Mtd. in desp. (Jhansi)—pp. 159 ; 160.

Morrissy, Dennis, Pte., (H. M. 86th Reg.)
  Wd. at Calpee.—p. 123.

Mortars.
  At Rathghur—pp. 4 ; 21.
  At Jhansi—p. 43.

Mow, village of.
  On Ram Gunga—p. 27.

Mowraneepore.
  Party of 14th Irregulars halt at—xxi.
  Tessildar of—xxii, xxvi.

Muddenpore.
  See Mudinpore.

Mudinpore.
  Pass of—p. 20.
  Sir H. Rose marches against—p. 21.
  Village of—p. 23.
  The pass cleared—*ib.*
  Casualties at—p. 25.

Muhoba.
  Fugitives from Nowgong at—xxv ; xxvi ; xxvii ; xxxii ; xxxiv ; xxxv.

Mukun Khan, Bargeer, (3rd Cav., H. C).
  Wd., R. Betwa.—cvii.

Mullvibill, Thomas, Pte., (H. M. 86th Reg.)
  Wd. at Jhansi—p. 58.

Mundesore.
  Brigr. Stuart's Report on operations at—lxvii.
  Evacuated by rebels—lxxi.
  Maj. Orr's Report on operations at—lxxiii.
  Casualties at—lxxvi - lxxviii.

Mundesore, Shazadah of.
  Flees from Rathghur—p. 7.
  Styled "King," *ib.* ; horse of—p. 8.

Mungul Khan.
  Chaprassi—x.

Mungul Persad, Naick (25th B. N. I.)
  Wd. at Jhansi—p. 59.

Mundlaysir.
  xlvi.
  Elephants sent to—l.
  Advance of British towards—li ; liv ; lvii ; lxv ; lxvi.
  Eng. fugitives quit—lxv.

Muntuoo.
  Situation of—xxxii.
  Its zemindar treats Eng. fugitives well—*ib.* xxxvi.

Muntuvo.
  See Muntuoo.

Murdan Singh, Duffadar, (1st Cav., H. C.)
  Wd. at Barodia—p. 15.

Murphy, James, Corp. (H. M. 86th Reg.)
  Wd. at Jhansi—p. 57.

Murphy, James, Pte. (H. M. 86th Reg.)
  Wd. at Jhansi—p. 58.

Murphy Peter, Pte., (H. M. 86th Reg.)
  Wd. at Jhansi—p. 58.

Murphy, P., Pte. (H. M. 95th Reg.)
  Mtd. in desp., (Gwalior)—p. 175.

Murray, Mrs.
  Bravery of, at Gwalior—xl.

Murray, W., Capt. (Cmdg. 4th Cav., H. C.)
  Wd. at Jhansi—p. 61.
  At Koonch—pp. 73 ; 74.
  Mtd. in desp.—p. 75.
  At Diapoora—p. 107.
  At Mundesore—lxviii ; lxxiv.
  Mtd. in desp.—lxxv.

INDEX

Mustijab Khan, Ressaldar Major. (Cav., H. C.)
Mtd. in desp. (Calpee)—117.

Mutineers.
See *Regiments, Mutinous.*

Mutlow, Mark.
Father-in-law to Mrs. Mutlow— xiv.

Mutlow, Mrs.
Her statement regarding the Mutiny at Jhansi—xii—xiv.

Mutha.
Attacked by rebels—p. 87 ; 88 ; 90.

Muttra.
Road from Etowa to—pp. 87.
Attack on—p. 109.

Myboob Khan, Tpr., (3rd Cav., H. C.)
Recmd. for "Order of British India"— p. 169.

Myers, John, Sgt. (H. M. 14th Lt. Dragns.)
Wd., R. Betwa—cvii.

Mytab Khan, Tpr., (3rd Cav., H. C.)
Recmd. for "Order of British India "— p. 169

N

Naghojee, Sepoy, (3rd Inf., H. C.)
Mortally wd. at Jhansi—p. 61.

Nagode.
English fugitives reach—xxx ; xxxi ; xxxvi.

Nagpore.
lxxxviii.

Nagupoora.
First Brig. at—p. 66.

Nahar Khan, Duffadar, (3rd Cav., H. C.) —
Recmd. for "Order of British India "— p. 169.

Naher, Mr. and Mrs. and children.
Take refuge at Parnasa—lxv.

Nana Sahib.
Propaganda in favour of—p. 83.
Partizans of—p. 93.
Orders as to disposal of—xci.

Nannoo Sing, Tpr., (1st Cav., H. C.)
Wd. at Koonch—p. 79.

Narradoo, Pte. (Madras S. M.)
Kld. at Jhansi—p. 59.

Narrain Salvee, Pte. (24th B. N. I.)
Wd. at Calpee—p. 124.

Narrain, Sepoy, (5th Inf., H. C.)
S.-s., Calpee—p. 125.

Narut.
Pass of –p. 20.
Defended by Rajah of Banpore—p. 21.
Feint against—*ib.*
Abandoned—p. 24.

Napier, R., Brigr.
At Morar—p. 135.
His report—pp. 136, 153—6.
"Special mention" (Morar)—pp. 138 ; 140 ; 151.
Takes over Sir H. Rose's command— p. 153 ; 167 ; 169.
Report on Jowra-Alipore—p. 163 ; xcii.

Naven, Peter, Pte., (H. M. 86th Reg.)
Wd. at Jhansi—p. 58.

Nawal Khan, Sowar (Meade's Horse).
Wd. (Jowra-Alipore)—p. 167.

Naylor, Dr.
Mtd. in desp. (Calpee)—p. 119.

Neave, Wyndham, Lt., (H. M. 71st Reg.)
Kld. at Morar, his gallantry—p. 137.
Mtd. in desp.— pp. 154 ; 170.

Nebonuggra.
Mutineers driven from—p. 27.

Need, A., Capt. (H. M. 14th Lt. Dragns.)
S.-s. (Koonch)—pp. 77 ; 105 ; 116 ; 117.
Captures ordnance before Calpee—p. 118.
Leads charge on the Betwa—xcv.
Rescued by Lt. Leith—xcix.
Mtd. in desp.—ci.

Neemuch.
News of mutiny at, reaches Mhow—xliv, xlv.
Road to, from Mhow, open—lii ; lxviii ; lxix.
Garrison relieved—lxxi.

Nelson, Hugh, Pte., (H. M. 95th Reg.)
Wd. at Gwalior—p. 172.

Nerbudda Field Force.
Casualties of, at Rathghur—p. 9 ; lxxx.

Neville, Capt., (R.E.)
Kld. at Barodia, his excellent services—pp. 12, 13 ; 15.

Nevin, Edw., Pte., (H. M. 86th Reg.)
Wd. at Jhansi—p. 58.

Newport, Ens. (3rd B. E. R.)
Mtd. in desp. (Jhansi)—pp. 54, 57.

Newton, Mr. & Mrs.
At Jhansi—xii.

Newton, John, Q. M. Sgt., (12th N. I.)
Spared with his family, by mutineers—iii.

Nia Bustie.
At Jhansi, shelled—p. 44.

Nicholas, John, Pte., (H. M. 86th Reg.)
Wd. at Calpee—p. 123.

Nicholl, Capt., (Commiss. of Ordn.)
Supplies stores to Sir H. Rose—p. 105.

Nicholson, Samuel, Pte., (H. M. 71st Highland Lt. Inf.)
Wd. at Gwalior—p. 170.

Nijim Hossein.
Revenue tahsildar—xii.

Nimaur.
English fugitives take refuge in—lxv.

Nolin, James, Pte., (H. M. 86th Reg.)
Mortally wd. at Jhansi—p 58.

Noonee.
Village of—p. 21.

Noor Khan, Tpr., (3rd Cav., H. C.)
Recmd. for "Order of British India"—p. 169.

Noreonlee, Camp.
Rebels at—p. 6.

Norman, H. W., Maj.
(Dep. Adjt.-Gen. of the Army)—pp. 19, 26, 39, 81, 128.

Novell, Pte., (H. M. 14th Lt. Dragns.)
Remd. for V. C. (Jowra-Alipore)—p. 165.

Nowgong.
Documents at, destroyed—iii.
Mutiny at—xv ; lxxxiv ; xcv.

Nujmodeen Khan, Tpr., (25th B. N. I.)
Wd. (Gwalior)—p. 170.

Nujoo Khan, Tpr., (1st Cav., H. C.)
Wd. at Koonch—p. 79.

Nurut.
Pass of—pp. 20, 23.

Nureeawallee.
Rebels abandon—p. 14.

Nursingur, Rajah of.
Applied to for help by Holkar—lxii.

Nursoo, Gun Lascar, (1st Co. Arty), H. C.)
Wd. at Koonch—p. 79.

Nusur Nulla Khan, Tpr., (1st Cav., H. C.)
Wd. at Jhansi—p. 61.

Nutteh Khan, Tpr. (3rd Cav., H. C.)
Recmd. for "Order of British India,"—p. 169.

Nuttoo Khan, Tpr., (Cav., H. C.)
Mtd. in desp. (Calpee)—p. 117.

Nyagong, Rajah of.
Furnishes escort to fugitive English—xxvii.

O

Oakes, T., Maj., (Cmdg. Cav. Brig.,) Saugor F. F.
Mtd. in desp.—p. 33.
Despatch from—p. 36.
Commends officers—p. 37.

O'Connor, Timothy, Pte., (H. M. 86th Reg.)
Wd. at Jhansi—p. 58.

Odepore.
Rebels at—p. 2.

Ogilvie, Capt. (Asst. Com. Gen.)
Supplies stores to Sir H. Rose—p. 105.

O'Hallaren, Patrick, Pte. (3rd B. E. R.)
Wd. at Jhánsi—p. 60.

Ommaney, Capt., (R. A.)
Cmds. Coy. of R. A. at Jhansi—p. 44.
Mtd. in desp.—p. 53.
His battery at Koonch—pp. 67, 69.
At Calpee—p. 101.
Mtd. in desp. (May 23rd, 1858)—p. 121.
Cmdg. Arty. at Calpee—p. 132.
His battery at the Betwa—xcvii ; cii.

Omra.
Camp—cxiii.

O'Neil, John, Pte., (H. M. 14th Lt. Dragns.)
S.-s, (Koonch)—p. 77.

Onow.
Gate at Jhansi—p. 49.

Oojein.
Value of rupee at—lii.
Seindiah's minister at—lxii.

Oomagee, Pte., (Bombay S. M.)
Wd. at Jhansi—p. 59.

Oomed Sing.
Brings message to Mhow from Holkar—li.

Oomree.
Maj. Orr at—p. 66.
Second Brigade at—p. 74.

Oorcha.
Ranee of Jhansi attacks—lxxxvi.

Opium.
Use of, by natives to stimulate courage—pp. 47, 94, 98.
Resulting dejection—p. 102.

Orai.
Camp—p. 80.
Fugitives from, at Gwalior—ii.

Oram, Robt., Pte., (H. M. 86th Reg.)
Wd. at Jhansi—p. 58.

Oraye.
Road from, to Calpee—pp. 84, 85.

Orcha.
Gate, at Jhansi—vi.

Ordiel Tewary, Pte., (25th B. N. I.)
Wd. at Calpee—p. 123.

Ordnance and Stores.
Captured from rebels—pp. 118, 151, 153; xcv, ci.

Orr, S., Maj., Cmdg. 3rd Cav. H. C.
At Goraria—lxix.

Orr, Surg. (4th Cav., H. C.)
Mtd. in desp. (Koonch)—p. 76.
Ditto   (Mundesore)—lxxv.

Orr, W. A., Maj., (Cmdg. Hyd. F.F.)
   Reconnoitres passes—p. 21.
   Pursues rebels—p. 23.
   Mtd. in desp.—pp. 24 ; 25.
   Destroys fortified house (Jhansi)—p. 50.
   Mtd. in desp. (Jhansi)—p. 53.
   Defeats the Rajahs—p. 65.
   Marches to Koonch—p. 66.
   His report referred to—p. 68.
   The report—p. 73.
   At Golowlee—p. 86.
   His force in Tehree—p. 90.
   At Muttra—p. 109.
   Mtd. in desp. (May 18th, 1858)—p. 121.
   Ordered to Punear—p. 133.
   Punear occupied—p. 150.
   Marches on Mundlaysir—li, lxiv.
   Advance of—lxvi.
   At Mundesore—lxvii ; lxviii.
   Mtd. in desp.—lxxi.
   His personal combats—lxxii.
   His report on operations—lxxiii—vi.
   At the Betwa—xcvii.
   Mtd. in desp.—cii.

Orri.
   Road to, from Koonch—p. 75.

Oude, (Oudh).
   p. 83.

Oude Artillery.
   Found at Rathghur—p. 8.

Oude.
   Cavalry of, believed to have joined rebels—p. 129.

Overing, Edwin, Pte., (H. M. 14th Lt. Dragns.)
   Wd. (Gwalior)—p. 170.

Owen, Lt.-Col., (1st Bombay Lancers.)
   Mtd. in desp. (Gwalior)—pp. 145 ; 148.
   "Special mention"—p. 174.

Owens, Hugh, Pte., (H. M. 86th Reg.)
   Wd. at Jhansi—p. 58.

P

Palmer, Capt. (R. A.)
   Commands Company at Banda—p. 36.
   Mtd. in desp., ib.

Pandoo Juddoum, Pte. (25th B. N. I.)
   Wd. at Jhansi—p. 59.

Pandoo Mengia, Naick, (25th B. N. I.)
   Kld. at Jhansi—p. 59.

Park, A. A., Lt. (24th B. N. I.)
   Kld. at Jhansi—p. 48 ; 61.

Park, Lt. (3rd B. E. R.)
   Mtd. in desp. (Jhansi)—pp. 54 ; 56.

Parkins, William, Sgt. (H. M. 14th Lt. Dragns.)
   Wd. (the Betwa)—cviii.

Parnasa.
   English fugitives at—lxv.

Parton, James, Pte. (H. M. 14th Lt. Dragns.)
   Wd. (the Betwa)—cviii.

Partridge, Lt. (23rd B. N. I. doing duty 5th Inf., H. C.)
   Mtd. in desp. (Koonch)—pp. 74 ; 76.

Pathans.
   In rebel garrison at Rathghur—pp. 7 ; 14.
   Among rebels—p. 50.

Pearce, Henry, Pte. (H. M. 14th Lt. Dragns.)
   Wd. at Koonch—p. 77.

Pearce, William, Pte. (H. M. 14th Lt. Dragns.)
   Wd. (the Betwa)—cviii.

Pearson, James, Pte. (H. M. 86th Reg.)
   Wd. at Jhansi—p. 58.

Pearson, John, Pte. (H. M. 8th Hussars.)
Wd. at Gwalior—p. 171.

Peeplia.
Rebels routed at—lxviii.

Peer Buccus, Pte. (4th B. N. I.)
Severely burnt, (the Betwa)—cix.

Peer Khan, Tpr. (1st Cav., H. C.)
Kld. at Calpee—p. 125.

Peishwa.
Army of the, so-called—pp. 71, 104.

Pelley, Capt. (Cmdg. 10th B. N. I.)
Mtd. in desp., (Kotah-ka-Serai)—p. 162; 176.

Pennells, Peter, Pte. (H. M. 14th Lt. Dragns.)
Wd. at Koonch—p. 77.

Pertheepal Sing, Golandauz, (1st Co. Arty., H. C.)
Wd. at Jhansi—p. 61.

Pettman, Lt. (B. H. A.)
Mtd. in desp.—p. 43.

Phool Bagh.
Palace at Gwalior—pp. 139, 144, 145, 147.
Captured—pp. 149, 174.
Mentioned—pp. 150, 157, 159, 160, 161.

Pickaring, Thos., Sgt., (H. M. 86th Reg.)
Wd. at Jhansi—p. 57.

Pike, William, Pte., (H. M. 95th Reg.)
Wd. at Gwalior—p. 172.

Pinkney, Capt., (Pol. Agt. at Jhansi.)
Services at Mudinpore—p. 24.
Mtd. in desp. (Calpee)—p. 105.

Pittma R., Lt., (1st Tp. H. A.)
Wd. at Barodia—p. 15.

Platt, Bvt.-Col. (Cmdg. 23rd N. I.)
Hears of outbreak at Indore—xlii.
Prepares for defence of Mhow—*ib*, xliv.
Murdered by his men—xliii, lv, lvii.
His undue confidence—xlv, xlvi, xlvii, liv.

Poharee.
Camp—p. 168.

Pohooj.
River—pp. 129, 132.

Ponton, J., Gnr. (4—2 Artillery.)
Wd. at Jhansi—p. 57.

Pooch.
Situation of—p. 65.

Poona.
Rafts brought from—p. 86.
Sir H. Rose's baggage reaches—p. 107.

Poorbess.
At Nowgong—xv, xviii.

Poore, Capt. (H. M. 8th Hussars.)
"Special mention," (Kotah-ka-Serai)—p. 176.
At Gwalior—cxv, cxvi.

Poorun, Pte. (Madras S. M.)
Wd. at Jhansi—p. 59.

Poorun Moochee, Pte. (26th B. N. I.)
Wd. at Jhansi—p. 59.

Pope, Lt. (Cmdg. No. 1. Madr. H. F. Batty.)
Mtd. in desp.—p. 36.

Powys, Lt. (6th N. I.)
Kld. by mutineers at Jhansi—ii, iv, viii.
Also his family—iii, ix.

Powys, Lt., (Canal Dept.)
At Jaitpore—xxix.

Postance, Mr. (Dep. Com. of Ordnance.)
At Mhow—xlviii.
Mtd. in desp.—liii.

Potter, Corp. (Arty.)
At Mhow—xlix.

Pran Singh.
Demands money from fugitives—xxviii.

Prendergast, Lt.
Mtd. in desp.—lxxi.
Wd. (Mundesore)—lxxi, lxxvii.

Prendergast, Lt. (Madras S. M.)
Mtd. in desp., (the Betwa)—ci.

Prendergast, Thos., Pte. (H. M. 86th Reg.)
Wd. at Jhansi—p. 58.

Prettijohn, Capt., (H. M. 14th Lt. Dragns.)
Wd. (Mudinpore)—p. 25.
Mtd. in desp. (Koonch)—p. 69.
At Jowra-Alipore—p. 163.
Mtd. in desp.—p. 165.
Leads charge at the Betwa—xcviii ; xcix.
Mtd. in desp. (Betwa)—cii.

Price, John, Pte. (H. M. 14th Lt. Dragns.)
Wd. (the Betwa)—cvi

Prior, Capt. (12th Lancers.)
Mtd. in desp.—p. 37.

Punear.
Maj. Orr at—pp. 133 ; 150.
Road from Gwalior to—p. 150.

Punnah.
Rajah of, loyal—lxxxvi.
P. mentioned—lxxx, lxxxiii, lxxxv.

Puray Doobay, Pte. (25th B. N. I.)
Kld. at Calpee—p. 123.

Purcell, Mr.
Murdered at Jhansi—vii.
Also his brother—ix.

Purrayta.
Hyd. Contingent at—p. 74.

Pursad Moorie, Pte. (25th B. N. I.)
Kld. at Jhansi—p. 59.

Puttan.
Village of, captured—p. 3.

R

Rabuccus, Sepoy, (50th N. I.)
Loyalty of—xxx.

Raines, J. A. R., Lt.-Col., (H. M. 95th Regt.)
At Gwalior—p. 143.
Turns captured guns on rebels—pp. 144 ; 145.
Repulses rebels—p. 146.
Leads charge—p. 148.
Comds. Inf. at Kotah-ka-Serai -p. 157.
His report of the assault—p. 160.
Commends gallantry of his men- p. 16.
Wd. at Gwalior—p. 171.
" Second special mention" (Gwalior)—p. 174.
" Special mention—p. 176.
At Gwalior—cxv.
Supplementary report from—cxviii.

Raite, Sgt., (Arty.)
At Muntuoo—xxxii.
At Nowgong—xxxiv.
With Lt. Townsend—xxxv.
Commended to Nawab at Banda—xxxvi.

Raj Ahmed, Bheestie, (5th Inf., H. C.)
Wd. (the Betwa) cix.

Rajahme, Sepoy, (3rd Inf., H. C.)
S.-s., Calpee —p. 125.

Rajpootana.
Brigade leaves, for Goonah—p. 64.

Rajpootana Field Force.
p. 134 ; commended by Sir H. Rose—p. 152 ; xciii.

Rajpore.
Ford at—xcvi.
Rebels' last stand at, (Betwa)—c.

Rajumah, Gun Lascar, (1st Co. Arty., H. C.)
Kld. at Koonch—p. 79.

Rajwas.
 Contemplated attack on rebels at—lxii.

Rama Mooray, Pte. (25th B. N. I.)
 Kld. at Calpee—p. 123.

Ramas Khan, Tpr. (1st Cav., H. C.)
 Wd. at Rathghur—p. 9.

Rambuccus, Pte., (25th B. N. I.)
 Wd. at Jhansi—p. 59.

Ramchunder Maney, Pte. (25th B. N. I.)
 Wd. (the Betwa)—cvii.

Ramchunder Mohothoy, Pte. (25th B. N. I.)
 S.-s., (Koonch)—p. 76.

Ramchunder Rao.
 See *Bhao Rao Ramchunder*.

Ramdeen, Tpr. (4th Cav., H. C.)
 Kld. at Calpee—p. 125.

Ramdeen Havildar, (24th B. N. I.)
 Wd. at Jhansi—p. 61.

Ramdeen, Havildar, (5th Inf., H. C.)
 Wd. at Jhansi—p. 62.

Ramdeen, Sepoy, (3rd Inf., H. C.)
 Wd. at Jhansi—p. 61.

Ramdeen, Sepoy, (3rd Inf., H. C.)
 Slightly burnt, (the Betwa)—cix.

Ramdeen Ahier, Naick, (Bombay S. M.)
 Wd. at Jhansi—p. 59.

Ramdeen Lodh, Pte. (25th B. N. I.)
 Wd. at Jhansi—p. 59.

Ramdual, Havildar, (2nd Co. Arty., H. C.)
 Kld. at Jhansi—p. 61.

Ramdyal, Sepoy, (5th Inf., H. C.)
 Wd. at Jhansi—p. 62.
 S.-s, (Calpee)—p. 125.

Ramgopal Dilchit.
 Moofedar of Bellaree—xxvi.

Ram Gunga.
 Defeat of rebels on the left bank of— p. 26.

Ramjee Sabday, Pte., (24th B. N. I.)
 Wd. at Jhansi—p. 61.

Ramjee Yadow, Pte., (24th B. N. I.)
 Wd. at Jhansi—p. 61.

Ramlall Tewarry, Pte., (25th B. N. I.)
 Wd., (Gwalior)—p. 170.

Rampura.
 Rajah of, friendly to English—p. 129.

Rampursaud, Sepoy, (3rd Inf., H. C.)
 Kld. at Jhansi—p. 61.

Ramsey, Hempell, Sapper, (21st Coy., R. E.)
 Wd. at Jhansi—p. 57.

Ram Sing, Pte. (4th B. N. I.)
 Wd., the Betwa—cix.

Ramswamy, Lc.-Naique, (Madras S. M.)
 Wd. at Rathghur—p. 9.

Ramswamy, Pte. (Madras S. M.)
 Wd. at Rathgur—p. 9.

Ranee of Jhansi.
 —See *Jhansi*.

Ransem, Thos., Pte. (H. M. 14th Lt. Dragns.)
 Kld. (R. Betwa)—cvii.

Rao Ramchunder.
 Brings letter to Mhow from Holkar— lix.

Rao Sahib.
 Rebel leader—p. 83.
 Orders as to disposal of,—xci, xcii. (See also, *Banda, Nawab of*.)

Rathghur.
Rebels resolve to defend Fort—p. 2.
Their motive—*ib.*
Nature and situation of the Rock—*ib.*
The Fort attacked by Sir H. Rose—p. 3.
Rebels open fire from Fort—p. 4.
The Eedgha captured by Brigr. Steuart—p. 4.
Tower at the main gate captured—p. 5.
Artillery open fire against East curtain of Fort—*ib.*
Rebel force from jungle attack videttes—*ib.*
Driven back and pursued—*ib.*
Rebels make unsuccessful night attack—p. 6.
Rebels attack convoy near Rathghur—*ib.*
Attempted rebel sortie driven back—*ib.*
British force enters the Fort—*ib.*
Flight of rebels—pp. 6-7.
Chief rebels captured—p. 7.
Fugitive rebels cut up by pursuing cavalry—*ib.*
Leading rebels hanged—*ib.*
Valuable stores found at—p. 8.
Effigy of European woman's head found—*ib.*
Humanity of British Troops to women and children of rebels—*ib.*
Rebel standards captured—*ib.*
Siege of by Scindiah—*ib.*
List of casualties at—p. 9.
Horses kld. and wd. at—p. 10.

Read, Lt. (10th B. N. I.)
His services at Gwalior—p. 144.
Mtd. in desp. (Gwalior)—p. 175.
Ditto —cxviii.

Red-hot shot.
Used at Jhansi—p. 44.

Redmayne, W. L., Lt., (H. M. 14th Lt. Dragns.)
Kld. at Mundesore—r.
His gallantry—lxxv; lxxvi.

Redstone, Edward, Pte., (H. M. 71st Reg.)
S.—s. (Koonch)—p. 78.

REGIMENTS, Artillery. Not specified.
Two 6-pndrs. at Rathghur—p. 3.
At Mudinpore—pp. 21, 23.
Casualties—p. 25.
Before Jhansi—pp. 41-45, 45, 49, 50.
Casualties—pp. 57, 62.
At Koonch—pp. 66, 67, 69.
Near Golowlee—p. 88.
Before Calpee—p. 89.
At Russulpore—p. 93.
Before Calpee—pp. 94, 95, 98, 100, 110-11.
Casualties—p. 112.
Mortar Battery—p. 113.
Casualties—pp. 123, 125.
March on Gwalior—pp. 130, 139.
At Gwalior—pp. 141, 142, 148.
Casualties—p. 170.
At the Betwa—xcvii, c, cii.

Bengal Artillery.
At Mundesore—lxx.
Casualties—lxxviii—xxviii.

Bhopal Artillery.
Guns of, at Mudinpore—p. 21.
Guns of, at Jhansi—pp. 65, 92.

Bombay Artillery.
At Rathghur—pp. 3, 4, 5.
At Barodia—pp. 11, 13.

Bombay Horse Artillery.
At Rathghur—p. 4.
Casualties—pp. 9, 10.
At Barodia—pp. 11, 12.
Casualties—p. 15.
(Horses)—p. 16.
Before Jhansi—pp. 40, 41.
Casualties—pp. 59, 62.
At Koonch—pp. 66, 69-70, 75.
At Mutha—p. 87.
At Calpee—pp. 95, 100, 101, 116, 118.

REGIMENTS, Artillery—*contd.*

Bombay Horse Artillery—*contd.*

Casualties at Calpee—pp. 122-123.
Proceed to Gwalior—pp. 132, 136.
"Eagle" Troop of —p. 138.
At Morar— p. 140.
At Gwalior——pp. 143, 145 ; 147, 149.
At Morar—pp. 153, 155.
At Kotah-ka-Serai—pp. 157, 162.
At Jowra-Alipore—pp. 163-164.
Casualties—pp. 166-167, 171.

Bombay Light Field Artillery.

At Rathghu—pp. 4, 6.
At Barodia—pp. 11, 13.
Casualties (Barodia)—p. 16.
At Mudinpore—pp. 21, 23.
At Koonch—p. 69.
At Mutha—p. 87.
At Calpee—pp. 95, 98, 100, 103.
At. Muttra—p. 109.
At Calpee— pp. 112-115, 115, 117.
In pursuit of rebels—p. 129.
March on Gwalior—p. 130.
Escort Siege Train—p. 133.
At Gwalior—pp. 135, 136-137, 139, 145, 147.
At Morar - pp. 153, 155.
At Mundesore—lxxii, lxxiv.
Casualties at Mundesore—lxxvii—viii.

Horse Artillery.

At Mudinpore—p. 21.
At Allahgunge—pp. 26, 27.
Casualties—p. 29.
At Jheeghun—pp. 29-30.
At Banda—pp. 31, 32.
E. Troop (Native) at Banda—pp. 31, 35.
Casualties—p. 38.
A. Troop (European) at Banda—pp. 31 35.
Casualties— p. 38.
At the Betwa—xcvii, xcix.
Casualties—cx.

REGIMENTS, Artillery—*contd.*

Hyderabad Contingent Artillery.

At Rathghur—p. 4.
Casualties—p. 9.
Casualties at Jhansi—p. 61.
At Koonch—pp. 73, 74.
Casualties—p. 79.
At Mutha—p. 87.
At Morar—pp. 140, 153.
At Mundesore –lxxiv.

Madras Field Artillery.

At Banda—p. 31.

Madras Foot Artillery.

Casualties at Banda (*nil*)—p. 38.

Reserve Artillery.

Casualties at the Betwa—cvii, cx.

Royal Artillery.

At Banda - pp. 31, 32, 36.
At Koonch— pp. 67, 69, 75.
At Calpee—pp. 95, 101.
At Diapoora—pp. 107-108.
At Muttra—p. 109.
Casualties—pp. 123, 126.
In garrison at Calpee—p. 132.

Siege Train under Lt. Mallock.

At Rathghur—pp. 3, 4, 19.
At Mudinpore—pp. 21, 23.
At Jhansi—p. 43.
At Calpee—p. 95.
Proceeds to Gwalior—pp. 133, 135, 136.
At the Betwa—xcvii.

Cavalry.

H. M. 8th Hussars.

At Gwalior—pp. 143, 145.
Escort Scindiah—pp. 151, 156, 157.
Charge of—p. 158.
Casualties (Gwalior)—pp. 171, 176.
Statement regarding their charge before Gwalior—cxiv—cxvii.

9th Lancers.

At Allahgunge—pp. 26, 27.
Casualties—p. 29.

REGIMENTS, Cavalry—*contd.*

H. M. 12th Lancers.
At Banda—p. 31.
Gallantry of—p. 32.
Capture gun—p. 36.
In pursuit—p. 37.
Casualties—p. 38.

H. M. 14th Light Dragoons.
Two troops under Maj. Scudamore at Rathghur—pp. 4, 5.
Videttes of, on R. Beena—p. 7.
Casualties at Rathghur—pp. 9, 10.
Three Tps. at Barodia—pp. 11, 12.
Casualties (horses)—p. 16.
Two Tps. under Maj. Scudamore at Malthone—p. 21.
Two Tps. under Sir H. Rose at Mudinpore—pp. 21-23.
Casualties at Mudinpore—p. 25.
Sent to invest Jhansi—p. 40.
In pursuit of Ranee of J.—p. 49.
Kill 200 rebels—p. 50.
Casualties at Jhansi—pp. 59, 62.
In action at Koonch—p. 67.
Charge the rebels at K.—pp. 68, 69, 74—75.
Casualties at Koonch—pp. 76—77, 78.
Rout rebel cavalry near Golowlee—p. 86.
At Mutha—p. 87.
Sun-stroke among, at Calpee—p. 90.
Praised by Sir H. Rose—p. 92.
At Calpee—pp. 95, 96.
In pursuit of rebels—pp. 101, 103, 116.
Detachment of, in rear-guard action near Etora—p. 107—108.
In action near Muttra—p. 109.
In advance on Calpee—p. 114.
Casualties at Calpee—pp. 122—123, 125—126.
Ordered to reinforce Lt.-Col. Robertson—pp. 129-130.
March on Gwalior—pp. 132, 135, 136.
In pursuit of rebels—pp. 138, 139.
Three Tps. stay at Morar—p. 140.
At Gwalior—pp. 145, 147.
Their steadiness commended—p. 149.

REGIMENTS, Cavalry—*contd.*

H. M. 14th Light Dragoons—*contd.*
Escort Scindiah to his palace—p. 151.
At Morar—pp. 153-155.
In pursuit of rebels—p. 163.
Dismounted party kill twenty rebels—p. 165.
Casualties at Jowra-Alipore—pp. 166-167.
Casualties at Gwalior—p. 170.
At Mundesore—lxvii, lxviii.
Gallant charge—lxix, lxx.
In pursuit of rebels—lxxiv, lxxv.
Casualties at Mundesore—lxxvi—lxxvii.
Their gallant charge on the Betwa commended by the G. G. and the C-in-C—xciv-xcix.
In action on the Betwa—p. xcvii.
Charges made by—xcix.
Cross the river and sabre rebels—c-ci.
Commended—ci-ciii.
Casualties on the Betwa—cvii—cviii, cx.

1st Bombay Lancers.
At Gwalior—pp. 145, 147.
Charge of—pp. 148, 157.
Casualties (Gwalior)—pp. 171, 174.

3rd Bombay Light Cavalry.
Reconnoitre Rathghur—p. 2.
Under Capt. Forbes—pp. 3, 5.
Proceed to Barodia—p. 11.
Cross the Beena—p. 12.
At Barodia—p. 14.
Casualties—p. 15.
At Mudinpore—p. 21.
Casualties—p. 25.
To invest Jhansi—pp. 40, 49.
At Goonah—pp. 64, 65.
At Calpee—p. 95.
At Diapoora—p. 107.
Casualties at Calpee—pp. 124, 126, 132.
At Morar—p. 140.
At Jowra-Alipore—pp. 163, 164.
Casualties—p. 167.

REGIMENTS, Cavalry—*contd.*

Hyderabad Contingent, 1st Cavalry.

Casualties at Rathghur—pp. 9, 10.
Ditto at Barodia—p. 16.
Ditto at Mudinpore—p. 25.
Gallantry in pursuit of rebels at Jhansi—p. 50.
Casualties at Jhansi—p. 61.
Led by Lt. Dowker in action at Koonch—p. 73.
Casualties at Koonch—p. 79.
In pursuit of rebels, under Lt. Dowker—p. 116.
Commended by Maj. Gall—p. 118.
Casualties at Calpee—p. 125.
Under Brigr.-Gen. Napier at Morar—p. 140.
At Mundesore—lxviii, lxxiii.
Under Lt. Johnstone on the Betwa—cii.
Casualties on the Betwa—cix; cx.

Hyderabad Contingent, 2nd Cavalry.

Gallant charge of, at Banda—p. 31!; 33; 34.

Hyderabad Contingent, 3rd Cavalry.

In action at Barodia—p. 12.
Casualties at Barodia—p. 16.
In action at Koonch—p. 68.
Capture gun from rebels—p. 69.
Casualties at Koonch—pp. 76, 78.
In action at Mutha—p. 87.
Under Capt. Abbott, before Calpee—pp. 96-97, 109, 113, 116.
Charge rebels at Calpee—p. 117.
Casualties during action, *ib.*
Ditto before Calpee—pp. 123, 125.
At Morar—p. 140.
At Jowra-Alipore—pp. 163-164.
Commended—p. 166.
Men recommended for "Order of British India"—pp. 168-169.
Casualties at Gwalior—p. 170; lxiv.
In action at Mundesore—lxvii.

REGIMENTS, Cavalry—*contd.*

Hyderabad Contingent, 3rd Cavalry—*contd.*

Under Lt. Clerk—lxviii.
Under Maj. S. Orr., charge of—lxix.
Casualties at Mundesore—lxxviii.
Under Lt. Johnstone at the Betwa—cii.
Casualties at the Betwa—cvii; cx.

Hyderabad Contingent, 4th Cavalry.

Under Capt. Abbott, at Mudinpore—p. 23.
Gallantry of, at Jhansi—p. 50.
Casualties—p. 61.
Under Capt. Murray at Koonch—p. 73.
Casualties at Koonch—p. 79.
Ditto at Calpee—p. 125; lxxiii.
Ditto at the Betwa—cix, cx.

Hyderabad Contingent, unspecified Cavalry.

At Rathghur—p. 7.
At Barodia—p. 11.
In advanced and rear guard of Sir H. Rose'e attack on pass of Mudinpore—pp. 21, 23.
At Jheeghun—p. 29.
Casualties—p. 30.
Under Maj.-Gen. Whitlock, at Banda—p. 31.
Gallantry at Banda—pp. 34—35.
Casualties at Banda—p. 38.
Under Brigr. Stuart in advance on Jhansi—p. 40.
In right attack on Jhansi—pp. 46-47.
In pursuit of rebels at Jhansi—p. 49.
In garrison at Jhansi—p. 65.
In action at Mutha—p. 87.
Ditto before Calpee—p. 95; 97; 101.
In pursuing column under Lt.-Col. Robertson—pp. 103, 129.
In rear-guard action near Diapoora—p. 107.
In 1st Brigr. at Calpee—p. 114.
Casualties at Calpee—pp. 126, 132.

REGIMENTS, Cavalry—*concld.*

Hyderabad Contingent unspecified Cavalry—*contd.*

Under Brigr.-Gen. Napier in pursuit of rebels—pp. 153, 154, 163.
Charge at Jowra-Alipore, under Capt. Abbott—p. 164.
Casualties at Jowra-Alipore—pp. 166-7.
At Mundesore, under Maj. Orr.—lxvii, lxxi.
In action on the Betwa—xcvii ; xcix ; c.

Meade's Horse.

At Morar—pp. 140, 150.
At Jowra-Alipore—p. 163.
Casualties—p. 167.

2nd Punjab Cavalry.

At Allahgunge—p. 27.
Casualties—p. 29.

Towana Horse.

At Calpee—p. 110.
Casualties—p. 112 ; 153 ; 154.

Engineers.

Royal Engineers.

Company under Capt. Fenwick at Jhansi—p. 53.
Casualties in 21st Co. at Jhansi—pp. 57, 62.
21st Co. under Lt. Gosset, at Koonch—p. 73.
Casualties at Koonch—pp. 76, 78 ; 95.
Under Lt. Edwards at Calpee—p. 99.
Commended by Sir H. Rose—*ib.*
With 1st Brig. at Calpee—pp. 113, 114.
Casualties at Calpee—pp. 123, 125.
In garrison at Calpee—p. 132.
At Morar, under Brigr. Napier—p. 140.

Bombay Sappers and Miners.

Assist in capture of Eedgha (Rathghur)—p. 4.
Casualties at Rathghur—p. 9.
Ditto at Jhansi—pp. 59, 62.
In garrison at Jhansi—p. 65.
Ordered to march on Gwalior—p. 130.

REGIMENTS, Engineers—*contd.*

Madras Sappers and Miners.

Under Lt.-Col. Liddell at attack on Rathghur—p. 3.
Cut road to Battery—*ib.*
Casualties at Rathghur—p. 9.
March under Sir H. Rose against Barodia—p. 11.
Commended for service at Rathghur—p. 15.
Casualties at Jhansi—pp. 59, 62 ; 114.
March against Gwalior under Sir H. Rose—p. 132.
March from Morar—p. 139.
Directed to make bridge across canal at Gwalior—p. 141.
Commended for zeal and intelligence—p. 142.
In attack on Morar—pp. 153, 154.
Their eminent services—lxxii.
At Goraria—*ib.*

Sappers and Miners (unspecified).

Under Sir H. Rose in attack on Pass of Mudinpore—p. 21.
Under Maj.-Gen. Whitlock in advance on Banda—pp. 31.

Infantry.

H. M. 71st.

Guard convoy of treasure and stores for Jhansi—pp. 64 ; 65.
Losses by sun-stroke before Koonch—pp. 68, 82.
Casualties from all causes before Koonch—p. 78.
Suffer greatly from effects of heat—p. 82.
Their admirable fire at Mutha—pp. 87 ; 95.
Occupy Muttra—p. 109.
Repulse rebels with heavy loss—*ib.*
Advance on Calpee in 1st Brig. under Brigr. Stuart—p. 114.
Casualties in operations against Calpee—pp. 124, 126.

REGIMENTS, Infantry—*contd.*
71st Highland Light Infantry—*contd.*

Ordered to reinforce Lt.-Col. Robertson and March on Gwalior—p. 130.
As skirmishers before Gwalior—p. 137.
Capture nullahs—*ib.*
Commended by Sir H. Rose—*ib.*
Their gallant spirit when prostrated by sun-sickness—p. 138.
March for Kotah-ka-Serai—p. 139.
In 2nd Brig. under Brigr.-Genl. Napier, at Morar—p. 153.
Clear the ravines of rebels, before Gwalior—pp. 154, 155.
Casualties, before Gwalior—p. 170.

H. M. 86th Reg.

Gallantry of, at Jhansi—pp. 46, 54, 55.
Casualties of, at Jhansi—pp. 57, 58, 62.
In action at Koonch—pp. 67, 68.
Casualties of, at Koonch—pp. 76, 78.
In action at Calpee—pp. 112, 113.
Drive mutineers from Rehree—p. 114.
Casualties at Calpee—pp. 123, 125.
Reinforce Lt.-Col. Robertson's column—pp. 129, 130.
Advance on Morar—p. 135.
Take Cantonments—p. 137.
Advance on Kotah-ka-Serai—p. 139.
Prostrated by sun-sickness—pp. 140, 141.
Capture guns at Gwalior—p. 143.
Further advance—pp. 145, 146.
First attack on Goraria—lxx.
Second attack—*ib.*
Casualties near Mundesore—lxxvii.
In action on the R. Betwa—xcvii, cvii, ciii.
Casualties on the Betwa—cvii, cx.

H. M. 88th Reg.

Reinforces Sir H. Rose—pp. 93, 94.
Weakened by sun-stroke—p. 96.
At Calpee—p. 110.
Enfield rifles used by—pp. 111; 114.

REGIMENTS, Infantry,—*contd.*
H. M. 95th Reg.

At Gwalior—pp. 141, 143.
Work captured guns—p. 144; 145; 146 147.
Charge of—p. 148.
Commended—pp. 157, 159
Casualties (Kotah-ka-Serai)—pp. 160, 161, 162.
Casualties (Gwalior)—pp. 171, 172, 174.

H. M. Rifle Brigade.

At Calpee—pp. 98, 113.

3rd Bombay European Reg.

Make reconnaissance at Rathghur—p. 2.
As skirmishers—p. 3.
Drag guns—p. 4.
Capture fort at Rathghur—p. 6.
Humanity of—p. 8.
Casualties of, at Rathghur—pp. 9, 11.
As skirmishers at Barodia—p. 12.
Commended by Sir Hugh Rose—p. 14.
Casualties of, at Barodia—p. 15.
At Mudinpore—p. 21.
Storm a hill—pp. 22, 23.
Casualties of, at Mudinpore—p. 25.
Persevering gallantry of, at Jhansi—p. 46.
Further services of, at Jhansi—p. 47.
Occupy the fortress—pp. 49, 56.
Casualties of, at Jhansi—pp. 60, 63.
Ditto of, at Koonch—p. 78.
Attack rebels in ambush at Calpee—p. 97.
Check rebels at Etora—p. 108.
At Deopore—p. 110.
At Calpee—pp. 112, 114.
Casualties of, at Calpee—pp. 124, 126.
At Calpee—p. 132.
Under Col. Riddell—p. 133.
Under Brigr.-Genl. Napier at Morar—p. 140.
In action on the Betwa—xcvii, c.
Casualties—cviii, cx.

REGIMENTS, Infantry—contd.

10th Bombay Native Infantry.
At Gwalior—p. 143.
Gallant charge—p. 144.
Capture an arsenal—p. 146; 147; 148.
Commended—pp. 157, 159.
Casualties (Kotah-ka-Serai)—pp. 160; 161; 162.
Casualties (Gwalior)—p. 172.
Capture of guns—cxviii.

24th Regt. Bombay Native Infantry.
Under Sir H. Rose at Rathghur—p. 2.
Occupy " Eedgha " at Rathghur—p. 4.
Storm tower at main gate—p. 5.
Casualties at Rathghur—p. 9.
In feint against pass of Narut—p. 21.
At Jhansi—p. 48.
Casualties at siege storm of Jhansi—pp. 61, 62.
Eight Cos. in garrison at Jhansi—p. 65. (Six)—p. 92.
Casualties at Koonch—p. 78.
In rear-guard action near Deopore—p. 107.
Occupy Muttra—p. 109.
Repel attack—p. 110.
Casualties at Calpee—pp. 124, 126; 132.
At Morar under Brigr. Napier—p. 140.
In action on the Betwa—xcvii.
Casualties on the Betwa—cix, cx.

25th Bombay Native Infantry.
Casualties at Jhansi—pp. 59, 62.
Under Lt.-Col. Robertson at Koonch—p. 67.
Thanked for their gallantry—ib.
With Sir H. Rose at Koonch—p. 68.
Casualties at Koonch—pp. 76, 78.
March to assistance of Maj. Forbes—p. 87.
Great sufferings from solar heat—p. 88.
In action before Calpee—pp 94, 95.
Protect camp at Calpee—p. 96.
Gallant charge of—99.

REGIMENTS, Infantry—contd.

25th Bombay Native Infantry—contd.
Specially mentioned for distinguished conduct—ib.
In pursuit of rebels—p. 100.
In pursuing column under Lt.-Col. Robertson—p. 103; 129.
In action at Calpee—pp. 113, 114.
Greatly distinguish themselves—p. 115.
Casualties at Calpee—pp. 123, 125.
Reinforce Lt.-Col. Robertson—p. 130.
Three days without a meal—p. 132.
Advance against Gwalior—p. 135.
Reinforce left attack—p. 136.
Enfilade rebel entrenchments—p. 137.
Reinforce Brigr. Smith—p. 139.
Support H. M. 86th Reg.—pp. 143, 146.
Ordered to attack barracks—p. 147.
Capture the fort at Gwalior—p. 150.
Casualties at Gwalior—p. 170.
In two attacks on Goraria—lxx.
Their admirable conduct mentioned—lxxii, lxxiii.
Casualties at Mundesore—lxxvii, lxxviii.
In action on the Betwa—xcvii, cii, civ.
Assist in capture of Kooshabore—ciii.
Casualties on the Betwa—cvii, cx.

Hyderabad Contingent, 3rd Inf.
Casualties at Jhansi—pp. 61-62.
At Koonch—p. 73.
Casualties at Calpee—p. 125.
Ditto at Mundesore—lxxviii.
At the Betwa—cix, cx.

Hyderabad Contingent 5th Inf.
Casualties at Jhansi—p. 62.
At Koonch—pp. 73, 74.
Casualties—p. 79.
Ditto at Calpee—p. 125.
Ditto. at Mundesore—lxxviii; cix; cx.

Hyderabad Contingent, unspecified Inf.
At Mudinpore—pp. 21, 22.
Under Dr. Vaughan—p. 72.
At Mutha—p. 87; 153.

REGIMENTS, Infantry - concld.

3rd Madras European Reg.
At Banda—p. 31.
Commended—p. 33.
Casualties—p. 38.

1st Reg., Madras Native Inf.
At Banda—p. 31.
Casualties—p. 38.

38th Reg., Native Inf.
At Golowlee—p. 87.

50th Reg., Native Inf.
At Banda—p. 31.
Casualties (*nil*)—p. 38.

Miscellaneous.
Bhopal.
Regt. of, placed at Sir H. Rose's disposal —p. 3.
Capture village of Puttan—*ib.*
Repulse rebels—p. 6.
Rebels escape through their lines at Rathghur—pp. 6, 7.
Contingent under Col. Travers, - xlvi.

Sikh Battalion.
Reinforces Sir H. Rose—pp. 93, 95.
At Calpee—p. 114.

Sikh Horse.
Under Col. Riddell—133.

Sikh Inf.
Under Col. Riddell—p. 133.

Sikh Police Corps.
Reinforce Sir H. Rose—p. 110.

Bhopal.
Troops at Rathghur—p. 7.

Camel Corps.
Reinforces Sir H. Rose—pp. 93, 95.
At Calpee—p. 97.
Charge of—pp. 98 ; 110.
Casualties—pp. 124, 126.

REGIMENTS, Mutinous.
1st Light Cavalry.
Maj. Harris shot and cut down by, at Mhow—xlvii.
Col. Platt trusts the Regt.—liv.
Is murdered, with other officers, by them—lvii.

5th Bengal Irregular Cavalry.
With the Nawab of Banda—p. 83.
Their commander killed—p. 97.
At Morar—p. 136.

14th Bengal Irregular Cavalry.
Let Infantry begin mutiny at Jhansi and Nowgong—i.
Their reason—*ib.*, ii.
Under Lt. Ryves—iii.
Officers of—v.
Save officers—vi.
At Nowgong—xv, xxi.

12th Native Infantry.
Seventh Company mutiny at Jhansi—i.
Their records lost—iii.
Seize magazine—v, vi.
Become mutinous at Nowgong—xv.
Profess affection for British—xvi, xx.
Set fire to their lines—xxv ; xxxiv.

23rd Native Infantry.
Mutiny of, at Mhow—xlii.
Kill their officers—xliii.
Their mess-house burned—xlvi ; lvii.

34th Native Infantry.
Bundelcund men discharged from—xvii.

52nd Native Infantry.
Cut up at Mudinpore—p. 23.
Their losses at Koonch—p. 70.
In rebel army at Calpee—p. 83.

Rehree.
Situation of—p. 89.
Attack on—pp. 93, 94, 100.
Rebel battery at—pp. 110, 111.

Reilly, Daniel, Pte. (H. M. 86th Reg.)
Wd. at Koonch—p. 76.

Reilly, J., Lt., (H. M. 8th Hussars.)
Died, s.-s.—p. 171.
"Special mention," (Kotah-ka-Serai)—p. 176.
In charge at Gwalior—cxv.
Account of his death—cxvi.

Relly, James, Pte. (3rd E. R.)
Wd. at Mudinpore—p. 25.

Remington, Lt.
At Muhoba—xxix, xxx.

Remmington, Maj.
Commands Horse Arty. at Allahgunge—pp. 26, 27.
Mtd. in desp.—p. 28.

Rewah.
Force raised t—xxxi.
Threatened by rebels—lxxx.
Rajah of, loyal—lxxxvi.
Under control of Sir R. Hamilton—lxxxviii.

Reynolds, John, Pte. (3rd B. E. R.)
Died, s.-s., Calpee—p. 124.

Rheman Khan, Pte. (24th B. N. I.)
S.-s. (Koonch)—p. 78.

Rhow.
Near Indore—liv.

Ribbons, George, Corp. (H. M., 14th Lt. Dragns.)
S.-s. (Koonch)—p. 77.

Rich, Maj. (H. M., 71st Regt.)
At Muttra—p. 109.
Mtd. in desp. (May 18, 1858)—p. 121.
At Morar—p. 137.
Pursues rebels—p. 154.
Mtd. in desp. ib.—p. 155.

Richards, Lt. (2nd Punj. Cav.)
Aids in capture of guns at Allahgunge—p. 27.

Rickards, Maj. (Pol. Agent, Bhopal.)
Wd. at Calpee—p. 105.
Sir H. Rose's indebtedness to—ib.

Riddell, Col.
Guards ford—p. 102.
Comdg. moveable column (Gwalior)—pp. 133, 134.
His advance delayed—p. 150.

Ridler, John, Pte. (H. M. 14th Lt. Dragns.)
Wd., (the Betwa)—cviii.

Rielly, Daniel.
See *Reilly*.

Rifle Pits.
At Rathghur—p. 3.

Rifles.
See *Enfield Rifles*.

Rijwass.
Sir H. Rose's force at—p. 21.

Ritchie, Field Surg.
Mtd. in desp. (Calpee)—p. 119.

Roach, Patrick, Pte. (H. M. 86th Reg.)
Wd. at Jhansi—p. 58.

Roberts, H. S., Maj.-Gen.
Comdg. Rajpootana F. F.—p. 156.
Captures Koteh—xci.
At Gwalior—xciii.
Comdg. Northern Div. of Army—cxiii.

Roberts, Walter, Pte. (H. M. 14th Lt. Dragns.)
Wd. (R. Betwa)—cvii.

Robertson, G. H., Maj. (Lt.-Col.)
Comdg. 25th B. N. I., mtd. in desp. (Jhansi)—p. 53.
At Koonch—p. 67.
Mtd. in desp. (Koonch)—p. 73.
"Special mention"—pp. 99, 103.
Report from, referred to—p. 114.
His knowledge of natives—p. 129.
Reinforced, ib., again—p. 130.
Commandant of Gwalior—p. 149.
"5th special mention"—p. 173.
At Mundesore—lxvii.
At Goraria—lxx.
Mtd. in desp.—lxxii.
Wd. at Mundesore—lxxvi.
At the Betwa—cii.

Robinson, George, Pte. (H. M. 14th Lt. Dragns.)
Wd. (the Betwa)—cviii.

Robinson, Henry, Pte. (H. M. 95th Reg.)
Wd. at Gwalior—p. 172.

Robinson, Capt. (3rd B. E. R.)
Mtd. in desp. (Jhansi) - pp. 54, 56.
Leads column at Jhansi—*ib*.

Rodden, Edward, Pte. (H. M. 95th Reg.)
Wd. at Gwalior—p. 172.

Roderick, Bugler (Arty.)
Wd. at Nowgong—xxxii; xxxv; xxxvi.

Roe, Lt. (12th Lancers.)
Acts as Brigr.-Maj.—p. 37.
Mtd. in desp.—*ib*.

Roger, Pte. (3rd B. E. R.)
Mtd. in desp. (Jhansi)—p. 56.

Roghooje Powar, Jemadar (25th B. N. I.)
Wd. at Jhansi—p. 59.

Rohilcund.
Page 83.
C.-in-C. in—p. 104.

Rohillas.
Among rebels—p. 49.
Disaffected—p. 93.

Roome, Lt.
Cmds. 10th B. N. I. at Gwalior—pp. 144, 146, 148.
"Special mention" (Gwalior)—p. 174.

Rose, Alexander, Sgt. (H. M. 71st Reg.)
S.-s. (Koonch)—p. 78.
Died, s.-s., Calpee—p. 124.

Rose, Capt. (Aide-de-Camp to Sir H. Rose.)
Mtd. in desp. (Barodia)—pp. 12, 18.
Saves a life at Jhansi—p. 48.
Mtd. in desp. (Betwa)—cii.

Rose, Sir Hugh, Maj.-Gen., Comdg. C. I. F. F.

Letters and Despatches from—
To Adjt.-Gen. of the Army (Camp Saugor, Feb. 7, 1858)—p. 2.
To Col. Green, C.B., Adjt.-Gen. of the Army—p. 10.
To Maj.-Gen. Mansfield, Chief of Staff, (Camp before Jhansi, March 26, 1858)—p. 19.
To Chief of the Staff, (Camp Mote, April 30, 1858)—p. 39.
To Maj.-Gen. Sir William Mansfield, Chief of the Staff, (camp Golowlee, May 24, 1858)—p. 64.
To Maj.-Gen. Sir Wm. M. Mansfield, Chief of the Staff of the Army in India, (Gwalior, June 22, 1858)—p. 81.
To Maj.-Gen. Sir William Mansfield, Chief of the Staff of the Army, India, (Poonah, Oct. 13, 1858)—p. 129.
List of officers and soldiers of C. I. F. F. and Rajpootana F. F. "mentioned" and "specially mentioned" by him for good service before Gwalior—p. 172.
To Col. Birch, Sec. to Govt. of India, Mil. Dept., (Camp Sirrus, March 19, 1858)—lxxxi.
To Maj.-Gen. Whitelock, Comdg. Saugor Field Divn, (Sirrus Ghat, March 19, 1858)—lxxxiii.
To the Chief of the Staff, (Camp Pooch, April 30, 1858)—xcv.
To the Chief of the Staff, (Camp Soopowlie, June 14, 1858)—cxi.

[**Rathghur.**]
Refers to report of Jan. 31, 1858—p. 2.
Approaches Rathghur—*ib*.
Extricates flankers from unfavourable position—*ib*.
Reconnoitres the surrounding country—*ib*.
Invests as far as possible, the rock of—3.
Records services of Regt of Bhopal—*ib*.

[Rathghur]—(*Contd.*)
Attacks the Fort under cover of a feint—3.
Leads troops through jungle to the Fort—*ib*.
Directs road to be cut to battery—*ib*.
And Rifle pits—*ib*.
Thanks battery and its Cmndr.—p. 4.
Personally superintends two simultaneous attacks—*ib*.
Orders capture of tower at main gate—*ib*.
Conducts attack on rebels on banks of the Beena—p. 5.
Hears of rebel attack on convoy—p. 6.
Makes over prisoners to Sir R. Hamilton—p. 7.
Also the Native letters, etc., found in the Fort—p. 8.
Enjoins the troops to spare women and children—*ib*.
Commends the services of officers and men—*ib*.
Submits a return of Oude artillery found in Fort—*ib*.
Returns thanks to His Excellency and Lord Elphinstone—p. 9.

[Barodia.]
Marches from Rathghur—11.
Orders of march adopted—*ib*.
Opens fire on rebel ambuscade—*ib*.
Drives rebels from jungle—p. 12.
Commends officers—*ib*.
Conducts further attack on rebels—*ib*.
Commends officers and men—p. 13.
Orders shelling of Fort—*ib*.
Barodia occupied—p. 14.
Marches back to Rathghur—*ib*.
Describes result of victory—*ib*.
Commends officers and men—pp. 14, 15.
Encloses list of casualties—p. 15.

[Pass of Mudinpore.]
Marches from Garakota to Saugor—p. 19.
Is detained at Saugor—*ib*.
Expects resistance to advance on Jhansi—p. 20.

[Pass of Mudinpore]—(*Contd.*)
Determines to force his way—*ib*.
Describes the three passes—pp. 20-21.
Requests Maj. Orr to reconnoitre them—p. 21.
Marches to Rijwass—*ib*.
Selects Mudinpore for attack—*ib*.
Makes feint against Narut—*ib*.
Leaves small garrison at Barodia—*ib*.
Marches against the pass—*ib*.
Drives rebels from a glen—p. 22.
Orders hill to be stormed—*ib*.
Sends Capt. Abbott to clear the pass—p. 23.
The pass gained—*ib*.
Describes rebel fortifications—p. 23.
Orders advance of siege train—*ib*.
Orders pursuit of rebels—*ib*.
Commends officers—p. 24.

[Jhansi.]
Arrives at Simra with 2nd Brigade—p. 40.
Sends Brigr. Steuart to invest Jhansi—*ib*.
Is delayed in reaching Jhansi—*ib*.
Makes repeated reconnaissances—*ib*.
Describes the fortress and city—pp. 40-41.
Establishes Flying Camps—p. 41.
Selects site for breaching battery—*ib*.
Desires preservation of the Palace—p. 42.
Constructs batteries on rocky ridge—p. 43.
Occupies the Jokun Bagh—p. 44.
Constructs other batteries—*ib*.
Describes damage done in Jhansi by cannonade—*ib*.
Consents to escalade—p. 45.
Postpones date of storming—*ib*.
Establishes telegraph on hill—*ib*.
Issues order for assault of city walls—*ib*.
Commends conduct of attack—p. 46.
Orders houses to be loopholed—*ib*.
Visits the right attack—*ib*.

[Jhansi]—(Contd.)

Passes through the breach with Lt.-Col. Turnbull—p. 47.
The latter killed—*ib*.
Orders clearance of part of the city—p. 47.
Allows soldiers to hoist Union Jack on Palace—p. 48.
Hears of attack on Flying Camp—*ib*.
Moves available troops against rebels on hill—*ib*.
Postpones attack on rest of city—p. 49.
Receives false alarm of approach of enemy—*ib*.
Occupies the rest of the city—*ib*.
Sends force in pursuit of flying rebels—*ib*.
Makes honourable mention of officers—p 50.
Describes great strength of Jhansi—p. 51.
Eulogises conduct of troops—pp. 51-52.
Orders destitute women and children at Jhansi to be fed—*ib*.
His obligations to officers—p. 53.

[Koonch.]

Marches from Jhansi on Calpee—p. 64.
Leaves garrison at Jhansi—p. 65.
Joins Maj. Gall at Pooch—*ib*.
Learns that rebels had occupied Koonch—*ib*.
Sends Maj. Orr against rebel Rajahs—*ib*.
Makes flank march to North-West—p. 66.
Comes within sight of Koonch—*ib*.
Determines to storm the town—p. 67.
The town occupied—*ib*.
Commends troops—*ib*.
Ditto —p. 69.
Discontinues pursuit in consequence of great heat—p. 70.
Describes results of rebel defeat at Koonch—pp. 70-71.
Commends officers—p. 72.
And Medical Department—p. 73.

[Calpee.]

Describes serious consequences of great heat—pp. 81-82.
And scarcity of water—p. 82.
Describes rebels' sources of strength—pp. 82-83.
Accidental frustration of his tactical plans—p. 84.
His original instructions—*ib*.
His letter to Col. Maxwell miscarries—*ib*.
Determines to march to Golowlee—pp. 84-85.
Orders 2nd Brig. to Banda—p. 85.
His plan foiled—*ib*.
Delays one day at Etowa—*ib*.
Reaches Golowlee—p. 86.
Sends instructions to Col. Maxwell—*ib*.
Effects junction of Bengal and Bombay troops—*ib*.
Marches to assistance of Maj. Forbes—p. 87.
Prevents evacuation of Mutha—*ib*.
Husbands the strength of his men—p. 88.
Commends officers—*ib*.
Gives details of plan of attack on Calpee—p. 89.
Compelled to modify his plan—p. 90.
Describes effects of great heat—*ib*.
Gives details of the difficulties he had to face—p. 91.
His eulogy of the troops under his command—p. 92.
Calls upon Col. Maxwell for reinforcements—p. 93.
Selects position for battery at Russulpore—*ib*.
Maintains his ground against rebel attacks—p. 94.
Receives notice of general attack by rebels—*ib*.
Gives details of his dispositions—p. 95.
Advance in force of rebels reported—p. 96.
His tactics against the attack—*ib*.

[Calpee] - (Contd.)
  Goes to the rescue of Brigr. Stuart with Camel Corps—p. 97.
  Charges and routs rebels—p. 98.
  Commends officers—*ib.*
  Decides on immediate attack on Calpee—p. 100.
  Leads troops through ravines—p. 101.
  And takes possession of Calpee—*ib.*
  Describes contents of Arsenal at Calpee—p. 102.
  Sends Lt.-Col. Robertson in pursuit of enemy—p. 103.
  Eulogises his troops—*ib.*
  Tenders his thanks to the G.-G., Lord Elphinstone, and Sir H. Somerset—p. 104.
  His indebtedness to officers of the Civil Service—pp. 104—105.
  Excuses tardy despatch of report—p. 106.
  His five attacks of sun-sickness—*ib.*
  Temporary loss of his baggage—p. 107.

[Gwalior.]
  Receives conflicting reports of flight of rebels—p. 129.
  Gives troops a short rest—*ib.*
  Reinforces Lt.-Col. Robertson—*ib.;* p. 130.
  Hears of rebel attack on Scindiah—*ib.*
  The seriousness of the situation—p. 131.
  Proceeds by forced marches to Gwalior—p. 132.
  Joins Brigr. Stuart's column—*ib.*
  Praises Hyderabad Contingent—p. 133.
  His plan of attack on Gwalior—*ib.*
  His lack of a map of Gwalior—pp. 133, 134.
  Orders Brigr. Smith to Kotah-ka-Serai—p. 134.
  Marches against the Morar Cantonments—*ib.*
  Reaches Bahadurpore—*ib.*
  Immediately attacks Morar—p. 135.
  Commends officers—p. 137.
  Praises the gallantry of his troops—p. 137.

[Gwalior] - (Contd.)
  Reconnoitres Gwalior—p. 139.
  Marches to Kotah-ka-Serai—p. 140.
  Receives report from Brigr. Smith—*ib.*
  Selects position for siege guns—p. 141.
  Orders attack on enemy's left flank—p. 143.
  Describes view of Gwalior from the heights—p. 144.
  Determines on immediate advance—*ib.*
  His dispositions for attack—pp. 145—147.
  Gives orders for general attack on Gwalior—p. 147.
  Enters the town with Lt.-Col. Raines—p. 148.
  Reaches Scindiah's Palace—p. 149.
  Sends patrols to clear the streets—*ib.*
  Orders investment of Fort—*ib.*
  Discusses Tantia Topee's character—p. 150.
  Requests Brigr. Napier to pursue enemy—p. 151.
  Receives Scindiah, and escorts him to his Palace—*ib.*
  His appreciation of Scindiah—*ib.*
  Praises the devotion of his troops—p. 152.
  Their exploits—pp. 152, 153.
  He gives over his command to Brigr. Napier—p. 153.
  His supplementary "Special Mentions" of officers—pp. 175—177.
  Letters to, from Maj.-Gen. Mansfield, on reduction of Jhansi—lxxix.
  Acknowledges instructions from Governor General—lxxxii.
  Letter from Maj.-Gen. Whitlock to—lxxxiii.

[The Betwa.]
  Announces his victory—xcv.
  Hears of Tantia Topee's force—xcvi.
  Marches to Bupoba—*ib.*
  Comments on the weakness of his force—xcvii.
  Sends Maj. Orr to watch enemy—*ib.*

[The Betwa]—(*Contd.*)
>Prepares for the attack—*ib*.
Describes engagement—xcviii-xcix.
Commends officers—xcix.
Orders pursuit of routed enemy—xcix-c.
Eulogises the conduct of his troops—ci.
Honourably mentions officers and men—*ib*.
Rectifies omission of names of officers—cxi.

Rose, W., Lt., (25th B. N. I.)
>Mtd. in desp. (Morar)—137.
Captures the Fort of Gwalior, and is killed—pp. 150, 170.
"Special mention,"—p. 173.

Ross, Maj.
>Comdg. Camel|Corps—p.p. 97.
"Special mention,"—pp. 98 ; 101.
Mtd. in desp. (May 22, 1858),—p. 122.

Rowjee, Horse-keeper (Arty.)
>Wd. at Mudinpore—p. 25.

Rugoonath Sing, Sepoy (5th Inf., H. C.)
>Fatally burnt, (the Betwa)—cix.

Ruheem Ali Nurut.
>Reinforces rebels—p. 129.

Rumzad Khan Havildar (25th B. N. I.)
>"Special mention," (Gwalior)—p. 175.

Runjeet Khan, Duffadar (4th Cav., H. C.)
>Kld. at Jhansi—p. 61.

Rupee, Company's.
>Fall of value of—lii.

Russulpoor.
>British Battery at—p. 93.
Co. of H. M. 86th Reg. at —p. 94.
Situation of—p. 110 ; 111.

Rutherford, Wm., Pte. (H. M. 71st Reg.)
>Died, s.-s. (Koonch)—p. 78.

Ryall, Lt. (Adjt. 2nd Cav., H. C.)
>Mtd. in desp.—p. 34.

Ryan, John, Pte. (H. M. 86th Reg.)
>Wd. at Jhansi—p. 58.

Rymattalah Khan, Tpr. (1st Cav., H. C.)
>Wd. at Barodia—p. 16.

Ryves, Lt. (12th N. I.)
>Supposed escape of—iii.
At Jhansi—xxi.

S

Saadut Khan.
>Mutineer, reward for his head—lxii.

Sadoolla Khan, Tpr. (3rd Cav., H. C.)
>Recmd. for " Order of British India,"—p. 169.

Sage, Brigr. (Cmdg. at Saugor.)
>Gives stores to Sir H. Rose—p. 105.

Saheb Rai.
>Aids British fugitive—iv.

Sahibood-deen.
>Khansamah, his account of mutiny at Jhansi—ix—xii.

Saibgunge.
>Mutineers driven from—p. 27.

Saligram Sing, Sepoy.
>Wd. at Nowgong—xxxii.

Sallow Khan, Tpr. (3rd Cav., H C.)
>Recmd. for " Order of British India,"—p. 169.

Salone.
>District of—xxxv.

Salpoora Hills.
>lxxxviii.

Salt Customs, Police.
>In action at Mudinpore—p. 21.
Rebels mistaken for them—p. 22.

Samajee Alrajee, Subadar (24th B. N. I.)
Wd. at Jhansi—p. 61.

Sanderson, Asst. Surg. (1st Cav., H. C.)
Mtd. in desp. (Koonch)—p. 76.

Sandwith, Capt. (3rd B. E. R.)
Wd. at Jhansi—pp. 48; 60.
Mtd. in desp.—pp. 54, 56.

"Sandy Plain."
Near Calpee—pp. 89, 94.

Sappe, F., Sgt. (Bombay S. M.)
Wd. at Rethghor—p. 9.

Sappery, Charles, Trumpeter, (Meade's Horse.)
Recmd. for "Order of Merit"—p. 165.

Sarel, Capt. (17th Lancers.)
Mtd. in desp.—p. 28.

Saugor.
Rebels try to prevent relief of—pp. 2, 11.
Sir H. Rose anxious to relieve—p. 8.
Communications with, open—p. 14.
Halt of 2nd Brig.—C. I. F. F. at—p. 19.
Sir H. Rose at—p. 40.
Road to, from Mhow, closed—lii.
Burwa-Saugor road—lxxxv.

Saugor Field Force.
—pp. 35, 36.
Casualties in, (April 19, 1858)—p. 38.

Schwabbe, Rev. Mr. (Prot. Chapl.).
Mtd. in desp. (Calpee)—p. 120.

Scinde.
River—pp. 129, 132.

Scindiah.
Device of, on s—p. 102.
Reported safe at Gwalior—p. 130.
His defeat at Bahadurpore—ib.; p. 135.
Flees to Agra—p. 130.
Importance of his dominions—

Scindiah—(Contd.)
Sheds prepared by, at Morar—p. 139.
Returns to Gwalior—p. 151.
Character of—ib.
Offers rewards to British troops—p. 152.
His dread of a mutiny at Gwalior—xxxvii.
Brigr. Ramsay's opinion of—xxxix.

Scindiah, Agent of.
Acts as guide at Morar—p. 136.
His incorrect information—p. 149.

Scot, P. G., Capt.
His Report of the mutiny at Jhansi—i—iii.
And of mutiny at Nowgong—xv.

Scott, Capt., (Paymaster of the Force.)
"Special mention" (Gwalior)—p. 173.
Mtd. in desp. (Jhansi)—cxi.

Scott, Lt., (H. M. 71st Reg.)
In pursuit of rebels—p. 154.
Mtd. in desp. (Gwalior)—p. 155.

Scott, Mr.
Murdered at Jhansi—vii.
Also his family—ix.

Scudamore, Maj., (Cmdg. H. M. 14th Lt. Dragns.)
At Rathghur—p. 4.
Conducts feint against Malthone—p. 21.
Mtd. in desp.—p. 24.
In command of flying camp at Jhansi—p. 41.
Mtd. in desp. (Jhansi)—pp. 52, 53.
At Koonch—p. 74.
At Muttra—p. 109.
Mtd. in desp. (Gwalior)—p. 155.
Cmdg. flying camp—cxvii.

Secunder Ali Beg. Ressaldar, (3rd Cav., H. C.)
Mtd. in desp. (the Betwa)—civ.
Wd. *ib.;* cvii.

Seehore.
Road to, from Mhow, closed—lii.
Col. Durand at—lx.

See Kundar Ali Beg.
See *Secunder*.

Seepree.
p. 133.
Brigr. Smith|at—p. 134.

Seetal Coonby, Pte. (25th B.|N. I.)
Kld. at Jhansi—p. 59.

Seetal Pursad, Havildar (24th B. N. I.)
Kld. at Jhansi—p. 61.

Seetaram.
Loyal native, promoted by| Maj. Kirke—xix ; xxxiii-iv.

Seetul, Driver (4th Co. 2nd| Batt. Arty.)
Mortally wd. at Gwalior—p. 170.

Seetul Pandy, Havildar (5th Inf., H. C.)
S.-s., Calpee—p. 125.

Seeumber Ahire, Pte. (25th B. N. I.)
Wd. at Gwalior—p. 170.

Sehore.
See | *Seehore*.

Sen Amee Aheer, Pte., (25th B. N. I.)
Wd. "Special mention", (Gwalior)—p. 175.

Sende Nuddee.
Crossed by British troops—p. 27.

Seuroho.
Village—xxxv.

Serai.
Fort of—p. 19.
Capture of—p. 20.
Rebels retire to—p. 23.
Occupied by Sir H. Rose—p. 24.

Sewa Juddoo, Bheestee, (10th N. I.)
Wd. at Gwalior—p. 172.

Sewajpore.
Brig. R. Walpole marches from, (Apl. 22nd, 1858)—p. 26.

Sewell, S. W., Ens. (H. M. 86th Regt.)
Mtd. in desp. Jhansi—pp. 53, 55.
Wd. at Jhansi—pp. 55, 57.

Sew Goo Kaum Pte., (Bombay S. M.)
Kld. at Jhansi—p. 59.

Sexton, J. M., Lt. and Adjt. (H. M. 95th Reg.)
Cmds. guns at Gwalior—p. 144.
Mtd. in desp. (Gwalior) pp. 162, 174.
Wd. at Gwalior—p. 171.
(Kotah-ka-Serai)—p. 176.
At Gwalior—cxviii.

Sexton, R. Paymaster Sgt. (H. M. 14th Lt. Dragns.)
S.-s., Koonch—p. 77.

Shab Baz Khan, Tpr. 4th Cav., H. C.)
Kld. the (Betwa)—cix.

Shaghur.
District of—p. 20.
The territory annexed—p. 24.
Occupied by detachment—xc.

Shaghur, Rajah of.
Defends Mudinpore—p. 21.
Aids rebels—p. 65.
Orders as to disposal of—xci.

Shah Ahmed, Bheestie (5th Inf., H. C.)
Severely|burnt,'(the Betwa)—cix.

Shahjeanpore.
Scindiah's minister at—lxii.

Shah Mirza Beg Bahadoor, Ressaldar Maj. (Cav., H. C.)
Mtd. in desp. (Calpee)—p. 117.

Shaick Dawood, Havildar, (Lt. Comp., 25th N. I.)
His daring act at Jhansi—p. 55.

Shair Ali, Tpr., (3rd Cav., H. C.)
Wd. at Calpee—p. 123.

Shaik Balla, Sepoy (3rd Inf., H. C.)
S.-s., Calpee—p. 125.

Shaik Cammoo, Sepoy (3rd Inf., H. C.)
S.-s., Calpee—p. 125.

Shaik Gholam Nubbi, Duffadar, (3rd Cav., H. C.)
Recmd. for " Order of British India," p. -169.

Shaik Jumla Mahomed, Tpr., (4th Cav., H. C.)
Kld. at Koonch—p. 79.

Shaik Kubeeroodean, Tpr., (3rd Cav., H. C.)
Recmd. for " Order of British India"—p. 169.
Wd. (Gwalior)—p. 170.

Shaik Lyfoolah, Tpr., (1st Cav., H. C.)
Wd. at Barodia—p. 16.

Shaik Raj Bup., Pte., (24th B. N. I.)
Kld. at Calpee—p. 124.

Shaik Rymon, Tpr., (1st Cav., H. C.)
Wd. at Rathghur—p. 9.

Shaikh Kyrashtee, Tpr. (1st Nat. Lt. Cav.)
Wd. at Gwalior—p. 171.

Shaikh Noor Mahomed Tpr. (1st Nat. Lt. Cav.)
Wd. at Gwalior—p. 171.

Shaikh Meeran, Tpr. (3rd Cav., H. C.)
Recmd. for " Order of British India "—p. 169.

Shaikh Mahomed, Tpr. (3rd Cav., H. C.)
Recmd for " Order of British India "—p. 169.

Shaikh Oomur, Tpr. (3rd Cav., H. C.)
Recmd. for " Order of British India "—p. 169.

Shaikh Sillar Bux, Tpr. (1st Nat. Lt. Cav.)
Wd. at Gwalior—p. 171.

Shakespear.
Mr. and family, safety of—lviii.

Shakespeare, Lt. (2nd Madras Cav.)
" Special mention"—p. 175.

Shan, James, Pte. (H. M. 95th Reg.)
Wd. (Kotah-ka-Serai)—p. 160.

Shan, Joseph, Pte. (H. M. 95th Reg.)
Wd. at Gwalior—p. 172.

Sharp, William, Pte., (H. M. 71st Highland Lt. Inf.)
Wd. (Koonch)—p. 7.

Shean, John, Pte., (3rd B. E. R.)
Wd. at Jhansi—p. 60.

Sheddon, Wm., Sgt. (H. M. 71st Lt. Highland Inf.)
S.-s., at Gwalior—p. 170.

Sheer Ghat.
Ford at—p. 102.
Reported flight of rebels towards—p. 129.

Shells.
Brass, made by natives—p. 102.

Sheik Baboo, Sepoy (3rd Inf. H. C.)
Mortally wd. at Jhansi—p. 62.

Sheik Banbun, Bheestie (3rd Inf., H. C.)
Slightly burnt, (the Betwa)—cix.

Sheik Boodun, Bheestie (5th Inf. H. C.)
Severely burnt, (the Betwa)—cix.

Sheik Chand, Sepoy (3rd Inf., H. C.)
Wd. at Jhansi—p. 61.

Sheik Mahomed Yacoob, Tpr., (1st Cav., H. C.)
Kld. (the Betwa)—cix.

Sheik Wuzzeer Ali, Tpr. (4th Cav., H. C.)
Wd. at Jhansi—p. 61.

Sheik Yacoob, Bheestie (5th Inf., H. C.)
Wd. (the Betwa)—cix.

Sher Ali, Tpr., (3rd Cav., H. C.)
Wd., mtd. in desp. (Calpee)—p. 117.

Sherghur.
British troops at—p. 110.

Sheriff, Maj.
Influence of at Gwalior—xl.

Sherlock, H., Asst. Surg. (H. M. 8th Hussars.)
Wd. at Gwalior—p. 171.
" Special mention"—p. 177.
Charges with squadron—cxvi.

Shew Churn Sing, Pte., (25th B. N. I.)
Kld. at Calpee—p. 123.

Shitah Khan, Tpr., (4th Cav., H. C.)
Wd. at Koonch—p. 79.

Shock Lall, Naick, (1st Nat. Lt. Cav.)
Wd. at Gwalior—p. 171.

Shorten, Steven, Gnr. (3rd Tp., H. A.)
Wd. at Gwalior—p. 171.

Sikhs.
In (12th N. I.) at Nowgong—xvii, xviii.
Mutiny—xxii, xxxiv.

Simpson, Lt., (23rd Beng. N. I.)
Mtd. in desp. (Jhansi), wd.—p. 50.
Saved from mutineers by sepoys—xliv.

Simpson, G., Lt. (4—2 Artillery.)
Wd. at Jhansi—p. 57.

Simra.
2nd Brig., under Sir H. Rose, arrives at —p. 40.

Simrole.
Bhopal Congt. retreat on—xlvi, liv.

Sinclair, J. deC., Capt. (Cmdg. Arty.)
lxxiv.
Mtd. in desp. (Mundesore)—lxxv.

Sinclair. John, Capt. (3rd Inf., H. C.).
At Mudinpore—p. 22.
Mtd. in desp.—p. 25.
Mortally wd. at Jhansi—pp. 50, 61.
lxxiv.
At Goraria—lxxiv—v.
Mtd. in desp.—*ib.*

Sinclair John, Pte., (3rd B. E. R.).
Wd. at Jhansi—p. 60.

Sinclare, Capt.
See *Sinclair,' John,* Capt.

Sind, River.
Difficult ghat on—p. 64.

Sirrus, Camp.
lxxxi.

Sirrus ghat.
lxxxiii.

Sirdar Khan, Pay-Havildar.
Loyal conduct of—xxxiii.

Sirsie.
Action near, (Apl. 22, 1858)—p. 26.

Skene, Maj.
Supdt. at Jhansi—i.
His wife and children—ii.
Murdered—iii.

Skene, Maj.—*contd.*
Closes town gates—vi.
Manner of his death—viii.
His warning to the Mutineers,—*ib.* ix, x.

Smalley, Mrs.
Death of—p. xxviii.

Smalley, Mr., Band-master (12th N. I.)
At Nowgong—xxiv, xxix, xxx.
Death of his child—xxxi.

Smith Capt., (H. M., 95th Reg.)
At Gwalior—p. 145.

Smart, Roland, Pte. (H. M. 14th Dragns.)
Died s.-s., Calpee—p. 122.

Smith, Abraham, Pte. (H. M. 14th Lt. Dragns.)
Wd. the Betwa—cviii.

Smith, Charles, Pte. (H. M. 14th Lt. Dragns.)
Wd. the Betwa—cviii.

Smith, Edw., Corpl. (H. M. 14th Lt. Dragns.)
Wd. at Jhansi—p. 59.

Smith, James, Sapper (21st Coy., R. E.).
Wd. at Jhansi—p. 57.

Smith John, Pte. (3rd B. E. R.)
Wd. at Jhansi—p. 60.

Smith, M. W., Brigr.
In cmd. of Rajpootana F. F.—p. 133.
At Seepree—p. 134.
At Kotah-ka-Serai—p. 139.
Reinforced—*ib.;* 140 ; 141.
Occupies heights before Gwalior—p. 143.
Attacks the Phool Bagh—147.
Mtd. in desp.—p. 149.
His force commended—p. 152.
His report of operations—pp. 156—159.
Cmdg. attack on Kotah-ka-Serai—p. 160.

Smith, M. W. Brigr.—*contd.*
"Second special mention," (Gwalior)—p. 173.
"Special mention,"—p. 175.
Supplementary report from—cxiii.

Smith, Samuel, Pte. (H. M. 14th Lt. Dragns.).
Wd. at Koonch—p. 77.
The Betwa—cviii.

Smith, Thos., Corp. (H. M. 8th Hussars)
Wd. at Gwalior—p. 171.

Smith, Thos., Pte. (3rd B. E. R.)
Wd. at Jhansi—p. 171.

Smith, William, Pte. (H. M. 14th Lt. Dragns.)
S.-s., (Koonch)—p. 77.

Smithy, Chas. Pte. (3rd B. E. R.)
Wd. at Jhansi—p. 60.

Sohaie.
Mtd.—p. 89.

Somerset, Sir Henry.
Sir H. Rose's indebtedness to—p. 104.

Soobanee Ragura, Pte. (24th B. N. I.)
Wd. at Jhansi—p. 61.

Soojab Khan, Subadar, (3rd Bom. Lt. Cav.)
Recmd. for "Order of Merit"—p. 165.

Soojut Khan, Subadar.
Mtd. in desp. (Barodia)—p. 13.

Soorowlee.
Village near Golowlee—p. 95.

Sowna, R.
At Mundesore—lxvii, lxviii, lxix.

Soyrage.
Fort of, see *Serai*, Fort of.

Spies.
Use of—p. 84.

Spillett, Silas, Pte. (9th Lancers.)
Wd. near Allahgunge—p. 29.

Stack, Dr. (H. M. 86th Reg.)
Kld. at Jhansi—pp. 73, 120.

Standards.
Rebel, captured at Rathghur—p. 8.

Staple, George, Pte. (14th Lt. Dragns.)
Wd. (Jowra-Alipore)—p. 166.

Star Fort.
British at Jhansi take refuge in—xix.

Steadman, James, Pte. (H. M. 14th Lt. Dragns.)
Kld. at Koonch—p. 77.

Steavens, Robt., Col.-Sgt. (3rd B. E. R.)
Wd. at Jhansi—p. 60.

Steel, William, Pte. (H. M. 71st Reg.)
S.-s., (Koonch)—p. 78.

Steen, John, Pte. (3rd F. R.)
Wd. at Mudinpore—p. 25.

Stent, George, Pte. (H. M. 14th Lt. Dragns.)
S.-s., (Koonch)—p. 77.

Steuart, C., Brigr.
In command of troops at Rathghur—p. 4.
Pursues rebels—p. 5.
Repels sortie—p. 6.
Commends officers—p. 8.
Left in charge of Rathghur—pp. 11, 14.
Cmds. 2nd Brig. at Jhansi—p. 45.
Reports exhaustion of his men—p. 49.
Watches the Betwa—ib.
Mtd. in desp. (Jhansi)—p. 53.
Report of (Jhansi)—pp. 55—57.
At Jhansi—p. 65.
At Chomair—pp. 66, 68, 74.
Detained at Koonch—p. 84.
Invalided—pp. 85—86.
With Sir R. Hamilton—xcii.

Steuart, Maj. (H. M. 86th Reg.)
At Koonch—pp. 67, 68.

Stewart, Capt.
Influence of, at Gwalior—xl.

Stewart, D. M., Maj.
Asst. Adjt.-Gen of the Army—cx.

Stewart, Maj. (H. M. 86th Reg.)
Before Calpee—p. 94.

Stewart, Mr.
Escapes from Jhansi in disguise—iii.

Stewart, Surg. (H. M. 14th Dragns.)
Mtd. in desp. (Calpee)—pp. 118—119.
Ditto.—p. 165.

Stewart, R., Pte. (3rd B. E. R.)
Wd. at Rathghur—p. 9.

Stock, Thos., Surg. (H. M. 86th Reg.)
Mtd. in desp. (Jhansi)—p. 55.
Kld.—ib.; p. 57.

Strickland, Rev. Mr. (R. C. Chapl.)
Mtd. in desp. (Calpee)—p. 120.

Strutt, Lt.
Comds. No. 4 Battery Bombay Arty. at Barodia—p. 11.
His good practice at Jhansi—p. 45.
Mtd. in desp. (Koonch)—p. 73.
At Calpee—p. 115.
(Morar)—pp. 136—137.
At Goraria—lxxiii.

Stuart, Alex., Pte. (H. M. 71st Reg.)
Died, s.-s. (Koonch)—78.

Stuart, C. S., Brigr.-Gen.
Cmds. 1st Brig. at Jhansi—p. 45.
Success of left attack under—pp. 45; 49.
Mtd. in desp.—p. 53
His report of operations of 1st Brigade before Jhansi—pp. 54—55.
At Golowlee—p. 38.
"Special mention,"—ib.
At Calpee—pp. 95-96.
Reinforced—p. 97.

Stuart, C. S., Brig.-Gen.—*contd.*
  Critical position of—p. 98.
  Leads right attack against Calpee—pp. 100-101.
  His report on action on the Jumna—pp. 112—16.
  Mtd. in desp. (May 23, 1858)—p. 121.
  Reinforces Lt.-Col. Robertson—p. 130.
  At Indoorkee—p. 132.
  Marches against Morar Cantonments—p. 134.
  At Morar—p. 135.
  Before Gwalior—p. 143.
  "Special mention"—p. 173.
  Storms Chandaree—lxxxiv—lxxxv.
  With 1st Brig. at the Betwa—xcviii.
  Mtd. in desp.—ci.
  His report—cii.

Stuart, John, Corp. (3rd B. E. R.)
  Wd. at Jhansi—p. 60

Stuart, Maj. (H. M. 86th Regt.)
  Mtd. in desp. (Jhansi)—p. 53.
  Leads attack—pp. 54, 55.
  Mtd. in desp. (Calpee)—p. 115.
    Ditto. (May 20 and May 22, 1858)—p. 121.

Suadut Khan, Tpr. (3rd Cav. H. C.)
  Recmd. for "Order of British India"—p. 169.

Sucalee.
  2nd Brig. reaches—p. 85.

Sudden, Hugh, Pte. (H. M. 14th Lt. Dragns.)
  Died, s.-s., Calpee—123.

Sudder Bazar.
  At Mhow—xlix.

Sudnee, Pte. (Bombay S. M.)
  Wd. at Jhansi—p. 59.

Sudun Khan, Tpr. (4th Cav., H. C.)
  Wd. at Koonch—p. 79.

Sufdar Ali Beg, Rissaldar (1st Cav., H. C.)
  Kld. at Koonch—p 79

Sullivan, C., Pte. (H. M. 86th Reg.)
  Mortally wd. at Jhansi—p. 57.

Sumowlee.
  2nd Brig., C. I. F. F. rest at—p. 163.

Sumsagee Israel, Subadar (24th B. N. I.)
  S.-s., (Koonch)—p. 78.

Sundee.
  Camp—p. 80.

Sunker Argoonhotry, Pte. (25th B. N. I.)
  Wd. at Calpee—p. 123.

Sunnow.
  Hyd. Contingent at—p. 74.

Sun-stroke.
  Casualties due to—
    pp. 68, 70, 72, 75, 76, 77, 78, 79, 82, 85, 88, 90, 91, 92, 98, 100, 103, 106, 118, 120, 122—125, 126, 140, 162, 166, 170-171.
  Effect of—p. 98.

Supree.
  lxxxix.

Surroop Sing, Tpr. (3rd Bombay Lt. Cav.)
  Kld. at Calpee—p. 124.

Suttle, James, Pte. (H. M. 95th Reg.)
  Wd. (Kotah-ka-Serai)—pp. 160, 171.

Swan, James, Pte. (H. M. 95th Reg.)
  Wd. at Gwalior—p. 172.

Swany, George, Pte. (H. M. 86th Reg.)
  Wd. at Jhansi—p. 58.

Sweeny, Stephen, Sgt. (H. M. 14th Lt. Dragns.)
  S.-s. (Koonch)—p. 77.

Syed Sharief, Tpr. (2nd Cav., H. C.)
Recmd. for promotion—p. 51.

Syeed Oosman, Tpr. (3rd Cav., H. C.)
Recmd. for "Order of British India"—p. 169.

Syud Jaffer, Sepoy (3rd Inf., H. C.).
S.-s., Calpee—125.

Syud Noor Ali, Jemadar (4th Cav., H. C.).
Wd. at Jhansi—p. 61.
(Betwa)—cix.

T.

Tackeerah, Maistry (1st Co. Arty., H. C.)
Wd. at Koonch—p. 79.

Tackoor, Sepoy (5th Inf., H. C.)
Died, s.-s., Calpee—p. 125.

Tahool Khan, Tpr. (4th Cav. H. C.)
Recmd. for promotion—p. 51.

Tajie Mahomed Khan, nephew of.
Kld. at Barodia—p. 14.

Takoor, Sepoy (5th Inf., H. C.)
Wd. at Koonch—p. 79.

Takoor Aheer, Pte. (25th B. N. I.)
Kld. at Calpee—p. 123.

Takoor Sing, Sepoy (5th Inf., H. C.)
Wd. at Koonch—p. 79.

Tantia Topee.
Tidings of—p. 49.
Occupies Koonch—65.
His flight—pp. 70, 73.
His intrigue against Scindiah—p. 130.
Its danger—p. 131.
His character—p. 150.
Ranee of Jhansi asks assistance from—lxxxvi.
Besieges Chirkaree—xc.
Flight of—xci.
Orders as to disposal of—*ib*.

Tantia Topee—*contd.*
At Koonch—xcii.
Hanged—xciii, xciv.
Organizes Army of the Peishwa—xcv, xcvi.
At the Betwa—c.

Taptee, R.
lxxxviii.

Taylor, Ens.
Murdered by mutineers at Jhansi, (various accounts of his death)—i, vi, ix, xiii, xxi.

Teerana.
The Komsidar of—lxii.

Tegmal Sing, Tpr. (1st Cav., H. C.)
Wd. and recmd. for promotion—p. 5!.

Tehree.
Troops from, mistaken for enemy—p. 49.
Situation of—p. 86.
Attacked—pp. 88, 90.
Village of—pp. 95, 96, 97.
Attacked—p. 100.
See also *Bigaroo*.

Tel Bate.
1st Brig. at—xc.

Telegraph.
Established near Jhansi—p. 45.

Ternan, Capt. (Dep. Commr. of Jaloun.)
Mtd. in desp. (Calpee)—p. 105.

Thain, Lt. (Sub-Asst. Com. Gen.)
Mtd. in desp. (Mundesore)—lxxi.

Thakoor Pursaud, Pte. (10th N. I.)
Wd. at Gwalior—p. 172.

Thal-Behut.
Fort of—pp. 20, 24.

Theobald, Mr.
Takes refuge at Parnasa—p. lxv.

Thompson, Capt. (H. M. 14th Lt. Dragns.)
At Koonch—p. 68.
At Morar—p. 136.
" Special mention "—p. 138.

Thompson, Qr. Mr. (Artillery).
Mtd. in desp. (Rathghur), his battery thanked—p. 4.
Wd.—p. 9.
Mtd. in desp.—p. 17.

Thomson, Gnr. (Bombay Arty.)
Mtd. in desp. (Mundesore)—lxx.

Thwaites, Joseph, Pte. (H. M. 14th Dragns.)
Died, s.-s., Calpee—p. 122.

Tierney, Mrs.
At Kubrai—xxix.
With her children at Muntuoo—xxxii.

Todd, Capt. (Brigade Maj., 2nd Brig.)
Mtd. in desp. (Jhansi)—pp. 54, 57.
Koonch—p. 73.
Letter to—p. 107.
Mtd. in desp. (Calpee)—pp. 120, 166.
Letter to—p. 168.

Tollen, Wm., Pte. (3rd B. E. R.)
Wd. at Jhansi—p. 60.

Tombs, Lt.-Col.
Commds. Horse Arty. at Allahgunge—pp. 26, 27.
Mtd. in desp.—p. 28.

Tookajee Rao Holkar.
See *Holkar*.

Tooka Ram, Pte. (24th B. N. I.)
Wd. at Jhansi—p. 61.

Tookunndeo Sookul, Pte. (24th B. N. I.).
Mortally wd. at Jhansi—p. 61.

Toolja Ram, Tpr. (1st Cav., H. C.)
Wd. at Jhansi—p. 61.

Toorab Khan, (12th N. I.)
Mutineer—xxv.

Tootle, William, Pte. (3rd B. E. R.)
Died, s.-s., Calpee—p. 124.

Topley, F. G., Pte. (H. M. 14th Dragns.)
Kld. at Koonch—p. 77.

Tounsend, Dennis, Pte. (H. M. 14th Lt. Dragns.)
Wd. at Koonch—p. 77.

Townsend, Mrs.
xxxvi.

Townsend, S., Sec. Lt.
In command of battery at Nowgong—xvi.
Is warned of mutiny—xviii, xxii; xxiii xxv; xxvi.
Attacked by natives and killed during retreat from Nowgong, xxviii, xxxiii.
His gallantry—*ib*, xxxv—vi.
Death of—xxxv.

Train Singo, Tpr. (1st Cav., H. C.)
Recmd. for promotion—p. 51.

Travers, Col., (Bhopal Contgt.)
Announces retreat to Simrole—xlvi; liv; lvii.

Travers, W. H. T. C., Lt. (H. M. 14th Lt. Dragns.)
S.-s., (Koonch)—p. 77.

Traylen, G., Pte. (H. M. 14th Lt. Dragns.)
Wd. mortally at Rathghur—p. 9.

Trower, Capt. (23rd N. I.)
At Mhow—xlii, xlviii, lii.
Volunteers under—lii.

Trueman, Ens. (3rd B. E. R.)
Mtd. in desp. (Calpee)—p. 115.
Ditto (May 22, 1858)—p. 121.

Tuft, George, Pte. (H. M. 8th Hussars.)
S.—s., Gwalior—p. 171.

Turnbull, Capt.
Mtd. in desp. (Jumna)—p. 111.

Turnbull, Sydney, Lt.-Col., (Comdg. Arty.)
At Rathghur—p. 4.
Reports breach practicable—p. 6.
Mtd. in desp.—p. 8.
His horse kld.—p. 11.
Leads Cavalry at Barodia—p. 12.
Services of—p. 13.
Mtd. in desp.—p. 17.
Mortally wd. at Jhansi—p. 47.
Mtd. in desp.—*ib.*
His death—p. 59.
At the Betwa—c.
Mtd. in desp.—ci, cvii.

Turnbull, Capt.
Mtd. in desp. (Calpee)—p. 103.

Turnbull, Lt.
Murdered at Jhansi—ii, iv, ix.

Turner, James, Pte. (H. M. 14th Lt. Dragns.)
S.-s., (Koonch)—p. 77.

Turner, John, Pte. (H. M. 86th Reg.)
Fatally wd. at Jhansi—p. 58.

Twearry Hossein.
Tessildar of Mowraneepore—xxii.

U

Ugber Sing, Pte. (25th B. N. I.)
Kld. at Jhansi—p. 59.

Ummeer Sing, Tpr. (4th Cav. H. C.)
Kld. at Jhansi—p. 61.

Union Jack.
Given to grandfather of husband of Ranee of Jhansi—p. 48.

Unooman Sing, Jamadar (4th Cav., H. C.)
Wd. at Jhansi—p. 61.

Ussud Ali Khan, Tpr. (1st Cav., H. C.)
Wd. (the Betwa)—cix.

V

Vahay, Thos., Pte. (H. M. 86th Reg.)
Wd. (R. Betwa)—cvii.

Valaitees.
In rebel garrison at Rathghur—pp. 5, 7, 14.
The term explained—pp. 42 ; 48 ; 49 ; 65.
Their losses at Koonch—p. 71 ; 83.
In Sind—pp. 102, 142, xcv, xcix.

Vanketsowarry, Pte. (Madras S. M.)
Wd. at Jhansi—p. 59.

Vass, Francis, Tpr., (3rd Lt. Cav.)
Mtd. in desp.—p. 13.
Wd. at Barodia—p. 15.

Vaughan, Dr. (Staff Surg.)
Mtd in desp. (Jhansi)—p. 53.
Leads an attack at Mudinpore—p. 72.
Mtd. in desp. (Calpee)—p. 120.

Veeraswammy, Pte. (Madras S. M.)
Wd. at Jhansi—p. 59.

Velaitees.
See *Valaitees.*

Vialles, Maj., (H. M. 95th Reg.)
At Gwalior—pp. 145, 161.
Mtd. in desp.—p. 162.
"Special mention,"—p. 174.
Mtd. in desp. (Kotah-ka-Serai)—p. 176.

Viner, Alexander, Pte. (H. M. 14th Dragns.)
Died, s -s., Calpee—p. 122.

W

Waite, John, Pte. (H. M. 14th Lt. Dragns.)
Wd., the Betwa—cviii.

Waldren, James, Pte. (H. M. 86th Reg.)
Wd. at Jhansi—p 58.

Wallace, M., Gnr. (1st Tp., H. A.)
Wd. at Rathghur - p. 9.

Waller, Lt., (25th Bombay N. I.).
Captures, with Lt Rose, the Fort of Gwalior—p. 150.
"Special mention,"—p 173.

Wallidad Khan.
Executed—p. 7.

Walpole, R., Brigr.
Report on action at Allahgunge—pp. 26—29.

Walsh, John, Sgt. (3rd B. E. R.)
Wd. at Jhansi—p. 60.

Ward, Joseph, Sgt. (H. M. 8th Hussars.)
Wd. at Gwalior—p. 171.

Ward, Peter, Pte. (H. M. 14th Lt. Dragns.)
Wd. at Koonch—p. 77.

Ward, Richard, Pte. (H. M. 86th Reg.)
Wd. fatally at Jhansi—p. 58.

Warner, Capt.
Mtd. in desp.—p. 28.

Water, scarcity of.
Between Jhansi and Calpee—p. 82.

Watkin, William, Pte. (H. M. 14th Lt. Dragns.)
Kld. (the Betwa)—cviii.

Watson, James, Pte. (3rd B. E. R.)
Kld. (the Betwa)—cviii.

Watson, William, Pte. (H. M. 71st Highland Lt. Inf.)
Wd. at Gwalior—p. 170.

Webb, Asst. Surg., (R. A.)
Mtd. in desp.—p. 36.

Webb, Henry, Pte. (H. M. 86th Reg.)
Fatally wd. at Jhansi—p. 58.

Webber, Lt. (R. E.).
Mtd. in desp. (Jhansi)—pp. 53, 55.

Western, Maj. (Dep. Commr. of Saugor.)
Sir H. Rose indebted to—p. 105.

Westmacott, Lt. (23rd Beng. N. I., doing duty with 4th Cav., H. C.)
Mtd. in desp. (Koonch)—p. 76.
At Mhow—xlii.

Westwacott, Lt. (1st Cav., H. C.)
Mtd. in desp. (Rathghur)—p. 5.
Again - p. 7.
Wd. at (Barodia)—pp. 15, 17.

Wetherall, F. R., Col. (Chief of Staff, C. I. F. F.).
Mtd. in desp. (Koonch)—pp. 72, 73, 100.
S.-s., (Calpee)—*ib.*, p. 110.
Mtd. in desp.—p. 119.
His horse wd.—p. 126.

Wharton, James, Gnr. (R. A.)
Died s.-s., Calpee—p. 123.

Wheelaham, Wm., Pte. (H. M. 86th Reg.)
Wd. at Jhansi—p. 58.

Wheeler, Sir H. M., Maj.-Genl.
His confidence in Capt. Dunlop—ii.
Satisfied with Maj. Kirke's report—xviii.

Wheeler, Wm., Pte. (3rd B. E. R.)
Mortally wd. at Jhansi—p. 60.

Wheler, Brigr.-Genl.
Reports heavy loss of rebels—p. 52.
Supplies stores to Sir H. Rose—p. 105.

Whitaker, Saml., S. S. Maj. (H. M. 14th Lt. Dragns.)
Wd. at Koonch—p. 76.

"White Turret."
At Jhansi—pp. 40, 44.

White, Wm., Pte. (H. M. 86th Reg.)
Kld. at Jhansi—p. 58.

Whitlock, G. C., Maj.-Genl.
Cmdg. Saugor Field Div., his report of engagement at Jheeghun—pp. 29—30.
———— ——— Banda—pp. 31—34 ; 38. lxxx ; lxxxiii ; lxxxviii — xcii.

Whirlpool, Pte. (3rd B. E. R.)
Mtd. in desp. (Jhansi)—p. 56.

Widut Sing, Tpr. (1st Cav., H. C.)
Wd. at Koonch—p. 79.

Wilbraham, John, Pte. (H. M. 14th Lt. Dragns.)
Vertigo at Koonch—p. 76.

Wilkinson, Capt. (9th Lancers.)
Captures guns at Allahgunge—p. 27.

Wilkinson, William, Pte. (3rd B. E. R.)
Wd. at Jhansi—p. 60.

Williams, Lt. (Sub. Asst. Com.-Genl.)
Mtd. in desp (Kotah-ka-Serai)—p. 158.
"Special mention"—p. 176.

Williams, A., Pte. (H. M. 14th Lt. Dragns.)
Wd. (the Betwa)—cviii.

Williams, James, Pte. (H. M. 14th Lt. Dragns.)
Wd. (Gwalior)—p. 170.

Williams, Joseph, Pte. (H. M. 14th Lt. Dragns.)
Wd. (the Betwa)—cviii.

Williams, Patrick, Pte. (3rd B. E. R.)
Wd. at Jhansi—p 60.

Wilson, Sgt. (H. M. 71st Reg.)
Wd., "special mention," Morar—p. 137.

Wilson, Chas. H., Line Serjeant.
Kld. at Koonch—p. 76

Wilson, James, Sgt. (H. M. 71st Highland Lt. Inf.)
Wd. (Gwalior)—p. 170.

Wilton, Mr.
Attempts escape—v.
Murdered at Jhansi with family—ix.

Wingfield, H., Pte., (3rd B. E. R.)
Wd. at Barodia—p. 15.

Winton, Pte. (H. M. 14th Lt. Dragns.)
Mtd in desp. (Calpee)—p. 118.

Wolfe, Alleyn. Sgt. (H. M. 86th Reg.)
Mtd. in desp. (Jhansi)—p. 55.

Women.
In rebel batteries at Jhansi—p. 43.

Wood, George, Pte. (H. M. 14th Lt. Dragns.)
S.-s. (Koonch)—p 77.

Wood, H. H. A., Capt., (Asst. Adjt. Gen., C. I. F. F.)
Documents signed by—pp. 9, 16, 25, 62, 78, 79, 126, cx.
Mtd. in desp —p. 18.
(Jhansi) - p. 53.
(Koonch)—p. 72.
Services of, at Mutha—p. 89.
Mtd. in desp (Calpee)—p. 119.
(Gwalior)—p. 172.
(The Betwa)—cii.

Wood, T., Pte. (Camel Corps.)
Wd. at Calpee—p. 124.

Woodburn, Gen., (Col.)
Elephants sent to—l ; lv ; lvii.
His dragoons—lviii.
His advance hindered—lxv.

Woolaston, J., Pte. (3rd B. E. R.)
Wd. mortally at Rathghur—p. 9.

Woolcomb, Capt., (Bombay Arty.)
His battery at Barodia—p. 11.
Mtd. in desp. (Jhansi)—pp. 50, 53.
His battery at Koonch—p. 67.
  Ditto   Goraria—lxix.
Mtd. in desp.—lxxii ; lxxiii ; lxxiv.
His battery at the Betwa—xcvii, cii.

Wooree Sing, Tpr. (3rd Bombay Lt. Cav.)
Kld. at Calpee—p. 124.

Worall, Col. Sgt. (Camel Corps.)
Wd. at Calpee—p. 124.

Wright, S., Pte. (3rd B. E. R.)
Wd. at Barodia—p. 15.

Wycherley, R., Pte. (14th Lt. Dragns.)
Wd. at Rathghur—p. 9.

Y

Youart, Wm., Pte. (H. M. 86th Reg.)
Wd. at Jhansi—p. 58.

Young, D. B., Lt., (25th B. N. I.)
Wd. at Mundesore—p. 166.

Z

Zoolicar Ali Beg., Rissaldar (1st Cav., H. C.)
Wd. at Koonch—p. 79.

CALCUTTA : PRINTED BY SUPDT. GOVT. PRINTING, INDIA, 8, HASTINGS STREET.